Lecture Notes in Computer Science 11897

More information about this series at http://www.springer.com/series/7410

Ilsun You (Ed.)

Information Security Applications

20th International Conference, WISA 2019
Jeju Island, South Korea, August 21–24, 2019
Revised Selected Papers

 Springer

Editor
Ilsun You ⓘ
Soonchunhyang University
Asan, Korea (Republic of)

ISSN 0302-9743   ISSN 1611-3349 (electronic)
Lecture Notes in Computer Science
ISBN 978-3-030-39302-1   ISBN 978-3-030-39303-8 (eBook)
https://doi.org/10.1007/978-3-030-39303-8

LNCS Sublibrary: SL4 – Security and Cryptology

This Springer imprint is published by the registered company Springer Nature Switzerland AG
The registered company address is: Gewerbestrasse 11, 6330 Cham, Switzerland

Preface

Over the past few decades, digital advancements have continuously become an essential aspect in almost all parts of the workplace. However, along with advancement comes major threat to individuals, businesses, and government where information is one the most valuable assets. Accordingly, compromise of these assets could lead to a disastrous effect. Therefore, it is of paramount importance to continuously study and developed new techniques to maintain information security.

The World Conference on Information Security Application (WISA) is one of the main security research venues, hosted by the Korea Institute of Information Security and Cryptography (KIISC), sponsored by the Ministry of Science, ICT and Future Planning (MSIP), and co-sponsored by the Electronics and Telecommunication Research Institute (ETRI), the Korea Internet and Security Agency (KISA), and the National Security Research Institute (NSR). The conference is one of the Korean flagships in the field of information security. In 2019, WISA celebrated its 20th anniversary with the goal: "Towards the Best Contributor to Information Security Applications." It continues to serve as an open forum for the exchanging and sharing of common research interests and results of research, development, and application in information security areas.

This volume is composed of the extended version of papers presented at the 20th World Conference on Information Security Applications (WISA 2019) held in Jeju Island, South Korea, during August 21–24, 2019. This year's conference was technically supported by Korea University, Soonchunhyang University, Soongsil University, Pukyong National University, and Chugnam University. The purpose of the WISA 2019 was to continue bringing together researchers and engineers in security areas, providing them with the opportunity to meet and discuss new ideas and technologies about information security and applications. The primary focus of this year's conference was on systems and network security including all other technical and practical aspects of security application.

A total of 29 outstanding papers covering areas such as application and game security, network security, blockchain, AI and machine learning, cryptography, IoT security, and hardware security were accepted for presentation at WISA 2019. Moreover, invited keynote talks by Prof. Wenjing Lou (Virginia Tech) and Prof. Adrian Perrig (ETH Zürich), as well as tutorial talks by Dr. Yousung Kang (ETRI), Dr. John Choi (MarkAmy), CEO Louis Hur, and CIS Team Manager Seungjun Lee (NSHC) augmented the conference.

With the great effort of the Organizing Committee and reviewers, support of the sponsor and co-sponsors, and active participation of all the participants, WISA 2019 was a great success during the celebration of its 20th anniversary. We would like to acknowledge the contribution of each invidual Program Committee member as well as our sincere gratitude to all the reviewers, authors, and participants for their unending support.

October 2019   Ilsun You

Organization

General Chair

Kyung-Hyune Rhee   Pukyong National University, South Korea

Program Committee Chair

Ilsun You   Soonchunhyang University, South Korea

Program Committee

Ioannis Agrafiotis	Oxford University, UK
Pelin Angin	Middle East Technical University, Turkey
Joonsang Baek	University of Wollongong, Australia
Sang Kil Cha	KAIST, South Korea
Xiaofeng Chen	Xidian University, China
Jin-Hee Cho	Virginia Tech, USA
Seong-Je Cho	Dankook University, South Korea
Dooho Choi	ETRI, South Korea
Hsu-Chun Hsiao	National Taiwan University, Taiwan
Qiong Huang	South China Agricultural University, China
Xinyi Huang	Fujian Normal University, China
Eul Gyu Im	Hanyang University, South Korea
Yeongjin Jang	Oregon State University, USA
Hiroaki Kikuchi	Meiji University, Japan
Joongheon Kim	Chung-Ang University, South Korea
Jong Kim	POSTECH, South Korea
Jongkil Kim	University of Wollongong, Australia
Byoungyoung Lee	Seoul National University, South Korea
Kyu Hyunng Lee	University of Georgia, USA
Manhee Lee	Hannam University, South Korea
Shengli Liu	Shanghai Jiao Tong University, China
Kazuhiro Minami	Institute of Statistical Mathematics, Japan
Aziz Mohaisen	University of Central Florida, USA
Kirill Morozov	University of North Texas, USA
Masakatsu Nishigaki	Shizuoka University, Japan
Yasuyuki Nogami	Okayama University, Japan
Jason Nurse	University of Kent, UK
Kazumasa Omote	University of Tsukuba, Japan
Ki-Woong Park	Sejong University, South Korea
Marcus Peinado	Microsoft, USA
Kui Ren	ZheJiang University, China

Junghwan Rhee	NEC Laboratories, USA
Ulrich Rührmair	LMU Munich, Germany
Kouichi Sakurai	Kyushu University, Japan
Junji Shikata	Yokohama National University, Japan
Dongwan Shin	New Mexico Tech, USA
Sang Uk Shin	Pukyong National University, South Korea
SeongHan Shin	AIST, Japan
Gang Tan	Pennsylvania State University, USA
Toshihiro Yamauchi	Okayama University, Japan
Kuo-Hui Yeh	National Dong Hwa University, Taiwan
Siu Ming Yiu	The University of Hong Kong, Hong Kong, China
Mengyu Yu	Roosevelt University, USA

Organizing Committee Chair

JungTaek Seo	Soonchunhyang University, South Korea

Organizing Committee

Hyobeom Ahn	Kongju National University, South Korea
Young Kyun Cha	Korea University, South Korea
Hangbae Chang	Chung-Ang University, South Korea
Sangwoo Cho	NSR, South Korea
Youngchul Choi	SGA Solutions Co., Ltd., South Korea
Dong-Guk Han	Kookmin University, South Korea
Seokhie Hong	Korea University, South Korea
Junbeom Hur	Korea University, South Korea
Louis Hur	NSHC, South Korea
Souhwan Jung	Soongsil University, South Korea
Hyungwoo Kang	Financial Supervisory Service, South Korea
Howon Kim	Pusan National University, South Korea
HyoungChun Kim	NSR, South Korea
Hyoungshick Kim	Sungkyunkwan University, South Korea
Ikkyun Kim	ETRI, South Korea
Jincheol Kim	KEPCO KDN Co., Ltd., South Korea
Jongsung Kim	Kookmin University, South Korea
Kwang Ho Kim	Chungbuk National University, South Korea
Seungjoo Kim	Korea University, South Korea
Sung Cheol Kim	KEPCO KDN Co., Ltd., South Korea
Tai Hyo Kim	Formal Works Inc., South Korea
Jin Kwak	Ajou University, South Korea
Hun Yeong Kwon	Korea University, South Korea
Kookheul Kwon	KINAC, South Korea
Taekyoung Kwon	Yonsei University, South Korea
Changhoon Lee	Seoul National University of Science and Technology, South Korea

DongHwi Lee	Dongshin University, South Korea
Im-Yeong Lee	Soonchunhyang University, South Korea
Jong-Hyouk Lee	Sangmyung University, South Korea
June Kyung Lee	NAONWORKS, South Korea
Kyung-Ho Lee	Korea University, South Korea
Mun-Kyu Lee	Inha University, South Korea
Sung-Jae Lee	KISA, South Korea
Duk Ryeouk Moon	KOEN, South Korea
Joong-Chan Na	ETRI, South Korea
Hyung Geon Oh	NSR, South Korea
Jin Young Oh	KISA, South Korea
Namje Park	Jeju National University, South Korea
Young-Ho Park	Sejeong Cyber University, South Korea
HwaJeong Seo	Hansung University, South Korea
Seung-Hyun Seo	Hanyang University, South Korea
Tae Shik Shon	Ajou University, South Korea
Wontae Sim	KISA, South Korea
Kyungho Son	Kangwon National University, South Korea
Yoojae Won	Chungnam National University, South Korea
San-Soo Yeo	Mokwon University, South Korea
Jeong Hyun Yi	Soongsil University, South Korea
Okyeon Yi	Kookmin University, South Korea
Kangbin Yim	Soonchunhyang University, South Korea
Jonghee M. Youn	Yeungnam University, South Korea

Contents

Security With AI and Machine Learning

IoT Security

Application and Game Security

Show Me Your Account: Detecting MMORPG Game Bot Leveraging Financial Analysis with LSTM

Kyung Ho Park[1], Eunjo Lee[2], and Huy Kang Kim[1(✉)]

[1] Graduate School of Information Security, Korea University,
Seoul, Republic of Korea
{kyungho96,cenda}@korea.ac.kr
[2] NCSOFT, Seoul, Republic of Korea
gimmesilver@ncsoft.com

Abstract. With the rapid growth of MMORPG market, game bot detection has become an essential task for maintaining stable in-game ecosystem. To classify bots from normal users, detection methods are proposed in both game client and server-side. Among various classification methods, data mining method in server-side captured unique characteristics of bots efficiently. For features used in data mining, behavioral and social actions of character are analyzed with numerous algorithms. However, bot developers can evade the previous detection methods by changing bot's activities continuously. Eventually, overall maintenance cost increases because the selected features need to be updated along with the change of bot's behavior.

To overcome this limitation, we propose improved bot detection method with financial analysis. As bot's activity absolutely necessitates the change of financial status, analyzing financial fluctuation effectively captures bots as a key feature. We trained and tested model with actual data of Aion, a leading MMORPG in Asia. Leveraging that LSTM efficiently recognizes time-series movement of data, we achieved meaningful detection performance. Further on this model, we expect sustainable bot detection system in the near future.

Keywords: MMORPG · Game bot detection · LSTM neural networks

1 Introduction

Online game plays a huge role in modern leisure. With 44.6 billion US dollars of market share estimated by 2022, Massively Multiplayer Online Role-Playing Game (MMORPG) takes significant position in global market [12]. MMORPG is a game genre that users have own characters to play various activities in a virtual world. They combat with monsters, accumulate game assets, even chat or date with others. As various activities exist, in-game ecosystem shows similar pattern as a real world. [2] Interestingly, people in a real world and MMORPG users

© Springer Nature Switzerland AG 2020
I. You (Ed.): WISA 2019, LNCS 11897, pp. 3–13, 2020.
https://doi.org/10.1007/978-3-030-39303-8_1

pursue a common goal: a wealth. In a real world, diligent workers accumulate wealth from salaries. Similarly, heavy users in a virtual world gather game assets and become wealthy. Wealth in a game makes character stronger, and stronger character gives more fun to player. Reflecting that players want better game assets, some corporate-like entities even created Real Money Trading (RMT), a transaction of game assets with real money [4]. However, money-related issues created illegal activities. Some malicious users developed automated program, called a game bot.

Game bot is an automated program playing game autonomously instead of human users. Without any touch of human, bots automatically move around virtual world. They behave in programmed way, repetitively do patterned actions to collect game asset. Bots normally gather wealth faster than normal players because program does not get tired [9]. Leveraging this efficiency, corporate-like entities called Gold Farmer Group (GFG) started to operate thousands of bots at the same time. GFGs collect enormous amount of in-game cash or rare items, and sell it to buyers with real money [1].

Game companies should detect these bots and provide adequate actions because bots create deprivation of normal users. If some users purchase items with real money and become powerful easily, normal users would depreciate their effort of growing characters. Moreover, in-game economy goes unstable with affluent assets created by bots. GFG especially collects a huge amount of game assets, and creates an inflation and overflow of asset. Inflated assets easily break balance among users and skew the game design. As a result, bots make gaming experience of normal users feel depreciated, leave the game, and eventually create loss to game company.

To counteract malicious activities of bots, academia and industry have developed bot detection methods in two main streams: client-side detection and server-side detection. Client-side method detects bots by implementing challenge-response program or security solution. For challenge-response method, game client asks question that humans can easily solve. As bots are not programmed to answer unexpected questions, characters with wrong response are classified as bots. Security solutions such as GameGuard or Warden are specially developed client-side program for bot detection. However, both methods are inadequate to apply at industry level. Challenge-response methods like CAPTCHA excessively drop user's game experience, as they feel disturbed during the play. Security solutions frequently collide with vaccine programs, create crash of the system [14].

To overcome limits of client-side methods, server-side methods have been proposed. Server-side methods capture unique characteristic of bots leverage data mining. Past works suggested numerous methods with data mining algorithms, but there were several hurdles. First of all, previous methods optimized detection model in a certain game, thus hard to generalize. Models performed well in selected game, but hard to be utilized in other games as well. Moreover, bot developers could neutralize detection methods if they recognize detection thresholds. As bot developers figured out patterns of bot detection, they started to make bots mimicking human user's behavior. For sustainable, generalized, and secured bot detection, it is necessary to develop improved method.

In this work, we propose bot detection method to jump over limitations of previous works. To design sustainable and commonly applicable detection method, we performed financial analysis to each character. Considering that bots eventually accumulate their wealth to specific character for RMT, we analyzed flow of in-game cash and assets. This generates effectiveness in two aspects. First, we can vividly capture bot's behavior as bots cannot repudiate financial patterns. If transactions among bots exist for accumulation, specific financial patterns must exist. Furthermore, financial analysis can be applied in different games as concept of cash or items generally exist. Most MMORPGs operate its own economy, and transactions occur among users. We can easily compare features used in financial analysis, and apply into different games.

Leveraging Recurrent Neural Networks (RNN) as algorithm, we trained model with game play log of Aion, a famous MMORPG developed by NCSOFT. We evaluated our model precisely captures financial pattern of bots, and provide improved detection method with following contributions below:

(1) Sustainability: As financial pattern of character is inevitable record, model effectively detects bots although bot behaves just like normal players or change its activity pattern.
(2) Generality: As model utilizes commonly used features in general MMORPG, game companies can easily apply model into multiple games.
(3) Individuality: Only once we train model with accumulated data, model classifies individual character as bot or normal user.
(4) Security: As neural network is a black-box model, bot developers are hard to recognize detection thresholds.

2   Literature Review

Among previous works, server-side method analyzes game play data to capture unique pattern of bots. We categorized features used in bot detection as Table 1, by dividing into two streams: sufficient condition and necessary condition. The sufficient conditions are set of features that bot's activity probably creates, but not absolutely accompanies. As the sufficient conditions include distinctive pattern of bots, we can identify bots during certain period of time. However, analysis of the sufficient conditions require repetitive updates as these conditions are not consistent. If bot developers modify bot's behavior, model also necessitates update to capture changed pattern. On the other hand, the necessary conditions are features must happen as a consequence of bot's behavior. As bots are designed to accumulate wealth efficiently, specific actions such as transaction among bots absolutely happen. Although bot developers change bot's behavior, pattern of wealth accumulation itself still exists. Thus, we can detect bots leveraging necessary conditions in consistent way.

Table 1. Researches on server-side bot detection method

Category	Data type	Modeling	Reference
Sufficient condition	Behavioral action	Sequence pattern	[10]
		Self-similarity of action	[9]
		Action frequency	[13]
	Social action	Chat log analysis	[5]
		Party play log analysis	[6]
Necessary condition	Transaction	Network analysis	[11]
	Coordinates where asset increase or decrease	DBSCAN	[8]

Detection method with sufficient conditions analyzes two data types: behavioral action and social action. Behavioral actions describe how character performs physical activities such as moving, normal attack, or using skills. Lee *et al.* analyzed the full action sequence of users on big data analysis platform. They set specific behavior sequences and applied simple scoring algorithm and Naive Bayesian algorithm to classify bots from users [10]. In another method, Lee *et al.* captured similarity of character behavior to classify game bots. They divided sequence of behavior with time window, and embedded as a feature vector. They showed bots have similar behavior pattern during play time by applying logistic regression algorithm with self-similarity of characters [9].

Not only behavioral characteristics, social actions also illustrate distinguishable patterns. Thousands of users communicate and socialize with others. They chat, form a party to complete quests, or create guild for sense of belonging. Leveraging chat logs among users, Kang *et al.* derived lexical, syntactic, semantic features from chatting contents using text mining methods. As bots have similar pattern of chatting to evade detection rules, analyzing text features with machine learning algorithms showed such high performance [5]. Kang *et al.* also analyzed party play log for game bot classification. They focused that the party play in MMORPG requires strong interaction between game players in a short time, which creates different party play pattern between bots and normal users. By inspection that game parties composed of bots play in distinctive way, they established thresholds for bot detection statistical algorithms [6].

Above methods with sufficient conditions showed significant performance, but accompanied limitation of sustainability. If bot developers change pattern of game bots, detection methods are easily avoidable. In this circumstance, we should change detection rule or re-train model repetitively. Some bots in these days started to behave and socialize like normal users. Intelligent bots are programmed to generate plausible chats, or do actions like normal users. Furthermore, if game company updates in-game ecosystem, it might blur existing detection rules. As bots change their behavior or actions following update, detection methods also require update of its threshold. Therefore, we acknowledged necessity of sustainable detection method using different features.

To overcome this limitation, some researches suggested detection method with necessary conditions. Financial features such as character's asset level and transaction are actively used. Song and Kim captured geographical tendency that location of transaction among bots show similar pattern. They analyzed specific coordinates of financial transaction within a map, and applied Density-Based Spatial Clustering of Applications with Noise (DBSCAN) algorithm to identify bots from normal users [11]. Lee *et al.* build a topological network of all transactions in a virtual world, and figured out specific patterns of transactions among bots. Especially in GFG, they illustrated bots have different roles for efficient asset gathering, and proposed structure of network for clear understanding of bot ecosystem [8].

Analysis of necessary conditions showed financial features are meaningful to identify bots from normal users. However, bot developers still can hedge detection method by changing transaction medium. For instance, if bots send cash or items through mailing, it does not leave location coordinates of transaction. Topological network analysis revealed macroscopic understanding about transactions among bots, but hard to capture individual bots rapidly. Building a network requires heavy resources to analyze whole structure. Whole network also necessitates repetitive update following change of transaction patterns among bots.

To improve previous methods, we present a bot detection method leveraging financial analysis. In pursuit of sustainable detection method, we analyzed financial status of character, necessary conditions of bot's activity. Level of cash or number of items a character owns are examples of financial status. We utilized status data rather than other features, as status itself cannot be modified. Derived features such as transaction coordinates can be hedged or easily changed. But status itself is a consequence of transaction, thus inevitable by bot developers. To scrutinize individual bot's financial data, we employed Long Short-Term Memory neural networks (LSTM) as algorithm. As neural network requires less resource rather than topological network, it enables economic model establishment process. From following sections, we propose bot detection model validated with actual MMORPG play data.

3   Proposed Methodology

3.1   Data Collection

We collected the game play dataset from Aion, one of the most famous MMORPGs in the world. The dataset is accumulated during the first week of May, 2010. Through collection process, we complied the End User License Agreement (EULA) and related laws under consent of Aion users. Anonymous data are confidentially collected, and utilized only for analysis of this work.

Table 2. Feature types in Aion status log

Type	Detailed features
Identification	Character number, account number
Location	Location coordinates, map number
Playing information	Health point, magical point, experience point
Social information	Party identification number, alliance identification number
Financial information	Cash status, item status, inventory status

Feature Selection. To filter features with financial status, we dropped unnecessary information through feature selection. In log data, there exists status log which periodically shows character's information. Among various status features described in Table 2, we extracted financial information, which illustrates financial status of character.

Ground-Truth Confirmation. Confirming ground-truth is an essential process of bot detection. We labeled data as bot and normal user following judgement of game company, NCSOFT. Company operates human inspectors who observe doubtful characters by hand. To evade mistakes and bias of human observers, company carefully labels doubtful character only when multiple observers decided in a similar way. Company also collects reasons of decision for comprehensive understanding. If blocked character was actually a normal user, character label is updated as normal user again. As our ground-truth is constructed through these sophisticated labelling process, we regard solid ground-truth for detection model is confirmed.

3.2   Feature Engineering

Feature engineering process takes significant position in model performance. To make log-level raw data into trainable form, we managed two steps of feature engineering: eliminating non-influential features, sliding time window with scaling.

Table 3. Rules for identifying non-influential features

No	Rule	Description
1	Feature indifference	A value of a feature is indifferent at bot and normal user
2	Feature invariance	Summation of a feature is 0, and standard deviation of a feature is 0 at bot and normal user, respectively

Eliminating Non-influential Features. To scrutinize change of financial data, we eliminated features without meaningful level of change. To leverage deep neural networks on bot detection, model should learn different dynamics of data between bot and normal user. If a feature with similar pattern is provided to the model, it blurs weights and bias of neural network. Thus, we set rules described in Table 3 to filter non-influential features.

If a feature is caught in Rule 1, it implicates model cannot learn any different pattern. A feature with same value between bot and normal user does not make any different pattern, thus we dropped features fulfilling Rule 1. Rule 2 proves that feature value is 0, creating sparsity at the training data. If we map training data into vector space, a feature filled with zero value creates sparse input vector. As sparse input vector blurs computation of model parameters, we dropped features fulfilling Rule 2 to reduce sparsity. After applying two rules above, we extracted essential features shown in Table 4 from log-level raw data.

Table 4. List of essential features

No	Type	Feature	Description
1	Item	Number of items	Total number of items a character owns
2	Cash	Total cash	Total amount of cash a character owns
3		Cash in account	Amount of cash a character carries in inventory
4		Cash in character bank	Amount of cash a character stores in warehouse
5		Cash in vendor	Amount of operating cash handled by transaction vendors such as sales agent or auction house
6	Evaluated asset value	Evaluated asset value	Sum of monetary value of cash and all items evaluated by default price
7		Mailing asset value	Sum of monetary value of all items in sent and received by mail evaluated by default price
8		Evaluated asset value in character bank	Sum of monetary value of cash and all items stored in character's warehouse evaluated by default price
9		Evaluated asset in account bank	Sum of cash and monetary value of all items stored in account's warehouse evaluated by default price

Sliding Time Window with Scaling. Log-level raw data necessitates transformation process to be in trainable form. As deep neural networks effectively learn from fixed length of data, long time-series data require cutting process. We

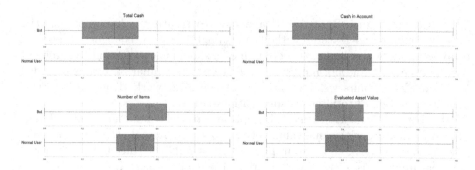

Fig. 1. Chosen boxplots of scaled feature distribution

set fixed length of time window, and generated training data by sliding along log-level raw data. Moreover, we applied scaling process to mitigate different scales of data. By calculating each feature with the equation below, we transformed data to be scaled between 0 and 1. Lastly, we labeled transformed data same as its original data.

$$X_{normalized} = \frac{X_i - Min(X_i)}{Max(X_i) - Min(X_i)}$$

We compared statistical difference of features to check whether they are distinct along with labels. As illustrated in Fig. 1, features such as total cash, cash in account, and number of items show different distribution at the same scale. Considering these differences, we clarified financial features can differentiate bots from normal users.

3.3 Modeling

We employed RNN as detection algorithm. RNN is one of deep neural networks that past computation result influences next computation of model parameters. Previous research on neural networks have shown RNN explores well with time-series data [3]. We analyzed financial data entangles temporal dynamics, thus utilized recurrent architecture to model. Among various types of RNN, we set LSTM neural networks considering its performance. We provided training data into LSTM network to identify bots and normal users. Training was performed along prefixed size of batches, and batch normalization was applied for better performance. For stabilized training, we also applied regularization techniques to evade the model's overfitting problem. After the training process finished, we validated the model with test dataset, and record its performance with four metrics: accuracy, precision, recall, and F1-score.

4   Experiment Result

To gain enough records of training, we separated monthly dataset into weekly basis. We randomly mixed data, and performed 10-fold cross validation for assured result. Table 5 shows the result of experiment with evaluation metrics.

Table 5. Bot detection experiment result

Experiment	Accuracy	Precision	Recall	F1 score
Week 1	0.9494	0.9385	0.9759	0.9490
Week 2	0.9401	0.9168	0.9831	0.9488
Week 3	0.9487	0.9237	0.9886	0.9551
Week 4	0.9509	0.9103	0.9861	0.9476
Average	0.9473	0.9223	0.9834	0.9501

We interpret trained model detects bots with reasonable performance. Experiment result shows relatively lower precision than recall, implicating existence of false positive error. Considering characteristics of bot detection, we evaluate this error is allowable. One of primary goals of bot detection is making a list of doubtful accounts rather than blocking accounts. If game company blocks normal user showing similar pattern as bots, it directly generates dissatisfaction or even annoy of user. Thus, bot detection prioritizes figuring out doubtful characters rather than direct blocking. In this viewpoint, we evaluate our model efficiently detects bots only with a few financial features. We expect ensembling our model with other methods would achieve more precise detection, which is further illustrated in following Discussion section.

5   Discussion

Ensembling for Precise Detection. Ensembling our model with other methods would build powerful bot detection system. To hedge risk of false positive error, bots are not decided by a single detection method. To reduce false positive errors, even human-based detection method in the past required many skilled observers. In similar way, we believe more detection methods are required to collaborate for industry-level application. For features of ensembling, we would leverage other necessary conditions of game bots. Transaction with other characters or Non-Player Characters (NPC) can be utilized as features. Considering more information of bots, detection model would be improved resulting powerful performance.

Applicability into Other MMORPGs. On following research, we would apply this model in other MMORPGs. With the growth of game industry, game companies operate multiple games at the same time. To put in game company's shoes, running different detection methods for different games is cost-ineffective. If detection method is applicable in multiple games, it creates economies of scale. We interpret features used in our model are commonly found. Previous research on bot network also suggested financial features are common traces of modern MMORPGs [7]. Therefore, we expect our model is applicable in other games to be used in industry-level practices.

6   Conclusion

In this work, we proposed employment of financial analysis to game bot detection in real MMORPG ecosystem. Previous studies showed efficient bot detection methods, but underlying problem was variance of bot's activity. If bot developers change activity or make them act like normal users, it becomes resource-consumable to update detection methods. To overcome this limitation, we utilized financial information of characters which are necessary conditions of bot's activity. Considering purpose of bots related to RMT, patterned change of financial status is inevitable for bot characters. Through experiments, our results reveal that financial information are highly related to bot's activity, suggesting effectiveness at bot detection. Leveraging time-series dynamics of financial data, our LSTM neural networks efficiently captured pattern of bots. We validated this efficiency with actual game data of Aion, a famous MMORPG developed by NCSOFT.

Our detection model establishes essential contributions. First and foremost, our model establishes sustainable detection method as bots are hard to evade patterned financial changes. Moreover, our model is applicable into other games as utilized features are common in modern MMORPG. Unlike macroscopic analysis of bot network, LSTM neural network is eligible to detect individual characters to generate list of doubtful characters. Finally, our model enhances security of detection as LSTM neural network is a black-box model making bot developers hard to predict detection thresholds. There still exists a room for improvement. With ensembling our model with other necessary conditions of game bot, we would like to achieve qualified bot detection system with powerful performance. To assure generality of our model, we plan to check model's performance on other actual MMORPG data. In pursuit of sustainable, and general bot detection, we will further research on financial analysis in MMORPG ecosystem.

Acknowledgements. This work was supported under the framework of international cooperation program managed by National Research Foundation of Korea (No. 2017K1A3A1A17092614).

References

1. Ahmad, M.A., Keegan, B., Srivastava, J., Williams, D., Contractor, N.: Mining for gold farmers: automatic detection of deviant players in MMOGs. In: 2009 International Conference on Computational Science and Engineering, vol. 4, pp. 340–345. IEEE (2009)
2. Castronova, E.: Virtual worlds: a first-hand account of market and society on the Cyberian Frontier. CESinfo Working Paper Series (2001)
3. Connor, J., Atlas, L.: Recurrent neural networks and time series prediction. In: IJCNN-91-Seattle International Joint Conference on Neural Networks, vol. 1, pp. 301–306. IEEE (1991)
4. Huhh, J.S.: Simple economics of real-money trading in online games (2008)
5. Kang, A.R., Kim, H.K., Woo, J.: Chatting pattern based game bot detection: do they talk like us? KSII Trans. Internet Inf. Syst. **6**(11), 2866–2879 (2012)
6. Kang, A.R., Woo, J., Park, J., Kim, H.K.: Online game bot detection based on party-play log analysis. Comput. Math. Appl. **65**(9), 1384–1395 (2013)
7. Kwon, H., Mohaisen, A., Woo, J., Kim, Y., Lee, E., Kim, H.K.: Crime scene reconstruction: online gold farming network analysis. IEEE Trans. Inf. Forensics Secur. **12**(3), 544–556 (2016)
8. Lee, E., Woo, J., Kim, H., Kim, H.K.: No silk road for online gamers!: Using social network analysis to unveil black markets in online games. In: Proceedings of the 2018 World Wide Web Conference on World Wide Web, pp. 1825–1834. International World Wide Web Conferences Steering Committee (2018)
9. Lee, E., Woo, J., Kim, H., Mohaisen, A., Kim, H.K.: You are a game bot!: Uncovering game bots in MMORPGs via self-similarity in the wild. In: NDSS (2016)
10. Lee, J., Lim, J., Cho, W., Kim, H.K.: In-game action sequence analysis for game BOT detection on the big data analysis platform. In: Handa, H., Ishibuchi, H., Ong, Y.-S., Tan, K.-C. (eds.) Proceedings of the 18th Asia Pacific Symposium on Intelligent and Evolutionary Systems. PALO, vol. 2, pp. 403–414. Springer, Cham (2015). https://doi.org/10.1007/978-3-319-13356-0_32
11. Song, H.M., Kim, H.K.: Game-bot detection based on clustering of asset-varied location coordinates. J. Korea Inst. Inf. Secur. Cryptol. **25**(5), 1131–1141 (2015)
12. Technavio Research: Global MMO Games Market 2018–2022 (2018). https://www.apnews.com/9e7c20b7267841efb0fb22b2bd9398e3. Accessed 27 May 2019
13. Thawonmas, R., Kashifuji, Y., Chen, K.T.: Detection of MMORPG bots based on behavior analysis. In: Proceedings of the 2008 International Conference on Advances in Computer Entertainment Technology, pp. 91–94. ACM (2008)
14. Woo, J., Kim, H.K.: Survey and research direction on online game security. In: Proceedings of the Workshop at SIGGRAPH Asia, pp. 19–25. ACM (2012)

Turn On the Lights: User Behavior in Game Environment Using CPTED

Jeongeun Seo, Minhee Joo, and Kyungho Lee

Korea University, 145 Anam-ro Seongbuk-gu, Seoul 02841, Republic of Korea
{sje5279,mhjoo9321,kevinlee}@korea.ac.kr

Abstract. The proliferation of the internet has allowed various online games such as Massive Multiplayer Online Role Playing Game (MMORPG) and First-Person Shooter (FPS) to garner much attention. Both MMORPG and FPS requires lower network latency, as the users are constantly required to assess and respond to the gaming environment and other users' decisions. Our study aims to investigate the users' psychological behavior by changing the gaming environment. We present CPTED as a risk control measure. Based on the principle of CPTED, two types of maps were designed and compared to analyze the game violence of users in each map. In order to compare the game violence of the users, 100 questionnaires were conducted. In this study, we used FAIR, a risk analysis model, to assess the threat and violence of the users.

Keywords: Online game security · Risk Management · CPTED · Crime Prevention Through Environmental Design · User behavior

1 Introduction

During the past decade, the inception of various ICT technologies have introduced online games on numerous platforms. With the popularity and rapid growth in the gaming industry, online games have been criticized for causing violent behaviors. Past studies have focused on the relationship between online games and the users' violent behavior, however, there has been a lack of study that focuses on the relationship between the gaming environment and user's behavior. As such, this study aims to investigate how the gaming environment may affect the user's behavior.

In recent years, first-person shooter (FPS) games have become a cultural phenomenon as Playerunknown's Battlegrounds (PUBG) sold more than 50 million copies and Fortnite: Battle Royale have generated over $2.4 billion (USD) in the year 2018 [1]. Well established video game franchises such as Call of Duty, Battlefield, and Fortnite have pursued a format that focuses on real-time environments. The environment's interaction with the players has a vital role in the gameplay and overall experience. Based on past studies, vacant building has been proven to increase the crime rates [2, 3].

This research was supported by the MSIT (Ministry of Science and ICT), Korea, under the ITRC (Information Technology Research Center) support program (IITP-2019-2015-0-00403) supervised by the IITP (Institute for Information & communications Technology Planning & Evaluation).

I. You (Ed.): WISA 2019, LNCS 11897, pp. 14–24, 2020.
https://doi.org/10.1007/978-3-030-39303-8_2

In this study, we use the risk management process and the Factor Analysis of Information Risk (FAIR) model to quantitatively analyze the risks. We also use Crime Prevention Through Environmental Design (CPTED) as a control measure to reduce the risk. We ascertain that the applying natural surveillance and access control, which are the two core components of CPTED, to the environment will have a relationship to the user's behavior. Moreover, we posit that applying CPTED will have a positive influence towards the user's state of mind.

Our study is structured as follows. Section 2 discusses the background of the risk management, FAIR Model and CPTED. Section 3 reviews the literature on user behavior in online gaming, environmental design for security, and 'Contagious Fire'. The proposed method of our study is explained in Sect. 4. Section 5 contains our findings and discussion. Finally, we present our findings in the conclusion.

2 Background

In this study, we use the Factor Analysis of Information Risk (FAIR) model, which helps organization analyze the risk through quantitative measures. We then apply Crime Prevention Through Environmental Design (CPTED) as a control measure to reduce the risk. Our paper presents a framework to assess and analyze how the user's behavior shifts when the environment changes.

2.1 Risk Management for the Security Domain

During the past few decades, the relevance and usefulness of risk management have strengthened, as risk management allows organizations to make rational decisions based on the assessed risks. Villa et al. [4] define risk priority areas into four areas for risk management: (i) the ability cope to unexpected losses, (ii) improving the knowledge and implementing protocols, (iii) focusing on risk communication, and (iv) learning from past events. Risk management is composed of risk assessment and risk analysis. According to NORSOK Standard Z-013 [5], risk assessment consists of six steps which are (i) establishment of the context, (ii) hazard identification, (iii) frequency estimation, (iv) consequence estimation, (v) establishment of the risk picture, and (vi) risk evaluation. Risk assessment constitutes of both quantitative and qualitative approaches to measure and assess the risk. In this paper, we use the Factor Analysis of Information Risk (FAIR) Model, which is a representative model of the strategic approach, to analyze the risks.

2.2 Factor Analysis of Information Risk (FAIR) Model

The Factor Analysis of Information Risk (FAIR) model is a risk management framework developed by Jack A. Jones [6]. The model calculates the risks based on the exact probability by factoring the frequency of events, data loss, and quantitative evaluation. The FAIR model helps assess and analyze the organization's risk by quantitatively measuring it. The FAIR model defines the risk with the probable frequency and probable magnitude of future loss within a given timeframe [7]. The Loss Event

Frequency (LEF) and Loss Magnitude (LM) are the two components that are considered when calculating the risk, as depicted in Fig. 1.

The LEF factors the Threat Event Frequency (TEF) and Vulnerability (Vul), while the LM factors the Primary Loss (PL) and Secondary Loss (SL). The TEF considers the Contact Frequency (CF) and Probability of Action (PoA). On the other hand, both the Threat Capability (TCap) and Resistance Strength (RS) are factored into the Vul. However, in our study we did not consider the Loss Magnitude.

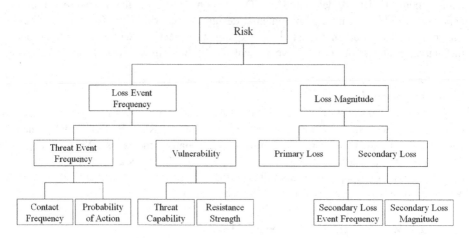

Fig. 1. The FAIR (Factor Analysis of Information Risk) Model assess the organization's risk by factoring in the Loss Event Frequency (LEF) and Loss Magnitude (LM).

2.3   CPTED (Crime Prevention Through Environmental Design)

Crime Prevention Through Environmental Design (CPTED) is an urban design technique to reduce crime rates by changing the physical environment. The technique relies on environmental design to build an environment with lower crime rates with less reliance on law enforcement. CPTED is a complex strategy that outlines the environmental design strategies into seven related area: (i) Defensible Space, (ii) Activity Program Support, (iii) Territoriality, (iv) Target Hardening, (v) Formal Organized Surveillance, (vi) Natural Surveillance, and (vii) Access Control as depicted in Fig. 2 [8–11]. Installing streetlights to the urban area have been proven to help create a more secure and safer community [12].

In this study, we use the risk management process and the Factor Analysis of Information Risk (FAIR) model to quantitatively analyze the risks. We also use CPTED as a control measure to reduce the risk.

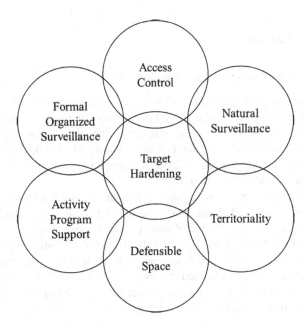

Fig. 2. The CPTED (Crime Prevention Through Environmental Design) is an urban design technique to reduce crime rates by changing the physical environment.

3 Related Works

3.1 User Behavior in Online Gaming

Past studies in online game have focused mostly on Massively Multiplayer Online Role-Playing Game (MMORPG) genres when observing the user's behaviors [13–16]. Qin [17] analyzed the relationship between the different social behaviors such as, role playing in online games and chatting. The study found that the environments within a game can change the social behaviors of the individuals. Gyarmat [18] proposed a network traffic model and user behavior model that recorded the trends of the MMORPG players based on the time zone.

3.2 Environmental Design for Security

Prior studies on city design and Natural Surveillance argues that the environment can have an influence on reducing crime rates [19, 20]. Jacobs [19] presented a solution to help solve the crimes through the urban redevelopment technique, which is part of a city design method. Jeffery [20] proposed that our approach to crime preventions focuses on models of deterrence and retribution, however, he contends that we should focus on preventative systems based on scientific principles. Desyllas et al. [21] states that building heights is one of the facts that effect the crime rates in urban environment. As such, defining boundaries and maintaining a positive image have been confirmed to help discourage offending. Through the design and management of the physical environment of buildings the public safety can improve, while reducing the fear of crime. Lee et al. [22] have found that installing closed-circuit television (CCTV) can help serve as a natural surveillance.

3.3   Shooting Performance and Contagious Fire

Knez and Niedenthal [23] conducted a psychological experiment with the lighting setting for the digital games, and they found that players lighting affects the cognition. By contrasting the lights with red and blue color hue, they found that the players registered the reddish light with warmer emotions and the blueish light to evoke a cool feeling. The study found that the individual's response time and performance to improve under the warmer lighting settings.

Police officers caught in a crossfire or lethal threat are sometimes unable to assess how many bullets were fired. Furthermore, recent police shootings have coined the term "contagious shooting", as the initial officer's shot triggers a cascade of shots from the other officers [24]. Officers will fire their shots when they panic as an unconscious response, and the number of shots will increase as the fear factors increase. In real-life situations, police officers have admitted that they are unaware of how many shots were fired during the crossfire as the immediate threat makes it difficult for the officers to assess how many rounds had been shot [25].

4   Proposal Method

This paper aims to measure the risk by applying the Risk Management model to the online game environments. Using AssaultCube, an open-source FPS game, we designed two maps for our experiment. The first map, Map1, is the default map provided by the AssaultCube. We changed the exposure rate of Map2 to create contrasting setting with the first map, Map1. To apply the CPTED method to the second map, Map2, we added fences to the environment, as depicted in Fig. 3. By applying contrasting settings to the two different maps, we wanted to observe if the Natural

Fig. 3. Two screenshots comparing the visual lighting with and without CPTED. Map2 (right) presents a brighter screen in comparison to Map1 (left), and Map2 includes fences to apply CPTED to the environment. (Color figure online)

Surveillance and Access Control would change the user's behavior. As mentioned in the aforementioned section, Natural Surveillance has been proven to reduce crime rates.

We carried out an experiment with a total of 100 graduate students majoring in the IT security domain at Korea University, Korea. We used two laptops with the identical model (LG14Z95), specifications, and settings. The players participating in the game used the same firearm, MF-577. The goal of the experiment was to demonstrate the potential relationship between the natural surveillance and user's behavior. The participants were given a brief description of the experiment, and a detailed explanation of the control setting was provided prior to the experiment. A survey was conducted after the experiment was conducted to the participants, as depicted in Table 1.

Table 1. The participants were asked to fill out a questionnaire that inquires about the user's demographic information and experience with Map1 and Map2.

Game preference questionnaire
Demographic-related items
- What is your gender?
- What is your age group do you belong to?
Items related to Map1
- How many bullets did you use?
- Select the words that best describe Map1. You can select multiple choices
Items related to Map2
- How many bullets did you use?
- Select the words that best describe Map2. You can select multiple choices
Items related to the map preference
- Which of the two maps did you prefer?
- Why did you choose the map?
- Is there anything you would have changed to Map1 or Map2?

The questionnaire survey consisted of questions that pertained to the different maps. We assured the participants that there are no right or wrong answers to ensure that the participants honestly answered the questions. The respondents were asked to recall the situations from the first and second gameplay. We asked the participants to select the words or phrases that best associated to their experiences. The participants were asked to select more than one answer, and they were asked to fill out the answers for both Map1 and Map2, as shown in Table 2.

The FAIR model, a risk analysis model, was used in our study to compare the threat and risk between to the two different maps. The model is able to measure the risk by factoring in the probable frequency and probable magnitude of future loss. The FAIR model is dived into LEF and LM.

Using the Risk Management Model we proposed a risk management procedure that consists of a five-step process. The first step is 'determining the scope' of the risk management. Then the risk analysis is the next step, which consists of 'identification of the assets', 'asset value', 'vulnerability evaluation', 'threat evaluation'. The 'risk assessment' assess and quantifies the risk. The CPTED is finally applied as a control measure, as illustrated in Fig. 4.

Table 2. The respondents were asked to select multiple answers that best reflected their thoughts and emotions from their game play from Map1 and Map2.

Positive	Negative
Open environment	Closed environment
Entertaining	Lack of entertainment
Thrilling	Boring
Bright	Dark
High replay value	Quit
Simple	Complex
Focused	Unfocused
Like	Dislike
Prefer	Do not prefer
Satisfied	Unsatisfied

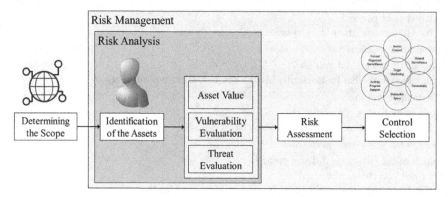

Fig. 4. The risk assessment proposed in this model of five steps: (i) determining the scope, (ii) identification of the assets, (iii) asset value, vulnerability evaluation, threat evaluation, (iv) risk assessment, and (v) control selection.

5 Result and Discussion

In our study, we consider the two principles, natural surveillance and access control, from CPTED. Map1 had a low exposure setting in comparison to Map2. By adjusting the brightness with the settings, we were able to apply natural surveillance to the Map2. As the brighter environment served as a natural surveillance to the participants. The fences that was installed within Map2 served as the access control, as shown in Fig. 3.

As mentioned in the previous section, we conducted a survey after the experiment. The participants consisted of 100 students who received graduate degrees or college degree. Over 28% of the respondents are female, and the 67.1% of the participants were in their 20s and 32.9% were in their 30. The first question in the survey inquired about the number of bullets the users have used.

Q3: How many bullets did you use in Map1?
Q5: How many bullets did you use in Map2?

Question 3, 5 were intended to measure the Threat Event Frequency (TEF). The item was designed to ask the users to identify how many bullets were shot. In our study, we divided the risks into five different levels: (i) Very High, (ii) High, (iii) Moderate, (iv) Low, and (v) Very Low. We based the five different levels on the number of bullets shots. When the number of bullets that were shot was greater or equal to 30, the participant's TEF was assigned a 'Very High' level. A 'High' level was assigned to the user when they shot less than 30 rounds of bullets, but greater or equal to 20. The 'Moderate' grade was assigned when the user fired less than 20 bullets, but fired greater or equal to 10 bullets. The 'Low' level was assigned to the users who shot less than 10 bullets, but shot greater or equal to 5 bullets. And the 'Very Low' grade was assigned to the users who had used less than 5 bullets.

Table 3. Threat Event Frequency was measured based on the number of bullets shot. A total of 50 rounds were assigned to each participants.

Threat Event Frequency (TEF)			
Criteria	Map1	Map2	Grade
$x \geq 30$ bullets per game			Very High (VH)
$20 \leq x < 30$ bullets per game			High (H)
$10 \leq x < 20$ bullets per game	V	V	Moderate (M)
$5 \leq x < 10$ bullets per game			Low (L)
$x < 5$ bullets per one game			Very Low (VL)

As illustrated through Table 2, we categorized the list of words that are associated positive and negative emotions. Each word was assigned a probability value that associated with either positive or negative values. Based on the words that the participant selected, we were able to calculate the value of the vulnerability (Vul), as shown in Table 4. In order to calculate the vulnerability, we assigned five different grade to the value: (i) Very High, (ii) High, (iii) Moderate, (iv) Low, and (v) Very Low.

Q4: Select the words that best describe Map1.
Q6: Select the words that best describe Map2.

Table 4. The vulnerability value for both Map1 and Map2.

Vulnerability (Vul)			
Criteria	Map1	Map2	Grade
$x < 30\%$	V		Very High (VH)
$30\% \leq x < 50\%$			High (H)
$50\% \leq x < 70\%$			Moderate (M)
$70\% \leq x < 90\%$		V	Low (L)
$90\% \leq x < 100\%$			Very Low (VL)

The results for the TEF from Map1 and Map2 were both assigned a 'Moderate' grade, as the participants fired less than 20 rounds of bullets and equal or greater than 10 bullets. The results of the two maps for the TEF is depicted in Table 3. On the other hand, the Vul for both Map1 and Map2 had very opposing results. The results from Map1 equates to 29% and the vulnerability value for Map2 was 70%. As such, Map1 was assigned a 'Very High' grade, while Map2 was assigned a 'Low' grade.

Based on the results from both the threat event frequency and vulnerability, we were able to calculate the risk. The participants assigned Map1 a 'Very High', however, Map2 had a very opposite grade by scoring a 'Low'. Based on the results we were able to ascertain that applying the CPTED method to the map provides a more positive ambiance to the overall gaming experience.

Based on the result of the TEF and Vul, we calculated the risks using a heat map both Map1 and Map2. The participants have assigned a 'Moderate' grade for the risk associated with Map1. Yet, Map2 scored a 'Low' as the environment reflected a more positive feeling towards the environment, as illustrated in Figs. 5 and 6.

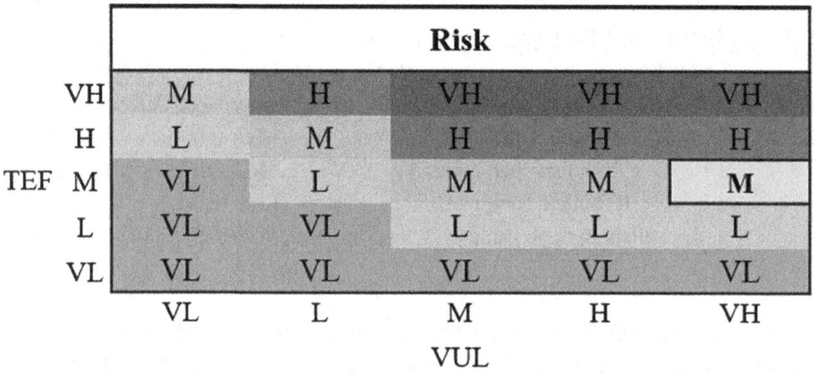

		Risk			
VH	M	H	VH	VH	VH
H	L	M	H	H	H
TEF M	VL	L	M	M	M
L	VL	VL	L	L	L
VL	VL	VL	VL	VL	VL
	VL	L	M	H	VH

VUL

Fig. 5. The heat map for Map1 was assigned a 'Moderate' grade based on the participants' response on the TEF and Vul.

		Risk			
VH	M	H	VH	VH	VH
H	L	M	H	H	H
TEF M	VL	L	M	M	M
L	VL	VL	L	L	L
VL	VL	VL	VL	VL	VL
	VL	L	M	H	VH

VUL

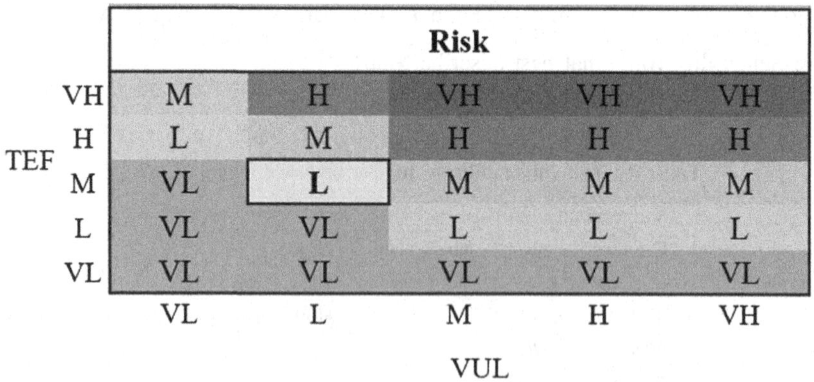

Fig. 6. The heat map for Map2 scored a 'Low' grade based on the participants' response on the TEF and Vul.

6 Conclusion

In recent years, many industries have been able to create virtual environments that can replicate environments that are similar to the reality [26]. It's also applied to the gaming industries. The environment has played a huge role in the user's gameplay with the technological advancements, as FPS have incorporated new formats to the game environment. However, academic literature on the security assessment for the environmental design in the virtual space is limited, as most of the studies have focused on how deterring criminal offences or reviewing the effectiveness of various security measures. Our study utilized the FAIR model to assess the risk and examines the environment with the virtual space by applying CPTED. We were able to introduce new obstacles and adjust the exposure and brightness within the environment, which helped us observe how the user's behavior changed when the natural surveillance and access control were applied.

Our study proposes a five-step risk management model that incorporates risk management and risk analysis. To the best of our knowledge, our paper is one of the first study to apply CPTED to a virtual environment. We believe our study was able to provide a better understanding and insight towards the FAIR model and CPTED.

References

1. Jason, M.B.: Fortnite drew imitators to survival games. Who will be the last one standing? New York Times 7 (2019)
2. Spelman, W.: Abandoned buildings: magnets for crime? J. Crim. Justice 21(5), 481–495 (1993)
3. Cui, L., Walsh, R.: Foreclosure, vacancy and crime. J. Urban Econ. 87, 72–84 (2015)
4. Villa, V., et al.: Towards dynamic risk analysis: a review of the risk assessment approach and its limitations in the chemical process industry. Saf. Sci. 89, 77–93 (2016)
5. NORSOK. Standard Z-013, Risk and Emergency Preparedness Analysis, 3rd edn. Standards Norway, Lysaker (2010)
6. Park, M., et al.: Situational awareness framework for threat intelligence measurement of android malware. JoWUA 9(3), 25–38 (2018)
7. Whitman, M.E., Mattord, H.J., Green, A.: Principles of Incident Response and Disaster Recovery. Cengage Learning, Boston (2013)
8. Moffatt, R.E.: Crime prevention through environmental design - a management perspective. Can. J. Criminol. 25, 19 (1983)
9. Sandhu, R.S., Samarati, P.: Access control: principle and practice. IEEE Commun. Mag. 32 (9), 40–48 (1994)
10. Brown, B.B., Bentley, D.L.: Residential burglars judge risk: the role of territoriality. J. Environ. Psychol. 13(1), 51–61 (1993)
11. Kelling, G.L., Coles, C.M.: Fixing Broken Windows: Restoring Order and Reducing Crime in Our Communities. Simon and Schuster, New York (1997)
12. Kim, D., Park, S.: Improving community street lighting using CPTED: a case study of three communities in Korea. Sustain. Cities Soc. 28, 233–241 (2017)
13. Hsu, S.H., Wen, M.-H., Wu, M.-C.: Exploring user experiences as predictors of MMORPG addiction. Comput. Educ. 53(3), 990–999 (2009)

14. Kang, A.R., et al.: I would not plant apple trees if the world will be wiped: analyzing hundreds of millions of behavioral records of players during an MMORPG beta test. In: Proceedings of the 26th International Conference on World Wide Web Companion. International World Wide Web Conferences Steering Committee (2017)

15. Kang, A.R., et al.: Rise and fall of online game groups: common findings on two different games. In: Proceedings of the 24th International Conference on World Wide Web. ACM (2015)

16. Chung, T., et al.: Unveiling group characteristics in online social games: a socio-economic analysis. In: Proceedings of the 23rd International Conference on World Wide Web. ACM (2014)

17. Qin, H., Rau, P.-L.P., Gao, S.-f.: The influence of social experience in online games. In: Jacko, J.A. (ed.) HCI 2011. LNCS, vol. 6764, pp. 688–693. Springer, Heidelberg (2011). https://doi.org/10.1007/978-3-642-21619-0_81

18. Gyarmati, L., Trinh, T.A.: Measuring user behavior in online social networks. IEEE Netw. **24**(5), 26–31 (2010)

19. Jacobs, J.: The Death and Life of Great American Cities - 1961. Vintage, New York (1992)

20. Jeffery, C.R.: Crime Prevention Through Environmental Design. Sage Publications, Beverly Hills (1977)

21. Desyllas, J., Connoly, P., Hebbert, F.: Modelling natural surveillance. Environ. Plan. **30**(5), 643–655 (2003)

22. Hee, L.J., Yook, L.J., Ryong, K.E., Gon, K.Y.: A study on the design of IoT-based CCTV using smarter devices. In: Proceedings of Symposium of the Korean Institute of Communications and Information Sciences, pp. 676–677. Korea Institute of Communication Sciences (2017)

23. Knez, I., Niedenthal, S.: Lighting in digital game worlds: effects on affect and play performance. Cyberpsychol. Behav. **11**(2), 129–137 (2008)

24. White, M.D., Klinger, D.: Contagious fire? An empirical assessment of the problem of multi-shooter, multi-shot deadly force incidents in police work. Crime Delinq. **58**(2), 196–221 (2012)

25. Michael, W.: Why did police officers fire 42 times to bring down a robbery suspect in queens? New York Times 2 (2019)

26. Chow, Y.-W., et al.: Video games and virtual reality as persuasive technologies for health care: an overview. JoWUA **8**(3), 18–35 (2017)

QR Code Watermarking for Digital Images

Yang-Wai Chow$^{(\boxtimes)}$, Willy Susilo, Joonsang Baek, and Jongkil Kim

Institute of Cybersecurity and Cryptology,
School of Computing and Information Technology, University of Wollongong,
Wollongong, Australia
{caseyc,wsusilo,baek,jongkil}@uow.edu.au

Abstract. With the growing use of online digital media, it is becoming increasingly challenging to protect copyright and intellectual property. Data hiding techniques like digital watermarking can be used to embed data within a signal for purposes such as digital rights management. This paper investigates a watermarking technique for digital images using QR codes. The advantage of using QR codes for watermarking is that properties of the QR code structure include error correction and high data capacity. This paper proposes a QR code watermarking technique, and examines its robustness and security against common digital image attacks.

Keywords: Data hiding · Discrete wavelet transform · Error correction · Images · QR code · Watermarking

1 Introduction

The extensive use, exchange and sharing of online digital media content has made the task of copyright and intellectual property protection increasingly challenging. Data hiding techniques like digital watermarking can be used for the purposes of digital rights management.

Digital watermarking is a widespread field that has been studied over many decades [4]. The idea behind watermarking is to embed additional data within a signal and be able to extract this data when required [5]. The embedding of additional data within the signal must be performed in a way that does not interfere with the normal usage of the signal. Furthermore, a successful watermark should be robust against signal alteration, up to a point at which the signal is damaged and loses its commercial value [13]. In light of this, there are four key properties that affect any watermarking system; namely, invisibility, capacity, robustness and security [4,12].

This paper investigates a QR code watermarking technique for digital images. The purpose of this approach is to capitalize on the inherent error correction properties of the QR code structure, along with its high data capacity. The QR code error correction mechanism allows a QR code to be correctly decoded

© Springer Nature Switzerland AG 2020
I. You (Ed.): WISA 2019, LNCS 11897, pp. 25–37, 2020.
https://doi.org/10.1007/978-3-030-39303-8_3

despite the presence of slight errors in the QR code, as long as the error does not exceed its error correction capacity. As such, by embedding a QR code as a watermark within a digital image, the watermark can potentially withstand distortions to the signal, provided the QR code can be reconstructed via the watermark extraction process.

There are two primary methods for embedding watermark data within digital images in an imperceptible manner. This can be done via the spatial domain or the frequency domain. There are a number of advantages of modifying coefficients in the frequency domain, for example, it incorporates features of the human visual system more effectively, it provides the ability to spread the embedded signal in the frequency domain, and it operates in the compressed domain which is also used by most compression standards [6]. Therefore, to make the watermark imperceptible, the proposed approach uses the Discrete Wavelet Transform (DWT) technique.

The aim of the proposed QR code watermarking approach, is to embed a QR code symbol within one of the DWT sub-bands of a digital image. Within the frequency domain, the strength of the embedded watermark can be adjusted based on the desired tradeoff between imperceptibility and robustness. This paper presents the proposed technique and examines its features with respect to the key watermarking properties. In addition, the paper demonstrates the robustness and security of the proposed QR code watermarking technique against common digital image attacks, like image compression, noise, cropping, sharpening and blurring, that may be carried out by an adversary.

2   Background and Related Work

2.1   The QR Code

A QR code symbol consists of a 2D array of light and dark squares, known as modules [7]. The QR code structure contains modules for encoding data and for function patterns. Function patterns consist of finder patterns, separators, timing patterns and alignment patterns. For example, there are three identical finder patterns located at the upper left and right, and lower left corner of the symbol. The finder patterns are for a QR code reader to recognize a QR code symbol and to determine its orientation.

In addition, the QR code structure has an inherent error correction mechanism that allows data to be recovered even if a certain number of modules have been corrupted. The data capacity of a QR code depends on its version and error correction level. There are forty different QR code versions and four error correction levels; namely, L (low), M (medium), Q (quartile) and H (high), which correspond to error tolerances of approximately 7%, 15%, 25% and 30% respectively.

2.2   Discrete Wavelet Transform (DWT)

The Discrete Wavelet Transform (DWT) is a technique that is widely used in image and signal processing. For digital images, the DWT technique involves the

Fig. 1. DWT at level 3.

decomposition of an image into frequency channels of constant bandwidth on a logarithmic scale [9,11].

When applying the DWT technique to a 2D image, the image is decomposed into four sub-bands, which are denoted as LL (low-low), LH (low-high), HL (high-low) and HH (high-high). Each sub-band in turn can be further decomposed at the next level, and this process can continue until the desired number of levels is achieved. In view of the fact that the human visual system is more sensitive to the LL sub-band (i.e. the low frequency component), to maintain image quality watermark information is typically embedded within one or more of the other three sub-bands [9]. Figure 1 gives a depiction how the DWT can decompose an image into sub-bands at 3 levels. For experiments in this paper, the watermark was embedded within the HH_3 sub-band.

2.3 Arnold Transform

The Arnold transform is a invertible transform that can be used for scrambling the pixels in a digital image. The transform scrambles the pixels within an image to disrupt the correlation between adjacent pixels. As such, the Arnold transform is commonly used as part of many watermarking schemes, as it distributes the pixels over the entire image [8]. The reason for doing this is so that any error introduced by distorting a watermarked image will be scattered over the image, and the watermark can still potentially be recovered despite the error.

2.4 Related Work

There have been a variety of different uses of QR codes in the area of computer security. In previous work, Chow et al. [3] proposed the use of QR codes for watermarking using two techniques in the frequency domain. Their proposed approach combined the use of the DWT with the Discrete Cosine Transform (DCT) for QR code watermarking. In other work on QR code watermarking, an authentication method for medical images using a QR code based zero watermarking scheme was proposed [14]. In the scheme, a patient's identification details and a link their data was encoded in the form of a QR code which served as the watermark.

Kang et al. [8] proposed a watermarking approach based on the combination of DCT, QR codes and chaotic theory. In their approach, a QR code image is encrypted with a chaotic system to enhance the security of the watermark, and embedded within DCT blocks after undergoing block based scrambling. In related work, a digital rights management method for protecting documents by repeatedly inserting a QR code into the DWT sub-band of a document was investigated [1]. Others have also proposed different QR code watermarking approaches, for example, by incorporating an attack detection feature to detect malicious interference by an attacker [15], or by embedding QR code watermarks using a just noticeable difference model to increase imperceptibility [10].

In related work on QR codes for security, Tkachenko et al. [16] described a modified QR code that could contain two storage levels. They called this a two-level QR code, as it had a public and a private storage level. The purpose of the two-level QR code was for document authentication. In addition, QR codes have also been used for secret sharing [2]. In this work, a method of distributing shares by embedding them into cover QR codes was proposed. These QR codes contained both public and private information, which allowed for the shares to be transmitted over public channels. The public information in the QR codes could be access by anyone, whereas only authorized individuals would be able to obtain the private information.

3   QR Code Watermarking

The aim of the QR code watermarking technique proposed in this paper is to embed a QR code watermark within a cover image, and to be able to extract the watermark. Figure 2 depicts the processes involved in the embedding and extraction processes. Details of the processes will be described in the respective subsections to follow.

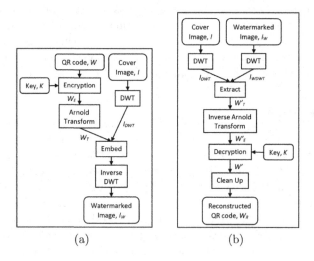

Fig. 2. Overview of the QR code watermarking processes; (a) embedding process; (b) extraction process.

3.1 Embedding Process

An overview of the embedding process is shown in Fig. 2(a). It can be seen from the figure that the embedding process accepts three inputs; a QR code, W, which is the watermark image; a key, K, for encryption; and a cover image, I. The output of the embedding process is a watermarked image, I_W.

It should be noted that K is a random bit string, which is used to encrypt and decrypt the watermark. The purpose of doing this is to ensure that even if an adversary can extract W, the adversary will not be able to obtain information about the contents of the watermark. The bits in K are to be XORed with the light and dark modules of W. As such, the length of the bit string must match the number of modules in W.

For the experiments in this paper, I was converted to DWT level 3 and the encrypted and scrambled watermark, W_T, was embedded within the HH_3 sub-band. The purpose of embedding information within the HH sub-band is due to the fact the human visual system is less sensitive to perturbations in this sub-band. The DWT coefficients C were modified based on Eq. 1 for the x and y pixels in W_T, where $W_{T,(x,y)} \in \pm 1$. The λ parameter can be adjusted to balance between watermark imperceptibility and robustness.

$$C'_{(x,y)} = C_{(x,y)} + \lambda W_{T,(x,y)} |C_{(x,y)}| \tag{1}$$

Prior to embedding the watermark, bits in the encrypted watermark were scrambled using Arnold transform. The reason for this is to distribute the watermark data over the entire image. In practice, this effectively reduces localized errors in the extracted watermark, which may result from distortions to I_W by an adversary. Algorithm 1 provides details of the steps involved in the embedding process.

Algorithm 1. Embedding algorithm

Input: A QR code, W, a cover image, I, and a key, K.
Output: A watermarked image, I_W

Step 1. Encrypt information in W by XORing the random bits in K with the modules in W to produce W_E.
Step 2. Generate a chaotic image W_T by scrambling the bits of the encrypted watermark W_E using Arnold transform over a number of iterations.
Step 3. Convert I to I_{DWT} by performing DWT to the desired level.
Step 4. Embed W_T in a I_{DWT} sub-band.
Step 5. Generate the watermarked image I_W by inversing DWT.

3.2 Extraction Process

Figure 2(b) provides an overview of the extraction process, which is very much the reverse of the embedding process. To extract the watermark image, the extraction algorithm requires the original cover image, I; the watermarked image, I_W; and the key, K, for decryption. The output of the algorithm is the reconstructed watermark, i.e. a reconstructed QR code, W_R.

Algorithm 2. Extraction algorithm

Input: The original cover image, I, the watermarked image, I_W, and the key, K.
Output: A reconstructed QR code, W_R

Step 1. Convert I to I_{DWT}, and I_W to $I_{W\,DWT}$, by performing DWT on the cover image and watermarked image respectively.
Step 2. Extract W_T' from differences in the specific sub-band (HH_3 in the experiments) of I_{DWT} and $I_{W\,DWT}$.
Step 3. Generate W_E' by inversing the Arnold transform.
Step 4. Decrypt W_E' using K to produce the extracted watermark image W'.
Step 5. Clean-up the W' and restore the QR code function patterns to produce W_R.

It should be noted that if I_W was distorted from attacks by an adversary, W' will result in a noisy image. Hence, a clean-up stage is required to restore the QR code. This is possible as long as information about the QR code is known; namely, the QR code version, error correction level, masking pattern and number of pixels per module. With this information, restoring the modules involves counting the total number of black and white bits for every module in W'. If there are more white bits, set the module color to white, and vice versa. Also, to ensure that the QR code is decodable, restore the QR code function patterns which may have been corrupted to produce the reconstructed QR code, W_R.

Any QR code reader should be able to decode W_R, as long as the error in W_R is below the error correction threshold of the QR code. Note that it is possible to only embed the data modules of W in I_W, since the function patterns are restored during the clean-up stage. However, in our experiments, we chose to embed the entire QR code because it provides information on the amount of noise in W', which results from distortions made to I_W. The steps involved in the extraction algorithm are provided in Algorithm 2.

4   Results and Discussion

This section presents results of experiments conducted to evaluate the proposed QR code watermarking technique. The experiments were performed using the OpenCV library on three well-known test images; namely, the Lena, Peppers and Mandrill images. These images can be seen in the tables of results shown in Tables 1, 2, and 3 respectively.

The images were all 512×512 in dimension. A QR code version 1 with error correction level H was used in the experiments. This QR code version is made up of 21×21 modules. Since the HH_3 sub-band of a 512×512 image has a 64 $\times$ 64 resolution, we converted each module in the QR code to consist of 3×3 pixels, resulting in a total QR code size of 63×63 pixels.

4.1 Imperceptibility and Capacity

Imperceptibility is the property whereby a human cannot perceive the difference between the original and watermarked signal. The Peak Signal-to-Noise Ratio (PSNR) metric was used as a measure of image quality and to indicate the perceptibility of distortions resulting from embedding a watermark within a cover image. Figure 3 shows a plot of the PSNR values for the test images that were obtained by varying the value of λ. Greater PSNR values indicate less difference between I and I_W. At low λ values, the human visual system is less sensitive to distortions cause by embedding the watermark. However, increasing the value of λ increases the distortion in the resulting image. When the distortion is clearly visible in I_W, the image looses its commercial value and usefulness.

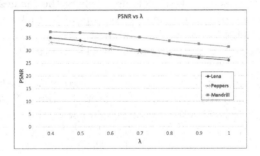

Fig. 3. PSNR values.

Capacity, or payload, is the amount of data that can be embedded by a watermarking scheme. The data capacity of the proposed watermarking technique is based on the capacity of the QR code version and error correction level of W. For a given QR code version, the higher the error correction level, the lower the data capacity, but the more robust the resulting watermark will be to errors. Hence, there is a tradeoff between data capacity and watermark robustness.

In addition, the size of W, is also governed by the size of I, since the watermark is to be embedded within a DWT sub-band of I. The higher the number of module in W, the more data the QR code can encode. However, this also means that for the watermark to be able to fit within a DWT sub-band, less pixels may have to be used to encode each module. The lower the number of pixels per module, the less robustness the watermark, because there is a higher potential for the pixels per module to the corrupted.

4.2 Robustness and Security

Robustness and security refer to a watermarking scheme's ability to withstand distortions to the watermarked signal. In the case of security, these distortions are intentional attacks by an adversary to impair the watermark [4,12]. The robustness and security of the proposed technique was examined by applying various attacks to the watermarked images; namely, JPEG compression, sharpening, blurring, salt-and-pepper noise, and cropping. These are common attacks that are typically used to evaluate watermarking techniques.

For the JPEG compression attack, the images was compressed to 50% quality using the OpenCV library. For the sharpening and blurring attacks, basic 3×3 convolution filters were used. The weights in sharpening filter were $\begin{bmatrix} 0 & -1 & 0 \\ -1 & 5 & -1 \\ 0 & -1 & 0 \end{bmatrix}$ and for blurring, a median filter $\begin{bmatrix} \frac{1}{9} & \frac{1}{9} & \frac{1}{9} \\ \frac{1}{9} & \frac{1}{9} & \frac{1}{9} \\ \frac{1}{9} & \frac{1}{9} & \frac{1}{9} \end{bmatrix}$ was used. For the salt-and-pepper noise attack, 1% of the pixels in the images were randomly overwritten with black or white pixels. Two cropping attacks were used, in the first, the image center was removed, while in the second attack, the corners of the image were removed. In both cropping attacks, a total of 25% of the images was removed.

To evaluate the amount of error in the extracted watermark and the reconstructed QR code, the Bit Error Rate (BER) and Module Error Rate (MER) metrics were used. The BER refers to the percentage of bits that were in error in the extracted watermark, W', whereas the MER is the percentage of incorrect QR code modules in the reconstructed QR code, W_R.

Tables 1, 2, and 3 demonstrate results of the various attacks on the respective test images. The results shown the tables, were obtained using $\lambda = 0.6$. For each test image and attack, the tables show the extracted watermark image and the BER, as well as the reconstructed QR code and the MER. As described in Sect. 3.2, the reconstructed QR code, W_R, was obtained after cleaning up the noise in W'. In addition, grey modules in the reconstructed QR code depict the modules that were incorrectly recovered. It should be noted that the error contained in all the reconstructed QR codes were within the error correction capacity, and thus, the reconstructed QR codes could correctly be decoded.

Table 1. Results on Lena.

Attack	Attacked Image	Extracted Watermark, W'	BER	Reconstructed QR Code, W_R	MER
Compression			21.10%		5.77%
Sharpening			16.61%		2.40%
Blurring			20.62%		4.33%
Noise			19.07%		3.85%
Cropping 1			17.74%		0.96%
Cropping 2			16.03%		1.44%

Table 2. Results on Peppers.

Attack	Attacked Image	Extracted Watermark, W'	BER	Reconstructed QR Code, W_R	MER
Compression			22.0%		4.81%
Sharpening			17.79%		5.29%
Blurring			24.04%		8.65%
Noise			19.18%		3.85%
Cropping 1			15.38%		1.44%
Cropping 2			15.92%		0.0%

Table 3. Results on Mandrill.

Attack	Attacked Image	Extracted Watermark, W'	BER	Reconstructed QR Code, W_R	MER
Compression			9.24%		0.0%
Sharpening			18.48%		3.85%
Blurring			21.31%		3.85%
Noise			12.44%		0.96%
Cropping 1			13.78%		0.0%
Cropping 2			14.0%		0.48%

5   Conclusion

This paper presents a QR code watermarking technique for digital images. The objective of the proposed watermarking technique is to embed a QR code within a cover image in an imperceptible manner. This was achieved by embedding a QR code within one the cover image's DWT sub-bands. The reason for using a QR code as a watermark is because the QR code structure incorporates an error correction mechanism that allows it to be correctly decoded even if it contains some error. In this paper, we discussed the properties of the proposed watermarking technique and demonstrated its robustness against common attacks that may be conducted by an adversary.

References

1. Cardamone, N., d'Amore, F.: DWT and QR code based watermarking for document DRM. In: Yoo, C.D., Shi, Y.-Q., Kim, H.J., Piva, A., Kim, G. (eds.) IWDW 2018. LNCS, vol. 11378, pp. 137–150. Springer, Cham (2019). https://doi.org/10.1007/978-3-030-11389-6_11
2. Chow, Y., Susilo, W., Tonien, J., Vlahu-Gjorgievska, E., Yang, G.: Cooperative secret sharing using QR codes and symmetric keys. Symmetry 10(4), 95 (2018). https://doi.org/10.3390/sym10040095
3. Chow, Y.-W., Susilo, W., Tonien, J., Zong, W.: A QR code watermarking approach based on the DWT-DCT technique. In: Pieprzyk, J., Suriadi, S. (eds.) ACISP 2017. LNCS, vol. 10343, pp. 314–331. Springer, Cham (2017). https://doi.org/10.1007/978-3-319-59870-3_18
4. Cox, I.J., Miller, M.L.: The first 50 years of electronic watermarking. EURASIP J. Adv. Signal Process. 2002(2), 820936 (2002). https://doi.org/10.1155/S1110865702000525
5. Hartung, F., Kutter, M.: Multimedia watermarking techniques. Proc. IEEE 87(7), 1079–1107 (1999). https://doi.org/10.1109/5.771066
6. Huang, J., Shi, Y.Q., Shi, Y.: Embedding image watermarks in DC components. IEEE Trans. Circuits Syst. Video Technol. 10(6), 974–979 (2000). https://doi.org/10.1109/76.867936
7. International Organization for Standardization: Information technology—automatic identification and data capture techniques—QR Code 2005 bar code symbology specification. ISO/IEC 18004:2006 (2006)
8. Kang, Q., Li, K., Yang, J.: A digital watermarking approach based on DCT domain combining QR code and chaotic theory. In: 2014 Eleventh International Conference on Wireless and Optical Communications Networks (WOCN), pp. 1–7, September 2014. https://doi.org/10.1109/WOCN.2014.6923098
9. Lai, C.C., Tsai, C.C.: Digital image watermarking using discrete wavelet transform and singular value decomposition. IEEE Trans. Instrum. Meas. 59(11), 3060–3063 (2010). https://doi.org/10.1109/TIM.2010.2066770
10. Lee, H.C., Dong, C.R., Lin, T.M.: Digital watermarking based on JND model and QR code features. In: Pan, J.S., Yang, C.N., Lin, C.C. (eds.) Advances in Intelligent Systems and Applications. Smart Innovation, Systems and Technologies, vol. 21, pp. 141–148. Springer, Heidelberg (2013). https://doi.org/10.1007/978-3-642-35473-1_15

11. Mallat, S.: A theory for multiresolution signal decomposition: the wavelet representation. IEEE Trans. Pattern Anal. Mach. Intell. **11**(7), 674–693 (1989). https://doi.org/10.1109/34.192463

12. Panah, A.S., Schyndel, R.V., Sellis, T., Bertino, E.: On the properties of non-media digital watermarking: a review of state of the art techniques. IEEE Access **4**, 2670–2704 (2016). https://doi.org/10.1109/ACCESS.2016.2570812

13. Podilchuk, C.I., Delp, E.J.: Digital watermarking: algorithms and applications. IEEE Signal Process. Mag. **18**(4), 33–46 (2001). https://doi.org/10.1109/79.939835

14. Seenivasagam, V., Velumani, R.: A QR code based zero-watermarking scheme for authentication of medical images in teleradiology cloud. Comput. Math. Methods Med. **2013**(516465), 16 (2013). https://doi.org/10.1155/2013/516465

15. Thulasidharan, P.P., Nair, M.S.: QR code based blind digital image watermarking with attack detection code. AEU Int. J. Electron. Commun. **69**(7), 1074–1084 (2015). https://doi.org/10.1016/j.aeue.2015.03.007. http://www.sciencedirect.com/science/article/pii/S1434841115001004

16. Tkachenko, I., Puech, W., Destruel, C., Strauss, O., Gaudin, J., Guichard, C.: Two-level QR code for private message sharing and document authentication. IEEE Trans. Inf. Forensics Secur. **11**(3), 571–583 (2016). https://doi.org/10.1109/TIFS.2015.2506546

Network Security and Blockchain

FSF: Code Coverage-Driven Fuzzing for Software-Defined Networking

Hyuntae Kim, Seongil Wi, Hyunjoo Lee, and Sooel Son[(✉)]

KAIST, Daejeon, Korea
{kimht_,seongil.wi,sn220865,sl.son}@kaist.ac.kr

Abstract. A Software-Defined Networking (SDN) controller plays a key role for assuring the security and robustness of its underlying network system. Previous studies focus on eliciting bugs in such SDN controller via penetration testing or fuzzing without considering code coverage feedback from a target controller under testing. We propose FSF, a code coverage-driven SDN fuzzer. We designed and implemented a fuzzing algorithm to take into account coverage differences incurred by mutated OpenFlow (OF) messages. FSF demonstrated its superiority in increasing the code coverage of a target controller and generated unique 146 tests that trigger bugs in the latest version of Floodlight, a well-known open-source SDN controller.

1 Introduction

Recent years have seen a surging interest in *software-defined networking (SDN)*. SDN is an innovative methodology to build a networking system wherein network controlling attributes are abstracted by software referred to as an SDN controller. SDN has been applied in diverse fields, such as cellular networks [4,31], IoT [11, 23], and broadband access [6,29] infrastructures, offering its own benefits for large enterprises and telecommunication networks.

Meanwhile, the growing popularity of adopting SDN calls into question the security of SDN systems. Yoon *et al.* pointed out that emerging SDN stacks have introduced new attack vectors due to their design decisions on facilitating dynamic network flows and topology managements [32]. Previous studies also introduced SDN security challenges [18,26] and manifested concrete attack scenarios [5].

Security researchers have conducted fuzzing and penetration testing to automatically gauge the security of off-the-shelf and open-source SDN systems [9,15,20,30]. Notably, DELTA [20] and BEADS [15] conducted fuzz testing by randomly mutating seed traffic, which are generated by executing the pingall and iperf commands from hosts. However, these approaches did not leverage any feedback information from a controller under testing, thereby solely depending on the input and output behaviors of the controller. They generated tens of thousands of testing strategies, i.e., test cases, which were chosen at the discretion of the testing analyst without any runtime feedback from a controller.

© Springer Nature Switzerland AG 2020
I. You (Ed.): WISA 2019, LNCS 11897, pp. 41–54, 2020.
https://doi.org/10.1007/978-3-030-39303-8_4

Consequently, the generated test cases do not trigger diverse inherent behaviors of the controller.

In this paper, we design and implement FSF, the first *code coverage-driven SDN fuzzer*. FSF is designed to find bugs in a target SDN system by feeding unexpected test inputs to the south bound communication channels between an SDN controller and SDN switches. The crux of our approach is to leverage the code coverage information obtained from an SDN controller to guide the test case generation.

We evaluated FSF using Floodlight, a popular open-source SDN controller, to vet its capabilities of increasing testing code coverage and discovering SDN controller bugs. FSF outperformed DELTA, a previous state-of-the-art SDN fuzzing tool, in covering code coverage and produced discovered 146 of unique test inputs that trigger bugs residing in the controller.

Our main contributions are as follows.

1. We present a novel code coverage-driven fuzz testing algorithm tailored for testing an SDN system. The proposed technique leverages the coverage information from a controller to evolve test cases during a fuzzing campaign.
2. We implement the proposed algorithm in our prototype and evaluate it on the latest version of Floodlight. FSF produced unique 146 tests that trigger critical bugs, which affect the daily operations of an entire SDN system. To the best of our knowledge, our tool is the first feedback-driven SDN fuzzer.

2   Background and Motivation

Software-Defined Networking. A network system consists of two main planes: a data plane that forwards network packets between routers, and a control plane that computes network paths that forward packets. In traditional networks, the data plane and the control plane tightly coupled within a single device, which makes it hard to insert new functionalities or updates forwarding rules into the device. SDN has emerged to overcome this problem. It conceptually separates the control plane from the data plane, and they communicate with a protocol called OpenFlow [3] to exchange the routing information. Changing the flow table with a logically centralized controller is straightforward, thus easing the management of a network system.

SDN Fuzz Testing. *Fuzzing* or *fuzz testing* is a software testing technique that detects software security vulnerabilities and was first used by Miller in the early 1990s [22]. Fuzzing feeds adversarial inputs to a program under test and monitors resulting crashes [7,13,27,28,33].

Many studies have applied SDN fuzzing to enhance the security of SDN systems [9,15,20,30]. SDN fuzzing differs from general fuzz testing schemes. Due to the intrinsic nature of a SDN system that consists of diverse architectural components and their complicated interconnections, the following questions should be addressed when designing a fuzzing algorithm: (1) which components provide an input (*testing source*)? (2) which components take this input (*testing target*)? (3) which bugs or threats the algorithm find (*detection criteria*)?

DELTA [20], for example, implements a black box fuzzing technique that tests an entire SDN system (testing target) consisting of SDN applications, control channels, and hosts (testing source). In particular, their testing source mutates SDN control flow sequences and input values of the control flow. It employs seven detection criteria, including controller crash and switch-performance degradation. Another SDN fuzzer is BEADS [15]. BEADS drops, duplicates, delays, and changes OpenFlow packets from malicious switches and injects ARP packets from malicious hosts to test the controller. They validate OpenFlow error messages, network state, pair-wise connectivity, controller resource usage, and switches based on the detection criteria.

Limitations of Previous SDN Fuzzers. Previous fuzzers expose some of the erroneous behaviors of the SDN system, but their approaches have the limitation of only observing the input and output behaviors of the controller as a black box. They limit the mutations of the input data without runtime feedback or controller internal information (e.g., code coverage) that can evolve test inputs to trigger unexpected behaviors. In fact, none of the previous SDN testing methods has applied this feedback information to the mutations. Thus, the generated test input often fails to cover the diverse operations of an SDN controller. For example, to modify an ongoing OpenFlow message, BEADS uses the following strategy; modifies a *specific field* of a *specific type* of a OpenFlow message to a *specific value*. Since there is no automatic guidance or feedback to systematically select these values (field, type, modification values), they blindly select values that are likely to trigger inherent bugs. As a result, their approaches are not general to elicit diverse unexpected SDN controller behaviors.

3   Threat Model

In this paper, we assume a *southbound interface (SBI) attacker*. An SBI is an interface between an SDN controller and its connected switches. An SBI attacker is capable of compromising a switch or performing a man-in-the-middle attack that feeds malicious OpenFlow messages to the controller on the SBI. Several previous studies have shown the feasibility of compromising practical SDN switches by exploiting network operating systems using outdated software [24,25]. Once an attacker compromises a switch, she is able to generate an arbitrary Open-Flow message as controller input. It is also feasible for an SBI attacker to perform an MITM attack by exploiting the communication channel between the control plane and the data plane. The OpenFlow specification [3] recommends the use of SSL/TLS protection to protect OpenFlow messages. However, many existing controllers are packaged with the default setting that disables the SSL/TLS support to ease the initial deployment. Furthermore, the protection is frequently disabled due to its noticeable performance degradation [5,10].

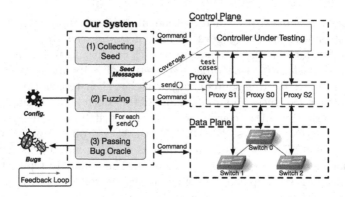

Fig. 1. FSF architecture.

4   Design

This section provides an overview of FSF and then describes each procedure for leveraging the coverage feedback from an SDN controller under testing, which makes FSF distinctive from other fuzzing tools, including DELTA and BEADS.

4.1   Overview

Figure 1 depicts the overall architecture of FSF. At a high level, it takes a set of user-configurable parameters. FSF then initiates a fuzz testing campaign. Once the campaign is completed, FSF reports a set of discovered bugs. FSF conducts a fuzz testing campaign in tandem with an SDN testing environment. The testing environment consists of a controller under testing, a set of SDN switches (data plane), and proxies that connect between the switches and their controller. FSF orchestrates these testing components to conduct a coverage-driven fuzzing testing campaign.

Testing Infrastructure. We implemented a *proxy* for each channel between the controller and its connected switches. Thus, each of these proxies is able to model the capability of an SBI attacker (Sect. 3).

A proxy has two roles: (1) forwarding benign OpenFlow messages, and (2) sending manipulated OpenFlow messages to a controller. The first role is required to maintain the continuous connections between the controller and its switches, which is an intrinsic characteristic of an SDN system. The proxy simply forwards incoming OpenFlow messages to avoid tampering with any ongoing transactions originating from benign switches. The second role models the capability of an SBI attacker. In the proxy, FSF mutates OpenFlow messages according to a given mutation policy and then sends these messages to elicit erroneous behaviors in the controller. The user-provided configuration parameters govern the distinction between benign and malicious switches. For instance, when Switch 1 in Fig. 1 is configured as a malicious switch, its corresponding Proxy 1 feeds diverse tests to elicit malicious behaviors in the controller.

Testing Procedure. Given a configuration file, FSF conducts three phases. Phase I collects seed messages by monitoring ongoing messages or by generating arbitrary OpenFlow messages (Sect. 4.2). Based on the collected seed messages, Phase II conducts a fuzzing campaign (Sect. 4.3). Specifically, it splits seed messages into several message sets, where the length of each is governed by a given configuration parameter. For each message set, FSF randomly mutates those messages in the set and feeds the mutated set to the controller. It then obtains the instruction coverage of the controller and leverages the feedback for subsequent fuzzing iterations. Phase III determines whether each mutated message set triggers bugs residing in the controller, thus serving as a bug oracle (Sect. 4.4).

4.2 Collecting Seed Messages

FSF begins a fuzzing campaign by collecting seed messages, which are observed from configured proxies. Because our testing target is an SDN controller, we only consider OpenFlow messages from a malicious switch to the controller. To diversify seed messages, we first identified what types of OpenFlow messages belong to switch-to-controller flows. According to the OpenFlow v1.3 specification [3], of 30 message types, 15 types are switch-to-controller OpenFlow messages. Note that DELTA [20] and BEADS [15] only covered six message types out of these 15 types (40%), which the `pingall` and `iperf` commands are able to trigger.

FSF considers all the 15 types of switch-to-controller messages. This means that FSF covers more diverse code spots in a target controller, thereby increasing the possibility of eliciting unexpected behaviors. We collect seed messages through three methods: (1) capturing packets in the stand-by state; (2) capturing packets after executing pre-defined commands to the control plane or data plane; and (3) generating packets according to the OpenFlow grammar specification.

Stand-By State. A proxy gathers seed messages by capturing network packets when a controller is in the stand-by state, awaiting incoming OpenFlow messages. In this state, the controller is involved only in (1) handshaking procedures that establish connections between the controller and its switches and in (2) checking the stability of established connections.

Commands Sent to the Control or Data Plane. To collect diverse seed messages, FSF lets the controller and its switches execute pre-defined commands. It then captures the packets caused by the exercised commands. FSF sends commands to the controller via its REST API. For instance, FSF inserts a flow rule to a switch and then removes it to generate `FLOW_REMOVED` messages. It also performs commands to the data plane using switch command-line interface (CLI) or host CLI. For instance, FSF asks a switch to disconnect a connection and reconnect it on a specific switch port to capture a `PORT_STATUS` message.

Generating Packets. The aforementioned methods are unable to cover the remaining four types. For these messages, FSF generates random messages according to the OpenFlow v1.3 specification [3]. When generating these messages, FSF identifies data fields to fill as well as their constraints and then assigns random values to generate seed messages.

Algorithm 1. Feedback-driven SDN Fuzzing Algorithm.

```
 1  function Fuzzing(conf, seed_msgs, controller, proxy, switch)
 2      cov_base ← ResetComponent(controller, proxy, switch)
 3      for i ← 0 to conf.size_q do
 4          subset ← RandomSample(seed_msgs, conf.size_s)
 5          Q.enqueue(subset, 0)
 6      while Q ≠ ∅ do
 7          subset, counter ← Q.dequeue()
 8          test_cases ← MutateSubset(subset)
 9          proxy.send(test_cases)
10          unseen_msgs ← GetUnseenMsgs()
11          found_bug, cov ← Evaluate(controller, proxy, switch)
12          bugs.append(found_bug)
13          if cov_base < cov then
14              mutated_m, non_mutated_m ← SplitMsgs(test_cases)
15              Q.enqueue(mutated_m.append(unseen_msgs, conf.size_s),0)
16              Q.enqueue(non_mutated_m.append(unseen_msgs, conf.size_s),0)
17              cov_base ← cov
18          else if counter < conf.threshold_c then
19              Q.enqueue(subset, counter + 1)
20      return bugs
```

4.3 Coverage-Driven SDN Fuzzing

Given a set of seed messages, FSF performs code coverage-driven fuzz testing by leveraging the coverage feedback from a target SDN controller. Algorithm 1 describes the overall fuzzing procedure. The underlying idea is to discard messages that caused no increase of code coverage and to give more chances to messages that already increased code coverage. Our assumption is that a message that helped increase code coverage is likely to be a good seed for further mutations, increasing code coverage.

The algorithm starts with a configuration file (*conf*), seed messages (*seed_msgs*), and instances of a controller, proxies, and switches.

FSF begins by resetting all the components in a testing environment and computing the baseline code coverage of the *controller* in Ln 2. Lns 4–5 initialize a test queue Q by assigning multiple input subsets, each of which contains randomly sampled messages from *seed_msgs*. Ln 5 enqueues each subset with its counter value, which is later used for discarding subsets tested multiple times. The size of Q and *subset* is configurable by setting $conf.size_s$ and $conf.size_q$.

For each iteration, FSF mutates a message subset dequeued from Q, sends the mutated messages in this subset, and evolves the message set by leveraging the feedback of a code coverage difference from the target controller, as Lns 6–19 show. The MutateSubset function in Ln 8 mutates randomly chosen messages in the subset. There are various ways to mutate messages such as flipping multiple bytes or inserting dummy bytes but, based on the results of our empirical study (Sect. 5.1), we selected the flipping multiple bits operation. Ln 9 sends messages in *test_cases* to the controller one by one. Note that there exist certain messages that require the precedence of a request from the controller (e.g., MULTIPART_REPLY). To address this, FSF invokes a REST API to incur the corresponding request (e.g., MULTIPART_REQUEST) from the SDN controller before sending a response message from the proxy as its replying message.

The GetUnseenMsgs function in Ln 10 collects previously unobserved messages. The unseen messages are switch-to-controller messages that occur after performing Ln 9. Their contents are unique so that FSF has not observed beforehand. Adding unseen messages to test cases improves the diversity of seed messages on which the mutations are performed. Therefore, we put these unseen messages in the queue later in Lns 15 and 16. Ln 11 performs an evaluation to determine whether bugs are triggered through the implemented bug oracle (Sect. 4.4) and to measure the cumulative code coverage in the controller.

If the mutated *test_cases* successfully hits new code space in the controller, FSF enqueues it to Q (Ln 13–17). As *test_cases* consists of mutated and non-mutated messages, FSF splits them by invoking the SplitMsgs function in Ln 14. Ln 15 enqueues the purely mutated messages (*mutated_m*) to Q. Because the size of the *mutated_m* is smaller than the $conf.size_s$, the number of ($conf.size_s$-$len(mutated\_m)$) of *unseen_msgs* is randomly selected and appended to *mutate_m*. The same process is used to enqueue non-mutated messages (*non_mutated_m*) because there is a chance that they contribute to increasing the code coverage when they are mutated later (Ln 16). We designed the algorithm to refine messages by separating mutated messages from non-mutated messages since non-mutated messages were already tried in previous iterations. Thus, we create a new message set by adding several unseen messages to mutated messages, which help the odd of increasing code coverage. At the same time, it gives another chance to non-mutated messages by creating a new message set with additional unseen messages.

If the *test_cases* does not touch any new code spots, FSF does not discard it immediately. We give it more chances to be used in further testing by putting them to Q with an increased counter, as shown in Ln 19. The value of the counter threshold $conf.size_s$ is also determined by a given configuration file.

4.4 Bug Oracle

The bug oracle determines whether test inputs trigger bugs or not by monitoring the components of the testing environment. We describe four standards to implement a bug oracle.

Controller Process Termination. FSF checks whether the controller process has terminated or crashed. In SDN, because multiple switches are continuously connected to an SDN controller, the controller's abrupt termination causes a denial of service for the entire SDN network.

Control Plane Resource Exhaustion. FSF also checks whether the CPU usage of the control plane process suddenly surges after sending testing messages. The abrupt increased usage when compared to a benign baseline indicates an opportunity for a denial of service, which impairs the controller's ability to deal with OpenFlow messages. Therefore, a bug that exhausts the CPU usage of the control plane can drop the QoS of the entire network.

Benign Switch Disconnection. We consider whether a benign switch is disconnected from the controller. A benign switch, e.g., switch 0 in Fig. 1, is a switch that is not compromised by the SBI attacker. When a mutated switch-to-controller message from a compromised switch contributes to other unrelated switch-to-controller channels being disconnected, the bug oracle considers it a DoS for benign switches.

Inter-host Communication Disconnection. The final bug oracle standard is a pair-wise connectivity test to check whether the data plane network works well. In particular, our testing scheme uses `pingall` command from the hosts to check that all hosts are reachable from all other hosts. This is effective in detecting message spoofing attacks and connectivity attacks.

5   Evaluation

We evaluated FSF using a real-world SDN system. We preliminary analyzed the efficacy of deployed mutation operations (Sect. 5.1), and measured the performance of FSF for improving testing code coverage (Sect. 5.2) and finding bugs (Sect. 5.3).

Experimental Setup. We evaluated FSF on the latest version (v1.2) of Floodlight [1]. We setup our system within a Virtual Box with an Intel core i7-9700K CPU and 9 GB of RAM. To measure the instruction coverage of the controller under testing, we used JaCoCo [2], a Java code coverage library. JaCoCo conducts online instrumentation in which instrumentation code is inserted in Java byte code when Java classes are loaded into main memory. We set the timeout to be 24 h for each fuzz testing campaign, and measured the cumulative instruction coverage of the controller during the testing time.

5.1   Operation Significance

To compare the efficacy of different mutation operations, we implemented a base fuzzer that only uses five mutation operations but leverages no feedback from the controller. This fuzzer takes following procedures: (1) setting the proxy to mutates observed switch-to-controller messages with a 10% probability; (2) it periodically generating multiple switch-to-controller messages according to the procedure described in Sect. 4.2.

Mutation Operations. We designed five mutation operations as follows. Note that each operation is designed to explore the diverse control flow of the controller under testing.

(a) *Flipping multiple bits*: it selects and flips multiple random bits. The number of bits to be mutated is randomly chosen from 1 to one tenth of all available bits.
(b) *Flipping multiple bytes*: it selects and flips the selected bytes. The number of mutated bytes is randomly selected from 1 to 10.

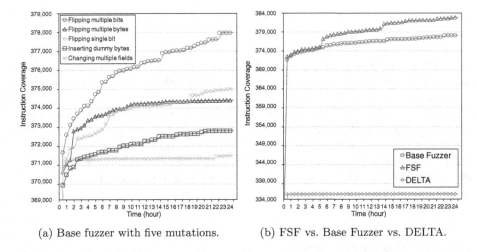

(a) Base fuzzer with five mutations.   (b) FSF vs. Base Fuzzer vs. DELTA.

Fig. 2. The instruction coverage of different fuzzers running for 24 h.

(c) *Flipping single bit*: it flips one randomly chosen bit in the message.

(d) *Inserting dummy bytes*: it inserts random bytes at the random position within the message. The length of the dummy is randomly chosen from one byte to 71,680 bytes.

(e) *Changing multiple fields*: it selects multiple random message fields, and change the selected field values to random values while preserving the type constraints according to the OpenFlow specification [3]. The number of mutated fields is randomly set from 1 to 20% of all available fields.

We compared the instruction coverage of the controller when each single mutation operation was applied. The objective here is to gauge how each mutation affects on increasing the instruction coverage of the SDN controller under testing.

Figure 2a shows the instruction coverage of preliminary base fuzzer with five operations for 24 h. Note that the *flipping multiple bits* operation touched the most number of instructions, 377,970 instructions in total. Based on the above observation, we adopted the *flipping multiple bits* operation to FSF.

We further analyzed root causes of observed coverage differences among the different mutation strategies. Floodlight internally uses `OpenFlowJ`, which parses a given OpenFlow messages according to the OpenFlow protocol specification. When a received message does not meet this specification, `OpenFlowJ` raises an exception, hindering to reach a deeper code region. Furthermore, each message field in a OpenFlow message requires a different primitive type, such as `uint8`, `uint32`, and `uint64`. Non-compliance of such primitive type requirements will also cause low code coverage. The three mutations of *changing multiple fields*, *flipping multiple bytes*, and *inserting dummy bytes* are more likely to generate OpenFlow messages that do not satisfy the specification nor the primitive type constraints. For instance, *flipping multiple bytes* often breaks a required type constraint. For example, the `Capabilities` field value in a `FEATURES_REPLY` message should have one of the following values: 0x00000000,0x00000001, 0x00000002, 0x00000004, 0x00000008, 0x00000020, 0x00000040, and 0x00000100. When flipping multiple bytes of this message, this mutation is able to generate a message with 0x00000011, which is not a valid OpenFlow message.

Flipping multiple bits is a simple but effective mutation strategy in practice. It is widely used in many fuzzers [12,14,33]. As shown in Fig. 2a, *flipping multiple bits* also was the most effective mutation strategy than other ones in terms of improving code coverage. Bit flipping causes no significant change in its target field, thus resulting in a high chance of not violating the aforementioned constraints. Also, *flipping multiple bits* is better than *flipping single bit* in generating more diverse tests.

5.2   Coverage Improvement

We compared the coverage improvement of FSF with that of two other fuzzers: (1) a preliminary base fuzzer with the *flipping multiple bits* operation (Sect. 5.1), and (2) DELTA [20], a state-of-the-art SDN security assessment framework. Unfortunately, the DELTA project [20] did not contain a fuzz testing function at the time of writing. The project does, however, support penetration testing, a key task of DELTA with 40 known attack scenarios. To compare our tool with DELTA, we measured the number of covered instructions after conducting penetration testing.

Figure 2b shows the instruction coverage of different fuzzers. We observed that FSF and the base fuzzer significantly outperformed DELTA on instruction coverage. Recall from Sect. 4.2, both fuzzers leverage all of the switch-to-controller OpenFlow message types, while DELTA only relies on a set of limited known attack scenarios. Therefore, we concluded that it is important to have a diverse set of seed messages to conduct comprehensive testing of an SDN system.

We also observed that FSF touched 4,835 more instructions than base fuzzer. As stated in Sect. 5.1, the main difference between the preliminary base fuzzer and FSF is the existence of a coverage feedback loop. Therefore, we note that the difference in the instruction coverage comes from the coverage feedback iteration.

5.3   Bugs Found

We further analyzed FSF in terms of its bug finding ability. Recall from Sect. 4.4 that we consider four types of bugs as our detection criteria: (1) controller process termination, (2) control plane resource exhaustion, (3) benign switch disconnection, and (4) inter-host communication disconnection. Table 1 summarizes the number of test instances that trigger bugs residing in the target SDN controller. We counted the number of distinct tests that trigger the bugs based on two different metrics that each column represents.

The second column in Table 1 shows the number of mutated message sets that trigger the corresponding bug. In total, 1 controller process termination,

Table 1. The number of test instances that trigger bugs.

Bug oracle	Total test instances	Unique test instances
Controller process termination	1	0
Control plane resource exhaustion	0	0
Benign switch disconnection	198	132
Inter-host communication disconnection	18	14

198 benign switch disconnection, and 18 inter-host communication disconnection bugs with their test instances were reported during the 24 h of a fuzzing campaign. We observed that FSF successfully triggered three types of bugs. Benign switch disconnection imposes a DoS for other benign switches. Hosts can not communicate with each other when disconnection occurs. Furthermore, the controller process crashes cause a DoS for the entire SDN network.

As a postmortem analysis, we extracted mutated message sets (i.e., *test_cases*) that successfully triggered bugs, send each of it in initial testing infrastructure, and see whether same bugs were triggered or not. Additionally, we minimize the reproducible *test_cases* by leveraging delta debugging [30,34] technique to get a minimized message set that causes the same bug. Finally, we compare minimized subsequence with each other in terms of sequence length, message type, and message length to count the number of unique message sets. As the third column in Table 1 shows, FSF found unique 146 test instances.

We further analyzed the 14 minimized unique instances that triggered the inter-host communication disconnection and identified two unique bugs via conducting postmortem analyses on the controller source with the input instances. One bug caused the failure of `ping` operations between hosts under benign switches. When a malicious switch sends an identified attack payload, this packet contributes hosts under benign switches to disconnecting from the network, causing a remote denial of service. Another bug caused not only the failure of `ping` operations but also the flooding of `PACKET_OUT` messages, demonstrating a feasible denial of service. Both bugs got assigned CVE numbers and have remained in the reserved status at the time of writing. On the other hand, the instances triggered the controller termination was not reproducible in the postmortem analysis.

6 Discussion

FSF only supports the latest version of Floodlight. However, it is straightforward to apply it to other types of SDN controllers, e.g., POX, ONOS, ODL, because the core idea of FSF in leveraging code coverage of the controller is indeed platform agnostic.

FSF only adopted the *flipping multiple bits* mutation. However, we believe that consolidating multiple mutations will bring a better result in terms of finding bugs as well as improving code coverage. Also, deploying combinatorial testing [8] that mutates fields with only known interesting values helps prune unnecessary test cases, enabling an efficient fuzzing campaign.

Note that the mutation ratio for the *flipping multiple bits* mutation is an important parameter to effectively trigger bugs [7]. Thus, exploring optimal mutation ratios for a fuzzing campaign can be a promising future direction of research.

We only implemented the bug oracles that detect the availability of an underlying SDN network. However, the bug oracles can be extended to check the confidentiality [21] and integrity of a target SDN network.

7   Related Work

SDN Attacks and Defenses. Many previous studies have presented attacks and defenses that can occur in SDN [5,16,17,19,26]. Benton *et al.* [5] presented the feasibility of an MITM attack in control channels due to the lack of SSL/TLS adoptions by vendors. Kazemian *et al.* [16] proposed an SDN system hardening tool. They identify all state changes in the communication channel, and check network policies in real time based on the header space analysis.

There exist previous survey studies to summarize the various SDN security issues [17,19,30,32]. Scott-Hayward *et al.* [30] proposed possible DoS attacks due to the limitations due to the design decisions, including centralized controllers and network flow tables. Flow Wars [32] presented a survey for the possible attacks with its attack vectors. They found 14 attacks and 22 concrete attack scenarios. For each attack classification, they suggested defense mechanisms.

SDN Fuzzing. Based on these SDN security problems, prior studies have been actively conducted on implementing automated testing tools to identify vulnerabilities [9,15,20,30]. DELTA [20] deploys a blackbox fuzz testing technique. It models the fuzzing input source to be malicious applications, control channels, or hosts. The input sources mutate SDN control flow sequences or input values of such control flows. BEADS [15] assumes malicious switches and hosts. It supports various mutations, including dropping, duplicating, delaying, and changing OpenFlow messages as well as ARP injection operations to elicit erroneous behaviors in an SDN system. AIM-SDN [9] focuses on identifying problematic data inconsistencies between data stores, which may exist in an SDN system. It uses REST API and SBI to perform fuzz testing to find data inconsistency problems.

Acknowledgements. We thank anonymous reviewers for their helpful feedback. This work was supported by Institute for Information & communications Technology Promotion (IITP) grant funded by the Korea government (MSIT) (No.2018-0-00254, SDN security technology development).

References

1. Floodlight. http://www.projectfloodlight.org/floodlight
2. JaCoCo: Java code coverage library. https://www.jacoco.org/jacoco/
3. Openflow switch specification: Version 1.3.1. https://www.opennetworking.org/wp-content/uploads/2013/04/openflow-spec-v1.3.1.pdf
4. Basta, A., Kellerer, W., Hoffmann, M., Morper, H.J., Hoffmann, K.: Applying NFV and SDN to LTE mobile core gateways, the functions placement problem. In: Proceedings of the Workshop on All Things Cellular: Operations, Applications and Challenges, pp. 33–38 (2014)
5. Benton, K., Camp, L.J., Small, C.: Openflow vulnerability assessment. In: Proceedings of the ACM SIGCOMM Workshop on Hot Topics in Software Defined Networking, pp. 151–152 (2013)
6. Bertaux, L., et al.: Software defined networking and virtualization for broadband satellite networks. IEEE Commun. Mag. **53**(3), 54–60 (2015)
7. Cha, S.K., Woo, M., Brumley, D.: Program-adaptive mutational fuzzing. In: Proceedings of the IEEE Symposium on Security and Privacy, pp. 725–741 (2015)
8. Cohen, D.M., Dalal, S.R., Parelius, J., Patton, G.C.: The combinatorial design approach to automatic test generation. IEEE Softw. **13**(5), 83–88 (1996)
9. Dixit, V.H., Doupé, A., Shoshitaishvili, Y., Zhao, Z., Ahn, G.J.: AIM-SDN: attacking information mismanagement in SDN-datastores. In: Proceedings of the ACM Conference on Computer and Communications Security, pp. 664–676 (2018)
10. Durner, R., Kellerer, W.: The cost of security in the SDN control plane. In: Proceedings of the ACM CoNEXT Student Workshop (2015)
11. Flauzac, O., González, C., Hachani, A., Nolot, F.: SDN based architecture for IoT and improvement of the security. In: Proceedings of the IEEE International Conference on Advanced Information Networking and Applications Workshops, pp. 688–693 (2015)
12. Hocevar, S.: zzuf. https://github.com/samhocevar/zzuf
13. Holler, C., Herzig, K., Zeller, A.: Fuzzing with code fragments. In: Proceedings of the USENIX Security Symposium, pp. 445–458 (2012)
14. Householder, A.D., Foote, J.M.: Probability-based parameter selection for black-box fuzz testing. Technical report, CMU/SEI-2012-TN-019, CERT (2012)
15. Jero, S., Bu, X., Nita-Rotaru, C., Okhravi, H., Skowyra, R., Fahmy, S.: BEADS: automated attack discovery in openflow-based SDN systems. In: Dacier, M., Bailey, M., Polychronakis, M., Antonakakis, M. (eds.) RAID 2017. LNCS, vol. 10453, pp. 311–333. Springer, Cham (2017). https://doi.org/10.1007/978-3-319-66332-6_14
16. Kazemian, P., Chang, M., Zeng, H., Varghese, G., McKeown, N., Whyte, S.: Real time network policy checking using header space analysis. In: Proceedings of the USENIX Symposium on Networked Systems Design and Implementation, pp. 99–111 (2013)
17. Klöti, R., Kotronis, V., Smith, P.: Openflow: a security analysis. In: Proceedings of the IEEE International Conference on Network Protocols, pp. 1–6 (2016)
18. Kreutz, D., Ramos, F., Verissimo, P.: Towards secure and dependable software-defined networks. In: Proceedings of the ACM SIGCOMM Workshop on Hot Topics in Software Defined Networking, pp. 55–60 (2013)
19. Kreutz, D., Ramos, F.M., Verissimo, P., Rothenberg, C.E., Azodolmolky, S., Uhlig, S.: Software-defined networking: a comprehensive survey. Proc. IEEE **103**(1), 14–76 (2015)

20. Lee, S., Yoon, C., Lee, C., Shin, S., Yegneswaran, V., Porras, P.A.: DELTA: a security assessment framework for software-defined networks. In: Proceedings of the Network and Distributed System Security Symposium (2017)
21. Lei, X., Huang, J., Hong, S., Zhang, J., Gu, G.: Attacking the brain: races in the SDN control plane. In: Proceedings of the USENIX Security Symposium, pp. 451–468 (2017)
22. Miller, B.P., Fredriksen, L., So, B.: An empirical study of the reliability of UNIX utilities. Commun. ACM **33**(12), 32–44 (1990)
23. Ojo, M., Adami, D., Giordano, S.: A SDN-IoT architecture with NFV implementation. In: Proceedings of the IEEE Globecom Workshops, pp. 1–6 (2016)
24. Pickett, G.: Abusing software defined networks. In: Proceedings of the Black Hat EU (2014)
25. Pickett, G.: Staying persistent in software defined networks. Black Hat Briefings (2015)
26. Porras, P., Shin, S., Yegneswaran, V., Fong, M., Tyson, M., Gu, G.: A security enforcement kernel for openflow networks. In: Proceedings of the ACM SIGCOMM Workshop on Hot Topics in Software Defined Networking, pp. 121–126 (2012)
27. Rawat, S., Jain, V., Kumar, A., Cojocar, L., Giuffrida, C., Bos, H.: VUzzer: application-aware evolutionary fuzzing. In: Proceedings of the Network and Distributed System Security Symposium (2017)
28. Rebert, A., Cha, S.K., Avgerinos, T., Foote, J., Warren, D., Grieco, G., Brumley, D.: Optimizing seed selection for fuzzing. In: Proceedings of the USENIX Security Symposium, pp. 861–875 (2014)
29. Rückert, J., Bifulco, R., Rizwan-Ul-Haq, M., Kolbe, H.J., Hausheer, D.: Flexible traffic management in broadband access networks using software defined networking. In: Proceedings of the IEEE Network Operations and Management Symposium, pp. 1–8 (2014)
30. Scott, C., et al.: Troubleshooting blackbox SDN control software with minimal causal sequences. ACM SIGCOMM Comput. Commun. Rev. **44**(4), 395–406 (2015)
31. Trivisonno, R., Guerzoni, R., Vaishnavi, I., Soldani, D.: SDN-based 5G mobile networks: architecture, functions, procedures and backward compatibility. Trans. Emerg. Telecommun. Technol. **26**(1), 82–92 (2015)
32. Yoon, C., et al.: Flow wars: systemizing the attack surface and defenses in software-defined networks. IEEE/ACM Trans. Netw. **25**(6), 3514–3530 (2017)
33. Zalewski, M.: American Fuzzy Lop. http://lcamtuf.coredump.cx/afl/
34. Zeller, A.: Yesterday, my program worked. Today, it does not. Why? In: Proceedings of the ACM SIGSOFT Software Engineering Notes, pp. 253–267 (1999)

DroPPPP: A P4 Approach to Mitigating DoS Attacks in SDN

Goksel Simsek, Hakan Bostan, Alper Kaan Sarica[✉], Egemen Sarikaya,
Alperen Keles, Pelin Angin, Hande Alemdar, and Ertan Onur

Middle East Technical University, Ankara, Turkey
{goksel.simsek,hbostan,e1942358,e2036143,e2310241,pangin,
alemdar,eonur}@ceng.metu.edu.tr

Abstract. Software-Defined Networking (SDN) has proven itself a useful technology for establishing and managing configurable, dynamic networks with the rapid deployment of services in the past decade. Despite
these advantages, the fact that the functionality of SDN relies heavily
on the controller with a much less capable data plane creates a single point of failure, which leaves the network susceptible to denial of
service (DoS) attacks mainly targeting the controller to affect the operation of the whole network. An effective approach for mitigating DoS
attacks in SDN requires identifying and stopping attacks as close to
their source as possible, which will require involvement of the data plane
in the mitigation strategy. In this work we propose DroPPPP, a DoS
prevention approach for SDN that operates in the data plane using the
P4 programming language. We demonstrate through experiments in the
Mininet that lightweight processing of the packets in the data plane
with DroPPPP negates significant overheads through reducing the traffic between switches while keeping the controller's CPU usage at 0% and
below 50% during spoofing and volumetric attacks.

Keywords: Software-Defined Networking · Denial of service · P4

1 Introduction

Software Defined Networking (SDN) [5] is a popular network architecture that
distinguishes itself from traditional networks in that it separates the control
plane and the data plane. In SDN, there is a centralized controller that creates
and maintains network control functions such as forwarding decisions. The centralized aspect of the structure of the SDN provides a better network view and
flexibility to the network manager. However, denial of service (DoS) attacks can
exploit this centralization, which makes the network more vulnerable to these
attacks compared to the traditional networks. Since the controller is responsible
for all control functions, it is easy for DoS attacks to overwhelm the controller,
especially using source IP and MAC spoofing-based attacks, which make it difficult to trace the origin of the attack and enforce appropriate thresholds to

© Springer Nature Switzerland AG 2020
I. You (Ed.): WISA 2019, LNCS 11897, pp. 55–66, 2020.
https://doi.org/10.1007/978-3-030-39303-8_5

only block malicious traffic, while allowing for legitimate traffic to pass through. If a packet does not match with any flow rule in the flow tables, the switch sends a packet_in message to the controller. The controller determines the action and sends a packet_out message to the corresponding switches. Communications between switches and the controller will increase significantly during a DoS attack, which affects the performance of the whole network. Considering the stated severe impacts of DoS attacks on SDN, early detection and prevention of DoS attacks as close to their origin as possible is a significant task.

P4, which stands for "Programming Protocol Independent Packet Processors" [1], is a recently introduced domain-specific programming language that allows forwarding and processing packets in the data plane without requiring intervention from the control plane. Although there are some limitations of the capabilities of P4, bringing computations to the data plane results in a significant performance gain. In this work, we propose DroPPPP, an approach for detecting and mitigating DoS attacks in the data plane using P4 switches, which are switches with limited computation capability that support the domain-specific P4 language. We utilize the flexibility of P4 switches and decrease the communication overhead between switches while maintaining the controller's CPU usage at 0% and below 50% during spoofing and volumetric attacks. Experiments with an SDN simulated in the Mininet environment demonstrate the efficacy of the approach with reduced round trip times and packet loss rates for the legitimate traffic under DoS attacks. To the best of our knowledge, this is the first work utilizing P4 to detect and prevent spoofing-based DoS attacks in SDN.

2   Related Work

As a variety of SDN architectures arose in the past few years, various approaches for mitigation or/and detection of DoS attacks on SDN's were developed. Detection of DDoS attacks against SDN controllers is done via the usage of the entropy of destination IP addresses in the study of Mousavi et al. [9]. Yet, attacks cannot be detected when destination addresses are spoofed as entropy will rise higher. DoS detection is done via Self Organizing Maps, a machine learning algorithm, in the work of Braga et al. [2]. Flow table entries in the switches are collected and from these flow entries, some features are extracted. At each predetermined time interval, flow entries in the switches are pulled and high attack rates may cause flooding of the channel between the controller and the switch. For the detection of TCP SYN flooding attacks in SDN, uncompleted TCP handshake processes are tracked in SLICOTS [8]. Host MAC addresses are used in blocking when uncompleted connection requests directed to a host are above a previously defined threshold. Host legitimacy is not considered, hence blockage applies to all hosts. In FlowSec [6], the bandwidth between the controller and the switches is observed. The controller receives a lower rate of packets when the bandwidth exceeds a previously defined threshold. Legitimate traffic is also affected in this approach. A DoS attack is not the only reason for a high traffic rate. The controller queue is maintained by a threshold value in the work of Raj et al. [12].

Packets that are from the same source and have the same destination IP are counted and the hosts that exceed a previously defined threshold are blocked based on their IP addresses when the number of packets in the controller queue exceeds the threshold. This method cannot detect spoofed IP addresses. Closest to our approach is that of DosDefender, which tracks hosts attached to each switch [4]. The controller stores the MAC and IP addresses, the number of ports each host uses and the switch ports that the hosts are connected to. At each arrival of a packer_in message, IP and MAC addresses are checked by the controller to their correspondence of the stored addresses. In case of spoofing, detection is provided via mismatching of the addresses and packets are blocked based on the switch port connected. Although DoS attacks may be detected by this approach, every connection results in additional delay, also it requires the controller to track all hosts in the network. In PacketChecker [3], legitimate packet_in requests are separated from malicious requests by storing and using switch ports and host MAC bindings. When the port MAC binding table does not contain the source MAC address of the packet, the packet is dropped. Yet, as dropping the packets is done at the controller; the bandwidth between the controller and the switches and the switch resources are still devoured by the spoofed packets.

3   Proposed Approach

3.1   Spoof Detection

Our proposed approach for mitigating DoS attacks in SDN is based on the observation that the attacks targeting the controller in SDN will mostly utilize source IP and MAC spoofing techniques in order to fill up the forwarding tables and cause increased communication between the switches and the controller to install forwarding rules for previously unseen traffic [4]. If we are able to detect that a specific host is using spoofing, blocking traffic from that host as appropriate will provide a first line of defense against the malicious traffic to be created in the network. In these networks, each switch or forwarding element in the data plane will be connected to hosts and other switches through its various ports. When a packet arrives at a specific port of a switch, the switch will be able to identify which host/switch the packet is sourced from. By dropping malicious traffic close to its origin, directly at the data plane through identification of spoofing at the switches, we protect the controller resources from being exhausted.

Algorithm 1 summarizes our main processing logic for spoofing detection. For every switch, we define an attack flag for every port that connects a host at the other end. When a switch receives a packet, it first checks whether it came from a port connected to a switch or a host. If it came from a switch, we apply the forwarding logic to it. Otherwise, it came from a host, and we further process the packet to check for an attack. In the processing procedure, the switch first reads the timestamp of the last attack packet received and the attack flag for that port. If the attack flag is set (i.e., there is currently an attack on that port) and the difference between the timestamps of last attack and the current packet is less than 1 s, the packet is dropped without further processing. Otherwise the switch calculates a hash value from the packet's source MAC address and source IP address, in order to identify the host connected to that port. Then, the calculated hash value is compared with the previously stored hash value for that port. If they match, all is OK, so the switch performs forwarding on the packet. If the stored hash value is zero, this is the first time we have received any packets from that port, or the value has been cleared after an attack is finished. Therefore, we bind/match the calculated hash with the port that the packet came from. Moreover, we clear the attack flag of the port and update the last attack time of the port (in case it is the end of an attack). If the stored value is not 0 and the hashes do not match, we say we detected an attack. When hashes do not match, we first read the last attack time for the port. If the time difference between the current packet and the last attack time is less than 5 s, then we set the attack flag, update the last attack time of the port and drop the packet. If the time difference is greater than 5 s, we assume that the attack has ended and bind/match the new hash value with the port and clear the attack flag. Then we perform forwarding. Processing logic handles the attack detection and port blocking and forwarding logic as explained above. The switch uses three registers (array-like structures) to perform attack detection logic. The first register is called r_known_hosts, and it is used to store hashed values of source IP (srcIP) and source MAC (srcMAC) of each host connected to a port. The second register is r_attack_time. It stores the timestamp of the last detected attack packet. The third register is r_port_attack_flag and it stores a flag for each port of the switch, indicating an ongoing attack on that port. Two match-action tables are used to perform forwarding. The first table is called ip_forward_table. It performs the longest prefix matching on the destination IP address of the packet. Matched values are used to call ip_forward action. The table is filled by the controller at the startup. The second table is neighbor_table and it is used to determine if a port is connected to another switch or a host. host_action is performed if the port is connected to a host and switch_action if the port is connected to a switch. The table is filled by the controller at the startup. After all, processing is done by deparser, which puts the headers back together and then outputs the packet from the port specified as the result of the forwarding logic in the previous step.

3.2   Volumetric Attack Detection

We perform volumetric attack detection based on the packet rates of the hosts connected to the switches. In many DoS attacks, the number of packets sent per second is abnormally high compared to normal network traffic. Similar to the spoofing approach, if we can detect an unusual amount of packets being sent from a host, we can block the traffic from that host to stop the attack. We employ a Two Rate Three Color Marker (RFC 2698) to identify the hosts exceeding specific packet rates and block their traffic. Two Rate Three Color Marker uses two rates to color (i.e. mark) packets. One of the used rates is Peak Information Rate (PIR), and the other is Committed Information Rate (CIR). It

---

Algorithm 1. Packet Processing Algorithm

Input: hdr(header), $attack\_time\_array$(last attack times), $port\_attack\_flag\_array$, $global\_time$(current time), $known\_hosts\_array$(hashes of $sourceIP$ and $sourceMAC$ of each host), $ingress\_port$, $ip\_forward\_table$, $neighbor\_table$

1: $action \leftarrow$ Action applied in $neighbor\_table$
2: **if** $action =$ "$host\_action$" **then**
3:     **if** hdr is valid **then**
4:        $port\_attack\_flag \leftarrow port\_attack\_flag\_array[ingress\_port]$
5:        $attack\_time \leftarrow attack\_time\_array[ingress\_port]$
6:        **if** $port\_attack\_flag = 1$ **and** $global\_time - attack\_time < 1000000$ **then**
7:           Drop the packet
8:        **else**
9:           $known\_hosts \leftarrow known\_hosts\_array[ingress\_port]$
10:          $HP \leftarrow$ Calculate the hash of the packet
11:          $bound\_hash \leftarrow$ Read hash from $known\_hosts$ corresponds to the port
12:          **if** $HP \neq bound\_hash$ **and** $bound\_hash \neq 0$ **then**
13:             **if** $global\_time - attack\_time < 5000000$ **then**
14:                $port\_attack\_flag \leftarrow 1$
15:                $port\_attack\_flag\_array[ingress\_port] \leftarrow port\_attack\_flag$
16:                $attack\_time\_array[ingress\_port] \leftarrow global\_time$
17:                Drop the packet
18:             **else**
19:                $bound\_hash \leftarrow 0$
20:                $port\_attack\_flag \leftarrow 0$
21:                $port\_attack\_flag\_array[ingress\_port] \leftarrow port\_attack\_flag$
22:             **end if**
23:          **end if**
24:       **end if**
25:       **if** $bound\_hash = 0$ **then**
26:          $known\_hosts\_array[ingress\_port] \leftarrow HP$
27:          $attack\_time\_array[ingress\_port] \leftarrow global\_time$
28:          $port\_attack\_flag\_array[ingress\_port] \leftarrow 0$
29:       **end if**
30:       **if** $attack\_flag = 0$ **then**
31:          Apply $ip\_forward\_table$
32:       **end if**
33:    **end if**
34: **else if** $action =$ "$switch\_action$" **then**
35:    Apply $ip\_forward\_table$
36: **end if**

---

compares the rate of the incoming packets to PIR and CIR to color each packet. A packet is marked GREEN if it does not exceed both PIR and CIR, YELLOW if it only exceeds CIR and RED if it exceeds the PIR.

In P4 we use a meter providing the implementation of the Two Rate Three Color Marker, and marked packets from each port according to their rates. If a packet is marked GREEN, it is forwarded without further processing. If a packet is marked YELLOW, it is still forwarded normally but an information message is sent to the controller in case it wants to take further action. If a packet is marked RED, it is dropped immediately and a message is sent to the controller. The two rates of the meter are set by the controller using the Thrift API of the switch implementation. Rates are given as a list of size two. The first element corresponds to the CIR and its burst size and the second element corresponds to the PIR and its burst size. The CIR and PIR are represented as packets/microseconds and burst sizes are represented as packet counts. For example 0.000001:1 denotes a rate of 1 packet/s with a burst size of 1 packet.

4   Evaluation

4.1   Experiment Setups

We simulate our experiment setups using the Mininet environment [7]. Switches use the "simple_switch" implementation of the P4's behavioral model v2 (BMv2) [11].

Spoof Detection Setup. In this setup, we use a linear topology with five linearly connected switches, all connected to a single controller. Each switch also has five hosts connected to it. A forwarding table consists of the IP ranges of hosts in the topology and the corresponding port numbers of the switch to perform forwarding. We perform our experiments on two different scenarios. In the first scenario, a host connected to the first switch sends pings to a host connected to the last switch, while an attacker who is connected to the second switch performs a spoofing-based denial of service (DoS) attack targeting the same host at the last switch. In the second scenario, a host connected to the first switch sends pings to a host connected to the last switch, but this time the attacker is also connected to the first switch.

Volumetric Attack Detection Setup. In this experimentation setup, we use a topology named France–D-B-L-N-C-A-N-N that is provided by [10]. There are 25 nodes in this topology, and we use nodes as switches. For every switch, we assign a random number of hosts in the interval of 1–3. In order to simulate a volumetric DDoS attack, we select 50% of hosts as attackers, 40% of them as casuals, and 10% of them as idle. We run a ping command on both attackers and casuals. Attackers target the same victim host in every experiment. Meanwhile, casual hosts randomly talk with each other and the victim host. As the name implies, idle hosts sleep during the experimentation and do not consume any resources.

4.2   Results

We have performed our experiments on a computer with an Intel Core i5-6500 CPU running at 3.60 GHz × 4. Each experiment has been repeated 50 times.

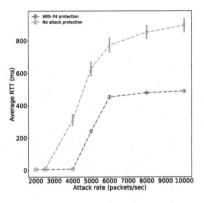

(a) Average RTT in Scenario-1.

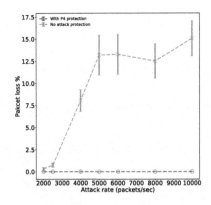

(b) Average packet loss in Scenario-1

Fig. 1. Average RTT and packet loss statistics in the Scenario-1.

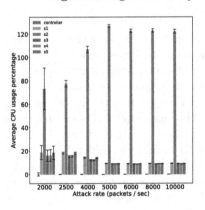

(a) CPU load for protected system.

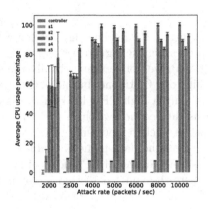

(b) CPU load for unprotected system.

Fig. 2. The CPU load distribution of the switches and the controller in the Scenario-1.

Spoof Detection Results. In spoof detection experiments, the attacker performs random source IP spoofing and flooding with a different rate of packets per second. The ping command sends 1000 packets, and we repeat the experimentation when the command is finished. In each experiment, we consider two different P4 application setups. The first P4 application does not have data-plane spoof detection. In the latter application, we have our proposal that performs spoof detection on the data-plane. In Fig. 1(a), we measure the average RTTs on the Scenario-1, with and without spoof detection on the data-plane. When the spoof detection is disabled, there is an increase in the RTTs after 3000 packets/second. We also observe that after 5000 packets/second, RTTs of both setups increase.

The reason for the increase in the RTTs in both setups can be seen in Fig. 2. As the attack rate gets faster, the CPU loads of switches also increase. In this

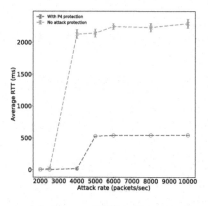
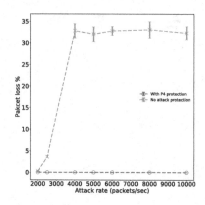

(a) Average RTT in Scenario-2.   (b) Average packet loss in Scenario-2

Fig. 3. Average RTT and packet loss statistics in Scenario-2.

context, high CPU load means that the switch is rather busy with the DoS attack than processing the regular packets, which therefore increases the average RTTs. In Fig. 2(b), we notice that not only the switch that encounters the attack first has a high of a CPU load, but all of the switches do. On the contrary, In Fig. 2(a), there is only a high CPU load on the first switch that detects the DoS attack, which is the second switch in the topology. The reason of this phenomenon is the cost of packet processing to detect an attack. As a result, when the spoof detection on the data-plane is enabled, the RTTs remain considerably low and stable since the overall CPU load of the system is noticeably smaller than the case where the spoof detection is not provided. Furthermore, it is essential to provide a low packet loss ratio during the DoS attack. In Fig. 1(b), we explore the packet loss ratios of both of the setups. We see that even under a heavy load, the packet loss remains zero when the spoof detection on the data-plane is enabled. On the other hand, when the spoof detection is not employed, we observe that the system suffers moderate packet loss as the overall load of the system is considerably high.

In Fig. 3(a), we evaluate the average RTTs on Scenario-2. If we compare Fig. 1(a) and Fig. 3(a), we can see that the system is more vulnerable to the place of the attacker when there is no spoof detection on the data-plane, as the average RTT is almost three times Scenario-1's results. On the contrary, when the spoof detection is enabled, we observe that the RTTs are approximately the same. Furthermore, in Fig. 3(b), the packet loss is greater compared to Fig. 1(b) when the spoof detection on the data-plane is not provided. In Fig. 4, we explore the reason why the RTT, and loss increased almost four times, and two times respectively when there is no spoof detection. In this experiment, we see the effect of having one more hop on the path between the victim and the attacker. Allowing a DoS attack even one more hop decreases the performance significantly, and the quality of service of hosts on and before the first switch which embraces the attack on the path to the target. In both of the scenarios, our

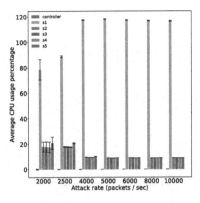

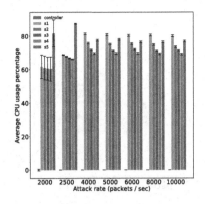

(a) CPU load for protected system.   (b) CPU load for unprotected system.

Fig. 4. CPU load distribution of the switches and the controller in Scenario-2.

spoof detection implementation does not make use of the controller. Therefore, we have the CPU load of the controller near zero. However, we observe that the CPU load of the switch embracing the attack is very high due to the packet processing cost to determine an attack.

Volumetric Attack Results. In volumetric attack detection experiments, we have 25 switches and 50 hosts in total. We randomly assign 25 of the hosts as attackers, 20 of the hosts as casuals and set five of the hosts as idle. The attacker hosts send 5000 packets to the same victim. The casual hosts randomly select another casual and send 100 packets. We perform two different experiments on this setup. The first experiment is measuring the impact of different CIR-PIR thresholds. In order to simulate their effectiveness, we set the attacker's rate as 240 packets per second since it is average considering the CIR-PIR thresholds. In the second experiment, we explore the effect of different attack rates. We set the CIR and PIR thresholds as 240 and 340 packets per second respectively. In both of the experiments, we set the packet rate of the casual hosts as 25 packets per second. Moreover, we repeat every experiment 30 times.

In Fig. 5(a) we measure average RTTs with and without volumetric attack protection in data-plane. When there is no protection, the RTTs of casual hosts are high while the attackers experience a relatively low RTT. The reason why the causal hosts experience high RTTs is without data-plane protection attackers are able to consume resources easily. We present the packet losses of casual hosts and attackers in Fig. 5(b). We observe that without attack protection, casual hosts and attackers experience similar packet losses. When the protection is enabled, attackers' packet loss increase dramatically while causal hosts packet loss decreases. Furthermore, there is a sharp drop after 200–300 CIR - PIR interval. From this phenomenon, we can conclude that the attackers' packet rate on the victim's switch is around 300 packets/s.

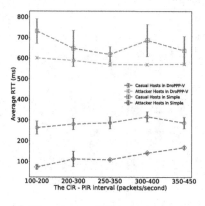
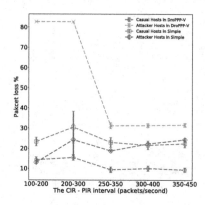

(a) The average RTTs measurements.   (b) The average packet loss statistics.

Fig. 5. The average RTT and packet loss statistics in CIR-PIR threshold experiments.

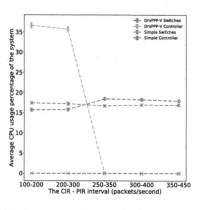
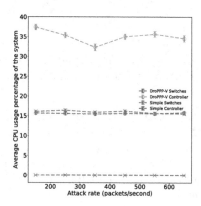

(a) The average CPU load statistics in the (b) The average CPU load statistics with
CIR-PIR threshold experiments.   different attack rates.

Fig. 6. The CPU load distribution of the switches and the controller in the Scenario-2.

In Fig. 6(a), we show the CPU usages of switches and the controllers with different CIR-PIR thresholds. CPU consumptions of switches are quite close to each other in both cases, with and without data-plane protection. To be precise, when the attack rate is greater than the CIR of the switch, the DroPPP-V switches consume slightly less CPU and when attack rate is smaller than the CIR of the switch, they consume more CPU. Moreover, when the attack rate is greater than the CIR, CPU consumption of the DroPPP-V controller is quite high. This is because the switches inform the controller when they detect an attack. To reduce high CPU consumption, more intelligent data plane algorithm should be employed. For instance, instead of warning the controller every time

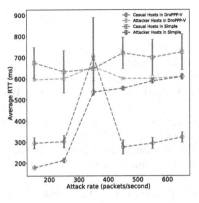

(a) The average RTTs measurements.

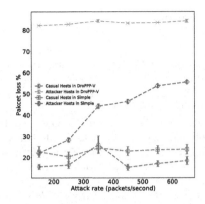

(b) The average packet loss statistics.

Fig. 7. The average RTT and packet loss statistics with different attack rates.

traffic exceeds CIR, switches can collect traffic information and inform the controller periodically. When we examine the CPU consumption of the system as we increase attack rate we can see that the CPU consumptions of the simple switch and the DroPPP-V switch are really close. Results are shown in Fig. 6(b).

In Fig. 7(a), we inspect the RTTs of casual hosts and attackers as we increase the attack rate. When the attack rate is between the CIR and PIR, the load on the switch is essentially doubled since it both forwards the packet and sends an information packet to the controller. Consequently, we observe a peak on both RTT and packet loss. Packet loss with increasing attack rates is presented in Fig. 7(b). Volumetric attack protection lowers the packet loss of casual hosts while increasing the packet loss of attackers.

5 Conclusion

In this paper, we proposed DroPPPP, a novel approach for mitigating spoofing-based DoS attacks in SDN, which reduces the overall workload of the switches by processing the packets in the data plane using P4 as we maintain the CPU load of the controller below 50% all the time. Our experiments showed that our approach increases the network's performance under a DoS attack, especially by decreasing packet loss significantly in both scenarios that we experimented with, while creating tolerable overhead when there is no attack. In the volumetric experiments, our controller only collects the warning statistics but do not perform any actions. Furthermore, switches always warn the controller when the CIR threshold is exceeded. This kind of behavior dramatically increases the CPU load of both the switches and the controller. Therefore, we plan to extend and design a more intelligent switch, and controller structure as future work. Moreover, we intend to implement In-band Network Telemetry (INT) with P4 to gather more extensive information about the network and use this information to block detected DoS attacks at the border switches.

References

1. Bosshart, P., et al.: P4: programming protocol-independent packet processors. SIGCOMM Comput. Commun. Rev. **44**(3), 87–95 (2014)
2. Braga, R., Mota, E., Passito, A.: Lightweight DDoS flooding attack detection using NOX/OpenFlow. In: IEEE Local Computer Network Conference, pp. 408–415, October 2010
3. Deng, S., Gao, X., Lu, Z., Gao, X.: Packet injection attack and its defense in software-defined networks. IEEE Trans. Inf. Forensics Secur. **13**(3), 695–705 (2018)
4. Deng, S., Gao, X., Lu, Z., Li, Z., Gao, X.: Dos vulnerabilities and mitigation strategies in software-defined networks. J. Netw. Comput. Appl. **125**, 209–219 (2019)
5. Kreutz, D., Ramos, F.M.V., Veríssimo, P.E., Rothenberg, C.E., Azodolmolky, S., Uhlig, S.: Software-defined networking: a comprehensive survey. Proc. IEEE **103**(1), 14–76 (2015)
6. Kuerban, M., Tian, Y., Yang, Q., Jia, Y., Huebert, B., Poss, D.: FlowSec: DOS attack mitigation strategy on SDN controller. In: IEEE International Conference on Networking, Architecture and Storage (NAS), Long Beach, CA, USA, 8–10 August 2016, pp. 1–2. IEEE Computer Society (2016)
7. Lantz, B., Heller, B., McKeown, N.: A network in a laptop: rapid prototyping for software-defined networks. In: Proceedings of the 9th ACM SIGCOMM Workshop on Hot Topics in Networks, pp. 19:1–19:6. Hotnets-IX, ACM, New York (2010)
8. Mohammadi, R., Javidan, R., Conti, M.: SLICOTS: an SDN-based lightweight countermeasure for TCP SYN flooding attacks. IEEE Trans. Netw. Serv. Manag. **14**(2), 487–497 (2017)
9. Mousavi, S.M., St-Hilaire, M.: Early detection of ddos attacks against software defined network controllers. J. Netw. Syst. Manag. **26**(3), 573–591 (2018)
10. Orlowski, S., Pióro, M., Tomaszewski, A., Wessäly, R.: SNDlib 1.0-survivable network design library. In: Proceedings of the 3rd International Network Optimization Conference (INOC 2007), Spa, Belgium, April 2007. Extended version accepted in Networks 2009. http://sndlib.zib.de
11. p4lang: p4lang/behavioral-model. https://github.com/p4lang/behavioral-model
12. Raj, A., Bhat, A.S., Namboothiri, L.V.: Effective threshold defence against DoS attack on SDN controller. Int. J. Pure Appl. Math. **119**(10), 691–698 (2018)

A Secure and Self-tallying E-voting System Based on Blockchain

Gongxian Zeng, Meiqi He, and Siu Ming Yiu[(⊠)]

The University of Hong Kong, Pokfulam, Hong Kong
{gxzeng,mqhe,smyiu}@cs.hku.hk

Abstract. E-voting has been studied for many years. Recently, researchers find that blockchain can provide an alternative secure platform for e-voting systems, because of its properties of tamper resistance and transparency. However, existing schemes either require centralized authorities to tally ballots or can only handle a limited number of voters. This paper tries to propose a self-tallying e-voting system, i.e., the public can verify the validity of all ballots and tally the ballots. To achieve this goal, technically, we design a new method on blockchain that can generate and distribute random numbers for ballot security and these random numbers will be cancelled out when multiplying all ballots to allow counting the ballots. Secondly, we adopt non-interactive zero knowledge proof to make sure these ballots are valid. Our scheme is proved to be secure.

Keywords: E-voting · Blockchain · Self-tallying · Zero-knowledge proof

1 Introduction

Voting plays an important role in a society. Paper-based voting systems waste a lot of papers and require a lot of manpower to finish tallying. Thus, electronic voting (e-voting) system was proposed. There are many e-voting systems, such as homomorphic encryption based voting [5], mix-net based voting [2], zero knowledge proof based voting [4] and signature based voting [6]. These systems have their advantages but many e-voting systems require a trusted bulletin board to record ballots, which is required to be append-only and tamper resistant. Recently, *blockchain* attracts a lot of attention as an e-voting platform since it satisfies the requirements of being a secure bulletin board. Also, the smart contract built on blockchain can help to do some important computation in a transparent way since the binary code is accessible in the chain. It is reported that the e-voting scheme in [7] that is based on blockchain, costs about only $0.7 per voter using Ethereum [13] (a blockchain platform) while it costs $2.77 using paper or DRE (direct-recording electronic machine) with paper in California, USA [1]. It is believed that blockchain based e-voting systems can be more secure and economic. Some business companies also try to consider e-voting using blockchain. For example, *Voatz*, a blockchain-based app, is offered to be a voting

© Springer Nature Switzerland AG 2020
I. You (Ed.): WISA 2019, LNCS 11897, pp. 67–76, 2020.
https://doi.org/10.1007/978-3-030-39303-8_6

option for West Virginia (U.S.) voters who are serving in the military overseas[1]. In academia, blockchain-based e-voting also attracted a lot of attention.

Table 1. Overview of some schemes

Requirements		Bin Yu [14]	OVN [7]	Our
Ballot result unknown	for administrator	✗	✓	✓
	for others	✓	✓	✓
Voter anonymity		✓	✗	✓
Interim result unavailable	for administrator	✗	✓	✓
	for others	✓	✓	✓
Double-voting resistance		✓	✓	✓
Public verifiability		✓	✓	✓
Self tallying		✗	✓	✓
Platform independent		✓	✓	✓

Recently, Yu et al. [14] proposed a platform independent e-voting scheme based on blockchain, which implies that changes in the underlying blockchain protocols would not affect the voting system. However, in their scheme, there is a powerful "voting administrator", who generates the public and secret keys for ballot encryption and decryption so that he can know the interim result easily. Thus, if the administrator colludes with one of the candidates, the candidates can adjust his/her strategy in time according to the interim result.

In 2017, McCorry et al. [7] proposed a decentralized and self-tallying e-voting protocol using blockchain without a tallying authority, called open vote network. It achieves a good security and anonymity. However, the computation overhead is large. It requires $O(n)$ multiplication operations for a voter to compute a public parameter (the reconstructed key), where n is the total number of voters. If leveraging the computation to the chain, e.g. using smart contract, it would cost too much blockchain computation resource and only supports at most 50 voters' reconstructed keys in one Ethereum transaction, because of the gas limit of Ethereum, which limits the number of voters.

This paper tries to improve the work of [7] and propose a better self-tallying e-voting system with no powerful central authorities nor trusted third parties. We also assume that some independent parties own high performance computational devices, for example the voting administrator, who could help tallying and verify all ballots but whom we do not trust. Thus, we focus on the weak devices of the common voters. An overview of comparison of existing schemes is shown in Table 1. It shows that our scheme satisfies all important security requirements. To achieve these goals, we propose a method based on blockchain to cancel

---

[1] https://www.wvnews.com/news/wvnews/history-making-mobile-voting-app-for-overseas-military-now-in/article_0402b7dd-af11-56ed-a42d-5981a214f9c0.html.

out random numbers in the ballots when multiplying them and design a zero knowledge proof to prove that the ballots are generated as stipulated.

2   Preliminary

2.1   Zero Knowledge Proof

We use $PoK\{\lambda : \Gamma = \gamma^{\lambda}\}$ to denote a non-interactive proof of knowledge of a (secret) λ. Thus, $PoK\{\exists x : t_1 = g_1^x \wedge t_2 = g_2^x\}$ denotes the proof of equality and knowledge of two discrete logarithms and $PoK\{\exists x : (t_1 = g_1^x \wedge t_2 = g_2^x) \vee (t_3 = g_3^x \wedge t_4 = g_4^x)\}$ denotes the proof of the knowledge of x for disjunctive of equality. For more details, you can refer to [11].

2.2   Decision Diffie-Hellman Assumption

In 1996, researchers [12] proposed the 3DDH assumption based on DDH assumption. Our ballot security is also based on 3DDH assumption, so we introduce it here.

Definition 1. *(3DDH) Given q is the order of group $\mathcal{G}$ and g is the generator, it is difficult to distinguish $(g^x, g^y, g^z, g^{xy}, g^{xz}, g^{yz}, g^{xyz})$ from $(g^x, g^y, g^z, g^{xy}, g^{xz}, g^{yz}, R)$, where $x, y, z \in Z_q^*$ and $R \in \mathcal{G}$.*

2.3   Blockchain and Bitcoin Puzzle

Blockchain is a public ledger to record all transactions, which are contained in sequenced blocks, using proof of work (PoW) [9] or other methods to achieve a consensus to maintain the chain. PoW requires block creators (or called miners) to solve a puzzle, so that $H(puz \parallel m \parallel r) \leq 2^{\lambda-d}$ (i.e., the hash value must contain a certain number of leading zeros), where H is a secure hash function, puz is the hash value of the last block, m contains the miner's public key and a new set of transactions to be committed to the blockchain, λ is the security parameter, d is the difficulty parameter and r is a nonce that all miners are searching for.

3   Our Proposed Scheme

3.1   Main Steps

In our scheme, there are n voters and a voting administrator. Here we only consider two candidates: candidate "0" and candidate "1" for ease of understanding, but it can be easily extended to multiple candidates.

Initialization. The voting administrator initializes a voting. He initializes the public parameters $(\mathcal{G}, g, h)$ where g and h are generators of Group $\mathcal{G}$ and $\log_g h$

is unknown for anybody. Also he initializes a hash function, $f: \mathcal{G} \rightarrow \{0,1\}^*$. He is going to launch a smart contract to define voting time and collect the ballots.

Registration. The voting administrator would collect the necessary information about the voters to check their eligibility. If the voter is eligible, he would get four coins (three for voting parameters and one for ballots). All voters would use them in an anonymous way, like zerocoin [8] or zerocash [10].

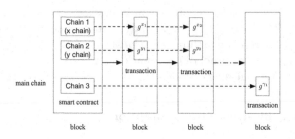

Fig. 1. Conceptual chains

Generating Voting Parameters. As shown in Fig. 1, in our scheme, there would be three conceptual chains besides the main chain to collect the ballots (Chain 1 and Chain 2 are denoted as x chain and y chain respectively). For every voter, he needs to solve puzzles in Chain 1 and Chain 2 first. Similar to the Bitcoin puzzle, here every voter needs to find a number $r = g^{\xi}$ so that:

$$Hash(puz||r||tx) \leq 2^{\lambda} \tag{1}$$

where puz would be the hash of previous transaction, tx would be a transaction to send one coin anonymously to the voter administrator and ξ would be x value or y value. Thus, if the voter finds a ξ to some puzzle, he sends a transaction to the chain and g^{ξ} would be public in the block. For transactions with the same order number in Chain 1 and Chain 2 (e.g. they are both i^{th} transactions), the random numbers are denoted as g^{x_i} and g^{y_i} respectively. For the voter who has x_i, he is responsible for sending g^{γ_i} to Chain 3, where $\gamma_i = f(g^{x_i y_i})$. It also need an anonymous coin.

Casting Ballots. Suppose that the $voter_m$ knows x_i and y_j, he computes his ballot in this way: $B_m = (g^{y_i})^{x_i}/(g^{x_j})^{y_j} \cdot g^{v_m} = g^{x_i y_i - x_j y_j + v_m}$ where $v_m \in \{0,1\}$. And then, he generates a non-interactive zero knowledge proof. The details are introduced in Sect. 3.2. Then the $voter_m$ packs all of them together and sends it to the voting smart contract with the last one coin anonymously.

Tallying. When all voters finish voting, it begins to tally. Not only the voting administrator but also anybody else can do it. It only needs to multiply all ballots. We can get $\prod_{m=1}^{n} B_m = g^{\sum_{i=1}^{n} x_i y_i - \sum_{j=1}^{n} x_j y_j + \sum_{m=1}^{n} v_m} = g^{\sum_{m=1}^{n} v_m}$. Then, we can use exhaustive search to work out how many ballots are voted for candidate "1". After that, the publics can check if all ballots are valid and check if the result is right.

3.2   Generating Non-interactive Zero Knowledge Proof

In this section, we are going to introduce the details of generating a non-interactive zero knowledge proof to prove that the ballots are valid and are generated as stipulated.

Now, for a $voter_m$, he uses two groups of parameters: $(g^{x_i}, g^{y_i}, g^{\gamma_i})$ and $(g^{x_j}, g^{y_j}, g^{\gamma_j})$, and he knows $(x_i, y_j, \gamma_i, \gamma_j)$. To avoid others to know what parameters the voter uses to encrypt the ballot, we allow the voter to choose other $(k-2)$ groups of (g^x, g^y, g^γ). Thus, there are k groups in total. We denote them as (t_{l1}, t_{l2}, t_{l3}) for simplicity where $l \in \{1, \ldots, k\}$.

Step One. We have committed the value γ_i and γ_j on the blockchain. We have also committed the value $R = \gamma_i \cdot \gamma_j$ on the blockchain. The next problem is how to compute a variable securely, of which the discrete logarithm is R.

First, we consider g^{γ_i}. The voter computes $\alpha_1 = h^{z_1}$ and $\alpha_2 = g^{\gamma_i z_1}$, where z_1 is a random number, chosen by $voter_m$. Consider this boolean expression $e_{1l}^\gamma = ((\alpha_2 = (t_{l3})^{s_1}) \wedge (\alpha_1 = h^{s_1}))$. If the expression is true, it implies that the voter knows s_1. We can hide which t_{l3} we use by using the disjunctive proofs in [11]: $PoK\{\exists s_1 : e_{11}^\gamma \vee \cdots e_{1k}^\gamma\}$. It means that among the given k groups, there is a t_{l3}, with which base the logarithm of α_2 is the same to the logarithm of α_1 with base h. Assume that the $voter_m$ knows the γ_i value of the dth group (t_{d1}, t_{d2}, t_{d3}) and let $s_1 = z_1$. Proof is generated as follows.

$$
\begin{array}{l}
\text{For } l \neq d: \\
\quad (c_l, r_l) \xleftarrow{\$} \{0,1\}^*, \; k_{l1} = (t_{l3})^{r_l}(\alpha_2)^{c_l}, \; k_{l2} = h^{r_{l1}}(\alpha_1)^{c_l}, \\
\text{For } l = d: \\
\quad w \xleftarrow{\$} \{0,1\}^*, \; k_{l1} = (t_{l3})^w, \; k_{l2} = h^w, \; c \leftarrow Hash(\alpha_1, \alpha_2, \{t_{l3}, k_{l1}, k_{l2}\}_{l \in \{1,\ldots,k\}}), \\
\quad c_d = c - \sum_{l \neq d} c_l, \; r_d = w - s_1 \cdot c_d, \\
\quad proof_1^\gamma = (\alpha_1, \alpha_2, \{c_l, r_l\}_{l \in \{1,\ldots,k\}})
\end{array}
$$

We do something similar for g^{γ_j}. The voter computes $\alpha_3 = h^{z_2}$ and $\alpha_4 = g^{\gamma_j z_2}$ where z_2 is a random number chosen by $voter_m$. We have boolean expression $e_{2l}^\gamma = ((\alpha_4 = (t_{l3})^{s_1}) \wedge (\alpha_3 = h^{s_1}))$ and $PoK\{\exists s_1 : e_{21}^\gamma \vee \cdots e_{2k}^\gamma\} \rightarrow proof_2^\gamma = (\alpha_3, \alpha_4, \{c_l, r_l\}_{l \in \{1,\ldots,k\}})$.

Finally, $voter_m$ computes $\alpha_5 = g^{\gamma_i \gamma_j z_1 z_2}$, $\alpha_6 = h^{z_1 z_2}$ and $\alpha_7 = g^{z_1 z_2}$, we have the following proofs:

$$
\begin{aligned}
PoK\{\exists (s_2, s_3, s_4) : &(\alpha_5 = (\alpha_2)^{s_2}) \wedge (\alpha_4 = g^{s_2}) \\
&\wedge (\alpha_6 = (\alpha_1)^{s_3}) \wedge (\alpha_3 = h^{s_3}) \\
&\wedge (\alpha_6 = h^{s_4}) \wedge (\alpha_7 = g^{s_4})\}
\end{aligned} \tag{2}
$$

The voter knows $s_2 = \gamma_j z_2$, $s_3 = z_2$ and $s_4 = z_1 z_2$, so he generates the proof in the following way:

$$
\begin{array}{l}
(w_1, w_2, w_3) \xleftarrow{\$} \{0,1\}^*, \\
k_1 = (\alpha_2)^{w_1}, \; k_2 = g^{w_1}, \; k_3 = (\alpha_1)^{w_2}, \; k_4 = h^{w_2}, \; k_5 = h^{w_3}, \; k_6 = g^{w_3}, \\
c \leftarrow Hash(\alpha_1, \ldots, \alpha_7, k_1, \ldots, k_6), \; r_1 = w_1 - s_2 * c, \; r_2 = w_2 - s_3 \cdot c, \; r_3 = w_3 - s_4 \cdot c, \\
proof^* = \{\alpha_5, \alpha_6, \alpha_7, c, r_1, r_2, r_3\}
\end{array}
$$

Thus, we get $proof^*$. Now, we have generated a variable α_5, of which logarithm with base α_7 is R. Although we do not reveal R directly, the following things are convincing: (i) the discrete logarithm of α_2 is the multiplication result of the logarithms of g^{γ_i} and α_1; (ii) the discrete logarithm of α_4 is the multiplication result of the logarithms of g^{γ_j} and α_3; (iii) the discrete logarithm of α_5 is the multiplication result of the logarithms of g^{α_2} and α_4; (iv) the discrete logarithm of α_7 with base g is the multiplication result of the logarithms of α_1 and α_3 with base g. It implies that the discrete logarithm of α_5 with base α_7 is $R = \gamma_i \cdot \gamma_j$. The next step is to generate a intermediate variable β.

Step Two. We discuss the proof for x part first. The $voter_m$ computes $\alpha_8 = g^{Ry_i}$ and $\alpha_9 = g^{Rx_iy_i}$ and we have the following boolean expression: $e_l^x = (((\alpha_9 = (\alpha_8)^{s_5}) \wedge (t_{l1} = g^{s_5}) \wedge (\alpha_{12} = h^{s_5}) \wedge (\alpha_8 = (t_{l2})^{s_6}) \wedge (\alpha_5 = (\alpha_7)^{s_6}))$. The expression means that $\alpha_9 = (t_{l2})^{s_5 s_6}$ and the discrete logarithm of α_{12} is also s_5, where s_5 is the logarithm of t_{l1} with base g and s_6 is R. We also adopt the disjunctive proofs here: $PoK\{\exists(s_5, s_6) : e_1^x \vee \ldots \vee e_k^x\}$. Thus, it is convincing that α_9 is derived from some g^y and its discrete logarithm of g^y is Rx, where x is the discrete logarithm of some g^x in the blockchain. Assume that the $voter_m$ knows the x value of the dth group (t_{d1}, t_{d2}, t_{d3}). Let $s_5 = x_i$ and $s_6 = R$.

For $l \neq d$:

$(c_l, r_{l1}, r_{l2}) \xleftarrow{\$} \{0,1\}^*$, $k_{l1} = (\alpha_8)^{r_{l1}}(\alpha_9)^{c_l}$, $k_{l2} = (g)^{r_{l1}}(t_{l1})^{c_l}$, $k_{l3} = h^{r_{l1}}(\alpha_{12})^{c_l}$, $k_{l4} = (t_{l2})^{r_{l2}}(\alpha_8)^{c_l}$, $k_{l5} = (\alpha_7)^{r_{l2}}(\alpha_5)^{c_l}$,

For $l = d$:

$(w_1, w_2) \xleftarrow{\$} \{0,1\}^*$

$k_{l1} = (\alpha_8)^{w_1}$, $k_{l2} = g^{w_1}$, $k_{l3} = h^{w_1}$ $k_{l4} = (t_{l2})^{w_2}$, $k_{l5} = (\alpha_7)^{w_2}$,

$c \leftarrow Hash(\alpha_5, \alpha_7, \alpha_8, \alpha_9, \alpha_{12}, \{t_{l1}, t_{l2}, k_{l1}, \ldots, k_{l5}\}_{l \in \{1, \ldots, k\}})$

$c_d = c - \sum_{l \neq d} c_l$, $r_{d1} = w_1 - s_5 \cdot c_d$, $r_{d2} = w_2 - s_6 \cdot c_d$

$proof^x = (\alpha_8, \alpha_9, \alpha_{12}, \{c_l, r_{l1}, r_{l2}\}_{l \in \{1, \ldots, k\}}^x)$

Thus, we get $proof^x$. Similarly, we can generate proof for y value. The voter computes $\alpha_{10} = g^{Rx_j}$ and $\alpha_{11} = g^{Rx_jy_j}$ and we have following expression: $e_l^y = (((\alpha_{11} = (\alpha_{10})^{s_7}) \wedge (t_{l2} = g^{s_7}) \wedge (\alpha_{13} = h^{s_7}) \wedge (\alpha_{10} = (t_{l1})^{s_8}) \wedge (\alpha_5 = (\alpha_7)^{s_8}))$. Then $PoK\{\exists(s_7, s_8) : e_1^y \vee \ldots \vee e_k^y\} \rightarrow proof^y = (\alpha_{10}, \alpha_{11}, \alpha_{13}, \{c_l, r_{l1}, r_{l2}\}_{l \in \{1, \ldots, k\}}^y)$ We have the intermediate variable $\beta = \alpha_9/\alpha_{11} = g^{R(x_iy_i - x_jy_j)}$, of which the logarithm with base g is $R(x_iy_i - x_jy_j)$. We can know the logarithm of β with base B_m or B_m/g is R, so we can prove that the B_m is computed as stipulated.

Step Three. We want to get $PoK\{\exists s_9 : ((\beta = (B_m)^{s_9}) \wedge (\alpha_5 = (\alpha_7)^{s_9})) \vee ((\beta = (B_m/g)^{s_9}) \wedge (\alpha_5 = (\alpha_7)^{s_9}))\}$. Then for the $voter_m$, he knows $s_9 = R$. Assume that he chooses $v_m = 0$, then he generates proofs as follows:

$$
\begin{aligned}
&(w, c_2, r_2) \xleftarrow{\$} \{0,1\}^* \\
&k_1 = (B_m)^w, \ k_2 = (\alpha_7)^w, \ k_3 = (B_m/g)^{r_2}\beta^{c_2}, \ k_4 = (\alpha_7)^{r_2}(\alpha_5)^{c_2} \\
&c \leftarrow Hash(\alpha_5, \alpha_7, B_m, \beta, k_1, \ldots, k_4) \\
&c_1 = c - c_2, \ r_1 = w - s_9 \cdot c_1 \\
&proof^\# = \{c_1, r_1, c_2, r_2\}
\end{aligned}
$$

Then, we get $proof^\#$. Then, the final proof is $proof = (proof_1^\gamma, proof_2^\gamma, proof^*, proof^x, proof^y, proof^\#)$.

4 Analysis

4.1 Analysis of Generating Voting Parameters

Due to the randomness of the puzzle solution, the result of $g^{x_i y_i - x_j y_j}$ would also be a random number if $i \neq j$ from the view of other people except the exact voter. But if $i = j$, the ballot would be $g^{x_i y_i - x_j y_j + v} = g^v$, which is very easy to know which candidate the voter votes for. We call it a collision. As we know, the problem of no collisions is the same as the problem of giving two permutations of n different numbers such that the same number appears in the different places. The probability is approximately $1/e$. If someone claims that his blocks in x chain and y chain have the same order number, we need to restart the parameters generation. The expected number of occurrences is $e \approx 2.7$, so it is estimated that we need to generate the random numbers about 3 times on average to satisfy the requirements. It also implies that adding some more chains would decrease the chance of collisions.

4.2 Security Features of Our Voting System

Voter Anonymity. In our scheme, we send anonymous coins to the voting administrator when generating the voting parameters or casting ballots, like zerocoin or zerocash, which provides a strong privacy of the coin owner. Except the voter, nobody else can know who generates these parameters and casts the ballot. In the casting ballot phase, we use k groups to generate the proof. The idea is similar to ring signature so that it is difficult to guess who is the voter. Thus our scheme provides a strong anonymity.

Interim Result Unavailable. It is tricky to know vote result of each ballot and the random numbers would only be cancelled out after all ballots are multiplied together. Thus it is different to know interim results during the voting.

Double-Voting Resistance. It is required to send a coin in anonymous way to the voting administrator and every voter has only one voting coin (the other three coin are for generating voting parameters, so it is easy to make them different technically). Since the blockchain is designed to be resistant to double spending attack, so our scheme is double-voting resistance.

Public Verifiability. Everyone can check whether the zero knowledge proofs in each ballot are valid or not and everyone can also check whether the final tally results are right or not. Thus, our scheme is publicly verifiable.

Ballot Security. If a common attacker can know which candidate the ballot is voted for, then given $(g^{x_i}, g^{y_i}, g^{x_j}, g^{y_j})$, he can distinguish $g^{x_i y_i - x_j y_j}$ from $g^{x_i y_i - x_j y_j + 1}$, which implies that the 3DDH problem is solvable. It is believed that 3DDH problem is difficult, so there is no such an attacker. For more details, you can refer to the following lemma. For the two voters who share the same groups with Ballot generator, they can collude to decrypt the exact vote of this ballot. However, the analysis in voter anonymity implies that this kind of attack is risky and ineffective. Therefore, the ballots on the public ledger are secure.

In the following, we are going to analyze the security of ballot formally. In our scheme, $g^R = g^{\gamma_i \gamma_j}$ is not given directly because we want to preserve the anonymity of the scheme. And it is a secret number from the view of a common attacker or other voters. In the following lemma, we are going to consider the ballot security only. Thus, for simplicity, we will give this information to the distinguisher.

Lemma 1. *For a group $\mathcal{G}$ with order q, given $(g^a, g^b, g^c, g^d, g^r, g^{rab}, g^{rcd}, \Omega)$, where a, b, c, d, r are chosen randomly from Z_q^*, it is difficult to decide whether $\Omega = g^{ab-cd}$ or $\Omega = g^{ab-cd+1}$.*

Proof. First, we define a game with respect to the above lemma.

Definition 2. *(Game$_1$) For a group $\mathcal{G}$ with order q, the challenger $\mathcal{C}_1$ chooses a value $\zeta \in \{0, 1\}$ and computes $(g^a, g^b, g^c, g^d, g^r, g^{rab}, g^{rcd}, \Omega)$, where a, b, c, d, r are chosen randomly Z_q^*. If $\zeta = 0$, $\Omega = g^{ab-cd}$ and if $\zeta = 1$, $\Omega = g^{ab-cd+1}$. He sends the tuple to the distinguisher $\mathcal{D}_1$. The distinguisher $\mathcal{D}_1$ is to guess the value ζ'. If $\zeta = \zeta'$, $\mathcal{D}_1$ wins and the game output 1, otherwise, $\mathcal{D}_1$ loses and the game output 0. The probability that $\mathcal{D}_1$ wins is defined as $Pr[output(Game_1) == 1]$.*

Thus, the advantage that $\mathcal{D}_1$ wins is: $Adv(Game_1^{\mathcal{C}_1, \mathcal{D}_1}) = |Pr[output(Game_1) == 1] - 1/2|$. We say that if a distinguisher can have non-negligible advantage in $Game_1$, then he can also have non-negligible advantage in $Game_2$ defined in Definition 3. To be exact, we have $Adv(Game_1^{\mathcal{C}_1, \mathcal{D}_1}) \leq Adv(Game_2^{\mathcal{C}_2, \mathcal{D}_2})$.

Definition 3. *(Game$_2$) For a group $\mathcal{G}$ with order q, the challenger $\mathcal{C}_2$ chooses a value $\zeta \in \{0, 1\}$ and computes $(g^a, g^b, g^r, g^{rab}, \Omega)$, where a, b, r are chosen randomly from Z_q^*. If $\zeta = 0$, $\Omega = g^{ab}$ and if $\zeta = 1$, $\Omega = g^{ab+1}$. Then he sends the tuple to the distinguisher $\mathcal{D}_2$. The distinguisher $\mathcal{D}_2$ is to guess the value ζ'. If $\zeta = \zeta'$, $\mathcal{D}_2$ wins and the game output 1, otherwise, $\mathcal{D}_2$ loses and the game output 0. The probability that $\mathcal{D}_2$ wins is defined as $Pr[output(Game_1) == 1]$.*

The advantage that $\mathcal{D}_2$ wins is $Adv(Game_2^{\mathcal{C}_2, \mathcal{D}_2}) = |Pr[output(Game_2) == 1] - 1/2|$. Next, we prove $Adv(Game_1^{\mathcal{C}_1, \mathcal{D}_1}) \leq Adv(Game_2^{\mathcal{C}_2, \mathcal{D}_2})$. For a distinguisher $\mathcal{D}_2$ in $Game_2$, when he receives $(g^a, g^b, g^r, g^{rab}, \Omega)$ from challenger. He chooses c, d randomly and computes $(g^c, g^d, (g^r)^{cd}, \Omega' = \Omega \cdot g^{cd})$. He sends

$(g^a, g^b, g^c, g^d, g^r, g^{rab}, g^{rcd}, \Omega')$ to the distinguisher $\mathcal{D}_1$. Then, $\mathcal{D}_1$ outputs ζ' and $\mathcal{D}_2$ also outputs ζ'. It is easy to know that $\mathcal{D}_2$ wins if $\mathcal{D}_1$ wins. So, we have $Adv(Game_1^{\mathcal{C}_1, \mathcal{D}_\infty}) \leq Adv(Game_2^{\mathcal{C}_2, \mathcal{D}_2})$.

We now explain $Adv(Game_2^{\mathcal{C}_2, \mathcal{D}_2})$ is negligible. First, we have two tuples:

$$tuple_1 = (g, g^a, g^b, g^r, g^{ar}, g^{br}, g^{abr}, g^{ab})$$
$$tuple_2 = (g, g^a, g^b, g^r, g^{ar}, g^{br}, g^{abr}, R)$$

where $a, b, r \in Z_q^*$ and $R \in \mathcal{G}$ are chosen randomly. If we set $h = g^r, s = r^{-1}$, we have

$$tuple_1' = (h^s, h^{sa}, h^{sb}, h, h^a, h^b, h^{ab}, h^{abs})$$
$$tuple_2' = (h^s, h^{sa}, h^{sb}, h, h^a, h^b, h^{ab}, R)$$

Thus, it is difficult to distinguish $tuple_1'$ and $tuple_2'$ by 3DDH assumption, which implies it is difficult to distinguish $tuple_1$ and $tuple_2$. Also, we have

$$tuple_3 = (g, g^a, g^b, g^r, g^{ar}, g^{br}, g^{abr}, g^{ab}g)$$
$$tuple_4 = (g, g^a, g^b, g^r, g^{ar}, g^{br}, g^{abr}, R'g)$$

where R' is chosen randomly from $\mathcal{G}$. Similarly, it is also difficult to distinguish $tuple_3$ and $tuple_4$. We know that $tuple_2$ and $tuple_4$ are indistinguishable, so it is difficult to distinguish $tuple_1$ and $tuple_3$. Therefore, we have $Adv(Game_2^{\mathcal{C}_2, \mathcal{D}_2}) \leq \epsilon$ where ϵ is a negligible function. Hence, the lemma is true, which implies that in our scheme, it is difficult to know which candidate the ballots are voted for.

4.3 Multiple Candidates

In reality, there are more than two candidates. To solve this problem, we can prepare multiple bits. For example, there are three candidates, we have two bits v_1 and $v_2 \in \{0, 1\}$. Then, "00", "10" and "01" represent candidate 0, 1 and 2. Thus, the ballot have two parts, B_1 for v_1 and B_2 for v_2. We just need to change the boolean expressions of the zero knowledge. Thus, when tallying, multiply B_1's and B_2's together respectively. Therefore, the logarithm of production of B_1's is the votes for candidate 1 and the logarithm of production of B_2's is the votes for candidate 2. And the left are for candidate 0.

5   Conclusions and Future Work

In this work, we consider a self-tallying e-voting system without the requirement of having a powerful centralized authorities nor trusted third parties. To achieve this goal, we use a new kind of construction to cancel all random numbers in the ballots, which is used to encrypt the vote result. As a result, our scheme can reduce the time of generating a ballot with proofs. It still remains some problems for further research. Similar to [7], our scheme also requires all voters to cast their ballots. If one of them does not do it, then our scheme would not work. We notice that an accumulator is often used in zero knowledge proof to reduce the size and more advanced zero knowledge proof techniques are adopted in practical use or proposed, e.g. zk-SNARK used in [10] and bulletproofs [3]. It is another research interest to consider to improve the overhead of zero knowledge proofs using these techniques.

Acknowledgements. This project is partially supported by the RGC CRF funding (CityU, C1008-16G) of the HKSAR Government and by HITSZ, Shenzhen, China while SM Yiu visited HITSZ.

References

1. Caceo election costs study (2017). http://results.caceoelectioncosts.org/. Accessed 27 Sept 2018
2. Adida, B.: Helios: web-based open-audit voting. In: USENIX Security Symposium, vol. 17, pp. 335–348 (2008)
3. Bünz, B., Bootle, J., Boneh, D., Poelstra, A., Wuille, P., Maxwell, G.: Bulletproofs: short proofs for confidential transactions and more. In: Bulletproofs: Short Proofs for Confidential Transactions and More. IEEE (2018)
4. Chow, S.S., Liu, J.K., Wong, D.S.: Robust receipt-free election system with ballot secrecy and verifiability. In: NDSS, vol. 8, pp. 81–94 (2008)
5. Katz, J., Myers, S., Ostrovsky, R.: Cryptographic counters and applications to electronic voting. In: Pfitzmann, B. (ed.) EUROCRYPT 2001. LNCS, vol. 2045, pp. 78–92. Springer, Heidelberg (2001). https://doi.org/10.1007/3-540-44987-6_6
6. Li, C.T., Hwang, M.S., Lai, Y.C.: A verifiable electronic voting scheme over the internet. In: Sixth International Conference on Information Technology: New Generations, ITNG 2009, pp. 449–454. IEEE (2009)
7. McCorry, P., Shahandashti, S.F., Hao, F.: A smart contract for boardroom voting with maximum voter privacy. In: Kiayias, A. (ed.) FC 2017. LNCS, vol. 10322, pp. 357–375. Springer, Cham (2017). https://doi.org/10.1007/978-3-319-70972-7_20
8. Miers, I., Garman, C., Green, M., Rubin, A.D.: Zerocoin: anonymous distributed e-cash from bitcoin. In: 2013 IEEE Symposium on Security and Privacy (SP), pp. 397–411. IEEE (2013)
9. Nakamoto, S.: Bitcoin: a peer-to-peer electronic cash system (2008)
10. Sasson, E.B., et al.: Zerocash: decentralized anonymous payments from bitcoin. In: 2014 IEEE Symposium on Security and Privacy (SP), pp. 459–474. IEEE (2014)
11. Shahandashti, S.F., Hao, F.: DRE-ip: a verifiable e-voting scheme without tallying authorities. In: Askoxylakis, I., Ioannidis, S., Katsikas, S., Meadows, C. (eds.) ESORICS 2016. LNCS, vol. 9879, pp. 223–240. Springer, Cham (2016). https://doi.org/10.1007/978-3-319-45741-3_12
12. Steiner, M., Tsudik, G., Waidner, M.: Diffie-Hellman key distribution extended to group communication. In: Proceedings of the 3rd ACM Conference on Computer and Communications Security, pp. 31–37. ACM (1996)
13. Wood, G.: Ethereum: a secure decentralised generalised transaction ledger. Ethereum Project Yellow Pap. **151**, 1–32 (2014)
14. Yu, B., et al.: Platform-independent secure blockchain-based voting system. In: Chen, L., Manulis, M., Schneider, S. (eds.) ISC 2018. LNCS, vol. 11060, pp. 369–386. Springer, Cham (2018). https://doi.org/10.1007/978-3-319-99136-8_20

Cryptography

An Extended CTRT for AES-256

SeongHan Shin[1]($\boxtimes$), Shota Yamada[1], Goichiro Hanaoka[1], Yusuke Ishida[2], Atsushi Kunii[2], Junichi Oketani[2], Shimpei Kunii[2], and Kiyoshi Tomomura[2]

[1] National Institute of Advanced Industrial Science and Technology (AIST), 2-4-7 Aomi, Koto-ku, Tokyo 135-0064, Japan
`seonghan.shin@aist.go.jp`
[2] ZenmuTech Inc., 2-8-1 Nishigotanda, Shinagawa-ku, Tokyo 141-0031, Japan

Abstract. At CRYPTO 2000, Desai proposed a simple and faster AONT based on the CTR mode of encryption (called, CTRT) and proved its security in the ideal cipher model. Though AES-128 whose key length $k = 128$ and block length $l = 128$ can be used in CTRT as a block cipher, AES-256 cannot be used in CTRT due to its intrinsic restriction of $k \leq l$. According to a recent ECRYPT-CSA report, AES-256 is strongly recommended rather than AES-128 for long term protection (security for thirty to fifty years) and post-quantum security. In this paper, we propose an extended CTRT (named as XCTRT) suitable for AES-256. By thoroughly evaluating all the tricky cases, we prove that XCTRT is secure in the ideal cipher model under the same AONT security definition of Desai. Also, we discuss the security result of XCTRT in concrete parameter settings. After showing performance measurements of XCTRT, we can say that our XCTRT has high speed encoding/decoding performance and is quite practical to be deployed in the real-world applications (e.g., cloud storage service).

Keywords: AONT · CTRT · AES · Security proof · Implementation · Performance evaluation

1 Introduction

In 1979, Shamir [13] and Blakley [3] independently proposed a (t, n)-threshold secret sharing scheme that distributes a message m into a set of n shares such that at least t ($\leq$ n) shares can reconstruct the message m, but less than t shares do not reveal any information on m in the information-theoretical sense.

In this regard, AONT (All-or-Nothing Transform) can be understood as a (n, n)-threshold secret sharing scheme. The concept of AONT was proposed by Revist [12] as a pre-processing step to an ordinary encryption mode for block ciphers in order to slow down brute-force key searching attacks. Specifically, AONT is an unkeyed, invertible and randomized transformation with the property that it is impossible to invert unless all output blocks are known. In [12], Rivest proposed the first AONT (Package Transform (PT)) based on a block

© Springer Nature Switzerland AG 2020
I. You (Ed.): WISA 2019, LNCS 11897, pp. 79–91, 2020.
https://doi.org/10.1007/978-3-030-39303-8_7

cipher where each share is an output block of the underlying block cipher. Later, Boyko [4] formalized several security definitions for AONTs in a strong sense that each output bit is treated as one share, and then proved that OAEP [2] satisfies these definitions in the random oracle model. At CRYPTO 2000, Desai [6] suggested a new security definition for AONTs regarding key privacy and a new characterization of AONTs so that the resulting all-or-nothing encryption paradigm yields secure (block cipher) encryption modes. Also, Desai proposed a simple (and faster than PT) AONT based on the CTR mode of encryption (called, CTRT) and proved its security in the ideal cipher model. In [11], Resch and Plank proposed a file dispersal scheme (AONT-RS) by combining a variant of Rivest's AONT with Reed-Solomon coding [10] to achieve high security and low computation/storage costs. This AONT-RS was applied to a commercial service of IBM Cloud Object Storage [1]. Recently, Chen et al. [5] proposed a generalized AONT-RS to deal with small ciphertexts.

In this paper, we focus on AONTs based on a block cipher (particular, CTRT [6]). As a default block cipher, AES [8] has been widely used in almost all security protocols/applications (e.g., TLS, SSH, IPsec, Kerberos, WEP/WPA, ZigBee and EMV).

1.1 Motivation and Our Contributions

When instantiating the block cipher with AES [8], CTRT [6] can use AES-128 whose key length $k = 128$ and block length $l = 128$. If AES-256 is directly used in CTRT, the first 128-bit of the last block reveals an information on the secret key K. From this reason, Desai proved the security of CTRT with a restriction of $k \leq l$. According to a recent ECRYPT-CSA report [7], AES-128 is recommended for near term protection (security for at least ten years), but on the other hand AES-256 is recommended for long term protection (security for thirty to fifty years) and post-quantum security.

In this paper, we propose an extended CTRT (for short, XCTRT) which can use a block cipher with a longer secret key than a block size ($k = 2l$).[1] The main idea of XCTRT is that our XCTRT encoding algorithm generates each one block of the pseudo-ciphertext from two consecutive blocks of the input message. This construction, in fact, complicates a security proof of XCTRT much more than that of CTRT. By thoroughly evaluating all the tricky cases, we prove that XCTRT is secure in the ideal cipher model under the same AONT security definition of [6]. Also, we discuss the security result of XCTRT in concrete parameter settings. After showing implementation details and performance measurements of XCTRT, we can say that our XCTRT has high speed encoding/decoding performance and is quite practical to be deployed in the real-world applications.

---

[1] This indicates that XCTRT complements CTRT with respect to the usage of AES. That is, AES-128 can be used in CTRT and AES-256 can be used in XCTRT.

2   Preliminaries

2.1   Block Cipher

A block cipher with key length k and block length l is a map $F : \{0,1\}^k \times \{0,1\}^l \to \{0,1\}^l$ such that $F_K(\cdot) \overset{\text{def}}{=} F(K, \cdot) : \{0,1\}^l \to \{0,1\}^l$ is a bijective map for any $K \in \{0,1\}^k$. Since F_K is a permutation, we can define $F_K^{-1} : \{0,1\}^l \to \{0,1\}^l$. We also define F^{-1} as $F^{-1}(K, y) \overset{\text{def}}{=} F_K^{-1}(y)$.

In the ideal cipher model, we assume that we have an oracle access to (F, F^{-1}), where F is a randomly sampled permutation on $\{0,1\}^l \to \{0,1\}^l$. In this paper, we analyze the security of our AONT scheme in the ideal cipher model. We then replace it with AES when we implement our scheme and evaluate its performance.

2.2   Syntax of AONT

The syntax of (un-keyed) AONT is defined by a pair of algorithms $\Pi = (\mathcal{E}, \mathcal{D})$, which we call "transformation algorithms" here.

Definition 1 (Transformation Algorithms). *The pair of algorithms $\Pi = (\mathcal{E}, \mathcal{D})$ is called transformation algorithms with block length l if it satisfies the following conditions for some natural numbers n and m.*

- *$\mathcal{E}$, the encoding algorithm, is a probabilistic algorithm that takes a message $x \in \{0,1\}^{nl}$ as input and outputs a pseudo-ciphertext $y \in \{0,1\}^{ml}$.*
- *$\mathcal{D}$, the decoding algorithm, is a deterministic algorithm that takes a pseudo-ciphertext $y \in \{0,1\}^{ml}$ as input and outputs either a message $x \in \{0,1\}^{nl}$ or a special symbol $\perp$ to indicate that the pseudociphertext is invalid.*

As for the correctness, we require that $x = \mathcal{D}(\mathcal{E}(x))$ holds with probability 1. Furthermore, both algorithms in Π are allowed to access the ideal block cipher (F, F^{-1}).

As one can see from the syntax, both algorithms in Π do not take any secret/encryption key as an input. However, since we allow them to access the oracles (F, F^{-1}), they may use the ideal block cipher internally.

2.3   Security Definition for AONT

Here, we define the security of AONT following Desai [6], who gave the security proof for CTRT under the same security definition. Our extension of CTRT to be given in Sect. 3 satisfies the same security notion (see Sect. 4).

Definition 2 (Security for AONT). *Let $\Pi = (\mathcal{E}, \mathcal{D})$ be transformation algorithms with block length l. We then define a random variable $\mathrm{Exp}_\Pi^{\mathrm{aon}}(A)$ for an* *adversary A through the following security game:*

$(x, s) \leftarrow A^{F,F^{-1}}(\text{find}); //(s \text{ is the state information})$

$\quad y_0 \leftarrow \mathcal{E}(x);$

$\quad y_1 \xleftarrow{\$} \{0,1\}^{|y_0|}; // (y_b = y_b[1] \| \cdots \| y_b[m] \text{ where } y_b[i] \in \{0,1\}^k)$

$\quad b \xleftarrow{\$} \{0,1\};$

$\quad b' \leftarrow A^{\mathcal{Y},F,F^{-1}}(\text{guess}, s); // \mathcal{Y} \text{ takes an index } j \in [m] \text{ and returns } y_b[j]$

$\text{return } (b' \overset{?}{=} b),$

In the above experiment, the adversary can access $\mathcal{Y}$ at most $m - 1$ times. Let us define the advantage of A as follows:

$$\text{Adv}_\Pi^{\text{aon}}(A) \overset{\text{def}}{=} 2 \cdot \Pr\left[\text{Exp}_\Pi^{\text{aon}}(A) = 1\right] - 1,$$

$$\text{Adv}_\Pi^{\text{aon}}(t, m, p) \overset{\text{def}}{=} \max_A \{\text{Adv}_\Pi^{\text{aon}}(A)\} \tag{1}$$

where max in Eq. (1) is taken over all adversaries with computational time at most t and the number of oracle queries (to either F or F^{-1}) being at most p.

We set the key length k of block cipher to be the security parameter. We say that AONT is secure if $\text{Adv}_\Pi^{\text{aon}}(A)$ is negligible in the security parameter for any PPT adversary A.

We remark that the queries made by A are with respect to block indices of $\mathcal{Y}$ as in [6]. For example, we do not consider adversaries who can see substrings of y_i with length less than k for all i. As in [6], security against such an adversary is outside the scope of this paper. We refer to [4] for a stronger security definition and [6] for further discussions.

3   An Extended CTRT (XCTRT)

In this section, we propose an extended version of Desai's CTRT [6] (for short, XCTRT) which can use a block cipher with a longer secret key than a block size. Concretely, we will set $k = 2l$ where k is the key length of the block cipher and l is the block length to be encrypted.

XCTRT. Our XCTRT consists of an encoding algorithm $\mathcal{E}-\text{XCTRT}$ and a decoding algorithm $\mathcal{D}-\text{XCTRT}$, both of which are defined as follows.

Algorithm 1. $\mathcal{E}$–XCTRT	Algorithm 2. $\mathcal{D}$–XCTRT
Input: $x[1] \parallel \cdots \parallel x[n]$	**Input:** $y[1] \parallel \cdots \parallel y[m]$
$\quad K \leftarrow \{0,1\}^k$	$\quad K = y[1] \oplus \cdots \oplus y[m]$
$\quad$ **for** $i = 1, \cdots, n$ **do**	$\quad$ **for** $j = 1, \cdots, m-1$ **do**
$\quad\quad x'[i] = x[i] \oplus F_K(i)$	$\quad\quad x'[2j-1] = $ (The left l-bit of $y[j]$)
$\quad$ **end for**	$\quad\quad x'[2j] = $ (The right l-bit of $y[j]$)
$\quad$ **for** $j = 1, \cdots, m-1$ **do**	$\quad$ **end for**
$\quad\quad y[j] = x'[2j-1] \parallel x'[2j]$	$\quad$ **for** $i = 1, \cdots, n$ **do**
$\quad$ **end for**	$\quad\quad x[i] = x'[i] \oplus F_K(i)$
$\quad y[m] = K \oplus y[1] \oplus \cdots \oplus y[m-1]$	$\quad$ **end for**
Output: $y[1] \parallel \cdots \parallel y[m]$	**Output:** $x[1] \parallel \cdots \parallel x[n]$

Here, we set $k = 2l$ (where $k, l \in \mathbb{N}$), $|x| = nl$ ($n \in 2\mathbb{N}$), $|y| = mk$, and $m = \frac{n}{2} + 1$. We note that K is used as a secret key for a block cipher F and the key length is $k = |K|$. The block length of the input message is $l = |x[i]|$ ($i \in \mathbb{N}, i \leq n$) and the block length of the output is $k = 2l = |y[j]|$ ($j \in \mathbb{N}, j \leq m$).

In CTRT [6], each one block of the pseudo-ciphertext is generated from each *one block* of the input except for the last block, whereas it is generated from *two blocks* of the input in our encoding algorithm above. This difference stems from the fact that the key length k of the block cipher equals to the block length l of messages to be encrypted in CTRT, whereas $k = 2l$ in our XCTRT. In the next section, we show that our construction is secure even with this modification.

4   Security Proof for XCTRT

The following theorem asserts that our XCTRT is secure as per Definition 2.

Theorem 1 (Security of XCTRT). *If $X + p \leq 2^{k-1}$ and $X = 2^l(4m - 7) - (2m - 4)(2m - 3)$, then our XCTRT construction satisfies*

$$\mathrm{Adv}_{\Pi}^{\mathrm{aon}}(t, m, p) \leq \frac{4m^2}{2^l} + \frac{5p}{2^{k+1}}$$

under the ideal cipher model where m is the number of output blocks and p is the number of queries that the adversary makes to the ideal cipher oracles (F, F^{-1}).

Here, we consider the conditions $X + p \leq 2^{k-1}$ and $X = 2^l(4m - 7) - (2m - 4)(2m - 3)$ that are necessary for the theorem to hold. Asymptotically, since m and p are polynomials in the security parameter, these conditions always hold. Furthermore, the term $\frac{4m^2}{2^l} + \frac{5p}{2^{k+1}}$ in the right hand side of the equation in the theorem is negligible since m and p are polynomials in the security parameter. When setting concrete parameters, one should be careful so as to satisfy the conditions $m^2 \ll 2^l$ and $p \ll 2^k$.

Proof. We show an upper bound on the advantage of an adversary A against the security of XCTRT. Recall that we defined the advantage of the adversary as $\mathrm{Adv}_{\Pi}^{\mathrm{aon}}(A) \overset{\mathrm{def}}{=} 2 \cdot \Pr[\mathrm{Exp}_{\Pi}^{\mathrm{aon}}(A) = 1] - 1$ in Definition 2. Let us denote the event that $\mathrm{Exp}_{\Pi}^{\mathrm{aon}}(A) = 1$ occurring by AC (Adversary is Correct) in the following.

Let $K^\star$ be the key chosen in the security game when $b = 0$. We define Bad as the event such that A makes a query for $F_{K^\star}(\cdot)$ or $F_{K^\star}^{-1}(\cdot)$ when $b = 0$. We also define FBad (resp., GBad) as the event such that Bad occurs in find (resp., guess) stage. We denote the number of queries to the oracles in the find (resp., guess) stage to be p_F (resp., p_G). By definition, we have $p = p_F + p_G$.

The upper bound on $\Pr[AC]$ can be given as follows:

$$\Pr[AC] = \Pr[AC \wedge \overline{\mathsf{Bad}}] + \Pr[AC \wedge \mathsf{Bad}]$$
$$\leq \Pr[AC \wedge \overline{\mathsf{Bad}}] + \Pr[\mathsf{Bad}] \leq \Pr[AC \wedge \overline{\mathsf{Bad}}] + \Pr[\mathsf{FBad}] + \Pr[\mathsf{GBad}]$$
$$= \Pr[AC \wedge \overline{\mathsf{Bad}}] + \Pr[\mathsf{FBad}] + \Pr[\mathsf{GBad} \wedge \mathsf{FBad}] + \Pr[\mathsf{GBad} \wedge \overline{\mathsf{FBad}}]$$
$$\leq \Pr[AC \wedge \overline{\mathsf{Bad}}] + 2\Pr[\mathsf{FBad}] + \Pr[\mathsf{GBad}|\overline{\mathsf{FBad}}]$$

where the second inequality follows from $\mathsf{Bad} = \mathsf{FBad} \cup \mathsf{GBad}$ and the union bound, the third inequality follows from $\Pr[\mathsf{E} \wedge \mathsf{F}] \leq \Pr[\mathsf{F}]$ for any events E and F. We therefore have

$$\Pr[AC] \leq \Pr[AC \wedge \overline{\mathsf{Bad}}] + 2\Pr[\mathsf{FBad}] + \Pr[\mathsf{GBad}|\overline{\mathsf{FBad}}]. \tag{2}$$

To finish the proof, we give bounds on each term in the right hand side of the equation above. To do so, we will prove Lemmas 1, 2, and 3 in the following.

Lemma 1.
$$\Pr[AC \wedge \overline{\mathsf{Bad}}] \leq \frac{1}{2} + \frac{m^2}{2^l} + \frac{p}{2^{k+1}}.$$

Proof. Let us define the left l-bit (resp., right l-bit) of $(x[2i-1]\|x[2i]) \oplus y_b[i]$ to be $z[2i-1]$ (resp., $z[2i]$) for $1 \leq i \leq m-1$. We define Cl_1 as the event such that $z[i] = z[j]$ holds for some $i, j \in [2(m-1)]$ with $i \neq j$. Note that by the definition of XCTRT, Cl_1 never occurs when $b = 0$ since we have $z[i] = F_{K^\star}(i)$ and $F_{K^\star}$ is a permutation in this case. We show an upper bound on $\Pr[\mathsf{Cl}_1]$.

$$\Pr[\mathsf{Cl}_1] = (1/2) \cdot \Pr[\mathsf{Cl}_1|b=0] + (1/2) \cdot \Pr[\mathsf{Cl}_1|b=1]$$
$$= (1/2) \cdot \Pr\left[\begin{array}{c|c} \exists i, j \in [2(m-1)] & \\ \text{s.t. } i \neq j \wedge z[i] = z[j] & b=1 \end{array}\right]$$
$$\leq (1/2) \cdot \sum_{i,j \in [2(m-1)], i \neq j} \Pr[z[i] = z[j]|b=1]$$
$$= (1/2) \cdot \binom{2(m-1)}{2} \cdot 2^{-l} \leq \frac{m^2}{2^l}.$$

In the above, the first equality follows from the security definition, the second equality from the definition of Cl_1, the first inequality follows from the union bound, and the third equality follows from the fact that each $z[i]$ is distributed uniformly at random over $\{0,1\}^l$ since so is $y[i]$ in the case of $b = 1$.

We also define Cl_2 as the event such that $b = 1$ and A makes a query to either $F_{K'}$ or $F_{K'}^{-1}$, where we define $K' \stackrel{\text{def}}{=} y_b[1] \oplus y_b[2] \oplus \cdots y_b[m]$. Since K' is distributed uniformly at random over $\{0,1\}^k$ when $b = 1$ and A makes at most p queries to its oracles, we can bound the probability of Cl_2 occurring by $p \cdot 2^{-k}$. From the above discussion, we have

$$\Pr[\mathsf{Cl}_2 \wedge \overline{\mathsf{Bad}}] = (1/2) \cdot \Pr[\mathsf{Cl}_2 \wedge b = 0] + (1/2) \cdot \Pr[\mathsf{Cl}_2 \wedge b = 1] = p \cdot 2^{-k-1}.$$

We then evaluate $\Pr[\mathsf{AC} \wedge \overline{\mathsf{Bad}}]$ as

$$
\begin{aligned}
\Pr[\mathsf{AC} \wedge \overline{\mathsf{Bad}}] &= \Pr[\mathsf{AC} \wedge \overline{\mathsf{Bad}} \wedge b = 0] + \Pr[\mathsf{AC} \wedge \overline{\mathsf{Bad}} \wedge b = 1] \\
&= \Pr[\mathsf{AC} \wedge \overline{\mathsf{Bad}} \wedge b = 0] + \Pr[\mathsf{AC} \wedge b = 1] \\
&= \Pr[\mathsf{AC} \wedge \overline{\mathsf{Bad}} \wedge b = 0] + \Pr[\mathsf{AC} \wedge (\overline{\mathsf{Cl}}_1 \wedge \overline{\mathsf{Cl}}_2) \wedge b = 1] \\
&\quad + \Pr[\mathsf{AC} \wedge (\mathsf{Cl}_1 \vee \mathsf{Cl}_2) \wedge b = 1] \\
&\leq \Pr[\mathsf{AC} \wedge \overline{\mathsf{Bad}} \wedge b = 0] + \Pr[\mathsf{AC} \wedge (\overline{\mathsf{Cl}}_1 \wedge \overline{\mathsf{Cl}}_2) \wedge b = 1] + \Pr[\mathsf{Cl}_1 \vee \mathsf{Cl}_2] \\
&\leq \Pr[\mathsf{AC}|\overline{\mathsf{Bad}} \wedge b = 0] \cdot \Pr[\overline{\mathsf{Bad}} \wedge b = 0] \\
&\quad + \Pr[\mathsf{AC}|(\overline{\mathsf{Cl}}_1 \wedge \overline{\mathsf{Cl}}_2) \wedge b = 1] \cdot \Pr[(\overline{\mathsf{Cl}}_1 \wedge \overline{\mathsf{Cl}}_2) \wedge b = 1] + \Pr[\mathsf{Cl}_1] + \Pr[\mathsf{Cl}_2] \\
&\leq \Pr[\mathsf{AC}|\overline{\mathsf{Bad}} \wedge b = 0] \cdot \Pr[b = 0] + \Pr[\mathsf{AC}|(\overline{\mathsf{Cl}}_1 \wedge \overline{\mathsf{Cl}}_2) \wedge b = 1] \cdot \Pr[b = 1] \\
&\quad + \Pr[\mathsf{Cl}_1] + \Pr[\mathsf{Cl}_2] \\
&\leq \frac{1}{2} \left(\Pr[\mathsf{AC}|\overline{\mathsf{Bad}} \wedge b = 0] + \Pr[\mathsf{AC}|(\overline{\mathsf{Cl}}_1 \wedge \overline{\mathsf{Cl}}_2) \wedge b = 1] \right) + \frac{m^2}{2^l} + \frac{p}{2^{k+1}},
\end{aligned}
$$

where the second equality follows since Bad does not occur when $b = 1$, and the second inequality follows from Bayes' theorem and the union bound.

In order to finish the proof of the lemma, it suffices to prove

$$\Pr[\mathsf{AC}|\overline{\mathsf{Bad}} \wedge b = 0] + \Pr[\mathsf{AC}|(\overline{\mathsf{Cl}}_1 \wedge \overline{\mathsf{Cl}}_2) \wedge b = 1] = 1.$$

By the definition of AC, the first term in the left hand side above is the probability that A outputs 0 under the condition $(\overline{\mathsf{Bad}} \wedge b = 0)$, whereas the second term is the probability that A outputs 1 under the condition $(\overline{\mathsf{Cl}}_1 \wedge \overline{\mathsf{Cl}}_2 \wedge b = 1)$. It suffices to show that the view of the adversary conditioned on $(\overline{\mathsf{Bad}} \wedge b = 0)$ is completely the same as that conditioned on $(\overline{\mathsf{Cl}}_1 \wedge \overline{\mathsf{Cl}}_2 \wedge b = 1)$. We first observe that when $b = 0$, $\{y_0[j]\}_{j \in [2(m-1)]}$ is distributed uniformly at random under the condition that $z[i] \neq z[j]$ for $i \neq j$, since y_0 is generated by the encoding algorithm honestly and F is a permutation. By definition, $\{y_1[j]\}_{j \in [2(m-1)]}$ follows the same distribution when $\overline{\mathsf{Cl}}_1$. We then fix the values of $y_b[1], \ldots, y_b[m-1]$. We observe that $y_0[m]$ is distributed uniformly at random so that A has not queried to $F_{K'}$ nor $F_{K'}^{-1}$ because we assumed $\overline{\mathsf{Bad}}$. We can also observe that $y_1[m]$ follows the same distribution since we assumed Cl_2. This completes the proof of the lemma.

Lemma 2.

$$\Pr[\mathsf{FBad}] \leq \frac{p_F}{2^{k+1}}.$$

Proof. Recall that FBad is the event such that $b = 0$ holds and A makes a query to either F_{K^*} or $F_{K^*}^{-1}$. We observe that the number of keys K for which A makes a query of the form $F(K, \cdot)$ or $F^{-1}(K, \cdot)$ is bounded by p_F. Furthermore, the information of K^* is not revealed to A in find stage, since A is not given pseudo-ciphertext at this point. The above observation along with the fact that K^* is chosen uniformly at random from $\{0, 1\}^k$ implise $\Pr[\mathsf{FBad}] \leq \Pr[b = 0] \cdot \frac{p_F}{2^k} = \frac{p_F}{2^{k+1}}$. This completes the proof of the lemma.

Lemma 3. *We have*

$$\Pr[\mathsf{GBad}|\overline{\mathsf{FBad}}] \leq \frac{p_G}{2^{k-1}},$$

where $X + p \leq 2^{k-1}$ *and* $X = 2^l(4m - 7) - (2m - 4)(2m - 3)$.

Proof. We first evaluate the probability such that the first query in guess stage made by A is either to F_{K^*} or $F_{K^*}^{-1}$. In order to do so, we analyze the distribution of K^* from the view of A that is given y_b and under the condition $\overline{\mathsf{FBad}}$.

In the following, let $\tilde{y}$ ($|\tilde{y}| = nl$) be the substring of the challenge pseudo-ciphertext y given to A by the game. A can obtain partial information of K^* from $\tilde{y}$. Without loss of generality, we assume $y = y_0$. We first observe that if $\tilde{y}$ is obtained by removing $y[m]$ from y (namely, if A does not query m to $\mathcal{Y}$), A cannot obtain any information about K^*. Therefore, we can assume that $\tilde{y}$ is obtaind from y by removing $y[j]$ ($1 \leq j \leq m - 1$) from it. First, since

$$F_{K^*}(2i - 1) \parallel F_{K^*}(2i) = (x[2i - 1] \parallel x[2i]) \oplus y[i], \tag{3}$$

the adversary knows the values of $\mathbf{S} = \{F_{K^*}(2a - 1), F_{K^*}(2a) \mid (1 \leq a \leq m - 1) \land (a \neq j)\}$. Furthermore, since A knows $y[j']$ for $j \neq j$, it can obtain K^* once it obtains $y[j]$[2]. Namely, from the view of A, knowing $y[j]$ is equivalent to knowing K^*. By the construction of $\mathcal{E}-\mathrm{XCTRT}$, we have

$$y[j] = (x[2j - 1] \oplus F_K(2j - 1)) \parallel (x[2j] \oplus F_K(2j)). \tag{4}$$

Here, $x[2j - 1]$ and $x[2j]$ are known to A since they are chosen by A itself. Therefore, in Eq. (4), only $F_K(2j - 1)$ and $F_K(2j)$ are unknown to A. Since F is modeled as an ideal cipher and thus $F_{K^*}(\cdot)$ is a permutation, we have $F_{K^*}(2j - 1) \notin \mathbf{S}$, $F_{K^*}(2j) \notin \mathbf{S}$, and $F_{K^*}(2j - 1) \neq F_{K^*}(2j)$. Therefore, the number of possible $y[j]$ (or equivalently, the number of possible K^*) is

$$(2^l - 2(m - 2))(2^l - 2(m - 2) - 1) = 2^k - X.$$

Namely, even though K^* is chosen uniformly at random from the set $\{0, 1\}^k$, whose size is 2^k, A can reduce the number of possible K^* by using the information from $\tilde{y}$ down to $2^k - X$. Furthermore, A can remove the keys that are used in the find stage from the candidates. As a result, the number of possible K^* is

---

[2] The only unknown term in $K = y[1] \oplus \cdots \oplus y[j] \oplus \cdots \oplus y[m]$ is $y[j]$.

further reduced to $2^k - X - p_F$. Let GBad_i be the event that GBad happens in the i-th query in the **guess** stage. We then have

$$\Pr[\mathsf{GBad}|\overline{\mathsf{FBad}}] \leq \Pr[\mathsf{GBad}_1|\overline{\mathsf{FBad}}] + \sum_{i=2}^{p_G} \Pr[\mathsf{GBad}_i|\overline{\mathsf{GBad}}_{i-1} \wedge \overline{\mathsf{FBad}}].$$

From the discussion above, we have $\Pr[\mathsf{GBad}_1|\overline{\mathsf{FBad}}] \leq \frac{1}{2^k - X - p_F}$. After the first query, the number of possible K^* will further decrease and we have $\Pr[\mathsf{GBad}_i|\overline{\mathsf{GBad}}_{i-1} \wedge \overline{\mathsf{FBad}}] \leq \frac{1}{2^k - X - p_F - (i-1)}$. Therefore, it holds

$$\Pr[\mathsf{GBad}|\overline{\mathsf{FBad}}] \leq \sum_{i=1}^{p_G} \frac{1}{2^k - X - p_F - (i-1)} \leq \frac{p_G}{2^k - X - p} \leq \frac{2p_G}{2^k}.$$

In the above, the second inequality follows from $p_F + i - 1 < p$ for $i \leq p_G$ and the third inequality follows from $X + p \leq 2^{k-1}$. This completes the proof of the lemma.

By combining Eq. (2) and Lemmas 1, 2, and 3, Theorem 1 follows.

5   Discussion

5.1   An Upper Bound on Input Message Length

From Theorem 1, we can see that the advantage of an adversary becomes larger as the number of output blocks m increases. In other words, the security of XCTRT decreases as the length of the input/output becomes longer. Here, we discuss how long input messages we can take in our XCTRT without affecting the security in practical parameter settings.

Let us recall that the advantage of an adversary is $\frac{4m^2}{2^l} + \frac{5p}{2^{k+1}}$ in the theorem. Here, p is the number of queries made by A and can be considered as the computational power of the adversary A. k and l are the key length and the block length of the block cipher, respectively. Let us set $m = 2^b$ and $p = 2^c$ and evaluate both terms. We have

$$\frac{4m^2}{2^l} + \frac{5p}{2^{k+1}} \approx \begin{cases} \frac{4m^2}{2^l}, & \text{if } \frac{4m^2}{2^l} \geq \frac{5p}{2^{k+1}}, \\ \frac{5p}{2^{k+1}}, & \text{otherwise} \end{cases},$$

where we ignore smaller term in each case. We then take logarithm of both sides in the above equation to obtain

$$\log_2\left(\frac{4m^2}{2^l} + \frac{5p}{2^{k+1}}\right) \approx \begin{cases} 2b - l + 2, & \text{if } b \geq \frac{c-k+l}{2} - \frac{3-\log_2 5}{2}, \\ c - k - 1 + \log_2 5, & \text{otherwise.} \end{cases} \tag{5}$$

Now, we discuss the security by setting concrete parameters. Since we will instantiate the block cipher with AES-256, we set $k = 256$ and $l = 128$ that satisfy $k = 2l$. We also set the number of oracle queries made by A to be $p = 2^{100}$

($c = 100$), which seems to be sufficiently large to capture the computational power of current real-world adversaries. In this parameter setting, we have $b \geq \frac{c-k+l}{2} - \frac{3-\log_2 5}{2}$ and thus we have $\log_2 \left(\frac{4m^2}{2^l} + \frac{5p}{2^{k+1}} \right) \approx 2b - 126$ from Eq. (5). We then set the upper bound on the advantage for an adversary to be 2^{-30}. To retain this security level, it suffices to satisfy $2b - 126 \leq -30 \Leftrightarrow b \leq 48$. Since the input message length is $|x| = nl = 2l(m-1) = 2^{b+8} - 2^8$, we conclude that our XCTRT remains secure as long as the message length is up to 2^{55}. This is about 4 petabytes, which is significantly large data size to be processed at once. This implies that the XCTRT construction is secure, as long as it is not required to deal with exceptionally huge data (larger than 4 petabytes message size) at once.

5.2   A Comparison of CTRT and XCTRT

In this subsection, we compare CTRT and XCTRT with respect to a relation between the number of output blocks m and the advantage of an adversary A in practical parameter settings.

Let us remind that the advantage of A is upper bounded by $\frac{4m^2}{2^l} + \frac{5p}{2^{k+1}}$ in XCTRT, and by $\frac{m^2+8p}{2^k}$ in CTRT (Theorem 2 of [6]). We set $k = l = 128$ for CTRT because AES-128 can be used as the block cipher, and set $k = 2l = 256$ for XCTRT because the block cipher can be instantiated with AES-256. As discussed in Sect. 1.1, AES-256 cannot be used in CTRT due to its intrinsic restriction $k \leq l$. We also set the number of oracle queries made by A to be $p = 2^{100}$, as in Sect. 5.1.

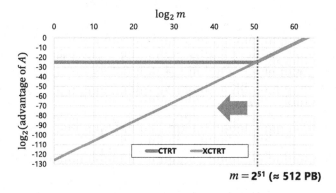

Fig. 1. A comparison of CTRT and XCTRT where $p = 2^{100}$, and AES-128 (resp., AES-256) is used in CTRT (resp., XCTRT)

With this parameter setting, we show a graphical comparison of CTRT and XCTRT with respect to a relation between m and the advantage of A in Fig. 1. When the number of output blocks $m \geq 2^{51}$, the advantage of A is almost same

Table 1. Measurement results of XCTRT encoding/decoding (in average)

Input message size	Processing time [ms]		Speed [MB/s]	
	Encoding	Decoding	Encoding	Decoding
4 KB	0.14	0.09	27	43
8 KB	0.13	0.10	59	82
16 KB	0.11	0.10	137	159
32 KB	0.14	0.11	230	288
64 KB	0.17	0.14	362	453
128 KB	0.19	0.15	664	847
256 KB	0.27	0.27	921	937
512 KB	0.82	0.39	611	1,293
1 MB	0.74	0.73	1,359	1,365
2 MB	1.39	1.33	1,436	1,501
4 MB	2.90	2.84	1,379	1,410
8 MB	5.87	5.59	1,362	1,431
16 MB	12.72	12.89	1,258	1,242
32 MB	22.36	21.86	1,431	1,464
64 MB	42.37	42.07	1,510	1,521
128 MB	84.46	85.11	1,516	1,504
256 MB	168.08	166.91	1,523	1,534
512 MB	335.80	336.43	1,525	1,522
1 GB	673.13	679.81	1,521	1,506

in both CTRT and XCTRT. When $m < 2^{51}$, the advantage of A in CTRT is fixed to be $\approx 2^{-25}$ whereas the advantage of A in XCTRT decreases linearly along with the decrease of m. From this, it is clear that our XCTRT guarantees a higher level of security, compared to CTRT, as the number of output blocks m decreases ($m < 2^{51}$).

6   Implementation and Performance Evaluation

Implementation Details. By instantiating the block cipher with AES-256, we implemented XCTRT on a PC whose OS is Microsoft Windows 10 Pro, OS version is 10.0.16299 N/A build 16299, processor and memory are Intel64 Family 6 Model 94 Stepping 3 GenuineIntel 3408 Mhz (Intel® Core™ i7-6700 CPU @ 3.40GHz) and 16 GB RAM, respectively. The implementation environment is as follows. We used C++ language and Visual Studio 2017 Version 15.4.1 as an integrated development environment where 'VC++ Version 19.11.25547 for x64' compiler and optimization options /GL /Ox /Ot /Oi are utilized. In our implementation, we used Cryptography API: Next Generation (CNG) [9] of Windows API which automatically enables AES-NI (Advanced Encryption Standard New Instructions) for AES hardware acceleration.[3]

Performance Measurement. We measure performance of XCTRT encoding/decoding in order to confirm that our software implementation of XCTRT is practical enough to be deployed in the real-world applications.

For each input message size, we run XCTRT encoding/decoding 10 times from which an average processing time (excluding a maximum value and a minimum value) is obtained. We show measurement results of XCTRT encoding/decoding in Table 1.[4] For example, both the XCTRT encoding and decoding algorithms only take less than 680 ms to process an input message of 1 GB size. Thus, we can say that our XCTRT has high speed encoding/decoding performance and is quite practical.

References

1. IBM Cloud Object Storage. https://www.ibm.com/cloud/object-storage
2. Bellare, M., Rogaway, P.: Optimal asymmetric encryption. In: De Santis, A. (ed.) EUROCRYPT 1994. LNCS, vol. 950, pp. 92–111. Springer, Heidelberg (1995). https://doi.org/10.1007/BFb0053428
3. Blakley, G.R.: Safeguarding cryptographic keys. In: Proceedings of the 1979 AFIPS National Computer Conference, pp. 313–317. AFIPS Press (1979)
4. Boyko, V.: On the security properties of OAEP as an all-or-nothing transform. In: Wiener, M. (ed.) CRYPTO 1999. LNCS, vol. 1666, pp. 503–518. Springer, Heidelberg (1999). https://doi.org/10.1007/3-540-48405-1_32
5. Chen, L., Laing, T.M., Martin, K.M.: Revisiting and extending the AONT-RS scheme: a robust computationally secure secret sharing scheme. In: Joye, M., Nitaj, A. (eds.) AFRICACRYPT 2017. LNCS, vol. 10239, pp. 40–57. Springer, Cham (2017). https://doi.org/10.1007/978-3-319-57339-7_3
6. Desai, A.: The security of all-or-nothing encryption: protecting against exhaustive key search. In: Bellare, M. (ed.) CRYPTO 2000. LNCS, vol. 1880, pp. 359–375. Springer, Heidelberg (2000). https://doi.org/10.1007/3-540-44598-6_23
7. ECRYPT-CSA: Algorithms, Key Size and Protocols Report, February 2018. http://www.ecrypt.eu.org/csa/documents/D5.4-FinalAlgKeySizeProt.pdf
8. FIPS PUB 197: Advanced Encryption Standard (AES), November 2001. https://csrc.nist.gov/csrc/media/publications/fips/197/final/documents/fips-197.pdf
9. Microsoft: Cryptography API: Next Generation. https://docs.microsoft.com/en-us/windows/desktop/seccng/cng-portal

---

[3] Though resistance to side-channel attacks lies outside the scope of this paper, it might be interesting to consider such property for software/hardware implementations of XCTRT.

[4] Only when the input size is 512 KB, the speed of encoding is quite slower than that of decoding. As a future work, we'd like to clarify an exact reason of this strange phenomenon.

10. Reed, I.S., Solomon, G.: Polynomial codes over certain finite fields. J. Soc. Ind. Appl. Math. **8**(2), 300–304 (1960)
11. Resch, J.K., Plank, J.S.: AONT-RS: blending security and performance in dispersed storage systems. In: FAST 2011, pp. 191–202. USENIX (2011)
12. Rivest, R.L.: All-or-nothing encryption and the package transform. In: Biham, E. (ed.) FSE 1997. LNCS, vol. 1267, pp. 210–218. Springer, Heidelberg (1997). https://doi.org/10.1007/BFb0052348
13. Shamir, A.: How to share a secret. Commun. ACM **22**(11), 612–613 (1979)

A Blind Ring Signature Based on the Short Integer Solution Problem

Huy Quoc Le[1]($\boxtimes$) (iD), Dung Hoang Duong[2], and Willy Susilo[2]

[1] Graduate School of Mathematics, Kyushu University,
744 Motooka, Nishi-ku, Fukuoka-shi, Fukuoka-ken 819-0395, Japan
q-le@math.kyushu-u.ac.jp
[2] Institute of Cybersecurity and Cryptology,
School of Computing and Information Technology, University of Wollongong,
Northfields Avenue, Wollongong, NSW 2522, Australia
{hduong,wsusilo}@uow.edu.au

Abstract. A blind ring signature scheme is a combination of a ring signature and a blind signature, which allows not only any member of a group of signers to sign on a message on behalf of the group without revealing its identity but also the user who possesses the message to blind it before sending to the group to be signed. Blind ring signature schemes are essential components in e-commercial, e-voting etc. In this paper, we propose the first blind ring signature scheme based on lattices. More precisely, our proposed scheme is proven to be secure in random oracle model under the hardness of the short integer solution (SIS) problem.

1 Introduction

Ring signatures were first introduced by Rivest et al. [19] in 2001. In such a scheme, a signer within a group can form a ring consisting of members in the group to sign a message on behalf of this ring, without using the secret keys of those members. A verifier can easily verify that the signature belongs to the ring using the ring public keys, but cannot reveal the identity of the signer, hence ensures the anonymity of the signer. Ring signatures can be used for whistle blowing [19] or anonymous membership authentication for ad hoc groups [5]. They can be used to derive other primitives such as deniable ring authentication [23] or perfect concurrent signatures [24]. Due to flexibility (forming a ring and signing messages without a group leader) and anonymity property of ring signatures, there have been recently found interesting applications of ring signatures in cryptocurrencies [21]. Another important kind of protocol that provides anonymity is blind signatures, first proposed by Chaum [6] for untraceable payments in 1983. Blind signatures allow a person to get a message signed by a signer without revealing any information about the message to the signer, and hence which provide the anonymity of the signed message. It therefore makes blind signatures useful in electronic auctions and electronic voting systems.

In some real-life applications, such as banking, we must make a single e-bank system more scalable by supporting many banks and adding some other

© Springer Nature Switzerland AG 2020
I. You (Ed.): WISA 2019, LNCS 11897, pp. 92–111, 2020.
https://doi.org/10.1007/978-3-030-39303-8_8

properties like strong anonymity of the signing banks and unlinkability of two different signatures. It's therefore necessary to combine blind and ring signatures into one, called *blind ring signatures*. Clearly, blind ring signatures find applications in various real-life scenarios that are required a combination of ring signatures and blind signatures; for examples, multi authority e-voting and distributed e-cash systems. Some examples of such contexts can be found such as in [9, 12, 26].

With the threat of Shor's quantum algorithms [22], the research community has been moving towards to post-quantum cryptography [4] in which lattice-based cryptography is one of the most promising candidates due to its high asymptotic efficiency and parallelism, as well as security under worst-case intractability assumptions. At ASIACRYPT 2009, Lyubashevksy [14] constructed a lattice-based identification scheme based on ideal lattices, and obtained a signature scheme via Fiat-Shamir's transformation [7]. Lyubashevsky later improved to a new signature scheme [15] whose security is based on the SIS problem. At AfricaCrypt 2013 [1], Aguilar-Melchor et al. proposed the first lattice-based ring signature scheme. Their construction is based on the scheme of Lyubashevsky [14] over ideal lattices. In 2018, Wang et al. [25] proposed a construction of ring signature from an improved scheme of Lyubashevsky [15]. Regarding blind signatures, the first scheme based on ideal lattices was introduced by Rückert [20] at Asiacrypt 2010. Recently, in 2018, Zhang et al. [27] also gave a new post-quantum construction for blind signature.

In this paper, inspired from the work of Rückert [20] and two aforementioned works on ring signature [25] and blind signature [27], we construct, for the first time, a blind ring signature scheme based on lattices. The scheme is provably secure (i.e., anonymous, blind and one-more unforgeable) in the random oracle model under the hardness of the SIS problem. Our work exploits the rejection sampling technique [15] and the trapdoor technique [8], which are fundamental tools used in lattice-based cryptography.

2   Preliminaries

Notations. For a positive integer l, we write $[l]$ for the set $\{1, 2, \cdots, l\}$. A column vector is denoted by small bold letter, e.g., vector $\mathbf{v}$. A matrix is denoted by bold capital letter, e.g., $\mathbf{A}$. Sometimes we write a_i, the i-th component of a vector $\mathbf{a} = (a_1, \cdots, a_n)$, by $\mathbf{a}[i]$. The notation $\mathbf{A}[i]$ is also used to stand for the i-th column of a matrix $\mathbf{A}$. The Gram-Schmidt orthogonal matrix of a matrix $\mathbf{A}$ will be written as $\tilde{\mathbf{A}}$. By notation "$x := a$" we mean that the variable x is assigned the value a or x is defined as a. We write $a \leftarrow_\$ A$ to say that a is sampled uniformly at random from the discrete set A; while if $\mathcal{D}$ is a probability distribution, then $a \leftarrow \mathcal{D}$ means that a is sampled according to $\mathcal{D}$. In case $\mathcal{A}$ is an algorithm, we write $a \leftarrow \mathcal{A}$ to say that a is an output of $\mathcal{A}$.

A *lattice* is a set of all integral combinations of given linearly independent vectors. Formally, given a matrix $\mathbf{A} = [\mathbf{a}_1, \cdots, \mathbf{a}_m] \in \mathbb{R}^{n \times m}$ such that $\mathbf{a}_i$'s are linearly independent, a lattice of *basis* $\mathbf{A}$ is the set $\mathcal{L}(\mathbf{A}) := \{\sum_{i \in [m]} \mathbf{a}_i z_i : z_i \in$

$\mathbb{Z}$}. For such a lattice, we call n the *dimension* of $\mathcal{L}(\mathbf{A})$. Take for example, for a random matrix $\mathbf{A} \leftarrow_\$ \mathbb{Z}^{n \times m}$, the following are also lattices, called *q-ary lattices*:

$$\Lambda = \{\mathbf{v} \in \mathbb{Z}^m : \mathbf{v} = \mathbf{A}\mathbf{z} \pmod{q} \text{ for some } \mathbf{z} \in \mathbb{Z}^n\},$$

$$\Lambda_q^\perp(\mathbf{A}) = \{\mathbf{z} \in \mathbb{Z}^m : \mathbf{A}\mathbf{z} = \mathbf{0} \pmod{q}, \text{ where } \mathbf{A} \leftarrow_\$ \mathbb{Z}^{n \times m}\}. \tag{1}$$

The *first minimum* of a lattice $\mathcal{L}$ is defined as $\lambda_1(\mathcal{L}) := \min_{\mathbf{v} \in \mathcal{L} \setminus \{\mathbf{0}\}} \|\mathbf{v}\|$. The *i-th minimum* of a lattice $\mathcal{L}$ of dimension n is denoted by and defined as $\lambda_i(\mathcal{L}) := \min\{r : \dim(\text{span}(\mathcal{L} \cap \mathcal{B}_n(0, r))) \geq i\}$, where $\mathcal{B}_n(0, r) = \{\mathbf{x} \in \mathbb{R}^n : \|\mathbf{x}\| \leq r\}$. The γ-SIVP problem is, given a basis $\mathbf{A}$ of a lattice $\mathcal{L}(\mathbf{A})$, to search for a set of n linearly independent lattice vectors $\mathbf{S} \subset \mathcal{L}(\mathbf{A})$ such that $\|\mathbf{S}\| \leq \gamma\lambda_n(\mathbf{A})$.

The security of our blind ring signature scheme will be based on the average-case assumption of the short integer solution (SIS) problem.

Definition 1 (SIS Problem). *Given a random matrix* $\mathbf{A} \leftarrow_\$ \mathbb{Z}_q^{n \times m}$, *a vector* $\mathbf{u} \leftarrow_\$ \mathbb{Z}_q^n$ *and a positive real number* β, *the inhomogeneous small integer problem* $\mathsf{ISIS}_{q,n,m,\beta}$ *is to find a vector* $\mathbf{z} \in \mathbb{Z}^m \setminus \{\mathbf{0}\}$ *such that* $\mathbf{A}\mathbf{z} = \mathbf{u}$ *(mod q) and* $\|\mathbf{z}\| \leq \beta$. *In the case* $\mathbf{u} = \mathbf{0}$, *we have the homogeneous small integer problem, named* $\mathsf{SIS}_{q,n,m,\beta}$.

One can prove that the hardness of SIS and ISIS are essentially equivalent for typical parameters [18, Chapter 4]. The $\mathsf{SIS}_{q,n,m,\beta}$ problem can be seen as an average-case short vector problem on the q-ary lattice $\Lambda_q^\perp(\mathbf{A})$ defined as in Eq. (1) which requires to find a sufficiently short nonzero vector in $\Lambda_q^\perp(\mathbf{A})$. The SIS problem was first introduced in by Ajtai in his seminal work [2]. He proved that solving the SIS problem can be reduced to solving certain worst-case problems in lattices. Then Micciancio and Regev [17] gave a more tighten reduction saying that for large enough q, solving SIS as hard as solving $\tilde{O}(\beta\sqrt{n})$-SIVP problem in all lattices in dimension n.

Definition 2 (Discrete Gaussian Distribution, Definition 4.2 of [15]). *The discrete Gaussian distribution over* $\mathbb{Z}^m$ *centered at some* $\mathbf{v} \in \mathbb{Z}^m$ *with standard deviation* σ *is defined as* $\mathcal{D}_{\mathbf{v},\sigma}^m(\mathbf{x}) := \rho_{\mathbf{v},\sigma}^m(\mathbf{x})/\rho_{\mathbf{v},\sigma}^m(\mathbb{Z}^m)$, *where* $\rho_{\mathbf{v},\sigma}^m(\mathbf{x}) :=$ $\left(\frac{1}{\sqrt{2\pi\sigma^2}}\right)^m e^{\frac{-\|\mathbf{x}-\mathbf{v}\|^2}{2\sigma^2}}$ *and* $\rho_{\mathbf{v},\sigma}^m(\mathbb{Z}^m) := \sum_{\mathbf{x} \in \mathbb{Z}^m} \rho_{\mathbf{v},\sigma}^m(\mathbf{x})$.

Some basic facts relating to the discrete Gaussian distribution are summarized in the following lemmas:

Lemma 1 (Lemma 4.3 in [15]).

(i) *For any* $k > 0$, $\Pr[|z| > k\sigma, z \leftarrow \mathcal{D}_\sigma^1] \leq 2e^{\frac{-k^2}{2}}$,

(ii) *For any* $\mathbf{v} \in \mathbb{Z}^m$, *and any* $\sigma, r > 0$, $\Pr[|\langle \mathbf{x}, \mathbf{v} \rangle| > r : \mathbf{x} \leftarrow \mathcal{D}_\sigma^m] \leq 2e^{-\frac{r^2}{2\|\mathbf{v}\|^2\sigma^2}}$.

Remark 1. In Lemma 1(i), if $k = 12$ then $|z| > 12\sigma$ with probability at most 2^{-100}. Similarly, in Lemma 1(ii), if we choose $r = 12\|\mathbf{v}\|\sigma$ then $|\langle \mathbf{x}, \mathbf{v} \rangle| \geq 12\|\mathbf{v}\|\sigma$ with probability at most 2^{-100}.

Lemma 2 (Lemma 4.4 in [15]). *For any $\eta > 0$, we have $\Pr[\|\mathbf{z}\| > \eta\sigma\sqrt{m}, \mathbf{z} \leftarrow \mathcal{D}_\sigma^m] \leq \eta^m e^{\frac{m}{2}(1-\eta^2)}$.*

Remark 2. In Lemma 2, the function $\eta^m e^{\frac{m}{2}(1-\eta^2)}$ is decreasing either in m (if η fixed) or in η (if m fixed). See Table 1 for example. Clearly we need $\eta > 1$ as small as possible. Hence, with typical large enough m, one usually chooses $\eta \in [1.1, 1.3]$.

Table 1. Some specific values for $\eta^m e^{\frac{m}{2}(1-\eta^2)}$

	$m = 50$	$m = 100$	$m = 200$
$\eta = 1.1$	0.61601	0.37947	0.14399
$\eta = 1.3$	0.01605	0.00026	0.00000007
$\eta = 3$	9.7×10^{-64}	9.9×10^{-127}	9.7×10^{-253}

Lemma 3 (Lemma 4.5 in [15]). *For any $\mathbf{v} \in \mathbb{Z}^m$, if $\sigma = \alpha\|\mathbf{v}\|$ where $\alpha > 0$, we have $\Pr\left[\mathcal{D}_\sigma^m(\mathbf{x})/\mathcal{D}_{\mathbf{v},\sigma}^m(\mathbf{x}) \leq e^{12/\alpha + 1/(2\alpha^2)} : \mathbf{x} \leftarrow \mathcal{D}_\sigma^m\right] \geq 1 - 2^{-100}$.*

Remark 3. In Lemma 3, if we choose, $\alpha = 12$, i.e., $\sigma = 12\|\mathbf{v}\|$ then $\mathcal{D}_\sigma^m(\mathbf{x})/\mathcal{D}_{\mathbf{v},\sigma}^m(\mathbf{x}) \leq e^{1+1/288}$ with probability at least $1 - 2^{-100}$.

Definition 3 (Statistical Distance, Definition 8.5 in [16]). *Let X and X' be two random variables over a countable set S. We define the statistical distance between X and X' by $\Delta(X, X') := \frac{1}{2}\sum_{x \in S} |\Pr[X = x] - \Pr[X' = x]|$.*

Lemma 4 (Triangular Inequality). *Let X_1, X_2 and X_3 be three random variables over a countable set S. We have $\Delta(X_1, X_3) \leq \Delta(X_1, X_2) + \Delta(X_2, X_3)$.*

Lemma 5 (Rejection Sampling, Theorem 4.6 in [15]). *Given a subset $V = \{\mathbf{v} \in \mathbb{Z}^m : \|\mathbf{v}\| \leq T\}$ and a real number $\sigma = \omega(T \log \sqrt{m})$. Define on V a probability distribution $h : V \to \mathbb{R}$. Then there exists a universal upper bound $M = O(1)$ such that the outputs of the following two algorithms $\mathcal{A}$ and $\mathcal{B}$ have a negligible statistical distance of $\Delta(\mathcal{A}, \mathcal{B}) := 2^{-\omega(\log m)}/M$:*

1. *$(\mathcal{A})$: $\mathbf{v} \leftarrow h$, $\mathbf{z} \leftarrow \mathcal{D}_{\mathbf{v},\sigma}^m$, output $(\mathbf{z}, \mathbf{v})$ with probability $\min(\frac{\mathcal{D}_\sigma^m(\mathbf{z},)}{M\mathcal{D}_{\mathbf{v},\sigma}^m(\mathbf{z})}, 1)$.*
2. *$(\mathcal{B})$: $\mathbf{v} \leftarrow h$, $\mathbf{z} \leftarrow \mathcal{D}_\sigma^m$, output $(\mathbf{z}, \mathbf{v})$ with probability $1/M$.*

Moreover, the probability that $\mathcal{A}$ outputs something is at least $(1 - 2^{-\omega(\log m)})/M$. Particularly, if $\sigma = \alpha T$ for any $\alpha > 0$ then $M = e^{12/\alpha + 1/(2\alpha^2)}$, $\Delta(\mathcal{A}, \mathcal{B}) = 2^{-100}/M$, and the probability that $\mathcal{A}$ outputs something is at least $(1 - 2^{-100})/M$.

In order to construct the blind ring signature, we exploit the **trapdoor technique** proposed in [8, Subsection 5.3] to generate necessary keys.

TrapGen(1^n). The algorithm on input the security parameter n, chooses a prime $q = poly(n)$ and an integer $m > 5n \log q$ to output a matrix $\mathbf{A} \in \mathbb{Z}_q^{n \times m}$ and $\mathbf{B_A} \in \mathbb{Z}_q^{m \times m}$ with $\|\tilde{\mathbf{B}}_\mathbf{A}\| \leq K := m^{1+\epsilon}$ for any $\epsilon > 0$, where *the distribution of $\mathbf{A}$ is statistically close to the uniform over $\mathbb{Z}_q^{n \times m}$* and the matrix $\mathbf{B_A}$ is a good basis of the lattice $\Lambda_q^\perp(\mathbf{A}) = \{\mathbf{v} \in \mathbb{Z}^m : \mathbf{Av} = \mathbf{0} \pmod{q}\}$.

We generalize the trapdoor inversion algorithm SampleISIS in [8, Subsection 5.3] to have the following algorithm:

SampleKey($\mathbf{A}, \mathbf{B_A}, \sigma, \mathbf{T}$). The algorithm takes as input $\mathbf{A} \in \mathbb{Z}_q^{n \times m}$, $\mathbf{B_A} \in \mathbb{Z}_q^{m \times m}$ outputted by TrapGen(1^n), a real number $\sigma \geq K \cdot \omega(\sqrt{\log n})$ and matrix $\mathbf{T} \in \mathbb{Z}_q^{n \times k}$, and returns a random (column) matrix $\mathbf{S} \in \mathbb{Z}^{m \times k}$ such that the j-th column $\mathbf{S}[j] \in D = \{\mathbf{s} \in \mathbb{Z}^m : \|\mathbf{s}\| \leq \sigma \sqrt{m}\}$ for all $j \in [k]$ and that $\mathbf{AS} = \mathbf{T} \pmod{q}$ with overwhelming probability. The distribution of $\mathbf{S}[j]$ for all $j \in [k]$ is $\mathcal{D}_{\mathbb{Z}, \sigma}^m$ statistically close to the uniform distribution over D.

In this work, we also exploit the **commitment function** com maps a pair of two strings $(\mu, \mathbf{t}) \in \{0, 1\}^* \times \{0, 1\}^n$ (called *committed string*) to a *commitment string* $C := \text{com}(\mu, \mathbf{t}) \in \{0, 1\}^n$ to hide the value of the message μ. For security goal, we need com to have two properties: *statistically hiding* and *computationally binding*. The first property ensures that any computationally unbounded algorithm is not able to statistically distinguish two commitment strings C and C' obtained from two distinct committed pairs $(\mu, \mathbf{t}) \neq (\mu', \mathbf{t}')$. The second property says that given a commitment string C obtained from the committed pair of strings $(\mu, \mathbf{t})$ (i.e., $C := \text{com}(\mu, \mathbf{t})$), no polynomia-time algorithm can find another pair $(\mu', \mathbf{t}')$ with $\mu' \neq \mu$ such that $C = \text{com}(\mu', \mathbf{t}')$. See [11,13,20] for more details.

3   Blind Ring Signature Schemes

A blind ring signature consists of four algorithms called Setup, KeyGen, Sign and Verify.

- Setup(1^λ) is a probabilistic polynomial-time algorithm which takes as input the security parameter λ and outputs a set of public parameters $\mathcal{P}$.
- KeyGen($\mathcal{P}$) is a probabilistic polynomial-time algorithm which takes as input the set of public parameters $\mathcal{P}$ to output a pair of public key (verification key) and secret key (signing key) (pk, sk) corresponding to a signer of the ring $R = \{\mathcal{S}_1, \cdots, \mathcal{S}_l\}$. We denote the set of public keys of the ring R by PK.
- Sign($\mathcal{P}, \text{sk}_j, \mu, PK$) is an interactive polynomial-time protocol of two parties: one is a user and another is a ring of signers $R = \{\mathcal{S}_1, \cdots, \mathcal{S}_l\}$. The user, say $\mathcal{U}(\mathcal{P}, PK, \mu)$, chooses a message μ that is blinded as μ^* before sending μ^* to the ring R to be signed. The ring R, in turn, will choose a member, say $\mathcal{S}_j$, who possess the secret key sk_j, written $\mathcal{S}_j(\mathcal{P}, \text{sk}_j)$, as the real signer interacting with the user. Finally, the signer obtains the *blinded signature* Σ^*

on μ^* and outputs his *view*, denoted $\mathcal{V}$, (it may that $\mathcal{V} \neq \Sigma^*$), while the user will output the *real* (or *final*) *signature* Σ on the original message μ by un-blinding Σ^*. The user may get an invalid signature denoted by a failure symbol $\perp$.

- Verify$(\mathcal{P}, \mu, \Sigma, PK)$ is a deterministic polynomial-time algorithm which takes as input the set of common parameters $\mathcal{P}$, the set of public keys PK, the message μ and the signature Σ on μ, then outputs 1 if the signature is valid and 0 otherwise.

A blind ring signature scheme must have the following properties: *Correctness, Anonymity, Blindness* and *One-more Unforgeability*. We will make these properties clearer below.

Correctness. *Correctness* requires that the verifier always outputs 1 if it receives a valid signature. Formally, it must hold that

$$\Pr[\mathsf{Verify}(\mathcal{P}, \mu, \Sigma, PK) = 1 : \Sigma \leftarrow \mathsf{Sign}(\mathcal{P}, \mathsf{sk}_j, \mu, PK), \Sigma \neq \perp] = 1.$$

A relaxation for the correctness is that if $\Sigma \leftarrow \mathsf{Sign}(\mathcal{P}, \mathsf{sk}_j, \mu, PK), \Sigma \neq \perp$ then $\mathsf{Verify}(\mathcal{P}, \mu, \Sigma, PK) = 1$ with overwhelming probability. (In our case the probability will be at least $1 - 2^{-100}$.)

Anonymity. The anonymity property ensures that a user is impossible to know which member of the ring was the true signer engaging in the blind ring signature protocol. The definition of the anonymity property is given in the game below. In this game, the attacker acts as a malicious user.

1. **Setup.** The adversary $\mathcal{A}$ outputs the set of common parameters $\mathcal{P}$, the ring of signers $R = \{\mathcal{S}_1, \cdots, \mathcal{S}_l\}$, its public keys PK, two distinct indexes $i_0, i_1 \in [l]$, two secret keys $\mathsf{sk}_{i_0}, \mathsf{sk}_{i_1}$ and a message μ. They are sent to the challenger $\mathcal{C}$.
2. **Challenge.** The challenger $\mathcal{C}$ chooses a random bit $b \in \{0, 1\}$, then runs Sign on the input $(\mathcal{P}, \mathsf{sk}_{i_b}, \mu, PK)$ to get a blinded signature $\Sigma^*_{i_b}$ on μ. The blinded signature $\Sigma^*_{i_b}$ will be given to the adversary $\mathcal{A}$.
3. **Output.** The adversary outputs a bit b' as a guess of b. He wins the game if $b' = b$.

We say that the blind ring signature achieves anonymity if any adversary $\mathcal{A}$ succeeds in guessing b with probability negligibly close to $1/2$. In other words, the advantage of $\mathcal{A}$ in distinguishing Σ_{i_0} and Σ_{i_1} is negligible.

Blindness. Blindness is a fundamental property of a blind ring signature saying that all members in the ring do not learn any information about the message received from the user that they are having to sign. The property can be modelled as a game between an adversary $\mathcal{A}$ and a challenger $\mathcal{C}$. In this game, the adversary $\mathcal{A}$ plays the role of a dishonest ring of signers R who tries to differentiate two given messages to know which one is being signed.

1. **Setup.** The adversary $\mathcal{A}$ chooses a security parameter λ and chooses a universal set of signers to generate the ring $R^* = \{\mathcal{S}_1, \cdots, \mathcal{S}_L\}$. Then it calls

---

Algorithm 1. BRS.Setup(1^n)

Input: Security parameter n.
Output: The set of public parameters $\mathcal{P}=(n, m, q, k, \kappa, \sigma, H, \sigma_1, \sigma_2, \sigma_3, M_1, M_2, M_3, \mathbf{T}, \eta)$
1: Generate parameters as in Table 2
2: An one-way and collision-resistant hash function $H : \{0,1\}^* \to \{\mathbf{c} \in \{-1,0,1\}^k :$ $\|\mathbf{c}\|_1 \leq \kappa\}$
3: A commonly-used matrix $\mathbf{T} \leftarrow_\$ \mathbb{Z}_q^{m \times k}$
4: Output all as the set $\mathcal{P}$

Algorithm 2. BRS.KeyGen ($\mathcal{P}$)

Input: $\mathcal{P}=(n, m, q, k, \kappa, \sigma, H, \sigma_1, \sigma_2, \sigma_3, M_1, M_2, M_3, \mathbf{T}, \eta)$
Output: A key pair $(\mathbf{A}, \mathbf{S})$
1: Run TrapGen(1^n) to get $\mathbf{A} \in \mathbb{Z}_q^{n \times m}$ and $\mathbf{B}_A \in \mathbb{Z}_q^{n \times m}$ is a trapdoor of $\mathbf{A}$; /* *the distribution of $\mathbf{A}$ is statistically close to the uniform over* $\mathbb{Z}_q^{n \times m}$ */
2: $\mathbf{S} \leftarrow$ SampleKey($\mathbf{A}, \mathbf{B}_A, \sigma, \mathbf{T}$), i.e., $\mathbf{AS} = \mathbf{T} \pmod q$ where $\mathbf{S} \in D_d :=$ $\{-d, \cdots, 0, \cdots, d\}^{m \times k}$, $d = \sigma\sqrt{m}$; /* *the distribution of $\mathbf{S}$ is $\mathcal{D}_{\mathbb{Z},\sigma}^{m \times k}$ statistically close to the uniform over D_d* */
3: **return** Public key $\mathbf{A}$ and secret key $\mathbf{S}$

Setup(1^λ) to get the set of public parameters $\mathcal{P}$ according to the security parameter λ and KeyGen($\mathcal{P}$) to output the key pairs $(\mathsf{pk}_i, \mathsf{sk}_i)_{i \in [L]}$ for each signer $\mathcal{S}_i$, $i \in [L]$. The adversary $\mathcal{A}$ knows $\mathcal{P}$ and $(\mathsf{pk}_i, \mathsf{sk}_i)_{i \in [L]}$.

2. **Challenge.** The adversary $\mathcal{A}$ chooses a subring $R \subset R^*$, and its corresponding public keys PK, and two messages $\mu_0 \neq \mu_1$, then he sends them to the challenger $\mathcal{C}$. The challenger $\mathcal{C}$ will flip a coin $b \in \{0, 1\}$ and sets up a blind ring signature protocol taking μ_b and the ring R as input. The adversary $\mathcal{A}$ chooses a signer $\mathcal{S}_j$ in the ring R to sign the hidden form of μ_b and acts as the signer in the protocol. Eventually, $\mathcal{A}$ gets the view $\mathcal{V}_b$ and also the "unblinded" signature $\Sigma_b \neq \bot$. If $\Sigma_b = \bot$, the game is restarted.

3. **Guess.** The adversary $\mathcal{A}$ outputs one value $b' \in \{0, 1\}$. The adversary wins the game if $b' = b$.

We say that a ring signature scheme is *blind* if for any adversary $\mathcal{A}$ the success probability in the game is only negligibly larger than $1/2$.

One-More Unforgeability. The one-more unforgeability property guarantees that from at most q_S real interactions of the blind ring signature protocol, the user has no capacity of producing $q_S + 1$ valid and different ring signatures. The property is defined by the game below. In this game, the forger will act the behaviour of a malicious user.

1. **Setup.** The forger $\mathcal{F}$ chooses a security parameter λ and chooses a universal set of signers to generate the ring $R^* = \{\mathcal{S}_1, \cdots, \mathcal{S}_L\}$. The challenger $\mathcal{C}$ calls Setup(1^λ) to get the set of public parameters $\mathcal{P}$ and KeyGen($\mathcal{P}$) to output the key pairs $(\mathsf{pk}_i, \mathsf{sk}_i)_{i \in [L]}$ for each signer $\mathcal{S}_i$, $i \in [L]$. Then $\mathcal{C}$ sends to the forger

$\mathcal{F}$ the set $\mathcal{P}$ and the set of public keys $\{\mathsf{pk}_i\}_{i\in[L]}$. The set $\{\mathsf{sk}_i\}_{i\in[L]}$ is kept secret.

2. **Queries.** The forger $\mathcal{F}$ adaptively makes queries to the challenger:
   - q_H hash queries to the random oracle which models the hash function H in the real protocol. For each hash query from the adversary, the challenger has to reply with a consistently random value.
   - q_S blind signing queries, each is of the form (μ_i, R_i) where $R_i \subset R^*$. For each signing query, the challenger must answer with a valid blind ring signature.

3. **Output.** The forger $\mathcal{F}$ outputs $q_S + 1$ tuples $\{(\mu_i, R_i, \Sigma_i)\}_{i\in[q_S+1]}, R_i \subset R^*$. He wins the game if $\{\Sigma_i\}_{i\in[q_S+1]}$ are all valid and $(\mu_i, R_i) \neq (\mu_j, R_j)$ for all $i, j \in [q_S + 1]$ and $i \neq j$.

We say that a blind ring signature scheme is *one-more unforgeable* if in the game, $\Pr[\mathcal{F} \text{ wins}]$ is negligible.

Remark 4. For simplicity, in the proof for the one-more unforgeability property of our proposed scheme, we assume that $R_i = R^*$ for all $i \in [q_S + 1]$, that is, the forger does not want to change the ring of signers at all.

4   Our Blind Ring Signature Scheme

We will present our blind ring signature (named BRS) scheme. The security of BRS bases on the average-case assumption of the SIS problem. The scheme follows the 4-move framework for blind ring signature as reviewed in Sect. 3. It consists of four algorithms (see Algorithms 1–3 and Fig. 1) described as follows:

- We suppose that n is the security parameter. BRS.Setup(1^n) is called to output a common set of parameters $\mathcal{P}$ (see Algorithm 1). We will mention the role of these parameters and how to set them in Subsect. 6.
- Given a matrix $\mathbf{T} \leftarrow_\$ \mathbb{Z}_q^{n\times k}$, to generate public key $\mathbf{A}_i \leftarrow_\$ \mathbb{Z}_q^{n\times m}$ and secret key $\mathbf{S}_i \in \mathbb{Z}_q^{m\times k}$ for each signer $\mathcal{S}_i$ in a ring $R = \{\mathcal{S}_1, \cdots, \mathcal{S}_l\}$ of l members such that $\mathbf{T} = \mathbf{A}_i\mathbf{S}_i$, we run l times BRS.KeyGen (see Algorithm 2) which exploits the preimage sample functions (trapdoor functions) mentioned in Subsect. 2. The secret key $\mathbf{S}_i$ follows a discrete Gaussian distribution $\mathcal{D}_\sigma^{m\times k}$ and its security is guaranteed by the hardness assumption of the ISIS problem.
- The signing algorithm (BRS.Sign) (see Fig. 1) is an interactive protocol between a user $\mathcal{U}$ and a ring $R = \{\mathcal{S}_1, \cdots, \mathcal{S}_l\}$. The user $\mathcal{U}$ knows the set of public keys PK and he wants the ring R to sign the message μ. Here we describe the protocol in the case that the ring secretly delegates some signer $\mathcal{S}_j \in R$ to interact with the user. We relatively split the signing interaction into five main phases:

The member $\mathcal{S}_j(\mathcal{P}, \mathbf{S}_j)$ is the signer	The user $\mathcal{U}(\mathcal{P}, PK, \mu)$
Phase 1: for $i \in [l]$: $\mathbf{s}_i \leftarrow_\$ \mathcal{D}^m_{\sigma_2}$ $\mathbf{x} = \sum_{i \in [l]} \mathbf{A}_i \mathbf{s}_i \pmod{q}$	
	$\mathbf{x} \longrightarrow$ **Phase 2:** for $i \in [l]$: $\mathbf{a}_i \leftarrow \mathcal{D}^m_{\sigma_3}$ $\mathbf{b} \leftarrow \mathcal{D}^k_{\sigma_1}, \mathbf{t} \leftarrow_\$ \{0,1\}^n,$ $\mathbf{w} = \sum_{i \in [l]} \mathbf{A}_i \mathbf{a}_i, C := \mathrm{com}(\mu, \mathbf{t})$ $\mathbf{u} = \mathbf{x} + \mathbf{w} + \mathbf{Tb} \pmod{q}$ $\mathbf{c} = H(\mathbf{u}, C, PK), \mathbf{e} = \mathbf{c} + \mathbf{b}$ Outputs $\mathbf{e}$ with probability $$\min\left\{ \frac{\mathcal{D}^k_{\sigma_1}(\mathbf{e})}{M_1 \cdot \mathcal{D}^k_{\mathbf{c},\sigma_1}(\mathbf{e})}, 1 \right\}$$
Phase 3: for $i \in [l] \setminus \{j\}$: $\mathbf{y}_i = \mathbf{s}_i$ for j: $\mathbf{y}_j = \mathbf{s}_j + \mathbf{S}_j \mathbf{e}$ Output $\mathbf{y}_j$ with probability $$\min\left\{ \frac{\mathcal{D}^m_{\sigma_2}(\mathbf{y}_j)}{M_2 \cdot \mathcal{D}^m_{\mathbf{S}_j \mathbf{e}, \sigma_2}(\mathbf{y}_j)}, 1 \right\}$$	$\longleftarrow \mathbf{e}$

	$\Sigma^* = \{\mathbf{y}_i\}_{i \in [l]} \longrightarrow$ **Phase 4:**
	for $i \in [l]$: $\mathbf{z}_i = \mathbf{y}_i + \mathbf{a}_i$
	    accepts $\mathbf{z}_i$ with probability
	$$\min\left\{ \frac{\mathcal{D}^m_{\sigma_3}(\mathbf{z}_i)}{M_3 \cdot \mathcal{D}^m_{\mathbf{y}_i, \sigma_3}(\mathbf{z}_i)}, 1 \right\}$$
	That is,
	if $(\exists i_0 \text{ s.t. } \|\mathbf{z}_{i_0}\| > \eta \sigma_3 \sqrt{m})$:
	    result $:= ((\mathbf{a}_i)_{i \in [l]}, \mathbf{b}, \mathbf{c}, C)$
	else: result $:=$ accept
	Output: $(\mu, \Sigma = ((\mathbf{z}_i)_{i \in [l]}, \mathbf{c}, \mathbf{t}))$
	or $\perp$ when result $\neq$ accept

Phase 5:
if (result $\neq$ accept):
    Parse result$= ((\mathbf{a}_i)_{i \in [l]}, \mathbf{b}, \mathbf{c}, C)$
    $\mathbf{w} = \sum_{i \in [l]} \mathbf{A}_i \mathbf{a}_i, \mathbf{v} = \sum_{i \in [l]} \mathbf{A}_i \mathbf{y}_i$
    $\mathbf{u} = \mathbf{x} + \mathbf{w} + \mathbf{Tb} \pmod{q}$
    $\mathbf{u}' = \mathbf{w} + \mathbf{v} - \mathbf{Tc} \pmod{q}$
    if ($\mathbf{e} - \mathbf{b} = \mathbf{c} = H(\mathbf{u}, C, PK)$
        and $\mathbf{c} = H(\mathbf{u}', C, PK)$
        and $\exists i_0$ s.t. $\|\mathbf{y}_{i_0} + \mathbf{a}_{i_0}\| > \eta \sigma_3 \sqrt{m})$:
            Restart the protocol
Output: the view $\mathcal{V} = (\mathbf{x}, \mathbf{e}, (\mathbf{s}_i, \mathbf{y}_i)_{i \in [l]})$
	$\longleftarrow$ result

Fig. 1. The signing protocol BRS.Sign$(\mathcal{P}, \mathbf{S}_j, \mu, PK)$, $j \in [l]$, $PK = \{\mathbf{A}_i\}_{i \in [l]}$

- <u>Phase 1:</u> The signer samples randomly a list $\{\mathbf{s}_i\}_{i \in [l]}$ according to the distribution $\mathcal{D}^m_{\sigma_2}$ to compute and then sends the *commitment* $\mathbf{x} = \sum_{i \in [l]} \mathbf{A}_i \mathbf{s}_i$ to the user.

- **Phase 2:** The user chooses blind factors $\mathbf{a}_i \leftarrow \mathcal{D}_{\sigma_3}^m$ for all $i \in [l]$ and $\mathbf{b} \leftarrow \mathcal{D}_{\sigma_1}^k$. He also chooses a random binary vector $\mathbf{t} \leftarrow_\$ \{0,1\}^n$ then uses the commitment function com to compute the commitment string $C :=$ com$(\mu, \mathbf{t}) \in \{0,1\}^n$. Afterward, he computes $\mathbf{u} = \mathbf{x} + \sum_{i \in [l]} \mathbf{A}_i \mathbf{a}_i + \mathbf{T}\mathbf{b}$ then hash it with C using the hash function H where $H : \{0,1\}^* \to D_c :=$ $\{\mathbf{c} \in \{-1,0,1\}^k : \|\mathbf{c}\|_1 \leq \kappa\}$ to get the *challenge* $\mathbf{c}$. To blind the message, the user uses the rejection sampling technique to get the *blinded challenge* $\mathbf{e}$. Finally, the user sends $\mathbf{e}$ to the ring.
- **Phase 3:** This is the signing phase in which the signer $\mathcal{S}_j$ considers $\mathbf{s}_i$'s sampled in Phase 1 as the partial signatures of other members in the ring on the message μ, while he uses his secret key $\mathbf{S}_j$ to compute his himself partial signature $\mathbf{y}_j = \mathbf{s}_j + \mathbf{S}_j \mathbf{e}$ on μ. In order to make sure that no information of his secret key $\mathbf{S}_j$ is leaked, the signer also exploits the rejection sampling such that $\mathbf{y}_j$ follows the same distribution $\mathcal{D}_{\sigma_2}^m$ as $\mathbf{s}_j$. Finally, he sends the *blinded signature* $\{\mathbf{y}_i\}_{i \in [l]}$ to the user.
- **Phase 4:** In this phase, the user computes $\mathbf{z}_i = \mathbf{y}_i + \mathbf{a}_i$ for all $i \in [l]$. The rejection sampling is used here to ensure that $\mathbf{z}_i$ is independent of $\mathbf{y}_i$ for blindness. If $\|\mathbf{z}_i\| \leq \eta\sqrt{m}\sigma_3$ for all $i \in [l]$ then the user outputs $(\mu, \Sigma = ((\mathbf{z}_i)_{i \in [l]}, \mathbf{c}, \mathbf{t}))$ as the *final signature*; otherwise, he returns "$\perp$". Note that, it is a must for the user to send result to the signer as a confirmation of the validity of the final signature (if result := accept) or as a requirement to restart the protocol (if result := $((\mathbf{a}_i)_{i \in [l]}, \mathbf{b}, \mathbf{c}, C)$).
- **Phase 5:** In this phase, if the signer gets result $\neq$ accept, he will check up some conditions before he restarts the protocol from the beginning. This helps to detect the case that an adversarial user tries to restart the signing protocol despite having obtained a valid signature. If the signer gets the validity confirmation from the user, he finally outputs the *view* $\mathcal{V} = (\mathbf{x}, \mathbf{e}, (\mathbf{s}_i, \mathbf{y}_i)_{i \in [l]})$.

- BRS.Verify$(\mathcal{P}, \mu, \Sigma, PK) = 1$ iff $\|\mathbf{z}_i\| \leq \eta\sqrt{m}\sigma_3$ for all $i \in [l]$ and $\mathbf{c} =$ $H(\sum_{i \in [l]} \mathbf{A}_i \mathbf{z}_i - \mathbf{T}\mathbf{c} \pmod{q}, \text{com}(\mu, \mathbf{t}), PK)$; and BRS.Verify$(\mathcal{P}, \mu, \Sigma, PK) = 0$ otherwise. (See Algorithm 3.)

5 Correctness and Security Analysis of BRS

5.1 Correctness

Theorem 1 (Correctness). *Our BRS scheme is correct after at most e^2 repetitions with probability at least $1 - 2^{-100}$.*

Proof (of Theorem 1). Given the pair $(\mu, \Sigma = ((\mathbf{z}_i)_{i \in [l]}, \mathbf{c}, \mathbf{t}))$ is the output of the user in BRS.Sign$(\mathcal{P}, \mathbf{S}_j, \mu, PK)$ as in Fig. 1, the set of public keys $PK = \{\mathbf{A}_i\}_{i \in [l]}$, and parameters $\mathcal{P}$, we will prove that $H(\sum_{i \in [l]} \mathbf{A}_i \mathbf{z}_i - \mathbf{T}\mathbf{c} \pmod{q},$ com$(\mu, \mathbf{t}), PK) = \mathbf{c}$.

Algorithm 3. BRS.Verify($\mathcal{P}, \mu, \Sigma, PK$)

Input: $\mathcal{P}, \mu, \Sigma = ((\mathbf{z}_i)_{i \in [l]}, \mathbf{c}, \mathbf{t})$, $PK = \{\mathbf{A}_i\}_{i \in [l]}$
Output: 1 or 0
1: $\mathbf{u} = \sum_{i \in [l]} \mathbf{A}_i \mathbf{z}_i - \mathbf{T}\mathbf{c}$ (mod q)
2: $\mathbf{c}' = H(\mathbf{u}, \text{com}(\mu, \mathbf{t}), PK)$
3: **if** $\mathbf{c}' = \mathbf{c}$ and $\|\mathbf{z}_i\| \leq \eta\sqrt{m}\sigma_3$ for all $i \in [l]$ **then**
4:     **return** 1
5: **else**
6:     **return** 0
7: **end if**

Without caring the restarts appear in rejection samplings, we have

$$\sum_{i \in [l]} \mathbf{A}_i \mathbf{z}_i - \mathbf{T}\mathbf{c} \ (\text{mod } q) = \sum_{i \in [l]} \mathbf{A}_i(\mathbf{y}_i + \mathbf{a}_i) - \mathbf{T}(\mathbf{e} - \mathbf{b}) \ (\text{mod } q)$$

$$= \sum_{i \in [l] \setminus \{j\}} \mathbf{A}_i \mathbf{s}_i + \mathbf{A}_j(\mathbf{s}_j + \mathbf{S}_j \mathbf{e})$$

$$+ \sum_{i \in [l]} \mathbf{A}_i \mathbf{a}_i - \mathbf{T}(\mathbf{e} - \mathbf{b}) \ (\text{mod } q)$$

$$= \sum_{i \in [l]} \mathbf{A}_i \mathbf{s}_i + \sum_{i \in [l]} \mathbf{A}_i \mathbf{a}_i + \mathbf{T}\mathbf{b} \ (\text{mod } q)$$

$$= \mathbf{x} + \mathbf{w} + \mathbf{T}\mathbf{b} \ (\text{mod } q).$$

Hence $H(\sum_{i \in [l]} \mathbf{A}_i \mathbf{z}_i - \mathbf{T}\mathbf{c} \ (\text{mod } q), \text{com}(\mu, \mathbf{t}), PK) = \mathbf{c}$. Note that, with overwhelming probability, $\|\mathbf{z}_i\| \leq \eta\sqrt{m}\sigma_3$ for all $i \in [l]$ by Lemma 2.

Now we analyze the rejection sampling technique to bound the number of restarts of our BRS protocol. Recall that, by Remark 3, we have

$$\frac{\mathcal{D}_\sigma^m(\mathbf{x})}{M \cdot \mathcal{D}_{\mathbf{v},\sigma}^m(\mathbf{x})} \leq \frac{e^{1+1/288}}{M},$$

with probability at least $1 - 2^{-100}$ if $\sigma = 12\|\mathbf{v}\|$. Being used in the rejection sampling, we need $\mathcal{D}_\sigma^m(\mathbf{x})/(M \cdot \mathcal{D}_{\mathbf{v},\sigma}^m(\mathbf{x})) \leq 1$. Since M should be as small as possible, it is sufficient to choose $M = \exp\left((24\|\mathbf{v}\|\sigma + \|\mathbf{v}\|^2)/(2\sigma^2)\right) \approx e^{1+1/288}$, with $\sigma = 12\|\mathbf{v}\|$. Now we apply above analyses to the rejection samplings in our BRS scheme. Remark that in Phase 2 of our scheme, as the user utilizes the rejection sampling locally to output $\mathbf{e}$, the restarts of this phase does not impact to the correctness of the scheme. We just care about the restarts happening in Phase 3 and Phase 5. Hence, after at most $M_2 \cdot M_3 \approx e^2$ restarts, the BRS scheme can successfully output a valid blind ring signature. □

Remark 5. In the proof of Theorem 1, we use $\mathbf{e} = \mathbf{c} + \mathbf{b}$ obtained in Phase 2 of BRS.Sign. Assume that $\mathbf{e} = \mathbf{c}' + \mathbf{b}'$ for some $\mathbf{b} \neq \mathbf{b}'$, $\mathbf{c} \neq \mathbf{c}'$, then also

$$\sum_{i \in [l]} \mathbf{A}_i \mathbf{z}_i - \mathbf{T} \mathbf{c}' \pmod{q} = \sum_{i \in [l]} \mathbf{A}_i (\mathbf{y}_i + \mathbf{a}_i) - \mathbf{T}(\mathbf{e} - \mathbf{b}') \pmod{q}$$

$$= \mathbf{x} + \mathbf{w} + \mathbf{T} \mathbf{b}' \pmod{q}.$$

Thus, if $\mathbf{e} - \mathbf{b}' = \mathbf{c}' = H(\mathbf{x} + \mathbf{w} + \mathbf{T} \mathbf{b}' \pmod{q}, \mathsf{com}(\mu, \mathbf{t}), PK)$, then $H(\sum_{i \in [l]} \mathbf{A}_i \mathbf{z}_i - \mathbf{T} \mathbf{c}' \pmod{q}, \mathsf{com}(\mu, \mathbf{t}), PK) = \mathbf{c}'$. This remark will be used in the proof of Theorem 4.

5.2   Anonymity

Recall that, in the anonymity game (see Subsect. 3), the adversary $\mathcal{A}$ receives a set of public keys $PK = \{\mathsf{pk}_i\}_{i \in [l]}$ and he adaptively make queries to the blind ring signature with a message μ and the indexes $i_0, i_1 \in [l]$ to get a signature Σ which depends on the random bit $b \in \{0, 1\}$ chosen by the challenger. The adversary wins the game if he guesses exactly the bit b. The following theorem says that the advantage of the attacker in guessing b is actually negligible.

Theorem 2 (Anonymity). *Given the ring of signers $R = \{\mathcal{S}_1, \cdots, \mathcal{S}_l\}$, and the set of key pairs $\{(\mathbf{A}_i, \mathbf{S}_i)\}_{i \in [l]}$, a message μ, two distinct indexes $i_0, i_1 \in [l]$ and a random bit $b \in \{0, 1\}$. Consider the anonymity game as in Subsect. 3. Let X_0 and X_1 two random variables representing the blinded signatures obtained by the blind ring signature protocol BRS.Sign with respect to $b = 0$ and $b = 1$, respectively. Then there exist a universal constant $M_2 > 0$ such that*

$$\Delta(X_0, X_1) \le \frac{2^{1 - \omega(\log m)}}{M_2}.$$

Proof (of Theorem 2). In the game, the challenger chooses randomly $b \in \{0, 1\}$ and runs BRS.Sign using the signer $\mathcal{S}_{i_b}$ corresponding to the private key $\mathbf{S}_{i_b}$, then we will get the blinded signature $(\mathbf{y}_1, \cdots, \mathbf{y}_{i_b} \cdots, \mathbf{y}_l)$, where $\mathbf{y}_{i_b} := \mathbf{S}_{i_b} \mathbf{e} + \mathbf{s}_{i_b}$ outputted with probability $\min\{\mathcal{D}_{\sigma_2}^m(\mathbf{y}_{i_b}) / (M_2 \cdot \mathcal{D}_{\mathbf{S}_{i_b} \mathbf{e}, \sigma_2}^m(\mathbf{y}_{i_b})), 1\}$ and $\mathbf{y}_i := \mathbf{s}_i \leftarrow \mathcal{D}_{\sigma_2}^m$ for all $i \in [l] \setminus \{i_b\}$.

Assume that the adversary gets the signature $(\mathbf{y}_1, \cdots, \mathbf{y}_{i_b} \cdots, \mathbf{y}_l)$ by choosing each element $\mathbf{y}_i$ from $\mathcal{D}_{\sigma_2}^m$ with probability $1/M_2$. We denote by Y the random variable according to the signature obtained by this way. Then using Lemma 5 we have

$$\Delta(X_0, Y) \le \frac{2^{-\omega(\log m)}}{M_2} \text{ and } \Delta(X_1, Y) \le \frac{2^{-\omega(\log m)}}{M_2}.$$

Hence $\Delta(X_0, X_1) \le \Delta(X_0, Y) + \Delta(X_1, Y) \le \frac{2^{1 - \omega(\log m)}}{M_2}$ still negligible. $\square$

5.3   Blindness

Theorem 3 (Blindness). *Our BRS scheme is blind provided that com is hiding and the hash function H is one-way.*

Proof (of Theorem 3). It is easy to see that the blindness of our BRS scheme is guaranteed by the rejection sampling technique and the hiding property of the commitment com.

As per the game of blindness in Subsect. 3, when the dishonest signer gives two messages μ_0 and μ_1 to the challenger, the challenger will chooses randomly a bit $b \in \{0, 1\}$. Then the signer and the challenger initiates the blind ring signature protocol having interaction with only one of two users $\mathcal{U}(\mathcal{P}, PK, \mu_0)$ and $\mathcal{U}(\mathcal{P}, PK, \mu_1)$. We show that the signer actually does not know which user he is interacting with, that is, the view $\mathcal{V} = (\mathbf{x}, \mathbf{e}, (\mathbf{s}_i, \mathbf{y}_i)_{i \in [l]})$ that the signer has is independent of the message being signed. More precisely, $\mathbf{e}$ and $(\mathbf{y}_i)_{i \in [l]}$ is independent of the message being signed. Indeed, let $\mathcal{V}_0 = (\mathbf{x}_0, \mathbf{e}_0, (\mathbf{s}_{0,i}, \mathbf{y}_{0,i})_{i \in [l]})$ and $\mathcal{V}_1 = (\mathbf{x}_1, \mathbf{e}_1, (\mathbf{s}_{1,i}, \mathbf{y}_{1,i})_{i \in [l]})$ be views respectively corresponding to users $\mathcal{U}(\mathcal{P}, PK, \mu_0)$ and $\mathcal{U}(\mathcal{P}, PK, \mu_1)$. Then, the rejection sampling in Phase 2 ensures that both $\mathbf{e}_0$ and $\mathbf{e}_1$ are distributed according to the same distribution $\mathcal{D}_{\sigma_1}^k$. Similarly, by the rejection sampling in Phase 3, both $\mathbf{y}_{0,i}$ and $\mathbf{y}_{1,j}$ for all $i, j \in [l]$ follow the same distribution $\mathcal{D}_{\sigma_2}^m$. The distributions of $\mathbf{e}$ and $\mathbf{y}_{0,i}$ are independent of choosing the message to be signed.

Regarding two unblinded signatures $\Sigma_0 = ((\mathbf{z}_{b,i})_{i \in [l]}, \mathbf{c}_b, \mathbf{t}_b)$ corresponding to the users $\mathcal{U}(\mathcal{P}, PK, \mu_b)$, $b = 0, 1$. Again, by the rejection sampling used in Phase 4, the malicious signer is impossible to distinguish $(\mathbf{z}_{0,i})_{i \in [l]}$ from $(\mathbf{z}_{1,i})_{i \in [l]}$. Certainly, the signer does not learn anything about the original message μ being signed from the challenges $\mathbf{c}_0$, $\mathbf{c}_1$ due to the property of the hash function H. Also, the distribution of $\mathbf{t}_b$ is independent of μ.

Finally, we concern the restart might happen in Phase 5. Again, by the hiding property of the commitment com and since the user samples fresh values $\mathbf{t}$, $\mathbf{a}$ and $\mathbf{b}$ after every such a restart, we have that each rerun of the protocol is independent of the previous runs. (See similar arguments to a blind signature scheme in [20].)   □

5.4   One-More Unforgeability

Before stating the main theorem of this subsection, we adopt the following lemma:

Lemma 6 (Lemma 5.2 in [15]).   *Given a matrix $\mathbf{A} \in \mathbb{Z}_q^{n \times m}$ where $m > 64 + n \log q / \log(2d+1)$, randomly chosen $\mathbf{s} \leftarrow_{\$} \{-d, \cdots, 0, \cdots, d\}^m$. Then with probability at least $1 - 2^{-100}$, there exists another $\mathbf{s}' \leftarrow_{\$} \{-d, \cdots, 0, \cdots, d\}^m$ such that $\mathbf{As} = \mathbf{As}' \pmod{q}$.*

For notational convenience, we call the (q_H, q_S, δ)-forger $\mathcal{F}$ a polynomial-time algorithm $\mathcal{F}$ that successfully breaks the one-more unforgeablity of our BRS protocol with non negligible probability δ, making at most q_H hash queries and at most q_S sign queries to the scheme. The following theorem says that if there exists such a forger then one can construct an algorithm being able to solve an SIS problem.

Theorem 4 (One-more   Unforgeability).   *Consider   the   BRS   scheme described in Sect. 4. Suppose that the commitment function com used in the BRS scheme is binding. If there is a (q_H, q_S, δ)-forger $\mathcal{F}$ who breaks the one-more unforgeablity of our BRS protocol then there is a polynomial-time* algorithm $\mathcal{G}$ which can solve an $\mathsf{SIS}_{q,n,ml,\beta}$ problem with $\beta = \max\{(2l\eta\sigma_3 + 2\sigma\sqrt{\kappa})\sqrt{m}, (2l\eta\sigma_3 + l\eta\sigma_2)\sqrt{m}\}$ with probability at least

$$\delta_{overall} \geq \min\left\{\frac{1}{4s}(1-\zeta)\left(1-\frac{1}{|D_c|}\right)\left(\frac{\delta - \frac{1}{|D_c|}}{q_H} - \frac{1}{|D_c|}\right), \delta\left(1-\frac{1}{|D_c|}\right)\right\},$$

where ζ is the probability of a restart in the scheme, $s := q_S + 1$.

Proof (of Theorem 4).

In the following, we will describe an algorithm $\mathcal{G}$ using $\mathcal{F}$ as a black-box routine to solve an $\mathsf{SIS}_{q,n,ml,\beta}$ problem as $\mathcal{G}$ desires:

1. **Setup.** First of all, $\mathcal{G}$ chooses a security parameter n and a set of signers to generate the ring $R = \{\mathcal{S}_1, \cdots, \mathcal{S}_l\}$. Then $\mathcal{G}$ calls BRS.Setup(1^n) to get the set of public parameters $\mathcal{P}$ and then calls BRS.KeyGen($\mathcal{P}$) to output the key pairs $(\mathbf{A}_i, \mathbf{S}_i)_{i\in[l]}$ for each signer $\mathcal{S}_i$, $i \in [l]$. After that, $\mathcal{G}$ sends to the forger $\mathcal{F}$ the set $\mathcal{P}$ and the set of public keys $PK := \{\mathbf{A}_i\}_{i\in[l]}$. The set of secret keys $\{\mathbf{S}_i\}_{i\in[l]}$ is kept secret. The goal of $\mathcal{G}$ is to solve the following $\mathsf{SIS}_{q,n,ml,\beta}$ problem:

$$\text{Find } \|\widehat{\mathbf{z}}\| \leq \beta \text{ such that } \mathbf{A}\widehat{\mathbf{z}} = \mathbf{0} \pmod{q}, \text{ where } \mathbf{A} := [\mathbf{A}_1\|\cdots\|\mathbf{A}_l]. \quad (2)$$

2. **Queries.** The forger $\mathcal{F}$ adaptively makes q_H hash queries to the random oracle which models the hash function H in the real protocol and q_S blind signing queries. The algorithm $\mathcal{G}$ creates and maintains a list L_H consisting of random oracle queries $(\mathbf{u}, C) \leftarrow_\$ \mathbb{Z}_q^n \times \{0,1\}^*$ and their corresponding hash value $\mathbf{c} \in D_c$, where $D_c := \{\mathbf{c} : \mathbf{c} \in \{-1,0,1\}^k, \|\mathbf{c}\|_1 \leq \kappa\}$. Furthermore, $\mathcal{G}$ randomly preselects $\mathcal{R} := \{\mathbf{r}_1, \cdots, \mathbf{r}_{q_H}\} \leftarrow_\$ D_c$ as a set of replies of H and also chooses a random tape ρ. The solver $\mathcal{G}$ runs $\mathcal{F}(\mathcal{P}, PK, \rho)$ as a black-box routine as follows:
   - **Random Oracle Queries.** Whenever $\mathcal{G}$ receives a query $(\mathbf{u}, C)$, it will check whether the query is in the list L_H or not. If yes, $\mathcal{G}$ sends the corresponding hash value $\mathbf{c}$ to the forger $\mathcal{F}$. Otherwise, $\mathcal{G}$ opts the first unused $\mathbf{r}_i, i \in [q_H]$ from $\mathcal{R}$, assigns $\mathbf{c} := \mathbf{r}_i$, stores the query-hash value pair $((\mathbf{u}, C), \mathbf{c})$ in L_H and sends $\mathbf{c}$ to the forger.
   - **Signing Queries.** The forger $\mathcal{F}$ plays the role of the user, processing q_S times the interactive blind ring signature protocol, while the solver $\mathcal{G}$ acts as the signer of the ring. If $\mathcal{F}$ wants to have the signature of a message μ, the solver $\mathcal{G}$ chooses some signer $\mathcal{S}_i$ from the ring R and runs the BRS.Sign algorithm in Fig. 1 to produce the required signature.
3. **Output.** After at most q_S signing queries, with non-negligible probability δ, the forger $\mathcal{F}$ eventually outputs $s := q_S + 1$ blind ring signatures

$$(\mu_1, (\mathbf{z}_{1,i})_{i\in[l]}, \mathbf{c}_1, \mathbf{t}_1), \cdots, (\mu_s, (\mathbf{z}_{s,i})_{i\in[l]}, \mathbf{c}_s, \mathbf{t}_s),$$

where $\mu_1, \cdots, \mu_s$ are s distinct messages. At the moment, the algorithm $\mathcal{G}$ predicts randomly an index $k \in [s]$ satisfying that $\mathbf{c}_k = \mathbf{r}_i$ for some $i \in [q_H]$.

Afterward, $\mathcal{G}$ samples new fresh random oracle answers $\{\mathbf{r}'_i, \cdots, \mathbf{r}'_{q_H}\} \leftarrow_\$ D_c$ and then invokes $\mathcal{F}(\mathcal{P}, PK, \rho)$ again with $\mathcal{R}' := \{\mathbf{r}_1, \cdots, \mathbf{r}_{i-1}, \mathbf{r}'_i, \cdots, \mathbf{r}'_{q_H}\}$. Among other values, the forger $\mathcal{F}$ outputs $(\mu'_k, (\mathbf{z}'_{k,i})_{i \in [l]}, \mathbf{c}'_k, \mathbf{t}'_k)$. If $\mathbf{c}_k \neq \mathbf{c}'_k$ then $\mathcal{G}$ returns

$$((\mathbf{z}_{k,i})_{i \in [l]} - \mathbf{S}_j \mathbf{c}_k, (\mathbf{z}'_{k,i})_{i \in [l]} - \mathbf{S}_j \mathbf{c}'_k) \text{ for all } j \in [l],$$

in order to solve the SIS problem. If $\mathbf{c}_k = \mathbf{c}'_k$, the solver $\mathcal{G}$ retries $\mathcal{F}(\mathcal{P}, PK, \rho')$ at most q_H^s times with a different random tape ρ'.

Analysis. The environment of $\mathcal{F}$ is perfectly simlulated by $\mathcal{G}$ and restarts happen with the same probability ζ as in the real scheme. Obviously, there is at least one signature not coming from a real interaction. The algorithm $\mathcal{G}$ guesses correctly the index of this signature with probability at least $1/s$. And $\mathbf{c}_k$ is a random oracle answer with probability $1/|D_c|$. Note that, with probability $1/2$, there is at least one of the reruns of $\mathcal{F}$ gives the same index pair (i, k) such that $\mathbf{r}_i = \mathbf{c}_k$. Therefore, we can assume that the index pairs in two runs are the same.

Applying the forking lemma [3, Lemma 3.1] with noting that restarts happen with probability ζ, we have that $\mathcal{F}$ is again successful in breaking the one-more unforgeability and outputs one more new signature $(\mu'_k, (\mathbf{z}'_{k,i})_{i \in [l]}, \mathbf{c}'_k, \mathbf{t}'_k)$ with probability $\delta_{frk} \geq (1 - \zeta)(\delta - 1/|D_c|)((\delta - 1/|D_c|)/q_H - 1/|D_c|)$ using the same random oracle query as in the first run. Thus we have

$$\left(\sum_{i \in [l]} \mathbf{A}_i \mathbf{z}_{k,i} - \mathbf{T}\mathbf{c}_k \ (\text{mod } q), \text{com}(\mu_k, \mathbf{t}_k)\right) = \left(\sum_{i \in [l]} \mathbf{A}_i \mathbf{z}'_{k,i} - \mathbf{T}\mathbf{c}'_k \ (\text{mod } q), \text{com}(\mu'_k, \mathbf{t}'_k)\right).$$

Since then, we have that

$$\sum_{i \in [l]} \mathbf{A}_i \mathbf{z}_{k,i} - \mathbf{T}\mathbf{c}_k \ (\text{mod } q) = \sum_{i \in [l]} \mathbf{A}_i \mathbf{z}'_{k,i} - \mathbf{T}\mathbf{c}'_k \ (\text{mod } q).$$

Equivalently,

$$\sum_{i \in [l]} \mathbf{A}_i (\mathbf{z}_{k,i} - \mathbf{z}'_{k,i}) + \mathbf{T}(\mathbf{c}'_k - \mathbf{c}_k) = \mathbf{0} \ (\text{mod } q). \tag{3}$$

Plugging $\mathbf{T} = \mathbf{A}_{i_0} \mathbf{S}_{i_0} \ (\text{mod } q)$ for some $i_0 \in [l]$ into Eq. (3), we have

$$\sum_{i \in [l] \backslash i_0} \mathbf{A}_i (\mathbf{z}_{k,i} - \mathbf{z}'_{k,i}) + \mathbf{A}_{i_0} (\mathbf{z}_{k,i_0} - \mathbf{z}'_{k,i_0} + \mathbf{S}_{i_0}(\mathbf{c}'_k - \mathbf{c}_k)) = \mathbf{0} \ (\text{mod } q). \tag{4}$$

Set the matrix

$$\mathbf{A} := [\mathbf{A}_1 \| \cdots \| \mathbf{A}_{i_0-1} \| \mathbf{A}_{i_0} \| \mathbf{A}_{i_0+1} \| \cdots \| \mathbf{A}_l],$$

and

$$\begin{aligned}\widehat{\mathbf{z}} :=& [\mathbf{z}_{k,1} - \mathbf{z}'_{k,1}, \cdots, \mathbf{z}_{k,i_0-1} - \mathbf{z}'_{k,i_0-1}, \mathbf{z}_{k,i_0} - \mathbf{z}'_{k,i_0} + \mathbf{S}_{i_0}(\mathbf{c}'_k - \mathbf{c}_k), \\ & \mathbf{z}_{k,i_0+1} - \mathbf{z}'_{k,i_0+1}, \cdots, \mathbf{z}_{k,l} - \mathbf{z}'_{k,l}],\end{aligned}$$

from Eq. (4) we have $\mathbf{A}\widehat{\mathbf{z}} = \mathbf{0} \ (\text{mod } q)$.

The next step is to prove that $\hat{\mathbf{z}} \neq \mathbf{0}$ with probability non- negligible. In fact, by Lemma 6, there is another secret key $\mathbf{S}'_{i_0}$ such that $\mathbf{A}\mathbf{S}_{i_0} = \mathbf{A}\mathbf{S}'_{i_0} \pmod{q}$ in which $\mathbf{S}_{i_0}$ and $\mathbf{S}_{i_0}$ have all the same columns but the i-th column with i is the position that $\mathbf{c}_k[i] \neq \mathbf{c}'_k[i]$. Clearly, if $\mathbf{z}_{k,i_0} - \mathbf{z}'_{k,i_0} + \mathbf{S}_{i_0}(\mathbf{c}'_k - \mathbf{c}_k) = \mathbf{0}$ then $\mathbf{z}_{k,i_0} - \mathbf{z}'_{k,i_0} + \mathbf{S}'_{i_0}(\mathbf{c}'_k - \mathbf{c}_k) \neq \mathbf{0}$. Thus with probability at least $1/2$ we get $\hat{\mathbf{z}} \neq \mathbf{0}$. Note that $\|\mathbf{z}_{k,i}\| \leq \eta\sigma_3\sqrt{m}$, $\|\mathbf{S}_i\| \leq \sigma\sqrt{m}$ and $\|\mathbf{c}_k\| \leq \sqrt{\kappa}$ for all $i \in [l]$. Hence, $\|\mathbf{z}_{k,i} - \mathbf{z}'_{k,i}\| \leq 2\eta\sigma_3\sqrt{m}$ for all $i \in [l]$,. Thus, $\|\hat{\mathbf{z}}\| \leq (2l\eta\sigma_3 + 2\sigma\sqrt{\kappa})\sqrt{m}$. Therefore, we have the success probability of $\mathcal{G}$ in solving the SIS problem (2) in this case is at least

$$\delta_{solve} \geq \frac{1}{4s}\delta_{frk} \geq \frac{1}{4s}(1 - \zeta)(\delta - 1/|D_c|)((\delta - 1/|D_c|)/q_H - 1/|D_c|).$$

Now, taking restarts happen in Phase 5 into account, we will show that if the adversarial user can forge a valid signature through a Phase 5 restart help, then $\mathcal{G}$ can solve the SIS problem stated in Eq. (2). To trigger a restart in Phase 5, the forger sends to the signer $\mathsf{result} := ((\mathbf{a}_i)_{i \in [l]}, \mathbf{b}, \mathbf{c}, C)$ which, together with the view of the signer $\mathcal{V} = (\mathbf{x}, \mathbf{e}, (\mathbf{s}_i, \mathbf{y}_i)_{i \in [l]})$, satisfies all the following conditions:

$$\mathbf{e} - \mathbf{b} = \mathbf{c} = H(\mathbf{x} + \mathbf{w} + \mathbf{T}\mathbf{b} \pmod{q}, C, PK), \tag{5}$$

$$\mathbf{c} = H(\mathbf{w} + \mathbf{v} - \mathbf{T}\mathbf{c} \pmod{q}, C, PK), \tag{6}$$

$$\|\mathbf{y}_{i_0} + \mathbf{a}_{i_0}\| > \eta\sigma_3\sqrt{m} \text{ for some } i_0 \in [l], \tag{7}$$

where $\mathbf{x} = \sum_{i \in [l]} \mathbf{A}_i\mathbf{s}_i$, $\mathbf{w} = \sum_{i \in [l]} \mathbf{A}_i\mathbf{a}_i$, $\mathbf{v} = \sum_{i \in [l]} \mathbf{A}_i\mathbf{y}_i$. Assume that the adversary can obtain a valid signature $\Sigma^* = ((\mathbf{z}'_i)_{i \in [l]}, \mathbf{c}', \mathbf{t}')$ (with probability at least δ) from this restart. That is, for some $\mathbf{b}' \in \mathcal{D}^k_{\sigma_1}$ such that $\mathbf{e} = \mathbf{c}' + \mathbf{b}'$ we have,

$$\mathbf{e} - \mathbf{b}' = \mathbf{c}' = H(\mathbf{x} + \mathbf{w} + \mathbf{T}\mathbf{b}' \pmod{q}, C, PK), \tag{8}$$

$$\mathbf{c}' = H(\sum_{i \in [l]} \mathbf{A}_i\mathbf{z}'_i - \mathbf{T}\mathbf{c}' \pmod{q}, \mathrm{com}(\mu, \mathbf{t}'), PK), \tag{9}$$

$$\|\mathbf{z}'_i\| \leq \eta\sigma_3\sqrt{m} \text{ for all } i \in [l]. \tag{10}$$

With probability $1 - 1/|D_c|$ (how to compute this probability, see [10, Subsection 4.6.1 in Chapter 4])), we have $\mathbf{c}' = \mathbf{c}$. Then by Eqs. (6) and (9), we have

$$\mathbf{w} + \mathbf{v} \pmod{q} = \sum_{i \in [l]} \mathbf{A}_i\mathbf{z}'_i \pmod{q}.$$

That is,

$$\sum_{i \in [l]} \mathbf{A}_i(\mathbf{a}_i + \mathbf{y}_i) \pmod{q} = \sum_{i \in [l]} \mathbf{A}_i\mathbf{z}'_i \pmod{q}.$$

Define

$$\hat{\mathbf{z}} := [\mathbf{a}_1 + \mathbf{y}_1 - \mathbf{z}'_1, \cdots, \mathbf{a}_l + \mathbf{y}_l - \mathbf{z}'_l].$$

Table 2. Parameter setting for our BRS scheme

Parameters	Requirement	Description
n	–	security parameter
l	–	number of ring members
q	$poly(n)$, prime	modulo
m	$\max(64 + n\log q/\log(2d+1), 5n\log q)$	in Lemma 6, TrapGen
K	$m^{1+\epsilon}$, for any $\epsilon > 0$	in SampleKey
σ	$\geq K \cdot \omega(\sqrt{\log n})$	in SampleKey
d	$\sigma \cdot \sqrt{m}$	in BRS.KeyGen
k and κ	such that $2^\kappa \cdot \binom{k}{\kappa} \geq 2^{100}$	in the hash function H
η	$[1.1, 1.3]$	in Lemma 2
$M_1 = M_2 = M_3$	$\exp(1 + 1/288)$	in the rejection sampling
σ_1	$12\sqrt{\kappa}$	
σ_2	$12\sigma\eta\sigma_1\sqrt{mk}$	
σ_3	$12\eta\sigma_2\sqrt{m}$	
signature size	$lm\log(12\sigma_3) + n + \kappa$ bits	
secret key size	$lmk\log(2d+1)$ bits ◦	
public key size	$(lnm + nk)\log q$ bits	

We have $\mathbf{A}\hat{\mathbf{z}} = \mathbf{0} \pmod{q}$. If $\hat{\mathbf{z}} = 0$, i.e., $\mathbf{a}_i + \mathbf{y}_i = \mathbf{z}'_i$ for all $i \in [l]$, then we have $\|\mathbf{y}_i + \mathbf{a}_i\| \leq \eta\sigma_3\sqrt{m}$ for all $i \in [l]$ (due to Eq. (10)) which contradicts with Eq. (7). Hence, $\hat{\mathbf{z}} \neq \mathbf{0}$ and we have $\|\hat{\mathbf{z}}\| \leq (2l\eta\sigma_3 + l\eta\sigma_2)\sqrt{m}$. The success probability of $\mathcal{G}$ in case the forger can get a valid signature through a restart is $\delta_{restart} \geq \delta(1 - 1/|D_c|)$.

To sum up, we have proven that with overall success probability of $\delta_{overall} \geq \min(\delta_{solve}, \delta_{restart})$, the solver $\mathcal{G}$ can solve the $\mathsf{SIS}_{q,n,ml,\beta}$ problem where

$$\beta = \max((2l\eta\sigma_3 + 2\sigma\sqrt{\kappa})\sqrt{m}, (2l\eta\sigma_3 + l\eta\sigma_2)\sqrt{m}).$$

6   Parameter Setting

Basically, parameters in this work are set in a similar way to [27]. We need parameters n, q, k to make sure that the SIS problem is computationally infeasible to keep secret keys $\mathbf{S}_i$'s not to be recovered. To generate the key pairs, we invoke the trapdoor functions using the discrete Gaussian distribution D_σ with $\sigma \geq L \cdot \omega(\sqrt{\log n})$ and $L = m^{1+\epsilon}$ for any $\epsilon > 0$.

For security proofs, we need $m \geq 64 + n\log q/\log(2d+1)$ via Lemma 6. We also need $m \geq 5n\log q$ for TrapGen works. So we can choose $m \geq \max\{64 + n \cdot \log q/\log(2d+1), 5n\log q\}$. The parameter κ appearing in the hash function H should be chosen to satisfy $2^\kappa \cdot \binom{k}{\kappa} \geq 2^{100}$ in order to guarantee that the min-entropy of H is at least 100. As analyzed in Subsect. 5.1, we can set

$M_i := e^{1+1/288}$ for all $i \in [3]$. Accordingly, we then set $\sigma_1 = 12\|\mathbf{c}\| = 12\sqrt{\kappa}$, $\sigma_2 = 12\|\mathbf{S}_j\mathbf{e}\| = 12\sigma\eta\sigma_1\sqrt{mk} = 144\sigma\eta\sqrt{mk\kappa}$ and $\sigma_3 = 12\|\mathbf{y}_i\| = 12\eta\sigma_2\sqrt{m} = 1728mn^2\sigma\sqrt{k\kappa}$.

The real signature is $\Sigma = ((\mathbf{z}_i)_{i\in[l]}, \mathbf{c}, \mathbf{t}))$. Each component of $\mathbf{z}_i$ is of length at most $12\sigma_3$ with probability at least $1 - 2^{-100}$ by Lemma 1, so the signature bit-size is $lm \log(12\sigma_3) + n + \kappa$ bits. The secret key bit-size is $lmk \log(2d + 1)$. The public key bit-size is $(lnm + nk) \log q$.

The parameter setting is summarized in Table 2.

7   Conclusions and Future Works

In this paper, we proposed, for the first time, a lattice-based blind ring signature scheme. Our scheme is proven to fulfill the anonymity and the blindness properties due to being constructed with the reject sampling technique. Moreover, the scheme is one-more unforgeable in the random oracle model under the hardness of SIS problem.

There have been several recent results in improving lattice-based (ring) signatures both on signature sizes and the hardness assumption (e.g. from module lattices), which can be utilized to improve our scheme. We will leave to apply these improvements as future works. One more interesting approach should be our next work is to design a blind ring signature without using trapdoor functions but, for example, basing on the idea of [1]. Also, it is still open to construct a blind ring signature that is secure in the standard model.

Acknowledgment. The first author would like to thank Prof. Masaya Yasuda for his financial support. The authors would like to thank anonymous reviewers for their helpful comments.

References

1. Aguilar-Melchor, C., Bettaieb, S., Boyen, X., Fousse, L., Gaborit, P.: Adapting Lyubashevsky's Signature Schemes to the Ring Signature Setting. Cryptology ePrint Archive, Report 2013/281 (2013). https://eprint.iacr.org/2013/281
2. Ajtai, M.: Generating hard instances of lattice problems (extended abstract). In: Proceedings of the Twenty-Eighth Annual ACM Symposium on Theory of Computing, STOC 1996, pp. 99–108. ACM, New York (1996). http://doi.acm.org/10.1145/237814.237838
3. Bellare, M., Neven, G.: New Multi-Signature Schemes and a General Forking Lemma. http://soc1024.ece.illinois.edu/teaching/ece498ac/fall2018/forkinglemma.pdf
4. Buchmann, J., Ding, J. (eds.): PQCrypto 2008. LNCS, vol. 5299, 1st edn. Springer, Heidelberg (2008). https://doi.org/10.1007/978-3-540-88403-3
5. Bresson, E., Stern, J., Szydlo, M.: Threshold ring signatures and applications to ad-hoc groups. In: Yung, M. (ed.) CRYPTO 2002. LNCS, vol. 2442, pp. 465–480. Springer, Heidelberg (2002). https://doi.org/10.1007/3-540-45708-9_30

6. Chaum, D.: Blind signatures for untraceable payments. In: Chaum, D., Rivest, R.L., Sherman, A.T. (eds.) Advances in Cryptology, pp. 199–203. Springer, Boston, MA (1983). https://doi.org/10.1007/978-1-4757-0602-4_18

7. Fiat, A., Shamir, A.: How to prove yourself: practical solutions to identification and signature problems. In: Odlyzko, A.M. (ed.) CRYPTO 1986. LNCS, vol. 263, pp. 186–194. Springer, Heidelberg (1987). https://doi.org/10.1007/3-540-47721-7_12

8. Gentry, C., Peikert, C., Vaikuntanathan, V.: Trapdoors for hard lattices and new cryptographic constructions. In: Proceedings of the Fortieth Annual ACM Symposium on Theory of Computing, STOC 2008, pp. 197–206. ACM, New York (2008). http://doi.acm.org/10.1145/1374376.1374407

9. Ghadafi, E.M.: Sub-linear blind ring signatures without random oracles. In: Stam, M. (ed.) IMACC 2013. LNCS, vol. 8308, pp. 304–323. Springer, Heidelberg (2013). https://doi.org/10.1007/978-3-642-45239-0_18

10. Guo, F., Susilo, W., Mu, Y.: Foundations of security reduction. Introduction to Security Reduction, pp. 29–146. Springer, Cham (2018). https://doi.org/10.1007/978-3-319-93049-7_4

11. Halevi, S., Micali, S.: Practical and provably-secure commitment schemes from collision-free hashing. In: Koblitz, N. (ed.) CRYPTO 1996. LNCS, vol. 1109, pp. 201–215. Springer, Heidelberg (1996). https://doi.org/10.1007/3-540-68697-5_16

12. Herranz, J., Laguillaumie, F.: Blind ring signatures secure under the chosen-target-CDH assumption. In: Katsikas, S.K., López, J., Backes, M., Gritzalis, S., Preneel, B. (eds.) ISC 2006. LNCS, vol. 4176, pp. 117–130. Springer, Heidelberg (2006). https://doi.org/10.1007/11836810_9

13. Kawachi, A., Tanaka, K., Xagawa, K.: Concurrently secure identification schemes based on the worst-case hardness of lattice problems. In: Pieprzyk, J. (ed.) ASIACRYPT 2008. LNCS, vol. 5350, pp. 372–389. Springer, Heidelberg (2008). https://doi.org/10.1007/978-3-540-89255-7_23

14. Lyubashevsky, V.: Fiat-shamir with aborts: applications to lattice and factoring-based signatures. In: Matsui, M. (ed.) ASIACRYPT 2009. LNCS, vol. 5912, pp. 598–616. Springer, Heidelberg (2009). https://doi.org/10.1007/978-3-642-10366-7_35

15. Lyubashevsky, V.: Lattice Signatures Without Trapdoors. Cryptology ePrint Archive, Report 2011/537, Full version of paper appearing at Eurocrypt 2012 (2012). https://eprint.iacr.org/2011/537. Accessed 18 Oct 2017

16. Micciancio, D., Goldwasser, S.: Complexity of Lattice Problems: A Cryptographic Perspective. The Kluwer International Series in Engineering and Computer Science, vol. 671. Kluwer Academic Publishers, Boston (2002)

17. Micciancio, D., Regev, O.: Worst-case to average-case reductions based on Gaussian measures. SIAM J. Comput. 37(1), 267–302 (2007). https://doi.org/10.1137/S0097539705447360

18. Peikert, C.: A decade of lattice cryptography. Found. Trends Theor. Comput. Sci. 10(4), 283–424 (2016). https://doi.org/10.1561/0400000074

19. Rivest, R.L., Shamir, A., Tauman, Y.: How to leak a secret. In: Boyd, C. (ed.) ASIACRYPT 2001. LNCS, vol. 2248, pp. 552–565. Springer, Heidelberg (2001). https://doi.org/10.1007/3-540-45682-1_32

20. Rückert, M.: Lattice-based blind signatures. In: Abe, M. (ed.) ASIACRYPT 2010. LNCS, vol. 6477, pp. 413–430. Springer, Heidelberg (2010). https://doi.org/10.1007/978-3-642-17373-8_24

21. van Saberhagen, N.: Cryptonote v 2.0 (2013). https://cryptonote.org/whitepaper.pdf

22. Shor, P.W.: Algorithms for quantum computation: discrete logarithms and factoring. In: Proceedings 35th Annual Symposium on Foundations of Computer Science, pp. 124–134, November 1994. https://doi.org/10.1109/SFCS.1994.365700
23. Susilo, W., Mu, Y.: Non-interactive deniable ring authentication. In: Lim, J.-I., Lee, D.-H. (eds.) ICISC 2003. LNCS, vol. 2971, pp. 386–401. Springer, Heidelberg (2004). https://doi.org/10.1007/978-3-540-24691-6_29
24. Susilo, W., Mu, Y., Zhang, F.: Perfect concurrent signature schemes. In: Lopez, J., Qing, S., Okamoto, E. (eds.) ICICS 2004. LNCS, vol. 3269, pp. 14–26. Springer, Heidelberg (2004). https://doi.org/10.1007/978-3-540-30191-2_2
25. Wang, S., Zhao, R., Zhang, Y.: Lattice-based ring signature scheme under the random oracle model. Int. J. High Perform. Comput. Netw. 11(4), 332–341 (2018). https://doi.org/10.1504/IJHPCN.2018.093236
26. Wu, Q., Zhang, F., Susilo, W., Mu, Y.: An efficient static blind ring signature scheme. In: Won, D.H., Kim, S. (eds.) ICISC 2005. LNCS, vol. 3935, pp. 410–423. Springer, Heidelberg (2006). https://doi.org/10.1007/11734727_32
27. Zhang, P., Jiang, H., Zheng, Z., Hu, P., Xu, Q.: A new post-quantum blind signature from lattice assumptions. IEEE Access 6, 27251–27258 (2018). https://doi.org/10.1109/ACCESS.2018.2833103

A Note on the Invisibility and Anonymity of Undeniable Signature Schemes

Jia-Ch'ng Loh[1], Swee-Huay Heng[1(✉)], Syh-Yuan Tan[2], and Kaoru Kurosawa[3]

[1] Faculty of Information Science and Technology, Multimedia University,
Melaka, Malaysia
jasonlohjc@gmail.com, shheng@mmu.edu.my
[2] School of Computing, Newcastle University, Newcastle upon Tyne, UK
syh-yuan.tan@newcastle.ac.uk
[3] Department of Computer and Information Sciences, Ibaraki University,
Hitachi, Ibaraki 316-8511, Japan
kaoru.kurosawa.kk@vc.ibaraki.ac.jp

Abstract. Undeniable signature is a special featured digital signature which can only be verified with the help of the signer. Undeniable signature should satisfy invisibility which implies the inability of a user to determine the validity of a message and signature pair as introduced by Chaum et al. Galbraith and Mao later proposed the notion of anonymity which implies the infeasibility to determine which user has issued the signature. They also proved that the notions of invisibility and anonymity are equivalent when the signers possess the same signature space, such that if an undeniable signature possesses invisibility, then it also possesses anonymity, and vice versa. In this paper, we show that in contradiction to the equivalency result established by Galbraith and Mao, there exist some undeniable signature schemes that possess invisibility but not anonymity. This motivates us to find out whether there is a limitation on Galbraith and Mao's equivalency result or the schemes are actually flawed. Our analysis shows that the anonymity property requires all signers to possess the same signature space but the invisibility property does not. This conforms to the equivalency result and implies that an undeniable signature scheme can be invisible but not anonymous if the signers possess the different signature spaces. Our result invalidates two past cryptanalysis on undeniable signature schemes.

Keywords: Anonymity · Invisibility · Undeniable signature

1 Introduction

The notion of undeniable signature was introduced by Chaum and van Antwerpen [7]. Unlike ordinary digital signature, undeniable signature has a distinctive feature, i.e., without the help of the signer, the verifier will not be able to verify the validity of the undeniable signature. Since it was introduced, there are various applications using it such as licensing software [7], electronic cash [25],

© Springer Nature Switzerland AG 2020
I. You (Ed.): WISA 2019, LNCS 11897, pp. 112–125, 2020.
https://doi.org/10.1007/978-3-030-39303-8_9

electronic voting and auctions [26,27]. There are also some variants of undeniable signature proposed such as convertible undeniable signature [3], designated verifier signature [17], and designated confirmer signature [5,23].

Convertible undeniable signature was proposed by Boyar et al. [3]. It is an extension of undeniable signature that allows the signer to transform an undeniable signature into a universally verifiable ordinary digital signature. There are two types of convertible undeniable signature, namely, selectively convertible and universally convertible. Selectively convertible undeniable signature allows the signer to convert only a specific undeniable signature into a universally verifiable one by releasing a token. In universally convertible undeniable signature, the signer releases part of his secret to convert the undeniable signature into the ordinary digital signature. Designated confirmer signature was introduced by Chaum [5], where it allows an undeniable signature to be verified with the help of the signer or the designated confirmer. On the other hand, the designated verifier signature was introduced by Jakobsson et al. [17], where it allows an undeniable signature to be verified by the designated verifier or the signer only.

As previous works were all built in the paradigm of conventional public key cryptography, Libert et al. [22] introduced the paradigm of identity-based undeniable signature, where it addressed the certificate generation and management issues by deriving the signer's public key from the signer's publicly verifiable information, and computing the signer's private key through a trusted third party. Identity-based undeniable signature was further enhanced by Duan [8] with the paradigm of certificateless undeniable signature in 2008 which addressed the issue of private key escrow problem in identity-based cryptography.

The notion of invisibility was introduced as the main security property for undeniable signature and designated confirmer signature by Chaum et al. [6]. Invisibility implies the inability of a user to determine whether a given message and signature pair is valid. It was later formalised by Camenisch and Michels [4] and generalised by Galbraith and Mao [9]. These two definitions of invisibility were also proven to be equivalent by Galbraith and Mao [9]. Galbraith and Mao [9] also introduced the notion of anonymity as the most relevant security property for undeniable signature and designated confirmer signature in multi-user settings. Anonymity implies that given an undeniable signature and public keys of two or more possible signers, it is infeasible to determine which user has issued the signature. They also claimed that the notions of invisibility and anonymity are equivalent if all signers are sharing the same signature space by providing a formal security proof. Huang et al. [16] later formalised invisibility and anonymity in convertible setting where the adversary has some additional accessible oracles and restrictions. They then provided the proof of equivalency between invisibility and anonymity using the same approach as Galbraith and Mao [9]. Since then, the notions of invisibility and anonymity have been regarded by researchers as equivalent, where one proves either of the security properties and the other security property follows [10,18,20–22].

The first provably secure convertible undeniable signature scheme based on RSA was proposed by Kurosawa and Takagi [19]. It was later revisited by Phong et al. [24] who showed that Kurosawa and Takagi's convertible undeniable signature scheme [19] did not satisfy anonymity, and thus invisibility is not satisfied too. Meanwhile, an identity-based convertible undeniable signature scheme based on pairings was proposed by Wu et al. [30]. It was later revisited by Behnia et al. [1] who showed that there exists an adversary who can break the anonymity and thus the invisibility of the scheme. A convertible undeniable signature scheme without random oracle was later proposed by Huang and Wong [12]. However, it was pointed out by Schuldt and Matsuura [28] that their schemes did not satisfy anonymity. The full version [13] of Huang and Wong's convertible undeniable signature scheme [12] was later published and they remarked that their scheme possesses invisibility only. Besides, Huang et al. [14] proposed a designated confirmer signature scheme, and they later highlighted that it did not satisfy anonymity in the full version [11] as well.

1.1 Our Contributions

We revisit three cryptanalysis [1, 24, 28] on undeniable signature schemes and show that two [1, 24] of them did not make a correct conclusion for the cryptanalysed schemes [13, 14, 29] on the equivalency of anonymity and invisibility. We also revisit a designated confirmer signature scheme [11] and show that it faces the same issue as in the cryptanalysed schemes. More precisely, these four schemes do not possess anonymity but they are invisible as the validity of the message and signature pair is not revealed. These observations contradict to the well accepted fact that invisibility is equivalent to anonymity. It is thus interesting to find out whether this phenomenon is caused by a limitation on Galbraith and Mao's security model or the schemes are actually flawed. We first show that the equivalency result of invisibility and anonymity is not applicable in the four schemes due to the signature space for each signer is different as opposed to the requirement placed in Galbraith and Mao's equivalency result [9]. Next, we show that invisibility does not require signers to have a common signature space but anonymity does. Therefore, the four schemes [11, 13, 14, 29] are invisible but not anonymous and the two cryptanalysis [1, 24] inadequately applied Galbraith and Mao's equivalency theorem on them.

1.2 Organisation of the Paper

The organisation of the paper is as follows. In Sect. 2, we review some preliminaries and recall the definitions of undeniable signature, convertible undeniable signature, and designated confirmer signature. We also review the security model of invisibility and anonymity, and the equivalency between them. In Sect. 3, we review the past attacks on some existing undeniable signature schemes. In Sect. 4, we show that the past attacks are not entirely correct by providing a detailed discussion. Finally, we conclude this paper in Sect. 5.

2 Preliminaries

2.1 Bilinear Pairings [2]

A brief review on the properties of bilinear pairings is discussed here. Let $\mathbb{G}$ and $\mathbb{G}_T$ be cyclic groups of prime order p and a generator $g \in \mathbb{G}$. The map $\hat{e} : \mathbb{G} \times \mathbb{G} \rightarrow \mathbb{G}_T$ is a bilinear map which satisfies the following properties:

- Bilinearity: for all $(x, y) \in \mathbb{G}$ and $(a, b) \in \mathbb{Z}_p$, we have $\hat{e}(x^a, y^b) = \hat{e}(x, y)^{ab}$.
- Non-degeneracy: if g is a generator of $\mathbb{G}$, then $\hat{e}(g, g)$ is a generator of $\mathbb{G}_T$ which also implies $\hat{e}(g, g) \neq 1$.
- Computability: there exists an efficient algorithm to compute $\hat{e}(x, y)$ for all $x, y \in \mathbb{G}$.

2.2 Undeniable Signature Scheme

An undeniable signature is a special featured digital signature which is only verifiable with the help of the signer. An undeniable signature scheme consists of the following algorithms and protocols [9]:

- *KeyGen*: On input a security parameter 1^k, it outputs a signer's public and private key pair (pk, sk).
- *Sign*: On input a message and a signer private key (m, sk), it outputs an undeniable signature σ.
- *Confirmation/Disavowal Protocol*: An interactive protocol that runs between the signer and the verifier on common input (pk, m, σ). The signer uses sk to check the validity of σ, then the signer proves to the verifier that σ is valid on m under pk, and the verifier outputs "1" if σ is a valid signature of m and outputs "0" otherwise.

Correctness. Every valid (invalid) undeniable signature can always be proven valid (invalid) with *Confirmation/Disavowal Protocol*.

2.3 Convertible Undeniable Signature Scheme

A convertible undeniable signature scheme consists of the same algorithms and protocols as in undeniable signature scheme with the following additional algorithms which allow selectively conversion and universally conversion [16]:

- *Selective-Convert*: On input (sk, m, σ), it computes a selective token π^S which can be used to publicly verify (m, σ) on pk.
- *Selective-Verify*: On input (pk, m, σ, π^S), it outputs $\perp$ if π^S is an invalid token on pk. Else, it outputs "1" if (m, σ, pk) is valid and outputs "0" otherwise.
- *Universal-Convert*: On input sk, it computes a universal token π^U which can be used to publicly verify every σ generated by sk.

– $Universal\text{-}Verify$: On input (pk, m, σ, π^U), it outputs $\perp$ if π^U is an invalid token on pk. Else, it outputs "1" if (m, σ, pk) is valid and outputs "0" otherwise.

Completeness and **Soundness**. **Completeness** is defined as that a valid (invalid) undeniable signature can always be proven valid (invalid) and **Soundness** is defined as that a valid (invalid) undeniable signature cannot be proven as invalid (valid).

2.4 Designated Confirmer Signature Scheme

A designated confirmer signature scheme consists of the same algorithms and protocols as in undeniable signature scheme with the additional algorithm, $DCKeyGen$, and an additional input, the confirmer's public key pk_c, into $Sign$ and $Confirmation/Disavowal\,Protocol$ [5]:

– $DCKeyGen$: On input a security parameter 1^k, it outputs a confirmer's public and private key pair (pk_c, sk_c).
– $Sign$: On input (m, sk, pk_c), it outputs a designated confirmer signature σ.
– $Confirmation/Disavowal\,Protocol$: An interactive protocol that runs between the signer/confirmer and the verifier on common input (pk, pk_c, m, σ). The signer/confirmer uses sk/sk_c to check the validity of σ, the output is a non-transferable proof ("1"/"0") that shows σ is valid/invalid on (m, pk, pk_c).

Correctness. Same as in Sect. 2.2.

2.5 The Notions of Invisibility and Anonymity

The notion of invisibility was first introduced by Chaum et al. [6]. It was later formalised by Camenisch and Michels [4] to distinguish whether a signature is corresponding to either message m_0 or m_1. Galbraith and Mao then generalised the notion of invisibility to distinguish a signature from a random element. Besides, Galbraith and Mao also proposed the notion of anonymity [9] to distinguish a signature which is either valid on public key pk_0 or pk_1, and they claimed that anonymity rather than invisibility should be considered as the main security property for undeniable signature in the multi-user setting. The notions of invisibility and anonymity were further studied by Huang et al. [16] in order to cover the convertible undeniable signature scheme.

Invisibility. This security property requires that given (m, σ) and a signer's public key pk, there is no computational way to decide whether (m, σ) is valid on pk or not without the help of the signer. Its security model is defined as the following game between an adversary $\mathcal{A}_I$ and a challenger $\mathcal{C}$ [9,16].

- **Setup:** C first runs $KeyGen(1^k) \rightarrow (pk, sk)$ and sends pk to $\mathcal{A}_I$.
- **Queries I:** $\mathcal{A}_I$ is able to make queries to sign oracle and confirmation/disavowal oracle. $\mathcal{A}_I$ can also make query to selective convert oracle if the scheme is convertible.
- **Output I:** At some point, $\mathcal{A}_I$ outputs a challenge message $\hat{m}$ to request a challenge signature $\hat{\sigma}$. If the scheme is deterministic, $\hat{m}$ is restricted where it must not have been submitted to sign oracle during **Queries I**. $\mathcal{A}_I$ submits a challenge message $\hat{m}$. C responds by randomly choosing $b \in \{0, 1\}$ and generates $\hat{\sigma} = Sign_{sk}(\hat{m})$ if $b = 0$. Otherwise, C returns a random element that is chosen from the same signature space as in $\hat{\sigma} = Sign_{sk}(\hat{m})$.
- **Queries II:** Once $\mathcal{A}_I$ obtains $\hat{\sigma}$, $\mathcal{A}_I$ can still make queries to the accessible oracles as in **Queries I**. The restrictions defined in **Output I** still hold with an additional restriction that any $(\hat{m}, \cdot)$ in the equivalence class of $(\hat{m}, \hat{\sigma})$ is not allowed to be submitted to confirmation/disavowal oracle and selective convert oracle.
- **Output II:** $\mathcal{A}_I$ outputs a guess b' and wins the game if $b' = b$.

The advantage of $\mathcal{A}_I$ has in the above game is defined as $\mathrm{Adv}(\mathcal{A}_I) = |Pr[b = b'] - \frac{1}{2}|$.

Definition 1. *An undeniable signature, convertible undeniable signature, or designated confirmer signature scheme is (t, q, ε)-invisible if there is no probabilistic polynomial time (PPT) adversary $\mathcal{A}_I$ can have success probability more than ε in its game with at most q queries to its accessible oracles in time t.*

Anonymity. This security property requires that given a valid (m, σ) and two possible signers' public keys (pk_0, pk_1), there is no computational way to decide who the real signer is. Its security model is defined as the following game between an adversary $\mathcal{A}_A$ and a challenger C [9,16].

- **Setup:** C first runs $KeyGen(1^k) \rightarrow (pk_0, sk_0)$ and $KeyGen(1^k) \rightarrow (pk_1, sk_1)$ and sends (pk_0, pk_1) to $\mathcal{A}_A$.
- **Queries I:** $\mathcal{A}_A$ is able to make queries to all the accessible oracles as in Sect. 2.5.
- **Output I:** $\mathcal{A}_A$ outputs a challenge message $\hat{m}$ to request for a challenge signature $\hat{\sigma}$ with the same restriction as in Sect. 2.5. C responds by randomly choosing a challenge bit $b \in \{0, 1\}$ and generates a challenge signature $\hat{\sigma} = Sign_{sk_b}(\hat{m})$ that is valid on either pk_0 or pk_1. In either case, $\hat{\sigma}$ is returned to $\mathcal{A}_A$.
- **Queries II:** Same as in Sect. 2.5.
- **Output II:** $\mathcal{A}_A$ outputs a guess b' and wins the game if $b' = b$.

The advantage of $\mathcal{A}$ has in the above game is defined as $\mathrm{Adv}(\mathcal{A}_A) = |Pr[b = b'] - \frac{1}{2}|$.

Definition 2. *An undeniable signature, convertible undeniable signature, or designated confirmer signature scheme is (t, q, ε)-anonymous if there is no PPT adversary $\mathcal{A}_A$ can have success probability more than ε in its game with at most q queries to its accessible oracles in time t.*

The Equivalence of Invisibility and Anonymity. The equivalence of invisibility and anonymity in undeniable signature and designated confirmer signature schemes was introduced by Galbraith and Mao [9], and further studied by Huang et al. [16] for the convertible variant. The equivalency shows that if an undeniable signature scheme possesses invisibility, then it also possesses anonymity, and vice versa. This is highlighted by Galbraith and Mao [9] and Phong et al. [24] that invisibility implies anonymity if and only if all signers are sharing the same signature space, especially in RSA based undeniable signature in order to ensure the signature length does not reveal the identity of the signer. We only include Theorem 1 which states that, if a scheme possesses invisibility then it also possesses anonymity, as given by Galbraith and Mao [9]. We omit Theorem 2 which states that, if a scheme possesses anonymity then it also possesses invisibility, as it is not referred in our subsequent discussion.

Theorem 1 [9,16]. *If an undeniable signature, convertible undeniable signature, or designated confirmer signature scheme possesses invisibility, then it also possesses anonymity.*

Proof. Suppose there exists an adversary $\mathcal{D}_A$ who can reveal the signer's public key of the signature in the game of anonymity, then there is an adversary $\mathcal{D}_I$ who can use $\mathcal{D}_A$ to have the advantage in the game of invisibility and thus the scheme is not invisible.

- **Setup:** The input to $\mathcal{D}_I$ is pk_0, and we run $KeyGen(1^k) \rightarrow (pk_1, sk_1)$ to produce another public and private key pair (pk_1, sk_1). $\mathcal{D}_I$ keeps sk_1 and flips a coin $b' \in \{0, 1\}$. If $b' = 0$, the input to $\mathcal{D}_A$ is (pk_0, pk_1), otherwise the input is (pk_1, pk_0).
- **Queries I:** Queries made by $\mathcal{D}_A$ with respect to pk_0 are all passed on as $\mathcal{D}_I$ queries, and queries with respect to pk_1 are handled by $\mathcal{D}_I$ using the knowledge of sk_1.
- **Output I:** At some point, $\mathcal{D}_A$ outputs a challenge message $\hat{m}$, $\mathcal{D}_I$ passes $\hat{m}$ as his own challenge as well. If the challenge bit $b = 0$, $\mathcal{D}_I$ receives a challenge signature $\hat{\sigma} = Sign_{sk_0}(\hat{m})$, or $\hat{\sigma}$ which with negligible probability, is valid on an arbitrary message if $b = 1$.
- **Queries II:** $\mathcal{D}_A$ can continue to make his queries to $\mathcal{D}_I$ as in **Queries I** with the restrictions covered in the adversaries' own challenges, such as $\hat{m}$ is not allowed to query for confirmation/disavowal oracle.
- **Output II:** At the end, $\mathcal{D}_A$ outputs a guess b''. If $b'' = b'$, $\mathcal{D}_I$ outputs 0 as his guess and 1 otherwise.

Note that in the case $b = 0$, where $\hat{\sigma} = Sign_{sk_0}(\hat{m})$. Since $\mathcal{D}_A$ can reveal the signer, $\mathcal{D}_A$ outputs $b'' = b'$ to $\mathcal{D}_I$ then $\mathcal{D}_I$ can always output 0. At this point, $\mathcal{D}_I$ wins the game with the help of $\mathcal{D}_A$ which denotes as:

$$\Pr[b'' = b' | b = 0] = \frac{1}{2} + \text{Adv}(\mathcal{D}_A)$$

However, in the case $b = 1$, $\hat{\sigma}$ is a random element which indicates an invalid signature (with the negligible chance that it is valid on $\hat{m}$). It follows by b' is independent of $\hat{\sigma}$, hence $\Pr[b'' \neq b'|b = 1] \approx \frac{1}{2}$. Therefore, the advantage of $\mathcal{D}_I$ is defined as follows:

$$\text{Adv}(\mathcal{D}_I) = \Pr[b'' = b'|b = 0]\frac{1}{2} + \Pr[b'' \neq b'|b = 1]\frac{1}{2} - \frac{1}{2}$$

$$= (\frac{1}{2} + \text{Adv}(\mathcal{D}_A))\frac{1}{2} + \frac{1}{2}\frac{1}{2} - \frac{1}{2}$$

$$= \frac{1}{2}\text{Adv}(\mathcal{D}_A)$$

□

Theorem 2 [9,16]. *If an undeniable signature, convertible undeniable signature, or designated confirmer signature scheme possesses anonymity, then it also possesses invisibility.*

3   Revisiting the Cryptanalysis on Some Undeniable Signature Schemes

In this section, we first briefly describe the attack mounted by Behnia et al. [1] on Wu et al.'s identity-based convertible undeniable signature scheme [30], followed by the attack by Phong et al. [24] on Kurosawa and Takagi's convertible undeniable signature scheme [19], and the attack by Schuldt and Matsuura [28] on Huang and Wong's convertible undeniable signature scheme [12]. Besides, we also briefly describe Huang et al.'s designated confirmer signature scheme [11] which possesses invisibility but not anonymity. We show that these schemes satisfy invisibility, but not anonymity.

3.1   Identity-Based Convertible Undeniable Signature Scheme of Wu et al.

In the identity-based convertible undeniable signature scheme of Wu et al. [30], the public parameter $PM = (\hat{e}, g, P_{pub} = g^s, H_1, H_2, H_3)$ and the signer's private key $sk = (SK_{ID} = H_1(ID)^s, VK_{ID} = H_1(ID||``Undeniable")^s)$. The undeniable signature $\sigma = (U, V, W)$ is given by

$$U = \hat{e}(VK_{ID}, H_2(m))$$
$$V = g^v$$
$$W = SK_{ID} \cdot H_3(U, V)^v$$

where v is the random salt.

Behnia et al. showed that this scheme did not satisfy anonymity [1]. Indeed, given $\sigma = (U, V, W)$, one can identify the signer by checking the validity of σ using Eq. (1) with the signer identity ID:

$$\hat{e}(W, g) = \hat{e}(H_1(ID), P_{pub}) \cdot \hat{e}(H_3(U, V), V) \tag{1}$$

They therefore concluded that invisibility in Wu et al.'s scheme is broken too following the equivalency result of Galbraith and Mao [9].

3.2 Undeniable Signature Scheme of Kurosawa and Takagi

In the undeniable signature scheme of Kurosawa and Takagi [19], the signer's public key $pk = (x, h_1, h_2, H, N_1, N_2)$ and the private key $sk = d$. The undeniable signature $\sigma = (e, y, x', \omega)$ is given by

$$y^e = x \cdot h_2^{H(x')} \mod N_2 \tag{2}$$

where e is a random exponent and (x', ω) are commitment values of a message m. Note that y must satisfy Eq. (2) with respect to the signer's public key $pk = (x, h_1, h_2, H, N_1, N_2)$. The signer randomly chooses $y' \in Z_{N_1}^*$, and $x' \in Z_{N_1}$ is computed such that

$$(y')^{N_1} = x' h_1^{H(m)} \mod N_1 \tag{3}$$

and $N_1 \cdot d = 1 \mod lcm(p_1 - 1, q_1 - 1)$ with the signer private key $sk = d$ and $N_1 = p_1 \cdot q_1$.

Phong et al. showed that this scheme did not satisfy anonymity [24]. Indeed, given $\sigma = (e, y, x', \omega)$, one can identify the signer by checking the validity of (e, y) on x' using Eq. (2) and pk. Phong et al. [24] then claimed that Kurosawa and Takagi's scheme did not possess invisibility too following the equivalency result of Galbraith and Mao [9], even if the signers share a common signature space.

3.3 Convertible Undeniable Signature Scheme of Huang and Wong

In the undeniable signature scheme of Huang and Wong [12], the signer's public key $pk = (Y, u)$ and the private key $sk = x$. The undeniable signature $\sigma = (\delta, \gamma, \theta)$ is given by

$$\delta = H(m)^{\frac{1}{(x+s)}} \tag{4}$$

$$\gamma = Y^s \tag{5}$$

$$\theta = u^s \tag{6}$$

where s is the random salt and H is a programmable hash function.

Schuldt and Matsuura showed that this scheme did not satisfy anonymity [28]. Indeed, given $\sigma = (\delta, \gamma, \theta)$, one can identify the signer by checking the validity of (γ, θ) using Eq. (7) with $pk = (Y, u)$:

$$\hat{e}(\gamma, u) = \hat{e}(Y, \theta) \tag{7}$$

This issue was also highlighted in the full version [13] of the convertible undeniable signature scheme by Huang and Wong [12] but no solution is given.

3.4   Designated Confirmer Signature Scheme of Huang et al.

In the designated confirmer signature scheme of Huang et al. [15], the same signature structure as in Sect. 3.3 was adopted. A slight difference is in the signer's public key $pk = u$ and there is confirmer's public key $pk_c = Y$. The elements of undeniable signature $\sigma = (\delta, \gamma, \theta)$ are as in Eqs. (4), (5) and (6) respectively.

Huang et al. highlighted in the full version of their paper that this scheme did not satisfy anonymity [11]. Indeed, given a designated confirmer signature $\sigma = (\delta, \gamma, \theta)$, one can identify the signer and the confirmer using the same Eq. (7) with (pk, pk_c). Huang et al. claimed that their scheme is not anonymous but it is invisible.

3.5   Invisibility of the Above Schemes

On the other hand, we can show that all the above schemes satisfy invisibility. Let us recall the invisibility game in Sect. 2.5 where the adversary $\mathcal{A}_I$ is required to guess whether a given $\hat{\sigma}$ is valid on $\hat{m}$ or a random element (invalid on $\hat{m}$). Note that during **Output I**, $\mathcal{A}_I$ submits a challenge message $\hat{m}$ to request a challenge signature $\hat{\sigma}$, where $\hat{\sigma}$ is valid on $\hat{m}$ if the challenge bit $b = 0$ or a random element if $b = 1$. However, Wu et al.'s scheme [30] shows that when the challenge bit $b = 1$, only the signature element $\hat{U}$ is random while $(\hat{V}, \hat{W})$ are not, such that $\hat{V} = g^v$ and $\hat{W} = SK_{ID} \cdot H_3(\hat{U}, \hat{V})^v$ where $v \in \mathbb{Z}_q$.

$$\text{If } b = 0, \hat{\sigma} = (\hat{U}, \hat{V}, \hat{W})$$

$$\text{If } b = 1, \hat{\sigma} = (random, \hat{V}, \hat{W})$$

Therefore, when $b = 1$, $\hat{\sigma} = (\hat{U}, \hat{V}, \hat{W})$ can be partially verified with Eq. (1) using the signer's identity ID and $(\hat{V}, \hat{W})$. This observation agrees with the claim of Behnia et al. [1] that the scheme did not possess anonymity, but the claim on invisibility is wrong as Eq. (1) cannot verify the validity of the challenge signature. In precise, $\mathcal{A}_I$ receives $\hat{\sigma}$ from the challenger which is valid on $\hat{m}$ if $b = 0$ or a random element (invalid on $\hat{m}$) if $b = 1$. In either case, $\mathcal{A}_I$ always output 0 as Eq. (1) always holds.

The same issue lies in Kurosawa and Takagi's scheme. Even if the signature element $x' \in Z_{N_1}$ is a random element, a valid y can be generated such that $y^e = x \cdot h_2^{H(x')} \mod N_2$ where e is a randomly selected value. At the end, a challenge signature $\hat{\sigma} = (\hat{e}, \hat{y}, \hat{x}', \hat{\omega})$ can still be partially verified with Eq. (2) using the signer's public key $pk = x$ and $(\hat{e}, \hat{y}, \hat{x}')$ in either case of $b = 0$ or $b = 1$. Apparently, the validity of $(\hat{m}, \hat{\sigma})$ cannot be decided as $\hat{m}$ is perfectly bonded in $\hat{x}'$ which is only verifiable with the knowledge of random value y'. This shows that Eq. (2) only reveals the identity of the signer but then invisibility still holds.

Likewise, the same issue happens in the security proofs of Huang and Wong's scheme [13] and Huang et al.'s scheme [11]. Even though the signature element $\hat{\delta}$ is a random value, $\hat{\gamma} = Y^s$ and $\hat{\theta} = u^s$ are still correctly generated. At the end, a challenge signature $\hat{\sigma} = (\hat{\delta}, \hat{\gamma}, \hat{\theta})$ can always be partially verified with Eq. (7) using the signer's public key (Y, u) (and confirmer's public key $pk_c = Y$ in Huang et al.'s scheme). Therefore, the invisibility is still intact as Eq. (7) reveals only the identity of the signer (and the confirmer in Huang et al.'s scheme).

4   Discussion

4.1   What Is Lacking in the Above Schemes?

We observe that each signer in the above schemes has their own respective signature spaces because of the condition that a valid signature must satisfy Eqs. (1), (2) and (7) respectively, depending on their respective public keys (signer identity).

More precisely, in the scheme of Wu et al. in Sect. 3.1, $\sigma = (U, V, W)$ must satisfy Eq. (1) which depends on ID. Therefore, the valid σ depends on ID. Hence the signature space is different if ID is different.

In the scheme of Kurosawa and Takagi in Sect. 3.2, $\sigma = (e, y, x', \omega)$ must satisfy Eq. (2) which depends on $pk = (x, h_1, h_2, H, N_1, N_2)$. Therefore, obviously the valid σ depends on $pk = (x, h_1, h_2, H, N_1, N_2)$. Hence the signature space is different if $pk = (x, h_1, h_2, H, N_1, N_2)$ is different.

Similarly, in the schemes of Huang and Wong, and Huang et al. in Sects. 3.3 and 3.4 respectively, $\sigma = (\delta, \gamma, \theta)$ must satisfy Eq. (7) which depends on $pk = (Y, u)$ and $(pk = u, pk_c = Y)$ respectively. Therefore, the valid σ depends on $pk = (Y, u)$ or $(pk = u, pk_c = Y)$. Hence the signature space is different if $pk = (Y, u)$ or $(pk = u, pk_c = Y)$ is different.

Let us now consider the proof of Theorem 1 which is given in Sect. 2.5. The following scenario may happen in the above schemes due to that the signers are having different signature spaces. We look at this in general without referring to a specific scheme. Suppose that $b = 1$. Then in Output I, D_I receives $\hat{\sigma}$ from his challenger, and sends it to D_A, where $\hat{\sigma}$ is randomly chosen from the signature space Σ_0 of pk_0. Now if the signature space Σ_1 of pk_1 is different from Σ_0, then D_A would be able to see that $\hat{\sigma} \in \Sigma_0$ but $\hat{\sigma} \notin \Sigma_1$. This means that

$$\Pr[b'' = b' \mid b = 1] \neq 1/2.$$

This is the part where the one-way equivalency from invisibility to anonymity cannot be achieved in the above schemes, i.e. invisibility does not imply anonymity if the signature space of the signers is different.

Thus, we may conclude that invisibility is preserved in the above schemes even though anonymity is broken mainly due to the signature space issue, i.e., each signer in the above schemes has their own respective signature spaces which is different. We note that this observation does not contradict to Galbraith and Mao's equivalency result [9] which stated that invisibility implies anonymity and vice versa, if and only if all signers are sharing the same signature space.

4.2 How to Improve These Schemes?

The above problem does not occur if the signature space of each signer is the same. Therefore, in the design of a provably secure undeniable signature scheme which fulfils both invisibility and anonymity, the designer must take into serious consideration on the signature space of each signer such that the scheme design must ensure that all signers are sharing the same signature space.

5 Conclusion

In this paper, we discovered that the past attacks on some existing undeniable signature schemes are not entirely correct as the invisibility of these schemes is still intact although the anonymity is broken. Thus, we managed to partially falsify the previous cryptanalysis mounted on Wu et al.'s Scheme by Behnia et al. and Kurosawa and Takagi's Scheme by Phong et al. We further pointed out that Galbraith and Mao's equivalence theorem is not applicable on these schemes due to the different signature spaces owned by each signer. We also showed that Huang and Wong, and Huang et al.'s schemes faced the similar issue. Our finding can be served as a reminder to researchers to exercise extreme caution in the design of a provably secure undeniable signature scheme which fulfils both invisibility and anonymity.

Acknowledgement. The authors would like to acknowledge the Malaysia government's Fundamental Research Grant Scheme (FRGS/1/2018/ICT04/MMU/01/01) for supporting this work.

References

1. Behnia, R., Tan, S.-Y., Heng, S.-H.: Cryptanalysis of an identity-based convertible undeniable signature scheme. In: Phan, R.C.-W., Yung, M. (eds.) Mycrypt 2016. LNCS, vol. 10311, pp. 474–477. Springer, Cham (2017). https://doi.org/10.1007/978-3-319-61273-7_23
2. Boneh, D., Franklin, M.: Identity-based encryption from the weil pairing. In: Kilian, J. (ed.) CRYPTO 2001. LNCS, vol. 2139, pp. 213–229. Springer, Heidelberg (2001). https://doi.org/10.1007/3-540-44647-8_13
3. Boyar, J., Chaum, D., Damgård, I., Pedersen, T.: Convertible undeniable signatures. In: Menezes, A.J., Vanstone, S.A. (eds.) CRYPTO 1990. LNCS, vol. 537, pp. 189–205. Springer, Heidelberg (1991). https://doi.org/10.1007/3-540-38424-3_14
4. Camenisch, J., Michels, M.: Confirmer signature schemes secure against adaptive adversaries. In: Preneel, B. (ed.) EUROCRYPT 2000. LNCS, vol. 1807, pp. 243–258. Springer, Heidelberg (2000). https://doi.org/10.1007/3-540-45539-6_17
5. Chaum, D.: Designated confirmer signatures. In: De Santis, A. (ed.) EUROCRYPT 1994. LNCS, vol. 950, pp. 86–91. Springer, Heidelberg (1995). https://doi.org/10.1007/BFb0053427
6. Chaum, D., van Heijst, E., Pfitzmann, B.: Cryptographically strong undeniable signatures, unconditionally secure for the signer. In: Feigenbaum, J. (ed.) CRYPTO 1991. LNCS, vol. 576, pp. 470–484. Springer, Heidelberg (1992). https://doi.org/10.1007/3-540-46766-1_38

7. Chaum, D., van Antwerpen, H.: Undeniable signatures. In: Brassard, G. (ed.) CRYPTO 1989. LNCS, vol. 435, pp. 212–216. Springer, New York (1990). https://doi.org/10.1007/0-387-34805-0_20

8. Duan, S.: Certificateless undeniable signature scheme. Inf. Sci. **178**(3), 742–755 (2008)

9. Galbraith, S.D., Mao, W.: Invisibility and anonymity of undeniable and confirmer signatures. In: Joye, M. (ed.) CT-RSA 2003. LNCS, vol. 2612, pp. 80–97. Springer, Heidelberg (2003). https://doi.org/10.1007/3-540-36563-X_6

10. Galindo, D., Herranz, J., Kiltz, E.: On the generic construction of identity-based signatures with additional properties. In: Lai, X., Chen, K. (eds.) ASIACRYPT 2006. LNCS, vol. 4284, pp. 178–193. Springer, Heidelberg (2006). https://doi.org/10.1007/11935230_12

11. Huang, Q., Wong, D.S., Susilo, W.: Efficient designated confirmer signature and DCS-based ambiguous optimistic fair exchange. IEEE Trans. Inf. Forensics Secur. **6**(4), 1233–1247 (2011). https://doi.org/10.1109/TIFS.2011.2161290

12. Huang, Q., Wong, D.S.: New constructions of convertible undeniable signature schemes without random oracles. Cryptology ePrint Archive, Report 2009/517 (2009). https://eprint.iacr.org/2009/517

13. Huang, Q., Wong, D.S.: Short and efficient convertible undeniable signature schemes without random oracles. Theor. Comput. Sci. **476**, 67–83 (2013). https://doi.org/10.1016/j.tcs.2013.01.010. http://www.sciencedirect.com/science/article/pii/S0304397513000601

14. Huang, Q., Wong, D.S., Susilo, W.: A new construction of designated confirmer signature and its application to optimistic fair exchange. In: Joye, M., Miyaji, A., Otsuka, A. (eds.) Pairing 2010. LNCS, vol. 6487, pp. 41–61. Springer, Heidelberg (2010). https://doi.org/10.1007/978-3-642-17455-1_4

15. Huang, Q., Wong, D.S., Susilo, W.: The construction of ambiguous optimistic fair exchange from designated confirmer signature without random oracles. Inf. Sci. **228**, 222–238 (2013)

16. Huang, X., Mu, Y., Susilo, W., Wu, W.: Provably secure pairing-based convertible undeniable signature with short signature length. In: Takagi, T., Okamoto, T., Okamoto, E., Okamoto, T. (eds.) Pairing 2007. LNCS, vol. 4575, pp. 367–391. Springer, Heidelberg (2007). https://doi.org/10.1007/978-3-540-73489-5_21

17. Jakobsson, M., Sako, K., Impagliazzo, R.: Designated verifier proofs and their applications. In: Maurer, U. (ed.) EUROCRYPT 1996. LNCS, vol. 1070, pp. 143–154. Springer, Heidelberg (1996). https://doi.org/10.1007/3-540-68339-9_13

18. Kurosawa, K., Heng, S.-H.: 3-move undeniable signature scheme. In: Cramer, R. (ed.) EUROCRYPT 2005. LNCS, vol. 3494, pp. 181–197. Springer, Heidelberg (2005). https://doi.org/10.1007/11426639_11

19. Kurosawa, K., Takagi, T.: New approach for selectively convertible undeniable signature schemes. In: Lai, X., Chen, K. (eds.) ASIACRYPT 2006. LNCS, vol. 4284, pp. 428–443. Springer, Heidelberg (2006). https://doi.org/10.1007/11935230_28

20. Laguillaumie, F., Vergnaud, D.: Short undeniable signatures without random oracles: the missing link. In: Maitra, S., Veni Madhavan, C.E., Venkatesan, R. (eds.) INDOCRYPT 2005. LNCS, vol. 3797, pp. 283–296. Springer, Heidelberg (2005). https://doi.org/10.1007/11596219_23

21. Laguillaumie, F., Vergnaud, D.: Time-selective convertible undeniable signatures. In: Menezes, A. (ed.) CT-RSA 2005. LNCS, vol. 3376, pp. 154–171. Springer, Heidelberg (2005). https://doi.org/10.1007/978-3-540-30574-3_12

22. Libert, B., Quisquater, J.-J.: Identity based undeniable signatures. In: Okamoto, T. (ed.) CT-RSA 2004. LNCS, vol. 2964, pp. 112–125. Springer, Heidelberg (2004). https://doi.org/10.1007/978-3-540-24660-2_9

23. Okamoto, T.: Designated confirmer signatures and public-key encryption are equivalent. In: Desmedt, Y.G. (ed.) CRYPTO 1994. LNCS, vol. 839, pp. 61–74. Springer, Heidelberg (1994). https://doi.org/10.1007/3-540-48658-5_8

24. Phong, L.T., Kurosawa, K., Ogata, W.: New RSA-based (selectively) convertible undeniable signature schemes. In: Preneel, B. (ed.) AFRICACRYPT 2009. LNCS, vol. 5580, pp. 116–134. Springer, Heidelberg (2009). https://doi.org/10.1007/978-3-642-02384-2_8

25. Pointcheval, D.: Self-scrambling anonymizers. In: Frankel, Y. (ed.) FC 2000. LNCS, vol. 1962, pp. 259–275. Springer, Heidelberg (2001). https://doi.org/10.1007/3-540-45472-1_18

26. Sakurai, K.: A bulletin-board based digital auction scheme with bidding down strategy-towards anonymous electronic bidding without anonymous channels nor trusted centers. In: Proceedings of CRYPTEC 1999 (1999)

27. Sakurai, K., Miyazaki, S.: An anonymous electronic bidding protocol based on a new convertible group signature scheme. In: Dawson, E.P., Clark, A., Boyd, C. (eds.) ACISP 2000. LNCS, vol. 1841, pp. 385–399. Springer, Heidelberg (2000). https://doi.org/10.1007/10718964_32

28. Schuldt, J.C.N., Matsuura, K.: An efficient convertible undeniable signature scheme with delegatable verification. In: Kwak, J., Deng, R.H., Won, Y., Wang, G. (eds.) ISPEC 2010. LNCS, vol. 6047, pp. 276–293. Springer, Heidelberg (2010). https://doi.org/10.1007/978-3-642-12827-1_21

29. Schuldt, J.C., Matsuura, K.: Efficient convertible undeniable signatures with delegatable verification. IEICE Trans. Fundam. Electron. Commun. Comput. Sci. **94**(1), 71–83 (2011)

30. Wu, W., Mu, Y., Susilo, W., Huang, X.: Provably secure identity-based undeniable signatures with selective and universal convertibility. In: Pei, D., Yung, M., Lin, D., Wu, C. (eds.) Inscrypt 2007. LNCS, vol. 4990, pp. 25–39. Springer, Heidelberg (2008). https://doi.org/10.1007/978-3-540-79499-8_4

Zero-Knowledge Proof System for Fully Anonymous Attribute Based Group Signatures from Lattices with VLR

Maharage Nisansala Sevwandi Perera$^{(\boxtimes)}$, Toru Nakamura,
Masayuki Hashimoto, and Hiroyuki Yokoyama

Adaptive Communications Research Laboratories,
Advanced Telecommunications Research Institute International (ATR), Kyoto, Japan
{perera.nisansala,tr-nakamura,masayuki.hashimoto,hr-yokoyama}@atr.jp

Abstract. Signature schemes with Verifier-Local Revocation (VLR) fail to achieve stronger anonymity notion, full-anonymity. In full-anonymity, it is free to corrupt the secret signing keys. Secret signing keys of VLR schemes consist of tokens which can be used to identify the users. Thus VLR schemes restrict corrupting secret signing keys. VLR schemes can achieve full-anonymity by separating tokens from secret signing keys. However, separation of tokens gives space to signers to replace tokens with fake values. Generating signatures with fake tokens can be prevented with a suitable proof system. This paper proposes a new zero-knowledge protocol to support provers to convince verifiers, that attributes used for creating the signature are valid and have naive tokens. Moreover, this paper offers a new Attribute-Based Group Signature (ABGS) scheme, that uses the proposed protocol and achieves full anonymity.

Keywords: Attribute-Based Group Signatures · Verifier-Local Revocation · Zero-knowledge proof · Full anonymity · Lattice-based cryptography

1 Introduction

Attribute-Based Group Signatures (ABGS) allow a verifier to request a signature from a group who possesses specific attributes [14]. Thus, only a group member possessing required attributes can sign anonymously on behalf of the group. ABGS schemes belong to the family of Digital Signature (DS) schemes such as Group Signature (GS) schemes and Ring Signature (RS) schemes. ABGS scheme is a combination of Group Signature Schemes and Attribute-Based Signatures.

Group Signatures were first introduced by Chaum and Van Heyst [2], and since then, different lines of works were presented to achieve security and efficiency. However, due to the two characteristics; *Anonymity* and *Traceability* of naive group signature schemes, most of the researchers interested in applying Group signatures in real-life systems. The anonymity allows any group member

© Springer Nature Switzerland AG 2020
I. You (Ed.): WISA 2019, LNCS 11897, pp. 126–140, 2020.
https://doi.org/10.1007/978-3-030-39303-8_10

to output a signature while hiding his identity among the group members. The traceability grants an authorized person to cancel the anonymity of a valid signature. Thus, group signature schemes produce signatures which are anonymous to the verifiers (outsiders) and known to the authorities.

Attribute-Based Signatures (ABS), which is a generalization of the digital signatures, allows a user to generate a signature over some specified attributes while being anonymous. In an ABS scheme, a user can generate a signature only if he possesses the attributes required in a given policy. Thus, the signer should possess the necessary attributes to create a signature, and the verifier may check whether the signature is generated by satisfying the policy requirements. The security of ABS ensures the privacy of the signer. Thus, the signer should not reveal any information related to the attributes. ABS schemes were first introduced by Maji et al. [21] in a preliminary version. Later, other ABS schemes [4,5,7,9,10,17,18,25] presented improvements like pairing efficiency, constant-size signatures, user-control linkability, and decentralized-traceability.

Khader proposed the first Attribute-Based Group Signature (ABGS) scheme [14]. In their scheme, the verifier can determine the role of the signer. Again, Khader presented another ABGS scheme with a revocation method [13]. However, both schemes are not secure under quantum attacks as they both were constructed using bilinear mappings. Recently, Kuchta et al. [15] and Zhang et al. [27] presented ABGS schemes from lattices. While Kuchta's work focuses on member registration, Zhang's work produces an ABGS scheme with revocation. In Zhang's scheme [27], a member revocation method called *Verifier-local Revocation* (*VLR*) is used to manage member revocation and attribute revocation.

VLR, which requires only to update the verifiers with revocation messages when a member is revoked, seems to be the most efficient revocation method at present. In group signature schemes, every member of a group has a token, and when he is revoked, this token is added to a list called *revocation list* (*RL*). The verifiers can check the validity of the signer using RL. In the same way, in ABGS schemes, every attribute of a member is assigned a token. Thus, when an attribute of a member is revoked, the related token is added to RL. Thus, any member with revoked attributes which are required in the policy cannot generate a valid signature.

The tokens of members are usually generated as a part of the secret signing keys in almost all the group signature schemes with VLR [16]. Thus, the adversary can attack the system if he knows the secret signing keys of the members. He can execute the verification algorithm with the tokens which he can obtain from the secret signing keys, and identify the signer. Thus, the scheme in [27] achieves weaker security notion called *selfless-anonymity* as most of the VLR group signature schemes. In selfless-anonymity, we assume that the adversary cannot get any secret signing keys. Thus, the schemes with VLR achieve the selfless-anonymity. On the other hand, VLR group signature schemes like [11,23] provided solutions to achieve stronger security than the selfless-anonymity for VLR group signature schemes. However, still, there is no Attribute-Based VLR Group Signature scheme that achieves *full-anonymity*. The full-anonymity proposed in [1] is believed to be the stronger version of anonymity. It requires to ensure the anonymity of a group signature scheme even all the member secret signing keys are exposed to an outsider.

To achieve full anonymity for ABGS with VLR, we require tokens to be independent of secret signing keys. Moreover, to prevent forging tokens, the signers should convince the verifiers that the tokens of the possessing attributes are valid, without disclosing them. As a result, we require a new zero-knowledge protocol to support such schemes.

Contribution

First, we propose a new zero-knowledge protocol which is built on the protocols given in [3,20,27]. Then we construct our new ABGS scheme based on the threshold-ABS scheme given in [3]. The construction of the protocol relies on the hardness of SIS and LWE lattice problems. We use decomposition, extension, masking, and permutation techniques to hide the secret data and convince the verifier that the signer has valid information. Using the Fiat-Shamir heuristic [6], we can make our new interactive protocol to non-interactive protocol.

In our scheme construction, we separate the token generation from the secret signing keys of the attributes. Since the tokens are independent of the secret signing keys, even though the secret signing keys are revealed to the adversary, he cannot attack the anonymity of the scheme. On the other hand, because of the independence of the tokens, members can fake the tokens of the attributes. To prevent such kind of forge, we require the signers to prove the nativity of the tokens while hiding them. Thus, the signers should convince the verifiers that he has relevant attributes, his attribute tokens are not being revoked, and those tokens are valid in zero-knowledge. We ensure that our new zero-knowledge protocol can satisfy those requirements.

2   Preliminary

2.1   Notation

We denote matrices by upper-case bold letters such as $\mathbf{A}$ and vectors by lower-case bold letters such as $\mathbf{v}$. Concatenation of matrices are denoted by $[\mathbf{A}|\mathbf{B}]$ and vectors by $[\mathbf{v}\|\mathbf{y}]$. For any integer $k \geq 1$, a set of integers $\{1, 2, \ldots, k\}$ is denoted by $[k]$. If S is a finite set, we present its size by $|S|$. $S(k)$ indicates its permutations of k elements and $b \hookleftarrow D$ denotes that b is sampled from a uniformly random distribution D. The standard notations of $\mathcal{O}$ and ω are used to classify the growth of functions. All algorithms are of base 2.

2.2   Discrete Gaussian Distribution

We consider a discrete Gaussian distribution for a lattice as in [3,23].

The Gaussian function centered in a vector $\mathbf{c}$ with parameter $s > 0$ is defined as $\rho_{s,\mathbf{c}}(\mathbf{x}) = exp^{-\pi\|(\mathbf{x}-\mathbf{c})/s\|^2}$. With respect to a lattice Λ the discrete Gaussian distribution is defined as $D_{\Lambda,s,\mathbf{c}}(\mathbf{x}) = D_{s,\mathbf{c}}(\mathbf{x})/D_{s,\mathbf{c}}(\Lambda) = \rho_{s,\mathbf{c}}(\mathbf{x})/\rho_{s,\mathbf{c}}(\Lambda)$ for all $\mathbf{x} \in \Lambda$.

2.3 Lattices, Hardness of Lattices, and Lattice Related Algorithms

For n, m, and prime $q \le 2$, let $\mathbf{B} = [\mathbf{b}_1| \cdots |\mathbf{b}_m] \in \mathbb{Z}_q^{n \times m}$ be linearly independent vectors in $\mathbb{Z}_q^n$. The n-dimensional lattice $\Lambda(\mathbf{B})$ for $\mathbf{B}$ is defined as

$$\Lambda_q^{\perp}(\mathbf{B}) = \{\mathbf{x} \in \mathbb{Z}^m \mid \mathbf{Bx} = \mathbf{0} \mod q\},$$

$$\Lambda_q^{\mathbf{u}}(\mathbf{B}) = \{\mathbf{x} \in \mathbb{Z}^m \mid \mathbf{Bx} = \mathbf{u} \mod q\},$$

where $\mathbf{u} \in \mathbb{Z}_q^n$.

Definition 1 (Learning With Errors (LWE)). *For integers $n, m \ge 1$, and $q \ge 2$, a vector $\mathbf{s} \in \mathbb{Z}_q^n$, and the Gaussian error distribution χ, the distribution $A_{s,\chi}$ is obtained by sampling $\mathbf{a} \in \mathbb{Z}_q^n$ uniformly at random and choosing $e \leftarrow \chi$, and outputting the pair $(\mathbf{a}, \mathbf{a}^T \cdot \mathbf{s} + e)$. LWE problem (decision-LWE problem) requires to distinguish LWE samples from truly random samples $\leftarrow \mathbb{Z}_q^n \times \mathbb{Z}_q$.*

For a prime power q, $b \ge \sqrt{n}\omega(\log n)$, and distribution χ, solving $LWE_{n,q,\chi}$ problem is at least as hard as solving $SIVP_\gamma$ (*Shortest Independent Vector Problem*), where $\gamma = \tilde{\mathcal{O}}(nq/b)$ [8,24].

Definition 2 (Small Integer Solution (SIS)). *For uniformly random matrix $\mathbf{A} \in \mathbb{Z}_q^{n \times m}$, SIS requires to find non-zero vector $\boldsymbol{x} \in \mathbb{Z}^m$, such that $\mathbf{A} \cdot \boldsymbol{x} = 0$ mod q and $\|\boldsymbol{x}\|_\infty \le \beta$.*

Lattice Related Algorithms:

- GenTrap(n, m, q) takes integers $n \ge 1, q \ge 2$, and sufficiently large $m = O(n \log q)$, and outputs a matrix $\mathbf{A} \in \mathbb{Z}_q^{n \times m}$ and a trapdoor matrix $\mathbf{R}$. The distribution of the output $\mathbf{A}$ is negl(n)-far from the uniform distribution.
- SampleD($\mathbf{R}$, $\mathbf{A}$, $\mathbf{u}$, σ) takes as inputs a vector $\mathbf{u}$ in the image of $\mathbf{A}$, a trapdoor $\mathbf{R}$, and $\sigma = \omega(\sqrt{n \log q \log n})$, and outputs $\mathbf{x} \in \mathbb{Z}^m$ sampled from the distribution $D_{\mathbb{Z}^m,\sigma}$, such that $\mathbf{A} \cdot \mathbf{x} = \mathbf{u} \mod q$.

2.4 Attribute Based Group Signature Schemes

According to the Dalia Khader's proposal [14], an ABGS scheme consists of five algorithms, namely, Setup, KeyGen, Sign, Verify, and Open. The ABGS scheme with VLR given in [27] has only former four algorithms as it employs the *implicit tracing algorithm* to track the attributes, which are used to generate a signature. The implicit tracing algorithm, which is embedded in VLR schemes, requires to execute Verify for all the user attributes until all the attributes are traced. The algorithms of a VLR-ABGS scheme are as follows.

- Setup: On input the security parameter, this algorithm sets other public parameters and defines the universal set of attributes. Then it assigns vectors for each attribute and returns all the setup parameters and set of attributes as a public parameter.
- KeyGen: On input the public parameter and the maximum number of group members, this algorithm generates a group public key and group manager's secret key. Moreover, it generates secret keys and tokens for all the attributes of all the group members. Finally, it returns the group public key, group manager's key, all the user secret signing keys, and user tokens.
- Sign: For a given policy and a message, any member who can satisfy the conditions of the policy generates a signature with his secret signing key.
- Verify: For a given message, a policy and a signature, the verifier validates the signature on the message and policy and outputs 1 or 0.

2.5   Full-Anonymity

We say that an ABGS scheme is fully anonymous if no polynomial bounded adversary has a non-negligible advantage against the challenger in the bellow game.

- Init: The challenger runs Setup and KeyGen to obtain a group public key, a group manager secret key, and keys and tokens of all the attributes of all the users. Then challenger gives the group public key and all the secret signing keys of all the users to the adversary.
- Query Phase 1: The adversary requests indices of the signer and the attributes for a particular signature. He sends the signature, a message, and a policy to the challenger.
- Challenge: The challenger outputs a message, a policy, and two indices with two sets of attributes. The challenger selects one index with the related attribute set and generates a challenging signature. Then he sends the challenging signature to the adversary.
- Query Phase 2: The adversary can query the opening of any signature as in Query Phase 1 except for the challenging signature.
- Guessing: The adversary guesses the index, which is used to generate the challenging signature. If he can guess correctly, then he wins the game.

3   Zero-Knowledge Argument of Knowledge Proof System

In this section, we propose an efficient proof of knowledge protocol which enables a prover $\mathcal{P}$ to convince the verifier $\mathcal{V}$ that he indeed a group member with a set of attributes that satisfies the given predicate Γ, and his attribute tokens are valid and are not in the revocation list RL.

We concern on statistical zero-knowledge argument systems (interactive protocols). Interactive protocols have two properties called *soundness property* and *zero-knowledge property.* While the soundness property only holds for *computationally bounded* cheating provers, the zero-knowledge property holds against *any* cheating verifiers [20].

We are engaging with *string commitment scheme*, which uses a string as the committed value and which satisfies the above requirements. Kawachi et al. [12] presented a more straightforward construction from lattices for string commitment scheme **COM**. Later, using the Kawachi's string commitment scheme, Ling et al. [19] proposed a Stern type zero-knowledge proof of knowledge for lattices. The security of their protocol is based on the hardness of the underlying ISIS (Inhomogeneous SIS) problem. In other words, to break their protocol, an attacker needs to solve the underlying ISIS problem. Ling et al. [19] achieved security by using a technique called *Decomposition-Extension.*

3.1 Techniques

We define some techniques that were used in the existing protocols [16,20,27], and which we use in the construction of our protocol.

- **Decomposition-Extension Technique**
  Let $k = \lfloor \log \beta \rfloor$ and the sequence of integers $\beta_1, \ldots, \beta_k$ be as follows.
  $\beta_1 = \lceil \beta/2 \rceil; \beta_2 = \lceil (\beta - \beta_1)/2 \rceil; \beta_3 = \lceil (\beta - \beta_1 - \beta_2)/2 \rceil; \ldots; \beta_k = 1$.
  Ling et al. [19] observed that an integer $z \in [0, \beta]$, if and only if there exists $z_1, \ldots, z_k \in \{0, 1\}$ such that $z = \sum_{j=1}^{k} \beta_j z_j$.
  The above observation allows the prover to efficiently decompose $\mathbf{z} \in [-\beta; \beta]^m$ into $\tilde{\mathbf{z}}_1, \ldots, \tilde{\mathbf{z}}_k \in \{-1, 0, 1\}^m$ such that $\sum_{j=1}^{k} \beta_j \tilde{\mathbf{z}}_j = \mathbf{z}$. To extend a vector $\tilde{\mathbf{z}}$ to $\mathbf{z} \in \mathsf{B}_{3m}$, where B_{3m} is a set of vectors in $\{-1, 0, 1\}^{3m}$ having exactly m coordinates equal to -1, m coordinates equal to 0, and m coordinates equal to 1, we select a random vector $\hat{\mathbf{z}} \in \{-1, 0, 1\}^{2m}$, and output $\mathbf{z} = (\tilde{\mathbf{z}} \| \hat{\mathbf{z}})$. Here $\hat{\mathbf{z}} \in \{-1, 0, 1\}^{2m}$ has $(m - \lambda_{-1})$ coordinates equal to -1, $(m - \lambda_0)$ coordinates equal to 0, and $(m - \lambda_1)$ coordinates equal to 1.
- **Matrix-Extension Technique**
  For a given matrix $\bar{\mathbf{A}}$ the extended matrix $\bar{\mathbf{A}}^*$ is obtained by appending $2m$ *zero − columns* to the matrix $\bar{\mathbf{A}}$. For instance, if the given matrix $\bar{\mathbf{A}} = [\mathbf{A}|\mathbf{A}_0|\mathbf{A}_1|\ldots|\mathbf{A}_\ell] \in \mathbb{Z}_q^{n \times (2+\ell)m}$, then the extended matrix $\bar{\mathbf{A}}^* \in \mathbb{Z}_q^{n \times (2+2\ell)3m}$ is obtained as

$$\bar{\mathbf{A}}^* = [\mathbf{A}|0^{n \times 2m}|\mathbf{A}_0|0^{n \times 2m}|\ldots|\mathbf{A}_\ell|0^{n \times 2m}|0^{n \times 3m\ell}].$$

Using the above techniques, in Stern protocol, the prover $\mathcal{P}$ can convince the verifier $\mathcal{V}$ that $\mathbf{z} \in [-\beta, \beta]^m$ and $\mathbf{A}\mathbf{z} = \mathbf{A}^* \sum_{j=1}^{k} \beta_j \mathbf{z}_j = \mathbf{u} \mod q$ by demonstrating below two statements.

1. For each j, a random permutation of $\mathbf{z}_j$ belongs to B_{3m}. Thus, $\mathbf{z}_j \in \mathsf{B}_{3m}$ and $\tilde{\mathbf{z}}_j \in \{-1, 0, 1\}^m$. This will convince that $\mathbf{z} \in [-\beta, \beta]^m$.
2. $\mathbf{A}^* \sum_{j=1}^{k} \beta_j (\mathbf{z}_j + \mathbf{r}_j) - \mathbf{u} = \mathbf{A}^* \sum_{j=1}^{k} \beta_j \mathbf{r}_j \mod q$, where $\mathbf{A}^*$ is the extended matrix of $\mathbf{A}$ and $\mathbf{r}_1, \ldots, \mathbf{r}_k \in \mathbb{Z}_q^{3m}$ are uniformly "masking" vectors for $\mathbf{z}_j$. This convinces that $\mathbf{A}\mathbf{z} = \mathbf{A}^* \sum_{j=1}^{k} \beta_j \mathbf{z}_j = \mathbf{u} \mod q$.

- For permutations $\pi, \psi \in S_{3m}$; $\tau \in S_{2\ell}$, $\xi \in S_p$, and for a vector $\mathbf{z} = (\mathbf{z}_{-1}\|\mathbf{z}_0\|\mathbf{z}_1\|\ldots\|\mathbf{z}_{2\ell}) \in \mathbb{Z}_q^{(2+2\ell)3m}$ we define,

$$F_{\pi,\psi,\tau,\xi}(\mathbf{z}) = (\pi(\mathbf{z}_{\xi(-1)})\|\psi(\mathbf{z}_{\xi(0)})\|\psi(\mathbf{z}_{\xi,\tau(1)})\|\ldots\|\psi(\mathbf{z}_{\xi,\tau(2\ell)})).$$

$F_{\pi,\psi,\tau,\xi}(\mathbf{z})$ *rearranges* the order of $2+2\ell$ blocks $\mathbf{z}_{-1}, \mathbf{z}_0, \ldots, \mathbf{z}_{2\ell}$ according to ξ and the order of 2ℓ blocks $\mathbf{z}_1, \mathbf{z}_2, \ldots, \mathbf{z}_{2\ell}$ according to τ. Then it *permutes* block $\mathbf{z}_{-1}$ according to π and the other $(1+2\ell)$ blocks according to ψ.

- For a given $\bar{\mathbf{z}} = (\mathbf{x}\|\mathbf{y}\|d_1\mathbf{y}\|\ldots\|d_\ell\mathbf{y}) \in \mathbb{Z}^{(2+\ell)m}$, we say, $d \in \{0,1\}^\ell$, if $d^* = (d_1, \ldots, d_\ell, d_{\ell+1}, \ldots, d_{2\ell}) \in B_{2\ell}$ and the random permutation of d^* is in the set of $B_{2\ell}$, where d^* is the extension of d and $B_{2\ell}$ is the set of vectors in $\{0,1\}^{2\ell}$ having Hamming weight ℓ.

- We say, $\mathbf{z} \in \mathsf{VALID}(d^*)$ if $\mathbf{z} \in \{-1,0,1\}^{(2+2\ell)3m}$ and there exits $\mathbf{x}, \mathbf{y} \in B_{3m}$, such that $\mathbf{z} = (\mathbf{x}\|\mathbf{y}\|d_1\mathbf{y}\|d_2\mathbf{y}\|\ldots\|d_{2\ell}\mathbf{y})$.

Based on the above discussion, we build our ZK-proof system.

3.2   Underlying Interactive Protocol

For an attribute i that a user has, we assign a vector $\mathbf{z}_i$ sampled from $D_{\mathbb{Z}^{2m},\sigma}$, which satisfies $\|\mathbf{z}_i\|_\infty \leq \beta$. For an attribute i that the user does not have, we assign a vector $\mathbf{z}_i$ sampled from $D_{\mathbb{Z}^{2m},\sigma}$, which does not satisfy $\|\mathbf{z}_i\|_\infty \leq \beta$.

Suppose a user with index d possesses valid credentials for a set of attributes $S_d = \{\mathbf{u}_1, \mathbf{u}_2, \ldots, \mathbf{u}_a\}$ and the given predicate is $\Gamma = \{t, S \subseteq \mathrm{Att}, t \in \mathbb{N} \wedge (S = \mathbf{u}_1, \ldots, \mathbf{u}_p)\}$, where Att is the universal set of attributes $\{\mathbf{u}_1, \mathbf{u}_2, \ldots, \mathbf{u}_u\}$ and Γ requires the signer to satisfy at least t attributes out of S. Let $S_m = S \cap S_d$ and $S_r = S \backslash S_m$, where $|S_m| = t$ and $|S| = p - t$.

- The public parameters are: a matrix $(\mathbf{A}, \mathbf{A}_0, \mathbf{A}_1, \ldots, \mathbf{A}_\ell) \in \mathbb{Z}_q^{n \times (2+\ell)m}$, a set of vectors $\{\mathbf{u}_i\}_{i=1}^p$, a threshold predicate $\Gamma = (t, S)$, matrices $\{\mathbf{B}_i \in \mathbb{Z}_q^{m \times n}\}_{i=1}^p$, and vectors $\{\mathbf{b}_i \in \mathbb{Z}_q^m\}_{i=1}^p$, where $t \leq |S| = p$.

- The prover's witnesses are: the index $d \in \{0,1\}^\ell$, t vectors $\mathbf{z}_i = (\mathbf{x}\|\mathbf{y}\|d_1\mathbf{y}\|\ldots\|d_\ell\mathbf{y})\,\mathbf{u}_i \in S_m$, where $\|\mathbf{z}_i\|_\infty \leq \beta$, $p - t$ vectors $\mathbf{z}_i = (\mathbf{x}\|\mathbf{y}\|d_1\mathbf{y}\|\ldots\|d_\ell\mathbf{y})$ for $\mathbf{u}_i \in S_r$, p vectors $\mathbf{t}_i \in \mathbb{Z}^m$, and p vectors $\mathbf{e}_i \in \mathbb{Z}^m$.

- The prover's goal is to convince the verifier in zero knowledge that:
  - For $i \in [t]$, $\mathbf{A}_d\mathbf{z}_i = \mathbf{u}_i \mod q$ and $\|\mathbf{z}_i\|_\infty \leq \beta$, where $\mathbf{A}_d = [\mathbf{A}|\mathbf{A}_0 + \sum_{i=1}^\ell d_i\mathbf{A}_i]$.
  - For $i \in [p - t]$, $\mathbf{A}_d\mathbf{z}_i = \mathbf{u}_i \mod q$ and $\|\mathbf{z}_i\|_\infty \not\leq \beta$.
  - For $i \in [p]$, $\|\mathbf{e}_i\| \leq \beta$ and $\mathbf{B}_i \cdot (\mathbf{A} \cdot \mathbf{t}_i) + \mathbf{e}_i = \mathbf{b}_i \mod q$.
  - For $i \in [p]$, $(\mathbf{A} \cdot \mathbf{t}_i) + (\mathbf{A}'_d \cdot \mathbf{z}_i) = \mathbf{u}_i \mod q$, where $\mathbf{A}'_d = [0 \in \mathbb{Z}_q^{n \times m} \mid 0 \in \mathbb{Z}_q^{n \times m} + \sum_{i=1}^\ell d_i \cdot \mathbf{A}_i]$.

Both the prover $\mathcal{P}$ and the verifier $\mathcal{V}$ compute the following matrices.

- $\bar{\mathbf{A}}^* = [\mathbf{A}|0 \in \mathbb{Z}^{n \times 2m}|\mathbf{A}_0|0 \in \mathbb{Z}^{n \times 2m}|\ldots|\mathbf{A}_\ell|0 \in \mathbb{Z}^{n \times 2m}|0 \in \mathbb{Z}^{2 \times 3m\ell}] \in \mathbb{Z}_q^{n \times (2+2\ell)3m}$.

- $\{(\mathbf{B}_i^* = \mathbf{B}_i \cdot \mathbf{A}) \in \mathbb{Z}_q^{m \times m}\}_{i=1}^p$.
- $\{\mathbf{I}_i^* \in \{0,1\}^{m \times 3m}\}_{i=1}^p$. Each matrix is obtained by appending $2m$ $zero$ $-$ $columns$ to the identity matrix of order m.
- $\bar{\mathbf{A}}'^* = [0 \in \mathbb{Z}^{n \times 3m}|0 \in \mathbb{Z}^{n \times 3m}|\mathbf{A}_1|0 \in \mathbb{Z}^{n \times 2m}|\dots|\mathbf{A}_\ell|0 \in \mathbb{Z}^{n \times 2m}|0 \in \mathbb{Z}^{2 \times 3m\ell}] \in \mathbb{Z}_q^{n \times (2+2\ell)3m}$.

Then,

- For S_m, the prover $\mathcal{P}$ applies the Decomposition-Extension technique on $\mathbf{z}_i$, and generates masking terms $\{\mathbf{r}_{z(i)}^j\}$, where $i \in [t]$ and $j \in [k]$, such that the verifier can check
  $\bar{\mathbf{A}}^* \cdot (\sum_{j=1}^k \beta_j \cdot (\mathbf{z}_i^j + \mathbf{r}_{z(i)}^j)) - \mathbf{u}_i = \bar{\mathbf{A}}^* \cdot (\sum_{j=1}^k \beta_j \cdot \mathbf{r}_{z(i)}^j) \mod q$, where $\mathbf{z}_i^j \in$ VALID(d^*).
- For S_r, $\mathcal{P}$ decomposes, extends $\mathbf{z}_i$, and generates masking terms $\{\mathbf{r}_{z(i)}^j\}$, where $i \in [p-t]$ and $j \in [k]$, such that
  $\bar{\mathbf{A}}^* \cdot (\sum_{j=1}^k \beta_j \cdot (\mathbf{z}_i^j + \mathbf{r}_{z(i)}^j)) - \mathbf{u}_i = \bar{\mathbf{A}}^* \cdot (\sum_{j=1}^k \beta_j \cdot \mathbf{r}_{z(i)}^j) \mod q$.
- For S, $\mathcal{P}$ decomposes, extends both $\mathbf{t}_i$ and $\mathbf{e}_i$, and generates masking terms $\{\mathbf{r}_{t(i)}^j\}$, where $i \in [p]$ and $j \in [k]$, and $\{\mathbf{r}_{e(i)}^j\}$, where $i \in [p]$ and $j \in [k]$ respectively, such that
  $(\mathbf{B}_i^* \cdot (\sum_{j=1}^k \beta_j \cdot (\mathbf{t}_i^j + \mathbf{r}_{t(i)}^j)) + \mathbf{I}_i^* \cdot (\sum_{j=1}^k \beta_j \cdot (\mathbf{e}_i^j + \mathbf{r}_{e(i)}^j))) - \mathbf{b}_i = \mathbf{B}_i^* \cdot (\sum_{j=1}^k \beta_j \cdot \mathbf{r}_{t(i)}^j) + \mathbf{I}_i^* \cdot (\sum_{j=1}^k \beta_j \cdot \mathbf{r}_{e(i)}^j) \mod q$.
- Similarly, $(\mathbf{A} \cdot (\sum_{j=1}^k \beta_j \cdot (\mathbf{t}_i^j + \mathbf{r}_{t(i)}^j)) + \bar{\mathbf{A}}'^* \cdot (\sum_{j=1}^k \beta_j \cdot (\mathbf{z}_i^j + \mathbf{r}_{z(i)}^j))) - \mathbf{u}_i = \mathbf{A} \cdot (\sum_{j=1}^k \beta_j \cdot \mathbf{r}_{t(i)}^j) + \bar{\mathbf{A}}'^* \cdot (\sum_{j=1}^k \beta_j \cdot \mathbf{r}_{z(i)}^j) \mod q$.

Description of the Protocol

Commitments:

- Randomly sample masking terms $\{\mathbf{r}_{z(i)}^j \hookleftarrow \mathbb{Z}_q^{(2+2\ell)3m}, \mathbf{r}_{t(i)}^j \hookleftarrow \mathbb{Z}_q^m, \mathbf{r}_{e(i)}^j \hookleftarrow \mathbb{Z}_q^{3m}\}^{p \cdot k}$ for $i \in [p], j \in [k]$ and $\mathbf{r}_{d^*} \hookleftarrow \mathbb{Z}_q^{2\ell}$.
- Sample permutations $\{\pi_j, \psi_j \hookleftarrow S_{3m}, \phi_j, \hookleftarrow S_m, \varphi_j \hookleftarrow S_{3m}\}_{j=1}^{p \cdot k}, \tau \hookleftarrow S_{2\ell}$, and $\xi \hookleftarrow S_p$.

The prover $\mathcal{P}$ generates commitments CMT $= (\mathbf{c}_1, \mathbf{c}_2, \mathbf{c}_3)$, and sends to the verifier $\mathcal{V}$.

- $\mathbf{c}_1 = \mathbf{COM}(\tau, \xi, \{\pi_j, \psi_j, \phi_j, \varphi_j\}_{j=1}^{p \cdot k}, \{\bar{\mathbf{A}}^* \cdot (\sum_{j=1}^k \beta_j \mathbf{r}_{z(i)}^j)\}_{i \in [p]}, \{\mathbf{B}_i^* \cdot (\sum_{j=1}^k \beta_j \cdot \mathbf{r}_{t(i)}^j) + \mathbf{I}_i^* (\sum_{j=1}^k \beta_j \cdot \mathbf{r}_{e(i)}^j)\}_{i \in [p]}, \{\mathbf{A} \cdot (\sum_{j=1}^k \beta_j \cdot \mathbf{r}_{t(i)}^j) + \bar{\mathbf{A}}'^* (\sum_{j=1}^k \mathbf{r}_z^j)\}_{i \in [p]})$.
- $\mathbf{c}_2 = \mathbf{COM}(\tau(\mathbf{r}_{d^*}), \{\{F_{\pi_i^j, \psi_i^j, \tau, \xi}(\mathbf{r}_{z(i)}^j)\}_{j=1}^k\}_{i \in [p]}, \{\{\phi_i^j(\mathbf{r}_{t(i)}^j)\}_{j=1}^k\}_{i \in [p]}, \{\{\varphi_i^j(\mathbf{r}_{e(i)}^j)\}_{j=1}^k\}_{i \in [p]})$.
- $\mathbf{c}_3 = \mathbf{COM}(\tau(d^* + \mathbf{r}_{d^*}), \{\{F_{\pi_i^j, \psi_i^j, \tau, \xi}(\mathbf{z}_i^j + \mathbf{r}_{z(i)}^j)\}_{j=1}^k\}_{i \in [p]}, \{\{\phi_i^j(\mathbf{t}_i^j + \mathbf{r}_{t(i)}^j)\}_{j=1}^k\}_{i \in [p]}, \{\{\varphi_i^j(\mathbf{e}_i^j + \mathbf{r}_{e(i)}^j)\}_{j=1}^k\}_{i \in [p]})$.

Challenge: The verifier $\mathcal{V}$ randomly chooses a challenge $CH \leftarrow \{1, 2, 3\}$, and sends it to $\mathcal{P}$.

Response: Depending on the challenge CH, the prover $\mathcal{P}$ responses as below.

- $CH = 1$: Let $\mathbf{v}_{d^*} = \tau(d^*)$ and $\mathbf{w}_{d^*} = \tau(\mathbf{r}_{d^*})$.
  For $i \in [p]$ let
  $\{\mathbf{v}_{z(i)}^j = F_{\pi_i^j, \psi_i^j, \tau, \xi}(\mathbf{z}_i^j)\}_{j=1}^k, \{\mathbf{w}_{z(i)}^j = F_{\pi_i^j, \psi_i^j, \tau, \xi}(\mathbf{r}_{z(i)}^j)\}_{j=1}^k,$
  $\{\mathbf{v}_{t(i)}^j = \phi_i^j(\mathbf{t}_i^j)\}_{j=1}^k, \{\mathbf{w}_{t(i)}^j = \phi_i^j(\mathbf{r}_{t(i)}^j)\}_{j=1}^k,$
  $\{\mathbf{v}_{e(i)}^j = \varphi_i^j(\mathbf{e}_i^j)\}_{j=1}^k, \{\mathbf{w}_{e(i)}^j = \varphi_i^j(\mathbf{r}_{e(i)}^j)\}_{j=1}^k.$
  Output $RSP_1 = (\mathbf{v}_{d^*}, \mathbf{w}_{d^*}, \{\{\mathbf{v}_{z(i)}^j, \mathbf{w}_{z(i)}^j, \mathbf{v}_{t(i)}^j, \mathbf{w}_{t(i)}^j, \mathbf{v}_{e(i)}^j, \mathbf{w}_{e(i)}^j\}_{j=1}^k\}_{i\in[p]}).$
- $CH = 2$: Let $\mathbf{y}_{d^*} = d^* + \mathbf{r}_{d^*}$.
  For $i \in [p]$ let $\{\{\mathbf{y}_{z(i)}^j = \mathbf{z}_i^j + \mathbf{r}_{z(i)}^j\}_{j=1}^k, \{\mathbf{y}_{t(i)}^j = \mathbf{t}_i^j + \mathbf{r}_{t(i)}^j\}_{j=1}^k,$
  $\{\mathbf{y}_{e(i)}^j = \mathbf{e}_i^j + \mathbf{r}_{e(i)}^j\}_{j=1}^k\}.$
  Output $RSP_2 = (\tau, \xi, \{\pi_j, \psi_j, \phi_j, \varphi_j\}_{j=1}^{p \cdot k}, \mathbf{y}_{d^*}, \{\{\mathbf{y}_{z(i)}^j, \mathbf{y}_{t(i)}^j, \mathbf{y}_{e(i)}^j\}_{j=1}^k\}_{i\in[p]}).$
- $CH = 3$:
  Output $RSP_3 : (\tau, \xi, \{\pi_j, \psi_j, \phi_j, \varphi_j\}_{j=1}^{p \cdot k}, \mathbf{r}_{d^*}, \{\{\mathbf{r}_{z(i)}^j, \mathbf{r}_{t(i)}^j, \mathbf{r}_{e(i)}^j\}_{j=1}^k\}_{i\in[p]}).$

Verification: The verifier $\mathcal{V}$ checks the received response RSP as follows.

- $CH = 1$: Check that $\mathbf{v}_{d^*} \in B_{2\ell}$, $\mathbf{v}_{z(i)}^j$ is valid with respect to $\mathbf{v}_{d^*}$ (that is $\mathbf{v}_{z(i)}^j \in \mathsf{VALID}(\mathbf{v}_{d^*})$) for at least t set of vectors and all $j \in [k]$, $\mathbf{v}_{t(i)}^j \in B_m$, and $\mathbf{v}_{e(i)}^j \in B_{3m}$. Then check that,
  - $\mathbf{c}_2 = \mathbf{COM}(\mathbf{w}_{d^*}, \{\{\mathbf{w}_{z(i)}^j, \mathbf{w}_{t(i)}^j, \mathbf{w}_{e(i)}^j\}_{j=1}^k\}_{i\in[p]}),$
  - $\mathbf{c}_3 = \mathbf{COM}((\mathbf{v}_{d^*} + \mathbf{w}_{d^*}), \{\{(\mathbf{v}_{z(i)}^j + \mathbf{w}_{z(i)}^j), (\mathbf{v}_{t(i)}^j + \mathbf{w}_{t(i)}^j),$
    $(\mathbf{v}_{e(i)}^j + \mathbf{w}_{e(i)}^j)\}_{j=1}^k\}_{i\in[p]}).$
- $CH = 2$: Check that
  - $\mathbf{c}_1 = \mathbf{COM}(\tau, \xi, \{\pi_j, \psi_j, \phi_j, \varphi_j\}_{j=1}^{p \cdot k}, \{\bar{\mathbf{A}}^* \cdot (\sum_{j=1}^k \beta_j \mathbf{y}_{z(i)}^j) - \mathbf{u}_i\}_{i\in[p]},$
    $\{\mathbf{B}_i^*(\sum_{j=1}^k \beta_j \cdot \mathbf{y}_{t(i)}^j) + \mathbf{I}_i^*(\sum_{j=1}^k \beta_j \cdot \mathbf{y}_{e(i)}^j) - \mathbf{b}_i\}_{i\in[p]}$
    $\{\mathbf{A} \cdot (\sum_{j=1}^k \beta_j \cdot \mathbf{y}_{t(i)}^j) + \bar{\mathbf{A}}'^*(\sum_{j=1}^k \mathbf{y}_{z(i)}^j) - \mathbf{u}_i\}_{i\in[p]}),$
  - $\mathbf{c}_3 = \mathbf{COM}(\tau(\mathbf{y}_{d^*}), \{\{F_{\pi_i^j, \psi_i^j, \tau, \xi}(\mathbf{y}_{z(i)}^j)\}_{j=1}^k\}_{i\in[p]},$
    $\{\{\phi_i^j(\mathbf{y}_{t(i)}^j)\}_{j=1}^k\}_{i\in[p]}, \{\{\varphi_i^j(\mathbf{y}_{e(i)}^j)\}_{j=1}^k\}_{i\in[p]}).$
- $CH = 3$: Check that
  - $\mathbf{c}_1 = \mathbf{COM}(\tau, \xi, \{\pi_j, \psi_j, \phi_j, \varphi_j\}_{j=1}^{p \cdot k}, \{\bar{\mathbf{A}}^* \cdot (\sum_{j=1}^k \beta_j \mathbf{r}_{z(i)}^j)\}_{i\in[p]},$
    $\{\mathbf{B}_i^*(\sum_{j=1}^k \beta_j \cdot \mathbf{r}_{t(i)}^j) + \mathbf{I}_i^*(\sum_{j=1}^k \beta_j \cdot \mathbf{r}_{e(i)}^j)\}_{i\in[p]},$
    $\{\mathbf{A} \cdot (\sum_{j=1}^k \beta_j \cdot \mathbf{r}_{t(i)}^j) + \bar{\mathbf{A}}'^*(\sum_{j=1}^k \mathbf{r}_{z(i)}^j)\}_{i\in[p]}),$
  - $\mathbf{c}_2 = \mathbf{COM}(\tau(\mathbf{r}_{d^*}), \{\{F_{\pi_i^j, \psi_i^j, \tau, \xi}(\mathbf{r}_{z(i)}^j)\}_{j=1}^k\}_{i\in[p]}, \{\{\phi_i^j(\mathbf{r}_{t(i)}^j)\}_{j=1}^k\}_{i\in[p]},$
    $\{\{\varphi_i^j(\mathbf{r}_{e(i)}^j)\}_{j=1}^k\}_{i\in[p]}.$

$\mathcal{V}$ outputs 1 if and only if all the conditions hold, otherwise he outputs 0.

3.3   Analysis of the Protocol

Theorem 1. *Let* COM *be a statistically hiding and computationally binding string commitment scheme. Then our protocol in Sect. 3.2 is a zero-knowledge argument of knowledge for the relation* $R = (n, \ell, m, t, p, k, \beta)$ *with perfect completeness, soundness error 2/3, and communication cost* $(\mathcal{O}(p\ell m \log \beta) \log q$.

Completeness and Communication Cost. If the prover $\mathcal{P}$ is honest and follows the protocol, then the verifier $\mathcal{V}$ always outputs 1. Based on the previous discussion, the proposed protocol has perfect completeness. Moreover, according to [12], the commitment CMT has $3n \log q$ bits. The verifier $\mathcal{V}$ sends two-bit challenge $CH \in \{1, 2, 3\}$. The response RSP of $\mathcal{P}$ is a subset of the set of masking terms and permutations which sums overall communication cost of upper bound $\mathcal{O}(p\ell m \log \beta) \log q$.

We employ standard simulation and extraction techniques for Stern-like protocol [12,19,26] to prove that the proposed protocol is a ZKAoK. The detailed proof is given in the full version of this paper.

4   Proposed Attribute-Based VLR Group Signature Scheme

Let λ be the security parameter, and $N = 2^\ell = poly(\lambda)$ be the maximum number of members in a group. Let integer $n = poly(\lambda)$, the modulus $q = \mathcal{O}(\ell n^2)$, and the dimension $m = \lceil 2n \log q \rceil$. Gaussian parameter $\sigma = \omega(\log m)$. The infinity norm bound for signature is $\beta = \tilde{\mathcal{O}}(\sqrt{\ell n})$.

- Setup(1^λ): On input the security parameter λ, set the parameters *para* as above, and proceed as below.
  1. Define the universal set of attributes $Att = \{\mathbf{u}_1, \mathbf{u}_2, \ldots, \mathbf{u}_u\}$, where $\mathbf{u}_i \in \mathbb{Z}_q^n$ is uniform random and $|Att| = u$. Each attribute att_i is associated to a uniform random vector $\mathbf{u}_i$ via a list $attLst = \{(att_i, \mathbf{u}_i)\}_{i \in \{1,2,\ldots,u\}}$.
  2. Select a hash function $\mathcal{H} : \{0,1\}^* \to \{1, 2, 3\}^t$, to be modeled as a random oracle, where $t = \omega(\log n)$.
  3. Output the public parameters $PP = (para, Att, attLst, \mathcal{H})$.
- KeyGen(PP, N): The randomized algorithm KeyGen takes the public parameters PP and $N = 2^\ell$ as the inputs and works as follows.
  1. Generate the verification key $\mathbf{A}, \mathbf{A}_0, \mathbf{A}_1, \ldots, \mathbf{A}_\ell \in \mathbb{Z}_q^{n \times m}$ and a trapdoor $\mathbf{T_A} \in \mathbb{Z}_q^{m \times m}$ for the modified Boyen's signature scheme as in [22].
  2. For a member with an index $d \in \{0, 1, \ldots, N-1\}$ and a set of attributes $S_d = \{\mathbf{u}_{a_1}, \mathbf{u}_{a_2}, \ldots, \mathbf{u}_{a_s}\} \subseteq Att$ ($|S_d| = s$), execute the following steps to generate keys and tokens for him.
     (a) Let $d[1] \ldots d[\ell] \in \{0, 1\}^\ell$ be the binary representation of d.
     (b) Compute $\mathbf{A}_d = [\mathbf{A} \mid \mathbf{A}_0 + \sum_{i=1}^\ell d[i] \cdot \mathbf{A}_i] \in \mathbb{Z}^{n \times 2m}$.
     (c) For all $j \in \{1, 2, \ldots, s\}$ sample $\mathbf{z}_{d,a_j} \hookleftarrow D_{\mathbb{Z}^{2m}, \sigma}$ as the secret key for an attribute $\mathbf{u}_{a_j}$ such that $\mathbf{A}_d \cdot \mathbf{z}_{d,a_j} = \mathbf{u}_{a_j}$ and $\|\mathbf{z}_{d,a_j}\| \leq \beta$.

(d) For the other attributes $u - s$ again sample fake credentials $\mathbf{f}_{d,f_j} \hookleftarrow D_{\mathbb{Z}^{2m},\sigma}$, such that $\mathbf{A}_d \cdot \mathbf{f}_{d,f_j} = \mathbf{u}_j$ and $\|\mathbf{f}_{d,f_j}\| \nleq \beta$.

(e) Hereafter we represent all the secret keys (fake or real) for attributes by $\mathbf{z}_{d,a_j}$.

(f) Get $\mathbf{A}'_d = [0 \in \mathbb{Z}_q^{n \times m} \mid 0 \in \mathbb{Z}_q^{n \times m} + \sum_{i=1}^{\ell} d[i] \cdot \mathbf{A}_i]$ by replacing $\mathbf{A}$ and $\mathbf{A}_0$ with zero matrices in the step (b).

(g) Compute $\mathbf{v}_{d_j} = \mathbf{A}'_d \cdot \mathbf{z}_{d_j} \in \mathbb{Z}^n$ for all the attributes.

(h) Run $\mathsf{SampleD}(\mathbf{T_A}, \mathbf{A}, \mathbf{u}_j - \mathbf{v}_{d_j}, \sigma)$ to obtain $\mathbf{t}_{d_j}$ for all the attributes.

(i) Let the secret signing key of d be $\mathbf{gsk}[d] = \{\mathbf{z}_{d_j}, \mathbf{u}_j\}_{j \in [u]}$ and the revocation token be $\mathbf{grt}[d] = \{\mathbf{u}^t_{d_j} = \mathbf{A} \cdot \mathbf{t}_{d_j}\}_{j \in [u]}$.

3. Output the group public key $\mathbf{gpk} = (\mathbf{A}, \mathbf{A}_0, \mathbf{A}_1, \ldots, \mathbf{A}_\ell, \mathbf{u}_1, \mathbf{u}_2, \ldots, \mathbf{u}_u)$, the group manager's secret key $\mathbf{gmsk} = \mathbf{T_A}$, the members' secret signing keys $\mathbf{gsk} = (\mathbf{gsk}[0], \mathbf{gsk}[1], \ldots, \mathbf{gsk}[N-1])$, and members' revocation tokens $\mathbf{grt} = (\mathbf{grt}[0], \mathbf{grt}[1], \ldots, \mathbf{grt}[N-1])$.

– $\mathsf{Sign}(PP, \Gamma, \mathbf{gpk}, \mathbf{gsk}[d], \mathbf{grt}[d], S_d, M)$: On input the group public key $\mathbf{gpk}$, and a message M, the user d in a possession of a secret signing key $\mathbf{gsk}[d]$, a revocation token $\mathbf{grt}[d]$, and a set of attributes $S_d \subseteq \mathsf{Att}$, generates a signature for a given threshold predicate $\Gamma = (t, S = \{\mathbf{u}_1, \mathbf{u}_2, \ldots, \mathbf{u}_p\} \subseteq \mathsf{Att})$, where $1 \leq t \leq |S| = p$, as below. Here, $\Gamma = (t, S)$ implies that the condition (policy) Γ requires the signer to posses at least t attributes out of the given set of attributes S, where the size of S is p.

1. Let $S_m \subseteq (S \cap S_d) \subseteq \mathsf{Att}$ be the matching attributes that the user d possesses, where $|S_m| = t$.

2. For the attributes $S \backslash S_m$ the user d has fake credentials.

3. For all the attributes $i \in p$,

   (a) Sample $\rho_i \overset{\$}{\leftarrow} \{0,1\}^n$, let $\mathbf{B}_i = \mathcal{G}(\bar{\mathbf{A}}, \mathbf{u}_i, M, \rho_i) \in \mathbb{Z}_q^{n \times m}$ ($\mathcal{G} : \{1,2,3\}^* \to \mathbb{Z}_q^{n \times m}$), where $\bar{\mathbf{A}} = [\mathbf{A}|\mathbf{A}_0|\ldots|\mathbf{A}_\ell]$.

   (b) Compute $\mathbf{b}_i = \mathbf{B}_i \cdot (\mathbf{A} \cdot \mathbf{t}_{d_i}) + \mathbf{e}_i \mod q$ ($\|\mathbf{e}_i\|_\infty \leq \beta$ with overwhelming probability).

4. Generate a non-interactive zero-knowledge argument of knowledge Π to prove that the prover d is indeed a valid group member possessing at least t non-revoked attributes among $S \subseteq \mathsf{Att}$. This is done by repeating the protocol given in Sect. 3, $\bar{t} = \omega(\log n)$ times with public inputs $(\mathbf{A}, \mathbf{A}_0, \mathbf{A}_1, \ldots, \mathbf{A}_\ell, \{\mathbf{u}_i\}_{i \in [p]}, \{\mathbf{B}_i\}_{i \in [p]}, \{\mathbf{b}_i\}_{i \in [p]})$ and witness $(d, \{\mathbf{z}_i\}_{i \in [p]}, \{\mathbf{t}_i\}_{i \in [p]}, \{\mathbf{e}_i\}_{i \in [p]})$.

   Then make it non-interactive via the Fiat-Shamir heuristic as a triple $\Pi = (\{\mathrm{CMT}^{(\bar{k})}\}_{k=1}^{\bar{t}}, \mathrm{CH}, \{\mathrm{RSP}^{(\bar{k})}\}_{k=1}^{\bar{t}})$, where $\mathrm{CH} = (\{Ch^{(\bar{k})}\}_{k=1}^{\bar{t}}) = \mathcal{H}(M, \mathbf{A}, \{\mathbf{A}_i\}_{i=0}^\ell, \{\mathbf{u}_i\}_{i=1}^p, \{\mathbf{B}_i\}_{i=1}^p, \{\mathbf{b}_i\}_{i=1}^p, \{\mathrm{CMT}^{(\bar{k})}\}_{k=1}^{\bar{t}})$.

5. Output a signature $\Sigma = (M, \{\rho_i\}_{i=1}^p, \{\mathbf{b}_i\}_{i=1}^p, \Pi)$.

– $\mathsf{Verify}(PP, \Gamma, \mathbf{gpk}, RL, M, \Sigma)$: This deterministic algorithm takes as inputs the group public key $\mathbf{gpk} = (\mathbf{A}, \mathbf{A}_0, \mathbf{A}_1, \ldots, \mathbf{A}_\ell, \mathbf{u}_1, \mathbf{u}_2, \ldots, \mathbf{u}_u)$, a threshold predicate $\Gamma = (t, S = \{\mathbf{u}_1, \mathbf{u}_2, \ldots, \mathbf{u}_p\} \subseteq \mathsf{Att})$, a signature Σ on a message M, and a list of revocation tokens $RL = \{\mathbf{u}^t_i = (\mathbf{u}^t_{i_1}, \mathbf{u}^t_{i_2}, \ldots, \mathbf{u}^t_{i_a})\}_{i \leq N} \subseteq \mathbf{grt}$, where $a \leq u$, and verifies the signature as below.

1. Pares the signature Σ as $(M, \{\rho_i\}_{i=1}^p, \{\mathbf{b}_i\}_{i=1}^p, \Pi)$.
2. Get $\{\mathbf{B}_i = \mathcal{G}(\bar{\mathbf{A}}, \mathbf{u}_i, M, \rho_i) \in \mathbb{Z}_q^{n \times m}\}_{i \in [p]}$.
3. Pares Π as $(\{\mathrm{CMT}^{(\bar{k})}\}_{k=1}^{\bar{t}}, \{Ch^{(\bar{k})}\}_{k=1}^{\bar{t}}, \{\mathrm{RSP}^{(\bar{k})}\}_{k=1}^{\bar{t}})$.
4. Return 0, if $(Ch_1, \ldots Ch_{\bar{t}}) \neq \mathcal{H}(M, \mathbf{A}, \{\mathbf{A}_i\}_{i=0}^\ell, \{\mathbf{u}_i\}_{i=1}^p, \{\mathbf{B}_i\}_{i=1}^p, \{\mathbf{b}_i\}_{i=1}^p,$ $\{\mathrm{CMT}^{(\bar{k})}\}_{k=1}^{\bar{t}})$.
5. For $i = 0$ to $\bar{t}$, run the verification steps of the protocol given in Sect. 3 with the public inputs $(\mathbf{A}, \mathbf{A}_0, \mathbf{A}_1, \ldots, \mathbf{A}_\ell, \{\mathbf{u}_i\}_{i \in [p]}, \{\mathbf{B}_i\}_{i \in [p]}, \{\mathbf{b}_i\}_{i \in [p]})$ to check the validity of $\mathrm{RSP}^{(\bar{k})}$ with respect to $\mathrm{CMT}^{(\bar{k})}$ and $Ch^{(\bar{k})}$. If any of the conditions does not hold, then return 0.
6. For each $\mathbf{u}_{i_x}^t$ in the given revocation list RL, where $x \leq u$ and $i \leq N$ compute $\mathbf{e}_i' = \mathbf{b}_i - \mathbf{B}_i \cdot \mathbf{u}_{i_x}^t \mod q$ to check whether there exists an index i such that $\|\mathbf{e}_i'\|_\infty \leq \beta$. If so return 0.
7. Return 1.

– Revoke($PP, \mathbf{gpk}, \mathbf{gmsk}, RL, d, S_r$): On input $\mathbf{gpk}$, the revocation list RL, the id d of the effecting member, and his revoking attribute set $S_r = \{\mathbf{u}_{d_1}^t = \mathbf{A} \cdot \mathbf{t}_{d_1}, \mathbf{u}_{d_2}^t = \mathbf{A} \cdot \mathbf{t}_{d_2}, \ldots, \mathbf{u}_{d_r}^t = \mathbf{A} \cdot \mathbf{t}_{d_r}\}$, where $r \leq u$, the group manager with $\mathbf{gmsk}$, do the following steps.
  1. Add all $\mathbf{u}_{d_i}^t$ to RL.
  2. Return RL.

5   Security Analysis of the Proposed Scheme

This paper provides a new ABGS scheme with VLR from lattices to achieve full-anonymity. The security of the scheme is proven in the random-oracle model under the hardness assumption of SIVP problem.

Theorem 2. *The proposed ABGS-VLR is correct with overwhelming probability. If the underlying non-interactive zero-knowledge (NIZK) protocol is simulation sound and zero-knowledge, then the proposed scheme is fully anonymous. Moreover, under the hardness of the $SIVP_{\mathcal{O}(\lambda)}$ problem our scheme is fully-traceable.*

In this paper we only prove the anonymity of the scheme. Proof of traceability of the scheme is provided in the full version of this paper.

Anonymity

In the anonymity game between a challenger and an adversary, first, the challenger generates keys and gives the public keys and all the users' secret signing keys to the adversary. The adversary can query signer's index of any signature. Later, he sends two challenging indices to the challenger. The challenger selects a bit randomly from the two indices, then generates and sends back a challenging signature. The adversary wins if he can guess the index which is used to generate the challenging signature without querying.

We prove that the proposed scheme is fully anonymous using the following two games between an adversary A and a challenger C.

Game 1. In this game, the challenger C sets everything honestly. The adversary is given the group public key and the secret signing keys of all the users. The challenger answers all the opening queries that the adversary makes. Finally, the challenger produces a signature Σ^* with the true identities $(i_0, i_1, S_0, S_1, \Gamma^*, M^*)$ that the adversary sent, and forwards Σ^* to the adversary.

Game 2. In this game, instead of generating an honest non-interactive zero knowledge argument Π, the challenger simulates the argument for the challenge signature Σ^*. Thus, Game 2 is the same as Game 1 except the simulated Π^*. Since the underlying argument system is statistically zero-knowledge, the distribution of simulated Π^* is statistically close to that of the legitimate Π. Thus Game 1 and Game 2 are indistinguishable.

Indistinguishability of above two games proves that our proposed scheme is fully anonymous.

6   Conclusion

In this paper, we considered a situation where the tokens of the attributes are generated independently to the secret signing keys of the attributes to achieve full anonymity. We presented a zero-knowledge protocol that enables provers to convince the validity of them, their attributes, and the tokens in such scenarios. Moreover, we presented a new ABGS scheme with VLR from lattices to achieve full anonymity.

References

1. Bellare, M., Micciancio, D., Warinschi, B.: Foundations of group signatures: formal definitions, simplified requirements, and a construction based on general assumptions. In: Biham, E. (ed.) EUROCRYPT 2003. LNCS, vol. 2656, pp. 614–629. Springer, Heidelberg (2003). https://doi.org/10.1007/3-540-39200-9_38
2. Chaum, D., van Heyst, E.: Group signatures. In: Davies, D.W. (ed.) EUROCRYPT 1991. LNCS, vol. 547, pp. 257–265. Springer, Heidelberg (1991). https://doi.org/10.1007/3-540-46416-6_22
3. El Bansarkhani, R., El Kaafarani, A.: Post-quantum attribute-based signatures from lattice assumptions. IACR Cryptology ePrint Archive 2016/823 (2016)
4. El Kaafarani, A., Chen, L., Ghadafi, E., Davenport, J.: Attribute-based signatures with user-controlled linkability. In: Gritzalis, D., Kiayias, A., Askoxylakis, I. (eds.) CANS 2014. LNCS, vol. 8813, pp. 256–269. Springer, Cham (2014). https://doi.org/10.1007/978-3-319-12280-9_17
5. El Kaafarani, A., Ghadafi, E., Khader, D.: Decentralized traceable attribute-based signatures. In: Benaloh, J. (ed.) CT-RSA 2014. LNCS, vol. 8366, pp. 327–348. Springer, Cham (2014). https://doi.org/10.1007/978-3-319-04852-9_17
6. Fiat, A., Shamir, A.: How to prove yourself: practical solutions to identification and signature problems. In: Odlyzko, A.M. (ed.) CRYPTO 1986. LNCS, vol. 263, pp. 186–194. Springer, Heidelberg (1987). https://doi.org/10.1007/3-540-47721-7_12

7. Gagné, M., Narayan, S., Safavi-Naini, R.: Short pairing-efficient threshold-attribute-based signature. In: Abdalla, M., Lange, T. (eds.) Pairing 2012. LNCS, vol. 7708, pp. 295–313. Springer, Heidelberg (2013). https://doi.org/10.1007/978-3-642-36334-4_19

8. Gentry, C., Peikert, C., Vaikuntanathan, V.: Trapdoors for hard lattices and new cryptographic constructions. In: ACM 2008, pp. 197–206. ACM (2008)

9. Ghadafi, E.: Stronger security notions for decentralized traceable attribute-based signatures and more efficient constructions. In: Nyberg, K. (ed.) CT-RSA 2015. LNCS, vol. 9048, pp. 391–409. Springer, Cham (2015). https://doi.org/10.1007/978-3-319-16715-2_21

10. Herranz, J., Laguillaumie, F., Libert, B., Ràfols, C.: Short attribute-based signatures for threshold predicates. In: Dunkelman, O. (ed.) CT-RSA 2012. LNCS, vol. 7178, pp. 51–67. Springer, Heidelberg (2012). https://doi.org/10.1007/978-3-642-27954-6_4

11. Ishida, A., Sakai, Y., Emura, K., Hanaoka, G., Tanaka, K.: Fully anonymous group signature with verifier-local revocation. In: Catalano, D., De Prisco, R. (eds.) SCN 2018. LNCS, vol. 11035, pp. 23–42. Springer, Cham (2018). https://doi.org/10.1007/978-3-319-98113-0_2

12. Kawachi, A., Tanaka, K., Xagawa, K.: Concurrently secure identification schemes based on the worst-case hardness of lattice problems. In: Pieprzyk, J. (ed.) ASIACRYPT 2008. LNCS, vol. 5350, pp. 372–389. Springer, Heidelberg (2008). https://doi.org/10.1007/978-3-540-89255-7_23

13. Khader, D.: Attribute based group signature with revocation. IACR Cryptology ePrint Archive 2007/241 (2007)

14. Khader, D.: Attribute based group signatures. IACR Cryptology ePrint Archive 2007/159 (2007)

15. Kuchta, V., Sahu, R.A., Sharma, G., Markowitch, O.: On new zero-knowledge arguments for attribute-based group signatures from lattices. In: Kim, H., Kim, D.-C. (eds.) ICISC 2017. LNCS, vol. 10779, pp. 284–309. Springer, Cham (2018). https://doi.org/10.1007/978-3-319-78556-1_16

16. Langlois, A., Ling, S., Nguyen, K., Wang, H.: Lattice-based group signature scheme with verifier-local revocation. In: Krawczyk, H. (ed.) PKC 2014. LNCS, vol. 8383, pp. 345–361. Springer, Heidelberg (2014). https://doi.org/10.1007/978-3-642-54631-0_20

17. Li, J., Au, M.H., Susilo, W., Xie, D., Ren, K.: Attribute-based signature and its applications. In: Proceedings of the 5th ACM Symposium on Information, Computer and Communications Security, pp. 60–69. ACM (2010)

18. Li, J., Kim, K.: Attribute-based ring signatures. IACR Cryptology ePrint Archive 2008/394 (2008)

19. Ling, S., Nguyen, K., Stehlé, D., Wang, H.: Improved zero-knowledge proofs of knowledge for the ISIS problem, and applications. In: Kurosawa, K., Hanaoka, G. (eds.) PKC 2013. LNCS, vol. 7778, pp. 107–124. Springer, Heidelberg (2013). https://doi.org/10.1007/978-3-642-36362-7_8

20. Ling, S., Nguyen, K., Wang, H.: Group signatures from lattices: simpler, tighter, shorter, ring-based. In: Katz, J. (ed.) PKC 2015. LNCS, vol. 9020, pp. 427–449. Springer, Heidelberg (2015). https://doi.org/10.1007/978-3-662-46447-2_19

21. Maji, H.K., Prabhakaran, M., Rosulek, M.: Attribute-based signatures. In: Kiayias, A. (ed.) CT-RSA 2011. LNCS, vol. 6558, pp. 376–392. Springer, Heidelberg (2011). https://doi.org/10.1007/978-3-642-19074-2_24

22. Micciancio, D., Peikert, C.: Trapdoors for lattices: simpler, tighter, faster, smaller. In: Pointcheval, D., Johansson, T. (eds.) EUROCRYPT 2012. LNCS, vol. 7237, pp. 700–718. Springer, Heidelberg (2012). https://doi.org/10.1007/978-3-642-29011-4_41

23. Perera, M.N.S., Koshiba, T.: Achieving almost-full security for lattice-based fully dynamic group signatures with verifier-local revocation. In: Su, C., Kikuchi, H. (eds.) ISPEC 2018. LNCS, vol. 11125, pp. 229–247. Springer, Cham (2018). https://doi.org/10.1007/978-3-319-99807-7_14

24. Regev, O.: On lattices, learning with errors, random linear codes, and cryptography. In: STOC, pp. 84–93. ACM Press (2005)

25. Shahandashti, S.F., Safavi-Naini, R.: Threshold attribute-based signatures and their application to anonymous credential systems. In: Preneel, B. (ed.) AFRICACRYPT 2009. LNCS, vol. 5580, pp. 198–216. Springer, Heidelberg (2009). https://doi.org/10.1007/978-3-642-02384-2_13

26. Stern, J.: A new paradigm for public key identification. IEEE Trans. Inf. Theory **42**(6), 1757–1768 (1996)

27. Zhang, Y., Gan, Y., Yin, Y., Jia, H.: Attribute-based VLR group signature scheme from lattices. In: Vaidya, J., Li, J. (eds.) ICA3PP 2018. LNCS, vol. 11337, pp. 600–610. Springer, Cham (2018). https://doi.org/10.1007/978-3-030-05063-4_46

Reversible Data Hiding in Homomorphic Encrypted Images Without Preprocessing

Hao-Tian Wu[1]([✉])[ID], Yiu-ming Cheung[2][ID], Zhenwei Zhuang[1], and Shaohua Tang[1,3]

[1] School of Computer Science and Engineering,
South China University of Technology, Guangzhou 510006, Guangdong, China
{wuht,csshtang}@scut.edu.cn, 641544825@qq.com
[2] Department of Computer Science, Hong Kong Baptist University,
Kowloon Tong, Hong Kong, China
ymc@comp.hkbu.edu.hk
[3] Peng Cheng Laboratory, Shenzhen 518055, Guangdong, China

Abstract. Recently, reversible data hiding in encrypted images (RDH-EI) has been developed to transmit additional data. Besides extracting the hidden data, the original or processed image should be obtained when needed. In this paper, a new RDH-EI method for homomorphic encrypted images is proposed by utilizing the additive homomorphism and self-blinding property in Paillier cryptosystem. Specifically, part of the hidden data may be extracted before image decryption while the rest can be extracted after image decryption. In addition, no preprocessing is required so that homomorphic processing can be performed before data embedding. The experimental results on test images validate that the proposed method is compatible with homomorphic image processing before data embedding. Compared with the state-of-the-art methods, higher embedding capacity can be obtained with the proposed method while the original or processed image can be correctly generated.

Keywords: Homomorphic encryption · Privacy protection · Reversible data hiding · Paillier cryptosystem

1 Introduction

Recently, reversible data hiding (RDH) has been proposed for the distortion sensitive applications (e.g., [1–11]), such as hiding data into medical images with the capability of recovering the original images [12]. Recently, RDH in encrypted images (RDH-EI) has been developed to transmit additional data along with encrypted images, such as in [13–28].

The work was partially supported by Natural Science Foundation of China under Grants 61772208, 61672444 and 61632013, and the Fundamental Research Funds for the Central Universities of China, and the Initiation Grant for Faculty Niche Research Areas (IG-FNRA) of HKBU with Grant: RC-FNRA-IG/18-19/SCI/03.

© Springer Nature Switzerland AG 2020
I. You (Ed.): WISA 2019, LNCS 11897, pp. 141–154, 2020.
https://doi.org/10.1007/978-3-030-39303-8_11

Depending on whether a preprocessing is performed to vacate room before encryption (VRBE), the RDH-EI methods can be classified into two categories. The first type creates embedding room in the plain-text domain (e.g., [15–21]), while the other type of RDH-EI methods directly modifies encrypted images for data embedding (e.g., [14,19]). By vacating room after encryption (VRAE), data hiding may be performed after other processing performed in the encryption domain (e.g., [29]) so that the processed image can be obtained after decryption. Depending on the embedding algorithms, data extraction may be performed in the encryption domain (e.g., [14]), or can be conducted jointly with image decryption (e.g., [13]), or even in both of the encryption and plain-text domains (e.g., [22,24]). In addition, it is preferred that data extraction is separable from image decryption (e.g., [14]) on the receiver side.

According to the encryption algorithms, the proposed RDH-EI methods can be classified into two categories. The first category is to encrypt digital images with a stream cipher, which has the advantage of fast implementation and no data expansion. However, the images encrypted with a stream cipher in [13–18] can hardly be processed in encryption domain. In the second category, "privacy homomorphism" is achieved so that an encrypted image can be processed in the encrypted domain. The disadvantages of this category include high complexity and data expansion compared with the size of plain-text data. The RDH-EI methods proposed in [22,24,25] fall into the second category.

In the past decades, significant progresses have been made in homomorphic encryption (e.g., [30–32]) to directly process data in encryption domain. Since there is no need to decrypt the cipher-texts for processing, user privacy and data integrity are protected. This property is very useful in modern communication systems, such as in cloud computing (e.g., [33,34]) and secure voting systems. Although it is still a challenge to implement complex computations in the fully homomorphic domain (e.g., [31]), quite a few signal processing techniques have been developed in additive homomorphic cryptosystems (e.g., [29]). Since data transmission is needed in these applications, conducting RDH in the homomorphic encryption domain can provide more functionalities, such as in [22–28]. However, preprocessing is required in most of the methods (e.g., [22,24,28]) so that the applicability is limited.

To improve the applicability of RDH-EI, a new RDH-EI method for homomorphic encrypted images is proposed in this paper by utilizing the additive homomorphism and self-blinding property in Paillier cryptosystem [30]. The proposed method can be regarded as an extension of the work in [28]. By combining the two data embedding algorithms proposed in [28], part of the hidden data may be extracted before image decryption while the rest can be extracted after image decryption. It is worthy to note that no preprocessing is required in the proposed method so that data embedding can be performed after homomorphic processing. The experimental results on a set of test images validate that the proposed method is compatible with homomorphic image processing before data embedding. Compared with the state-of-the-art methods, higher embedding capacity can be obtained with the proposed one while the original or processed images could be exactly recovered.

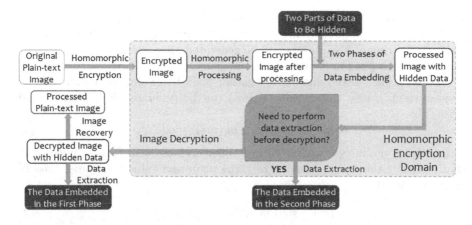

Fig. 1. A flowchart of the proposed method without preprocessing.

The rest of this paper is organized as follows. In the next section, the proposed method is presented by introducing two data embedding algorithms in Paillier cryptosystem. The experimental results on test images are given to demonstrate efficacy of the proposed method in Sect. 3. Finally, we summarize the paper and draw a conclusion in Sect. 4.

2   A Reversible Data Hiding Method Compatible with Homomorphic Processing

In this section, a new RDH-EI method is proposed, which is compatible with homomorphic image processing in encrypted domain. As shown in Fig. 1, no preprocessing is required so that an encrypted image can be directly processed in homomorphic encryption domain. Then two phases of data embedding are conducted for data extraction before and after decryption, respectively. Besides correctly extracting the hidden data, the processed plain-text image should be obtained after decryption. In the following, the two algorithms developed in [25] will be introduced, which are adopted in the proposed method for data embedding.

2.1   Value Expansion Algorithm

The value expansion algorithm is adopted in the first phase of the proposed method. After applying it, the plain-text of a cipher value is modified for data embedding while the hidden data can only be extracted after image decryption.

Additive Homomorphism in Paillier Cryptosystem. The Paillier cryptosystem [30] is based on the decisional composite residuosity problem. After encrypting a plain-text value m, a big integer $\mathbf{e_k}[m]$ is generated as the cipher value. Here $\mathbf{e_k}[\cdot]$ represents the encryption operation by using the encryption key $\mathbf{k}$, which can be publicly known after a Paillier cryptosystem is set up. For instance, a string of big integers will be generated after encrypting an image by converting each pixel in it into one big integer.

To add a plain-text value m_1 to another plain-text value m_2 within Paillier cryptosystem, a new cipher value $\mathbf{e_k}(m')$ can be generated from $\mathbf{e_k}(m_1)$ and $\mathbf{e_k}(m_2)$ by

$$\mathbf{e_k}(m') = (\mathbf{e_k}(m_1) \cdot \mathbf{e_k}(m_2)) \ mod \ N^2, \tag{1}$$

where N is a big integer generated in Paillier cryptosystem and included in $\mathbf{k}$. By decrypting the cipher value $\mathbf{e_k}(m')$, the plain-text value $(m_1 + m_2) \ mod \ N$ can be obtained, i.e.,

$$(m_1 + m_2) \ mod \ N = \mathbf{d_{\hat{k}}}[\mathbf{e_k}(m')] \tag{2}$$

where $\mathbf{d_{\hat{k}}}[\cdot]$ represents the decryption operation by using the private decryption key $\hat{\mathbf{k}}$.

Data Embedding by Value Expansion. A bit value $b \in \{0, 1\}$ can be embedded into the cipher value of a pixel value i by expanding its plain-text value. Suppose that $\mathbf{e_k}(i)$ is the cipher value of i. The following operation is conducted to embed a bit value b by modifying it to $\mathbf{e_k}(i')$ by

$$\mathbf{e_k}(i') = \begin{cases} (\mathbf{e_k}(i) \cdot \mathbf{e_k}(i) \cdot g) \ mod \ N^2, & \text{if } b = 1 \\ (\mathbf{e_k}(i) \cdot \mathbf{e_k}(i)) \ mod \ N^2, & \text{if } b = 0 \end{cases} \tag{3}$$

where g is the other value included in the public encryption key $\mathbf{k}$ of a Paillier cryptosystem and it can be used to replace the cipher value of integer 1 (i.e., $\mathbf{e_k}(1)$) in calculation. Consequently, a bit value 1 or 0 is embedded into the cipher value $\mathbf{e_k}(i')$ by applying Eq. (3). To extract the hidden bit value and recover i as well, $\mathbf{e_k}(i')$ needs to be decrypted. From additive homomorphism, we know that $\mathbf{d_{\hat{k}}}[\mathbf{e_k}(i')] = (2i + b) \ mod \ N$. For a grey-level pixel value, $i \in [0, 255]$ so that $2i + b \in [0, 511]$. When N is a big integer represented with hundreds of bits, $(2i + b) \ mod \ N = 2i + b$ so that the values of i and b can be obtained by

$$i = \lfloor \frac{\mathbf{d_{\hat{k}}}[\mathbf{e_k}(i')]}{2} \rfloor, \tag{4}$$

where $\lfloor \cdot \rfloor$ the represents the floor function, and

$$b = \mathbf{d_{\hat{k}}}[\mathbf{e_k}(i')] - 2i. \tag{5}$$

It can be seen that the redundancy of value representation in Paillier cryptosystem is exploited to achieve the reversibility of data embedding. For an integer within $[0, 255]$ and another integer in $[0, 511]$, their encrypted values are represented with the same bits. So the bit value embedded by applying Eq. (3) can be correctly extracted. To further exploit the redundancy to increase the data hiding rate, Eq. (3) can be iteratively applied. That is, for the resulting

$e_k(i')$ after embedding a bit value b (i.e., $d_{\hat{k}}[e_k(i')] = 2i + b$), another binary value b' can be further embedded by applying Eq. (3) to generate another cipher value $e_k(i'')$ so that $d_{\hat{k}}[e_k(i'')] = 2 \times (2i + b) + b'$. Given that

$$[2 \times (2i + b) + b'] \bmod N = 2 \times (2i + b) + b', \tag{6}$$

both b and b' can be correctly extracted from $e_k(i'')$. Meanwhile, the range of the corresponding plain-text value is changed from $[0, 255]$ to $[0, 511]$, then $[0, 1023]$, and so on. Since the big integer N included in the public key k is often represented in hundreds of bits, the operations of value expansion can be iterated for multiple times given that the expanded plain-text value does not exceed N. Therefore, up to 1015 bits can be reversibly hidden into a cipher pixel value when N is represented with 1024 bits.

2.2   Self-blinding Algorithm

The value expansion algorithm is suitable for data extraction after image decryption. In some cases, data extraction needs to be performed without image decryption. For instance, the image owner may want to send some extra information with encrypted images to the web server, but obviously the web server does not have the private decryption key $\hat{k}$. For data extraction without image decryption, the self-blinding property of Paillier cryptosystem is utilized in [22, 25] so that a cipher value is modified without changing its plain-text value. To keep the data embedded in the first phase unchanged, the self-blinding algorithm proposed in [25] is adopted in the second phase of the proposed method.

Property of Self-blinding in Paillier Cryptosystem. Due to the randomness in data encryption, a plain-text value may be encrypted into a lot of possible cipher-texts in Paillier cryptosystem. That is, the cipher value of a plain-text value m is not unique because multiple cipher values can be decrypted to the same plain-text value. More precisely, the self-blinding property in Paillier cryptosystem indicates that

$$d_{\hat{k}}[e_k(m)r^N \bmod N^2] = m \bmod N \tag{7}$$

where r is is a random element in $\mathbb{Z}_N^*$ that consists of all integers relatively prime with N. The self-blinding property indicates that every cipher value can be modified without changing its plain-text value.

Data Hiding with the Self-blinding Property. To embed a bit value b into a cipher value $e_k(i)$, the following condition should be met:

$$e_k(i) \bmod 2 = b. \tag{8}$$

If the condition in Eq. (8) does not hold (i.e., $e_k(i) \bmod 2 \neq b$), $e_k(i)$ should be changed to another cipher value. In that case, an integer r relatively prime with

N is chosen, and $\mathbf{e_k}(i)$ is multiplied by r^N to obtain $\mathbf{e_k}(i)r^N$. So another cipher value $\mathbf{e'_k}(i)$ can be generated by

$$\mathbf{e'_k}(i) = [\mathbf{e_k}(i) \times r^N] \bmod N^2. \tag{9}$$

From Eq. (7), we know $\mathbf{d_{\hat{k}}}[\mathbf{e_k}(i)r^N] = i \bmod N$ so that $\mathbf{d_{\hat{k}}}[\mathbf{e'_k}(i)] = i \bmod N$. The operation in Eq. (9) is iterated until $\mathbf{e'_k}(i) \bmod 2 = b$. If the condition cannot be met with r, another integer r' that is relatively prime with N can be used instead in Eq. (9) to generate new cipher values. The rationale of iteratively applying Eq. (9) to find a suitable cipher value is based on the randomness in Paillier encryption. For instance, one bit information can be embedded by switching between the odd and even cipher values of the same plain-text value by applying Eq. (9). Thanks to the self-blinding property, the corresponding plain-text value is unchanged while the only operation to extract the hidden bit value is conducted by

$$b' = \mathbf{e'_k}(i) \bmod 2, \tag{10}$$

where b' denotes the extracted bit value.

To increase the data embedding rate, multiple bits can be embedded into one cipher value. For instance, to embed a s-bit value $b_1 b_2 \ldots b_s$ into one cipher value $\mathbf{e_k}(i)$, another cipher value $\mathbf{e_k^s}(i)$ is generated so that

$$\mathbf{e_k^s}(i) \bmod 2^s = b_1 b_2 \ldots b_s. \tag{11}$$

In this case, a data hiding rate of s bpp is reached by iteratively applying Eq. (9) until the condition in Eq. (11) is met. In the experiments, a hiding rate up to 14 bpp was realized in a Paillier cryptosystem with a 1024-bit N. Note that the complexity of data embedding (i.e., searching for the appropriate cipher value corresponding to a given plain-text value) is exponentially increased with the hiding rate. Given the value of s is known, the hidden value can be extracted by

$$b'_1 b'_2 \ldots b'_s = \mathbf{e_k^s}(i) \bmod 2^s, \tag{12}$$

where $b'_1 b'_2 \ldots b'_s$ are the string of extracted bit values.

2.3 Adopting the Two Algorithms

After image processing in homomorphic encryption domain, the data to be extracted after decryption can be hidden by applying the value expansion algorithm in the first phase. Suppose that a t-bit binary value $a_1 a_2 \ldots a_t$ is to be embedded into $\mathbf{e_k}(m)$. Firstly, a cipher value $\mathbf{e_k}(m_1)$ is obtained after embedding a_1 into $\mathbf{e_k}(m)$ by applying Eq. (3). Then another cipher value $\mathbf{e_k}(m_2)$ is calculated after embedding a_2 into $\mathbf{e_k}(m_1)$ with Eq. (3), and so on, until the last cipher value $\mathbf{e_k}(m_t)$ is generated after embedding a_t into $\mathbf{e_k}(m_{t-1})$ with Eq. (3). As a result, the embedded bits can be sequentially extracted after decryption. For instance, the last embedded bit value a_t is extracted by

$$\begin{cases} i_t = \lfloor \frac{\mathbf{d_{\hat{k}}}[\mathbf{e_k}(m_t)]}{2} \rfloor \\ a_t = \mathbf{d_{\hat{k}}}[\mathbf{e_k}(m_t)] - 2 \cdot i_t \end{cases}. \tag{13}$$

For an integer l decreasing from $t - 1$ to 1, an embedded bit value a_l can be iteratively extracted by

$$\begin{cases} i_l = \lfloor \frac{i_{l+1}}{2} \rfloor \\ a_l = i_{l+1} - 2 \cdot i_l \end{cases}. \tag{14}$$

It can be deduced that the original pixel value $m = i_1$.

To embed data that can be extracted in encryption domain, the self-blinding algorithm is applied in the second phase so that the encrypted value $e_k(m_t)$ is modified to another encrypted value $e_k^*(m_t)$ without changing its plain-text value. For instance, a s-bit binary value $b_1 b_2 \ldots b_s$ were embedded in the experiments so that

$$e_k^*(m_t) \bmod 2^s = b_1 b_2 \ldots b_s. \tag{15}$$

By replacing $e_k^s(i)$ in Eq. (12) with $e_k^*(m_t)$, the embedded bits can be directly extracted without decrypting the cipher values. Therefore, the self-blinding algorithm can also be adopted before homomorphic processing, as shown in Fig. 1. In that case, the embedded data (e.g., by the image owner) can be extracted before homomorphic processing (e.g., by the web server). Even if the hidden message has not been extracted, the following homomorphic processing is not affected because the plain-text pixel values are unchanged after applying the self-blinding algorithm.

2.4 Procedure of the Proposed Method

The procedure of the proposed method can be divided into three stages (i.e., image encryption, image processing and image recovery). Compared with the flowchart as illustrated in Fig. 1, the steps of data embedding and extraction before homomorphic processing in encrypted domain has been appended.

Image Encryption Stage. Given a plain-text cover image I, public encryption key k (including the big integer N and g) of a Paillier cryptosystem, a piece of message D_{B1} to be sent to the web server, the following steps are carried out by the image owner:

(1) Encrypt I with k to produce an encrypted image $e_k(I)$;
(2) Apply Eq. (9) to each cipher pixel value in $e_k(I)$ except the last 4 cipher values to meet the condition in Eq. (11) so that s bits are embedded into one cipher pixel value;
(3) Represent s in four bits and embed them to the last 4 cipher pixel values by iteratively applying Eq. (9) to met the condition in Eq. (8), respectively. Thus the encrypted image with hidden data is generated and denoted as $e'_k(I)$.

Image Processing Stage. Given a message D_A to be extracted after image decryption and a message D_{B2} to be extracted without decryption, the following steps are carried out by the web server:

(1) Perform data extraction on the last 4 cipher pixel values in $\mathbf{e'_k(I)}$ by applying Eq. (10) so that the value of s is known;

(2) With the extracted value of s, extract D_{B1} from the rest cipher pixel values in $\mathbf{e'_k(I)}$ by using Eq. (12);

(3) Process $\mathbf{e'_k(I)}$ in encryption domain if needed so that a new encrypted image $\mathbf{e_k(I_c)}$ is generated;

(4) Embed D_A into $\mathbf{e_k(I_c)}$ by iteratively applying Eq. (3) to embed t bits into each cipher value so that another encrypted image $\mathbf{e_k(I'_c)}$ is generated;

(5) Embed D_{B2} into $\mathbf{e_k(I'_c)}$ by using Eq. (9) to embed s bits into one cipher value as shown in Eq. (15);

(6) Hide the value of s (represented in 4 bits) and the value of t (represented in 12 bits) into the last 16 cipher pixel values in $\mathbf{e_k(I'_c)}$ by iteratively applying Eq. (9) until the condition in Eq. (8) is met. Note that the last 16 cipher pixel values were excluded from being used in Step (5). Then the processed image with hidden data is generated and denoted as $\mathbf{e_k^*(I'_c)}$.

Image Recovery Stage. When the processed image with hidden data $\mathbf{e_k^*(I'_c)}$ is received, data extraction and image recovery are carried out as follows:

(1) Perform data extraction on the last 16 cipher pixel values in $\mathbf{e_k^*(I'_c)}$ with Eq. (10) to extract the values of s and t;

(2) With the extracted s, directly extract D_{B2} from the rest cipher pixel values in $\mathbf{e_k^*(I'_c)}$ in a way as shown in Eq. (12);

(3) Given the private decryption key $\hat{\mathbf{k}}$, a plain-text image $\mathbf{I}_c^d$ can be generated after decrypting $\mathbf{e_k^*(I'_c)}$;

(4) With the extracted t, extract the hidden bits (i.e., D_A) from $\mathbf{I}_c^d$ by using Eq. (13) and iteratively applying Eq. (14) ;

(5) Obtain the processed plain-text image $\mathbf{I}_c$ with every pixel value i_1 obtained by iteratively applying Eq. (14).

Note that the original plain-text image $\mathbf{I}$ is exactly recovered if no processing is performed in homomorphic encryption domain (i.e., $\mathbf{e'_k(I)}$ has not been changed to $\mathbf{e_k(I_c)}$ in Step (3) of Image Processing Stage).

3   Experimental Results

In the experiments, 8 gray-level images downloaded from USC-SIPI[1] with the size of 512×512 were used for performance evaluation, which are shown in Fig. 2. In implementing the Paillier cryptosystem, the bit length of N was set to 1024. Hereinafter, the algorithm presented in Sect. 2.1 is denoted by the value expansion (VE) algorithm, while the algorithm introduced in Sect. 2.2 is denoted by the self-blinding (SB) algorithm. The programs were developed with Java Eclipse SDK and run on a 64-bit PC with Intel Core CPU @3.2 GHz and 8G RAM.

---

[1] http://sipi.usc.edu/database/database.php?volume=misc

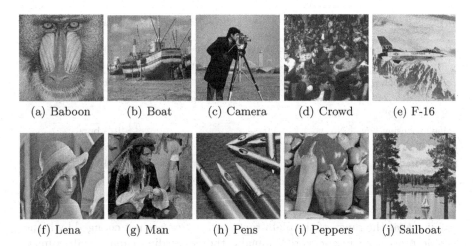

(a) Baboon	(b) Boat	(c) Camera	(d) Crowd	(e) F-16
(f) Lena	(g) Man	(h) Pens	(i) Peppers	(j) Sailboat

Fig. 2. 10 gray-level images used in the experiments with the size of 512×512.

3.1 Data Extraction in Different Scenarios

One feature of the proposed method is that the hidden data can be extracted in different scenarios (i.e., before homomorphic processing, after processing and before image decryption, after image decryption). For instance, a message can be transmitted to the web server by embedding it into the encrypted image with the self-blinding algorithm. While keeping the plain-text image unchanged, the hidden data can be extracted by applying modulo operation on the cipher pixel values. After conducting homomorphic processing on the cipher image, a secret message can be hidden into the processed image by using the value expansion algorithm, which is to be extracted by a receiver with the decryption key. In addition, another message can be further embedded by using the self-blinding algorithm, which is to be extracted without image decryption.

As the data embedded with the self-blinding algorithm can be directly extracted by applying the modulo operation, the to-be-hidden message can be previously encrypted with a secret key or a public key provided by the receiver. Thus the corresponding key (the same secret key or the corresponding private key of the receiver) is required to decrypt the extracted data. In this way, the content of the hidden message is protected to enhance security.

3.2 Embedding Capacity

According to the procedure in Sect. 2.4, the embedding capacity of the proposed method includes three parts, respectively for data extraction before processing, data extraction after processing and before decryption, and data extraction after image decryption. The embedding capacity before processing is equal to that of the self-blinding algorithm proposed in [25]. The highest hiding rate reported in [25] was 12 bpp, which was increased to 14 bpp in the experiments.

Table 1. Performance comparisons on embedding capacity with [22, 24, 25, 28]

Scheme/Algorithm	Preprocessing	Data extraction (for a 1024-bit N)	
		in encrypted domain	in plain-text domain
Combined scheme [22]	Yes	close to 1 bpp	0.5 bpp
MCG scheme [24]	Yes	about $\frac{12}{35}$ bpp (given 1 bpp in preprocessing)	
Self-blinding [25]	No	14 bpp	0
Value expansion [25]	No	0	1015 bpp
Hierarchical [28]	Yes	14 bpp	more than 1 bpp
Proposed Method	No	14 bpp (before processing) 14 bpp (after processing)	1014 bpp

Given that the range of the plain-text pixel values was not changed by homomorphic processing in encrypted domain, the embedding capacity after image decryption is equal to that of the value expansion algorithm proposed in [25]. For a 8-bit pixel value, a hiding rate up to 1015 bpp was achieved with the value expansion algorithm when the bit length of N was 1024. For correct decryption, a plain-text value should be less than N included in the public encryption key. When the expanded plain-text value was no more than 1023 bits, the embedded data were correctly extracted. Otherwise, the original pixel value could not be recovered and the hidden bit values were not be correctly extracted.

As the range of an expanded plain-text value is enlarged by applying the value expansion algorithm, a high hiding rate can still be achieved by applying the self-blinding algorithm on its cipher value. Since a cipher pixel value is generated by performing modulo N^2, the range of searching appropriate cipher values is unchanged. In the experiments, a hiding rate up to 14 bpp was obtained with the self-blinding algorithm after 1014 bits had been embedded into a cipher pixel value with the value expansion algorithm. Performance comparisons on embedding capacity between the proposed method with [22, 24, 25, 28] are shown in Table 1.

3.3   Compatibility with Homomorphic Processing

With the proposed method, the encrypted image can be used as normal because no preprocessing needs to be conducted. Meanwhile, applying the self-blinding algorithm does not affect the plain-text of an encrypted image so that the processed image can be obtained after decryption. For instance, two plain-text images "Man" and "Bird" as shown in Fig. 3(a) and (b) were encrypted within Paillier cryptosystem. Then the two cipher images are added by utilizing the additive homomorphism so that a sum cipher image was generated. By performing the arithmetic modulo 256 on the newly generated cipher image, an image as shown in Fig. 3(c) was obtained for exhibition. By applying the value expansion algorithm, totally 1014 bits were embedded into one cipher pixel value so that a sum cipher image with hidden data was generated. By applying the self-blinding algorithm, extra 14 bits were further hidden into each cipher pixel

(a) "Man" (size: 512×512) (b) "Bird" (size: 512×512) (c) After adding two ci-pher images

(d) After data embedding with the VE algorithm (1014 bpp) (e) After data embedding with the SB algorithm (14 bpp) (f) After image decryption and then being divided by 2

Fig. 3. A new image can be obtained by processing two images in Paillier cryptosystem, while different parts of the hidden data can be extracted from the sum cipher image.

value. The data hidden with the self-blinding algorithm were correctly extracted without image decryption, while those embedded with the value expansion algorithm were correctly extracted after image decryption. By dividing the recovered image (i.e., the one generated after data extraction in plain-text domain) by 2, an average image was obtained as shown in Fig. 3(f), which was identical to the one generated by adding the two plain-text images and then dividing the sum by 2. From this example, it can be seen that the proposed method is compatible with homomorphic image processing before data embedding.

3.4 Security Analysis

Since both of the value expansion and self-blinding algorithms are performed in homomorphic encryption domain, the security of the proposed method depends on that of the adopted Paillier cryptosystem. Normally, the parameter N in Paillier cryptosystem consists of hundreds of bits, making it hard to directly decrypt the encrypted data without the private decryption key. Moreover, applying the proposed method for reversible data hiding in encrypted images does not compromise the security of cryptosystem. Since only homomorphic addition operations are conducted with the value expansion algorithm, no information of the hidden message can be leaked before image decryption. To protect the data to be embedded with the self-blinding algorithm, the message can be previously encrypted (e.g., with the RC4 or RSA algorithm) before being embedded. After data extraction, the message can be obtained from the extracted data with the corresponding decryption key.

4   Conclusion

In this paper, we have presented a new reversible data hiding method in homomorphic encryption domain based on Paillier cryptosystem. As no preprocessing is required before image encryption, a cipher image can be used or processed as normal while extra data can be hidden within it afterwards. By applying the proposed method, the hidden data can be extracted before or after image decryption for different usages. The image owner, web server and administrator can transmit messages to each other by hiding them in encrypted images at acceptable computational cost. One limitation of the proposed method is that the encrypted image cannot be further processed after reversible data hiding, which will be studied in our future work.

References

1. Shi, Y.Q., Li, X., Zhang, X., Wu, H.T., Ma, B.: Reversible data hiding: advances in the past two decades. IEEE Access **4**, 3210–3237 (2016)
2. Cheung, Y.M., Wu, H.T.: A sequential quantization strategy for data embedding and integrity verification. IEEE Trans. Circuits Syst. Video Technol. **17**(8), 1007–1016 (2007)
3. Sachnev, V., Kim, H.J., Nam, J., Suresh, S., Shi, Y.Q.: Reversible watermarking algorithm using sorting and prediction. IEEE Trans. Circuits Syst. Video Technol. **19**(7), 989–999 (2009)
4. Wu, H.T., Cheung, Y.M.: Public authentication of 3d mesh models. In: Proceedings of 2006 IEEE/WIC/ACM International Conference on Web Intelligence, Hong Kong, pp. 940–948 (2016)
5. Wu, H., Cheung, Y.: A high-capacity data hiding method for polygonal meshes. In: Camenisch, J.L., Collberg, C.S., Johnson, N.F., Sallee, P. (eds.) IH 2006. LNCS, vol. 4437, pp. 188–200. Springer, Heidelberg (2007). https://doi.org/10.1007/978-3-540-74124-4_13
6. Wu, H.T., Huang, J.: Reversible image watermarking on prediction error by efficient histogram modification. Sig. Process. **92**(12), 3000–3009 (2012)
7. Ou, B., Li, X., Zhao, Y., Ni, R., Shi, Y.Q.: Pairwise prediction-error expansion for efficient reversible data hiding. IEEE Trans. Image Process. **22**(12), 5010–5021 (2013)
8. Wu, H.T., Dugelay, J.L., Shi, Y.Q.: Reversible image data hiding with contrast enhancement. IEEE Signal Process. Lett. **22**(1), 81–85 (2015)
9. Li, X., Zhang, W., Gui, X., Yang, B.: Efficient reversible data hiding based on multiple histograms modification. IEEE Trans. Inf. Forensics Secur. **10**(9), 2016–2027 (2015)

10. Dragoi, I.C., Coltuc, D.: Adaptive pairing reversible watermarking. IEEE Trans. Image Process. **25**(5), 2420–2422 (2016)

11. Wang, J., Chen, X., Ni, J., Mao, N., Shi, Y.Q.: Multiple histograms based reversible data hiding: framework and realization. IEEE Trans. Circuits Syst. Video Technol. https://doi.org/10.1109/TCSVT.2019.2915584

12. Wu, H.T., Huang, J., Shi, Y.Q.: A reversible data hiding method with contrast enhancement for medical images. J. Vis. Commun. Image Represent. **31**, 146–153 (2015)

13. Zhang, X.: Reversible data hiding in encrypted images. IEEE Signal Process. Lett. **18**(4), 255–258 (2011)

14. Zhang, X.: Separable reversible data hiding in encrypted image. IEEE Trans. Inf. Forensics Secur. **16**(5), 826–832 (2012)

15. Ma, K., Zhang, W., Sun, W.: Reversible data hiding in encrypted images by reserving room before encryption. IEEE Trans. Inf. Forensics Secur. **8**(3), 553–562 (2013)

16. Wu, X., Sun, W.: High-capacity reversible data hiding in encrypted images by prediction error. Sig. Process. **104**, 387–400 (2014)

17. Shiu, C.-W., Chen, Y.-C., Hong, W.: Encrypted image-based reversible data hiding with public key cryptography from difference expansion. Sig. Process. Image Commun. **39**, 226–233 (2015)

18. Cao, X., Du, L., Wei, X., Meng, D.: High capacity reversible data hiding in encrypted images by patch-level sparse representation. IEEE Trans. Cybern. **46**(5), 1132–1143 (2016)

19. Qian, Z., Zhang, X.: Reversible data hiding in encrypted image with distributed source encoding. IEEE Trans. Circuits Syst. Video Technol. **26**(4), 636–646 (2016)

20. Zhou, J., Sun, W., Dong, L., Liu, X., Au, O.C., Tang, Y.Y.: Secure reversible image data hiding over encrypted domain via key modulation. IEEE Trans. Circuits Syst. Video Technol. **26**(3), 441–452 (2016)

21. Puteaux, P., Puech, W.: An efficient MSB prediction-based method for high-capacity reversible data hiding in encrypted images. IEEE Trans. Inf. Forensics Secur. **13**(7), 1670–1681 (2018)

22. Zhang, X., Long, J., Wang, Z., Cheng, H.: Lossless and reversible data hiding in encrypted images with public key cryptography. IEEE Trans. Circuits Syst. Video Technol. **26**(9), 1622–1631 (2016)

23. Xu, D., Wang, R.: Separable and error-free reversible data hiding in encrypted imagesn. Sig. Process. **123**, 9–21 (2016)

24. Xiang, S., Luo, X.: Reversible data hiding in homomorphic encrypted domain by mirroring ciphertext group. IEEE Trans. Circuits Syst. Video Technol. **28**(11), 3099–3110 (2018)

25. Wu, H.T., Cheung, Y.M., Huang, J.: Reversible data hiding in Paillier Cryptosystem. J. Vis. Commun. Image Represent. **40**, 765–771 (2016)

26. Wu, X., Chen, B., Weng, J.: Reversible data hiding for encrypted signals by homomorphic encryption and signal energy transfer. J. Vis. Commun. Image Represent. **41**, 58–64 (2016)

27. Wu, H.T., Cheung, Y.M., Yang, Z., Tang, S.: A high-capacity reversible data hiding method for homomorphic encrypted images. J. Vis. Commun. Image Represent. **62**, 87–96 (2019)

28. Wu, H.T., Yang, Z., Cheung, Y.M., Xu, L., Tang, S.: High-capacity reversible data hiding in encrypted images by bit plane partition and MSB prediction. IEEE Access **7**, 62361–62371 (2019)

29. Barni, M., Kalker, T., Katzenbeisser, S.: Inspiring new research in the field of signal processing in the encrypted domain. IEEE Sig. Process. Mag. **30**(2), 16–16 (2013)

30. Paillier, P.: Public-key cryptosystems based on composite degree residuosity classes. In: Stern, J. (ed.) EUROCRYPT 1999. LNCS, vol. 1592, pp. 223–238. Springer, Heidelberg (1999). https://doi.org/10.1007/3-540-48910-X_16
31. Gentry, C.: Fully homomorphic encryption using ideal lattices. In: Proceedings of the 41st ACM Symposium on Theory of Computing, pp. 169–178 (2009)
32. Brakershi, Z., Vaikuntanathan, V.: Efficient fully homomorphic encryption from (standard) LWE. SIAM J. Comput. **43**(2), 831–871 (2014)
33. Haghighat, M., Zonouz, S., Abdel-Mottaleb, M.: Security and privacy in cloud computing: vision, trends, and challenges. IEEE Trans. Cloud Comput. **2**(2), 30–38 (2015)
34. Zhang, X., Yang, Z., Liu, Y., Tang, S.: Reliable task assignment for spatial crowdsourcing. IEEE Trans. Emerg. Top. Comput. **7**(1), 174–186 (2019)

Model Selection for Data Analysis in Encrypted Domain: Application to Simple Linear Regression

Mi Yeon Hong and Ji Won Yoon$^{(\boxtimes)}$

Korea University, Seoul, Republic of Korea
{hachikohmy,jiwon_yoon}@korea.ac.kr

Abstract. In the big data era, data scientists explore machine learning methods for observed data to predict or classify. For machine learining to be effective, it requires access to raw data which is often privacy sensitive. In addition, whatever data and fitting procedures are employed, a crucial step is to select the most appropriate model from the given dataset. Model selection is a key ingredient in data analysis for reliable and reproducible statistical inference or prediction. To address this issue, we develop new techniques to provide solutions for running model selection over encrypted data. Our approach provides the best approximation of the relationship between the dependent and independent variable through cross validation. After performing 4-fold cross validation, 4 different estimates of our model's errors are calculated. And then we use bias and variance extracted from these errors to find the best model. We perform an experiment on a dataset extracted from Kaggle and show that our approach can homomorphically regress a given encrypted data without decrypting it.

Keywords: Fully Homomorphic Encryption · TFHE · Model selection

1 Introduction

Vast quantities of data have recently been generated from the Internet, social network sites, health-care applications, and many other companies. This big data is a valuable asset in industry and academics because information obtained from various sources and channels can help for us to understand the underlying phenomena of human behaviors, society and even nature itself. In order to effectively analyze obtained big data, it is essential to build more specialized and advanced data storage management for handling such big data because traditional databases are developed for relatively small data. The cloud technology to store very large data is a solution to overcome the problems and limitations

This research is supported by the MSIP (Ministry of Science, ICT and Future Planning), Korea, under the IITP support program (2017-0-00545).
We thank Joonsoo Yoo and Jeonghwan Hwang for their assistance in this research.

I. You (Ed.): WISA 2019, LNCS 11897, pp. 155–166, 2020.
https://doi.org/10.1007/978-3-030-39303-8_12

of traditional databases in managing very large data both in terms of storage methods or access speeds. Many enterprises are trying to outsource their data solution to third party service providers (i.e. cloud computing) for saving the cost and increasing performance efficiency but this outsourced initiative in turn introduces a number of security and privacy concerns.

In order to remove the concerns in security and privacy for the outsourced data, there have been several methodologies to protect the privacy of the data. One of the solutions is the homomorphic encryption (HE) which protects confidential data, while allowing third parties to perform arithmetic computation on encrypted data without decryption. Recently, several libraries have been introduced and they are now used to apply for advanced data mining and machine learning algorithms. In this paper, as the other contemporary researches are done, we also use a well-known HE library which is called Fast Fully Homomorphic Encryption over the Torus(TFHE) library [1,2] to apply privacy preserving data analysis in encrypted domain.

However, we realized that current researches in HE based machine learning have focused only on the development of the known algorithms without the deep insightfulness in data and machine learning algorithm. In data analysis society, it is known that there exists no model that is universally suitable for any data and goal. Worse, an unsuitable choice of model or method can unfortunately lead to severely misleading conclusions, or disappointing predictive performances due to over-fitting or under-fitting. Therefore, a crucial step in data analysis is to find the optimal model which provides better performance in given dataset using the *model selection*. Since the machine learning or data analysis in a HE scheme is inheriting the one in un-encrypted domain, the *model selection* is still one of the key steps to obtain the better performance and to decrease the problem of the over-fitting or under-fitting in the HE scheme. However, despite of the importance of finding the optimal model, there are few researches which consider the *model selection* when data analysis is performed through Homomorphic Encryption scheme.

In this paper, the contributions are two-folds.

- We introduce the *model selection* for the linear regression which is one of the simplest but useful data mining methods.
- We introduce practical matrix inversion for the linear regression with the *model selection* since the *model selection* for the linear regression requires lots of matrix operations including matrix inversion and it is not straightforward to directly implement the matrix inversion.

2   Background

In this section, we give brief description of three key technologies: Homomorphic Encryption (HE), TFHE library and the *model selection*. After we first describe the basic concept of Homomorphic Encryption (HE), we explain the TFHE library which is one of the well-known HE libraries. Then we will explain basic description about the model selection which is one of critical issues in data analysis and applied statistics. In addition, Gauss-Jordan elimination will be described in the end of this section for explaining homomorphical operation in matrix inversion.

2.1 Homomorphic Encryption

Homomorphic encryption is an encryption scheme that allows some kind of computations on encrypted data. With HE, the sever can process user's data without decrypting it. It can be expressed as the following equation:

$$Enc(m_1) \star Enc(m_2) = Enc(m_1 \star m_2),$$

where Enc is the encryption algorithm, m_1, m_2 is the plaintext and $\star$ is the homomorphic operation.

The concept of privacy homomorphism was originally proposed as an a modification of the RSA cryptosystem, which explains the concept of preserving the computation between ciphertexts. However, this technique was not actually used because of the fatal safety problem that the secret key is exposed by the operation between two ciphertexts. Although various HE schemes and libraries have been introduced since then but when using randomized noise to encrypt a plaintext, the noise is amplified whenever the operation is performed which prevents the ciphertext from being normally decrypted if it exceeds a certain level.

The first working HE scheme was introduced in 2009 by Gentry [4] which reduced noise amplification problem that once allows an unlimited number of evaluation operations on the encrypted data and resulting output is within the ciphertext space so called Fully Homomorphic Encryption (FHE) scheme. Gentry uses a bootstrapping algorithm to eliminate the accumulated noise but it requires a lot of time because of the complexity of bootstrapping algorithm and the disadvantage that the capacity of the ciphertext increases because the plaintext has to be bit-by-bit encrypted. Thus, the bootstrapping part, which is the intermediate refreshing procedure of a processed ciphertext, is too costly in terms of computation.

2.2 TFHE Library

Chillotti et.al released TFHE(Fast Fully Homomorphic Encryption over the Torus) library which is designed from FHEW. The TFHE is basically a GSW-based library [5] with fast bootstrapped operations. It significantly improves the performance of the bootstrapping operation, which has the greatest effect on the performance of the fully homomorphic encryption algorithm, in 0.1 s by using a gate-by-gate bootstrapping procedure.

The library supports the homomorphic evaluation of the binary gates (AND, OR, XOR, NAND, NOR, etc...), as well as the negation and the MUX gate and these can be used for various operations. The gate-bootstrapping mode of TFHE has no restriction on the number of gates or on their composition therefore this allows to perform any computation over encrypted data. TFHE library provides 3 steps:

- Generate a secret key and a cloud key for encrypting data and exporting ciphertexts, respectively.
- Cloud key owner imports the cloud key and encrypted input data and then exports the results using homomorphic circuit.
- Secret key owner decrypts and prints the final answer.

2.3 Model Selection

When we consider a set of candidate models,
In machine learning, the *model selection* is a process to choose one of the most appropriate model among given multiple models. In addition, the *model selection* represents two different meanings because there are two meanings for the 'model' in machine learning society.

- **Model is considered as an algorithm:** the *model selection* chooses the most appropriate one between different machine learning approaches - e.g. SVM, KNN, logistic regression, etc.
- **Model is considered as an complexity:** the *model selection* chooses one between different hyper-parameters or sets of features for the same machine learning approach - e.g. deciding between the polynomial degrees or complexities for linear regression.

In this paper, we focus on *model selection* with varying complexity by adapting numerical solution for regression.
To fit regression models, we need to make a choice of degrees/orders. Polynomial regression is a form of linear regression in which the relationship between the independent variable x and dependent variable y is modeled as an m-th degree polynomial. It is represented by an equation of the general form:

$$y(x, \beta) = \beta_0 + \beta_1 x + \beta_2 x^2 + \cdots + \beta_m x^m = \sum_{i=0}^{m} \beta_i x^i \qquad (1)$$

where β is a set of polynomial coefficient. β is determined by fitting the polynomial to the training data by minimizing the errors to optimize between training dataset and the function $y(x, \beta)$. That is, obtaining optimal solution for the best model is to find optimal model order m^*.
Model fit according to m can be assessed by estimation errors. Errors are influenced by bias and variance, both bias and variance are affected by model complexity. If a model is too simple to explain the data, it is likely to have high bias and low variance called under-fitting. By contrast, over-fitting overly occurs when complex models have low bias and high variance. In machine learning, over-fitted model may fit perfectly on training data but is likely to fit very poorly with new data.
To avoid under-fitting and over-fitting, it is important to choose an appropriate model with optimal complexity. Therefore, we need to find a way to determine a suitable value among models with different complexities. A simple but useful

way is splitting dataset into training set to determine β and validation set to evaluate and optimize model complexity.

However, the dataset for training and testing in practice is limited. In order to build appropriate model with finite volume of dataset, one solution is to use cross validation. Cross validation like the K-fold cross validation splits the training set into K smaller sets and doing multiple iterations of training and evaluation.

2.4 Inverse of a Matrix by Gauss-Jordan Elimination

Given set of data, the least square in general uses the normal equation which requires matrix inverse. We propose Gauss-Jordan elimination method [6], which solves linear systems to find inverse of a matrix.

Suppose $\mathbf{A}$ is a square matrix and we look for its inverse matrix $\mathbf{A}^{-1}$ of the same size, such that $\mathbf{A}^{-1}\mathbf{A} = \mathbf{A}\mathbf{A}^{-1} = \mathbf{I}$ for an identity matrix $\mathbf{I}$. Given vectors $\mathbf{x}$ and $\mathbf{b}$, multiplying $\mathbf{A}\mathbf{x} = \mathbf{b}$ by $\mathbf{A}^{-1}$ gives $\mathbf{A}^{-1}\mathbf{A}x = \mathbf{A}^{-1}\mathbf{b}$. It is solved by $x = \mathbf{A}^{-1}\mathbf{b}$. But it is not necessary to compute $\mathbf{A}^{-1}$ and multiply with $\mathbf{b}$ because elimination goes directly to $\mathbf{x}$. The Gauss-Jordan is to solve $\mathbf{A}^{-1}\mathbf{A} = \mathbf{I}$, finding each column of $\mathbf{A}^{-1}$.

3   Methods

In TFHE library, HE scheme performs on a bit-by-bit arithmetic operation with binary (i.e. modulo 2) so all input data must be converted to binary numbers. We perform all operations with this library- e.g. addition, subtraction, multiplication, division and so on. Before we design matrix inverse and model selection algorithm, we introduce several operations notation consisting of boolean logic gates and its applications. Table 1 presents our notation of HE operations used in this study.

Table 1. The notation of HE operations

Operation	HE function	Notation
Addition	*HomAdd*	$\oplus$
Substraction	*HomSubt*	$\ominus$
Multiplication	*HomMulti*	$\otimes$
Division	*HomDiv*	$\oslash$
Mux	*bootsMUX*	$\odot$

3.1 Matrix Inverse with TFHE

For matrix inverse we can adapt Gauss-Jordan elimination algorithm to encrypted approximate inverse circuit. We start with an arbitrary square matrix and a same size identity matrix - i.e. all the elements along its diagonal are 1. And then we perform operations on the rows of the input matrix in order to transform it and obtain an identity matrix, and perform exactly the same operations on the accompanying identity matrix in order to obtain the inverse one. For a matrix $\mathbf{A}$ of size $n \times n$, an identity matrix of size $n \times n$ is appended to the matrix. After that the following two operations based on reduced row-echelon form are iterated on all rows to obtain the inverse:

- **(Phase 1) Normalize pivotal row:** A pivotal row p is selected and from the rows whose diagonal elements have not yet been used as a pivot and the value of the pivotal element is saved as P_p. Then the pivotal row is normalized by dividing the entire pivotal row by P_p. This transforms the pivotal element to unity 1 and the pivotal row of identity matrix element to $1/P_p$.
- **(Phase 2) Reduce non-pivotal rows:** Each non-pivotal row is reduced by saving the value of its pivotal column element and then recomputing all its row elements. This transforms its pivotal column element to zero and after it is performed on all non-pivotal rows, their pivotal column elements become 0.

After performing these phases on every row, treating each row once as a pivotal row, the original matrix becomes a unit matrix while the unit matrix becomes the inverse. Algorithm 1 shows how to construct matrix inverse with HE operations, as described above. We assumed $\mathbf{A}$ (i, j) is non-zero and determinant of matrix $\mathbf{A}$ is also non-zero. $BootsMUX(S, a, b)$ means mux gate that homomorphically outputs either the message of a or b depending on the boolean value in S, without decrypting any of the cipertxts. If $S = 1$, it represents a otherwise it represents b.

The classical Gauss-Jordan elimination method for matrix inverse involves augmenting the matrix with a unit matrix and requires a workspace twice as large as the original matrix as well as computational operations to be performed on both the original and the unit matrix therefore, it costs much time to execute results of matrix.

3.2 Model Selection with TFHE

To construct model selection algorithm, the proposed method using Eq. 1 is polynomial regression. This method uses the least-square procedure to fit the data to a higher order polynomial. The residuals between the model and the given dataset $(x_k, y_k)_{k=0}^{n-1}$ for all k are given by:

$$R(\beta_0, \cdots, \beta_m) = \sum_{k=0}^{n} \left(\sum_{i=0}^{m} \beta_i x_k^i - y_k \right)^2. \tag{2}$$

Algorithm 1. HE Algorithm for Gauss-Jordan elimination

- **Input:** n by n matrix $\mathbf{A}$
- **Output:** inverse of n by n matrix $\mathbf{A}$

1: assign the size of rows and columns of $\mathbf{A} \leftarrow [r, c]$
2: assign the size r of new identity matrix $\leftarrow \mathbf{F}$
3: **for** $j = 1$ to r **do**
4:   **for** $i = j$ to r **do**
5:     initialize $s \leftarrow 0$
6:     **for** $k = 1$ to r **do**
7:       $s \leftarrow \odot(\mathbf{A}(i,j), \mathbf{A}(j,k), s)$
8:       $\mathbf{A}(j,k) \leftarrow \odot(\mathbf{A}(i,j), \mathbf{A}(i,k), \mathbf{A}(j,k))$
9:       $\mathbf{A}(i,k) \leftarrow \odot(\mathbf{A}(i,j), s, \mathbf{A}(i,k))$
10:      $s \leftarrow \odot(\mathbf{A}(i,j), \mathbf{F}(j,k), s)$
11:      $\mathbf{F}(j,k) \leftarrow \odot(\mathbf{A}(i,j), \mathbf{F}(i,k), \mathbf{F}(j,k))$
12:      $\mathbf{F}(i,k) \leftarrow \odot(\mathbf{A}(i,j), s, \mathbf{F}(i,k))$
13:     **end for**
14:     $t = 1 \oslash \mathbf{A}(j,j)$
15:     **for** $k = 1$ to r **do**
16:       $\mathbf{A}(j,k) \leftarrow t \otimes \mathbf{A}(j,k)$
17:       $\mathbf{F}(j,k) \leftarrow t \otimes \mathbf{F}(j,k)$
18:     **end for**
19:     **for** $\mathbf{L} = 1$ to r **do**
20:       **if** $L = j$ **then**
21:         $t = -\mathbf{A}(L,j)$
22:         **for** $k = 1$ to r **do**
23:           $c \leftarrow t \otimes \mathbf{A}(j,k)$
24:           $d \leftarrow t \otimes \mathbf{F}(j,k)$
25:           $\mathbf{A}(L,k) \leftarrow \mathbf{A}(L,k) \oplus c$
26:           $\mathbf{F}(L,k) \leftarrow \mathbf{F}(L,k) \oplus d$
27:         **end for**
28:       **end if**
29:     **end for**
30:   **end for**
31: **end for**

The coefficients obtains its global minimum when the gradient of R is zero, that is, the partial derivatives of R must be zero for $0 \leq j \leq m$:

$$\frac{\partial R}{\partial \beta_j} = 2 \sum_{k=0}^{n-1} \left(\sum_{i=0}^{m} \beta_i x_k^i - y_k \right) x_k^j = 0. \tag{3}$$

It simplifies to

$$\sum_{i=0}^{m} \left(\sum_{k=0}^{n-1} x_k^{j+i} \right) \beta_i = \sum_{k=0}^{n-1} x_k^j y_k. \tag{4}$$

This is a linear system of $(m+1)$ equations in $(m+1)$ unknown coefficients and denote the form of

$$A^T A \beta = A^T y \tag{5}$$

where A is a matrix and the coefficient matrix of the normal equation is

$$A^T A = \begin{bmatrix} \sum_{k=0}^{n-1} 1 & \sum_{k=0}^{n-1} x_k & \cdots & \sum_{k=0}^{n-1} x_k^m \\ \sum_{k=0}^{n-1} x_k & \sum_{k=0}^{n-1} x_k^2 & \cdots & \sum_{k=0}^{n-1} x_k^{m+1} \\ \vdots & \vdots & \ddots & \vdots \\ \sum_{k=0}^{n-1} x_k^m & \sum_{k=0}^{n-1} x_k^{m+1} & \cdots & \sum_{k=0}^{n-1} x_k^{2m} \end{bmatrix}, A^T y = \begin{bmatrix} \sum_{k=0}^{n-1} y_i \\ \sum_{k=0}^{n-1} x_k y_k \\ \vdots \\ \sum_{k=0}^{n-1} x_k^m y_k \end{bmatrix} \tag{6}$$

The supposition that x_k are increasing guarantees that $A^T A$ is invertile so the coefficients of the polynomial are

$$\beta = (A^T A)^{-1} A^T y = \mathbb{A}^{-1} \times \mathbb{D} \tag{7}$$

then solving for β by Gauss-Jordan elimination method. The model selection algorithm for HE is presented in the following.

Algorithm 2. HE Algorithm for Model selection

- **Input:** dataset $\mathbf{x} = (\mathbf{x_1}, \mathbf{x_2}, \cdots, \mathbf{x_n})$, $\mathbf{y} = (\mathbf{y_1}, \mathbf{y_2}, \cdots, \mathbf{y_n})$
- **Output:** coefficients $\beta = (\beta_0, \beta_1, \cdots, \beta_n)$

1: Initialize all elements of matrix $\mathbb{A}$, $\mathbb{D}$ to 0
2: **for** $i = 0$ to number of $n - 1$ **do**
3:    **for** $j = 0$ to number of $n - 1$ **do**
4:       $\mathbb{A}_{i,j} \leftarrow \mathbb{A}_{i,j} \oplus x_{(i)} \otimes$ assigned $x_{(i)}^{th}$ power
5:       $\mathbb{D}_{i,j} \leftarrow \mathbb{D}_{i,j} \oplus x_{(i)} \otimes$ assigned $x_{(i)}^{th}$ power $\otimes y_{(i)}$
6:    **end for**
7:    Calculate inverse matrix of $\mathbb{A}$
8:    $\beta = Gauss - Jordan(\mathbb{A}) \otimes \mathbb{D}$
9: **end for**
10: **return** β

First, we initialized $\mathbb{A}$, $\mathbb{D}$ matrix elements to 0 and updated our elements using polynomial regression function that we've implemented. Then we compute the value of elements through homomorphic operations and multiply the solution of matrix inverse $\mathbb{A}$ with matrix $\mathbb{D}$.

4   Implementation

In this section, we present results of adopted version of model selection over encrypted data. The experimental environment setup is as follows- all computations were run on a computer with 16 GB RAM, Intel Core i7-8700 CPU 3.2 GHz, Ubuntu 18.04 and we used TFHE library version 1.0.1.

Table 2. Coefficients of the 1st to 4th degree polynomial representations

Value of coefficient	Degree of polynomial			
	1	2	3	4
β_0	1.4000	−1.6000	1.2000	−4.2000
β_1	0.6000	3.1714	−0.7619	80.6667
β_2		−0.4286	1.0714	−48.5000
β_3			−1.0667	11.8333
β_4				−1.0000

We implemented model selection algorithm with two datasets. For one thing, it is to figure out our HE Gauss-Elimination algorithm works correctly with various HE functions incorporated inside. For another thing, we expanded our scope to the real world dataset from the Kaggle [5].

4.1 Toy Dataset

First we use artificially created vectors x and y data to check performance and evaluation of our algorithm: $\mathbf{x} = [1, 2, 3, 4, 5]$, $\mathbf{y} = [1, 4, 2, 6, 3]$.

Figure 1 shows the fitting curve of each degree and the value of root mean square error according to the degree of polynomial. Table 2 also shows the coefficients for polynomials of various degree.

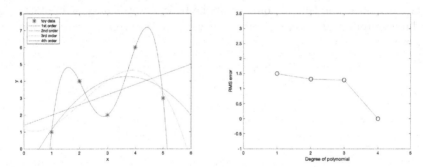

Fig. 1. Polynomial regression of toy dataset with HE model select algorithm and its RMS error

The values of the coefficients β is determined by fitting the polynomial to the data. It can be done by minimizing the error function, sum of squares of the error, that measures the gap between function $y(x, \beta)$ and given data points,

$$E(\beta) = \frac{1}{2} \sum_{n=1}^{N} \left(y(x_n, \beta) - t_n \right)^2 \tag{8}$$

where t_n is the corresponding target values. We use the root mean square error defined by

$$E_{RMS} = \sqrt{\frac{2E(\beta^+)}{N}} \tag{9}$$

$E(\beta^+)$ is derivatives with respect to the coefficients. As we can see figures above, for each choice of order we can evaluate the residual value of $E(\beta^+)$ for the given data. Toy dataset is too small to split training test set so we use all data into training set to measure best fit order. For 4th polynomial, RMS error goes to zero because the regression is tuned exactly to all data points. In that case, values of 2nd and 3rd give small error and we might suppose that the best predictor of new data would be when order is 3.

4.2 Real World Dataset

Kaggle's dataset is then used by users to find and publish datasets to create machine learning models for application extension. The dataset is limited to height and weight and consists of 1000×2 data. We sampled 100 data respectively and evaluated the polynomial regression coefficients for each degree.

We use K-fold cross validation, the purpose of using our dataset with this method is to predict weight changes by height and avoid underfitting and overfitting. If we randomly selected the values of the height and weight of the training and test set, we assumed each set represents the entire dataset. We performed 4-fold cross validation technique to estimate RMS errors.

Our approach to find the best fit of given dataset, when fitting the data in 1st to 4th order, it works well without any problem and its RMS error is equivalent in plaintext situation. But we found that the RMS error deviations in more than 5th dimension are very large. Figure 2 shows the RMS error of training and test dataset respectively.

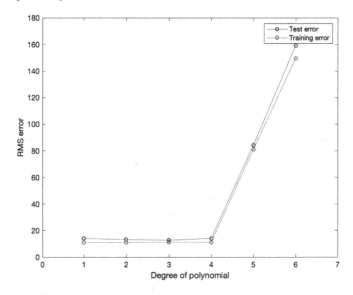

Fig. 2. RMS error value of polynomial regression with each order of height-weight dataset

We figured out the cause of this problem that our dataset contain features highly varying in magnitudes, units and ranges and to avoid this, we have to standardization our dataset before experiment. Standardization (or Z-score normalization) is the process of rescaling the features so that they'll have the properties of a Gaussian distribution with $\mu = 0$ and $\sigma = 1$ where μ is the mean and σ is the standard deviation from the mean. Figure 3 shows 5th and 10th order of polynomial regression.

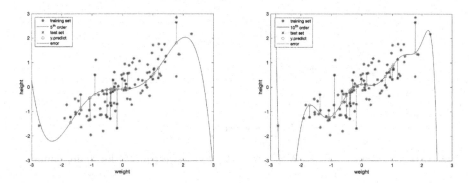

Fig. 3. 5th and 10th polynomial regression with standardized data

After 4-fold cross validation with training and test dataset, finding a model with the appropriate complexity for a dataset requires finding a balance between bias and variance. Complexity is varied by using model selection algorithm that range in model order from 1(least complex) to 12(most complex). We then calculate and display the squared bias, variance, and test set error for each of the estimators.

As the model complexity increases, the estimator variance (magenta curve) gradually increases. Additionally, as model complexity increases, the squared bias (red curve) decreases. Thus there is a tradeoff between bias and variance that comes with model complexity. The best model will have both low bias and low variance. In this Fig. 4, we notice the best estimator in terms of the intersection. The best estimator corresponds to a polynomial model of order of 4.

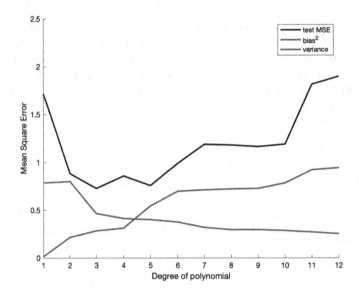

Fig. 4. Bias, variance and test MSE with HE Model selection (Color figure online)

5 Conclusion

In this paper, we introduced methods for constructing HE of Model selection and evaluated our algorithm with its application. Model selection methods are an essential tool for data analysis, especially for big datasets involving many predictors. Although we use only one feature as independent variable and we'll expand number of features to find optimized model complexity in further research. There still remains a variety of tasks that involve secure data outsourcing of cloud computing services. On the basis of our fundamental operations and the models, we will develop furthermore various machine learning methods under FHE in the future to solve the tasks.

References

1. Chillotti, I., Gama, N., Georgieva, M., Izabachène, M.: Faster fully homomorphic encryption: bootstrapping in less than 0.1 seconds. In: Cheon, J.H., Takagi, T. (eds.) ASIACRYPT 2016. LNCS, vol. 10031, pp. 3–33. Springer, Heidelberg (2016). https://doi.org/10.1007/978-3-662-53887-6_1
2. Chillotti, I., Gama, N., Georgieva, M., Izabachene, M.: Improving TFHE: faster packed homomorphic operations and e cient circuit bootstrapping. Cryptology ePrint Archive (2017)
3. Rivest, R.L., Adleman, L., Dertouzos, M.L.: On data banks and privacy homomorphisms. Found. Sec. Comput. **4**(11), 169–180 (1978)
4. Gentry, C., et al.: Fully homomorphic encryption using ideal lattices, vol. 9, pp. 169–178 (2009)
5. TFHE. https://tfhe.github.io/tfhe/. Accessed 15 Aug 2017
6. DasGupta, D.: In-place matrix inversion by modified Gauss-Jordan algorithm. Appl. Math. **4**(10), 1392–1396 (2013)

Timed-Release Encryption with Master Time Bound Key

Gwangbae Choi[(✉)] and Serge Vaudenay

LASEC - Security and Cryptography Laboratory,
Ecole Polytechnique Fédérale de Lausanne (EPFL), Lausanne, Switzerland
{gwangbae.choi,serge.vaudenay}@epfl.ch

Abstract. Timed-release encryption allows senders to send a message to a receiver which cannot decrypt until a server releases a time bound key at the release time. The release time usually supposed to be known to the receiver, the ciphertext therefore cannot be decrypted if the release time is lost. We solve this problem in this paper by having a master time bound key which can replace the time bound key of any release time. We first present security models of the timed-release encryption with master time bound key. We present a provably secure construction based on the Weil pairing.

Keywords: Timed-release encryption · Weil pairing · Bilinear Diffie-Hellman problem

1 Introduction

The concept of timed-release encryption was first proposed by May [16]. The idea is to introduce the concept of time into an encryption scheme, especially into the decryption algorithm. There are two distinct approaches. One is to focus on the amount of time it takes to decrypt and the other is to have a trusted server to unlock encryption in due time. As time is one of the important aspects in the real world, timed-release encryption can be used for several purposes [20] such as bidding in an auction, as a personal time capsule, key escrow, etc. It can also be used to store sensitive data which should not be accessible before some time.

The first category of timed-release encryptions uses time-lock puzzles [20], which involves heavy computation for the decryption. The second one involves a trusted server [3,6–8,10,13]. It requires a time bound key which is periodically released by the trusted server for the decryption.

The timed-release encryption with a time-lock puzzle was first introduced by Rivest et al. [20]. They showed that the approach which makes available only some part of the decryption key and makes a receiver to brute force the remaining part of the decryption key is not sufficient for the timed-release encryption because it is parallelizable, so it offers no guarantee of the amount of time required to decrypt. They proposed a construction based on a time-lock puzzle which requires some non-parallelizable sequential computations on a single

© Springer Nature Switzerland AG 2020
I. You (Ed.): WISA 2019, LNCS 11897, pp. 167–179, 2020.
https://doi.org/10.1007/978-3-030-39303-8_13

processor. Therefore, it has some guarantee that the receiver will spend at least some time doing sequential computations.

Timed-release encryption with a trusted server was first proposed by May [16] while introducing this concept. The first approach is to send a message and a release time to a trusted server who then transfers the message after the release time is passed. Then, Rivest et al. [20] proposed a construction in which the trusted server does not store any message but this scheme suffers from problems of anonymity and confidentiality. Di Crescenzo et al. [10] proposed a construction based on a conditional oblivious transfer which allows a sender to be anonymous. But the receiver cannot be anonymous and the trusted server is a subject to denial-of-service attack. Later, Blake and Chan [3] proposed a construction based on the identity-based encryption scheme by Boneh and Franklin [5] in which the trusted server interacts with neither the sender nor the receiver. As Blake and Chan did not provide any security notion, Cathalo et al. [6] proposed its security notions and improved its construction. Based on the construction of Blake and Chan, Hwang et al. [13] proposed a construction with pre-open capability which allows a receiver to decrypt before the release time by using the pre-open key. As security analysis of this construction was not sufficient, Dent and Tang [11] introduced additional security models for the construction of Hwang et al. On the other hand, Cheon et al. [8] proposed a construction of authenticated timed-release encryption. Later, Chalkias et al. proposed a more efficient timed-release encryption scheme [7]. In 2009, Nakai et al. [18] proposed a generic construction of the timed-release encryption with pre-open capability by using an identity-based encryption and a public key encryption. Their generic construction was improved by Matsuda et al. [15] in terms of efficiency. In 2010, Paterson et al. [19] proposed the time-specific encryption paradigm. In time-specific encryption, a ciphertext can only be decrypted during a chosen time interval rather than after a chosen time. Therefore, the time-specific encryption can be seen as the generalization of the timed-release encryption. Later, Kasamatsu et al. [14] showed how the time-specific encryption can be derived from forward-secure encryption.

The first approach does not require any trusted server, but the sender does not have the full control on the release time of the encrypted message since it depends on the computational power of the receiver and the time it started to decrypt. With the second approach, the release time can be fully controlled by the sender since it requires a time bound key which will be released by the trusted server at the release time. However, for the protocol to work, it is necessary to include a trusted server and thus it may lead to security vulnerabilities due to the addition of another participant in the protocol.

In this paper, we focus on the second approach and we will study another potential problem which did not consider in previous works. In the previous works, the release time was usually somehow known to the receiver and the receiver could execute the decryption algorithm with the time bound key of the corresponding release time. Then, what happens if the receiver loses the release time? The receiver obviously cannot deduce which time bound key should be used for the decryption. The receiver therefore cannot correctly decrypt the ciphertext since the time bound key of the release time is required for the decryption.

There already exist some easy ways to solve this problem. The sender for example can store the release time after the encryption, and sends it again to the receiver when the receiver asks the release time. This approach however cannot be an actual solution of the problem since an intuitive goal of timed-release encryption is to send a message for the time period when the sender and the receiver do not communicate. Another approach which does not require any communication between the sender and the receiver is to make the receiver to decrypt with all time bound keys. This solution however requires too much computation, compare to the normal decryption, and the receiver requires a way to check the correctness of the decrypted message.

The constructions with pre-open capability [13] might be a solution for the problem of losing the release time by giving the pre-open key which allows the decryption without the time bound key. The sender however needs to know the release time of the ciphertext to generate the corresponding pre-open key, it is equivalent to store the release time on the sender side. If the sender is storing the release time of the ciphertext, the sender can simply resend the release time to the receiver. The problem therefore becomes trivial. We hence consider the case neither the sender nor the receiver knows the release time.

Our Contributions and Structure

In this paper, we propose a better solution on this problem. We introduce a master time bound key which can be used as a valid time bound key for any release time. The receiver therefore can ask to the trusted server to decrypt a ciphertext of an unknown release time. This however can raise another problem with confidentiality of the message if the receiver needs to send the entire ciphertext to the trusted server for the decryption with master time bound time bound key. Our solution also solves this problem. A ciphertext of our construction consists of three elements. The receiver needs to send a single element to the trusted server to do the computation with master time bound key. Since this element is independent from the message, the trusted server cannot learn anything about the message.

The master time bound key moreover can be used when the trusted server terminates its service. Since a time bound key of the release time is needed for the decryption, the ciphertext whose release time is after the termination of the trusted server can never be decrypted. If it is more important not to lose the message than being decrypted before its release time, the trusted server needs to reveal its secret key or all future time bound keys to make the users able to decrypt their ciphertexts. If the trusted server reveals its secret key, receivers must implement another decryption algorithm which decrypts with the trusted server secret key instead of a time bound key. If the trusted server generates all future time bound keys (and possibly encrypt them with a timed-release encryption of another server), there might have a problem with the storage complexity if the amount of remaining time periods is huge. All of these solutions therefore require some additional works. However, if the trusted server has the master time bound key, it is enough if the trusted server releases the master time bound key at the end of its service. Moreover, the storage overhead is minimized since the size of master time bound key is equal to the size of time bound key.

Finally, our master time bound key can play the role of a backup solution to decrypt messages in emergency situations (e.g. sudden disappear of the trusted server).

In this paper, we propose a timed-release encryption scheme which has the master time bound key that can be used to decrypt a ciphertext of any time period. In Sect. 2, we show the notions that we will use in this paper. In Sect. 3, we define primitives of timed-release encryption. In Sect. 4, we propose a construction of timed-release encryption scheme with master time bound key.

2   Preliminaries

We denote a concatenation of two bit strings a and b as $a||b$ and an empty input or output by $\perp$. We write $x \xleftarrow{\$} G$ if x is uniformly chosen from a set G. We denote an empty string or algorithm by ε. For any probabilistic algorithm $f(x)$, we denote an instance of the algorithm $f(x)$ with a sequence of random coins γ as $f(x;\gamma)$. For any g in some group G, a subgroup generated by g is written as $\langle g \rangle$. Let $X : \Omega \to S$ and $Y : \Omega \to S$ be two random variables. Then, the statistical distance between two random variables X and Y is $d(X,Y) = \frac{1}{2}\sum_{s\in S}|\Pr[X = s] - \Pr[Y = s]|$. We denote the uniform distribution over a set G by $\mathcal{U}_G$.

Definition 1 (Weil pairing [21, III.8.1]). *Let K be a finite field and E be an elliptic curve over K. The Weil pairing $e : E[m] \times E[m] \longrightarrow \mu_m$, where $E[m]$ is m-torsion subgroup of E and μ_m is m-th roots of unity in the algebraic closure $\bar{K}$, satisfies the following properties.*

1. *Bilinear: $\forall P_1, P_2, Q_1, Q_2 \in E[m]$, $e(P_1 + P_2, Q_1) = e(P_1,Q_1)e(P_2,Q_1)$ and $e(P_1, Q_1 + Q_2) = e(P_1,Q_1)e(P_1,Q_2)$.*
2. *Non-degenerate: $\forall P \in E[m], \exists Q \in E[m]$ such that $e(P,Q) \neq 1$.*
3. *Alternating: $\forall P \in E[m], e(P,P) = 1$.*
4. *Galois invariant: $\forall \sigma \in G_{\bar{K}/K}, e(P^\sigma, Q^\sigma) = e(P,Q)^\sigma$.*

We note that the Weil pairing can be efficiently computed by the Miller's algorithm [17].

Definition 2 (Decisional bilinear Diffie-Hellman problem [5]). *Let $\mathsf{Gen}(1^\lambda) = \pi = (\lambda, K, E, m, e)$ be an algorithm which generates appropriate instance of the decisional bilinear Diffie-Hellman problem, given the security parameter λ, where K is a field, E is an elliptic curve over K, and $e : E[m] \times E[m] \longrightarrow \mu_m$ is a bilinear map.*

We say that the decisional bilinear Diffie-Hellman problem is hard for Gen if

$$Adv_{\mathcal{A}}^{DBDH}(\lambda) = \left| \Pr\left[DBDH\text{-}0_{\mathsf{Gen}}^{\mathcal{A}}(\lambda) = 1 \right] - \Pr\left[DBDH\text{-}1_{\mathsf{Gen}}^{\mathcal{A}}(\lambda) = 1 \right] \right|$$

is a negligible function in λ for all probabilistic and polynomial time algorithm $\mathcal{A}$ where DBDH-d is defined as follows for $d \in \{0, 1\}$.

Game: $DBDH\text{-}d^{\mathcal{A}}_{\mathsf{Gen}}(\lambda)$

1 $\pi \leftarrow \mathsf{Gen}(1^{\lambda})$

2 $(a_0, b_0, c_0) \xleftarrow{\$} \mathbb{Z}^3_m$

3 $(a_1, b_1, c_1) \xleftarrow{\$} \mathbb{Z}^3_m$

4 $(P, Q) \xleftarrow{\$} E[m] \times E[m]$

5 $d' \leftarrow \mathcal{A}(\pi, P, Q, a_0 P, b_0 P, c_0 P, a_0 Q, b_0 Q, c_0 Q, e(P, Q)^{a_d b_d c_d})$

6 **return** d'

3 Primitives of Timed-Release Encryption with Master Time Bound Key

In this section, we formally define the primitives of timed-release encryption with master time bound key. Our primitives are similar to the primitives in literatures [3,6,8,11,13]. The difference however is the key generation algorithm of the trusted server outputs the master time bound key along with the secret key and the public key.

Let S be a sender, R be a receiver and TS be a trusted server. We define a timed-release encryption scheme with master time bound key as follows:

Definition 3 (Timed-release encryption scheme with master time bound key). *A timed-release encryption scheme consists of the following algorithms:*

- Setup$(1^{\lambda}) = \pi$ *is a probabilistic polynomial time algorithm which generates a system parameter π given a security parameter λ.*
- KeyGen$_{TS}(\pi) = (sk_{TS}, pk_{TS}, mk_{TS})$ *is a probabilistic polynomial time algorithm of the trusted server TS which takes a system parameter π, and generates a secret key sk_{TS}, a public key of the trusted server pk_{TS} and a master time bound key mk_{TS}.*
- KeyGen$_R(\pi) = (sk_R, pk_R)$ *is a probabilistic polynomial time algorithm of the receiver R which takes a system parameter π, and generates a secret key sk_R and a public key of the receiver pk_R.*
- Broadcast$(sk_{TS}, t, \pi) = \tau_t$ *is a probabilistic polynomial time algorithm of the trusted server TS which takes a secret key of the trusted server pk_{TS}, scheduled broadcast time t and a system parameter π, and broadcasts time bound key τ_t.*
- Enc$(pk_{TS}, pk_R, m, t, \pi) = c$ *is a probabilistic polynomial time algorithm of the sender S which takes a trusted server public key pk_{TS}, a receiver public key pk_R, a message m, release time t, and a system parameter π, and outputs a ciphertext c.*
- Dec$(sk_R, \tau_t, c, \pi) = m$ *is a deterministic polynomial time algorithm of the receiver R which takes a receiver secret key sk_R, a time bound key at the*

release time t τ_t, a ciphertext c, and a system parameter π, and outputs a message m or $\perp$.

Then, we expect a timed-release encryption scheme to satisfy the following condition:

- *For any security parameter λ, for any system parameter π = Setup(1^λ), for any trusted server key pair $(sk_{TS}, pk_{TS}, mk_{TS})$ = KeyGen$_{TS}(\pi)$, for any receiver key pair (sk_R, pk_R) = KeyGen$_R(\pi)$, for any message m and for any time period t,*

$$\Pr_{\gamma_1, \gamma_2} \left[\text{Dec}(sk_R, \text{Broadcast}(sk_{TS}, t, \pi; \gamma_1), \text{Enc}(pk_{TS}, pk_R, m, t, \pi; \gamma_2), \pi) = m \right] = 1$$

and

$$\Pr_{\gamma} \left[\text{Dec}(sk_R, mk_{TS}, \text{Enc}(pk_{TS}, pk_R, m, t, \pi; \gamma), \pi) = m \right] = 1$$

The key generation algorithm of the receiver KeyGen$_R$ sometimes takes the trusted server public key pk_{TS} as input. We however define our KeyGen$_R$ to be independent from pk_{TS} as it was done in some constructions [15, 18]. If KeyGen$_R$ is dependent to pk_{TS}, the receiver needs to get the trusted server public key before the generation of its key pair. If they are independent, the receiver does not need any communication with the trusted server before the release time, it will be therefore more efficient.

The timed-release encryption has two security objectives. One is the confidentiality of the message until its release time against the receiver. The other is the anonymity of the sender and the receiver against the trusted server.

4   Construction with Master Time Bound Key

In this section, we propose a timed-release encryption scheme TRE which has the master time bound key. In addition, our construction does not require KeyGen$_R$ to be dependent to pk_{TS} and a hash function which maps to a point on the elliptic curve. Let h_κ be a collision-resistant hash function from $K^* \times E[q]$ to a set F, $\mathcal{E}$ be an asymmetric encryption scheme which consists of (KeyGen, Enc, Dec) with plaintext space $K \times F$, and f_π be a pseudorandom generator from μ_q to K, i.e. for $\omega \in \mu_q$ uniformly distributed, $f_\pi(\omega)$ is computationally indistinguishable from the uniform distribution over K. Then, our construction with plaintext space K^* is as follows. We note that our Broadcast is similar to KeyGen of the identity-based encryption scheme of Boneh and Boyen [4], which generates the secret key of a user which can be used to compute the inverse of the random value which is multiplied to the message, and TS-release of the timed-release encryption scheme of Cathalo et al. [6], which computes $g^{-(s+H(t))}$ where s is the secret key, $H(t)$ is the hash of a time period t and g is a generator of a group.

- **TRE.Setup(1^λ):** Pick two prime numbers p and q such that $q|(p \pm 1)$. Pick the finite field $K = \mathbb{F}_{p^2}$ and a supersingular elliptic curve $E(K)$ of cardinality $(p \pm 1)^2$. Then, compute q-torsion subgroup $E[q]$ and the Weil pairing $e : E[q] \times E[q] \longrightarrow \mu_q$ where μ_q is the group of q-th roots of unity in K. Pick κ from the key space of h and output $\pi = (\lambda, K, E, q, e, \kappa)$.

– TRE.KeyGen$_{\text{TS}}(\pi)$: Pick P and Q from $E[q]$ such that $|\langle P \rangle| = |\langle Q \rangle| = q$ and $P \notin \langle Q \rangle$, and pick a, b, c, d uniformly from $\mathbb{Z}_q^*$ until $\langle(1, a)\rangle$, $\langle(b, 1)\rangle$ and $\langle(c, d)\rangle$ are distinct subgroups of $\mathbb{Z}_q \times \mathbb{Z}_q$. Then, compute

$$mk_{\text{TS}} = (1 - ab)(bd - c)^{-1}(bP + Q),$$
$$sk_{\text{TS}} = (a, b, c, d, P, Q)$$

and

$$pk_{\text{TS}} = (pk_{\text{TS}}^{(0)}, pk_{\text{TS}}^{(1)}, pk_{\text{TS}}^{(2)}) = (P + aQ, bP + Q, cP + dQ),$$

and output sk_{TS}, pk_{TS} and mk_{TS}.

Property 1. $e(P, P) = e(Q, Q) = 1$, $e(P, Q)e(Q, P) = 1$ and $e(P, Q) \neq 1$. (See the proof below.)

Property 2. $e(pk_{\text{TS}}^{(0)}, pk_{\text{TS}}^{(1)}) = e(P, Q)^{1-ab} \neq 1$ because $\langle(1, a)\rangle$ and $\langle(b, 1)\rangle$ are distinct subgroups of $\mathbb{Z}_q \times \mathbb{Z}_q$.

– TRE.KeyGen$_{\text{R}}(1^\lambda)$: Generate a pair of secret and public keys (sk, pk) by calling $\mathcal{E}$.KeyGen(1^λ). Then, output $sk_{\text{R}} = sk$ and $pk_{\text{R}} = pk$.
– TRE.Broadcast(sk_{TS}, t, π): Pick s uniformly from $\mathbb{Z}_q^*$. Compute

$$\tau_t = \begin{cases} sP + (ab - 1)(c + bt)^{-1}Q, & \text{if } t = -d \\ (1 - ab)(d + t)^{-1}P + sQ, & \text{if } t = -cb^{-1} \\ s(d + t)^{-1}P + (s + ab - 1)(c + bt)^{-1}Q, & \text{otherwise.} \end{cases}$$

Property 3. $e(\tau_t, t \cdot pk_{\text{TS}}^{(1)} + pk_{\text{TS}}^{(2)}) = e(mk_{\text{TS}}, t \cdot pk_{\text{TS}}^{(1)} + pk_{\text{TS}}^{(2)}) = e(P, Q)^{1-ab}$ (See the proof below.)

– TRE.Enc$(pk_{\text{TS}}, pk_{\text{R}}, m, t, \pi)$: Output $\perp$ if $m \notin K^*$. Pick r_1 uniformly from $\mathbb{Z}_q^*$ and pick r_2 uniformly from K^*. Then, compute

$$ct_0 = m \cdot r_2,$$
$$ct_1 = r_1 t \cdot pk_{\text{TS}}^{(1)} + r_1 \cdot pk_{\text{TS}}^{(2)},$$
$$ct_2 = \mathcal{E}.\text{Enc}(pk_{\text{R}}, (r_2 + f_\pi(e(pk_{\text{TS}}^{(0)}, pk_{\text{TS}}^{(1)})^{r_1}), h_\kappa(ct_0, ct_1)))$$

and output $ct = (ct_0, ct_1, ct_2)$.

Property 4. $e(\tau_t, ct_1) = e(pk_{\text{TS}}^{(0)}, pk_{\text{TS}}^{(1)})^{r_1}$

– TRE.Dec$(sk_{\text{R}}, \tau_t, ct, \pi)$: Compute

$$(r_2', \sigma) = \mathcal{E}.\text{Dec}(sk_{\text{R}}, ct_2).$$

Output

$$m = ct_0 \cdot (r_2' - f_\pi(e(\tau_t, ct_1)))^{-1}$$

if $\sigma = h_\kappa(ct_0, ct_1)$, and output $\perp$ otherwise.

Proof of Property 1. $e(P,P) = e(Q,Q) = e(P+Q, P+Q) = 1$ comes from the alternating property of the Weil pairing. Hence, $1 = e(P+Q, P+Q) = e(P,Q)e(Q,P)$ due to bilinearity. Now, assume that there exists $P, Q \in E[q] \backslash \{O\}$ such that $P \notin \langle Q \rangle$ and $e(P,Q) = 1$. Then, we have $e(P, \alpha P + \beta Q) = e(P,Q)^{\beta} = 1$ for any $\alpha, \beta \in \mathbb{Z}_q$. Since q is prime, $\{\alpha P + \beta Q : \alpha, \beta \in \mathbb{Z}_q\} = E[q]$. Hence, it contradicts non-degeneracy, and such P and Q do not exist. Consequently, $e(P,Q) \neq 1$ and $e(P,Q)^{-1} = e(Q,P)$.   □

Proof of Property 3. When $t \neq -d$ and $t \neq -cb^{-1}$, we have

$$
\begin{aligned}
&e(\tau_t, t \cdot pk_{\mathrm{TS}}^{(1)} + pk_{\mathrm{TS}}^{(2)}) \\
&= e(s(d+t)^{-1}P + (s+ab-1)(c+bt)^{-1}Q, (c+bt)P + (d+t)Q) \\
&= e(s(d+t)^{-1}P, (d+t)Q)e((s+ab-1)(c+bt)^{-1}Q, (c+bt)P) \\
&= e(P,Q)^s e(Q,P)^{s+ab-1} \\
&= e(P,Q)^{1-ab}.
\end{aligned}
$$

When $t = -d$, we have

$$
\begin{aligned}
e(\tau_t, t \cdot pk_{\mathrm{TS}}^{(1)} + pk_{\mathrm{TS}}^{(2)}) &= e(sP + (ab-1)(c+bt)^{-1}Q, (c+bt)P) \\
&= e(P,Q)^{1-ab}.
\end{aligned}
$$

Similarly, when $t = -cb^{-1}$, we have

$$
\begin{aligned}
e(\tau_t, t \cdot pk_{\mathrm{TS}}^{(1)} + pk_{\mathrm{TS}}^{(2)}) &= e((1-ab)(d+t)^{-1}P + sQ, (d+t)Q) \\
&= e(P,Q)^{1-ab}.
\end{aligned}
$$

With mk_{TS}, we can also obtain same result regardless of t.

$$
\begin{aligned}
&e(mk_{\mathrm{TS}}, t \cdot pk_{\mathrm{TS}}^{(1)} + pk_{\mathrm{TS}}^{(2)}) \\
&= e((1-ab)(bd-c)^{-1}(bP+Q), (c+bt)P + (d+t)Q) \\
&= e((1-ab)(bd-c)^{-1}bP, (d+t)Q)e((1-ab)(bd-c)^{-1}Q, (c+bt)P) \\
&= e(P,Q)^{(1-ab)(bd-c)^{-1}(b(d+t)-c-bt)} \\
&= e(P,Q)^{1-ab}.
\end{aligned}
$$

□

By the choice of parameters, the q-th torsion subgroup $E[q]$ is a proper subset of E over K. Since $E[q] \cong \mathbb{Z}_q \times \mathbb{Z}_q$ [21], there exist $q+1$ distinct subgroups of order q in $E[q]$ and every element in $E[q] \backslash \{O\}$ generates a subgroup of order q. Therefore, we can deduce that $e(P,Q) = 1 \Longleftrightarrow P \in \langle Q \rangle$ for all $P, Q \in E[q]$. Hence, in TRE.KeyGen$_{\mathrm{TS}}$, $|\langle P \rangle| = |\langle Q \rangle| = q$ always holds and $P \notin \langle Q \rangle$ holds with probability of $\frac{q}{q+1}$ for any P and Q randomly chosen from $E[q]$, and $P \notin \langle Q \rangle$ can be easily verified by checking if $e(P,Q)$ is not equal to 1.

Assume that $\mathcal{E}.\mathsf{Dec}(sk, \mathcal{E}.\mathsf{Enc}(pk, m)) = m$ always holds for any message m and key pair (sk, pk) generated by using $\mathcal{E}.\mathsf{KeyGen}$ with some random coin. Then,

TRE.Dec is correct if $e(pk_{\text{TS}}^{(0)}, pk_{\text{TS}}^{(1)})^{r_1} = e(\tau_t, ct_1)$. From the choice of keys, we have

$$
\begin{aligned}
e(pk_{\text{TS}}^{(0)}, pk_{\text{TS}}^{(1)})^{r_1} &= e(P + aQ, bP + Q)^{r_1} \\
&= e(P, bP + Q)^{r_1} e(aQ, bP + Q)^{r_1} \\
&= e(P, bP)^{r_1} e(P, Q)^{r_1} e(aQ, bP)^{r_1} e(aQ, Q)^{r_1} \\
&= e(P, Q)^{r_1(1-ab)}.
\end{aligned}
$$

Since $ct_1 = r_1(t \cdot pk_{\text{TS}}^{(1)} + pk_{\text{TS}}^{(2)})$, the decryption is always correct.

4.1   Security Analysis

In this section, we will show the following results:

- Indistinguishability under chosen plaintext attacks (IND-CPA security) of $\mathcal{E}$ implies indsitinguishability under chosen plaintext attacks of trusted server[1] (IND-TS-CPA security) of TRE. This security does not depend on h_κ which could be set to a constant function;
- Indistinguishability under chosen ciphertext attacks (IND-CCA security) of $\mathcal{E}$ and the collision-resistance of h_κ imply indistinguishability under chosen ciphertext attacks of trusted server[1] (IND-TS-CCA security) of TRE;
- Hardness of the decisional bilinear Diffie-Hellman problem and the PRG property of f_π imply indistinguishability under chosen plaintext attacks of receiver for a selected release time[2] (IND-R-ST-CPA security) of TRE.

The detailed security definitions and the proofs of following theorems can be found from the full version of the paper [9].

Theorem 1 (IND-TS-CPA security). *Let $\mathcal{A}$ be an IND-TS-CPA adversary against TRE which runs in time η with advantage δ. Then, there exists an IND-CPA adversary $\mathcal{B}$ against $\mathcal{E}$. The advantage of $\mathcal{B}$ is at least δ and its time complexity is $\eta + \eta_e + \eta_{f_\pi}$ where η_e is the time to evaluate the pairing $e(\cdot, \cdot)$, η_e is the time to evaluate the pairing $e(\cdot, \cdot)$ and η_{f_π} is the evaluation time of f_π.*

Theorem 2 (IND-TS-CCA security). *Let $\mathcal{A}$ be an IND-TS-CCA adversary against TRE which runs in time η with advantage δ. Then, there exist an IND-CCA adversary $\mathcal{B}$ against $\mathcal{E}$ and a collision adversary $\mathcal{C}$ against h_κ. The advantage of adversary $\mathcal{B}$ is at least $\delta - \delta_{h_\kappa}$ and its time complexity is $\eta + \eta_e + \eta_{f_\pi} + \eta_{h_\kappa}$ where η_e is the time to evaluate the pairing $e(\cdot, \cdot)$, η_e is the time to evaluate the pairing $e(\cdot, \cdot)$, η_{f_π} is the evaluation time of f_π, η_{h_κ} is the evaluation time of h_κ and δ_{h_κ} is the advantage of $\mathcal{C}$.*

---

[1] An adversary can select pk_{TS}.

[2] An adversary needs to declare a release time that it wants to attack before getting any public key and can selects pk_{R}.

Theorem 3 (IND-R-ST-CPA security). *Let $\mathcal{A}$ be an IND-R-ST-CPA adversary against* TRE *which runs in time η with advantage δ. Then, there exist an algorithm $\mathcal{B}$ which solves the decisional bilinear Diffie-Hellman problem and a distinguisher $\mathcal{D}$ between $f_\pi(\mathcal{U}_{\mu_q})$ and $\mathcal{U}_K$. The advantage of $\mathcal{B}$ is at least $\delta - 3/q - \delta_{f_\pi}$ and its time complexity is $\eta + 3\eta_e + \eta_{\mathcal{E}.\mathsf{Enc}}$ where δ_{f_π} is the advantage of $\mathcal{D}$, η_e is the time to evaluate the pairing $e(\cdot, \cdot)$, and $\eta_{\mathcal{E}.\mathsf{Enc}}$ is the execution time of $\mathcal{E}.\mathsf{Enc}$.*

4.2 Decryption with Master Time Bound Key

The biggest difference between our construction and other constructions is the existence of the master time bound key. By using the master time bound key, a ciphertext of unknown release time can be decrypted. By our construction, a ciphertext consists of (ct_0, ct_1, ct_2). In order to decrypt a ciphertext, we need to compute $e(\tau_t, ct_1)$ should be computed. Due to Property 3, the master time bound key mk_{TS} can replace any time bound key. Indeed, the receiver only needs to ask the trusted server to compute $e(mk_{\mathrm{TS}}, ct_1)$ to decrypt the ciphertext. Since ct_1 is independent from the message, the trusted server cannot learn anything about the message while computing $e(mk_{\mathrm{TS}}, ct_1)$.

Similarly, the trusted server can terminate its service without any computational and storage overhead while preventing losing the encrypted data of users by revealing the master time bound key. Since the master time bound key can replace any time bound key, we do not need any extra algorithm for the decryption with mk_{TS}. This is an advantage for the trusted server as it does not need to provide any additional algorithm for the decryption with master time bound key.

On the other hand, the time bound key τ_t which is generated by TRE.Broadcast can be equal to the master time bound key mk_{TS} depending on the random value s. Therefore, the master time bound key can be broadcasted by the trusted server as a time bound key of a certain time period. However, it can happen with probability of at most $1/(q-1)$ where q is exponential in the security parameter λ, so it happens in negligible cases. The trusted server could also easily prevent this problem by comparing the time bound key with master time bound key before the broadcast.

4.3 Discussion

Since our construction uses an elliptic curve over an extension field $\mathbb{F}_{p^2}$, we first need to know what is the computational overhead compared to other constructions which work on $\mathbb{F}_p$. However, it is not easy to compare the exact overhead because some constructions [3,6–8,13] are based on the generic bilinear pairing, and some constructions [15,18] are based on the generic identity-based encryption. Therefore, their computational cost is dependent on the underlying bilinear pairing and the underlying identity-based encryption scheme. An identity-based encryption scheme is usually based on the bilinear pairing[3], and it always requires at least one evaluation of the bilinear pairing. One of most common instantiation of the bilinear pairing is to use the Weil pairing or the Tate pairing after applying a distortion map to one of two input points. Since the distortion map maps a point defined on the elliptic curve over a field $\mathbb{F}_p$ to $\mathbb{F}_{p^2}$, the computation of the Weil pairing or the Tate pairing is actually the computations on $\mathbb{F}_{p^2}$. Therefore, the asymptotic complexities of our construction and other constructions are similar as long as the bilinear pairing is the most complex computation.

Our construction can also be built on the top of generic bilinear pairings. Let G be an additive cyclic group, G_T be a multiplicative cyclic group, and $\hat{e} : G \times G \longrightarrow G_T$ be a bilinear pairing. If we define $P = (g, 0)$, $Q = (0, g)$ and $e(aP + bQ, cP + dQ) = e((ag, bg), (cg, dg)) = \hat{e}(ag, dg)\hat{e}(cg, bg)^{-1}$, we can obtain the same construction on the top of generic pairing. The computation of e however requires two evaluations of a generic bilinear pairing $\hat{e}$. As we mentioned in the previous paragraph, a generic bilinear pairing is usually instantiated with the Weil pairing or the Tate pairing. We therefore use the Weil pairing over $\mathbb{F}_{p^2}$ for the efficiency. We note that the construction with a generic pairing can be more efficient than our construction with the Weil pairing if one can instantiate a more efficient bilinear pairing.

In our construction, the encryption requires a single evaluation of the Weil pairing e. Since the encryption always requires to compute $e(pk_{\mathrm{TS}}^{(0)}, pk_{\mathrm{TS}}^{(1)})$, it can be precomputed by the trusted server and integrated into the trusted server public key. Therefore, we can make the encryption faster by replacing the trusted server public key pk_{TS} to $(e(pk_{\mathrm{TS}}^{(0)}, pk_{\mathrm{TS}}^{(1)}), pk_{\mathrm{TS}}^{(1)}, pk_{\mathrm{TS}}^{(2)})$.

5   Conclusion

In this paper, we proposed a timed-release encryption scheme which has the master time bound key. With master time bound key, a ciphertext can be decrypted even if the release time of the ciphertext is unknown. We also showed that our construction is IND-TS-CCA-secure and IND-R-ST-CPA-secure.

Acknowledgement. Gwangbae Choi is supported by the Swiss National Science Foundation (SNSF) Proejct funding no. 169110.

References

1. Agrawal, S., Boneh, D., Boyen, X.: Efficient lattice (H)IBE in the standard model. In: Gilbert, H. (ed.) EUROCRYPT 2010. LNCS, vol. 6110, pp. 553–572. Springer, Heidelberg (2010). https://doi.org/10.1007/978-3-642-13190-5_28
2. Agrawal, S., Boyen, X.: Identity-based encryption from lattices in the standard model. Manuscript, July 2009

---

[3] There also exist several identity-based encryption schemes which do not require a bilinear pairing [1,2,12], but we do not compare with them.

3. Blake, I.F., Chan, A.C.: Scalable, server-passive, user-anonymous timed release public key encryption from bilinear pairing. IACR Cryptology ePrint Archive (2004)

4. Boneh, D., Boyen, X.: Secure identity based encryption without random oracles. In: Franklin, M. (ed.) CRYPTO 2004. LNCS, vol. 3152, pp. 443–459. Springer, Heidelberg (2004). https://doi.org/10.1007/978-3-540-28628-8_27

5. Boneh, D., Franklin, M.K.: Identity-based encryption from the Weil pairing. SIAM J. Comput. **32**, 586–615 (2003)

6. Cathalo, J., Libert, B., Quisquater, J.-J.: Efficient and non-interactive timed-release encryption. In: Qing, S., Mao, W., López, J., Wang, G. (eds.) ICICS 2005. LNCS, vol. 3783, pp. 291–303. Springer, Heidelberg (2005). https://doi.org/10.1007/11602897_25

7. Chalkias, K., Hristu-Varsakelis, D., Stephanides, G.: Improved anonymous timed-release encryption. In: Biskup, J., López, J. (eds.) ESORICS 2007. LNCS, vol. 4734, pp. 311–326. Springer, Heidelberg (2007). https://doi.org/10.1007/978-3-540-74835-9_21

8. Cheon, J.H., Hopper, N., Kim, Y., Osipkov, I.: Timed-release and key-insulated public key encryption. In: Di Crescenzo, G., Rubin, A. (eds.) FC 2006. LNCS, vol. 4107, pp. 191–205. Springer, Heidelberg (2006). https://doi.org/10.1007/11889663_17

9. Choi, G., Vaudenay, S.: Timed-release encryption with master time bound key (full version). Cryptology ePrint Archive, Report 2019/904 (2019). https://eprint.iacr.org/2019/904

10. Di Crescenzo, G., Ostrovsky, R., Rajagopalan, S.: Conditional oblivious transfer and timed-release encryption. In: Stern, J. (ed.) EUROCRYPT 1999. LNCS, vol. 1592, pp. 74–89. Springer, Heidelberg (1999). https://doi.org/10.1007/3-540-48910-X_6

11. Dent, A.W., Tang, Q.: Revisiting the security model for timed-release encryption with pre-open capability. In: Garay, J.A., Lenstra, A.K., Mambo, M., Peralta, R. (eds.) ISC 2007. LNCS, vol. 4779, pp. 158–174. Springer, Heidelberg (2007). https://doi.org/10.1007/978-3-540-75496-1_11

12. Döttling, N., Garg, S.: Identity-based encryption from the Diffie-Hellman assumption. In: Katz, J., Shacham, H. (eds.) CRYPTO 2017. LNCS, vol. 10401, pp. 537–569. Springer, Cham (2017). https://doi.org/10.1007/978-3-319-63688-7_18

13. Hwang, Y.H., Yum, D.H., Lee, P.J.: Timed-release encryption with pre-open capability and its application to certified e-mail system. In: Zhou, J., Lopez, J., Deng, R.H., Bao, F. (eds.) ISC 2005. LNCS, vol. 3650, pp. 344–358. Springer, Heidelberg (2005). https://doi.org/10.1007/11556992_25

14. Kasamatsu, K., Matsuda, T., Emura, K., Attrapadung, N., Hanaoka, G., Imai, H.: Time-specific encryption from forward-secure encryption: generic and direct constructions. Int. J. Inf. Secur. **15**, 549–571 (2016)

15. Matsuda, T., Nakai, Y., Matsuura, K.: Efficient generic constructions of timed-release encryption with pre-open capability. In: Joye, M., Miyaji, A., Otsuka, A. (eds.) Pairing 2010. LNCS, vol. 6487, pp. 225–245. Springer, Heidelberg (2010). https://doi.org/10.1007/978-3-642-17455-1_15

16. May, T.C.: Timed-release crypto (1993). http://www.hks.net.cpunks/cpunks-0/1460.html

17. Miller, V., et al.: Short programs for functions on curves. Unpublished Manuscript 97 (1986)

18. Nakai, Y., Matsuda, T., Kitada, W., Matsuura, K.: A generic construction of timed-release encryption with pre-open capability. In: Takagi, T., Mambo, M. (eds.) IWSEC 2009. LNCS, vol. 5824, pp. 53–70. Springer, Heidelberg (2009). https://doi.org/10.1007/978-3-642-04846-3_5

19. Paterson, K.G., Quaglia, E.A.: Time-specific encryption. In: Garay, J.A., De Prisco, R. (eds.) SCN 2010. LNCS, vol. 6280, pp. 1–16. Springer, Heidelberg (2010). https://doi.org/10.1007/978-3-642-15317-4_1

20. Rivest, R.L., Shamir, A., Wagner, D.A.: Time-lock puzzles and timed-release crypto (1996)

21. Silverman, J.H.: The Arithmetic of Elliptic Curves, vol. 106. Springer, New York (2009). https://doi.org/10.1007/978-0-387-09494-6

Secret Sharing on Evolving Multi-level Access Structure

Sabyasachi Dutta[1]([✉]), Partha Sarathi Roy[2]([✉]), Kazuhide Fukushima[2], Shinsaku Kiyomoto[2], and Kouichi Sakurai[1]

[1] Faculty of Information Science and Electrical Engineering, Kyushu University, Fukuoka, Japan
saby.math@gmail.com, sakurai@inf.kyushu-u.ac.jp
[2] Information Security Laboratory, KDDI Research, Inc., Fujimino, Japan
{pa-roy,ka-fukushima,kiyomoto}@kddi-research.jp

Abstract. Secret sharing is a process that allows storing secret information in a distributed manner among several participants. In the original setting of secret sharing schemes, it was assumed that the total number of participants is fixed from the very beginning. However, to meet the state of the art needs, it is required to consider the scenario where any time a new participant can join and the total number of participants is (*possibly*) unbounded. Evolving secret sharing solves the problem. Secret sharing for evolving threshold access structure has been considered in the last few years. Here, we consider the Multi-level access structures. More specifically, we consider evolving compartmental and hierarchical access structures. We provide constructions with the estimation of share sizes.

Keywords: Evolving access structure · Compartmental access structure · Hierarchical access structure · Information theoretic security

1 Introduction

1.1 Background and Motivation

Secret sharing is a method to distribute a secret piece of information among n many parties so that any predefined "qualified" sets of parties can recover the secret information, whereas every predefined "unqualified" sets of parties do not get any information about the secret. Secret sharing schemes were proposed independently by Shamir [16] and Blakley [3] in 1979. The *monotone* collection of qualified sets of parties is called an *access structure*. Secret sharing was initiated on *threshold access structure*. More works on secret sharing can be found in [4,9, 10,18]. To address more practical needs, *compartmental* and *hierarchical* access structures are found to be very well fitted. Due to the potential applicability,

S. Dutta—Research is financially supported by National Institute of Information and Communications Technology (NICT), Japan under the NICT International Invitation Program.

hierarchical access structure has been studied extensively with the appearance of improved schemes or ones with additional functionality [2,6–8,14,15,18–21]. Recently, Shima and Doi [17] gave a scheme based on information dispersal technique. However, all the classical secret sharing schemes assume that the number of participants is fixed, as well as the access structure is well-defined beforehand. An access structure is called an *evolving* access structure if anyone (or both) of the above two presumptions fail to hold. So needless to say that the number of parties can be potentially infinite and existing classical methodology fails to provide a secret sharing scheme when the access structure is evolving.

1.2 Related Works

The classical secret sharing schemes assume that the number of participants and the access structure is known in advance. Komargodski, Naor and Yogev [11] introduced evolving secret sharing schemes where the dealer does not know in advance the number of participants that will participate, and moreover, there is no upper bound on their number. Thus, the number of participants could be potentially infinite and the access structure may change with time. Komargodski, Naor and Yogev [11] considered the scenario when participants come one by one and receive their share from the dealer; the dealer, however, cannot update the shares which have already been distributed. They showed that for every evolving access structure there exists a secret sharing scheme where the share size of the tth participant is 2^{t-1}. They also constructed (k, ∞)-threshold evolving secret sharing scheme for constant k in which the share size of the tth participant is $(k-1)\log t + \mathcal{O}(\log\log t)$. Furthermore, they have provided an evolving 2-threshold scheme which is nearly optimal in the share size of the tth participant viz. $\log t + \mathcal{O}(\log\log t)$.

The main technique that [11] used to significantly reduce the share size is introducing the concept of *generations*. Each generation consists of participants and the size of every generation grows exponentially with time. The sizes of generations are however prefixed depending on the threshold value k. Usage of Shamir secret sharing scheme helped to reduce share sizes exponentially.

Later, Komargodski and Paskin-Cherniavsky [12] applied the idea of evolving k-threshold schemes to evolving dynamic threshold schemes and provided a secret sharing scheme in which the share size of the tth participant is $\mathcal{O}(t^4 \log t)$ bits. Furthermore, they showed how to transform evolving threshold secret sharing schemes into robust schemes with the help of algebraic manipulation detection (AMD) codes [5]. Lastly, Beimel and Othman [1] considers the problem of ramp secret sharing for evolving threshold schemes and drastically reduced the share size to $\mathcal{O}(1)$. Beimel and Othman [1], defined evolving (a, b) ramp scheme as follows: Let $0 < b < a < 1$. Any set of participants whose maximum participant is the i-th participant and contains at least ai participants can reconstruct the secret; however, we also require that any set such that all its prefixes are not a b-fraction of the participants should not get any information on the secret.

Table 1. Comparative studies of share sizes

Scheme	Share size of tth participant
Compartmental access structure	
[11]	2^{t-1}
Proposed	$kt \cdot max\{l, \log(kt)\}$
Hierarchical access structure	
[11]	2^{t-1}
Construction-I	$(k_1 + k_2 + \cdots + k_m)t \cdot max\{l, \log(k_m t)\}$
Construction-II	$((k_1 + k_2 + \cdots + k_m)t - (m-1)) \cdot max\{l, \log(k_m t)\}$

k_i denotes the threshold of i-th compartment/level of compartmental/hierarchical access structure, respectively. $k = max\{k_1, k_2, \ldots, k_m\}$ & l is the length of secret.

1.3   Our Contribution

In this paper, we present the construction of secret sharing schemes for evolving compartmental and hierarchical access structures. In the case of hierarchical access structure, we present two schemes. The second one outperforms the first one in respect of share size. Moreover, we show that it is possible to have an ideal secret sharing scheme even with infinitely many parties.

Main challenge behind the constructions is to make compatible the concept of *generation* in case of multi-level access structures. We treat multi-level access structures as a combination of multiple threshold access structure to adopt the concept of *generation*.

1.4   Comparison with Existing Results

It is possible to realize evolving compartmental and hierarchical access structures by evolving general access structure of [11]. In Table 1, we have provided a comparative study between the proposed constructions and the construction of [11]. It is evident from the Table 1 that the proposed constructions reduce the share size exponentially in respect of [11].

2   Preliminaries

For a positive integer n the set $\{1, 2, \ldots, n\}$ is denoted by $[n]$. Let $\mathcal{P}_n = [n]$ be a set of n participants. Let $2^{\mathcal{P}_n}$ denote the power set of $\mathcal{P}_n$. A collection $\mathcal{A} \subset 2^{\mathcal{P}_n}$ is said to be *monotone* if $A \in \mathcal{A}$ and $A \subset B$ imply $B \in \mathcal{A}$.

Definition 1 *(Access structure).* $\mathcal{A} \subset 2^{\mathcal{P}_n}$ *is called a monotone access structure if the collection $\mathcal{A}$ is monotone. Any subset A of $\mathcal{P}_n$ which are in $\mathcal{A}$ are called qualified sets and $F \notin \mathcal{A}$ are called unqualified or forbidden.*

Definition 2 *(Threshold Access structure).* *Let $n \in \mathbb{N}$ and $0 < k \leq n$. A (k, n)-threshold access structure $\mathcal{A}$ on a participant set $[n]$ is defined by $\mathcal{A} = \{X \subset [n] : |X| \geq k\}$.*

We say that $\mathcal{P}_n$ is partitioned into m compartments $L_1, L_2, \ldots, L_m$ with $|L_i| = n_i$ for $i = 1, 2, \ldots, m$ if the following conditions hold:

- $\mathcal{P}_n = L_1 \cup \ldots \cup L_m$
- $L_i \cap L_j = \emptyset$ for all $i \neq j$.

Definition 3 (Compartmental Access Structure [4]). *The compartmental access structure $\mathcal{A}$ on $\mathcal{P}_n$ with disjoint compartments $L_1, L_2, \ldots L_m$ is defined as follows:*

$$\mathcal{A} = \{A \subseteq \mathcal{P} : |A \cap L_i| \geq k_i \text{ for } i = 1, 2, \ldots, m \land |A| = k \geq (\sum_{i=1}^{m} k_i)\}$$

Let us denote such an access structure explicitly as $\mathcal{A}(n, l, \{n_i\}, k, \{k_i\})$, or $\mathcal{A}$ in short.

We now give the definition of disjunctive hierarchical access structure [19] on a set $\mathcal{P}_n$ of n participants.

Definition 4 (Hierarchical Access Structure [19]). *Let a set of participants $\mathcal{P}_n = [n]$ be composed of m disjoint levels $\mathcal{L}_1, \mathcal{L}_2, \ldots, \mathcal{L}_m$ such that $\mathcal{P} = \cup_{i=1}^{m} \mathcal{L}_i$, where $\mathcal{L}_i \cap \mathcal{L}_j = \emptyset$ for all $1 \leq i \neq j \leq l$. With each level $\mathcal{L}_i$ a positive integer (threshold) k_i is associated such that $k_1 < k_2 < \cdots < k_m$ and $|\mathcal{L}_i| = n_i \geq k_i$. A disjunctive hierarchical access structure, denoted by $\bigsqcup_{i=1}^{l} (k_i, n_i)_{\mathcal{P}}$ is completely defined by the collection of minimal qualified sets $\mathcal{Q}_{min} \subset 2^{\mathcal{P}}$ where $U \in \mathcal{Q}_{min}$ means either*

- U contains exactly k_j members from $\mathcal{L}_j$ for some $1 \leq j \leq m$ or
- *if $j = max\{i : U \cap \mathcal{L}_i \neq \emptyset\}$ then U contains precisely k_j many members from $\cup_{i=1}^{j} \mathcal{L}_i$ such that for every c, $1 \leq c \leq j - 1$, $|U \cap (\cup_{i=1}^{c} \mathcal{L}_i)| \leq k_c$.*

Any subset of participants that contains at least one minimal qualified set is a qualified set. Collection of qualified sets will be denoted with Γ.

We now define restriction of an access structure to its first $m < n$ parties which in essence describes the qualified sets formed by the parties in $[m]$ in $\mathcal{A}$.

Definition 5 *(Restriction of Access structure).* *Let $\mathcal{A}_n$ be an access structure on a set of n participants $\mathcal{P}_n = [n]$ and let $1 \leq m \leq n - 1$. The restriction of the given access structure to the first m participants, denoted by $\mathcal{A}_n|_m$, is defined to be the collection $\mathcal{A}_n|_m = \{X \in \mathcal{A}_n : \{m + 1, m + 2, \ldots, n\} \cap X = \emptyset\}$.*

If it is clear from the context that $\mathcal{A}_n$ is an access structure on the participant set $[n]$ then we drop the suffix n and simply write $\mathcal{A}$.

Definition 6 *(Evolving Access structure).* *An infinite sequence of access structures $\{\mathcal{A}_i\}_{i \in \mathbb{N}}$ is called an evolving access structure if:*

1. *for every $i \in \mathbb{N}$, $\mathcal{A}_i$ is an access structure over $[i]$.*
2. *for every $i \geq 2$, $\mathcal{A}_i|_{i-1} = \mathcal{A}_{i-1}$.*

2.1   Secret Sharing Scheme

In a secret sharing scheme there is a dealer who has a secret s, a set of parties $[n]$ and an access structure $\mathcal{A}$. The dealer shares the secret among the parties in such a way that any qualified set of parties can recover the secret but any unqualified set of parties has no information about the secret.

Definition 7 *(Secret Sharing Scheme).* *A secret sharing scheme $\mathcal{S}$ for an access structure $\mathcal{A}$ consists of a pair of algorithms* (ShareGen, Reconst). *ShareGen is a probabilistic algorithm that gets as input a secret s (from a domain of secrets S) and a number n, and generates n shares $\Pi_1^{(s)}, \Pi_2^{(s)}, \ldots, \Pi_n^{(s)}$. Reconst is a deterministic algorithm that gets as input the shares of a subset B of parties and outputs a string. The requirements for defining a secret sharing scheme are as follow:*

1. *(Correctness) For every secret $s \in S$ and every qualified set $B \in \mathcal{A}$, it must hold that $Pr[\text{Reconst}(\{\Pi_i^{(s)}\}_{i \in B}, B) = s] = 1$.*
2. *(Security) For every unqualified set $B \notin \mathcal{A}$ and for any two distinct secrets $s_1 \neq s_2$ in S, it must hold that the two distributions $\{\Pi_i^{(s_1)}\}_{i \in B}$ and $\{\Pi_i^{(s_2)}\}_{i \in B}$ are identical.*

The *share size* of a secret sharing scheme $\mathcal{S}$ is the maximum number of bits each party has to hold in the worst case over all parties and all secrets.

Definition 8. *A secret sharing scheme is said to be ideal if its share size is equal to the secret size.*

Definition 9 *(Evolving Secret Sharing Scheme).* *Let $\mathcal{A} = \{\mathcal{A}_t\}_{t \in \mathbb{N}}$ be an evolving access structure. A secret sharing scheme $\mathcal{S}$ for $\mathcal{A}$ consists of a pair of algorithms* (ShareGen, Reconst). *ShareGen is a probabilistic algorithm and Reconst is a deterministic algorithm which satisfy the following:*

1. *ShareGen$(s, \Pi_1^{(s)}, \Pi_2^{(s)}, \ldots, \Pi_{t-1}^{(s)})$ gets as input a secret s from the domain of secrets S and the secret shares of parties $1, 2, \ldots, t-1$ and outputs the share of the tth party viz. $\Pi_t^{(s)}$.*
2. *(Correctness) For every secret $s \in S$, every $t \in \mathbb{N}$ and every qualified set $B \in \mathcal{A}_t$, it must hold that $Pr[\text{Reconst}(\{\Pi_i^{(s)}\}_{i \in B}, B) = s] = 1$.*
3. *(Security) For every $t \in \mathbb{N}$ and every unqualified set $B \notin \mathcal{A}_t$ and for any two distinct secrets $s_1 \neq s_2$ in S, it must hold that the two distributions $\{\Pi_i^{(s_1)}\}_{i \in B}$ and $\{\Pi_i^{(s_2)}\}_{i \in B}$ are identical.*

2.2   Evolving Secret Sharing [11]

General Construction. The authors in [11] gave a construction of secret sharing scheme for evolving general access structure. Let $\{\mathcal{A}_t\}_{t \in \mathbb{N}}$ denote an evolving access structure and $\{f_t\}_{t \in \mathbb{N}}$ be the sequence of monotone characteristic functions for the evolving sequence of access structures. Each $f_t : \{0,1\}^t \longrightarrow \{0,1\}$.

Suppose $s \in \{0, 1\}$ be the secret bit that needs to be shared. At time t, just before the tth party arrives, the dealer maintains a list of bits $w_{(b_1,...,b_i)}$ for all $i \in [t-1]$ where each b_i is either 0 or 1.

1. If $f_1(1) = 1$, set $w_1 = s$
   otherwise, set w_1 a random bit.
2. for every $i \geq 1$; set $w_{(b_1,...,b_{i-1},0)} = 0$.
3. If $f_t(b_1, \ldots, b_{t-1}, 1) = 1$ and $f_{t-1}(b_1, \ldots, b_{t-1}) = 0$:
   set $w_{(b_1,...,b_{t-1},1)} = w_{(b_1,...,b_{t-1})} \oplus \cdots \oplus w_{(b_1)} \oplus s$.
4. If $f_t(b_1, \ldots, b_{t-1}, 1) = 1$ and $f_{t-1}(b_1, \ldots, b_{t-1}) = 0$:
   set $w_{(b_1,...,b_{t-1},1)} = 0$.
5. If $f_t(b_1, \ldots, b_{t-1}, 1) = 0$:
   set $w_{(b_1,...,b_{t-1},1)}$ a uniform random bit.

Theorem 1 (Theorem 3.1 of [11]). *For every general evolving access structure the above algorithm gives a secret sharing scheme where the share size of tth party is bounded above by 2^{t-1}.*

(k, ∞)**-Threshold Secret Sharing.** Each party, when it arrives, is assigned to a generation. Party $t \in \mathbb{N}$ is assigned to generation $g = \log_k t$. The generations are growing in size: For $g = 0, 1, 2, \cdots$ the g-th generation begins when the k^g-th party arrives. Therefore, the size of the g-th generation (i.e. the number of parties that are members of this generation), is $size(g) = k^{g+1} - k^g = (k-1).k^g$. Let $s \in \{0, 1\}^l$ be the secret. When a generation g begins the dealer remembers k^g l-bit strings s_A for all $A = (c_0, \cdots, c_{g-1}) \in \{0, \cdots, k\}^g$ (where if $g = 0$ it remembers only the secret). Intuitively, each such s_A is an l-bit string that we share to the parties in generation g assuming that in generation $i \in \{0, \cdots, g-1\}$ c_i parties arrived. We explain how the dealer sets the value of s_A for $A = (c_0, \cdots, c_g)$. Notation: let $s_{prev(A)} = s$ if $g = 0$ and $s_{prev(A)} = s_{(c_0,\cdots,c_{g-1})}$ otherwise.

1. If $c_g = 0$, set $s_A = s_{prev(A)}$ and HALT.
2. If $c_0 + \cdots + c_g < k$, then the dealer:
   a. samples $r_A \longleftarrow \{0, 1\}^l$ uniformly at random.
   b. sets $s_A = s_{prev(A)} \oplus r_A$.
   c. shares the l-bits r_A among the parties in the g-th generation using Shamir's $(c_g, size(g))$-threshold secret sharing scheme.
3. If $c_0 + \cdots + c_g = k$, then the dealer shares the l-bit string $s_{prev(A)}$ among the parties in the g-th generation using Shamir's $(c_g, size(g))$-threshold secret sharing scheme.

Theorem 2 (Lemma 5.2 of [11]). *For every $k, l \in \mathbb{N}$ the above algorithm gives a secret sharing scheme for the evolving (k, ∞) access structure and an l-bit secret in which for every $t \in \mathbb{N}$ the share size of the tth party is bounded by $kt \cdot max\{l, \log kt\}$.*

The authors [11] further improved upon the share-size by a recursive argument and the summary of their findings is as follows.

Theorem 3 (Theorem 5.1 of [11]). *For every* $k, l \in \mathbb{N}$ *the above algorithm gives a secret sharing scheme for the evolving* (k, ∞) *access structure and an* l-*bit secret in which for every* $t \in \mathbb{N}$ *the share size of the* t^{th} *party is bounded by* $(k-1)\log t + 6k^4 l \log\log t \cdot \log\log\log t + 7k^4 l \log k$.

3 Evolving Compartmental Access Structure

A scheme presented in Section 3.1 of [11] for general access structures can be applied to construct secret sharing scheme for evolving compartmental access structures. However, the share size of the tth participant is 2^{t-1}. We present an efficient construction based a scheme of [4]. Moreover, most interestingly, we show that it is possible to have ideal secret sharing scheme even with infinitely many parties for a certain type of compartmental access structure. Classification of all such evolving access structures is an interesting issue but we do not pursue the question here.

Suppose, there are m compartments, namely, $L_1, L_2, \ldots, L_m$. We maintain the same notations as in Definition 3. Let s be a l-bit secret to be shared. The access structure is *evolving* in the sense that arbitrary number of parties can join one by one. Every party will be assigned exactly one level out of these m many levels. We note that m (number of levels) and k_i (threshold values) remain constant. In the following Fig. 1 we describe the scheme.

- **Initial Set-up:** Suppose, there are m compartments, viz. $L_1, L_2, \ldots, L_m$. Let s be a $l-$bit secret to be shared.
- **Sharing Phase:**
  1. The Dealer $\mathcal{D}$ shares s using (m, m) secret sharing scheme, where the shares are $s_1, s_2, \ldots, s_m$ s.t. $s = s_1 \oplus \cdots \oplus s_m$.
  2. Each party $t \in \mathbb{N}$, when it arrives, is assigned to a compartment, say, L_i.
  3. The dealer $\mathcal{D}$ distributes the share to t according to the Evolving k_i- threshold access structure.
- **Reconstruction Phase:**
  1. A qualified set $A = \bigcup_{i=1}^{m} A_i$, where $|A_i| \geq k_i$, will broadcast their shares.
  2. A_i will reconstruct s_i according to the Evolving k_i- threshold scheme.
  3. Reconstruct $s = s_1 \oplus \cdots \oplus s_m$.

Fig. 1. Secret sharing scheme for evolving compartmental access structure.

The correctness of reconstruction follows from the two facts: (1) correctness of individual (k_i, ∞)-secret sharing schemes for $i = 1, 2, \ldots, m$ whence the s_i's are reconstructed and (2) from the correctness of (m, m)-secret sharing scheme. Moreover, the security of the scheme also follows from the securities of underlying individual (k_i, ∞)-schemes and the security of (m, m)-secret sharing scheme. We also note that the share size of tth party is solely determined by the compartment he is assigned. It is easy to see that the share size of tth participant is bounded above by $kt \cdot max\{l, \log(kt)\}$ where $k = max\{k_1, k_2, \ldots, k_m\}$. From the discussion we now have the following theorem.

Theorem 4. *There exists a secret sharing scheme for evolving compartmental access structure parameterized by m and threshold values $k_1, \ldots, k_m$ such that the share size of tth party is bounded above by $kt \cdot max\{l, \log(kt)\}$ where $k = max\{k_1, k_2, \ldots, k_m\}$ and l denotes the bit-length of the secret.*

Remark 1. We note that the share size of the above construction can be reduced exponentially by applying Theorem 3.

Ideal Secret Sharing on Evolving Access Structure. We note that it is possible to have ideal secret sharing scheme for a particular type of evolving compartmental access structure namely, the *star-graph* access structure (see Fig. 2). The vertex v_0 itself constitutes one compartment (essential compartment) and rest of the vertices belong to another fixed compartment (ordinary compartment). New parties join the ordinary compartment and the minimal qualified sets are of the form $\{v_0, v_i\}$ for any $i \geq 1$, which are shown as the edges of the graph. The shares of the scheme are generated by one-time running an ideal secret sharing scheme for $(2, 2)$-threshold access structure. One share is assigned to v_0 and the other share is copied and assigned to every new v_i for $i \geq 1$.

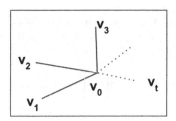

Fig. 2. Evolving star-graph access structure

4   Evolving Hierarchical Access Structure

Hierarchical access structure is defined in Definition 4. We consider *evolving*-ness of hierarchical access structure by allowing (possibly) infinitely many parties to join. But we keep the number of levels and corresponding threshold values fixed over time. Using a scheme of [11] for evolving general access structure we can have a secret sharing scheme for evolving hierarchical access structure with exponential share size. We give two constructions to reduce share sizes. The first construction is a direct construction and we improve our results in the second one.

Construction-I

The main idea of Construction-I is to view a participant belonging to i^{th} level L_i in $(m - i + 1)$ different ways - as a member of $L_1 \cup \ldots \cup L_i$ (with threshold value k_i) and as a member of $L_1 \cup \ldots \cup L_j$ (with threshold value k_j) for all $j = i + 1, \ldots, m$. Therefore, parties who belong to higher level has more shares to carry (Fig. 3).

- **Initial Setup:** Suppose, there are m levels, namely, $L_1, L_2, \ldots, L_m$, with threshold $k_1, k_2, \ldots, k_m$ s.t. $k_1 < k_2 < \ldots < k_m$. s is a l-bit secret to be shared.
- **Sharing Phase:**
  1. Each party $t \in \mathbb{N}$, when it arrives, is assigned to a level, say, L_i.
  2. The dealer $\mathcal{D}$ distributes the share to t according to the Evolving $k_i, k_{i+1}, \ldots, k_m$ threshold access structure, where $1 \le i \le m$.
- **Reconstruction Phase:**
  1. A minimal qualified set A will broadcast their shares in following manner:
  Case-I All the participants of A are from same level L_i.
     * Broadcast the share of Evolving k_i threshold access structure and reconstruct according to Evolving k_i threshold secret sharing scheme.
  Case-II Participants of A are from various level and the lowest level is L_j.
     * Broadcast the share of ShareGen(k_j, ∞) algorithm and reconstruct according to Reconst(k_j, ∞) algorithm.

Fig. 3. Construction-I: secret sharing scheme for evolving hierarchical access structure.

The correctness of reconstruction follows from the correctness of individual (k_i, ∞)-secret sharing schemes for $i = 1, 2, \ldots, m$. The security of the scheme also follows from the securities of underlying individual (k_i, ∞)-schemes. We also note that the share size of tth party is solely determined by the level he is assigned. It is easy to see that the share size of tth participant is bounded above by $(k_1 + k_2 + \cdots + k_m)t \cdot max\{l, \log(k_m t)\}$. From the discussion we now have the following theorem:

Theorem 5. *There exists secret sharing scheme for an evolving hierarchical access structure parameterized by number of levels m and the threshold values $k_1, \ldots, k_m$ with share size of tth party bounded by $(k_1 + \cdots + k_m)t \cdot max\{l, \log(k_m t)\}$, where l denotes the length of secret.*

Construction-II

Suppose, there are m levels, namely, $L_1, L_2, \ldots, L_m$, with threshold $k_1, k_2,$ $\ldots, k_m$ s.t. $k_1 < k_2 < \ldots < k_m$. s is a l-bit secret to be shared. Each party, when it arrives, is assigned to a generation and a level. Party $t \in \mathbb{N}$ is assigned to generation $g = \log_{k_m} t$ and in a level L_i. Here, we build upon the algorithm of Sect. 2.2 by using an IDEAL-HSS$(k_1, \ldots, k_m; (k-1)k^g)$, where IDEAL-HSS$(k_1, \ldots, k_m; (k-1)k^g)$ denotes an *ideal* Hierarchical Secret Sharing Scheme (e.g. [4,6,13]) with m levels among $(k-1)k^g$ participants where $k = k_m$. The details is given in the Construction-II (see, Fig. 4).

- **Initial Setup:** Suppose, there are m levels, namely, $L_1, L_2, \ldots, L_m$, with threshold $k_1, k_2, \ldots, k_m$ s.t. $k_1 < k_2 < \ldots < k_m$. s is a l-bit secret to be shared.
- **Sharing Phase:**
  1. If $c_g = 0$, set $s_A = s_{prev(A)}$ and HALT.
  2. If $c_0 + \cdots + c_g < k_i$, then the dealer:
     a. samples $r_A \longleftarrow \{0,1\}^l$ uniformly at random.
     b. sets $s_A = s_{prev(A)} \bigoplus r_A$.
     c. shares the l-bits r_A among the parties in the gth generation using Shamir's $(c_g, size(g))$-threshold secret sharing scheme.
  3. a. If $c_0 + \cdots + c_g = k_i$, where at least two c_i are non-zero, then the dealer shares the l-bit string $s_{prev(A)}$ among the parties in the gth generation using Shamir's $(c_g, size(g))$-threshold secret sharing scheme.
     b. If $c_0 + \cdots + c_g = k_i$, where only one c_i is non-zero, then the dealer shares the l-bit string $s_{prev(A)}$ among the parties in the gth generation using ShareGen of IDEAL-HSS$(k_1, \ldots, k_m; (k-1)k^g)$.
- **Reconstruction Phase:**
  1. A qualified set A will broadcast their shares in following manner:
  Case-I All the participants of A are from same generation g.
     * Broadcast the share corresponding to IDEAL-HSS$(k_1, \ldots, k_m; (k-1)k^g)$ and reconstruct by calling Reconst of IDEAL-HSS$(k_1, \ldots, k_m; (k-1)k^g)$.
  Case-II Participants of A are from various generations and the lowest level is L_j.
     * Broadcast the share of (k_j, ∞) threshold access structure and reconstruct according to Reconst of (k_j, ∞) algorithm.

Fig. 4. Construction-II: secret sharing scheme for evolving hierarchical access structure.

The correctness of reconstruction follows from the two facts: (1) correctness of IDEAL-HSS, when all the participants come from same generation, and (2) from the correctness of individual (k_i, ∞)-secret sharing schemes for $i = 1, 2, \ldots, m$, when participants come from various generation. The security of the scheme follows from the securities of underlying Shamir secret sharing scheme and IDEAL-HSS. We also note that the share size of tth party is solely determined by the level he is assigned. It is easy to see that the share size of tth participant is bounded above by $((k_1 + k_2 + \cdots + k_m)t - (m-1)) \cdot max\{l, \log(k_m t)\}$. From the discussion, we now have the following theorem:

Theorem 6. *There exists secret sharing scheme for an evolving hierarchical access structure parameterized by number of levels m and the threshold values $k_1, \ldots, k_m$ with share size of tth party bounded by $((k_1 + k_2 + \cdots + k_m)t - (m-1)) \cdot max\{l, \log(k_m t)\}$.*

5   Conclusion

In this paper, we have studied evolving secret sharing schemes for compartmental and hierarchical access structure for the first time. We, also, show that it is possible to have an ideal secret sharing scheme even with infinitely many parties. Classification of all such evolving access structures on which ideal secret sharing can be achieved remains an interesting open issue. The evolving schemes have a conceptual disadvantage: The dealer needs to remember all of the previously generated shares. This is a problem with the existing technique(s). How to make schemes more efficient from the dealer's perspective remain an interesting open question.

Acknowledgement. The authors are grateful to the anonymous reviewers for their kind comments and suggestions to improve the article.

References

1. Beimel, A., Othman, H.: Evolving ramp secret-sharing schemes. In: Catalano, D., De Prisco, R. (eds.) SCN 2018. LNCS, vol. 11035, pp. 313–332. Springer, Cham (2018). https://doi.org/10.1007/978-3-319-98113-0_17
2. Belenkiy, M.: Disjunctive multi-level secret sharing. IACR Cryptology ePrint Archive 2008, 18 (2008)
3. Blakley, G.R.: Safeguarding cryptographic keys. In: AFIPS 1979, pp. 313–317 (1997)
4. Brickell, E.F.: Some ideal secret sharing schemes. In: Quisquater, J.-J., Vandewalle, J. (eds.) EUROCRYPT 1989. LNCS, vol. 434, pp. 468–475. Springer, Heidelberg (1990). https://doi.org/10.1007/3-540-46885-4_45
5. Cramer, R., Dodis, Y., Fehr, S., Padró, C., Wichs, D.: Detection of algebraic manipulation with applications to robust secret sharing and fuzzy extractors. In: Smart, N. (ed.) EUROCRYPT 2008. LNCS, vol. 4965, pp. 471–488. Springer, Heidelberg (2008). https://doi.org/10.1007/978-3-540-78967-3_27
6. Ghodosi, H., Pieprzyk, J., Safavi-Naini, R.: Secret sharing in multilevel and compartmented groups. In: Boyd, C., Dawson, E. (eds.) ACISP 1998. LNCS, vol. 1438, pp. 367–378. Springer, Heidelberg (1998). https://doi.org/10.1007/BFb0053748

7. Guo, C., Chang, C.C., Qin, C.: A hierarchical threshold secret image sharing. Pattern Recogn. Lett. **33**(1), 83–91 (2012)
8. Herranz, J., Laguillaumie, F., Libert, B., Ràfols, C.: Short attribute-based signatures for threshold predicates. In: Dunkelman, O. (ed.) CT-RSA 2012. LNCS, vol. 7178, pp. 51–67. Springer, Heidelberg (2012). https://doi.org/10.1007/978-3-642-27954-6_4
9. Ito, M., Saito, A., Nishizeki, T.: Multiple assignment scheme for sharing secret. J. Cryptol. **6**(1), 15–20 (1993)
10. Karchmer, M., Wigderson, A.: On span programs. In: 1993 Proceedings of the Eighth Annual Structure in Complexity Theory Conference, pp. 102–111. IEEE (1993)
11. Komargodski, I., Naor, M., Yogev, E.: How to share a secret, infinitely. In: Hirt, M., Smith, A. (eds.) TCC 2016. LNCS, vol. 9986, pp. 485–514. Springer, Heidelberg (2016). https://doi.org/10.1007/978-3-662-53644-5_19
12. Komargodski, I., Paskin-Cherniavsky, A.: Evolving secret sharing: dynamic thresholds and robustness. In: Kalai, Y., Reyzin, L. (eds.) TCC 2017. LNCS, vol. 10678, pp. 379–393. Springer, Cham (2017). https://doi.org/10.1007/978-3-319-70503-3_12
13. Koyama, K.: Cryptographic key sharing methods for multi-groups and security analysis. IEICE Trans. **E66**(1), 13–20 (1983)
14. Pakniat, N., Noroozi, M., Eslami, Z.: Secret image sharing scheme with hierarchical threshold access structure. J. Vis. Commun. Image Represent. **25**(5), 1093–1101 (2014)
15. Roy, P.S., et al.: Hierarchical secret sharing schemes secure against rushing adversary: cheater identification and robustness. In: Su, C., Kikuchi, H. (eds.) ISPEC 2018. LNCS, vol. 11125, pp. 578–594. Springer, Cham (2018). https://doi.org/10.1007/978-3-319-99807-7_37
16. Shamir, A.: How to share a secret. Commun. ACM **22**(11), 612–613 (1979)
17. Shima, K., Doi, H.: A hierarchical secret sharing scheme based on information dispersal techniques. In: Lee, K. (ed.) ICISC 2018. LNCS, vol. 11396, pp. 217–232. Springer, Cham (2019). https://doi.org/10.1007/978-3-030-12146-4_14
18. Simmons, G.J.: How to (really) share a secret. In: Goldwasser, S. (ed.) CRYPTO 1988. LNCS, vol. 403, pp. 390–448. Springer, New York (1990). https://doi.org/10.1007/0-387-34799-2_30
19. Tassa, T.: Hierarchical threshold secret sharing. J. Cryptol. **20**(2), 237–264 (2007)
20. Tassa, T.: Generalized oblivious transfer by secret sharing. Des. Codes Crypt. **58**(1), 11–21 (2011)
21. Tentu, A.N., Paul, P., Vadlamudi, C.V.: Conjunctive hierarchical secret sharing scheme based on MDS codes. In: Lecroq, T., Mouchard, L. (eds.) IWOCA 2013. LNCS, vol. 8288, pp. 463–467. Springer, Heidelberg (2013). https://doi.org/10.1007/978-3-642-45278-9_44

Strengthened PAKE Protocols Secure Against Malicious Private Key Generator

SeongHan Shin[✉]

National Institute of Advanced Industrial Science and Technology (AIST),
2-4-7 Aomi, Koto-ku, Tokyo 135-0064, Japan
seonghan.shin@aist.go.jp

Abstract. At WISA 2015, Choi et al. [9] proposed an identity-based password-authenticated key exchange (iPAKE) protocol using the Boneh-Franklin IBE scheme. In this paper, we revisit the iPAKE protocol [9] (and its generic construction) that has been standardized in the international standard committee ISO/IEC JTC 1/SC 27. First, we show that the iPAKE protocol is insecure against passive/active attacks by a malicious PKG (Private Key Generator) where the malicious PKG can find out all clients' passwords by just eavesdropping the communications, and the PKG can share a session key with any client by impersonating the server. Then, we propose two strengthened PAKE (SPI and SPI-S) protocols that prevents such malicious PKG's passive/active attacks. Also, we discuss security of the SPI and SPI-S protocols, and compare relevant protocols in terms of efficiency and security.

Keywords: PAKE · IBE · Online/offline dictionary attacks

1 Introduction

The password-based authenticated key exchange protocols provide password authentication and establishment of session keys to be used for protecting subsequent communications. Since the appearance of EKE [4,5] (known as PAKE), such protocols have been extensively studied (see [1,13] and references therein) in order to be secure against passive/active attacks as well as offline dictionary attacks on human-memorable passwords, and have received much attention because password authentication is commonly used (and standardized in IEEE, ISO/IEC, IETF, ITU-T) and widely deployed in many real-world applications (e.g. TLS, SSH, IPsec, WEP/WPA, HTTP). At the same time, there are several attempts to strengthen security of the password-based authenticated key exchange protocols by combining other cryptographic primitives. In [16], Yi et al. proposed an identity-based PAKE protocol using IBE (Identity-Based Encryption). Recently, Choi et al. [9] proposed another identity-based PAKE (called, iPAKE) protocol using the Boneh-Franklin IBE scheme [6,7] and its generic construction. Concurrently, Hwang et al. [11] proposed identity-based

© Springer Nature Switzerland AG 2020
I. You (Ed.): WISA 2019, LNCS 11897, pp. 192–205, 2020.
https://doi.org/10.1007/978-3-030-39303-8_15

PAKE protocols constructed from IBS (Identity-Based Signature) [10]. In addition to the security of password authentication, these protocols [9,11,16] provide another layer of security meaning that it is not possible for an attacker who gets the password to impersonate the server.

1.1 Motivation and Our Contributions

Currently, the identity-based PAKE protocols [9,11] have been standardized in ISO/IEC JTC 1/SC 27 [12].[1] So, it is of significant importance to thoroughly analyze security of these protocols [9,11]. In this paper, we focus on the iPAKE protocol [9] using the Boneh-Franklin IBE scheme [6,7]. After describing the iPAKE protocol [9], we show that it is insecure against passive/active attacks by a malicious PKG (Private Key Generator) where the malicious PKG can find out all clients' passwords by just eavesdropping the communications, and the PKG can share a session key with any client by impersonating the server. Then, we propose two strengthened PAKE (SPI and SPI-S) protocols both of which provide security against passive/active attacks by a malicious PKG. Also, we discuss security of the SPI and SPI-S protocols, and compare the PAKE protocols using the BF-IBE scheme [6,7] (PAKE-CS [16], iPAKE [9], SPI, SPI-S) in terms of efficiency, number of passes and security against a malicious PKG.

2 Preliminaries

2.1 Notations

Let $k \in \mathbb{N}$ and $\lambda \in \mathbb{N}$ be the security parameters. Let $\{0,1\}^*$ be the set of finite binary strings and $\{0,1\}^k$ be the set of binary strings of length k. Let $A\|B$ be the concatenation of A and B. If U is a set, then $u \xleftarrow{\$} U$ indicates the process of selecting u at random and uniformly over U. If U is a function (whatever it is), then $u = U$ indicates the process of assigning the result to u. Let $\mathbb{D}_{pw}$ be a dictionary size of passwords. Let C and S be the identities of client and server, respectively, with each ID $\in \{0,1\}^*$.

Also, let $\mathbb{G}_1$ and $\mathbb{G}_2$ be two groups of order q for some large prime q. A bilinear map $e : \mathbb{G}_1 \times \mathbb{G}_1 \rightarrow \mathbb{G}_2$ has the following properties: (1) Bilinear: For all $g_1, g_2 \in \mathbb{G}_1$ and all $\alpha, \beta \in \mathbb{Z}_q^*$, $e(g_1^\alpha, g_2^\beta) = e(g_1, g_2)^{\alpha\beta}$; (2) Non-degenerate: For all pairs $g_1, g_2 \in \mathbb{G}_1$, $e(g_1, g_2) \neq 1$. If g is a generator of $\mathbb{G}_1$, then $e(g, g)$ is a generator of $\mathbb{G}_2$; and (3) Computable: There is an efficient algorithm to compute $e(g_1, g_2)$ for any $g_1, g_2 \in \mathbb{G}_1$.

---

[1] According to the ISO/IEC JTC 1/SC 27 meeting, these protocols [9,11] already became Korean key management standard in 2015, and have been applied to various applications (e.g. retails, smart home, payment).

2.2   Computational Assumptions

First, we define the Computational Diffie-Hellman (CDH) problem. Let $\mathcal{G}_1$ be the group generation algorithm that takes as input 1^λ and outputs a group description $(\mathbb{G}_1, q, g)$ where $\mathbb{G}_1$ is a finite cyclic group of prime order q with g as a generator.

Definition 1 (CDH Problem). *Let $\mathcal{G}_1$ be the group generation algorithm described above. A (t_1, ε_1)-CDH$_{\mathbb{G}_1}$ adversary is a probabilistic polynomial time (PPT) machine $\mathcal{B}$, running in time t_1, such that its success probability $\mathsf{Succ}_{\mathbb{G}_1}^{cdh}(\mathcal{B})$, given random elements g^α and g^β to output $g^{\alpha\beta}$, is greater than ε_1. We denote by $\mathsf{Succ}_{\mathbb{G}_1}^{cdh}(t_1)$ the maximal success probability over every adversaries, running within time t_1. The CDH problem states that $\mathsf{Succ}_{\mathbb{G}_1}^{cdh}(t_1) \leq \varepsilon_1$ for any t_1/ε_1 not too large.*

Next, we define the Bilinear Diffie-Hellman (BDH) problem. Let $\mathcal{G}_2$ be the BDH group generation algorithm that takes as input 1^λ and outputs a group description $(\mathbb{G}_1, \mathbb{G}_2, e, q, g)$ where $\mathbb{G}_1$ and $\mathbb{G}_2$ are two groups of prime order q, $e : \mathbb{G}_1 \times \mathbb{G}_1 \to \mathbb{G}_2$ is an admissible bilinear map and g is a generator of $\mathbb{G}_1$.

Definition 2 (BDH Problem). *Let $\mathcal{G}_2$ be the BDH group generation algorithm described above. A (t_2, ε_2)-BDH$_{\mathbb{G}_1, \mathbb{G}_2, e}$ adversary is a probabilistic polynomial time (PPT) machine $\mathcal{B}$, running in time t_2, such that its success probability $\mathsf{Succ}_{\mathbb{G}_1, \mathbb{G}_2, e}^{bdh}(\mathcal{B})$, given random elements g^α, g^β and g^γ to output $e(g, g)^{\alpha\beta\gamma}$, is greater than ε_2. We denote by $\mathsf{Succ}_{\mathbb{G}_1, \mathbb{G}_2, e}^{bdh}(t_2)$ the maximal success probability over every adversaries, running within time t_2. The BDH problem states that $\mathsf{Succ}_{\mathbb{G}_1, \mathbb{G}_2, e}^{bdh}(t_2) \leq \varepsilon_2$ for any t_2/ε_2 not too large.*

2.3   An Identity-Based Encryption Scheme

In this subsection, we define the syntax of identity-based encryption (IBE) and describe the Boneh-Franklin IBE (BF-IBE) scheme [6,7] that is the most efficient construction among IBE schemes (see [8]).

Definition 3 (Identity-Based Encryption). *An identity-based encryption (IBE) scheme is a quadruple of probabilistic polynomial time algorithms (Setup$_{\mathsf{IBE}}$, Extract, Encrypt, Decrypt) such that:*

- *The setup algorithm Setup$_{\mathsf{IBE}}$ takes as input 1^λ and outputs public parameters pp_{IBE} and a master secret key msk where (mpk, msk) is a pair of master public/secret keys and mpk is included in pp_{IBE}. Also, the public parameters include descriptions of a finite message space $\mathcal{M}$ and a finite ciphertext space $\mathcal{C}$. The pp_{IBE} will be publicly known, while the msk will be known only to the Private Key Generator (PKG).*
- *The key extraction algorithm Extract takes as input pp_{IBE}, msk and an identity $\mathsf{ID} \in \{0,1\}^*$, and outputs a private key d_{ID} corresponding to the user with this identity.*

- *The encryption algorithm* Encrypt *takes as input* pp_{IBE}, *an identity* ID *and a message* $M \in \mathcal{M}$, *and outputs a ciphertext* $C \in \mathcal{C}$.
- *The decryption algorithm* Decrypt *takes as input* pp_{IBE}, C *and a private key* d_{ID}, *and outputs* $M \in \mathcal{M}$.

It is required that $M = \mathsf{Decrypt}(pp_{\mathsf{IBE}}, C, d_{\mathsf{ID}})$ *for all* ID $\in \{0,1\}^*$ *and* $M \in \mathcal{M}$ *where* $C = \mathsf{Encrypt}(pp_{\mathsf{IBE}}, \mathsf{ID}, M)$.

2.4 Boneh-Franklin IBE (BF-IBE)

Here, we describe the Boneh-Franklin IBE (BF-IBE) scheme [6,7] that is proven to be IND-ID-CPA secure (i.e. semantic security against adaptively chosen identity and message attacks) in the random oracle model [3] under the BDH problem in Definition 2.

- The setup algorithm $\mathsf{Setup}_{\mathsf{IBE}}$ on input 1^λ outputs public parameters pp_{IBE} and a master secret key msk where $(\mathbb{G}_1, \mathbb{G}_2, e, q, g)$ is generated by calling the BDH group generation algorithm $\mathcal{G}_2$ on input 1^λ, and $G : \{0,1\}^* \to \mathbb{G}_1$ and $H : \mathbb{G}_2 \to \{0,1\}^k$ are descriptions of cryptographic hash functions. The message space $\mathcal{M} = \{0,1\}^k$ and the ciphertext space $\mathcal{C} = \mathbb{G}_1 \times \{0,1\}^k$. Let z be a random element from $\mathbb{Z}_q^*$ and set $(\mathsf{mpk}, \mathsf{msk}) = (g^z, z)$. It outputs $(pp_{\mathsf{IBE}}, \mathsf{msk}) = ((\mathbb{G}_1, \mathbb{G}_2, e, q, g, g^z, G, H), z)$.
- The key extraction algorithm Extract, on input pp_{IBE}, $\mathsf{msk}(= z)$ and an identity ID, computes $Q_{\mathsf{ID}} = G(\mathsf{ID})$ and outputs a private key $d_{\mathsf{ID}} \equiv Q_{\mathsf{ID}}^z$.
- The encryption algorithm Encrypt, on input pp_{IBE}, an identity ID and a message M, chooses a random element $r \xleftarrow{\$} \mathbb{Z}_q^*$ and computes $g_{\mathsf{ID}} = e(G(\mathsf{ID}), g^z)$, $U_1 \equiv g^r$ and $U_2 = M \oplus H(g_{\mathsf{ID}}^r)$. Then, it outputs a ciphertext $C = (U_1, U_2)$.
- The decryption algorithm Decrypt, on input pp_{IBE}, $C = (U_1, U_2)$ and a private key $d_{\mathsf{ID}}(\equiv Q_{\mathsf{ID}}^z)$, computes $\delta = e(d_{\mathsf{ID}}, U_1)$ and outputs $M = U_2 \oplus H(\delta)$.

The consistency of the BF-IBE scheme can be easily checked by

$$\delta = e(d_{\mathsf{ID}}, U_1) = e(Q_{\mathsf{ID}}^z, g^r) = e(Q_{\mathsf{ID}}, g)^{zr} = e(Q_{\mathsf{ID}}, g^z)^r = g_{\mathsf{ID}}^r. \tag{1}$$

3 The iPAKE Protocol

In this section, we describe the iPAKE protocol [9] which consists of **Initialization** and **Key Establishment** phases.

3.1 Initialization

In this phase, it executes the following three processes Setup, Extract and Registration.

3.1.1 Setup

The Setup on input 1^λ outputs public parameters pp and a master secret key msk by running the setup algorithm $\text{Setup}_{\text{IBE}}$ of Sect. 2.4 where $H', H_3 : \{0,1\}^* \to \{0,1\}^k$ are descriptions of additional cryptographic hash functions. It outputs $(pp, \text{msk}) = ((pp_{\text{IBE}}, H', H_3), z)$.

3.1.2 Extract

The Extract (run by PKG), on input the public parameters pp, the master secret key $\text{msk}(= z)$ and an identity S, computes $Q_S = G(S)$ and outputs a private key $d_S \equiv Q_S^z$ that is securely transmitted to the corresponding server S.

3.1.3 Registration

First, client C randomly chooses his/her password pw from a dictionary $\mathbb{D}_{pw}$ and sends $(C, H'(pw))$ to server S. Then, the server stores $(C, H'(pw))$ to a password file. This registration process should be done securely between client C and server S.

3.2 Key Establishment

In this phase, client C and server S execute the iPAKE protocol over insecure networks in order to share a session key. This phase of iPAKE has three steps as below.

Step 1. The client C runs the encryption algorithm Encrypt of Sect. 2.4 on input pp, an identity S and a message $H'(pw)$. Then, client C sends (C, U_1, U_2) to server S.

Step 2. After receiving a message (C, U_1, U_2) from client C, server S runs the decryption algorithm Decrypt of Sect. 2.4 on input pp, (U_1, U_2) and a private key d_S. If $(U_2 \oplus H(\delta)) \neq H'(pw)$, the server aborts the protocol. Otherwise, server S chooses a random element $y \xleftarrow{\$} \mathbb{Z}_q^\star$, and computes $Y \equiv g^y$ and $Z \equiv U_1^y$. Also, the server computes a session key $SK_S = H_3(C||S||sid||\delta||Z)$, where $sid = U_1||U_2||Y$, and then sends (S, Y) to the client.

Step 3. After receiving a message (S, Y) from server S, client C computes $Z \equiv Y^x$ and a session key $SK_C = H_3(C||S||sid||g_S^r||Z)$ where $sid = U_1||U_2||Y$.

4 Passive/Active Attacks on iPAKE

This section shows passive and active attacks by a malicious PKG (Private Key Generator) on the iPAKE protocol [9]. Also, these attacks can be applied to the generic construction of iPAKE (in Section 4 of [9]).

4.1   A Passive Attack on iPAKE

Here, we show that a malicious PKG can find out all clients' passwords by just eavesdropping the communications of the iPAKE protocol. After eavesdropping the first message (C, U_1, U_2) in the **Key Establishment** phase, the malicious PKG who has the master secret key z can decrypt the ciphertext (U_1, U_2) since $d_S \equiv (G(S))^z$. With all possible password candidates, the PKG can find out the client's password pw by performing offline dictionary attacks on $H'(pw) = U_2 \oplus H(e(d_S, U_1))$. Of course, these offline dictionary attacks can be used for all clients who registered to server S.

4.2   An Active Attack on iPAKE

Here, we show that a malicious PKG can share a session key with any client by impersonating the server in the iPAKE protocol. After receiving the first message (C, U_1, U_2) in the **Key Establishment** phase, the malicious PKG who has the master secret key z just executes **Step 2** except the check of $W \neq H'(pw)$ and then can share the same session key $SK_C = H_3(C||S||sid||\delta||Z)$ with client C. Note that in this active attack the PKG does not need to perform offline dictionary attacks at all.

5   A Strengthened PAKE (SPI) Protocol

In this section, we propose a strengthened PAKE (for short, SPI) protocol that provides security against passive/active attacks by a malicious PKG (Private Key Generator). The main idea of SPI is to double mask the password verification data on client C where the first mask is performed with a Diffie-Hellman public key and the second one is with an encryption algorithm Encrypt of BF-IBE [6, 7]. The SPI protocol consists of **Initialization** and **Key Establishment** phases.

5.1   Initialization

In this phase, it executes the following three processes Setup, Extract and Registration.

5.1.1   Setup
The Setup on input 1^λ outputs public parameters pp and a master secret key msk where $(\mathbb{G}_1, \mathbb{G}_2, e, q, g)$ is generated by calling the BDH group generation algorithm $\mathcal{G}_2$ on input 1^λ, h is another random generator of $\mathbb{G}_1$, and $G : \{0,1\}^* \to \mathbb{G}_1$, $H : \mathbb{G}_2 \to \{0,1\}^k$, $H_1 : \{0,1\}^* \to \mathbb{Z}_q^*$ and $H_2, H_3 : \{0,1\}^* \to \{0,1\}^k$ are descriptions of cryptographic hash functions. Also, it chooses a random element $z \overset{\$}{\leftarrow} \mathbb{Z}_q^*$ and sets $(\mathsf{mpk}, \mathsf{msk}) = (g^z, z)$. It outputs $(pp, \mathsf{msk}) = ((\mathbb{G}_1, \mathbb{G}_2, e, q, g, h, g^z, G, H, H_1, H_2, H_3), z)$.

5.1.2 Extract

The Extract (run by PKG), on input the public parameters pp, the master secret key $\mathsf{msk}(= z)$ and an identity S, computes $Q_\mathsf{S} = G(\mathsf{S})$ and outputs a private key $d_\mathsf{S} \equiv Q_\mathsf{S}^z$ that is securely transmitted to the corresponding server S.

5.1.3 Registration

First, client C randomly chooses his/her password pw from a dictionary $\mathbb{D}_{pw}$ and sends $(\mathsf{C}, h^{-H_1(pw)})$ to server S. Then, the server stores $(\mathsf{C}, h^{-H_1(pw)})$ to a password file. Note that password pw is kept by client C secretly, and $(d_\mathsf{S}, (\mathsf{C}, h^{-H_1(pw)}))$ are held by server S secretly. This registration process should be done securely between client C and server S.

5.2 Key Establishment

In this phase, client C and server S execute the SPI protocol over insecure networks (e.g. the Internet) in order to share a session key to be used for protecting subsequent communications. This phase of SPI has three steps as below (see also Fig. 1).

Step 1. The client C chooses two random elements $x, r \xleftarrow{\$} \mathbb{Z}_q^*$, and computes a Diffie-Hellman public value $X \equiv g^x$ and its masked value $W \equiv X \cdot h^{H_1(pw)}$ using the password pw. For the second mask, the client encrypts the value W by computing $g_\mathsf{S} = e\left(G(\mathsf{S}), g^z\right)$, $U_1 \equiv g^r$ and $U_2 = W \oplus H(g_\mathsf{S}^r)$. Then, client C sends (C, U_1, U_2) to server S.

Step 2. The server S chooses a random element $y \xleftarrow{\$} \mathbb{Z}_q^*$ and computes a Diffie-Hellman public value $Y \equiv g^y$. After receiving a message (C, U_1, U_2) from client C, server S decrypts the latter mask using its private key $d_\mathsf{S} \equiv Q_\mathsf{S}^z$ by computing $\delta = e(d_\mathsf{S}, U_1)$ and $W = U_2 \oplus H(\delta)$. Also, the server computes $X' \equiv W \cdot h^{-H_1(pw)}$ and a Diffie-Hellman key $K' \equiv (X')^y$. Then, server S computes its authenticator $V_\mathsf{S} = H_2(sid\|X'\|K')$ and a session key $SK_\mathsf{S} = H_3(sid\|X'\|K')$ where a session identifier $sid = \mathsf{C}\|\mathsf{S}\|U_1\|U_2\|Y$. Finally, the server sends $(\mathsf{S}, Y, V_\mathsf{S})$ to the client.

Step 3. After receiving a message $(\mathsf{S}, Y, V_\mathsf{S})$ from server S, client C first computes a Diffie-Hellman key $K \equiv Y^x$ and checks the validity of V_S. If $V_\mathsf{S} \neq H_2(sid\|X\|K)$ where $sid = \mathsf{C}\|\mathsf{S}\|U_1\|U_2\|Y$, the client aborts the protocol. Otherwise, client C computes a session key $SK_\mathsf{C} = H_3(sid\|X\|K)$.

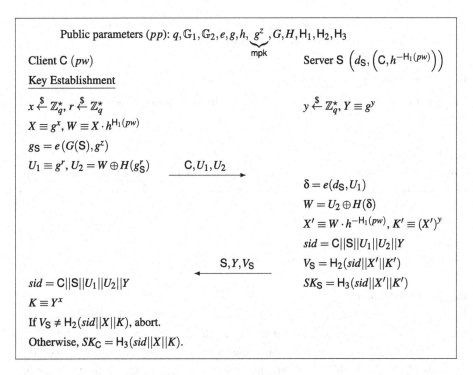

Fig. 1. A strengthened PAKE (for short, SPI) protocol secure against malicious PKG

From the above construction, one might think of using only one random element (x or r) instead of two random elements in **Step 1** for efficiency improvements. However, such constructions can result in offline dictionary attacks by a malicious PKG who has the master secret key z. For example, if the random element r is reused for K (i.e. $X \equiv g^r$) the malicious PKG can find out the password pw by performing offline dictionary attacks. This is the reason why we use two random elements x, r where x is used for the first mask and r is for the second mask in the SPI protocol.

6 A Strengthened PAKE (SPI-S) Protocol for Simultaneous Message Exchanges

In this section, we propose a strengthened PAKE (for short, SPI-S) protocol that not only provides security against passive/active attacks by a malicious PKG, but also allows simultaneous message exchanges between client C and server S. The latter feature is particularly important in a situation where network latency matters. Differently from SPI, we exploit the masking technique [2] of Diffie-Hellman public values for the first mask of password verification data. Actually, this masking technique makes it possible to remove the computation of V_S (in **Step 2** of the **Key Establishment** phase). The SPI-S protocol consists of **Initialization** and **Key Establishment** phases.

6.1   Initialization

In this phase, it executes the following three processes Setup, Extract and Registration.

6.1.1   Setup

This process is almost same as Setup of Sect. 5.1.1 except that h_1 and h_2 are two random generators of $\mathbb{G}_1$. It outputs $(pp, \mathsf{msk}) = ((\mathbb{G}_1, \mathbb{G}_2, e, q, g, h_1, h_2, g^z, G, H, \mathsf{H}_1, \mathsf{H}_2), z)$.

6.1.2   Extract

This process is the same as Extract of Sect. 5.1.2.

6.1.3   Registration

First, client C randomly chooses his/her password pw from a dictionary $\mathbb{D}_{\mathsf{pw}}$ and sends $(\mathsf{C}, h_1^{-\mathsf{H}_1(pw)}, h_2^{\mathsf{H}_1(pw)})$ to server S. Then, the server stores $(\mathsf{C}, h_1^{-\mathsf{H}_1(pw)}, h_2^{\mathsf{H}_1(pw)})$ to a password file. Note that password pw is kept by client C secretly, and $(d_\mathsf{S}, (\mathsf{C}, h_1^{-\mathsf{H}_1(pw)}, h_2^{\mathsf{H}_1(pw)}))$ are held by server S secretly. This registration process should be done securely between client C and server S.

6.2   Key Establishment

In this phase, client C and server S execute the SPI-S protocol over insecure networks (e.g. the Internet) in order to share a session key to be used for protecting subsequent communications. This phase of SPI-S has three steps as below (see also Fig. 2).

Step 1. This step is the same as **Step 1** of Sect. 5.2 except the computation of masked value $W \equiv X \cdot h_1^{\mathsf{H}_1(pw)}$. Then, client C sends (C, U_1, U_2) to server S.

Step 2. The server S chooses a random element $y \xleftarrow{\$} \mathbb{Z}_q^\star$, and computes a Diffie-Hellman public value $Y \equiv g^y$ and its masked value $Z \equiv Y \cdot h_2^{\mathsf{H}_1(pw)}$. Then, the server sends (S, Z) to the client without waiting for his/her message. After receiving a message (C, U_1, U_2) from client C, server S decrypts the latter mask using its private key $d_\mathsf{S} \equiv Q_\mathsf{S}^z$ by computing $\delta = e(d_\mathsf{S}, U_1)$ and $W = U_2 \oplus H(\delta)$. Also, the server computes $X' \equiv W \cdot h_1^{-\mathsf{H}_1(pw)}$, a Diffie-Hellman key $K' \equiv (X')^y$ and a session key $SK_\mathsf{S} = \mathsf{H}_2(sid\|X'\|Y\|K')$ where a session identifier $sid = \mathsf{C}\|\mathsf{S}\|U_1\|U_2\|Z$.

Step 3. After receiving a message (S, Z) from server S, client C computes $Y' \equiv Z \cdot h_2^{-\mathsf{H}_1(pw)}$, a Diffie-Hellman key $K \equiv (Y')^x$ and a session key $SK_\mathsf{C} = \mathsf{H}_2(sid\|X\|Y'\|K)$ where $sid = \mathsf{C}\|\mathsf{S}\|U_1\|U_2\|Z$.

Public parameters (pp): $q, \mathbb{G}_1, \mathbb{G}_2, e, g, h_1, h_2, \underbrace{g^z}_{\mathsf{mpk}}, G, H, \mathsf{H}_1, \mathsf{H}_2$

Client C (pw) $\qquad\qquad\qquad$ Server S $\left(d_{\mathsf{S}}, \left(\mathsf{C}, h_1^{-\mathsf{H}_1(pw)}, h_2^{\mathsf{H}_1(pw)}\right)\right)$

__Key Establishment__

$x \xleftarrow{\$} \mathbb{Z}_q^\star, r \xleftarrow{\$} \mathbb{Z}_q^\star \qquad\qquad\qquad y \xleftarrow{\$} \mathbb{Z}_q^\star, Y \equiv g^y$

$X \equiv g^x, W \equiv X \cdot h_1^{\mathsf{H}_1(pw)} \qquad\qquad Z \equiv Y \cdot h_2^{\mathsf{H}_1(pw)}$

$g_{\mathsf{S}} = e(G(\mathsf{S}), g^z)$

$U_1 \equiv g^r, U_2 = W \oplus H(g_{\mathsf{S}}^r)$

$$\xrightarrow{\quad C, U_1, U_2 \quad}$$

$$\xleftarrow{\quad S, Z \quad}$$

$\qquad\qquad\qquad\qquad\qquad\qquad \delta = e(d_{\mathsf{S}}, U_1)$

$\qquad\qquad\qquad\qquad\qquad\qquad W = U_2 \oplus H(\delta)$

$sid = \mathsf{C}||\mathsf{S}||U_1||U_2||Z \qquad X' \equiv W \cdot h_1^{-\mathsf{H}_1(pw)}, K' \equiv (X')^y$

$Y' \equiv Z \cdot h_2^{-\mathsf{H}_1(pw)}, K \equiv (Y')^x \qquad sid = \mathsf{C}||\mathsf{S}||U_1||U_2||Z$

$SK_{\mathsf{C}} = \mathsf{H}_2(sid||X||Y'||K) \qquad SK_{\mathsf{S}} = \mathsf{H}_2(sid||X'||Y||K')$

Fig. 2. A strengthened PAKE (for short, SPI-S) protocol for simultaneous message exchanges

7 Security of SPI and SPI-S

In this section, we discuss security of the SPI and SPI-S protocols against passive/active attacks by a malicious PKG (Private Key Generator), and server impersonation attacks after password compromise. Note that security against passive/active attacks by a malicious PKG is a stronger security guarantee than security against passive/active attacks by an outside attacker.

Let us consider passive/active attacks by a malicious PKG who not only has the master secret key msk in the SPI and SPI-S protocols, but also eavesdrops and completely controls the exchanged messages between client C and server S. If the PKG cannot compute an authenticated session key SK with the probability better than that of online dictionary attacks, we can say that the SPI and SPI-S protocols are secure against the malicious PKG's passive/active attacks.

7.1 Security of SPI

We start with the PKG's passive attacks in the SPI protocol where the PKG can get the messages (C, U_1, U_2), $(\mathsf{S}, Y, V_{\mathsf{S}})$, and then wants to compute the session key SK. That is, the PKG's goal is to derive the correct K from W and Y, because the only secret in the computation of SK is $K \equiv Y^x$. Though X' can be determined with all possible password candidates $pw' \in \mathbb{D}_{\mathsf{pw}}$, the only way for the PKG to extract K from W and Y is to compute Y^x. However, the probability for the PKG to compute Y^x is negligible in the security parameter for the underlying group since both x and y are random elements chosen from $\mathbb{Z}_q^*$. Therefore, the SPI protocol is secure against the PKG's passive attacks.

In the PKG's active attacks on the SPI protocol, there are two cases to be considered. When the PKG impersonates server S (as in the attack of Sect. 4.2), it can compute the same SK (to be shared with client C) if and only if the authenticator V_S is valid. For a valid authenticator V_S, the PKG has to compute the correct K' from W and Y after guessing a password $pw' \in \mathbb{D}_{pw}$ so that its probability is bounded by the probability of $pw' = pw$. Of course, the PKG can know whether pw' is equal to pw or not by seeing a subsequent message from client C. However, when $pw' \neq pw$, the probability for the PKG to compute the correct K' is negligible in the security parameter for the underlying group since the PKG has to guess the discrete logarithm x (chosen by client C) as well. That is, this server impersonation attack is restricted by the online dictionary attacks where the PKG can try a guessed password by communicating with the honest client C. When the PKG impersonates client C, it can compute the same SK (to be shared with server S) if and only if the received authenticator V_S is valid. For that, the PKG should have used the same password $pw' = pw$ in the computation of W. If V_S is not valid, the PKG can notice that the guessed password pw' is not equal to pw. However, when $pw' \neq pw$, the probability for the PKG to compute the correct K is negligible in the security parameter for the underlying group since the PKG has to guess an *entangled* discrete logarithm y' as well[2]. That is, this client impersonation attack is restricted by the online dictionary attacks where the PKG can try a guessed password by communicating with the honest server S. Therefore, the SPI protocol is secure against the PKG's active attacks.

We can prove a formal security of the SPI protocol by showing a reduction to the CDH problem in Definition 1. As a core proof technique, we embed a Diffie-Hellman instance (g^α, g^β) into the simulation of the SPI protocol. Specifically, we set $h = g^\alpha$ and introduce the other part g^β in the simulation of server S by computing a Diffie-Hellman public value $Y \equiv (g^\beta)^y$. After excluding all negligible success probabilities and online dictionary attacks, we can show that the CDH problem is solved by using an adversary who is attacking on the SPI protocol. Due to the lack of space, the details are omitted.

7.2   Security of SPI-S

Here, we start with the PKG's passive attacks in the SPI-S protocol where the PKG can get the messages (C, U_1, U_2), (S, Z), and then wants to compute the session key SK. That is, the PKG's goal is to derive the correct K from W and Z, because the only secret in the computation of SK is $K \equiv Y^x$. Though both X' and Y' can be determined with all possible password candidates $pw' \in \mathbb{D}_{pw}$, the only way for the PKG to extract K from W and Z is to compute Y^x. However, the probability for the PKG to compute Y^x is negligible in the security parameter

---

[2] In other words, the PKG should solve the discrete logarithm between two random generators g and h.

for the underlying group since both x and y are random elements chosen from $\mathbb{Z}_q^\star$. Therefore, the SPI-S protocol is secure against the PKG's passive attacks.

In the PKG's active attacks on the SPI-S protocol, there are two cases to be considered. When the PKG impersonates server S (as in the attack of Sect. 4.2), it can compute the same SK (to be shared with client C) if and only if the Diffie-Hellman key K' is equal to K. For that, the PKG has to compute the correct K' from W and Y after guessing a password $pw' \in \mathbb{D}_{pw}$ so that its probability is bounded by the probability of $pw' = pw$. Of course, the PKG can know whether pw' is equal to pw or not by seeing a subsequent message from client C. However, when $pw' \neq pw$, the probability for the PKG to compute the correct K' is negligible in the security parameter for the underlying group since the PKG has to guess the discrete logarithm x (chosen by client C) as well. That is, this server impersonation attack is restricted by the online dictionary attacks where the PKG can try a guessed password by communicating with the honest client C. When the PKG impersonates client C, it can compute the same SK (to be shared with server S) if and only if the Diffie-Hellman key K is equal to K'. For that, the PKG has to compute the correct K from X and Z after guessing a password $pw' \in \mathbb{D}_{pw}$ so that its probability is bounded by the probability of $pw' = pw$. Of course, the PKG can know whether pw' is equal to pw or not by seeing a subsequent message from server S. However, when $pw' \neq pw$, the probability for the PKG to compute the correct K is negligible in the security parameter for the underlying group since the PKG has to guess the discrete logarithm y (chosen by server S) as well. That is, this client impersonation attack is also restricted by the online dictionary attacks where the PKG can try a guessed password by communicating with the honest server S. Therefore, the SPI-S protocol is secure against the PKG's active attacks.

The security of the SPI-S protocol against the PKG's passive/active attacks can be formally proved by following the proof technique of [2] under the set password-based chosen-basis CDH problem since we applied the same masking technique of Diffie-Hellman public values as in [2].

Also, it is clear that the security of the SPI and SPI-S protocols against server impersonation attacks after password compromise is inherent to the security of the BF-IBE scheme in Sect. 2.4.

Table 1. Comparison of PAKE protocols using the BF-IBE scheme [6,7]

Protocols	Computation costs		Communication	# of	Security against a
	Client C	Server S	costs	passes	malicious PKG
PAKE-CS [16]	$1e + 5\mathsf{Exp}_{\mathbb{G}_1} +$ $1\mathsf{Exp}_{\mathbb{G}_2}$	$1e + 4\mathsf{Exp}_{\mathbb{G}_1}$	$\|C\| + \|S\| +$ $4\|\mathbb{G}_1\| + \|H\|$	2	No
iPAKE [9]	$1e + 2\mathsf{Exp}_{\mathbb{G}_1} +$ $1\mathsf{Exp}_{\mathbb{G}_2}$	$1e + 2\mathsf{Exp}_{\mathbb{G}_1}$	$\|C\| + \|S\| +$ $2\|\mathbb{G}_1\| + \|H\|$	2*	No
SPI (Sect. 5)	$1e + 3.17\mathsf{Exp}_{\mathbb{G}_1} +$ $1\mathsf{Exp}_{\mathbb{G}_2}$	$1e + 2\mathsf{Exp}_{\mathbb{G}_1}$	$\|C\| + \|S\| +$ $2\|\mathbb{G}_1\| + 2\|H\|$	2	Yes
SPI-S (Sect. 6)	$1e + 3.34\mathsf{Exp}_{\mathbb{G}_1} +$ $1\mathsf{Exp}_{\mathbb{G}_2}$	$1e + 2\mathsf{Exp}_{\mathbb{G}_1}$	$\|C\| + \|S\| +$ $2\|\mathbb{G}_1\| + \|H\|$	2	Yes

*As stated in [9], the iPAKE protocol can be constructed with a single pass.

8   Comparison

In this section, we compare the PAKE protocols using the BF-IBE scheme [6,7] (PAKE-CS [16], iPAKE [9], SPI of Sect. 5, SPI-S of Sect. 6) in terms of efficiency, number of passes and security against a malicious PKG.

We summarize the comparative result in Table 1 where $\mathsf{Exp}_{\mathbb{G}_1}$ (resp., $\mathsf{Exp}_{\mathbb{G}_2}$) indicates a modular exponentiation in $\mathbb{G}_1$ (resp., $\mathbb{G}_2$), and $|c|$ indicates a bit-length of c. The number of modular exponentiations for one simultaneous calculation of two bases (i.e. $g_1^{x_1} \cdot g_2^{x_2}$) is counted to 1.17 due to the Strauss's algorithm [14,15] (also known as Shamir's trick). If pre-computation is allowed, the computation cost of client C is reduced to $2\mathsf{Exp}_{\mathbb{G}_1}$ (resp., $2.17\mathsf{Exp}_{\mathbb{G}_1}$) in the SPI (resp., SPI-S) protocol. One can see that there is a trade-off between the SPI and SPI-S protocols with respect to computation costs of client C and communications costs. Though the iPAKE protocol [9] is more efficient than the SPI and SPI-S protocols with respect to both computation costs of client C and communications cost, it is not secure against passive/active attacks by a malicious PKG (as in Sect. 4).

References

1. Research papers on password-based cryptography. http://www.jablon.org/passwordlinks.html. Accessed 8 Aug 2019
2. Abdalla, M., Pointcheval, D.: Simple password-based encrypted key exchange protocols. In: Menezes, A. (ed.) CT-RSA 2005. LNCS, vol. 3376, pp. 191–208. Springer, Heidelberg (2005). https://doi.org/10.1007/978-3-540-30574-3_14
3. Bellare, M., Rogaway, P.: Random oracles are practical: a paradigm for designing efficient protocols. In: CCS 1993, pp. 62–73. ACM (1993)
4. Bellovin, S.M., Merritt, M.: Encrypted key exchange: password-based protocols secure against dictionary attacks. In: IEEE Symposium on Security and Privacy, pp. 72–84. IEEE (1992)
5. Bellovin, S.M., Merritt, M.: Augmented encrypted key exchange: a password-based protocol secure against dictionary attacks and password file compromise. In: CCS 1993, pp. 244–250. ACM (1993)
6. Boneh, D., Franklin, M.: Identity-based encryption from the weil pairing. In: Kilian, J. (ed.) CRYPTO 2001. LNCS, vol. 2139, pp. 213–229. Springer, Heidelberg (2001). https://doi.org/10.1007/3-540-44647-8_13
7. Boneh, D., Franklin, M.: Identity-based encryption from the weil pairing. SIAM J. Comput. **32**(3), 586–615 (2003)
8. Boyen, X.: A tapestry of identity-based encryption: practical frameworks compared. Int. J. Appl. Crypt. **1**(1), 3–21 (2008)
9. Choi, K.Y., Cho, J., Hwang, J.Y., Kwon, T.: Constructing efficient PAKE protocols from identity-based KEM/DEM. In: Kim, H., Choi, D. (eds.) WISA 2015. LNCS, vol. 9503, pp. 411–422. Springer, Cham (2016). https://doi.org/10.1007/978-3-319-31875-2_34
10. Galindo, D., Garcia, F.D.: A schnorr-like lightweight identity-based signature scheme. In: Preneel, B. (ed.) AFRICACRYPT 2009. LNCS, vol. 5580, pp. 135–148. Springer, Heidelberg (2009). https://doi.org/10.1007/978-3-642-02384-2_9

11. Hwang, J.Y., Kim, S.-H., Choi, D., Jin, S.-H., Song, B.: Robust authenticated key exchange using passwords and identity-based signatures. In: Chen, L., Matsuo, S. (eds.) SSR 2015. LNCS, vol. 9497, pp. 43–69. Springer, Cham (2015). https://doi.org/10.1007/978-3-319-27152-1_3

12. ISO/IEC JTC 1/SC 27: Information security, cybersecurity and privacy protection. https://www.iso.org/committee/45306.html. Accessed 8 Aug 2019

13. Jarecki, S., Krawczyk, H., Xu, J.: OPAQUE: an asymmetric PAKE protocol secure against pre-computation attacks. In: Nielsen, J.B., Rijmen, V. (eds.) EUROCRYPT 2018. LNCS, vol. 10822, pp. 456–486. Springer, Cham (2018). https://doi.org/10.1007/978-3-319-78372-7_15

14. Menezes, A.J., van Oorschot, P.C., Vanstone, S.A.: Handbook of Applied Cryptography, pp. 617–618. CRC Press (1996)

15. Straus, E.G.: Addition chains of vectors. Am. Math. Mon. **71**(7), 806–808 (1964)

16. Yi, X., Tso, R., Okamoto, E.: Identity-based password-authenticated key exchange for client/server model. In: SECRYPT 2012, pp. 45–54. Science and Technology Publications (2012)

Efficient Decentralized Random Commitment Key Generation for Mixnet Shuffle Proof

Jongkil Kim[✉], Joonsang Baek, Willy Susilo, and Yang-Wai Chow

Institute of Cybersecurity and Cryptology, School of Computing and Information Technology, University of Wollongong, Wollongong, Australia
{jongkil,baek,wsusilo,caseyc}@uow.edu.au

Abstract. In this paper, we propose a new commitment key generation method for the mixnet shuffle proof developed by Bayer-Groth in Eurocrypt' 12. The problem of the shuffle proof algorithm is that it gives too much power to a single authority: It has been shown that the authority, who creates commitment keys and generates proofs for verifying electronic voting (e-voting) results, also can produce malicious verification proofs by logging the exponents of commitment keys. We suggest a new way to decentralize the commitment key generation process by allowing multiple parties to jointly participate in the commitment key generation. Therefore, any of the parties, even who operating e-voting system, cannot know the exponents of commitment keys fully. Therefore, our suggestion distributes the power that is concentrated on the single authority and makes the verification process of the proof more sound and prudent.

Keywords: Multi-party computation · E-voting · Commitment

1 Introduction

1.1 Motivation

The e-voting becomes a popular voting method for modern governance. The growing mobility of citizens makes e-voting to an unavoidable trend for successful democratic decision. Advanced cryptographic primitives improve the anonymity and privacy of e-voting and enable people to make sure that their votes are secured and counted.

Recently, Lewis et al. [13] raised several concerns on e-voting processes based on Bayer-Groth proofs [14]. They claim that logging the random exponents of commitment keys in Bayer-Groth proofs can be used to manipulate e-voting results, which can pass verification. The problem that they pointed out may be debatable since it assumes that an authority, who governs and operates e-voting such as electoral commission, is untrusted. Moreover, their claim is not surprising since the shuffle and verification processes of mixnet depend on hardness of the

© Springer Nature Switzerland AG 2020
I. You (Ed.): WISA 2019, LNCS 11897, pp. 206–216, 2020.
https://doi.org/10.1007/978-3-030-39303-8_16

discrete logarithm problem. Knowing the exponents of commitment keys leads the security failures.

However, fair voting is critically important for the successful execution of democracy. In a critical national election such as the presidential election, a risk that compromising the voting result is huge. Distributing the concentration of power from a single authority to multiple parties makes people more convince on the process and outputs of the election. Enabling such distribution of power remains an important task to build a more trusted e-voting system.

1.2 Our Contribution

In this paper, as a solution to the Lewis et al.'s problem mentioned above, we propose a technique that generates the commitment keys in a decentralized way. Our technique enables that the multiple parties participate in generating the commitment keys of Bayer-Groth's suffle algorithm [14]. Particularly, our technique can be applied to efficiently distribute the power of the authority running e-voting. In our scheme, the random exponents of the commitment keys cannot be leaked unless all parties collude. Moreover, it allows anyone who is participated in commitment key generation to verify that the generated keys are valid even if the commitment variables are randomized.

Our technique relies on the discrete logarithm problem. Its main idea can be explained clearly in the most simple cases where there are only two parties "Alice" and "Bob" (although it can be easily extended to the multi-party case). We suppose that two parties, Alice and Bob, generate a commitment variable together. First, a given generator g for a cyclic group $\mathbb{G}$ of order q, Alice randomly selects a from Z_q^* and computes g^a. Bob, then, picks b at random and computes $(g^a)^b$, which is random due to randomness of the two variables a and b. But, the exponents ab will be hidden unless both Alice and Bob collude. This means that no one will know ab including Alice and Bob. However, this simple multi-party computation needs an additional verification process. Suppose that Alice has performed her computation first and has sent g^a to Bob. If Bob wants to cheat Alice, instead of computing $(g^a)^b$, Bob can compute g^b and set this as an output. But, in this case, Alice will not know whether the output was generated actually from g^{ab} or just from g^b. Moreover, Bob knows the exact power of the output, which is b.

Our solution avoids this fraud by allowing Alice to verify that the Bob's output is computed under Alice's random value, a. Therefore, instead of providing a sole output value, Bob needs to provide a proof. In particular, when Bob submits g^{ab}, he has to submit g^b too. Then, Alice who owns a will verify that the values are created correctly based on her submission by computing $(g^b)^a$.

2 Preliminaries

2.1 Commitment

For a cyclic group $\mathbb{G}$ of large prime order q, the general Pedersen commitment scheme [12] works as follows:

The key generation algorithm K chooses random generators $G_1, \ldots, G_n$ and H of the group $\mathbb{G}$ and sets the commitment key $ck = (G_1, \ldots, G_n, H)$. To commit to n elements $(a_1, \ldots, a_n) \in Z_q^n$, we pick randomness $r \in Z_q$ and compute $com_{ck}(a_1, \ldots, a_n; r) = H^r \prod_{i=1}^{n} G_i^{a_i}$. We can also commit to less than n elements; this is done by setting the remaining entries to 0. We will always assume that interested parties have verified that commitments belong to the group $\mathbb{G}$.

The commitment is computationally binding under the *discrete logarithm assumption*. The commitment scheme is perfectly hiding since the commitment is uniformly distributed in $\mathbb{G}$ no matter what the messages are.

2.2 Known Exponents Attacks on Commitment Keys [13]

The mixnet ZKP of Bayer and Groth [14] highly relied on the discrete logarithm (DL) assumption. Particularly, in their commitment scheme, logging exponents of commitment parameters result in the failure of the security. In other words, if a malicious authority generates commitment parameters $ck = \{H, G_1, \ldots, G_n\}$ where $G_i = H^{e_i}$ by using H and logging e_i, the malicious authority can generate a fake commitment result using those known exponents. For example, A commitment $com_{ck}(\boldsymbol{a}; r)$ can be computed using $com_{ck}(\boldsymbol{b}; r_0)$ by setting

$$r_0 = r + \sum_{i=1}^{n} e_i(a_i - b_i)$$

because

$$com_{ck}(\boldsymbol{a}; r) = H^r \prod_{i=1}^{n} G_i^{a_i}$$

$$= H^r \prod_{i=1}^{n} H^{a_i e_i}$$

$$= H^{r + \sum_{i=1}^{n}(a_i - b_i)e_i} \prod_{i=1}^{n} H^{b_i e_i}$$

$$= H^{r_0} \prod_{i=1}^{n} G_i^{b_i}$$

$$= com_{ck}(\boldsymbol{b}; r_0)$$

3 Proposed Technique

3.1 Overview

In the original generation of commitment keys, the single authority creates randomized values from Z_q^*. Given the group generator g, the authority can generate the random exponent r_i and compute g^{r_i} to compute commitment keys. Because this authority is also the one who generates proofs to verify the results, r_i can be used as a trapdoor to make cheat proofs when it is logged [13].

To prevent this flaw in the scheme, we suggest two steps to generate commitment keys between multiple parties. The first step is randomizing generators from g to g' and h', which are respectively for G_i and H, by participating multiple parties in the system. The second step is creating random commitment keys using the randomized generators. We accept that any party can record its random exponent, but do not allow the whole values of powers of randomized generators (accordingly, commitment keys) to be known to any of the involved parties unless all parties collude.

Moreover, our technique enables efficient and flexible generation of commitment parameters. The trivial approach is making all parties participate in the generation of each commitment key. In a real e-voting system, the number of commitment keys required to verfy the voting results is very large because the number of commitment keys is close to the square of total number of votes. Since the increasing number of e-votes, generating and managing a large number of commitment keys and its proofs in each party is not easy. Moreover, if the number of e-voters are larger than its anticipation, the system may require whole generation process, again to increase the acceptable voting numbers depending on the implementation design of voting system. Our stepwise approach enables the system not to be limited by this restriction.

3.2   Randomizing a Generator

The first step is randomizing a generator g to $g' = g^{\prod_{i=1}^{n} a_i}$ and $h' = g^{\prod_{i=1}^{n} b_i}$ where n is the total number of parties and a_i and b_i are their contribution to the randomization. Therefore, unless all parties collude, the discrete logarithms to the base g of g' and h' are not be computable. Moreover, each party can verify that their contribution on g' and h' using the proofs that each participating party provides along with their computation on g' and h'. We use h' to generate H and g' to generate $G_1, \ldots, G_n$. We also can use different randomized generators to break correlation between commitment keys in G_i (particularly, the first few commitment keys of G_i), instead of using g' for all G_i. In this section, we describe how to derive g', but the same technique can be used to generate h'.

Multi-party commitment key generation can be realized by the following four algorithms. We use $[k]$ to denote the set $\{1, \ldots, k\}$:

- **Setup**$(\lambda) \to pk$: The algorithm generates a cyclic group $\mathbb{G}$ of order q with the generator g. It sets $pk = (\mathbb{G}, q)$. It also sets $P_0 := \{g\}$.
- **KeyGen**$(pk, i) \to sk_i$: The algorithm takes as inputs pk and randomly selects a_i from Z_q^*. It outputs $sk_i = a_i$.
- **ParamGen**$_1(pk, sk_1, P_0) \to P_1$: Only for the first party, the algorithm takes as inputs a generator g from P_0 and a_1 from sk_1. It then computes the randomized generator $P_1 := g^{a_1}$ and outputs P_1.
- **ParamGen**$_2(pk, sk_k, P_{k-2}, P_{k-1}) \to P_k$ for $k \geq 2$: The algorithm takes as inputs the outputs from the previous parties. Particularly, it takes $g^{\prod_{i=1}^{k-2} a_i}$

from P_{k-2} and $\{g^{\prod_{i=1}^{k-1} a_i}, g^{(\prod_{i=1}^{k-1} a_i)/a_j}; j = [k-2]\}$ from P_{k-1}.

The kth party, who has $sk_k = a_k$, then computes (1) the randomized generator $(g^{\prod_{i=1}^{k-1} a_i})^{a_k}$ and (2) the proofs $(g^{\prod_{i=1}^{k-2} a_i})^{a_k}$ and $(g^{(\prod_{i=1}^{k-1} a_i)/a_j})^{a_k}$ for all $j \in [k-2]$. Therefore, it outputs

$$P_k = \{g^{\prod_{i=1}^{k} a_i}, g^{(\prod_{i=1}^{k} a_i)/a_j}; j = [k-1]\}.$$

- **Verification**$(sk_k, P_N) \rightarrow \{0,1\}$: The kth party takes as inputs from P_N where

$$P_N = \{g^{\prod_{i=1}^{N} a_i}, g^{(\prod_{i=1}^{N} a_i)/a_j}; j = [N-1]\}.$$

To verify the result, the algorithm takes $g^{\prod_{i=1}^{N} a_i}$ and the kth proof b_k, which is supposed to be $g^{\prod_{i=1}^{N} a_i/a_k}$. If $g^{\prod_{i=1}^{N} a_i}$ is identical to $(b_k)^{a_k}$, it outputs 1. Otherwise, it outputs 0 and aborts.

The verification over the final results can be performed by each party for the final outcome of commitment keys, which are generated by the Nth party in the generation. Table 1 shows the summary of randomization process of the generator g. The columns of the table show that the outputs of **ParamGen**. The row "Randomized generator" shows the randomized outcome of the generator contributed by each of N parties. It should be noted that the value is the last column in this row is the commitment key (i.e, G_i). The values in the following rows show the proofs.

Table 1. Randomizing g and the proofs associated to N parties

	Generator	P_1	P_2	P_3	$\ldots$	P_N
Randomized generator	g	g^{a_1}	$g^{a_1 a_2}$	$g^{a_1 a_2 a_3}$	$\ldots$	$g^{\prod_{i=1}^{N} a_i}$
Proofs for the 1st party			g^{a_2}	$g^{a_2 a_3}$	$\ldots$	$g^{(\prod_{i=1}^{N} a_i)/a_1}$
Proofs for the 2nd party				$g^{a_1 a_3}$	$\ldots$	$g^{(\prod_{i=1}^{N} a_i)/a_2}$
$\vdots$					$\ddots$	$\vdots$
Proofs for the $(N-1)$th party						$g^{(\prod_{i=1}^{N} a_i)/a_{N-1}}$

3.3 Random Generation over Commitment Keys

After the successful generation of a randomized generator $g' = g^{\prod_{i=1}^{N} a_i}$ and $h' = g^{\prod_{i=1}^{N} b_i}$, election board can randomly generate commitment keys such as $H, G_1, \ldots, G_n$ over the randomized generators. However, this randomization also needs to provide the proofs where the variables are generated over the g' and h'.

Let r_i be a random variable that be selected to randomize commitment keys. The participated party cannot distinguish $G_i = (g')^{r_i}$ from g^{r_i} because r_i is not given. One of the trivial approach is providing the proofs for each commitment keys. However, in this case, the number of elements, which have to be given for the proofs, is significantly large.

For example, 10 candidates of the election are participated in to generating g', and there exists 100,000 voters for the e-voting. In the worst case scenario, the number of total commitment keys required is 100,001 variables, $H, G_1, \ldots, G_{100,000}$. However, the size of the proofs is 10 times larger, which is one million variables since 100,001 proofs are required for each of 10 candidates. This results in a slow verification process since it means that each candidate requires to compute one 100,001 exponentiations over a group element to verify that the commitment keys are properly computed.

We subsequently reduce the number of proofs by multiplying commitment keys. For example, in our technique, each party only needs 99,999 multiplication between group elements and two exponentiation instead of 100,001 exponentiations. Moreover, the number of proofs is only four elements, two for H and the other two for $G_1 \ldots G_n$ for each party. Therefore, it significantly reduces the computation and storage requirements for the party. We also describe the **ParamGen** for $G_1, \ldots, G_n$ below.

The commitment keys ck and its proofs ck_{pr} can be generated by the following two algorithms:

- **ParamGen**$(pk, P_{N-1}, P_N, g', n) \to (ck, ck_{pr})$: The algorithm takes as inputs a generator g' and information of the group $\mathbb{G}$ from pk, P_{N-1} and P_N. It randomly selects random values $r_1, \ldots, r_n$ from Z_q^* and outputs commitment keys

$$ck := \{g'^{r_1}, \ldots, g'^{r_n}\}.$$

To prove that the algorithm generates ck in a correct manner, it computes $r = \sum_{i=1}^{n} r_i$. Then, it outputs

$$ck_{pr} := \{g'^r, g^{(\prod_{i=1}^{N} a_i)r/a_j}; j = [N]\}.$$

It should be noted that the algorithm can obtain $g^{(\prod_{i=1}^{N} a_i)/a_j}$ for $j = [N-1]$ from P_N. It also can get $g^{\prod_{i=1}^{N-1} a_i} (= g^{(\prod_{i=1}^{N} a_i)/a_N})$ from P_{N-1}.

- **Verification**$(sk_k, ck, ck_{pr}) \to \{0, 1\}$: The kth party takes as inputs commitment keys $ck = \{g'^{r_1}, \ldots, g'^{r_n}\}$ and its proofs $\{g'^r, g^{(\prod_{i=1}^{N} a_i)r/a_j}; j = [N]\}$. To verify the result, the algorithm compares the following:

$$\prod_{i=1}^{n} g'^{r_i} = g'^r \text{ and } (g^{(\prod_{i=1}^{N} a_i)r/a_k})^{a_k} = g'^r.$$

If both equalities hold, it outputs 1. Otherwise, it outputs 0 and aborts.

4   Implementation

We implement our commitment key generation algorithm to measure the computation overheads. We set q to 2048 bits prime and use the initial generator

$g = 2$. We use a big number (BN) library from OpenSSL [16]. C language is used to implement the algorithm. The algorithm implemented and tested in Virtual Machine having Ubuntu OS. Four processors and 8 GB are allocated to the VM. The machine hosting the VM is operated by Windows 10 Enterprise. The host machine has Intel i5-7440HQ CPU @ 2.80 GHz with 16 GB memory.

The computational overheads to randomize the generator are different for each participants. Because one who randomize the generator provide proofs for all previously participated parties, the computation overhead increases as shown in Table 2.

Table 2. Computation overheads to randomize a generator (by Time (ms))

Computing order	1st	10th	20th	30th	40th	50th
Time (ms)	5.00	35.41	68.35	101.07	134.83	165.90

After successfully randomizing the generator, the authority who operates e-voting system can generate commitment keys. Although generating commitment keys are not necessary to be a realtime operation, the reasonable generation times are important because the number of voters is usually large. We measure the execution times by the number of commitment keys in Table 3. Generating 10,000 commitment keys are taken around 30 s in a single core, which can be assumed reasonably fast.

Table 3. Commitment key generation time (ms) with the randomized generator

# of com. keys	1 party	20 parties	40 parties	60 parties	80 parties	100 parties
10	4.6	10.55	16.92	23.27	29.83	35.91
100	33.94	39.38	45.83	52.01	58.86	64.75
1000	323.51	329.35	335.23	338.88	347.22	352.74
10000	3218.8	3211.72	3208.8	3209.5	3211.98	3217.76

The verification time taking to check whether the commitment keys are generated properly or not is fast since we replace the unnecessary exponentiation over group element to multiplication between group elements. It can be verified within 100 ms for each party even the number of commitment keys are large (10,000). Table 4 shows the verification time by milliseconds.

5   Related Work

5.1   E-voting Requirements

The e-voting that guarantees untraceability dates back to 1981 when Chaum considered the basic ideas [3]. There have been numerous e-voting protocols

Table 4. Commitment key verification time (ms) (for each party)

# of com. keys	10	100	1000	10000
Time (ms)	14.69	15.47	20.67	96.91

and systems that realize them. Though many, no single system has successfully realized the ideal e-voting protocol. According to Wang et al. [11], there are three reasons why the realization of e-voting is a vexing problem. First, it is hard to agree on the requirements of the e-voting. Second, the e-voting system is huge and complex. Lastly, despite its complexity, the e-voting system should be usable for voters.

Although it is difficult to fully agree on what requirements should be satisfied for a particular e-voting system, a consensus view is that the most (or the majority) of the security requirements summarized in Table 5 should be addressed.

Table 5. Security requirements of the e-voting

Requirements	Meaning
Correctness	The votes should be counted correctly
Privacy	None of any voter's ballots should be known to anyone
Unreusability	No one can cast a vote twice
Eligibility	Only authorized voters can vote
Robustness	A system should function properly with certain amount of misbehaved voters
Verifiability	A voter can verify if his vote is being counted
Fairness	No partial results will be computed before the end of election
Receipt-freeness	A voter can neither obtain nor construct a receipt to prove his/her vote
Universal verifiability	Anyone can verify the final voting result is intact

5.2 Cryptographic Primitives for E-voting

To realize a secure e-voting system, many cryptographic primitives should be employed. We briefly summarize them as follows.

- Mixnet: The main idea of mixnet [3] is to break the link between the source and the destination by using a chain of mixes, each of which only knows the node that it immediately received the message from, and the immediate destination to send the message to. Each message is encrypted using public keys of several mixes and the order of encrypted message (ciphertext) is shuffled.

Upon receiving the ciphertext, each mix strips off its own layer of encryption to reveals where to send the message next. By passing through several mixes and being cascaded through several shuffle agents, the origin and the order of the ciphertext would not be revealed, and the authority will not be able to trace the ciphertext.

In the e-voting system utilizing the mixnet, ballots are encrypted and sent to mixes so that the authority is unable to link a ballot to a particular voter. It should be noted that in the mixnet, at least one mix is assume to be trustworthy in the sense that it would not collude in revealing the relationship between voters and their ballots. A "robust" mixnet should provide evidence that a voter's ballot is encrypted through the layers of mixes and is not discarded or replaced.

- Blind signature: In some e-voting system, the voter sends a ballot containing a token and their vote to the authority (through the anonymous channel). The authority needs to ensure that any eligible voters can vote and vote once only, on the basis that the token can be used only once. However, there is privacy concern that the voter's identity could be revealed when he/she obtains the token. In this case, one can use "blind signature" [4], whereby the voter as a requester can get a signature on the blinded token from the authority. The voter can should be able to cast a vote with un-blinded token.
- Homomorphic encryption: Homomorphic encryption [6,7] makes it possible to aggregate ciphertexts without decrypting them. When it is applied to the e-voting system, each encrypted ballot can be aggregated by an agent before being tallied at the authority [8].
- Zero-Knowledge Proof: Zero-Knowledge Proof (ZKP) allows a party to prove to another party that a given statement is true without revealing any secret associated with the statement. ZKP is an essential tool for the e-voting system since there are many occasions that need verification without revealing confidential information. One example is that voters need to verify their encrypted votes really encrypt the right form of votes without revealing the contents. Another example is that the mixes need to verify that re-encryption and shuffling is performed correctly without revealing anything [9,14].

5.3   Examples of e-voting System in Practice

As mentioned in the beginning of this section, e-voting system is huge and complex. However, various institutions across regions have made meaningful attempts to develop and test e-voting. In this paper, we briefly survey some notable systems reported in the literature.

Direct Recording Electronic Systems (DRE) [2] is a touch screen voting system, in which votes are recorded in a computer memory. Sensus [5] is a security-aware e-voting system, which employs the blind signature. It suffers from the vulnerability that some voters can cast their votes instead of those who did not vote. VoteBox [10] is a system that utilizes a distributed broadcast network and replicated log to provide robustness and audit when failure, misconfiguration, or tampering occurs. Its core technology includes homomorphic encryption. Helios

[1] is a web-based e-voting system in which ballots are encrypted and anonymously sent to the server using mixnet. It provides universal verifiability. sVoting [15] is the e-voting system operated by Swiss-post. It uses Bayer-Groth's shuffle algorithm to provide privacy and anonymity of voting with the verification.

6   Conculsion

In this paper, we proposed a new decentralized method to generate commitment keys for Bayer-Groth suffle proof. Previously, Bayer-Groth suffle proof allows an authority to cheat the proof by logging the exponents of commitment keys. If both proofs and commitment keys are generated by a single authority, this may arise the question on the correct verification of the voting results. We suggest a way to restrict the roles of a single authority and decentralize the process to create commitment keys. Moreover, all the participants can verify and check that their contributions to create commitment keys are valid. Therefore, our result leads more secure and prudent e-voting system.

References

1. Adida, B.: Helios: web-based open-audit voting. In: The International Conference on Security Symposium 2008, pp. 335–348 (2008)
2. Altun, A.A., Bilgin, M.: Web based secure e-voting system with fingerprint authentication. Sci. Res. Essays **6**(12), 2494–2500 (2011)
3. Chaum, D.: Untraceable electronic mail, return addresses, and digital pseudonyms. Commun. ACM **24**(2), 84–90 (1981)
4. Chaum, D.: Blind signatures for untraceable payments. In: Chaum, D., Rivest, R.L., Sherman, A.T. (eds.) Advances in Cryptology, pp. 199–203. Springer, Boston (1983). https://doi.org/10.1007/978-1-4757-0602-4_18
5. Cranor, L.F., Cytron, R.K.: Sensus: a security-conscious electronic polling system for the internet. In: The Hawaii International Conference on System Sciences, vol. 3, pp. 561–570 (1997)
6. Drucker, N., Gueron, S.: Achieving trustworthy homomorphic encryption by combining it with a trusted execution environment. J. Wirel. Mob. Netw. Ubiquit. Comput. Dependable Appl. **9**(1), 86–99 (2018)
7. Gentry, C.: A fully homomorphic encryption scheme. Ph.D. thesis, Stanford University (2009)
8. Kiayias, A., Yung, M.: The vector-ballot e-voting approach. In: Juels, A. (ed.) FC 2004. LNCS, vol. 3110, pp. 72–89. Springer, Heidelberg (2004). https://doi.org/10.1007/978-3-540-27809-2_9
9. Neff, C.: A verifiable secret shuffle and its application to e-voting. In: ACM Conference on Computer and Communications Security, pp. 116–125 (2001)
10. Sandler, D., Derr, K., Wallach, D.S.: VoteBox: a tamper-evident, verifiable electronic voting system. In: The International Conference on Security Symposium, pp. 349–364 (2008)
11. Wang, K., Mondal, S.K., Chan, K., Xie, X.: A review of contemporary e-voting: requirements, technology, systems and usability. Data Sci. Pattern Recogn. **1**(1), 31–47 (2017)

12. Pedersen, T.P.: Non-interactive and information-theoretic secure verifiable secret sharing. In: Feigenbaum, J. (ed.) CRYPTO 1991. LNCS, vol. 576, pp. 129–140. Springer, Heidelberg (1992). https://doi.org/10.1007/3-540-46766-1_9
13. Lewis, S.J., Pereira, O., Teague, V.: The use of trapdoor commitments in Bayer-Groth proofs and the implications for the verifiabilty of the Scytl-SwissPost Internet voting system (2019). https://people.eng.unimelb.edu.au/vjteague/UniversalVerifiabilitySwissPost.pdf
14. Bayer, S., Groth, J.: Efficient zero-knowledge argument for correctness of a shuffle. In: Pointcheval, D., Johansson, T. (eds.) EUROCRYPT 2012. LNCS, vol. 7237, pp. 263–280. Springer, Heidelberg (2012). https://doi.org/10.1007/978-3-642-29011-4_17
15. Swiss Post's e-voting solution. https://www.post.ch/en/business/a-z-of-subjects/industry-solutions/swiss-post-e-voting. Accessed 14 June 2019
16. OpenSSL - Cryptography and SSL/TLS Toolkit. https://www.openssl.org/. Accessed 14 June 2019

Security With AI and Machine Learning

Catching the Phish: Detecting Phishing Attacks Using Recurrent Neural Networks (RNNs)

Lukáš Halgaš[1(✉)], Ioannis Agrafiotis[1], and Jason R. C. Nurse[2]

[1] Department of Computer Science, University of Oxford, Oxford, UK
{lukas.halgas,ioannis.agrafiotis}@cs.ox.ac.uk
[2] School of Computing, University of Kent, Canterbury, UK
j.r.c.nurse@kent.ac.uk

Abstract. The emergence of online services in our daily lives has been accompanied by a range of malicious attempts to trick individuals into performing undesired actions, often to the benefit of the adversary. The most popular medium of these attempts is phishing attacks, mainly through emails and websites. In order to defend against such attacks, there is an urgent need for automated mechanisms to identify this malicious content before it reaches users. Machine learning techniques have gradually become the standard for such classification problems. However, identifying common measurable features of phishing content (e.g., in emails) is notoriously difficult. To address this problem, we engage in a novel study into a phishing content classifier based on a recurrent neural network (RNN), which identifies such features without human input. At this stage, we scope our research to emails, but our approach can be extended to apply to websites. Our results show that the proposed system outperforms state-of-the-art tools. Furthermore, our classifier is efficient and takes into account only the text and, in particular, the textual structure of the email. Since these features are rarely considered in email classification, we argue that our classifier can complement existing classifiers with high information gain.

Keywords: Phishing · Machine learning · Recurrent neural networks · Natural language processing · Web security

1 Introduction

Advances in computer security have raised confidence in internet safety leading to e-commerce, internet banking and other means of sending, managing and receiving money online. Unfortunately, the advent of online services has been accompanied by illicit attempts to sham such transactions to the benefit of malicious entities. Perhaps the most popular and easy to execute attack, which poses a threat to organisations, institutions and simple users, is *phishing*.

© Springer Nature Switzerland AG 2020
I. You (Ed.): WISA 2019, LNCS 11897, pp. 219–233, 2020.
https://doi.org/10.1007/978-3-030-39303-8_17

Phishing is a type of cyber-attack that communicates socially engineered messages to humans using digital channels in order to persuade them to perform certain activities to the attacker's benefit [12,16]. Email is the most common avenue for a phishing attack, with almost 91% of successful cyber-attacks/security breaches initiated by sending out spoofed emails [18]. The entire phishing operation can even be outsourced and automated [20], enabling the phishing threat to be, as it is, ubiquitous and continuous. Research has also found that it is increasingly difficult for humans to detect phishing attacks [10]. Therefore, there is a strong argument for automated mitigation methods to keep the user's exposure to the attacks at a minimum.

The dynamic nature of phishing, with new trends and challenges constantly emerging, motivates a more adaptive filtering approach. Machine learning (ML) has been utilised, as the de-facto standard for classification purposes over many fields, email classification included. Developing a ML-based classifier to underline the phishing filtering is the approach we investigate in this paper. Our classifier analyses the text of the email and, in particular, the email's language structure. It follows that our work is largely orthogonal to contemporary email classification systems which, to the best of the authors' knowledge, do not employ natural language processing. We propose a novel detection system for phishing emails based on recurrent neural networks (RNNs). Our evaluation indicates that the RNN system outperforms state-of-the-art tools.

In what follows, Sect. 2 presents alternative approaches to automated detection of phishing emails and literature on current machine learning approaches. Section 3 details our methodology and feature selection for the RNN, while Sect. 4 describes the system implementation. Section 5 discusses the evaluation of the system, and Sect. 6 concludes the paper.

2   Current Landscape on Mitigation Techniques to Phishing

Techniques to mitigate the phishing problem include human training, laboriously curated blacklists and two-factor authentication for affected resources. However, to combat the problem of large numbers and the dynamic nature of phishing, automated techniques to detect new threats is required. Our work focuses on automated detection of phishing emails. We note that diverse techniques to combat phishing at various levels of the attack can be found in the literature. We reduce our treatment to the algorithmic classification of emails as phish or ham.

Specialised algorithms to classify email as phishing, spam (unsolicited email) or ham (i.e., not spam) have been the focus of research since the beginning of unsolicited email. Classification of phishing email is subsumed in the more general problem of spam filtering. As such, most email classifiers, hence filters, treat relatively harmless spam equivalently to dangerous phishing emails. We challenge the conventional parity in Subsect. 3.3.

Phishing email and bulk spam email are distinct in intent and characteristics. While bulk spam uses sensationalistic language for advertising in personal inboxes, phishing emails mimic ham emails to raise confidence in its allegedly legitimate origin. Thus, Chandrasekaran et al. argue that filtering phishing emails needs to be treated separately from the bulk spam filtering [5]. Their classifier uses 23 *style marker features* including the number of words W, the number of characters C and the number of words per character W/C aliased as *vocabulary richness*, together with two structural attributes extracted from the email subject and body. The authors report results of up to perfect classification, with the accuracy dropping by 20% with the removal of the two structural features. Although the experiment used only a small corpus of 400 emails, the results demonstrate the importance of language and layout, or structure, of emails in phishing classification.

In practice, machine learning-based classifiers using a small set of characteristic features outperform those based on a broad set of general features. In the domain of phishing classification, for example, Fette et al. identified a subset of only ten features (of the hundreds of features commonly used to classify spam email), that best distinguish phishing emails from ham [6]. The resulting method outperformed the trained version of Apache's SpamAssassin [22] classifier at identifying phishing emails, with the false negative rate reduced by a factor of ten. This result demonstrates that having specialised features for the task, in prominence to general email classification features, improves phishing classification.

Bergholz et al. build on top of this work by introducing advanced features for phishing classification [3]. The authors note that improvement in classification through variation of the classifying algorithm itself is statistically insignificant. In conclusion, statistically significant improvement is possible by inventing better features. Bergholz et al. hence develop two sets of advanced features based on unsupervised learning algorithms to complement 27 basic features commonly used in spam detection. One set of the advanced features are based on a dynamic Markov chain (DMC) language model, and additional word-clusters, or email topics, are based on a latent Dirichlet allocation (LDA) model. The best results occur when the advanced features are used in conjunction with the basic features, achieving the state-of-the-art [3].

Toolan et al. analysed 40 basic features popularly used in email classification and ranked them based on their *information gain* to the classification task at hand [24]. The most informative features were vocabulary richness of the email body and the subject. Other popular features performed very poorly, indicating that our intuitive understanding of what constitutes a phishing email may be very wrong. This is illustrated by the failure to gain information from counting <form> elements or finding the word 'debit' in the subject. We may attribute the results to a shift in phishing trends, or to the failure of human experts to identify useful features. The authors also conclude that language modelling approaches to phishing classification are the most promising.

In line with the results and conclusions of previous work, we algorithmically design an advanced feature based on little human intuition. In particular, we train a recurrent neural network (RNN) as a language model to distinguish phishing from ham based on the text of the email only. We describe our advanced feature in detail in Sect. 4.

3   Methodology

The *classification* task is to identify which of a finite number k of categories, or classes $C = \{c_1, \ldots, c_k\}$, a sample $\boldsymbol{x}$ belongs to, i.e., deduce a classifier or mapping, $\boldsymbol{x} \mapsto c$. In our application to phishing, the classification is a mapping of email representations to the label set $\{phish, ham\}$.

The machine learning (ML) approach to classification is to automatically establish a function f that determines the desired class

$$\widehat{y} = f(\boldsymbol{x}) \in \{ham, phish\}$$

on the input of a representation $\boldsymbol{x}$ of an email. The function f is parameterised by values $\boldsymbol{\theta}$. During the training phase, the parameter values $\boldsymbol{\theta}$ are determined to reproduce a relation between the input $\boldsymbol{x}$ and class label y in agreement with a training set $\{(\boldsymbol{x}_0, y_0), \ldots, (\boldsymbol{x}_n, y_n)\}$ of pre-classified samples and a suitable optimisation criterion. In this sense, the ML approach is to extrapolate the relationship between the observed sample points and class labels to unlabelled input $\boldsymbol{x}$ and its predicted class $\hat{y} = f(\boldsymbol{x})$.

3.1   Feature Identification

An input $\boldsymbol{x}_{\mathrm{raw}}$ representing an email as a (very long) series of binary digits, comprising the raw source code of an email in binary format, is unwieldy for an algorithm to detect patterns. We hence use a more compact representation of the input as a feature vector $\boldsymbol{x} = \big(f_1(\boldsymbol{x}_{\mathrm{raw}}), \ldots, f_m(\boldsymbol{x}_{\mathrm{raw}})\big)$. Features should characterise an email with respect to the current classification problem. The relative inaccuracy of ML-based spam classifiers on the seemingly similar task of phishing classification illustrates the need for specialised features for this task [6].

Features are most often identified by experts, in line with their intuitive understanding of "phishiness" or "hamness". Toolan et al. [24] demonstrated that such intuitively sound features often fail to be relevant in phishing classification. On the other hand, structural features have empirically been indicative of emails being ham or phish [6]. Language modelling approaches to improving the state-of-the-art in phishing classification are considered the most worthwhile to research [24]. Naturally, we follow the language modelling approach to design a strong feature based on the structure and content of the email's body.

Natural language processing (NLP) is the field of Computer Science studying human-machine interactions and, in particular, establishing and exploiting language models. The rich structure and ambiguity of natural languages make it difficult to identify and extract complex language features, such as the tone of urgency in the email body. Previously, Verma et al. used pre-trained Word-Net hypernymy trees of sets of words conveying urgency or action, among other characteristics, to identify sentences and hence emails as actionable or informative [25].

In the unsupervised learning approach, the ML algorithm detects data patterns in the dataset without supervision or specific expert advice. That is, the training of the model determines, or learns, the features itself. Fortunately, the unsupervised learning algorithms form the state-of-the-art techniques in language modelling. It follows that our approach of training a language model as a feature is not susceptible to mistakes in expert feature identification.

3.2 Deep Learning

Neural networks (NNs) are a computational model, in the quintessential example of a multilayer perceptron resembling a hierarchical network of units, or neurones. The hierarchical structure intuitively gives NNs the capacity to extract high-level features from simple data, i.e., to disentangle and winnow the factor of variation in the NN's input. This intuition of NN structure makes NNs suitable for the task of *representation learning*, or automatic feature identification.

Recurrent neural networks (RNNs), the deepest of all learners, are a family of NNs specialised for processing sequential data. Like Markov chain models, RNNs have the advantage of processing data in sequence, thus accounting for the order of data. The input text is usually abstracted to a sequence of characters, words or phrases. Undoubtedly, the order of words is valuable in language modelling. RNNs form the backbone of the current state-of-the-art language models, so an RNN language model should form an accurate content-based classifier of emails.

The literature presents several applications of NNs to the related problem of classifying malicious URLs and websites [1,14,26,28]. Bahnsen et al. have used RNNs to classify web addresses as linking to phishing or legitimate websites [1]. The input was a sequence of the URL's characters only. Similarly, we use RNNs to classify emails as phishing or ham, with the input being a sequence of words only.

We alleviate the learning problem from language modelling to the binary classification of email to phish or ham. This classification can be trivially abstracted to predicting y, where $y = 1$ if *phish* and $y = 0$ if *ham*. We thus get a supervised learning problem with representation learning. This simpler task overcomes the often-prohibitive computational cost of training a full-blown language model. Inherently, the RNN classifier models a $y \sim \text{Bernoulli}(p_x)$ distribution using a sigmoid output unit

$$p_x = \sigma(z_x) := \frac{1}{1 + \exp(-z_x)} = \frac{\exp(z_x)}{\sum_{y'=0}^{1} \exp(y' z_x)}$$

where z_x is the output of the last linear layer, dependent on the RNN input x. Intuitively, this is the normalisation of the unnormalised probability distribution

$$\widetilde{p}_x(c) = \exp(c\, z_x)$$
$$\log \widetilde{p}_x(c) = c\, z_x$$

for $c \in \{0,1\}$. Then $p_x = p(y = 1 \mid \text{sequence of words of email } x) \in [0,1]$ gives the email label prediction $\widehat{y} = \arg\max_{c \in \{0,1\}} p(y = c \mid x) = \mathbb{1}\{z_x \geq 0\}$.

3.3 Precision/Accuracy Trade-Off

Commonly, misclassification of phishing and ham emails are considered to have different weights of error [4,6]. A false positive, or incorrectly labelling a legitimate email as phishing is considered to be a more severe error than a false negative, or misclassifying a phishing email as ham. This convention is an artefact of bulk spam filtering, where being exposed to harmless unsolicited advertising is smaller harm than having a legitimate email undelivered. Note that phishing filtering is a subproblem of spam filtering, with techniques as well as related conventions adapted from the more general problem.

It follows that many phishing classifiers emphasise the *precision* of the classifier together with its *accuracy* as criteria of classifier merit. However, a phishing email generally poses more harm than a bulk spam email. Despite the common practice in related work, we do not introduce different penalties to the various misclassification.

Nevertheless, our technique, as most ML-based techniques, is flexible to the trade-off of between accuracy and precision. The RNN classifier, described above, gives a probability value $p(y = 1 \mid x) \in [0,1]$ of the email x being phish. This output value can be viewed as the confidence of the email being phish, where a value close to 0.5 means low confidence in the classification. Thus, a simple method to increase precision, at the cost of lowering accuracy, is to increase the threshold value for labelling an email phish.

4   Design and Implementation

Our RNN classifier labels an input email as either a legitimate email or a phishing attempt. In this section, we describe the procedure of transforming the raw email source into a variable size vector of integers that is input to the RNN itself. The preprocessing of the emails is illustrated in Fig. 1. Use of the trained RNN classifier, also illustrated in the figure, is described in Sect. 5.

4.1   Preprocessing for the RNN Classifier

Our binary classification RNN model takes sequences of integer values as input and outputs a value between 0 and 1. We abstract the computer-native copy of an email as a sequence of bytes into the high-level representation as a sequence of

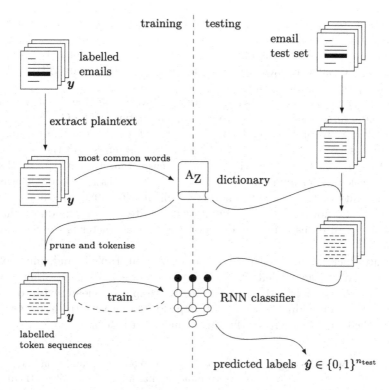

Fig. 1. Training and testing pipeline. We establish a dictionary of the most common words and train our recurrent neural network (RNN) classifier during the training phase. Preprocessing of the emails input into the RNN consists of extracting plaintext, which is then pruned and transformed into a sequence of tokens of manageable size.

symbol and word tokens, represented as unique integers. It is customary to 'feed' RNNs with an n-gram representation of the abstracted text. Due to the small size of our dataset, our dictionary of n-grams would contain very few repetitive phrases of n words for values $n \geq 2$. For the balance of token expressiveness, and vocabulary size, we choose to represent emails as sequences of 1-grams, or single-word tokens.

Note that our classifier only considers the text of emails in making its classification decision. Thus, useful features, such as those based on linked web address analysis, are entirely orthogonal to our classifier and thus are largely complementary. As an initial step in preprocessing of the classified email, we extract its text in plaintext format.

4.2   Tokenising the Text

We seek flexibility in tokenising the text through fine-tuning the parameters of the tokeniser, such as rules of what word or character sequences to represent by the same token. The naïve approach of splitting on whitespace characters does not generalise well to email tokenising. Incautious or malicious salting, e.g., inconsistent whitespace or the ubiquity of special characters, form words unique to an email. Considering such tokens would inherently lead to overfitting, based on the presence of unique traits.

Our approach to tokenising is that of adjusted word-splitting. First, we lower-case all characters in the email and remove all characters the RFC 3986 standard does not allow to be present in a URL, i.e., we only keep the unreserved a-z, 0-9, - . _ ~ and reserved : / ? # [ ] @ ! $ & ' ( ) * + , ; = characters and the percentage sign %. Although this step is motivated by the ease of later identifying URLs for the <url> token determination, we get the benefit of restricting our character base cardinality to 61. The 60th character, which RFC 3986 does not allow in URL, but we do not immediately replace with whitespace, is the quote character ", which is often used in emails. Note, the 61st character is the whitespace character.

We introduce four special tokens summed up in Table 1, and, nine tokens for the special characters left, replacing dots, quotes and seven other special characters with their respective tokens. Finally, we split the clean text into words, serving as their individual tokens, and prepend and append the start <s> and end <e> tokens, respectively, to the tidy sequence of tokens.

Table 1. As a preprocessing step, we abstract out web addresses and email addresses, as well as longer sequences of non-alphanumeric characters. We replace them with special tokens, summarised in the Table.

<url>	Replaces a URL beginning with http:// or https://
<www>	Replaces a URL beginning with the informal www.
<email>	Stands for an email address
<threespecial>	Groups together and replaces three or more consecutive non-alphanumeric characters, possibly separated by whitepace
<s>	Beginning, or start, of email
<e>	End of email

The final representation of the email includes only lowercase alphanumeric words and tokens. Using a list of allowed characters, we aggressively parse the text, mitigating the threat of the text exhibiting unexpected behaviour.

4.3 Recurrent Neural Network Classifier

Our model is a simple RNN, consisting of an encoding layer, two recurrent layers, and a linear output layer with a Softplus activation, as shown in Fig. 2. Challenges of training deep networks, of which RNNs are the deepest, motivate most of the design decisions presented in this section.

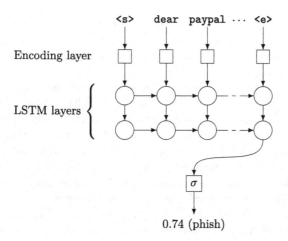

Fig. 2. Our recurrent neural network (RNN) classifier: The input is a sequence of tokens, each mapped to a learned vector representation. The output is a value between 0 and 1, with a value over 0.5 being classified as phish.

We implement our recurrent layers with the long short-term memory (LSTM) architecture [9]. LSTM is a gated recurrent neural layer architecture that, through its carefully designed self-loops, can learn long-range dependencies. We use a variation of the original concept with weights on the self-loop conditioned on the context [7]. Due to its carefully crafted architecture, LSTMs are resistant to the vanishing gradient problem [2]. As is the standard, we use the tanh nonlinear activation on the cells' output. We describe the choice of the size of the hidden layer in Subsect. 5.1, but we will choose the hidden state to be 200 variables large.

The output h_2 of the last LSTM cell of the second layer is input further up the model. So that our model outputs a single variable $p_{\hat{y}} \in (0, 1)$ as required. Since we are modelling a Bernoulli probability, we use the simplest linear layer

$$h_2 \mapsto w^{\mathsf{T}} h_2 + b = z,$$

consisting of a weight vector w and bias scalar b. The final output is obtained by mapping the linear layer output scalar through the logistic sigmoid function

$$p_{\hat{y}} = \sigma(z) := \frac{1}{1 + \exp(-x)} \in (0, 1)$$

to obtain the estimated probability of an email being phish.

4.4   Input Sequence Preprocessing

If we let every token in the dataset to have its unique embedding vector, not only would the encoding layer be huge, but our model predictions would not generalise well to any emails containing unknown words. We hence reduce the size of the *dictionary* considered by our model, in order to acquire round values, to the 4 989 most common words in the training and validation sets of emails as token sets. In other words, we do not consider repetitions of a word in a single email in determining the occurrence count.

Every token in the dictionary is assigned a unique index value. So that our vocabulary reduction is not too harsh, we unite tokens of similar meaning. We stem the words using the Snowball Stemmer, a more aggressive version of the popular Porter Stemmer [19]. We then add five more tokens, <unkalpha>, <unknnum>, <unk>, <cuts> and <cute>, to the dictionary. We summarise the new tokens in Table 2. The first three abstract out unknown words to the dictionary, such as those that consist of only alphabetical or numerical values, or fit none of the first two, respectively. We describe the final two tokens in Sect. 4.5 below. Note that the eleven special tokens described in Tables 1 and 2, together with the 4 989 most common word tokens form the complete dictionary of 5 000 tokens. The number is arbitrary.

Table 2. To make the set of tokens manageably small, we only keep the most common words and replace the rest with special tokens indicating that they are unknown to our dictionary. To make the size of the email representation manageable, we limit the size of emails to 1 000 tokens and replace the parts cut out with special tokens.

<unkalpha>	Words of alphabetical characters not in dictionary
<unknum>	Numbers not in dictionary
<unk>	Other unknown words
<cuts>	Beginning, or start, of a pruning cut
<cute>	End of a pruning cut

4.5 Cutout Pruning

Anomalous emails of very long sequence representations cause training inefficiency, amongst other problems, in evaluating very long-range dependencies. The problem is that such long emails cause unnecessary *'padding'* of other, shorter sequences, when employing gradient-based learning in batches, reducing stability and the speed of learning. Most notably, modern GPU architectures take time proportional to the maximum length of a sample in the batch to evaluate batched samples, as we do.

We hence compromise our email representation for excessively long emails via a simple pruning procedure. The idea is to cut out a sequence of size a third of our threshold of 1 000 tokens, and 'glue' the beginning and end of the email to the *cutout* sequence. The concept is to keep the beginning, most middle and ending parts of the email, skipping the uninformative bits of ham or phish emails. To allow our model to grasp the idea of the anomaly introduced in close-neighbour word dependencies, we add two tokens, <cuts> and <cute>, to the dictionary to represent a start or an end of a sequence caused by the pruning cut. Intuitively, we think of these tokens as *'glue'*.

Emails represented as sequences of indices of their respective tokens, in the range of the dictionary size $V = 5000$, are input or *'fed'* to the RNN. The first, *encoding* layer, encodes each index in sequence with its corresponding token embedding. The embedding vectors elements are initialised as random Gaussian $\mathcal{N}(0, 0.1^2)$ values and learned as parameters of the model.

5 Evaluation

Before presenting the results of our RNN classifier, we first introduce the email datasets used in the evaluation. Table 3 presents a summary of the datasets used. The first dataset, SA-JN, is a combination of all 6 951 ham emails from the SpamAssassin public corpus [22] and 4 572 phishing emails from the Nazario phishing corpus [15] collected before August 2007. SA-JN is a accessible dataset used in related work to evaluate comparable phishing detection solutions [3, 6, 25].

Our second dataset, En-JN, is a combination of the Enron email dataset combined with phishing emails from the Nazario phishing corpus. The Enron email dataset is generated by 158 employees of the Enron Corporation, and, to the best of the authors' knowledge, is the only large public dataset of real-world emails. We combine a randomly selected subset of 10 000 emails from the Enron dataset together with all 9 962 phishing emails from the Nazario phishing corpus.

Table 3. Decomposition of datasets used in evaluation.

Corpus	Size	Ham	Phishing	Source
SA-JN	11 523	6 951 (60%)	4 572 (40%)	SpamAssassin and Nazario
En-JN	19 962	10 000 (50%)	9 962 (50%)	Enron and Nazario

As is common practice in statistical learning, we split the data samples for training and evaluation. Separately, we sort the ham and phishing emails by the `datetime` stamp extracted from the email `Received` or `Received-Date` field (defined to be the maximum, or latest, timestamp where multiple `Received` or `Received-Date` fields are present). Consequently, we get two sorted lists, that we separately split into *training and validation*, and *testing* sets, with a 9-1 ratio twice. The respective 81% – 9% – 10% splits respect the received datetime stamps with the most recent 10% of the emails forming the testing set. The underlying reasoning is to approximate the real scenario of training the classifier on present data to predict future data. We then combine the ham and phishing sets, respecting the splits.

We evaluate our classifier against the most popular metrics in email classifications, which we introduce shortly. We then compare our language model to other content-based classifiers.

5.1 Training

The encoding itself accounts for $5000 \times 200 = 1$ mil parameters of the model. The challenge of training so many parameters of a network requires more advanced optimisation algorithms. We employ the following techniques for optimisation and regularisation of our model.

We initialise the weights of the LSTM cells to random orthogonal matrices with the gain set to 5/3 for the weights of the cell gate with tanh activations, and set the other weights, with sigmoid activations, to orthogonal matrices with gain 1 [21]. It is the perfect orthogonality of the weight matrices that motivated our choice for the embedding and LSTM to share the same unit size of 200.

As suggested by Jozefowicz et al. [11], we initialise the bias of the LSTM forget gate to 1, and initialise all other biases to 0 throughout the RNN. We initialise the weights outside of the recurrent layers by sampling from the Gaussian $\mathcal{N}(0, 0.1^2)$ distribution. The model contains dropout [23] of 0.2 on the embedding layer, a dropout of 0.5 between all recurrent states on top of each other, with no dropout in-between successive states of a recurrent layer, as proposed by Sutskever et al. [27]. We also add dropout of 0.5 at the final output of the recurrent layer.

The model is optimised using the Adam optimiser [13] against the binary cross-entropy loss function. We train the model with batches of size 200 samples. We shuffle the training dataset at the beginning of every epoch. To tackle the exploding gradient problem, we clip the gradient norm $\|g\|$ [17] with threshold 1. Finally, we stop training early with continuation of learning [8] by training over the validation set once.

5.2 Evaluation Metrics

Given that the datasets used for email classification vary significantly in how even their distributions are, the apparent *accuracy* measure is of limited value for comparison to other classifiers. We hence report the standard measures of *precision*, *recall*, the *F-measure*, *false positive* and *false negative rates* in addition to accuracy.

We note that email classification errors vary in importance. As an artefact of the problem of spam email classification, it is common practice to consider a false positive error to be more costly than a false negative misclassification. However, this is under the assumption of aggressive filtering of positives and harmless false negatives. In the domain of phishing emails, however, false negatives present significant danger and less aggressive filtering methods such as alerts and link-disabling are common.

We train the classifier over four epochs on the training dataset and one more epoch over the validation dataset. Because the model is expensive to train, in time and computational power, the results provided are of the single trained instance. We evaluate the model on the test set, which had been unseen during training, and is chronologically separated from training a validation set. This is because we split each dataset into training, validation and testing sets in chronological order.

Our classifier is most directly comparable to other text-based features, or sub-classifiers that analyse the text of the classified email only. We compare our work with the textAnalysis sub-classifier of the PhishNet-NLP email classifier by Verma et al. [25], and the state-of-the-art dynamic Markov chain (DMC) model proposed by Bergholz et al. [3]. We summarise the results in Table 4.

Table 4. Summary of our results in comparison to related work in popular metrics.

	corpus	accuracy	fp-rate	fn-rate	precision	recall	F-measure
textAnalysis	?-JN	78.54%	14.90%	22.90%	95.93%	77.10%	85.49%
DMC$_{text}$	SA-JN	99.56%	0.00%	4.02%	100.00%	95.98%	97.95%
Our RNN	SA-JN	98.91%	1.26%	1.47%	98.74%	98.53%	98.63%
Our RNN	En-JN	96.74%	2.50%	4.02%	97.45%	95.98%	96.71%

Our test dataset is well-separated from the training set. We could argue that the classification problem we evaluated our classifier against is unrealistically hard. Intuitively, messages arriving in a specific inbox would exhibit more pronounced patterns, and would thus be easier to classify correctly.

Verma et al. [25] propose that textAnalysis offers a classification value very independent from the other features, as only the text of the email is considered. For the same reason, our classifier should not copy the labels of other features present in classification, but rather provide an independent view on the classification at hand.

The RNN classifier outperforms the textAnalysis classifier and has comparable results to the state-of-the-art DMC$_{text}$ feature. We note that perfect classification is not possible in our setting, as two emails with the same token sequence will necessarily be labelled equally. Since both, ham and phishing email corpora contain empty emails with attachments, which have been removed, the emails are identical to our classifier. This proves inseparability of the emails with the word-sequence representation.

6   Conclusion

In this paper, we propose a novel automated system aiming to mitigate the threat of phishing emails with the use of RNNs. Our results suggest that the flexibility of RNNs gives our system an edge over the expert feature selection procedure, which is vastly employed in ML-based attempts at phishing mitigation.

We focused on the overlooked content source of email information and demonstrated its utility when considered in phishing threat mitigation. The nature of RNN and its training procedure make it suitable for the case of online learning deployment. Our classifier could theoretically change over time to capture new trends continuously and keep up accurate and precise classification through-out. Our results have demonstrated a wealth of potential in non-trivial feature identification for classifying emails since our system's performance surpasses the state-of-the-art systems which are based on features designed by human intu-ition.

Finally, it is worth noting that the general criticism of supervised learning extends to our case. Little information is provided by the RNN classifier on the nature of emails at successful classification. The proposed solution generalises easily to the case of inclusion of basic spam email, and is a prospect for further automated success.

References

1. Bahnsen, A.C., Bohorquez, E.C., Villegas, S., Vargas, J., González, F.A.: Clas-sifying phishing URLs using recurrent neural networks. In: Proceedings of the APWG Symposium on Electronic Crime Research, eCrime 2017. IEEE, April 2017. https://doi.org/10.1109/ECRIME.2017.7945048
2. Bengio, Y., Simard, P., Frasconi, P.: Learning long-term dependencies with gradient descent is difficult. IEEE Trans. Neural Netw. **5**(2), 157–166 (1994). https://doi.org/10.1109/72.279181
3. Bergholz, A., Chang, J.H., Paaß, G., Reichartz, F., Strobel, S.: Improved phishing detection using model-based features. In: Proceedings of the Fifth Conference on Email and Anti-Spam, CEAS 2008, August 2008
4. Bergholz, A., De Beer, J., Glahn, S., Moens, M.F., Paaß, G., Strobel, S.: New filtering approaches for phishing email. J. Comput. Secur. **18**(1), 7–35 (2010). https://doi.org/10.3233/JCS-2010-0371. Special Issue on EU-funded ICT research on Trust and Security
5. Chandrasekaran, M., Narayanan, K., Upadhyaya, S.: Phishing email detection based on structural properties. In: Proceedings of the 9th Annual NYS Cyber Security Conference, NYSCSC 2006, June 2006
6. Fette, I., Sadeh, N., Tomasic, A.: Learning to detect phishing emails. In: Proceed-ings of the 16th International Conference on World Wide Web, WWW 2007, pp. 649–656. ACM, May 2007. https://doi.org/10.1145/1242572.1242660
7. Gers, F.A., Schmidhuber, J., Cummins, F.: Learning to forget: continual prediction with LSTM. Neural Comput. **12**(10), 2451–2471 (2000). https://doi.org/10.1109/72.279181
8. Goodfellow, I., Bengio, Y., Courville, A.: Deep Learning. MIT Press, Cambridge (2016). https://www.deeplearningbook.org
9. Hochreiter, S., Schmidhuber, J.: Long short-term memory. Neural Comput. **9**(8), 1735–1780 (1997). https://doi.org/10.1162/neco.1997.9.8.1735
10. Iuga, C., Nurse, J.R.C., Erola, A.: Baiting the hook: factors impacting susceptibil-ity to phishing attacks. Hum.-Centric Comput. Inf. Sci. **6** (2016). https://doi.org/10.1186/s13673-016-0065-2
11. Jozefowicz, R., Zaremba, W., Sutskever, I.: An empirical exploration of recurrent network architectures. In: Proceedings of the 32nd International Conference on Machine Learning, ICML 2015, pp. 2342–2350, July 2015
12. Khonji, M., Iraqi, Y., Jones, A.: Phishing detection: a literature survey. IEEE Commun. Surv. Tutor. **15**(4), 2091–2121 (2013). https://doi.org/10.1109/SURV.2013.032213.00009

13. Kingma, D.P., Ba, J.L.: Adam: a method for stochastic optimization. arXiv preprint (2014). https://arxiv.org/abs/1412.6980
14. Mohammad, R.M., Thabtah, F., McCluskey, L.: Predicting phishing websites based on self-structuring neural network. Neural Comput. Appl. **25**(2), 443–458 (2014). https://doi.org/10.1007/s00521-013-1490-z
15. Nazario, J.: https://monkey.org/~jose/phishing/
16. Nurse, J.R.C.: Cybercrime and you: how criminals attack and the human factors that they seek to exploit. In: The Oxford Handbook of Cyberpsychology. Oxford University Press, Oxford, May 2019. https://doi.org/10.1093/oxfordhb/9780198812746.013.35
17. Pascanu, R., Mikolov, T., Bengio, Y.: On the difficulty of training recurrent neural networks. arXiv preprint (2012). https://arxiv.org/abs/1211.5063
18. PhishMe Inc.: 2016 enterprise phishing susceptibility and resiliency report (2016)
19. Porter, M.F.: Snowball: a language for stemming algorithms. https://snowballstem.org/
20. Ramzan, Z.: Phishing attacks and countermeasures. In: Stavroulakis, P., Stamp, M. (eds.) Handbook of Information and Communication Security, pp. 433–448. Springer, Heidelberg (2010). https://doi.org/10.1007/978-3-642-04117-4_23
21. Saxe, A.M., McClelland, J.L., Ganguli, S.: Exact solutions to the nonlinear dynamics of learning in deep linear neural networks. arXiv preprint (2013). https://arxiv.org/abs/1312.6120
22. SpamAssassin. https://spamassassin.apache.org/old/publiccorpus/
23. Srivastava, N., Hinton, G.E., Krizhevsky, A., Sutskever, I., Salakhutdinov, R.: Dropout: a simple way to prevent neural networks from overfitting. J. Mach. Learn. Res. **15**(1), 1929–1958 (2014)
24. Toolan, F., Carthy, J.: Feature selection for spam and phishing detection. In: 2010 eCrime Researchers Summit, pp. 1–12. IEEE, October 2010. https://doi.org/10.1109/ecrime.2010.5706696
25. Verma, R., Shashidhar, N., Hossain, N.: Detecting phishing emails the natural language way. In: Foresti, S., Yung, M., Martinelli, F. (eds.) ESORICS 2012. LNCS, vol. 7459, pp. 824–841. Springer, Heidelberg (2012). https://doi.org/10.1007/978-3-642-33167-1_47
26. Vinayakumar, R., Soman, K.P., Poornachandran, P.: Evaluating deep learning approaches to characterize and classify malicious URLs. J. Intell. Fuzzy Syst. **34**(3), 1333–1343 (2018). https://doi.org/10.3233/JIFS-169423
27. Zaremba, W., Sutskever, I., Vinyals, O.: Recurrent neural network regularization. arXiv preprint (2014). https://arxiv.org/abs/arXiv:1409.2329
28. Zhao, J., Wang, N., Ma, Q., Cheng, Z.: Classifying malicious URLs using gated recurrent neural networks. In: Barolli, L., Xhafa, F., Javaid, N., Enokido, T. (eds.) IMIS 2018. AISC, vol. 773, pp. 385–394. Springer, Cham (2019). https://doi.org/10.1007/978-3-319-93554-6_36

CAPTCHA Image Generation Using Style Transfer Learning in Deep Neural Network

Hyun Kwon[1], Hyunsoo Yoon[1], and Ki-Woong Park[2(✉)]

[1] School of Computing, Korea Advanced Institute of Science and Technology,
Daejeon, South Korea
[2] Department of Computer and Information Security, Sejong University,
Seoul, South Korea
woongbak@sejong.ac.kr

Abstract. CAPTCHA is widely used as a security solution to prevent automated attack tools on websites. However, CAPTCHA is difficult to recognize human perception when it gives a lot of distortion to have resistance against the automated attack. In this paper, we propose a method to deceive the machine while maintaining the human perception rate by applying the style transfer method. This method creates a style-plugged-CAPTCHA image by combining the styles of different images while maintaining the content of the original CAPTCHA sample. We used 6 datasets in the actual site and used Tensorflow as the machine learning library. Experimental results show that the proposed method reduces the recognition rate of the DeCAPTCHA system to 3.5% while maintaining human perception.

Keywords: Completely automated public turing test to tell computers and humans apart (CAPTCHA) · Deep neural network (DNN) · Convolutional neural network (CNN) · Image style transfer

1 Introduction

Recently, automated attacks are being made using machines with excellent computing performance. Because these automated attacks [16] become available for bulletin boards [15], unlimited subscriptions [4], spam messages [3], and DDoS attacks [7] on Web sites, security solutions [18, 26] are becoming more important to prevent automated attacks. Among security solutions, Completely Automated Public Turing test to tell Computers and Humans Apart (CAPTCHA) [26] is a typical solution to defend against such automated attacks. CAPTCHA is widely used to determine whether a user is a human or a machine through challenge response tests. This method consists of asking a question that the machine can not understand but the person understands the question. If the requester's response is determined to be correct, the service is provided. If the answer is incorrect, the service is rejected.

© Springer Nature Switzerland AG 2020
I. You (Ed.): WISA 2019, LNCS 11897, pp. 234–246, 2020.
https://doi.org/10.1007/978-3-030-39303-8_18

In order to make CAPTCHA images based on text [5] which are misrecognized by the machine, it is necessary to add some distortion such as rotation, size, and arc to text images. This distorted image can be understood by humans, but makes the machine hard to recognize. In addition, there is CAPTCHA based on audio and images. CAPTCHA based on audio [25] generates sounds with noise in numbers and letters so people can understand but machines do not understand. However, the audio method may have the disadvantage that the user system has to support the voice and the external sound. In this paper, we have studied CAPTCHA images based on text.

However, attack methods to break CAPTCHAs such as optical character recognition (ORC) [6] are being studied. Therefore, in order to avoid such attack methods, it is necessary to adjust the rotation, size, and position of letters, but when it is too much, there is a disadvantage that the usability is greatly reduced due to a distorted text image which is difficult to be recognized by human perception. Therefore, there is a need for a method that the machine recognizes incorrectly within the range of maintaining the human recognition rate.

Recently, deep neural network (DNN) [23] has provided good performance for image recognition [14], image generation [12], and image synthesis [21]. Especially, convolutional neural network (CNN) [20] shows good performance in image recognition field. It is possible to extract features from each feacture and synthesize different images. Among them, the style transfer method [11] can extract the representation of the content of the original sample and extract the representation of the style of another image. For example, it can create a new image that combines Obama's photo content with Rousseau's image style.

In this paper, we propose a style-plugged-CAPTCHA method to deceive the machine while maintaining the perception rate of human by applying style transfer learning to the CAPTCHA image dataset. The propose scheme generates a style-plugged-CAPTCHA image by extracting the content feature of the original sample and the style feature of the other image. The contribution of this paper is as follows.

- This paper propose the style-plugged-CAPTCHA method. We systematically organize the frameworks of the proposed scheme.
- We analyzed the degree of image distortion of the proposed method using CAPTCHA image datasets which is operated on actual site.
- We measured the recognition of the style-plugged-CAPTCHA images by comparing the original images with the DeCAPTCHA system in order to verify the performance of the proposed method.

The rest of this paper is structured as follows: In Sect. 2, we review the related work. The proposed scheme is presented in Sect. 3. In Sect. 4, we present and explain the experiment and evaluation. The proposed scheme is discussed in Sect. 5. Finally, Sect. 6 concludes the paper.

2   Related Works

The CAPTCHA system [13] was first introduced in 1997 as an Internet search site, AltaVista. Section 2.1 presents an overview of related research on CAPTCHA based on text. Section 2.2 provides an overview of CNN and Sect. 2.3 explains the image style transfer method.

2.1   A Review of CAPTCHA Based on Text

CAPTCHA based on text is a method using distorted text images that are correctly recognized by humans but misrecognized by machines. In order to prevent the machine from recognizing the CAPTCHA by the automated attack, the CAPTCHA system gives the rotation of the text image, resizes the letters, adds an arc, or overlaps the letters. Typically, there are three methods that CAPTCHA based on text. First, the connecting characters together (CCT) [9] method is giving overlap and noise of characters, and arc to text images in order to resistant to character segmentation and recognition by the automatic machine. Second, the hollow method [10] is designed to connect all texts together in a format that only displays the outline of the text. This method is resistant to the segmentation and recognition of the machine while enhancing human perception. Third, the character isolated method [8] is a method of displaying each character independently of each other, unlike the above-mentioned method. Therefore, the distortion of each character is severe compared to other methods.

This CAPTCHA based on text is disadvantageous in that it is degraded to human perception rate if it is too much distortion. Unlike the conventional method, the proposed method applies different image styles while maintaining human perception rate.

2.2   A Review of CNN Model

CNN [20] is a deeply neural network that is commonly used for visual imagery as a regularized version of a fully connected network. In particular, CNN has the advantage of reflecting information on spatial characteristics without loss. Since the input and output data are processed as three-dimensional data using the CNN, spatial information can be maintained. However, in the fully connected network, since only one-dimensional data is received, spatial information of the three-dimensional data is lost.

The structure of CNN consists of fully connected layer, convolution layer, and pooling. A fully connected layer means a layer of the form combined with all the neurons of the previous layer.

The convolution layer extracts the characteristics of the image using a filter in the input image. In the convolution layer, the value is obtained by multiplying the adjacent pixel by the convolution filter for the output data at each layer. The input and output data in the convolution layer are called a feature map.

The purpose of the pooling layer is to be used when performing subsampling or extracting data samples once again through the convolution process. Similar to the convolution layer, pooling uses only adjacent pixel values, but there is no computation. There are two types of pooling: max pooling and average pooling. The max pooling sets the largest pixel value in adjacent pixels to a new pixel value. On the other hand, the average pooling sets the average value of adjacent pixels to a new pixel value.

The parameters of CNN can be set by parameter of convolution filter number, filter window size, padding, and stride. In convolution filter number, it is important to keep the number of convolution filter relatively constant at each layer. In the filter window size, it can be used to emphasize the desired features by utilizing the non-ineariness in the intermediate stage when several small filters are overlapped. The padding means to increase the input data around a specific pixel value before performing the convolution to adjust the output data size and prevent loss of information. The stride is the parameter that controls the window's moving distance.

2.3   A Review of Image Style Transfer Method

Image style transfer [11] proposed a method of creating a new image by combining the content of the original image with the style of another image. This method uses a feature that allows CNN to extract information from the semantic image at high-level. This method reduces the two loss functions to create a new image. The first loss function represents a content representation of original image, meaning it maintains a specific content by increasing object information that represents the content of the image. The second loss function proposes a method of obtaining the information about the feature space of the texture of an other image. The proposed method is a method of applying image style transfer method to CAPTCHA image domain.

3   Proposed Method

To generate a style-plugged-CAPTCHA images, the proposed method accepts the original image and the other image as input values, and generates a new image that combines the content of the original image and the style of the other image, as shown in Fig. 1.

For this study, we used the style transfer architecture given in [11]. In the CNN model, this method extracts the content feature from the original image and extracts the style feature from the other image separately. First, in the case of a content feature, a feature map can be extracted through the convolution layer of the original image. As the layer becomes deeper, pixel level information disappears, but the semantic information of the input image remains. Therefore, we extract the content feature of the original image from the deep layer. Second, in case of style feature, it is based on gram matrix [17]. The gram matrix represents the correlation between the feature maps of each layer. By using correlation of feature maps of several layers, it is possible to obtain information

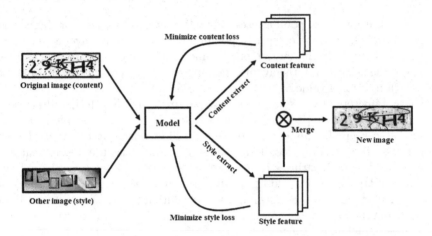

Fig. 1. Proposed architecture.

considering multiple scales of stationary information rather than layout information of image. The more deep layers are included, the more the image gets static information rather than layout information.

To generate the proposed CAPTCHA image, the method updates the noise image $\overrightarrow{x}$ through back propagation of the loss function $loss_T$. The loss function $loss_T$ is the sum of content loss $loss_{content}$ and style loss $loss_{style}$:

$$loss_T = loss_{style}(\overrightarrow{a}, \overrightarrow{x}) + \alpha \cdot loss_{content}(\overrightarrow{p}, \overrightarrow{x}), \tag{1}$$

where $\overrightarrow{a}$ means other image, $\overrightarrow{x}$ means noise image, which is a composite image, and $\overrightarrow{p}$ means original image. α is a weighted value over 1. The initial value is 1. First, the content loss $loss_{content}$ is calculated based on the content feature for the noise image $\overrightarrow{x}$, which is the image to be synthesized with the original image $\overrightarrow{p}$. The procedure is as follows. First, the original image $\overrightarrow{p}$ and noise image $\overrightarrow{x}$ are feed-forward through the network, respectively. Second, we obtain feature maps P and F in layer l as input values to original image $\overrightarrow{p}$ and noise image $\overrightarrow{x}$, respectively. Third, through the obtained feature maps P and F, the content loss is defined as follows.

$$loss_{content}(\overrightarrow{p}, \overrightarrow{x}, l) = \frac{1}{2} \sum_{i,j} (F_{ij}^l - P_{ij}^l)^2, \tag{2}$$

where P_{ij}^l is the activation i_{th} filter at position j in layer l and F_{ij}^l is the activation i_{th} filter at position j in layer l.

Second, style loss $loss_{content}$ is calculated based on the style feature for other image (style) $\overrightarrow{a}$ and noise image $\overrightarrow{x}$. The procedure is as follows. First, the other image $\overrightarrow{a}$ and noise image $\overrightarrow{x}$ are feed-forward through the network, respectively. Second, we obtain gram matric A and G in layer l as input values to other image $\overrightarrow{a}$ and noise image $\overrightarrow{x}$, respectively. Third, through the obtained gram matric A and G, the style loss is defined as follows.

$$E_l = \frac{1}{4N_l^2 M_l^2} \sum_{i,j} (G_{ij}^l - A_{ij}^l)^2, \qquad (3)$$

where A_{ij}^l and G_{ij}^l are the inner product between the vectorised feature maps i and j in layer l, N_l is the number of feature maps at layer l, and M_l is height $\times$ width of feature maps at layer l. In the case of the style feature, the total style loss $loss_{style}$ is as follows because it uses several layers simultaneously.

$$loss_{style}(\overrightarrow{a}, \overrightarrow{x}) = \sum_{l=0}^{L} w_l E_l, \qquad (4)$$

where w_l is weighting factors of the layer to the total loss. The details of the procedure for generating a proposed CAPTCHA image are given in Algorithm 1.

Algorithm 1. Style-plugged-CAPTCHA Image generation.

Input: original image $\overrightarrow{p}$, other image (style) $\overrightarrow{a}$, noise image $\overrightarrow{x}$, P_{ij}^l is the activation i_{th} filter at position j in layer l and F_{ij}^l is the activation i_{th} filter at position j in layer l, A_{ij}^l and G_{ij}^l are the inner product between the vectorised feature maps i and j in layer l, N_l is the number of feature maps at layer l, and M_l is height $\times$ width of feature maps at layer l, iterations r.

Style-plugged-CAPTCHA Image generation:

   $\overrightarrow{a} \leftarrow 0$

  for r step **do**

     $loss_{content}(\overrightarrow{p}, \overrightarrow{x}, l) \leftarrow \frac{1}{2} \sum_{i,j} (F_{ij}^l - P_{ij}^l)^2$

     $E_l \leftarrow \frac{1}{4N_l^2 M_l^2} \sum_{i,j} (G_{ij}^l - A_{ij}^l)^2$

     $loss_{style}(\overrightarrow{a}, \overrightarrow{x}) \leftarrow \sum_{l=0}^{L} w_l E_l$

     $loss_T \leftarrow loss_{content} + loss_{style}$

     Update $\overrightarrow{x}$ by minimizing $loss_T$ through back propagation such as $\overrightarrow{a} - \lambda \frac{\delta loss_T}{\delta \overrightarrow{a}}$

  end for

   $return \ \overrightarrow{a}$

4　Experiment and Evaluation

Through experiments, we show that the proposed scheme can generate a style transfer CAPTCHA image that is resist to the DeCAPTCHA and can maintain the human perception. We used the Tensorflow [2] library, a widely used open source library for machine learning, on a Intel(R) Core(TM) i5-8400 CPU 2.80 GHz server.

4.1　Experimental Method

In terms of experimental datasets, we used 6 different CAPTCHA datasets running on the web site and 100 data per dataset. The six Web sites are as follows: smart-mail.de, ArticlesFactory.com, nationalinterest.org, cesdb.com, mail.aol.com, and tiki.org.

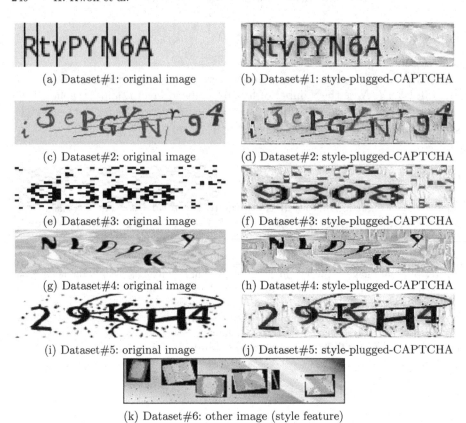

(a) Dataset#1: original image

(b) Dataset#1: style-plugged-CAPTCHA

(c) Dataset#2: original image

(d) Dataset#2: style-plugged-CAPTCHA

(e) Dataset#3: original image

(f) Dataset#3: style-plugged-CAPTCHA

(g) Dataset#4: original image

(h) Dataset#4: style-plugged-CAPTCHA

(i) Dataset#5: original image

(j) Dataset#5: style-plugged-CAPTCHA

(k) Dataset#6: other image (style feature)

Fig. 2. The sampling example of style-plugged-CAPTCHA for the original image of each dataset when selecting dataset #6 as the style image.

In terms of pretrained model and DeCAPTCHA, we used the VGG-19 model [24] as a pretrained model. Tables 1 and 2 show the structure and parameters for the VGG-19 model. As DeCAPTCHA, we used the gsc captcha breaker program [1]. The gsc captcha breaker is the software used in the website by segmenting and recognizing CAPTCHA images.

To generate the style transfer CAPTCHA, L-BFGS optimization [22] is used as box constrained optimization. The L-BFGS optimization is an efficient algorithm for solving a large scale problem. It is used to design and refine quadratic models for optimization functions. The iteration is 100 and weight of loss α is 1. For a given number of iterations, the proposed method updates the output $\overrightarrow{x}$ from the feedback of content loss and style loss. At the end of the iterations, the new image, $\overrightarrow{x}$, was evaluated in terms of human perception and the recognition rate of DeCAPTCHA. The recognition rate of DeCAPTCHA means the rate at which CAPTCHA is correctly recognized by gsc captcha breaker.

4.2 Experimental Results

Figure 2 shows an example of creating a style-plugged-CAPTCHA image for the original image of each dataset when selecting dataset 6 as the style image. In the figure, a style-plugged-CAPTCHA image is created that takes the style property of the other image while retaining the content of the original image. Especially, the style image is the same, but the degree of deformation of the style is slightly different according to the characteristics of the original image. However, it is seen that the recognition rate of a person is maintained because a lot of letters are not transformed by the human perception.

Figure 3 shows that a style-plugged-CAPTCHA image is generated for each dataset when the original sample and the other image are given a difference of 1 in the dataset order. In the figure, a style-plugged-CAPTCHA image is generated by extracting the style of the other image while maintaining the content of the original sample. For example, in datasets #3, #4, #5, and #6, the figure shows that the point-point portion of the style image is added to the style-plugged-CAPTCHA image. In addition, the newly created style-plugged-CAPTCHA image can be seen to remain in the human perception.

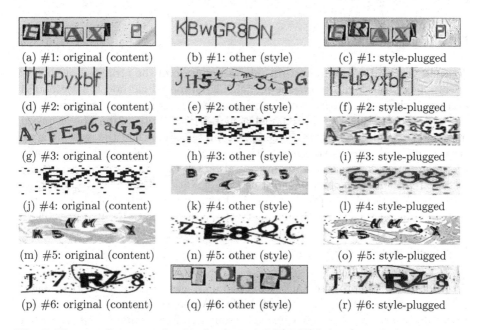

(a) #1: original (content)   (b) #1: other (style)   (c) #1: style-plugged

(d) #2: original (content)   (e) #2: other (style)   (f) #2: style-plugged

(g) #3: original (content)   (h) #3: other (style)   (i) #3: style-plugged

(j) #4: original (content)   (k) #4: other (style)   (l) #4: style-plugged

(m) #5: original (content)   (n) #5: other (style)   (o) #5: style-plugged

(p) #6: original (content)   (q) #6: other (style)   (r) #6: style-plugged

Fig. 3. The sampling example of style-plugged-CAPTCHA for the each dataset: Original is a original image, other is a other image, and style-plugged is a style-plugged-CAPTCHA.

Figure 4 shows the recognition rate for the original image and style-plugged-CAPTCHA by the DeCAPTCHA program for 100 samples per dataset. In the figure, the recognition rate of DeCAPTCHA is different for each dataset.

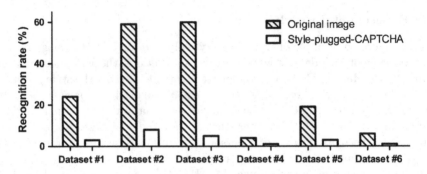

Fig. 4. DeCAPTCHA recognition rates.

Especially, when the style-plugged-CAPTCHA method is applied, the recognition rate of the DeCAPTCHA is significantly lowered for the style-plugged-CAPTCHA image due to the modulation on the style. Therefore, the style-plugged-CAPTCHA image has some resistance to the DeCAPTCHA system than the original image.

5   Discussion

Attack Method Consideration. The assumption of the proposed method is a white box attack that knows the model. The proposed method is a method of extracting the content feature of the original sample and the style feature of the other image from the pretrained model using L-BFGS optimization The proposed method gives more weight to the content representation than the existing style transfer method. Because the recognition rate of a person is reduced when there are many changes in a content representation, the weight is set higher in the content representation than in the style representation. Unlike the conventional CAPTCHA method, the proposed method proposes a method of changing the style by using the feature which can extract the feature in CNN. It is possible to generate CAPTCHA images more variously by changing the image style rather than changing characters.

Application. The proposed method is useful for generating CAPTCHA images in large quantities. If the amount of CAPTCHA images is limited, it is necessary to generate various CAPTCHA images through various combinations. In such a case, the proposed method can be used to generate CAPTCHA images of different styles. On the contrary, if the DeCAPTCHA system requires learning about various data, it can be used to improve the performance of the DeCAPTCHA system by generating various images generated through the proposed method and learning in advance.

Limitation. In the proposed method, if the weight of the style representation is increased, the image distortion may be increased. Also, if the other image of the style image is severely distorted, the content image may be affected. Therefore, it is necessary to consider when selecting a style image.

Also, since the proposed method does not attack the DeCAPTCHA system with a white box, it is not directly attacked. Therefore, it is necessary to compare the input and output values of the DeCAPTCHA system and extend it to the CAPTCHA method with optimal distortion while maintaining human recognition rate.

6 Conclusion

In this paper, we proposed a style-plugged-CAPTCHA image that change the style for the original image. The propose scheme generates a style-plugged-CAPTCHA image by extracting the content feature of the original sample and the style feature of the other image. These style-plugged-CAPTCHA image has some resistance to the DeCAPTCHA system. Experimental results show that the proposed method maintains the human recognition rate while decreasing the recognition rate to about 3.5% for the DeCAPTCHA system. The proposed scheme can also show the possibility of being applied to applications such as the data expansion. Future studies can be extended to more diverse datasets. It can also be applied to generate CAPTCHAs using the generative adversarial net method [19] instead of the L-BFGS algorithm.

Acknowledgement. This work was supported by the Institute for Information and Communications Technology Promotion (2018-0-00420, 2019-0-00426) and supported by the National Research Foundation of Korea (2017R1C1B2003957, 2017R1A2B4006026).

Appendix

Table 1. Model of VGG-19 [24]

Layer type	Model shape
Convolution+ReLU	[3, 3, 64]
Convolution+ReLU	[3, 3, 64]
Max pooling	[2, 2]
Convolution+ReLU	[3, 3, 128]
Convolution+ReLU	[3, 3, 128]
Max pooling	[2, 2]
Convolution+ReLU	[3, 3, 256]

(continued)

Table 1. (*continued*)

Layer type	Model shape
Convolution+ReLU	[3, 3, 256]
Convolution+ReLU	[3, 3, 256]
Convolution+ReLU	[3, 3, 256]
Max pooling	[2, 2]
Convolution+ReLU	[3, 3, 512]
Convolution+ReLU	[3, 3, 512]
Convolution+ReLU	[3, 3, 512]
Convolution+ReLU	[3, 3, 512]
Max pooling	[2, 2]
Convolution+ReLU	[3, 3, 512]
Convolution+ReLU	[3, 3, 512]
Convolution+ReLU	[3, 3, 512]
Convolution+ReLU	[3, 3, 512]
Max pooling	[2, 2]
Fully connected+ReLU	[4096]
Fully connected+ReLU	[4096]
Fully connected+ReLU	[1000]
Softmax	[1000]

Table 2. VGG-19 [24] model parameters.

Parameter	Values
Learning rate	0.01
Momentum/Dropout	0.9/0.5
Decay/Batch size	0.0005/256
Iteration/Epochs	370,000/74

References

1. GSA Captcha Breaker: GSA - Softwareentwicklung und Analytik GmbH (2017). https://captcha-breaker.gsa-online.de/
2. Abadi, M., et al.: Tensorflow: a system for large-scale machine learning. In: OSDI, vol. 16, pp. 265–283 (2016)
3. Alorini, D., Rawat, D.B.: Automatic spam detection on gulf dialectical Arabic Tweets. In: 2019 International Conference on Computing, Networking and Communications (ICNC), pp. 448–452. IEEE (2019)
4. Bukac, V., Stavova, V., Nemec, L., Riha, Z., Matyas, V.: Service in denial – clouds going with the winds. Network and System Security. LNCS, vol. 9408, pp. 130–143. Springer, Cham (2015). https://doi.org/10.1007/978-3-319-25645-0_9

5. Bursztein, E., Martin, M., Mitchell, J.: Text-based CAPTCHA strengths and weaknesses. In: Proceedings of the 18th ACM Conference on Computer and Communications Security, pp. 125–138. ACM (2011)
6. Swamy Das, M., Rao, K.R.M., Balaji, P.: Neural-based hit-count feature extraction method for Telugu script optical character recognition. In: Saini, H.S., Singh, R.K., Patel, V.M., Santhi, K., Ranganayakulu, S.V. (eds.) Innovations in Electronics and Communication Engineering. LNNS, vol. 33, pp. 479–486. Springer, Singapore (2019). https://doi.org/10.1007/978-981-10-8204-7_48
7. Demoulin, H.M., Pedisich, I., Phan, L.T.X., Loo, B.T.: Automated detection and mitigation of application-level asymmetric dos attacks. In: Proceedings of the Afternoon Workshop on Self-Driving Networks, pp. 36–42. ACM (2018)
8. Gao, H., Tang, M., Liu, Y., Zhang, P., Liu, X.: Research on the security of microsoft's two-layer captcha. IEEE Trans. Inf. Forensics Secur. **12**(7), 1671–1685 (2017)
9. Gao, H., Wang, W., Fan, Y., Qi, J., Liu, X.: The robustness of "connecting characters together" CAPTCHAs. J. Inf. Sci. Eng. **30**(2), 347–369 (2014)
10. Gao, H., Wang, W., Qi, J., Wang, X., Liu, X., Yan, J.: The robustness of hollow CAPTCHAs. In: Proceedings of the 2013 ACM SIGSAC Conference on Computer & Communications Security, pp. 1075–1086. ACM (2013)
11. Gatys, L.A., Ecker, A.S., Bethge, M.: Image style transfer using convolutional neural networks. In: Proceedings of the IEEE Conference on Computer Vision And Pattern Recognition, pp. 2414–2423 (2016)
12. Gregor, K., Danihelka, I., Graves, A., Rezende, D.J., Wierstra, D.: Draw: a recurrent neural network for image generation. arXiv preprint arXiv:1502.04623 (2015)
13. Hasan, W.K.A.: A survey of current research on captcha. Int. J. Comput. Sci. Eng. Surv. (IJCSES) **7**(3), 141–157 (2016)
14. He, K., Zhang, X., Ren, S., Sun, J.: Deep residual learning for image recognition. In: Proceedings of the IEEE Conference on Computer Vision and Pattern Recognition, pp. 770–778 (2016)
15. Holz, T., Marechal, S., Raynal, F.: New threats and attacks on the world wide web. IEEE Secur. Priv. **4**(2), 72–75 (2006)
16. Householder, A., Houle, K., Dougherty, C.: Computer attack trends challenge internet security. Computer **35**(4), sulp5–sulp7 (2002)
17. Johnson, J., Alahi, A., Fei-Fei, L.: Perceptual losses for real-time style transfer and super-resolution. In: Leibe, B., Matas, J., Sebe, N., Welling, M. (eds.) ECCV 2016. LNCS, vol. 9906, pp. 694–711. Springer, Cham (2016). https://doi.org/10.1007/978-3-319-46475-6_43
18. Kwon, H., Kim, Y., Yoon, H., Choi, D.: Optimal cluster expansion-based intrusion tolerant system to prevent denial of service attacks. Appl. Sci. **7**(11), 1186 (2017)
19. Kwon, H., Kim, Y., Yoon, H., Choi, D.: Captcha image generation systems using generative adversarial networks. IEICE Trans. Inf. Syst. **101**(2), 543–546 (2018)
20. LeCun, Y., Bottou, L., Bengio, Y., Haffner, P.: Gradient-based learning applied to document recognition. Proc. IEEE **86**(11), 2278–2324 (1998)
21. Li, C., Wand, M.: Combining Markov random fields and convolutional neural networks for image synthesis. In: Proceedings of the IEEE Conference on Computer Vision and Pattern Recognition, pp. 2479–2486 (2016)
22. Moritz, P., Nishihara, R., Jordan, M.: A linearly-convergent stochastic L-BFGS algorithm. In: Artificial Intelligence and Statistics, pp. 249–258 (2016)
23. Schmidhuber, J.: Deep learning in neural networks: an overview. Neural Netw. **61**, 85–117 (2015)

24. Simonyan, K., Zisserman, A.: Very deep convolutional networks for large-scale image recognition. ICLR 2015 (2015)
25. Soupionis, Y., Gritzalis, D.: Audio CAPTCHA: existing solutions assessment and a new implementation for VoIP telephony. Comput. Secur. **29**(5), 603–618 (2010)
26. von Ahn, L., Blum, M., Hopper, N.J., Langford, J.: CAPTCHA: using hard AI problems for security. In: Biham, E. (ed.) EUROCRYPT 2003. LNCS, vol. 2656, pp. 294–311. Springer, Heidelberg (2003). https://doi.org/10.1007/3-540-39200-9_18

A New Password Cracking Model with Generative Adversarial Networks

Sungyup Nam, Seungho Jeon, and Jongsub Moon[(✉)]

Graduate School of Information Security, Korea University, Seoul, South Korea
{synam,ohgnu90,jsmoon}@korea.ac.kr

Abstract. Owing to the generality and importance of the password as a means of authentication, many studies have addressed password-strength evaluation methods and password cracking methods. Recently, the generative adversarial networks approach to enhance password guessing (Pass-GAN) has been proposed as a password cracking method in research that is based on generative adversarial networks (GAN). The results of this study have received substantial attention. In this paper, we propose the use of a recurrent neural networks-based (RNN) GAN, which comprises the use of the improved Wasserstein GAN (IWGAN) cost function. These models that combine the RNN with IWGAN perform better than Pass-GAN. We have conducted experiments to compare the performance of our proposed model with that of PassGAN and analyzed the results. Using these analyses, we confirmed that our proposed models exhibited a password cracking performance improvement of 5–10% more than that of PassGAN.

Keywords: Password cracking · GAN · IWGAN · RNN · PassGAN · Hashcat

1 Introduction

Whenever we encounter problems related to authentication, we immediately consider passwords. Although many authentication methods can be applied to various devices, passwords are the simplest and most prevalent method. Due to the versatility of passwords, people usually have many passwords for their services or documents. Sometimes people forget some of their passwords and need to recover them with password cracking tools. Law enforcement agencies, such as police and prosecutors are often required to crack passwords while conducting investigations. For example, a password may be established for an MS Word file created by a criminal or a disk drive (HDD/SSD) may be encrypted with an encryption SW, such as VeraCrypt [15]. Research on technology for cracking passwords is important and necessary for solving the previous mentioned problems.

Three methods can be utilized to crack a password. The first method is a brute-force attack; the second method is a dictionary-based attack; and the last method is a hybrid attack [19].

© Springer Nature Switzerland AG 2020
I. You (Ed.): WISA 2019, LNCS 11897, pp. 247–258, 2020.
https://doi.org/10.1007/978-3-030-39303-8_19

The brute-force attack involves generating a password by combining a certain number of letters and numbers to satisfy password length and attacking until the same hash value is reached. The brute-force attack method, which is the easiest method among the password-cracking methods, has been rapidly improved by the recent development of graphics processing unit (GPU) technology. As the length of the password increases, however, the time required for a brute-force password attack considerably increases.

The second method is the dictionary-based attack [19], which is a method for cracking passwords using attack dictionaries. Leaked passwords are primarily used to create an attack dictionary, which can be produced by combinations of words from the Oxford dictionary and numbers that people may use as real passwords. The advantage of this method is that we can attempt to crack the password within a constant time using hash algorithms regardless of the password length. However, the attack range is limited by the number of password candidates that the attack dictionary holds, and the success of the password cracking depends on the quality of the attack dictionary.

The last method is the hybrid attack [19], which is an attack that increases the cracking performance of dictionary-based attacks by supporting the transformation of password candidates in attack dictionaries. The transformation of password candidates is conducted by adding masking information as a prefix (or postfix) of elements, such as the brute-force attack or applying various changing rules (for example, capitalization and changing character position) to characters.

The most commonly employed free tools for password cracking are John the Ripper (JTR) [1] and Hashcat [2], which support the three of previous mentioned attack methods. When cracking a password hash with using Hashcat or JTR, we usually apply built-in rules such as best64 to a leak password dictionary, such as RockYou [3,7], which demonstrated a reasonable performance in terms of the cracking success rate [18]. Rules such as best64 are a collection of patterns that are often used to create password candidates, which are employed to increase the number of cracked passwords. The use of rules to extend the scope of password cracking has two drawbacks. First, creating a rule file that reflects all password variants by analyzing the leaked passwords used by tens of millions of people is difficult. Second, because password cracking rules reflect an expert's personal experiences, the cracking performance of rules is not consistent.

Therefore, the password guessing study for identifying a suitable method using leaked passwords has been conducted. In the password guessing study, leaked password dictionaries are automatically analyzed, and we can generate an attack dictionary that contains password candidates that people may use. Two approaches exist for reducing the time required to analyze the leaked password patterns and quickly create a password candidate dictionary that can perform better in password attacks. The first approach is based on a probabilistic analysis and the second approach involves the use of deep learning models. We briefly review these approaches in the next chapter.

In this paper, we propose an improved deep learning based password guessing method that exhibits a better password cracking performance than that of the previous deep learning approach (PassGAN). Further, we explore various training parameter values to generate an effective password-guessing dictionary.

This paper is organized as follows: In Sect. 2, we provide a summary of the probabilistic approaches and the deep learning study as a password guessing method. In Sect. 3, we explain our approaches for improving the performance of PassGAN. In Sect. 4, we describe the experimental environment and deep learning training parameters. In Sect. 5, we explain the password-cracking performance test results. We conclude this study in Sect. 6.

2   Related Studies

In this section, we present a short review of password guessing methods. In the deep learning section, we will explain GAN with more detail than other deep learning methods.

Markov and Context-Free Grammar Approaches

In the probabilistic approach, a method that comprises the use of the Markov model was proposed. Narayanan et al. proposed a method for generating a pseudo password using the Markov model [17]. The key idea of this method is that the password space that people use most in the entire password search space is limited to passwords that are easy to remember when creating a password, and the passwords in this area adhere to a certain probability distribution of alphanumeric combinations. A password generation rule that expresses a combination of various alphabets and numbers as regular expressions and defines the probability of each combination was created. This early work has been subsequently extended by Ma et al. [16] and Dürmuth et al. [8].

The most important aspect of these studies is the application of the probabilistic context-free grammar (PCFG) concept to the password guessing method. This approach was first proposed by Weir et al. [21]. Until recently, research based on PCFG has been continuously extended and improved [14,22]. Considering the complexity of the current password, the grammatical structure includes not only simple alphabets and numerical combinations, but also complex combinations that use special characters and keyword-walk. The leaked password is then automatically analyzed to calculate the probability distribution for each grammar structure, and the probability information of the word used for each grammar element is also stored. Using the stored data, the PCFG generates a password in the order of the grammatical structure with high probability, such that the PCFG improves the crack efficiency over time. In the experiment, the password guessing method that comprises the use of PCFG exhibited a higher cracking success rate than the dictionary-based attack using Hashcat built-in rules. This method was effective in expanding the cracking range in the password space.

Deep Learning Approaches

A password guessing method that employ deep learning was proposed by Melicher et al. [6], who applied an RNN [13]. The RNN [13] is a deep learning method that exhibits excellent performance in the field of natural language processing and is utilized in various tasks, such as chat bots application, translation, and auto-completion. In the Melicher et al.'s method [6], leaked passwords are used as training data. After the training is completed, a guessing password is generated in character units. In the RNN model, a character that constitutes the password is based on the previously selected characters. This operation method is similar to the Markov process. In addition to Melicher et al. [6], there is Hitaj et al.'s PassGAN [12] as a deep learning–based password guessing method. Pass-GAN was developed using the Improved Wasserstein GAN (IWGAN), which is a relatively new model among the various GAN models. GAN, which is a deep learning model used in PassGAN, has recently become an important generation model. The goal of the first GAN model presented by Goodfellow et al. [10] was to generate samples that were likely to be included in the population throughout the training to obtain a distribution that is identical to the population in the high dimension. In contrast to the existing neural network model, GAN has unique structure. Two deep neural networks (DNNs) are employed, and each DNN is referred to as a generative DNN (denoted as G) and a discriminative DNN (denoted as D). The roles of G and D are defined as follows: D distinguishes between real data and the fake data generated by G, and G is trained to perform the role of generating fake data. In the case of G, the objective is to create perfect fake samples such that the D cannot distinguish between the actual sample and the sample generated by G. This problem is a minimax problem. Goodfellow et al. [10] have mathematically proven that this problem has a global optimum when the distribution of fake samples generated by G is identical to the distribution of the real data. The minimax problem can be expressed as follows:

$$\min_{G} \max_{D} V(D,G) = \mathop{\mathbb{E}}_{x \sim \mathbb{P}_{data}(x)} [log D(x)] + \mathop{\mathbb{E}}_{z \sim \mathbb{P}_z(z)} [log(1 - D(G(z)))] \qquad (1)$$

After Goodfellow et al. proposed the first GAN, various GAN models with better performance have been suggested. Among these GAN models, the Wasserstein GAN (WGAN) [4] and improved training of Wasserstein GAN (IWGAN) [11] presented a more stable method that enable the GAN model to find the global optimum. IWGAN was proposed by Gulrajani et al. [11], who introduced the concept of a gradient penalty instead of gradient clipping in WGAN and showed stable training of the GAN model without divergence. The IWGAN showed that the CNN based IWGAN model can be applied to a text generation area. PassGAN was derived from these experimental results.

PassGAN also uses leaked passwords (RockYou) as training data, and the role of D is to distinguish between the real password and fake password generated by G. G is trained to create passwords that are similar to the leaked passwords to deceive D. G can sample the fake passwords, which can deceive the D finally. The experiments showed that PassGAN can create passwords that Hashcat cannot generate.

3   Proposed Model

To improve the performance of password cracking, we approached it from two perspectives. The first perspective is to change the deep learning model in the discriminator and generator, while the second is the structural change in the PassGAN model.

Single Discriminator Model

PassGAN was developed based on the IWGAN, and the generator G and discriminator D use CNNs. The CNN model can be used for texture generation. However the CNN is not the best solution for text generation. Passwords have a certain order and rules for the characters that constitute passwords. For example, we consider the password "p@ssw0rd". If we know that @ and s appear after p, then we can guess that the next character will be s. This conjecture is possible because the characters used by people have a certain order, and preceding characters have a probabilistic effect on the selection of the following characters. In this field, RNN [13] is a suitable deep-learning model that exhibits good performance in processing such sequential data, and the LSTM [9] and GRU [5] are good cell types of RNN. As shown in Fig. 1b, it is expected that the password cracking performance will be improved by changing the deep learning model of the D and G from CNN to RNN without changing the PassGAN's structure. In addition, we denote this model as r-PassGAN.

Dual Discriminators Model

We propose a model that simultaneously changes the model of D and G from CNN to RNN and the structure of the GAN. The basic idea of changing the GAN structure is to use dual discriminators that use the IWGAN's cost function. The discriminators D1 and D2 perform the same functions as those in D2GAN, which was proposed by Nguyen et al. [20]. D1 attempts to detect the real passwords among the real and fake passwords, and D2 attempts to detect the fake passwords among the real and fake passwords. In the dual discriminators GAN model, the goal of generator G is to deceive both D1 and D2, such that the distribution of the real password and that of the fake passwords generated by G must be identical. D1 and D2 fall into an indistinguishable state where they cannot distinguish between a real password and a fake password. In the first dual discriminator model, the sum of each discriminator's costs is defined, and D1 and D2 are trained to minimize the sum of the costs. Generator G is trained to maximize the cost sum in contrast to the discriminators' costs (Algorithm 1). We denote this model as a dual discriminators combination PassGAN and abbreviate its name to r-PassD2CGAN (Fig. 1c).

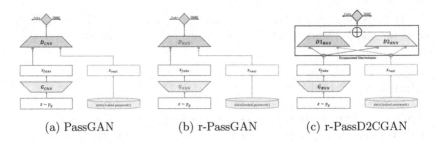

(a) PassGAN   (b) r-PassGAN   (c) r-PassD2CGAN

Fig. 1. PassGAN, r-PassGAN, r-PassD2CGAN block diagram

Algorithm 1. r-PassD2CGAN calculates each discriminator's gradient penalty. We use the default values of $\lambda = 10$, $n_{critic} = 10$, $n_{gen} = 40$, $\alpha = 0.0001$, $\beta_1 = 0.5$ and $\beta_2 = 0.9$.

Require: Gradient penalty coefficient λ, number of critic iterations per generator n_{critic}, number of generator iterations per discriminator n_{gen}, batch size m, and Adam hyperparameters α, β_1, and β_2.

Require: Initial D_1 and D_2 critic parameters w_0 and u_0, and initial generator parameter θ_0.

  while θ has not converged **do**
    for $t = 1, ..., n_{critic}$ **do**
      for $i = 1, ..., m$ **do**
        Sample real data $x \sim \mathbb{P}_r$, latent variable $z \sim p(z)$, and a random number
        $\epsilon \sim U[0, 1]$.
        $\tilde{x} \leftarrow G_\theta(z)$
        $\hat{x} \leftarrow \epsilon x + (1 - \epsilon)\tilde{x}$
        $\bar{x} \leftarrow \epsilon \tilde{x} + (1 - \epsilon)x$
        $L_{D_1}^{(i)} \leftarrow D_w(\tilde{x}) - D_w(x) + \lambda(\|\nabla_{\hat{x}} D_w(\hat{x})\|_2 - 1)^2$
        $L_{D_2}^{(i)} \leftarrow D_u(x) - D_u(\tilde{x}) + \lambda(\|\nabla_{\bar{x}} D_w(\bar{x})\|_2 - 1)^2$
        $L_{D2_{comb}}^{(i)} = L_{D_1}^{(i)} + L_{D_2}^{(i)}$
      end for
      $(w, u) \leftarrow \text{Adam}(\nabla_{(w,u)} \frac{1}{m} \sum_{i=1}^{m} L_{D2_{comb}}^{(i)}, w, u, \alpha, \beta_1, \beta_2)$
    end for
    for $t = 1, ..., n_{gen}$ **do**
      Sample a batch of latent variable $\{z^{(i)}\}_{i=1}^{m} \sim p_{(z)}$
      $\theta \leftarrow \text{Adam}(\nabla_\theta \frac{1}{m} \sum_{i=1}^{m} (-D_w(G_\theta(z)) + D_u(G_\theta(z)), \theta, \alpha, \beta_1, \beta_2)$
    end for
  end while

---

4   Experiments

Experiments for the performance comparison are designed to check whether the proposed models provides a better performance than that of PassGAN. In addition, the performance was evaluated with not only the simple crack-success-rate measurement but also the extensibility of the cracked password. The detailed experimental setup is described as follows:

Training Configuration

Training Parameters. The basic training parameters that were utilized in each model are identical to those of PassGAN (training values are defined in Algorithms 1). Only one G/D training ratio was set differently from that of PassGAN. We conducted experiments for obtaining the proper G/D training ratio of our models. The configuration of the optimized G/D ratio experiment is described as follows: The subjects of this experiment are two models that comprise RNN, with exception of PassGAN. The G/D training ratio is changed from 10:10 to 100:10. The data employed in the training is RockYou, and the training epoch is 20,000 (20k). To evaluate the experimental results, we applied the N-gram (N = 3, 4) Jensen–Shannon divergence (JSD) values of the RockYou versus the dictionary generated by each RNN–based model. As shown in Fig. 2, all models (r-PassGAN, r-PassD2CGAN) show similar patterns. The JSD is lowest at 40:10 and increases from 50:10.

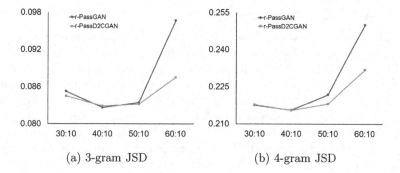

(a) 3-gram JSD   (b) 4-gram JSD

Fig. 2. N-gram JSD (N = 3, 4) by G/D ratio (X-axis: G/D training ratio; Y-axis: JSD value). The data employed in the training is a RockYou password dictionary of length 1–8. The lower is the JSD value, the closer is the value to the password distribution generated by human.

Training Data. The data applied in the training of the three deep-learning models, including PassGAN, are plain-text passwords from RockYou. Before training the models, the RockYou dictionary was refined. In this experiment, first, we excluded the unicode characters from the RockYou. Second, we analyzed the length of the passwords in the RockYou dictionary. We then used whole length of RockYou (about 14 million and password length: 1–32). For the performance evaluation of each model based on the password length, the passwords were divided into three sections based on length (1–8, 9–15, and 16–32), and the training dictionaries were created using RockYou for each password-length section. The purpose of experimenting by dividing the password into three sections by length is to identify which model has the best performance per password length section.

Password Cracking

The target of the password cracking was set to leaked passwords from the LinkedIn site. In the crack performance test of the RockYou dictionary trained models, 20% of LinkedIn leaked passwords with 1–32 character length were used as the cracking target. Unicode password also excepted like RockYou. When testing the cracking performance with Hashcat, we applied the best64 rule for two reasons. The first reason is to measure the cracking performance of the guessing password in conditions that are similar to the practical field, where the rules, such as best64 are applied to the password dictionary. The second reason is that considerable amount time is required to generate billions of passwords using the deep learning model. Thus, even if we generate a small number of passwords, we could successfully crack many passwords that are associated with a simple transformation by applying the best64 rule.

5   Evaluation

Dictionary Quality Perspective

The quality of the password-guessing dictionary was compared from two viewpoints. The first viewpoint considered the similarity between the dictionary generated by the model and the training dictionary created by people. The second viewpoint consider the number of unique guessing passwords in the dictionary generated by the model. If the model generates a large number of duplicated guessing passwords, the password cracking performance within a limited time is degraded. To measure the similarity, the JSD is applied as the evaluation criteria. The JSD value for each N-gram was compared with that of a human-made password dictionary (RockYou leaked-password dictionary). As shown in Fig. 3, RNN–based models have lower JSD values than the PassGAN in the case of all N-grams. RNN–based models are more similar to the human–generated password distribution in terms of an N-gram than the PassGAN.

In terms of the performance of the redundancy rate of the generated guess passwords, the RNN–based models exhibit a better performance than that of PassGAN. As the length of the generated password increases, the space for generating the password is exponentially widened, and thus, the difference in the redundancy rate of each model disappears in the case of the 16–32 password-length section. RNN–based models show a low password-generation redundancy even in a narrow password space, which facilitates efficient password cracking (Table 1).

Cracking Performance Perspective

The most interesting aspect of creating a password-guessing dictionary using our models that have been trained using a leaked-password dictionary is the number of target password have been successfully cracked and the contribution of our password–guessing dictionary to cracking the hashes that were not previously cracked. We discuss the cumulative password cracking performance and cracking area expansion capability of r-PassGAN and r-PassD2CGAN against PassGAN.

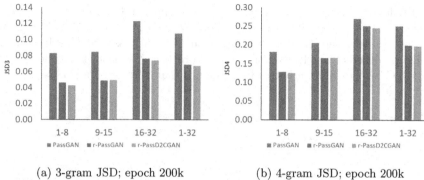

(a) 3-gram JSD; epoch 200k   (b) 4-gram JSD; epoch 200k

Fig. 3. N-gram JSD of generated password dictionary (X-axis: password length; Y-axis: JSD value)

Table 1. Redundancy rate of guessing password dictionary

Models	1–8	9–15	16–32	1–32
PassGAN	7.52%	0.55%	0.1%	4.08%
r-PassGAN	4.42%	0.15%	0.10%	2.02%
r-PassD2CGAN	4.34%	0.15%	0.09%	2.05%

Total Password Cracking. First, we demonstrate the cracking performance per training epoch. The result of RockYou's password length section shows only slight difference in the password cracking performance after all models have learned 100,000 (we denote 100k) times. RNN–based models show acceptable cracking password performance for all password lengths and training epochs.

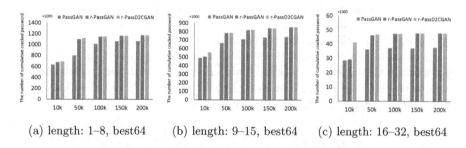

(a) length: 1–8, best64   (b) length: 9–15, best64   (c) length: 16–32, best64

Fig. 4. Total cumulative cracked password by training epoch.

Figure 5 shows the relationship between the number of password guessing and the number of cumulative password cracks. The number of cumulative password cracks tends to differ between the early training (10k epoch) model and the ending (200k epoch) model. When the training epoch is 10k, r-PassD2CGAN shows the highest cumulative cracks from the beginning, this tendency continues until the latter half of the crack. In the case of epoch 200k, only the difference between the PassGAN and two RNN models can be confirmed, with only a slight difference between the RNN models. The results of the password–length sections are slightly different. In the case of the password-length sections 9–15 and 16–32, r-PassD2CGAN exhibits a better performance than that of r-PassGAN.

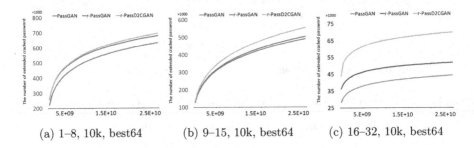

(a) 1–8, 10k, best64   (b) 9–15, 10k, best64   (c) 16–32, 10k, best64

Fig. 5. Total cumulative cracked password by the number of guessed passwords.

Cracking Extensibility. We show the experimental results of the password cracking space extension of each model's password-guessing dictionary. The experimental results of the password cracking space extensibility were analyzed from two perspectives. First, we analyzed the extension of the password dictionary generated by each model for the cracking space of the real password that was applied in each model training. We analyzed the ratio of the number of passwords that can be cracked by only the model against the password that the model did not crack for all proposed models.

The difference in the cracking results of the password dictionary generated by each model is shown in Table 2. This table shows that all proposed models have unique password cracking regions whereas the other models failed to crack. This finding is important because the use of all dictionaries created in each model can maximize the password cracking space. The model with the largest number of unique cracks is r-PassGAN, followed by r-PassD2CGAN and PassGAN. The difference between the RNN models is very small.

Table 2. Difference in each model's cracking result set.

Models	PassGAN	r-PassGAN	r-PassD2CGAN
PassGAN	0	107103	107406
r-PassGAN	235937	0	143182
r-PassD2CGAN	235127	142069	0

6   Conclusions

In this paper, we proposed two models that show better cracking performance than that of PassGAN, which was the first GAN–based password–guessing model. In our models, we employed the RNN as a basic DNN. Although the performance of the PassGAN was improved only by the change from CNN to RNN, we adopted a dual discriminator structure to obtain a substantially better performance. The G/D training ratio for the optimized training in the RNN–based IWGAN is experimentally derived. We show that the RNN–based models have an improved performance compared with PassGAN because cracking performance tests are conducted. Using the deep learning model to train the existing password dictionary and generate a guessing-password dictionary requires considerable amount time. However, time investment has the benefits of cracking using a guessing-password dictionary that is secured via these tasks.

Using the experimental results of this study, the selection of a password generation model for password cracking extension can be guided. If ample time is available but the available computing environment is undesirable, we recommend the use of only one RNN–based model to crack the password. In this case, the type of the RNN–based models is not important. If insufficient time is available and sufficient GPU power is available, we recommend the use of r-PassD2CGAN, which showed acceptable cracking performance with a small epoch, such as 10k. To maximize the number of cracked passwords, all models should be employed because each model has a unique cracked password.

References

1. John the Ripper password cracker. http://www.openwall.com/john/
2. Hashcat Advanced Password Recovery (1999). https://hashcat.net/wiki/
3. RockYou Online (2009). https://wiki.skullsecurity.org/Passwords
4. Arjovsky, M., Chintala, S., Bottou, L.: Wasserstein generative adversarial networks. In: Proceedings of the 34th International Conference on Machine Learning. Proceedings of Machine Learning Research, vol. 70, pp. 214–223. PMLR (2017)
5. Cho, K., van Merrienboer, B., Gülçehre, Ç., Bougares, F., Schwenk, H., Bengio, Y.: Learning phrase representations using RNN encoder-decoder for statistical machine translation. arXiv preprint arXiv:1406.1078 (2014)
6. Cranor, L.F., et al.: Fast, lean, and accurate: modeling password guessability using neural networks. In: 25th USENIX Security Symposium (USENIX Security 16), pp. 175–191. ACM Press (2016)
7. Cubrllovic, N.: Rockyou hack: from bad to worse (2009). https://techcrunch.com/2009/12/14/rockyou-hack-security-myspace-facebook-passwords
8. Dürmuth, M., Angelstorf, F., Castelluccia, C., Perito, D., Chaabane, A.: OMEN: faster password guessing using an ordered Markov enumerator. In: Piessens, F., Caballero, J., Bielova, N. (eds.) ESSoS 2015. LNCS, vol. 8978, pp. 119–132. Springer, Cham (2015). https://doi.org/10.1007/978-3-319-15618-7_10
9. Gers, F.A., Schmidhuber, J., Cummins, F.: Learning to forget: continual prediction with LSTM. Neural Computation (2000)

10. Goodfellow, I., et al.: Generative adversarial networks. In: Advances in Neural Information Processing Systems 27, pp. 2672–2680. Curran Associates, Inc. (2014)

11. Gulrajani, I., Ahmed, F., Arjovsky, M., Dumoulin, V., Courville, A.C.: Improved training of Wasserstein GANs. In: Advances in Neural Information Processing Systems 30, pp. 5767–5777. Curran Associates, Inc. (2017)

12. Hitaj, B., Gasti, P., Ateniese, G., Perez-Cruz, F.: PassGAN: a deep learning approach for password guessing. arXiv preprint arXiv:1709.00440 (2017)

13. Hochreiter, S., Schmidhuber, J.: Long short-term memory. Neural Comput. **9**, 1735–1780 (1997)

14. Houshmand, S., Aggarwal, S., Flood, R.: Next gen PCFG password cracking. IEEE Trans. Inf. Forensics Secur. **10**(8), 1776–1791 (2015)

15. IDRIX: Veracrypt (2017). https://www.veracrypt.fr/en/Home.html

16. Ma, J., Yang, W., Luo, M., Li, N.: A study of probabilistic password models. In: 2014 IEEE Symposium on Security and Privacy, pp. 689–704. IEEE (2014)

17. Narayanan, A., Shmatikov, V.: Fast dictionary attacks on passwords using time-space tradeoff. In: Proceedings of the 12th ACM Conference on Computer and Communications Security - CCS 2005 (2005)

18. NSAKEY: Hashcat: GPU password cracking for maximum win (2015). https://github.com/NSAKEY/nsa-rules

19. Tasevski, P.: Password attacks and generation strategies. Master's thesis, Tartu University: Faculty of Mathmematics and Computer Sciences (2011)

20. Nguyen, T.D., Le, T., Vu, H., Phung, D.: Dual discriminator generative adversarial nets. arXiv preprint arXiv:1709.03831 (2017)

21. Weir, M., Aggarwal, S., de Medeiros, B., Glodek, B.: Password cracking using probabilistic context-free grammars. In: 2009 30th IEEE Symposium on Security and Privacy, pp. 391–405. IEEE (2009)

22. Yazdi, S.H.: Probabilistic context-free grammar based password cracking: attack, defense and applications. Ph.D. thesis, Florida State University, Department of Computer Science (2015)

Is It Possible to Hide My Key into Deep Neural Network?

Taehyuk Kim[1,2], Taek-Young Youn[1,2], and Dooho Choi[1,2(✉)]

[1] University of Science and Technology, Daejeon, Republic of Korea
[2] Electronics and Telecommunications Research Institute, Daejeon, Republic of Korea
{taehyuk,taekyoung,dhchoi}@etri.re.kr

Abstract. The use of cryptographic functions has become vital for various devices, such as PCs, smart phones, drones, and smart appliances; however, the secure storage of cryptographic keys (or passwords) is a major issue. One way to securely store such a key is to register the key using secret data such as biometric data and then regenerate the key whenever it is needed. In this paper, we present a novel methodology for hiding cryptographic keys inside a deep neural network (DNN), and is termed as the DNN-based key hiding scheme. In this method, DNNs are constructed and trained with noisy data to hide the key within the network. To prove that our methodology works in practice, we propose an example of the DNN-based key hiding scheme and prove its correctness. For its robustness, we propose two basic security analysis tools to be able to check the example's security. To the best of our knowledge, this is the first attempt of its kind.

Keywords: Key hiding · Key generation · Deep neural network · Noisy data · Physical unclonable function

1 Introduction

In modern cryptography, Kerckhoffs's principle is one of the most important principles, which states that a cryptographic system should be secure, even if everything about the system, except the key, is public knowledge. In this statement, it is clear that one of the most important factors in determining the security of a cryptographic system is the cryptographic key. There are many methods for keeping and using keys safely. One traditional way to hide a key is to memorize the key and use it whenever necessary; however, this method involves several problems. Simply, it is possible to forget the key. Moreover, it is hard to memorize several keys; therefore, assuming that the same key is used repeatedly in multiple places, all keys are at risk if only one is leaked.

This work was supported by Institute for Information & communications Technology Planning & Evaluation (IITP) grant funded by the Korea government (MSIT) (No. 2019-0-00033, Study on Quantum Security Evaluation of Cryptography based on Computational Quantum Complexity).

I. You (Ed.): WISA 2019, LNCS 11897, pp. 259–272, 2020.
https://doi.org/10.1007/978-3-030-39303-8_20

Two methods for securely storing cryptographic keys are often used to address the problems mentioned above. One stores the cryptographic key in secure storage inside the device, for example, in hardware security modules (HSM) or trusted platform modules (TPM). The drawback of this hardware method is that it is more expensive than methods based on software. Additionally, if one loses an embedded secure storage device, the key is also lost. Another method registers the key using secret data with noise such as biometric data, then regenerates the key whenever it is needed. Representative methods include fuzzy extractor [1,2] and fuzzy commitment schemes [3], which employ error correction codes (ECC) as the main function.

Most key generation mechanisms use methods similar to the fuzzy extractor concept and use ECC as a key element. However, some authors have shown that key generation is possible without the use of ECC. For example, [4] presented a key binding mechanism without ECC that registers and regenerates keys using the fingerprint feature. Because ECC is not used, there is no security-performance tradeoff issue between the binding key size and key recovery rate. The authors bind a key bit by enrolling a transformed genuine fingerprint template (using the cancelable biometric trick) if the key bit was 1; otherwise, the key bit is bound by enrolling a transformed fake fingerprint feature template. Their key release mechanism subsequently extracts the key bit 1 if a transformed template (cancelable template) of the query fingerprint is well matched with the enrolled template.

On the continuation of the above idea without using ECC, you can raise the following question:

- **Is it possible to apply a machine learning technique such as deep neural networks to hide a key using noisy data?**

This paper confirms that the answer to this question is yes by introducing a novel concept for hiding cryptographic keys within deep neural networks. The feasibility of this method is demonstrated through implementation of an instance. Furthermore, we propose two basic security analysis methods to validate the robustness of our example implementation.

1.1   Our Contributions

The proposed approach for hiding a key within a deep neural network with noisy data is termed the deep neural network based (DNN-based) key hiding scheme. In this approach, it is first necessary to prepare appropriate noisy data for use as the secret input for extracting the key from the deep neural network. In Sect. 3.2, image data and physically unclonable function (PUF) data are used. The DNN-based key hiding scheme consists of a key hiding network & training and key reproduction, as follows:

- Key Hiding Network & Training
  - Deep neural network for extracting features from noisy data

- Learning network for hiding the key after binding extracted features and the key
- Training the above network to hide the key using the prepared noisy data for positive learning and other data for negative learning
  - Key Reproduction
    - Extracting the hidden key from the learned network using the prepared noisy data

To determine the practical correctness of this novel key hiding concept, we conduct experiments using an example DNN-based key hiding scheme.

In the proposed scheme, the secret information is the prepared noisy data used for extracting the key and training the key hiding network, and the public information is the trained DNN network that has optimal weights and biases. It is vital to prove that there is no potential for key leakage from this public information; therefore, we provide two basic tools to analyze the security of the DNN-based key hiding scheme and demonstrate that partial key information is revealed if the key hiding network is trained with weak data.

1.2 Organization of the Paper

The paper is organized as follows. In Sect. 2, we address related research. In Sect. 3, we define the novel key hiding scheme and present an instance to show the feasibility of this approach. In Sect. 4, we prove the correctness of our example through experimental results, and present two security analysis mechanisms to verify the robustness of the example. We describe several outstanding issues related to this new key hiding method in Sect. 5 and present our conclusions in Sect. 6.

2   Related Research

Juels et al. [3] proposed a fuzzy commitment scheme that enables dynamic key generation without storing the key in the device. Based on this scheme, the generalized fuzzy extractor method was proposed [1,2], which generates a key using noisy biometric data. Subsequently, the fuzzy vault scheme was proposed [5], which generates a key using fingerprints. Many other fuzzy extractor-based methods have since emerged, applying the schemes to several biometrics including fingerprints [6], irises [7,8], faces [9], and palmprints [10]. A more recent study has proposed fuzzy commitment using two noisy sources instead of biometrics [11].

Moreover, Jin et al. [4] proposed a new key binding scheme without using ECC. They employed cancelable biometrics to bind and release the cryptographic key, making the scheme robust to several attacks and eliminating the key size dependence on ECC. During key binding, the key bit is bound to features and a cancelable transform is applied to true fingerprint features with key bit 1 and synthetic features with key bit 0. Then, key bound cancelable templates are generated. During key release, more cancelable templates are generated from queried biometric data using cancelable transform. If both sets of cancelable templates are similar, the released key bit is 1; otherwise, it is 0.

2.1   Preliminary Concepts

Convolutional Neural Network. An artificial neural network (ANN) is employed in several fields including biometrics [12], finance [13], and language [14]. Various kinds of ANNs have been emerged and specialized to serve the purpose well. Convolutional neural networks (CNNs) [15] which constructed to process multiple layered images are one of them. CNNs are composed of two parts: feature extraction and classification. In feature extraction, unique features of the input data are found through a convolution layer and a pooling layer. The convolution layer performs a convolution operation using input data and a convolution filter set. This operation creates features that are activated by only highlighting the filter. The results of the operation pass through a rectified linear unit (ReLU) [16] and enter the pooling layer, which reduces the size of features from the convolutional layer. There are several types of pooling, with max pooling being the most common, which takes the greatest value from each chunk of features. The features generated from feature extraction are used for the classification, which consists of a fully connected layer and a loss layer. All neurons included in the fully connected layer are fully connected to the features. Thus, the activations of the fully connected layer are computed by matrix multiplication. Finally, the activations are transmitted to the loss layer and a softmax function is typically used for classification. In the loss layer, the deviation between the input label and predicted value is computed. To minimize the deviation, the weights are modified.

Logistic Regression with Neural Network. Logistic regression [17] is a machine learning algorithm most commonly used for binary classification. It results in a linear equation between the independent and dependent variables, which is a binary outcome employing the sigmoid function. Each independent variable x_i is multiplied by a corresponding weight value w_i and summed.

$$z = x_1 \cdot w_1 + x_2 \cdot w_2 + \cdots + x_i \cdot w_i$$

The result, z, is entered into the sigmoid function and the function outputs a value between 0 and 1. The weight values are modified to minimize the deviation between the output of the sigmoid function and the binary input label using cross entropy.

Physical Unclonable Function. A PUF provides a unique identity for a device. PUF generates unpredictable random bit strings using differences in the manufacturing process such as physical variations. There are two types of PUF: weak PUF and strong PUF [18].

3   DNN-Based Key Hiding Scheme

The goal of this section is to define the new key hiding concept, termed the DNN-based key hiding scheme, and verify the applicability of the scheme using a detailed example.

3.1   Proposed Methodology

We assume that noisy data such as biometric data, PUF data, or image data will be used to train the hiding network and extract the key from the network. Here, k is a randomly chosen cryptographic key. The DNN-based key hiding scheme consists of key hiding network & training and key reproduction. Detailed descriptions are given below.

Key Hiding Network and Training. In Fig. 1, d_i is noisy data where $i = 1, \ldots, n$ and n is the amount of noisy data. n can be 1 if we use only one type of noisy data. n is two in this paper because two types of noisy data are used (image data and PUF value). The feature generation layers in Fig. 1 represent a deep learning network for inducing features of the noisy data $d_1, \ldots, d_n$. The key hiding layers in Fig. 1 represent the learning network for binding the key k to the features extracted from the feature generation layers and hiding k in the network by training the key hiding network. The output in Fig. 1 represents an appropriate label for learning the network. The key hiding network is then trained using noisy data d_i and the output to hide k. After the training process, the network and its parameters are saved to use during key extraction.

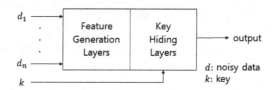

Fig. 1. Conceptual diagram of the key hiding network & training process

Key Extraction. Key extraction produces k hidden in the trained key hiding network (Fig. 2). The input for key extraction is noisy data and the output is k if the input is correct noisy data d_i where $i = 1, \ldots, n$. The feature generation layers in Fig. 2 are identical to those of the trained key hiding network. The key extraction layers are the same trained network as the key hiding layers of the trained key hiding network, excluding the process of binding k.

In Sect. 3.2, we present a practical example of our DNN-based key hiding scheme to verify the feasibility of this newly defined concept.

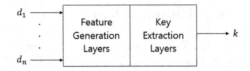

Fig. 2. Conceptual diagram of key extraction

3.2 Instantiation

Here, we introduce a practical example for the DNN-based key hiding scheme defined in Sect. 3.1, which is graphically described in Fig. 3. First, we prepare an image with a size of 16×16 pixels and a PUF value of 64 bits as noisy data d_1 and d_2. Notice that d_1 and d_2 are secret data, but deep neural networks and related parameters are public data in this example.

Key Hiding Network and Training. The feature generation layers consist of one convolutional layer, one max pooling layer, and a PUF binding layer, whereas the key hiding layers consist of a key binding layer and sk logistic regressions where sk is the bit size of the key $k = k_1 k_2 \cdots k_{sk}$. Let img and puf denote the image and PUF value used as input data in the layers.

A concrete description of the feature generation layers is as follows:

1. **Convolutional layer.** Employ filters w_{CNN} with a size of $7 \times 7 \times sk$ and a stride of 2 and apply the ReLU function.
2. **Max pooling layer.** Employ a window with a size of 2×2 and a stride of 2. Then, we obtain features $\{F_i\}_{i=1}^{sk}$ where the size of F_i is 8×8.
3. **PUF binding.** Let $F_i = [f_1, \ldots, f_{64}]$, $puf = [p_1, \ldots, p_{64}]$, and $pF_i = [pf_1, \ldots, pf_{64}]$ be an output of the PUF binding for $i = 1, \ldots, sk$. Compute $pf_i = (-1)^{(1-p_i)} \cdot f_i$, in which the sign of f_i is flipped if an i-th bit of the PUF is 0. Then, features $\{pF_i\}_{i=1}^{sk}$ are generated. Of the many different ways to bind a PUF value puf, we employ simple sign flipping, which produces good results in the experiments.

The key hiding layers are as follows:

1. **Key binding.** The inputs of key binding are $\{pF_i\}_{i=1}^{sk}$ and the outputs are $\{kF_i\}_{i=1}^{sk}$. Compute $kF_i = [(-1)^{(1-k_i)} \cdot pf_1, \ldots, (-1)^{(1-k_i)} \cdot pf_{64}]$ for each $i = 1, \ldots, sk$. This means that the sign of each element pf_j in pF_i is flipped if the i-th bit of the key k is 0 for $j = 1, \ldots, 64$ and $i = 1, \ldots, sk$.
2. **Logistic regression.** Generate logistic regressions $\{LR_i\}_{i=1}^{sk}$. In each logistic regression, there is a weight value w_{LR}^i, where $i = 1, \ldots, sk$, a sigmoid function, and cross entropy. The logistic regression LR_i takes a feature kF_i as an input. Let h_i denote an output of $kF_i \times w_{LR}^i$ and let y_i denote an output of $sigmoid(h_i)$.

Now, we describe the two types of training used to hide k in the DNN architecture.

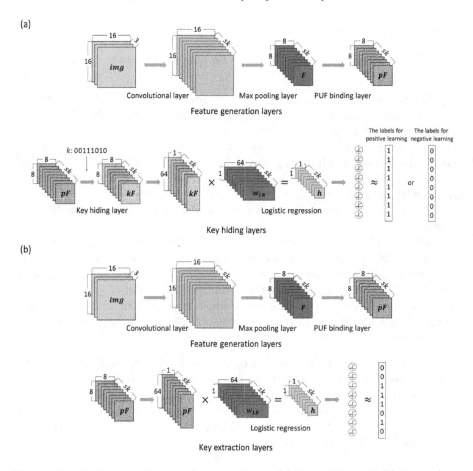

Fig. 3. Graphical description of our instantiation. (a) Key hiding and (b) Key extraction

- **Positive learning** is the learning process trained with label 1. The weight values $\{w_{LR}^i\}_{i=0}^{sk}$ in the logistic regression are optimized to minimize the deviation between y_i and the input label. The data used for positive learning are as follows:
    - Original images: Image d_1
    - Original outputs: PUF value d_2
    - Original key: Key k
- **Negative learning** is the learning process trained with label 0 in each logistic regression, and is very important in terms of the security of our instantiation. If the data used in negative learning are not appropriate, serious problems can arise (see Sect. 4). The data used for negative learning are as follows:
    - Color inverted images: Images created by flipping each bit of the binary representation of pixels in the original image

- Bit-flipped PUF value: value modified by flipping each bit of the original PUF d_2
- Bit-flipped Key: value modified by flipping the bit of the original key

Key Extraction. The key extraction function consists of the trained feature generation layers and sk trained logistic regressions from the trained key hiding network in Sect. 3.2. In the sk logistic regression part of Fig. 3(b), it predicts a key using features $\{pF_i\}_{i=1}^{sk}$, which are extracted from feature extraction layers and optimized weight values w_{LR}^i. Let y_i be the output of $sigmoid(pF_i \times w_{LR}^i)$ for $i = 1, \ldots, sk$. Then, y_i has a value between 0 and 1. We adopt a key decision criteria whereby if $y_i > 0.5$, an i-th bit of a key k' is 1; otherwise, it is 0. Finally, we obtain a key, k', which is the hidden key, k, if a valid image and a PUF value is entered.

Here, we explain why the right key, k, is produced for a valid image and PUF value. It should be remembered that we flip the sign of all elements of the feature pF_i when an i-th bit of the key k is 0 and train each feature in $\{kF_i\}_{i=1}^{sk}$ with the label 1. Assuming that we have the optimized w_{CNN} and w_{LR}^i, $i = 1, \ldots, sk$, let pF_i^h and pF_i^e denote an i-th feature, which is generated in the trained key hiding network and the key extraction, respectively, and k_i be i-the key bit of the key k for $i = 1, \ldots, sk$.

- $k_i = 0$: The sign of all elements of pF_i^h is flipped so that $kF_i = -pF_i^h$ and $sigmoid(kF_i \times w_{LR}^i) \approx 1$. In key extraction, however, as there is no process that flips the sign of the feature pF_i^e, the absolute values of $pF_i^e \times w_{LR}^i$ and $kF_i \times w_{LR}^i$ are almost equal, but the signs are opposite. Therefore, $sigmoid(pF_i^e \times w_{LR}^i)$ is close to 0. Following the key decision criteria, the extracted key bit is 0.
- $k_i = 1$: Contrary to 0, the sign of each element of pF_i^h does not change; therefore, $kF_i = pF_i^h$ and $sigmoid(kF_i \times w_{LR}^i) \approx 1$. In key extraction, the absolute values of $pF_i^e \times w_{LR}^i$ and $kF_i \times w_{LR}^i$ are almost equal and their signs are the same. Therefore, $sigmoid(pF_i^e \times w_{LR}^i)$ is close to 1. Following the key decision criteria, the extracted key bit is 1.

4   Analysis

4.1   Correctness

In this section, we show that our scheme can reliably extract a key regardless of key size and does not generate a valid key for incorrect input data. The data used in our experiments are as follows:

- Correct images: Same as the trained images used for hiding the key k
- False images: Different images from the trained image
- Correct PUF: Original PUF value used for hiding the key k
- False PUF: In our experiment, this is a collection of random bit strings that are different from the original PUF value

Each dataset consists of 1,000 images and/or PUF values. We implement the key hiding network using a TensorFlow [19]. Table 1 shows the experimental results. In case 1 of Table 1, the false reject ratio (FRR) is extremely low, indicating that our instantiation extracts the correct key when valid input data are entered. Moreover, the FRR shows a similar result for each key size 64, 128, and 256, indicating that our example reliably extracts the valid key regardless of key size. In case 2 and case 4, the false acceptance rate (FAR) is 0%. In case 3, FAR is approximately 0.8% when the key size is 256.

Table 1. Correctness

	Input data			Key size		
	Image	PUF		64	128	256
Case1	Correct images	Correct PUF	FRR	0.1	0.6	0.2
Case2	Correct images	False PUF	FAR	0.0	0.0	0.0
Case3	False images	Correct PUF		4.1	2	0.8
Case4	False images	False PUF		0.0	0.0	0.0

FRR(%): False Reject Ratio
FAR(%): False Acceptance Ratio

4.2 Robustness

In the previous section, we prove that our example can correctly hide a key then reliably extract it. Here, we introduce two security analysis tools to verify the robustness of our scheme and our experimental results. As explained previously, the public and secret information of our scheme is as follows:

– Public information: Key extraction functionality including deep neural network architecture and its weight values
– Secret information: Correct noisy data used to produce the hidden key during key extraction. Image data and PUF values are secret information in the example of Sect. 3.2

Two possible attack methods are suggested for determining the hidden key from the public information.

1. The attacker can investigate the potential for key leakage from the weight values in the key extraction
2. The attacker can collect many outputs of our key extraction functionality using random inputs, then attempt to find information about the hidden key from the statistical results of the output values

The two security analysis tools are based on these two attack methods.

Weight Sum Analysis. In the first attack method, an adversary analyzes the weight parameters in the key extraction functionality and attempts to find information related to the valid key. In our example of Sect. 3.2, the public parameters are w_{CNN} and w_{LR}. w_{CNN} is not related to the key; however, w_{LR}, which is the weight value of the key hiding layers, is closely related to the hidden key. Therefore, the attacker can exploit the weight values. Let $w_{LR}^i = (w_1^i, w_2^i, \ldots, w_{64}^i)$ be the weight value related to the i-th key bit extraction in (b) of Fig. 3 for $i = 1, \ldots, sk$. Now, we simply add all elements $(w_1^i, w_2^i, \ldots, w_{64}^i)$ in each weight value in $\{w_{LR}^i\}_{i=1}^{sk}$, and $\{weightSum_i\}_{i=1}^{sk}$ is the result.

$$weightSum_1 = (w_1^1 + w_2^1 + \ldots + w_{64}^1)$$
$$weightSum_2 = (w_1^2 + w_2^2 + \ldots + w_{64}^2)$$

$$\ldots$$

$$weightSum_{sk} = (w_1^{sk} + w_2^{sk} + \ldots + w_{64}^{sk})$$

Finally, the attacker estimates each key bit as follows (also see Algorithm 1):

- the i-th key bit is guessed as 1, if $weightSum_i > 0$
- the i-th key bit is guessed as 0, otherwise

Algorithm 1. Weight value sum analysis

---

input : $\{w_{LR}^i\}_{i=1}^{sk}$
output: An inferred key k'

for $i = 0$ **to** sk **do**
  $weightSum = 0$
  for $j = 0$ **to** 64 **do**
    | $weightSum = weightSum + w_j^i$
  end
  if $weightSum > 0$ **then**
    | $k_i' = 1$
  else
    | $k_i' = 0$
  end
end
return k'

We analyze our example from Sect. 3.2 with the experimental data used to verify its correctness. For a hidden key size of 64, the Pearson correlation is 0.09 between the guessed key string from Algorithm 1, which implies that the result of Algorithm 1 is similar to the randomly guessed key.

Here, we show an example whereby someone trains with data that is not the negative training data defined in Sect. 3.2, so partial information of the hidden key may be revealed from analysis of the Algorithm 1. We carelessly generate negative learning data as follows:

– Ingredients of weak negative learning
  • Original images: Same as the original images used in positive learning.
  • Bit-flipped PUF value: Value modified by flipping each bit of the original PUF used in positive learning.
  • Original key: Identical to the key trained in positive learning.

When applying the Algorithm 1 after this negative training, a Pearson correlation with the hidden key string is 0.84.

Statistical Analysis. The second analysis tool involves exploiting the key extraction functionality. An attacker can choose input data randomly and perform key extraction, resulting in outputs of 0 or 1 for each key bit. Assuming that they have multiple arbitrary input data and try the same attempt several times, they can create a collection of keys. The attacker then counts the number of 0 and 1 values at the i-th bit of all keys in the collection, with $zeroCount_i$ and $oneCount_i$ as the results. Then, they adopt a criteria whereby if $zeroCount_i > oneCount_i$, the i-th bit of the key is guessed as 0; otherwise, it is guessed as 1. Algorithm 2 describes this statistical analysis.

Again, the example from Sect. 3.2 is analyzed using the experimental data used to verify its correctness. A Pearson correlation between the key guessed and hidden is 0.1. It means there is no relation which could be latent risk of being attacked. Here, we show an example whereby if someone trains with data other than the negative training data defined in Sect. 3.2, a statistical attack using Algorithm 2 is possible. The following negative learning data is generated:

– Ingredients of weak negative learning
  • Original images: Same as the original images used in positive learning.
  • Random PUF value: Randomly generated value.
  • Original key: Same as the key used in positive learning.

The experimental results for this example show a Pearson correlation of 0.59 with the right key string. This implies that there is potential to reveal the hidden key.

5   Open Issues

To the best of our knowledge, this is the first attempt to hide a cryptographic key within a deep neural network. As such, there are many unsolved questions requiring further research. For example:

1. **Learning network issues**
   – Different learning network structures from that proposed in this paper
   – Application of our methodology to auto encoding
   – Other key binding mechanisms
   – Learning networks for hiding and generating a group key

Algorithm 2. Statistical analysis

---

input : Arbitrary images and PUF outputs
output: An inferred key k'

$\{zeroCount_i\}_{i=1}^{sk} = 0$
$\{oneCount_i\}_{i=1}^{sk} = 0$
while $i < iteration$ **do**
   $candKey = keyExtraction(img_i, puf_i)$
   for $i = 0$ **to** sk **do**
      if $candKey_i = 0$ **then**
       | $zeroCount_i = zeroCount_i + 1$
      else
       | $oneCount_i = oneCount_i + 1$
      end
   end
end
for $i = 0$ **to** sk **do**
   if $zeroCount_i ¿ oneCount_i$ **then**
      | $k'_i = 0$
   else
      | $k'_i = 1$
   end
end
return k'

---

2. **Noisy data issues**
   - Development of other noisy data
   - Application of our methodology to biometric information such as faces and irises.
   - Use of more than two factors
3. **Application issues**
   - Finding an adequate application scenario
   - Application potential to the low-cost IoT environment or smart phone application
   - Application to authorization of commercial machine learning engine
4. **Security issues**
   - Advanced security analysis for the proposed scheme
   - Formal security proof tool for the proposed scheme

6   Conclusion

In this paper, we present a novel approach for hiding cryptographic keys within the deep neural network, which we term the DNN-based key hiding scheme. To verify the feasibility of our new concept, we present a practical example of the DNN-based key hiding scheme and demonstrate its correctness. Lastly, we newly present two basic security analysis methods for checking its robustness and address several open issues for further study. To the best of our knowledge, this is the first attempt at such an approach.

References

1. Dodis, Y., Reyzin, L., Smith, A.: Fuzzy extractors: how to generate strong keys from biometrics and other noisy data. In: Cachin, C., Camenisch, J.L. (eds.) EUROCRYPT 2004. LNCS, vol. 3027, pp. 523–540. Springer, Heidelberg (2004). https://doi.org/10.1007/978-3-540-24676-3_31

2. Dodis, Y., Ostrovsky, R., Reyzin, L., Smith, A.: Fuzzy extractors: how to generate strong keys from biometrics and other noisy data. SIAM J. Comput. **38**(1), 97–139 (2008)

3. Juels, A., Wattenberg, M.: A fuzzy commitment scheme. In: Proceedings of the 6th ACM Conference on Computer and Communications Security, pp. 28–36 (1999)

4. Jin, Z., Teoh, A., Goi, B., Tay, Y.: Biometric cryptosystems: a new biometric key binding and its implementation for fingerprint minutiae-based representation. Pattern Recogn. **56**(13), 50–62 (2016)

5. Juels, A., Sudan, M.: A fuzzy vault scheme. Des. Codes Crypt. **38**(2), 237–257 (2006)

6. Nakouri, I., Hamdi, M., Kim, T.H.: Chaotic construction of cryptographic keys based on biometric data. In: 2016 International Conference on High Performance Computing & Simulation (HPCS), pp. 509–516 (2016)

7. Itkis, G., Chandar, V., Fuller, B.W., Campbell, J.P., Cunningham, R.K.: Iris biometric security challenges and possible solutions: for your eyes only? Using the iris as a key. IEEE Signal Process. Mag. **32**(5), 42–53 (2015)

8. Mariño, R.Á., Álvarez, F.H., Encinas, L.H.: A crypto-biometric scheme based on iris-templates with fuzzy extractors. Inf. Sci. **195**, 91–102 (2012)

9. Sutcu, Y., Li, Q., Memon, N.: Design and analysis of fuzzy extractors for faces. In: Optics and Photonics in Global Homeland Security V and Biometric Technology for Human Identification VI, pp. 509–516 (2009)

10. Leng, L., Teoh, A.: Alignment-free row-co-occurrence cancelable palmprint fuzzy vault. Pattern Recogn. **48**, 2290–2303 (2015)

11. Choi, D., Seo, S.H., Oh, Y.S., Kang, Y.: Two-factor fuzzy commitment for unmanned IoT devices security. IEEE Internet Things J. **6**, 335–348 (2019)

12. Conti, V., Rundo, L., Militello, C., Mauri, G., Vitabile, S.: Resource-efficient hardware implementation of a neural-based node for automatic fingerprint classification. J. Wirel. Mob. Netw. Ubiquit. Comput. Dependable Appl. (JoWUA) **8**, 19–36 (2017)

13. Li, Y., Ma, W.: Applications of artificial neural networks in financial economics: a survey. In: 2010 International Symposium on Computational Intelligence and Design, pp. 211–214 (2010)

14. De Mulder, W., Bethard, S., Moens, M.-F.: A survey on the application of recurrent neural networks to statistical language modeling. Comput. Speech Lang. **30**, 61–98 (2015)

15. Krizhevsky, A., Sutskever, I., Hinton, G.E.: ImageNet classification with deep convolutional neural networks. Advances in Neural Information Processing Systems, pp. 1097–1105 (2012)

16. Nair, V., Hinton, G.E.: Rectified linear units improve restricted Boltzmann machines. In: Proceedings of the 27th International Conference on Machine Learning (ICML-10), pp. 807–814 (2010)

17. Harrington, P.: Machine Learning in Action. Manning, Greenwich (2012)

18. Wallrabenstein, J.R.: Practical and secure IoT device authentication using physical unclonable functions. In: 2016 IEEE 4th International Conference on Future Internet of Things and Cloud (FiCloud), pp. 99–106 (2016)
19. Abadi, M., et al.: TensorFlow: a system for large-scale machine learning. In: 12th USENIX Symposium on Operating Systems Design and Implementation (OSDI 2016), pp. 265–283 (2016)

IoT Security

RC PUF: A Low-Cost and an Easy-to-Design PUF for Resource-Constrained IoT Devices

Sangjae Lee$^{(\boxtimes)}$, Mi-Kyung Oh, Yousung Kang, and Dooho Choi

Electronics and Telecommunications Research Institute,
Daejeon, Republic of Korea
{leestrike, ohmik, youskang, dhchoi}@etri.re.kr

Abstract. A physically unclonable function (PUF) is a security primitive that can generate device-specific cryptographic information by extracting the features of hardware uncertainty. Despite the advantages of PUFs introduced over the past decade, the majority of them have to be implemented on a separate chip or embedded as a part of a chip, making it difficult to use them in low-cost IoT devices. To increase the usability of PUFs in IoT devices, we propose a novel resistor-capacitor (RC) PUF that can be configured at low cost. The main feature of this RC-based PUF is that it extracts the small difference caused by charging and discharging of RC circuits and uses it as a response. Experimental results show that the proposed RC PUF has more than 49% uniqueness while maintaining over 98% reliability. It also reveals less than 1% stability at 10% voltage changes from 3.3 V to 3.0 V, representing very robust characteristics against voltage variations. For temperature changes from -30 °C to 70°, the stability is maintained below 4%.

Keywords: Physically unclonable function · Hardware security · Key · Resistor-capacitor · IoT

1 Introduction

Physically unclonable functions (PUFs) have emerged as a new alternative to meet the increasing demand for protection of embedded systems against security attacks such as replication of semiconductors, or stealing default ID/password or security keys stored in nonvolatile memory. A PUF generates device-specific information unique to a semiconductor or hardware by using the innate hardware uncertainty derived from the manufacturing process [1].

Based on these characteristics, a PUF can be used to generate and maintain secret credentials that are even unknown to semiconductor architectures or device programmers. Exploiting the PUF as a source of "secret" information, it can be used in applications such as secret key management, data privacy, device authentication, and intellectual property (IP) protection of FPGAs or chips [2].

Various types of PUF have been studied such as RO-based PUF [2–5], delay-based PUF [6], and SRAM PUF [7, 8] over the past decade. Please refer to [2] for a comprehensive overview on PUFs. The majority of such PUFs, however, must be fabricated as separate ASICs or FPGAs, or embedded in the chip at the design time.

© Springer Nature Switzerland AG 2020
I. You (Ed.): WISA 2019, LNCS 11897, pp. 275–285, 2020.
https://doi.org/10.1007/978-3-030-39303-8_21

In recent years, there have been attempts to implement a PUF using the components of the device itself such as dynamic RAM (DRAM) PUF [9, 10] and radio frequency (RF) PUF [11]. DRAM PUFs identified unexpected setup behavior in commercial off-the-shelf DRAMs that could be used as a PUF. RF PUFs identified the effect of variations in analog, RF, and mixed signal properties in wireless radios, where inherent RF properties were used to make a PUF without any additional hardware. Some studies have shown that it is possible to construct SRAM PUFs using existing off-the-shelf components [12]. The advantage of these PUFs is that they can be implemented without any extra hardware.

Another interesting approach to make a PUF is to use analog circuits as a PUF primitive [13]. This study demonstrated an analog PUF structure based on analog and mixed signal circuits. An input challenge was converted to an analog signal by digital-to-analog converters (DACs) and passed through low pass filters and amplifiers. The resulting signal was sampled by an analog-to-digital converter (ADC), and a response was generated from sampled bits.

The motivation for this work is similar with [11] in that we have to provide affordable PUF functionality for resource-constrained IoT devices without using previously mentioned on-chip/off-chip PUF-dedicated hardware. Focusing on the fact that resistors and capacitors have inherent tolerances that arise in the manufacturing process, we achieve PUF-like properties by combining those components with ADCs embedded in many commercial microcontrollers (MCUs). The proposed approach adopts analog circuits and an ADC as PUF primitives, which is similar to [13]. However, instead of exploiting amplifiers, only passive components are simply employed for analog circuits and DACs are not used.

In this paper, we propose a novel resistor-capacitor (RC) PUF that can be implemented using only one MCU equipped with on-board RC components. We first analyze the RC PUF operation and explain the RC PUF architecture, describing how to choose resistor and capacitor components and other parameters. Finally, we present experimental results to characterize the RC PUF with two types of RC circuits.

2   RC PUF Design

2.1   RC PUF Architecture

The basic structure of the RC PUF is shown in Fig. 1, where the RC PUF generates 1-bit response for a challenge consisting of multiple bits. The input challenge is shifted by 1 bit and the corresponding bit is applied sequentially to the digital output pin such as a general purpose I/O (GPIO). If the I/O voltage of the MCU is 3.3 V, the voltage applied to the input of the RC circuit becomes 3.3 V or ground (GND or 0 V) depending on the value of the output bit. The GPIO output or the input of the RC circuit (RCin) remains constant for a period of time for one bit, which is defined as "bit delay time." After the bit delay time has expired, the output changes by the next bit. Accordingly, the output of the RC circuit gradually increases (charge) or decreases (discharge).

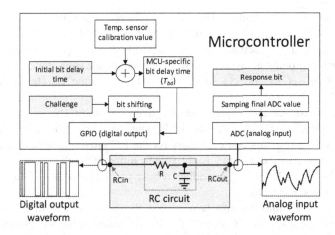

Fig. 1. Hardware and software block diagram of RC PUF.

After a challenge bit stream is passed to the GPIO, the last output voltage of the RC circuit (RCout) is sampled by the ADC and 1-bit response is extracted from the ADC value.

The key consideration in RC PUF design is that the input voltage of the RC circuit must be changed in a "transient-state" before the output of the RC circuit by a previous bit enters a "steady-state", i.e., fully charged (3.3 V) or discharged (GND). The bit delay time in Fig. 1 determines the change time of the input of the RC circuit. If the bit delay time is too long to make the RC circuit a "steady-state", the output of the RC circuit will be stuck at 3.3 V or GND for all input challenges. Hence, the effect of component tolerance almost disappears and it is not easy to differentiate response values between different challenges or devices. In the RC PUF, it is important to keep the bit delay time as small as possible because the longer the bit delay time is, the longer the response generation time in the RC PUF will be, which negatively affects applications that use the PUF. We note that the software delay function on MCUs can adjust this bit delay time from 1 microsecond to tens of microseconds.

Keeping in mind that the appropriate bit delay time determines the total performance of our RC PUF, we show how to select the parameters of the RC components. Physically, the bit delay time is related to the product of the resistance and the capacitance, i.e., $\tau = RC$ [18], where R is the resistance of the resistor and C is the capacitance of the capacitor. Therefore, the resistance and capacitance must be selected considering the limit of the bit delay time.

When selecting the capacitance, it is important to consider both probing analysis and reliability. Generally, the input capacitance of an oscilloscope probe ranges up to 100 pF [20]. If the capacitance of the RC circuit is too large (e.g., 1 uF), the input capacitance of the probe is too small compared to the capacitance of the RC circuit, and thus probing does not affect the rise and fall times of the RC circuit. This can allow the correct ADC input voltage to be read by probing and therefore make the RC PUF vulnerable to probing analysis. On the contrary, if the capacitance is too small (e.g., below tens of pF), probing increases the total capacitance of the RC circuit, making it difficult to estimate the original ADC value. However, experiments have shown that reliability is more severely affected if the capacitance is less than a few tens of pF. As a result, we choose the capacitance between 100 pF and 200 pF to ensure reliability while preventing probing analysis to some extent. Since the capacitance is determined, the resistance is set to 100 kΩ so that the bit delay time can be up to tens of microseconds.

Once the resistance and capacitance are fixed, we must choose the appropriate resistor and capacitor type for the RC PUF. The main concern when selecting RC components is that resistors and capacitors for the RC circuit have to be chosen such that the tolerance must be as large as possible to differentiate the response correlation between different PUFs, while providing robust properties against temperature and voltage variations and aging.

The RC PUF exploits commonly used thin film resistors and multilayer ceramic capacitors (MLCCs) for the RC circuit. For the capacitor of the RC circuit, we use a class 1 (C0G) capacitor with a 20% tolerance that is more robust to temperature variation and aging than class 2 or class 3 capacitors [15–17]. We then choose a resistor with a tolerance of 1% and a good temperature coefficient of 25 ppm for the RC circuit [14]. The selected resistor and capacitor can be purchased for less than 10 cents. Thus, the RC PUF can be implemented at a lower cost than other PUFs implemented as separate chips or built into SoCs, which usually cost several dollars. In addition, the RC circuit is separated from the microcontroller, eliminating the need to use a specific chip with a built-in PUF, which provides design flexibility.

Finally, we consider two approaches to generate the bit delay time for our RC PUF. One is to use the initial fixed bit delay time for all RC PUF instances. The other is to use its own bit delay time for each RC PUF, where temperature sensor calibration values are added to the initial fixed bit delay time to generate its own unique bit delay, as shown in Fig. 1. We note that the temperature sensor calibration value is stored in the MCU at the manufacturing process.

2.2 RC PUF Simulation

We perform a simulation to view the "transient-state" characteristics at the RC circuit output. We first analyze the behavior of the first-order RC circuit, as shown in Fig. 1. The basic representation of a first-order RC circuit is divided into two modes – rising (or charging) and falling (or discharging). The voltage change at the time of charging and discharging the RC circuit can be expressed as [18]

$$V_t = V_{max}\left(1 - e^{-\frac{t}{RC}}\right), \text{ when charging,} \tag{1}$$

$$V_t = V_0 e^{-\frac{t}{RC}}, \text{ when discharging,} \tag{2}$$

where R is the resistance of the resistor, C is the capacitance of the capacitor, V_{max} is the maximum voltage applied to the input of the RC circuit and V_0 is the initial input voltage of the RC circuit at the start of discharging.

As we mentioned earlier, the "transient-state" of the voltage change should be calculated for the proposed RC PUF behavior. To do this, we modify (1) and (2) to indicate charging and discharging behavior starting at the last voltage value of the previous "transient-state" when a new input value is applied to the RC circuit. Thus, the modified voltage can be derived as

$$V_{t+1} = V_t + V_{rise}\left(1 - e^{-\frac{T_{bd}}{RC}}\right), \text{ when charging,} \tag{3}$$

$$V_{t+1} = V_t e^{-\frac{T_{bd}}{RC}}, \text{ when discharging,} \tag{4}$$

where the difference between V_{max} and the voltage V_t at the start time of charging is $V_{rise} = V_{max} - V_t$, and T_{bd} is the bit delay time. As shown in (3) and (4), the voltage change up to the next time is affected by the previous voltage V_t. Figure 2 shows an example where bit values of '101' are sequentially applied to the input of the RC circuit, where the initial RC input voltage is $V_0 = 0$ V, and $V_{max} = 3.3$ V. The voltage change for the first bit '1' after T_{bd} is then calculated as follows according to (3).

$$V_1 = V_{max}\left(1 - e^{-\frac{T_{bd}}{RC}}\right). \tag{5}$$

When the RC input is changed by the second bit '0', the voltage change according to (4) is then given by

$$V_2 = V_1 e^{-\frac{T_{bd}}{RC}}. \tag{6}$$

Next, for the third bit '1', the voltage change is calculated by using (3) and (6), which can be written as

$$\begin{aligned} V_3 &= V_2 + (V_{max} - V_2)\left(1 - e^{-\frac{T_{bd}}{RC}}\right) \\ &= V_1 e^{-\frac{T_{bd}}{RC}} + \left(V_{max} - V_1 e^{-\frac{T_{bd}}{RC}}\right)\left(1 - e^{-\frac{T_{bd}}{RC}}\right), \end{aligned} \tag{7}$$

where V_1 is calculated in (5). It is observed from (6) and (7) that the voltage change due to the sequence of bit patterns accumulates the influence of the previous values.

In Fig. 2, the red line represents the simulated waveform of the RC PUF using the first-order RC circuit, where we used an arbitrary 32-bit challenge shown at the top of the figure. The resistance and capacitance in the RC circuit are determined as $R = 100$ kΩ and $C = 200$ pF, respectively. The maximum input voltage to the RC circuit is $V_{max} = 3.3$ V and the bit delay time is $T_{bd} = 4.3$ us for the simulation.

As expected, the output of the RC circuit changes according to the challenge bit pattern during the "transient-state". In the ideal case, the output value of the RC circuit according to the same bit pattern should be the same for different RC PUFs. However, the component tolerance, i.e., R and C, causes a difference in the sampled ADC value between different RC PUFs, leading to the responses being uncorrelated with each other.

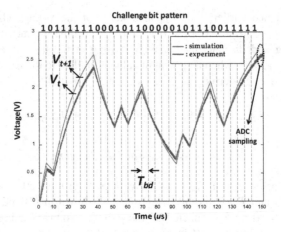

Fig. 2. Comparison of simulation and experimental waveforms.

2.3 RC PUF Implementation

We implemented a RC PUF board equipped with the RC circuit and one MCU with ADC functionality, as shown in Fig. 3. The resistance and capacitance of the RC circuit are the same as those used in the simulation. The supply voltage of the MCU is 3.3 V converted from USB 5 V voltage through a low-dropout regulator (LDO). Hence, the output voltage of the GPIO used as the input of the RC circuit is also 3.3 V. We also constructed a testbed using 100 RC PUF boards to measure the performance of the RC PUF.

In order to compare the simulation results with the experimental results, we run the RC PUF using the same challenge used in the simulation. We note from Fig. 2 that the waveform of the RC PUF is similar to the simulation waveform, and the implemented RC PUF works as expected when compared to the simulation. The difference between the simulation and the experimental waveform is considered to be caused by the component tolerance of RC and other on-board components.

Fig. 3. Implemented RC PUF (below) and testbed (upper).

3   Experimental Results

As described in Sect. 2, the sampled ADC value at the RC circuit output is used to generate a response bit. Since the ADCs embedded in the commonly used MCU normally support multiple bit resolution, e.g., 12-bit, we face the problem of determining which bit is used for a response bit among multiple bits. For example, the valid bit must be selected from bit 11 to bit 0, where bit 0 represents the least significant bit. The response bits between different PUFs for the same challenge are more likely to be the same as the selected bit position is closer to bit 11. Conversely, the error probability for the response value increases as the selected bit position approaches bit 0. Through several experiments, although bit 4 to bit 6 can be used as a response bit, we found that bit 5 is the most appropriate bit position considering the uniqueness and reliability of the implemented RC PUF board.

Once the ADC bit position is fixed, it is possible to evaluate the performance of the RC PUF. In order to characterize the RC PUF, we use three commonly employed performance metrics: uniqueness, reliability (also known as steadiness), and uniformity [4, 21].

Uniqueness represents the variations in the responses of multiple devices to the same challenge and can be referenced as extra-chip variation (EC), which is calculated as [4]

$$EC = \frac{1}{M(M-1)N} \sum_{i=1}^{M} \sum_{k=1,k \neq i}^{M} \sum_{j=1}^{N} \frac{HD(r_{i,j}, \overline{r_k})}{n} \times 100\%, \qquad (8)$$

where M is the number of devices, n is the length of response, $r_{i,j}$ is the j-th response sample from the i-th board, $\overline{r_k}$ is the mean value of the N responses from the k-th board, and HD represents the hamming distance. We note that the optimal value for uniqueness is 50%.

Reliability or *steadiness* represents the ability of a particular device to generate the same response and can be referenced as intra-chip variation (IC), which is given by [4]

$$IC_i(T, V) = \frac{1}{N} \sum_{j=1}^{N} \frac{HD(r_{i,j}, r_{i,ref})}{n} \times 100\%, \qquad (9)$$

where $r_{i,ref}$ is the mean value of responses of the i-th board. We note that this metric depends on the environmental parameters, such as temperature (T) and voltage (V). The percentage figure for reliability can be defined as

$$Reliability = 100 - IC_i(T, V). \qquad (10)$$

Obviously, the optimal value for reliability is 100%.

Uniformity is used to describe the distribution of 0 s and 1 s in a PUF response. The ideal uniformity is achieved when 0 s and 1 s occurs with equal probability in a PUF response. It can be expressed as follow [21]

$$U_i = \frac{1}{n} \sum_{l=1}^{n} r_{i,l} \times 100\%, \tag{11}$$

where U_i is the uniformity of i-th board and $r_{i,l}$ is the l-th bit of total n-bit response from the i-th board. The optimal value for uniformity is 50%.

3.1   Uniqueness, Reliability and Uniformity

For the uniqueness and reliability test, the RC PUF was evaluated with 32,768 random challenges, where each 32-bit challenge was repeated 100 times, and then majority voting was applied to determine the response bit.

First we tested the RC PUF by fixing the bit delay time (FD) to 2 us and 32 us to evaluate the performance change by the bit delay time. Next, we added 4-bit and 5-bit MCU-specific helper data to the initial bit delay time so that the newly generated bit delay times were between 8–24 us (VD4) and 1–32 us (VD5), respectively. For example, if we run RC PUF in FD mode, then the same bit delay time (T_{bd}) is used for all challenges in all RC PUF boards. However, for VD4 or VD5 modes, T_{bd} is unique among different RC PUF boards, but the same for all challenges in one RC PUF board.

As shown in Table 1, when the fixed bit delay time (FD) increases from 2 us to 32 us, the uniqueness and reliability are improved in the RC PUF. This is because the longer the operating time is, the more differences are accumulated due to the tolerance of the RC circuit. When using the MCU-specific bit delay time (VD4 and VD5), the RC PUF has more than 48% uniqueness as shown in Fig. 4, which is close to the ideal value of 50%, while achieving more than 98% reliability. Finally, uniformity over all delay mode is 50.1–50.3%, which is close to the optimal value of 50%.

We can see that the difference in ADC values between different PUFs is in the range of several tens to hundreds using different bit delay times, i.e., VD4 and VD5, resulting in a better uniqueness than using the same fixed delay time for all PUFs.

Table 1. Uniqueness and reliability of RC PUF.

Metric	Delay mode (bit delay time)			
	FD (2 us)	FD (32 us)	VD4 (8–24 us)	VD5 (1–32 us)
Uniqueness (%)	27.3	30.9	48.5	48.8
Reliability (%)	96.2	98.5	98.2	98.3
Uniformity (%)	50.3	50.3	50.2	50.1

3.2   Stability Against Voltage and Temperature Variations

For the stability of the RC PUF, we consider the environmental variations, e.g., temperature and voltage. We first extracted a 1024-bit reference response from 10 randomly selected RC PUF boards, where FD and VD4 bit delay cases under normal conditions (room temperature of 25 °C and supply voltage of 3.3 V) are considered. The stability was then calculated based on how many bit flips occurred compared with the reference response.

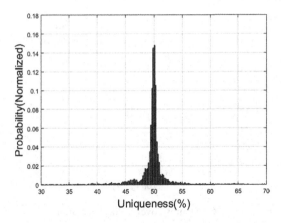

Fig. 4. Uniqueness for VD5.

To evaluate the stability under different temperatures, we used a temperature chamber, varying the temperature from −30 °C to 70 °C with 10 °C increments. Figure 5 shows that the stability is maintained within 2% at temperatures below 50 °C, but increases above 50 °C. This is because temperature has a more dominant effect on ADC accuracy than the effects of resistors and capacitors with a good temperature coefficient. Nevertheless, the worst case stability of 4% (FD) is an acceptable error rate that can be recovered using commonly used error correction codes [2].

The stability for voltage variations was measured in 0.05 V steps over a voltage range of 3.3 V–3.0 V. Figure 6 reveals less than 1% stability over the entire range, which corresponds to a bit flip of less than 10 bits of 1024 bits. The main reason of robust stability over voltage is that the power supply voltage of the MCU is equal to both the output voltage of the GPIO used as the input voltage of the RC circuit and the operating voltage of the ADC. Therefore, the ADC value is determined by the voltage change ratio, not the absolute voltage.

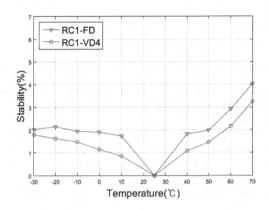

Fig. 5. Stability over temperature variation.

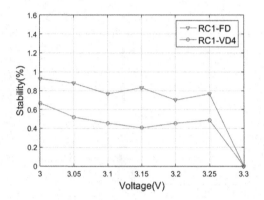

Fig. 6. Stability over voltage variation.

4 Conclusion

In this paper, we proposed a novel RC PUF that can be easily implemented using one MCU with ADC function and several low-cost resistors and capacitors. By appropriately selecting those components and using MCU-specific helper data, the proposed RC PUF achieved 48.8% uniqueness and 98.3% reliability. Due to the structural characteristics, our RC PUF shows less than 1% stability over 10% voltage variation. With regard to performance, price, and ease of implementation, the proposed RC PUF can be used as a security primitive for IoT devices.

Future works will include probing analysis and modeling attacks against the proposed RC PUF with various types of RC circuits. A generalized randomness test will also be included in our future works.

Acknowledgement. This work was supported by Institute of Information & communications Technology Planning & Evalution(IITP) grant funded by the Korea government (MSIT) (No.2018-0-00230, Development on Autonomous Trust Enhancement Technology of IoT Device and Study on Adaptive IoT Security Open Architecture based on Global Standardization [TrusThingz Project]).

References

1. Suh, G.E., Devadas, S.: Physical unclonable functions for device authentication and secret key generation. In: proceedings of 2007 44th ACM/IEEE Design Automation Conference, pp. 9–14. ACM (2017)
2. Herder, C., Yu, M.D., Koushanfar, F., Devadas, S.: Physical unclonable functions and applications: a tutorial. In: Proceedings of the IEEE, pp. 1126–1141. IEEE (2014)
3. Cao, Y., Zhao, X., Ye, W., Han, Q., Pan, X.: A compact and low power RO PUF with high resilience to the EM Side-channel attack and the SVM modelling attack of wireless sensor networks. Sensors **18**(2), 322 (2018)

4. Marchand, C., Bossuet, L., Mureddu, U., Bochard, N., Cherkaoui, A., Fischer, V.: Implementation and characterization of a physical unclonable function for IoT: a case study with the TERO-PUF. IEEE Trans. Comput.-Aided Design Integr. Circ. Syst. **37**(1), 97–109 (2018)

5. Clark, L.T., Medapuram, S.B., Kadiyala, D.K., Brunhaver, J.: ACRO-PUF: a low-power, reliable and aging-resilient current starved inverter-based ring oscillator physical unclonable function. IEEE Trans. Circ. Syst. I: Regul. Paper **64**(12), 3138–3149 (2017)

6. Tajik, S., et al.: Physical characterization of arbiter PUFs. In: Batina, L., Robshaw, M. (eds.) CHES 2014. LNCS, vol. 8731, pp. 493–509. Springer, Heidelberg (2014). https://doi.org/10.1007/978-3-662-44709-3_27

7. Gong, M., Liu, H., Min, R., Liu, Z.: Pitfall of the strongest cells in static random access memory physical unclonable functions. Sensors **18**(6), 1776 (2018)

8. Clark, L.T., Medapuram, S.B., Kadiyala, D.K., Brunhaver, J.: Physically unclonable functions using foundry SRAM cells. IEEE Trans. Circ. Syst. I: Regul. Papers **66**(3), 955–966 (2019)

9. Tehranipoor, F., Karimian, N., Yan, W., Chandy, J.A.: DRAM-based intrinsic physically unclonable functions for system-level security and authentication. IEEE Trans. Very Large Scale Integr. Syst. **25**(3), 1085–1097 (2017)

10. Schaller, A., et al.: Decay-based DRAM PUFs in commodity devices. IEEE Trans. Dependable Secure Comput. **16**(3), 462–475 (2018)

11. Chatterjee, B., Das, D., Maity, S., Sen, S.: RF-PUF: enhancing IoT security through authentication of wireless nodes using in-situ machine learning. IEEE Internet Things J. **6**(1), 388–398 (2019)

12. Oh, M., et al.: Secure key extraction for IoT devices integrating IEEE 802.15.4 g/k transceiver. In: proceedings of 2018 International Conference on Information and Communication Technology Convergence, pp. 833–835 (2018)

13. Deyati, S., Muldrey, B., Singh, A., Chatterjee, A.: Design of efficient analog physically unclonable functions using alternative test principles. In: proceedings of 2017 International Mixed Signals Testing Workshop. IEEE (2017)

14. Kuehl, R.: Stability of thin film resistors - prediction and differences base on time dependent Arrhenius law. Microelectron. Reliab. **49**(1), 51–58 (2009)

15. Kahn, M.: Multilayer ceramic capacitors – materials and manufacture. AVX Corporation (2012)

16. Rhan, J.: Not all caps are created equal. In: IEEE–Long Island Chapter–EMC Society (2015)

17. Pan, M., Randall, C.A.: A brief introduction to ceramic capacitors. IEEE Electr. Insul. Mag. **26**(3), 44–50 (2010)

18. Horowitz, P., Hill, W.: The Art of Electronics, 2nd edn, pp. 20–21. Cambridge University Press, Cambridge (1989)

19. Gu, C., Hanley, N., O'Neill, M.: Improved reliability of FPGA-based PUF identification generator design. ACM Trans. Reconfig. Technol. Syst. **10**(3), 20:1–20:23 (2017)

20. Davis, N.: An introduction to oscilloscope probes. https://www.allaboutcircuits.com/technical-articles/an-introduction-to-oscilloscope-probes (2017). Accessed 9 April 2019

21. Maiti, A., Gunreddy, V., Schaumont, P.: A Systematic method to evaluate and compare the performance of physical unclonable functions. In: Athanas, P., Pnevmatikatos, D., Sklavos, N. (eds.) Embedded Systems Design with FPGAs, pp. 245–267. Springer, New York (2013). https://doi.org/10.1007/978-1-4614-1362-2_11

On the Automation of Security Testing for IoT Constrained Scenarios

Sara N. Matheu[1]([✉])[iD], Salvador Pérez[1], José L. Hernández Ramos[2], and Antonio Skarmeta[1]

[1] Department of Information and Communications Engineering (DIIC), University of Murcia, 30100 Murcia, Spain
{saranieves.matheu,salvador.p.f,skarmeta}@um.es
[2] European Commission, Joint Research Centre (JRC), 21027 Ispra, Italy
jose-luis.hernandez-ramos@ec.europa.eu

Abstract. Due to the high increase of IoT technologies and devices, analyzing their security is crucial for their acceptance. Towards this end, an automated security testing approach should be considered as a cornerstone to cope with the business interests and the high fragmentation of new approaches. In particular, this work analyses the use of the Model-Based Testing (MBT) approach and specific technologies and tools to automate the generation of security tests. Then, we provide a detailed description of its application to the Elliptic Curve Diffie-Hellman over COSE (EDHOC) protocol, which is being defined within the scope of the Internet Engineering Task Force (IETF).

Keywords: IoT · Security testing · Security risk assessment · Model-Based Testing (MBT)

1 Introduction

Advances in Information and Communication Technologies, especially in the Internet of Things (IoT), have the potential to improve many facets of our life. However, despite the potential benefits, several obstacles limit a wide deployment [10]. One of the main barriers is related to the perceived threats to data security and privacy, and a widely held belief that these cannot be adequately addressed with current approaches. This situation gets worse with new protocols and techniques recently developed and non standardized, which are not widely adopted due to the lack of information related with the real security provided. In this scenario, being able to test and analyze the security vulnerabilities related with a specific device and protocol would provide a more harmonized IoT security view to be leveraged by end consumers [11].

Dealing with this problem, security testing attempts to verify that an implementation protects data and maintains functionality as intended, revealing flaws of the system under test (SUT). However, the existing dynamism inherent to IoT devices makes the testing process a long and tedious process, which requires

© Springer Nature Switzerland AG 2020
I. You (Ed.): WISA 2019, LNCS 11897, pp. 286–298, 2020.
https://doi.org/10.1007/978-3-030-39303-8_22

defining, modeling and implementing each test. This collides with new discovered vulnerabilities, updates or patches, that makes necessary repeating all the process, order to main the security level updated. In addition, the constraints inherent to some IoT devices in terms of memory or computation power, makes the process of programming the tests more difficult to be performed. Finally, as testing approaches are usually time-consuming and expensive, analyzing the security of recently developed approaches is totally discarded, and therefore they are not applied to critical environments that need a particular and well known security level. In this sense, an automated and cost-effective testing approach would also help to test the security level of non standardized protocols [2].

Following this line, the Model-Based Testing approach (MBT) [5] has shown its benefits and usefulness for systematic compliance testing of systems [3]. In this approach, the structure of the system is modelled by Unified Modelling Language (UML) class diagrams, while the system behavior is expressed in Object Constraint Language (OCL)[1]. In particular, this approach was explored in the context of the H2020 ARMOUR project, where we have proposed an integrated methodology for security risk assessment and testing as the main building blocks for cybersecurity certification [15,16]. The use of MBT is intended to automate the testing process to cope with the challenges described before. In this work, we analyze the benefits and limitations of the MBT approach when it is applied to analyze the security level of a SUT. Towards this end, we consider an IoT scenario based on the Elliptic Curve Diffie-Hellman over COSE (EDHOC) [22] protocol, which is employed as key agreement protocol. It should be noted that this proposal is based on the Concise Binary Object Representation (CBOR) [4] that is employed to encode the EDHOC messages, and the CBOR Object Signing and Encryption (COSE) [20] to protect them. This use of these standards aims to provide a lightweight key agreement approaches to be considered in IoT constrained scenarios.

The remainder of the paper is as follows: Sect. 2 reviews the main approaches related with IoT security testing, whereas Sect. 3 reviews the main security protocols at transport layer for IoT. Then, Sect. 4 describes the insights of the EDHOC protocol and Sect. 5 discusses and applies the MBT methodology to the EDHOC protocol described before. Finally, Sect. 6 concludes the paper with an outlook about our future work in this area.

2   Security Testing

The ISO 29119 standard defines security testing as *a type of testing that tries to evaluate the protection level of the system under test against unauthorized access, unwanted use and denial of service*. Testing security properties such as confidentiality, integrity, authentication, authorization, availability, and non-repudiation is crucial to ensure the development of trusted systems. In this sense, security testing identifies if a specific security property is correctly implemented. This can be achieved through a high number of security testing approaches. One of

---

[1] http://www.omg.org/spec/OCL/2.4.

the most basic testing approach is the penetration testing [1]. This type of testing is similar to an attack from a malicious third party, with limited information about the SUT and only able to interact with the system's public interfaces. However, this technique is generally manual and in some cases, combined with the usage of black-box vulnerability scanners. Also manually, code-based testing [8] detects vulnerabilities by looking at the code. Moreover, the regression testing [24] ensures that changes or updates do not cause unintended effects. In addition, fuzzing testing [9] is usually employed for injection attacks, since it consists on passing into a target system valid and invalid message sequences to check if the system breaks, and the associated reasons.

Compared to previous testing methods, Model-Based Testing (MBT) [5] is able to manage and accomplish testing tasks in a more cost effective and efficient way [3], due to the high abstraction level used for defining the tests. In addition, a large number of MBT tools have been developed to support the practice and utilization of MBT technologies in real cases [14]. A MBT model represents the system under test (SUT), its environment, or the test itself, which directly supports test analysis, planning, control, implementation, execution and reporting activities.

As already mentioned, following our proposed methodology in [16], the SUT is modeled by Unified Modeling Language (UML) class diagrams, while the system behavior is expressed in Object Constraint Language (OCL)[2], using the CertifyIt tool [5] to export the tests. The use of MBT and the mentioned tool are intended to automate the security testing to deal with the dynamic nature of IoT scenarios. In particular, if there is a security change, the tests can be redefined by changing the model, without the need to modify the real implementation.

3 Transport and Application Layer Security in IoT

Nowadays, the Constrained Application Protocol (CoAP) [23] is considered the main protocol for the application layer in IoT. From the security point of view, it specifies a binding to the Datagram Transport Layer Security (DTLS) [19] for protecting communications. DTLS is based on the TLS protocol [7], thus being a two-layer protocol. The lower layer consists of the Record protocol, which aims to encapsulate the corresponding messages of a protocol of the upper layer providing different functionality, such as the Handshake protocol or the Application Data protocol. In this sense, the Handshake protocol allows to establish certain security parameters (e.g., cryptographic algorithms or authentication schemes) between two entities. This way, they are able to calculate shared symmetric keys in order to protect mutual communications. Furthermore, the Application Data protocol enables the exchange of encrypted data between those two entities once the handshake process has been successfully completed.

A common feature of IoT scenarios is the presence of proxies to reduce the use of network bandwidth and the response time. In addition, communications

---

[2] http://www.omg.org/spec/OCL/2.4.

are usually performed through brokers, which follow the *publish/subscribe pattern*, with the purpose of keeping involved devices uncoupled. Accordingly, the protection of CoAP communications needs to be based on the establishment of different DTLS security associations, as shown in Fig. 1. In particular, DTLS security associations are established between IoT device - proxy, proxy - proxy and proxy - publish/subscribe broker, thus providing *"hop-by-hop security"* in contrast to *"end-to-end security"*. This fact implies that both the proxies and the brokers have access to all exchanged information, so that such intermediate entities are able to perform certain security attacks, such as *eavesdropping*, *message manipulation* or *message injection* [21].

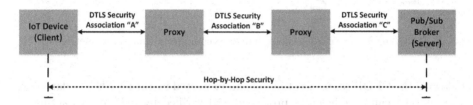

Fig. 1. DTLS security associations between an IoT device and a broker

In order to face this situation, security at the application layer emerges as a solution to mitigate such threats and guarantee *"end-to-end security"* in these networks. Additionally, this approach enables to protect communications independently of the underlying technology or protocol being used. In this sense, new proposals, such as EDHOC [22] and OSCORE [18], emerge as object-based security alternatives to the transport layer security (in particular, to the DTLS protocol) in order to protect data exchange in IoT networks. In this work, EDHOC has been used as an example to apply the testing approach, and it is described in the next section.

4   EDHOC

EDHOC [22] is a lightweight key exchange protocol that allows the establishment of symmetric keys between two entities, usually a client and a server. This protocol implements the Elliptic Curve Diffie-Hellman algorithm (ECDH) [17] with ephemeral keys in order to provide Perfect Forward Secrecy (PFS) [12]. In addition, EDHOC establishes two authentication modes with the purpose of confirming the identity of the involved entities, in particular, authentication based on public keys (i.e., raw public keys and certificates) and authentication based on a pre-shared key. This way, the authentication process and the shared key generation process remain independent of each other. Moreover, EDHOC defines a three-message exchange, which can be embedded as payload in an application protocol like CoAP. In this sense, note that other application protocols can be adopted to carry out this exchange. Furthermore, EDHOC messages are encoded

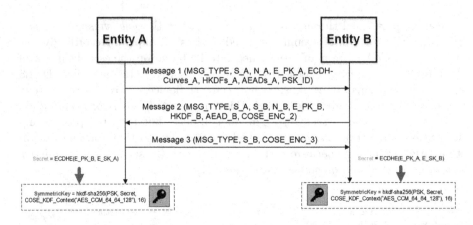

Fig. 2. EDHOC three-message exchange to compute a shared symmetric key

following the CBOR representation [4] and protected by the COSE standard [20], so that they can be efficiently processed and verified by IoT devices acting as clients, which usually present constrained resources (e.g., sensors). Accordingly, Fig. 2 shows the EDHOC three-message exchange carried out between the Entity A acting as a client and the Entity B acting as a server. In addition, it should be pointed out that authentication mode employed is based on a pre-shared key (PSK).

By using this authentication mode, the EDHOC exchange starts with the *Message 1*, which is sent by the Entity A and includes the message type (MSG_TYPE), a unique session identifier for this entity (S_A), a nonce (N_A), its ephemeral public key (E_PK_A), the supported cryptographic algorithms (i.e., the curves ($ECDH - Curves\_A$), KDF ($HKDFs\_A$) and AEAD ($AEADs\_A$) algorithms) and an identifier associated to the PSK (PSK_ID) used to perform the authentication process.

When the Entity B receives the *Message 1*, it validates the S_A and uses the PSK_ID to get the key pre-shared with the Entity A. Now, both parts can compute the shared secret using the Diffie-Hellman algorithm and the ephemeral keys. The Entity A runs the Diffie-Hellman algorithm with its ephemeral secret key (E_SK_A) and the E_PK_B. Similarly, Entity B runs such algorithm with its ephemeral secret key (E_SK_B) and the E_PK_A. After computing the secret, the Entity B sends the *Message 2*, which includes the corresponding MSG_TYPE, the S_A, a unique session identifier for this entity (S_B), a nonce (N_B), the ephemeral public key of this entity (E_PK_B), the selected cryptographic algorithms (i.e., the KDF ($HKDF\_B$) and AEAD ($AEAD\_B$) algorithms) and a COSE object ($COSE\_ENC\_2$) encrypted by using the PSK, the secret and the AEAD algorithm. The COSE object contains the *Message 1* and all data included in *Message 2*. Therefore, this COSE object enables to authenticates the Entity B, as well as to protect the integrity of messages 1 and 2.

When the Entity A receives the *Message 2*, it validates the S_B and decrypts the ($COSE\_ENC\_2$). If this process finishes successfully, this entity sends the *Message 3* including the corresponding MSG_TYPE, the S_B and a new COSE object encrypted by using the PSK ($COSE\_ENC\_3$) that contains the *Message 1*, the *Message 2* and all data included in *Message 3*. Thus, the $COSE\_ENC\_3$ is used for the Entity A authentication and for ensuring the integrity of all EDHOC messages. Once the Entity B obtains this third message, it validates the S_B and decrypts the $COSE\_ENC\_3$ in order to finish the EDHOC three-message exchange.

Once this message exchange has successfully completed, the shared symmetric key is computed by applying a key derivation function over the shared secret. In particular, the HMAC-based Extract-and-Expand Key Derivation Function (HKDF) [13] is used to carried out this derivation operation, due to it is proposed by the EDHOC specification. Specifically, symmetric key computation is performed as follows:

$$SymmetricKey = hkdf - sha256(PSK, Secret,$$
$$COSE\_KDF\_Context("AES\_CCM\_64\_64\_128"), 16)$$

where the *COSE_KDF_Context(AlgorithmID)* structure is defined by following the [20] and [22]:

$$COSE\_KDF\_Context(AlgorithmID) =$$
$$(AlgorithmID, (null, null, null),$$
$$16,'''', sha256(sha256(Message1|Message2)|Message3))$$

As it is shown, the HKDF makes use of the SHA-256 as hash function including the following parameters: the PSK, the $Secret$, a $COSE\_KDF\_Context(AlgorithmID)$ structure and the shared symmetric key length (16-byte length).

Finally, it should be noted that such $COSE\_KDF\_Context(AlgorithmID)$ structure includes a parameter called $AlgorithmID$, which indicates the algorithm that will be employed to protect application data. In this case, we establish this parameter to "AES_CCM_64_64_128".

5   Testing EDHOC Security

In this section we apply MBT to a particular scenario with EDHOC to get some insights about its security level. It should be noted that our approach is complementary to the use of formal verification techniques, as proposed in [6]. The exchange is performed between an IoT device (entity A) and a server (entity B), as shown in Fig. 2. It should be noted that for the implementation of EDHOC, we have developed our own library, while we have used the *erbium* library[3] for CoAP. Due to the limit of space, we have selected two security properties (authentication and confidentiality) to show with details how to generate the tests following the MBT approach.

---

[3] http://people.inf.ethz.ch/mkovatsc/erbium.php.

5.1   Identifying the Tests

The first step is to define the tests to be performed. Table 1 shows the details for the confidentiality and authentication tests. In the confidentiality, we perform the complete execution of the scenario (successful EDHOC exchange), in which a sniffer is added. After executing these tests we have the sniffer trace and the test status (PASS or FAIL). This output can be used to obtain valuable information, such as the PSK length used for the authentication, the shared secret length, PSK ID length, ciphersuite or the percentage of non encrypted data. These data are used to measure the security level provided by the protocol, so it can be compared with other mechanisms.

Table 1. Confidentiality and authentication tests

ID:C1 – Confidentiality
1. Device sends message 1 of EDHOC with a valid PSK_ID
2. Server answers with the message 2 of EDHOC
3. Device receives message 2 and answers with message 3 of EDHOC
4. Sniffer agent is listening the whole exchange
ID:A1 – Authentication
1. Attacker device sends message 1 of EDHOC with a non valid PSK_ID
2. Server is not able to find the associated PSK and sends an EDHOC error
ID:A2 – Authentication
1. Attacker device sends EDHOC message 1 with a valid PSK_ID (stolen)
2. Server answers with EDHOC message 2
3. Attacker receives message 2 and answers with EDHOC message 3 encrypted with non valid PSK
4. Server sends an EDHOC error
ID:A3 – Authentication
1. Device sends message 1 of EDHOC with a valid PSK_ID
2. Attacker server answers with EDHOC message 2; COSE object is encrypted with non valid key
3. Device is not able no decrypt the COSE, so it answer with an EDHOC error

According to Table 1, A1 and A2 tests are focused on the device. The former (A1) checks that an attacker device with a non valid PSK ID is unable to perform the complete EDHOC exchange, since the server will not find the associated PSK, answering with an error message. The latter (A2) checks that an attacker device with a stolen valid PSK ID is unable to perform EDHOC since it does not have the PSK associated to that PSK ID. In this way, when the attacker sends the third message encrypting the COSE object with a non valid PSK, the server detects it and stops the connection, sending an error message. Finally, the third test (A3) is focused on the server. This test checks that a server with a non valid

PSK is unable to perform EDHOC, in an analogous way to the previous test. When the server sends the second message, it has to encrypt the COSE object with the non valid PSK, so the device should detect it, stopping the connection and sending an error message.

5.2   Designing the Model and Operations

Once we have described the tests, the next step is to design the MBT model. We have defined 6 main entities as shown in Fig. 3: the server, the IoT device, the three messages that are part of the EDHOC exchange and a sniffer to use in the confidentiality tests.

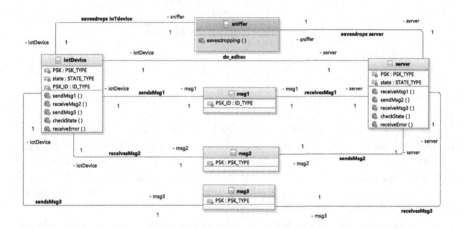

Fig. 3. MBT model for EDHOC

We also include the required fields to emulate the tests we have designed before. In this case, we need the *PSK* and *PSK_ID* to test the authentication. An extra field *STATE* is used to emulate the behavior of the protocol and to control the different steps. We define the enumerated type for these fields as:

- ID_TYPE: VALID_ID, NON_VALID_ID
- PSK_TYPE: VALID_PSK, NON_VALID_PSK
- STATE_TYPE: START,   SENT1,   SENT2,   SENT3,   RECEIVED1, RECEIVED2, RECEIVED3, ERROR

We model the operations required by EDHOC and test associated by using the OCL language. For each operation, we need to specify the parameters, the preconditions and the postconditions. The preconditions allow to control when this operation can be executed in the step sequence of the protocol, whereas the postconditions are used to emulate the protocol behavior.

EDHOC must start with the sendMsg1() operation (Table 2), and in turn, this operation can be only called at the start of the protocol. This is controlled using the *STATE* variable in the preconditions. This operation includes a parameter to allow to change the *PSK_ID* sent to the server in the message1 (*p_Id_type*). This operation changes the state of the IoT device to SENT1 and modifies the *PSK_ID* field of message1 accordingly to the parameter it has received.

Table 2. Operation sendMsg1()

Parameters	p_Id_type
Preconditions	self.state=STATE_TYPE::START
Postconditions	

```
/**@REQ:  IOT_SENT_MSG1*/
if  ( self . state=STATE_TYPE : : START)
    then
          self . state=STATE_TYPE : : SENT1
              and
          self . msg1 . PSK_ID=p_Id_type
          ----@AIM:  SENT_MSG1
else  false
endif  and  self . checkState ( self . state )
```

The operation receiveMsg1() can only be called if the IoT device has sent the first message, so we specify this in the preconditions (Table 3). It includes a parameter to show what is the value of the *PSK_ID* received (*p_Id_type*). In the postconditions, we control this value, acting accordingly; if the *PSK_ID* is invalid, we change the state to *ERROR*, whereas if it is valid, we change the state to *RECEIVED1*.

The rest of the operations (sendMsg2(), receiveMsg2(), sendMsg3(), receiveMsg3() and receiveError()), follow a similar procedure, modeling the strictly necessary behavior of EDHOC for defining the tests.

Finally, we have a special function checkState() that is an observer function. This type of functions do not have preconditions nor postconditions (only true). They are meant to be executed after every other operation to allow us to check everything is performed correctly through the observation of a variable, which is its only parameter. In this case, we use the *STATE* variable. It is worth noting that we use tags to label certain parts of the code. For example, in Table 3, we have a general tag at the beginning of the code (@*REQ: SERVER_RECEIVED_MSG1*) to specify that this part of the code is related with the reception of the first message by the server. Inside this operation, we have more specific tags such as—@*AIM: ERROR_PSK_ID* that indiccates that this part of the code is achieved when there is an error due to a non valid PSK_ID or—@*AIM: RECEIVED_MSG1_OK* that indicates that it is a correct reception of the first message of the protocol. These tags allow us to define the tests easily through the test purposes.

Table 3. Operation receiveMsg1()

Parameters	p_Id_type
Preconditions	*self.state=STATE_TYPE::START and* *self.iotDevice.state=STATE_TYPE::SENT1*
Postconditions	

```
/**@REQ:  SERVER_RECEIVED_MSG1*/
if ( self . state=STATE_TYPE : : START)  then
        ----@AIM:  RECEIVED_MSG1
        if ( self . msg1 . PSK_ID=ID_TYPE : :
            NON_VALID_ID  and  p_Id_type=
            ID_TYPE : : NON_VALID_ID )  then
                self . state=STATE_TYPE : : ERROR
                ----@AIM:  ERROR_PSK_ID
        else  if  ( self . msg1 . PSK_ID=ID_TYPE : :
            VALID_ID  and  p_Id_type=ID_TYPE : :
            VALID_ID )  then
                self . state=STATE_TYPE
                    : : RECEIVED1
                ----@AIM:
                    RECEIVED_MSG1_OK
            else  false
            endif
        endif
else  false
endif and  self . checkState ( self . state )
```

5.3   Describing the Test Purposes

Once we have a functional model, we create a test suite and define several test purposes following the test description we have done at the beginning of the process. More concretely, the test purpose language is based on regular expressions to conceive the testing scenarios in terms of states to be reached and operations to be called. The language relies on combining keywords, to produce expressions that are both powerful and easy to read by a test engineer. Instead of specifying all the protocol steps to reach a certain situation, we use different tags in the code. For example, in A2 (Listing 1.1), we use the tag *IOT_RECEIVED_MESSAGE2* to reach that section of the code instead of writing sendMsg1(), receiveMsg1(), etc. Once we reach the code in which the device receives the second message, we use the sendMsg3() with the *NON_VALID_PSK* parameter to emulate a message3 with an invalid PSK. Finally, we finalize the test specifying that the expected result is to reach the error tag *IOT_RECEIVED_ERROR* that is in the **receiveError()** function.

Listing 1.1. "Test purpose for A2"

```
use  any_operation  any_number_of_times  to_activate  behavior_with_tags  {
    AIM : IOT_RECEIVED_MSG2/RECEIVED_MSG2}
then  use  EDHOC1. sendMsg3 (NON_VALID_PSK)
then  use  any_operation  any_number_of_times  to_activate
    behavior_with_tags  {REQ: IOT_RECEIVED_ERROR}
```

5.4   Generating and Executing the Tests

For the test generation and execution, we use the CertifyIt tool to complete the middle steps of the tests. CertifyIt allows to check if the tests are performed correctly following the model description we have done. After this, the JUnit language is used to export the corresponding tests. The main goal of the use of JUnit is the systematic and automatic testing of security properties in IoT devices for improving efficiency and scalability. After the exportation, CertifyIt generates a JUnit test suite and an interface (called adapter) containing all the functions defined in the model, which must be implemented in order to link the real device and server with the test suite. The code in Listing 1.2 shows the JUnit test for the A2 test previously defined.

Listing 1.2. "JUnit test of A2"

```
public void testAuthN_iot2_4__4d_ef_bd_() throws Exception {
    adapter.EDHOC1iotDevicesendMsg1(iotDevice.EDHOC1, ID_TYPE.
        VALID_ID);
    adapter.EDHOC1iotDevicecheckState(iotDevice.EDHOC1, STATE_TYPE.
        SENT1);
    adapter.EDHOC1serverreceiveMsg1(server.server, ID_TYPE.
        VALID_ID);
    adapter.EDHOC1servercheckState(server.server, STATE_TYPE.
        RECEIVED1);
    adapter.EDHOC1serversendMsg2(server.server, PSK_TYPE.
        VALID_PSK);
        ...
```

The last step is to upload the EDHOC code into the devices and to execute the JUnit test suite in order to check if the real device passes the tests. This way, we obtain the related security information to analyze the security of the SUT.

As already mentioned, in case there is an update of the device (e.g., due to a security patching/update process), previous tests can be re-executed to get the security level of the update device. Furthermore, if a new vulnerability is discovered, only the MBT model and test purposes must be updated. Unless we add a new operation or variable, the implementation of the tests will be automatic, since we already have the adapter interface that copes with it. This is where the power of this testing approach lies. However, MBT and CertifyIt still have some weak points that makes the modeling quite difficult for some vulnerabilities, for example integrity. In this case, a different test for each field of the messages is required, and this can not be automated in the test purposes. Indeed, it should be noted that traditional MBT approaches are not focused on security testing; therefore, there is a real need to complement such technique with complementary testing methods to build a more comprehensive security testing solution to be used in the IoT context. This aspect represents part of our future work in this area.

6   Conclusions

The application of suitable mechanisms for testing security in IoT scenarios is crucial to ensure the development of new protocols and techniques. This work has presented some insights on the applicability of MBT approaches to EDHOC, which represents an emerging security proposal within the IETF. Indeed, EDHOC has been recently proposed as a lightweight and authenticated key exchange to be leveraged in constrained environments. According to our work, MBT has shown powerful benefits in terms of test automation and updating in case there is a security change. However, the lack of some features such as the automation of the test purposes generation and the inheritance, limits the power of the approach. Finally, the existence of an adapter interface helps to maintain the testing environment and the real device separated, so if there is a change in the tests, the code inside the device does not have to be re-uploaded. Based on this initial proposal, our future work is intended to integrate the security testing with the generation of security policies based on the results obtained, with the aim to enforce the security of the IoT devices.

Acknowledgments. This work was supported in part by the Spanish Ministry of Economy and Competitiveness and the ERDF funds cofinantiation through the PERSEIDES project under GrantTIN2017-86885-R and the USEIT project under Grant PCIN-2016-010, in part by the H2020-780139 SerIoT project, and in part by the FPU-16/03305 Research Contract of the Ministry of Education and Professional Training of Spain.

References

1. Arkin, B., Stender, S., McGraw, G.: Software penetration testing. IEEE Secur. Priv. **3**(1), 84–87 (2005). https://doi.org/10.1109/MSP.2005.23
2. Atapour, C., Agrafiotis, I., Creese, S.: Modeling advanced persistent threats to enhance anomaly detection techniques. J. Wirel. Mob. Netw. Ubiquit. Comput. Dependable Appl. (JoWUA) **9**(4), 71–102 (2018). https://doi.org/10.22667/JOWUA.2018.12.31.071
3. Bernabeu, G., Jaffuel, E., Legeard, B., Peureux, F.: MBT for global platform compliance testing: experience report and lessons learned. In: 25th IEEE International Symposium on Software Reliability Engineering Workshops, Naples, Italy (2014). https://doi.org/10.1109/ISSREW.2014.91
4. Bormann, C., Hoffman, P.: Concise Binary Object Representation (CBOR) (RFC7049) (2013). https://tools.ietf.org/html/rfc7049
5. Bouquet, F., Grandpierre, C., Legeard, B., Peureux, F., Vacelet, N., Utting, M.: A subset of precise UML for model-based testing. In: Proceedings of the 3rd International Workshop on Advances in Model-Based Testing - A-MOST 2007, pp. 95–104. ACM Press, London (2007). https://doi.org/10.1145/1291535.1291545 http://portal.acm.org/citation.cfm?doid=1291535.1291545
6. Bruni, A., Sahl Jørgensen, T., Grønbech Petersen, T., Schürmann, C.: Formal verification of ephemeral Diffie-Hellman over COSE (EDHOC). In: Cremers, C., Lehmann, A. (eds.) SSR 2018. LNCS, vol. 11322, pp. 21–36. Springer, Cham (2018). https://doi.org/10.1007/978-3-030-04762-7_2
7. Eric Rescorla: The Transport Layer Security (TLS) Protocol Version 1.3 (2018). https://tools.ietf.org/html/draft-ietf-tls-tls13-28
8. Felderer, M., Büchler, M., Johns, M., Brucker, A.D., Breu, R., Pretschner, A.: Chapter one - security testing: a survey. In: Advances in Computers, vol. 101,

pp. 1–51. Elsevier (2015). https://doi.org/10.1016/bs.adcom.2015.11.003. http://www.sciencedirect.com/science/article/pii/S0065245815000649

9. Godefroid, P., Levin, M.Y., Molnar, D.: SAGE - whitebox fuzzing for security testing. Queue **10**(1), 20:20–20:27 (2012). https://doi.org/10.1145/2090147.2094081

10. Jing, Q., Vasilakos, A.V., Wan, J., Lu, J., Qiu, D.: Security of the internet of things: perspectives and challenges. Wirel. Netw. **20**(8), 2481–2501 (2014)

11. Kammuller, F., Kerber, M., Probst, C.W., Kammueller, F., Kerber, M.: Insider threats and auctions: formalization, mechanized proof, and code generation. J. Wirel. Mob. Netw. Ubiquit. Comput. Dependable Appl. **8**(1), 44–78 (2017). https://doi.org/10.22667/JOWUA.2017.03.31.044

12. Krawczyk, H.: Perfect forward secrecy. In: van Tilborg, H.C.A. (ed.) Encyclopedia of Cryptography and Security, pp. 457–458. Springer, Boston (2005). https://doi.org/10.1007/0-387-23483-7_298

13. Krawczyk, H., Eronen, P.: HMAC-based Extract-and-Expand Key Derivation Function (HKDF) (RFC869) (2010). https://tools.ietf.org/html/rfc5869

14. Li, W., Le Gall, F., Spaseski, N.: A survey on model-based testing tools for test case generation. In: Itsykson, V., Scedrov, A., Zakharov, V. (eds.) TMPA 2017. CCIS, vol. 779, pp. 77–89. Springer, Cham (2018). https://doi.org/10.1007/978-3-319-71734-0_7

15. Matheu-Garcia, S.N., Hernandez-Ramos, J.L., Skarmeta, A.F.: Test-based risk assessment and security certification proposal for the internet of things. In: 2018 IEEE 4th World Forum on Internet of Things (WF-IoT), pp. 641–646. IEEE, Singapore, February 2018. https://doi.org/10.1109/WF-IoT.2018.8355193. https://ieeexplore.ieee.org/document/8355193/

16. Matheu-Garcia, S.N., Hernandez-Ramos, J.L., Skarmeta, A.F., Baldini, G.: Risk-based automated assessment and testing for the cybersecurity certification and labelling of IoT devices. Comput. Stand. Interfaces **62**, 64–83 (2019). https://doi.org/10.1016/j.csi.2018.08.003. https://www.sciencedirect.com/science/article/abs/pii/S0920548918301375?via%3Dihub

17. McGrew, D., Igoe, K., Salter, M.: Fundamental elliptic curve cryptography algorithms (2010). https://tools.ietf.org/id/draft-mcgrew-fundamental-ecc-04.html

18. Palombini, F., Seitz, L., Selander, G., Mattsson, J.: Object security for constrained RESTful environments (OSCORE) (2018). https://tools.ietf.org/html/draft-ietf-core-object-security-15

19. Rescorla, E., Modadugu, N.: Datagram transport layer security version 1.2 (2012). https://tools.ietf.org/html/rfc6347. Published: RFC 6347

20. Schaad, J.: CBOR Object Signing and Encryption (COSE) (RFC8152), July 2017. https://doi.org/10.17487/RFC8152. https://www.rfc-editor.org/info/rfc8152

21. Selander, G., Palombini, F., Hartke, K.: Requirements for CoAP end-to-end security (2017)

22. Selander, G., Mattsson, J., Palombini, F.: Ephemeral Diffie-Hellman Over COSE (EDHOC) (2019). https://tools.ietf.org/id/draft-selander-ace-cose-ecdhe-13.html

23. Shelby, Z., Hartke, K., Bormann, C.: The Constrained Application Protocol (CoAP) (RFC7252) (2014). https://tools.ietf.org/html/rfc7252

24. Yoo, S., Harman, M.: Regression testing minimization, selection and prioritization: a survey. Softw. Test. Verif. Reliab. **22**(2), 67–120 (2012). https://doi.org/10.1002/stv.430. http://doi.wiley.com/10.1002/stv.430

Cyber Deception in the Internet of Battlefield Things: Techniques, Instances, and Assessments

Jeman Park[1], Aziz Mohaisen[1(✉)], Charles A. Kamhoua[2],
Michael J. Weisman[2], Nandi O. Leslie[2], and Laurent Njilla[3]

[1] University of Central Florida, Orlando, USA
mohaisen@ucf.edu
[2] Army Research Laboratory, Adelphi, USA
[3] Air Force Research Laboratory, Rome, NY, USA

Abstract. The Internet of Battlefield Things (IoBT) is an emerging application to improve operational effectiveness for military applications. The security of IoBT is one of the more challenging aspects, where adversaries can exploit vulnerabilities in IoBT software and deployment conditions to gain insight into their state. In this work, we look into the security of IoBT from the lens of cyber deception. First, we formulate the IoBT domain as a graph learning problem from an adversarial point of view and introduce various tools through which an adversary can learn the graph starting with partial prior knowledge. Second, we use this model to show that an adversary can learn high-level information from low-level graph structures, including the number of soldiers and their proximity. For that, we use a powerful n-gram based algorithm to obtain features from random walks on the underlying graph representation of IoBT. Third, we provide microscopic and macroscopic approaches that manipulate the underlying IoBT graph structure to introduce uncertainty in the adversary's learning. Finally, we show our approach's effectiveness through analyses and evaluations.

Keywords: IoBT · Cyber deception · n-gram · Graph learning

1 Introduction

The Internet of Things (IoT) is one of the most rapidly growing technologies in recent years. IoT is expected to greatly change our lives, with many applications that allow billions of devices to interconnect, enabling them to share information through the networking medium. An area where the IoT technology promises significant change to the modus operandi is the *battlefield*, where soldiers and equipment are deployed in wartime. By adopting the IoT technology, various sensors attached to soldiers or equipment are able to share information, which maximizes strategic insight and awareness. The environment where the multiple

I. You (Ed.): WISA 2019, LNCS 11897, pp. 299–312, 2020.
https://doi.org/10.1007/978-3-030-39303-8_23

devices work in cooperation is called the Internet of Battlefield Things (IoBT) [4]. IoBT is expected to enhance combat power by utilizing various sensors that can complement the human's senses and provide further awareness.

However, the security in the emerging IoBT is still an open concern. Although the exclusion of human's interaction brings lots of convenience to individual soldiers using IoBT, intrusions by adversaries are one of the fundamental concerns in IoT in general, and IoBT in particular. Among many risks possible in the battlefield, an adversary might be able to get a deeper understanding of deployments, tactics, etc. by monitoring the IoBT and high-level features of its networks. In particular, even if the enemy does not fully gain control over the whole system of an IoBT, it is still possible for the attacker to obtain a "sketch" of information that can be meaningful in estimating various pieces of knowledge that guide his decisions. The state-of-the-art studies provide various techniques [8,15,19] which can be used to learn features of "networks" from the partial knowledge of the entire network, making such learning process possible.

In order to realize the full potential of IoBT in the field, it is important to understand the new types of threats associated with them. First and foremost, such an understanding is essential step towards building the appropriate mechanisms for countering such a threat with effective defenses. To this end, in this paper we have a first look at the security of IoBT. We abstract the objectives of an adversary into multiple tasks, and demonstrate how successful the adversary could be in realizing those tasks using partial knowledge of the IoBT network. In doing so, we utilize an advanced approach using n-gram features obtained from random walks on the underlying IoBT graph, and demonstrate that an adversary can learn essential information, such as the number of deployed soldiers and the proximity of soldiers and nodes, using this approach.

To counter those attacks, we further develop cyber deception mechanisms (and their associated justification) that look into manipulating the underlying IoBT network in microscopic or macroscopic fashion, and show such deception affects the learning ability of the adversary. Cyber deception in IoBT, to this end, is similar to its application in other arenas (e.g., honeypot), where we try to trick the adversary into misunderstanding the defender's capacity and the underlying system on the ground. To the best of our knowledge, our work presents the first such work that looks into formalizing threats in IoBT and designs quantifiable countermeasures through deception.

Contributions. (1) We formalize IoBT as a graph of graphs, whereby an adversary is interested in learning the number of assets (soldiers or equipment), their proximity, and their relationships. (2) We explore learning approaches, in which the adversary tries to achieve his objective with limited knowledge (by stitching pieces of information together in a machine learning model). (3) To defend against those attacks, our deception strategies involve the addition or removal of subgraphs, nodes, or edges. We provide a system-level justification of these deception techniques and analyze their effect on the IoBT mission, as well as the confidence of the adversary in achieving his goal.

2 Preliminaries and Settings

In this section, we review the preliminaries required for understanding the rest of this work. We start by introducing an abstract model of IoT in the battlefield, formally identify various objectives and associated threats.

2.1 IoT in the Battlefield

IoT has found applications in many fields, ranging from civilian to military. In the latter field of applications, the use of IoT for military applications is termed the Internet of Battlefield Things (IoBT). In IoBT, various "assets" or "things" are deployed in the field to achieve a certain mission. Those assets may include sensors, actuators, devices (computers, vehicles, robots, wearables, etc.), infrastructure, information sources, and (perhaps most importantly) humans. Those things are interconnected to form a network and thereby improve strategical efficiency of deployed soldiers and other assets. As shown in Fig. 1a, in modern warfare, various types of devices are deployed to collect and share information between various actors in the battlefield in collaborative way.

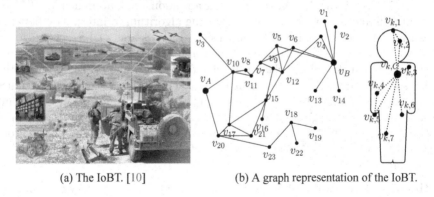

(a) The IoBT. [10]   (b) A graph representation of the IoBT.

Fig. 1. An example of Internet of Battlefield Things (IoBT) and associated graph. Copyright note: (a) is an illustration by Evan Jensen, US ARL, used with permission.

In general, graphs are a popular tool for analyzing network topology. Graph-based approaches visualize the network by representing each interface (device) as a node and the connection between devices as an edge in the network. Graph theory is often used to analyze attacks or defenses on the network [13]. In this regard, an IoBT network also can be viewed as a graph, corresponding to the various things (devices) in the network and their interconnections. As such, an IoBT is characterized as $G = (V, E)$, as shown in Fig. 1b (left). In this graph, each node $v_i \in V$ corresponds to an atomic level of a thing, including sensors, actuators, or devices in the IoBT, while each edge in the graph corresponds to a connection between two different things.

The physical IoBT network has multiple soldiers, the most valuable asset in the field. We express the network associated with each soldier (particularly the wearable, sensors, etc.) as $G_1, G_2, \ldots G_g \subset G$, where $G_i = (V_i, E_i)$, $V_i \subset V$ and $E_i \subset E$. Those various soldiers in the physical network and their associated on-body network correspond to a subgraph in G. Figure 1b (right) shows an example of a subgraph; for G_k corresponding to a soldier k, we use (V_k, E_k) where $v_{k,i} \in V_k \subset V$ can be a wearable device, such as a biochemical sensor, camera, or smart glass, worn by an individual soldier. That is, Fig. 1b (left) can be summarized as a whole graph which has each subgraph G_k^S as a node v_k. We make the distinction between edges in E as follows: edges that connect between devices are called *links* if they only connect within the same subgraph and *bridges* otherwise.

2.2 Threat Towards IoBT

While providing a strategic advantage, the IoBT can expose a vulnerability in the domain of military application. In the following, we give an example of the threat model that the adversary can deduce through the graph analysis.

Counting the Number of Soldiers (Equipment). Recently, it has been shown possible of exploring a whole graph—by identifying communities, nodes, and landmarks—from a given vertex using a random walk approach [8,14]. The random walk method allows a feature learning algorithm to interpolate between pure Breadth-First Search (BFS) and Depth-First Search (DFS). As such, an adversary can learn features of the whole graph, which makes an adversary successfully perform multi-label classification of the vertices and bridges between the vertices in a computationally efficient manner. Furthermore, these same studies show that even fragmentary information can allow attackers to infer significant information about the graph. By attacking a small portion of V and learning the features using a random walk strategy, we can deduce important information, such as the number of soldiers on the battlefield, which is equal to the number of subgraphs in G.

Estimating Proximity of Soldiers. In IoBT, devices carried by a soldier are used for data communication with nearby soldiers as well as the C&C. Each device may support short-range or long-range communication depending on its purpose. This intuitively shows that an individual (G_i) with many nearby soldiers has more bridges. As such, the adversary can use this information to estimate the proximity of each soldier and rank subgraphs based on the number of bridges they have.

2.3 n-gram Overview

A key building block in our analysis of our graph learning techniques and their effectiveness is the n-gram model. The n-gram is a method of analyzing the sequence of words (or events) in the text form in which each character represents a preassigned word. Let $\mathcal{C} = \{c_1, c_2, \ldots, c_\ell\}$ be a set of ℓ unique characters corresponding to the associated words set $\mathcal{W} = \{w_1, w_2, \ldots, w_\ell\}$. A string $\mathcal{S} = c_1 c_2 c_3 \ldots c_s$ can symbolize the sequence of words/events $w_1 w_2 w_3 \ldots w_s$, where

$c_i \in \mathcal{C}$ and $w_i \in \mathcal{W}$ for $1 \leq i \leq s$. With this approach, the original document D can be translated into the n-gram document D'.

The translated document D' is used for feature extraction and learning. Once D' is divided into multiple tokens with a length of n, the set of tokens T can have the unique feature of the original document D. Without losing generality, we can express our document as the sequence of states (nodes) observed in a random walk, and the n-grams as the sub-walks observed in this walk. The ultimate goal is to use the n-gram representation as features, and using those features to make a decision concerning the various learning activities above.

2.4 Cyber Deception: Key Idea and Objectives

Cyber deception is an emerging technology for defending and detecting the cyber attack, which deploys the traps within the existing network. The honeypot [18] is a representative example of cyber deception. It deploys a device that pretends to be a normal user on the network, which can then lead an adversary to attack it. During the attack, the honeypot extracts meaningful information about the attacker and the attack itself using security software.

Cyber deception can be applied to mitigate the threats to IoBT listed above. The common feature of the proposed malicious activities in Sect. 2.2 is that the adversary only with incomplete information extends his knowledge through random based exploration. If we are able to change the underlying state of the whole graph or subgraph of a system by adding/removing vertices or edges, the attacker will be unable to learn accurately those features of the system. For example, and without losing generality, if n vertices are added to the whole graph with i vertices, $G = (V, E)$, where $V = \{v_1, v_2, \ldots, v_i\}$, the resulting whole graph G' will have the set of vertices $V' = \{v_1, \ldots, v_i, \ldots, v_{i+n}\}$, which means the order of the graph changes from i to $i + n$.

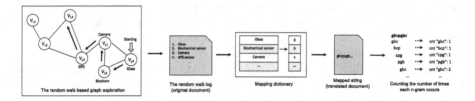

Fig. 2. The adversary's strategy using random walk and n-gram.

3   Methodology

3.1   Efficient Learning with n-gram

To obtain meaningful information from IoBT, it is important for an adversary to understand the features of the whole graph, representing the network among soldiers and equipment. However, due to the dynamics of the network, learning the graph is a nontrivial task for the attacker. Similar to Ad-hoc networks, for instance, when a soldier moves, the devices attached to the soldier can be connected to devices of other soldiers within close proximity at each point in time. This means that the shape of the graph can change according to the current distribution or movement on the field. Therefore, in a dynamic environment, an efficient analysis method is required for the attacker to understand the overall shape of the graph.

n-gram as a Feature Learning Technique. Here, we propose a n-gram based approach as a strategy of an adversary who knows only partially about the network to learn further features. Let G be the graph representation of the whole IoBT network, and G' be the partial graph that the adversary knows, where $G' \subset G$. The primary goal of the adversary is to extract meaningful features from G' that also can be applied to the analysis of G.

Figure 2 depicts the n-gram approach taken by the adversary. As a first step, with fragmentary information, the adversary can generate a training dataset to build a classifier for learning. By applying the random walk strategy in IoBT, and hoping from a node to another, the adversary can explore the graph from node to node that are directly connected. The history of the visited nodes is recorded by logging the type and label of each node. After this exploration, the list of recorded "device" is translated into a string by referring to a dictionary which maps each device type to the preassigned character; for example, biochemical sensor to 'b'. The resulting string is then transformed to the n-gram structure by extracting multiple tokens of length n ($n = 3$ in Fig. 2). At this point, the patterns of occurrences of n-grams are considered the features of the graph. Similar to other learning approaches from graphs, it is assumed that the part of the graph known to the adversary through exploration shares common characteristics with the whole graph. The tokens (n-grams) and the number of occurrences are then fed into the ML-based classifier for training.

Adversary Model. In this work, we assume that the adversary is capable of knowing the other devices connected to a device. In other words, it is a chain process that identifies devices connected to one device, selects one device among them, and then identifies the devices connected thereto. This assumption on the adversary's capability can be justifiable as it can be achieved in various ways. Considering that many sensors or equipment rely on the wireless network, for example, the adversary can eavesdrop the packet in the air and figure out the address information (source and destination). By doing so, even if the content of the packet is protected by the encryption, the adversary still can draw the graph of connections. In this work, we do not consider insider threat who can have enough knowledge of the whole network. We deal with an external adversary that has to infer about the whole with partial knowledge.

Graph Explorer with Random Walk Strategy. In this work, we implemented a graph explorer based on *node2vec* [8]. In *node2vec*, the 2nd order random walk strategy with two parameters is mixed with BFS and DFS. One, return parameter p, controls the likelihood of revisiting, while another, in-out parameter q, affects the direction of exploration, inward or outward from the starting node. This state-of-the-art strategy makes it possible to explore and learn the graph in a computationally efficient way while preserving the network neighborhoods of nodes. In our implementation, the graph explorer records the sequence of the visits by random walk and the index of the associated subgraph (e.g., $v_{k,4}, k$), which results in the ground-truth data for the adversary.

3.2   Cyber Deception in IoBT: Instantiations

Our cyber deception relies on changes in the shape of a graph, making it difficult for an attacker to extract accurate information from the graph for achieving his end goal. In our study, we consider cyber deception in two ways: microscopic (on each subgraph) and macroscopic (on the whole graph) approaches, which we elaborate in the following by explaining the changes in the graph and the concrete instantiations.

Microscopic Approach. Applying deception in subgraphs affects the number of devices and connections between those devices. By such a change in a subgraph, one can prevent an attacker from grouping devices and recognizing them as a community (soldier) using the proposed n-gram approach. In order to conduct this microscopic approach, we consider both adding/removing vertices (devices) and edges (links).

(1) Adding/Removing Vertices (Devices). In this approach, the change of vertices implies a change of the devices connected in a soldier's subgraph. The increase of vertices is achieved by providing soldiers with some duplicated or additional devices (e.g., sensors) for deception. Clearly, this approach would increase the cost of building the IoBT network with deception. On the other hand, removing vertices from the subgraph at the microscopic level can be easily done by turning some devices off periodically. Because it may affect the capability of the soldier (by, for example, reducing the cognitive ability of the soldier empowered by IoBT devices and sensors), the use of this deception approach should be considered carefully.

(2) Adding/Removing Edges (Links). The edges in the subgraph are connection between devices. Which device is connected to which device determines the topology of the subgraph (or soldier-level network). In other words, the change of links will increase the diversity of the topology. By adding an additional interface (physical or virtual) to the device, it is possible to provide devices with more connections (links) with the other devices. Conversely, it is also feasible to remove the links in a way that stops some interfaces, which results in the loss of some connections, corresponding to the removal of those links (at the risk of impeding the mission).

Macroscopic Approach. While making a change in each subgraph G_k is a microscopic approach, the macroscopic approach is to change the whole graph G itself. That is, macroscopic cyber deception means the change in the number of soldiers on the battlefield or the connection between soldiers.

(1) Adding/Removing Vertices (Soldiers). Adding a vertex in the whole graph will "generate" a virtual soldier on the battlefield, leading to adding G_k in G. To deceive the adversary, the added subgraph should have similar structure to those of real soldiers (e.g., nodes, edges, type of devices, topology distribution, etc.). This deception method can be realized by making each soldier carry two identical sets of devices where each set forms a different subgraph. Another way is to virtualize a device that a soldier wears in order to make it act as two independent devices. Although the latter one is more efficient in terms of reducing the number of devices that a soldier has to bring to the field (and their associated weight), such approach makes the assumption that those devices in general have the capabilities to support virtualization, which is a nontrivial task.

(2) Adding/Removing Edges (Bridges). This approach can be realized in a similar way to change the number of links above. A single device worn by an individual soldier can be made to communicate directly with a device outside its network. At the graph level, this method can make the device no longer included in the subgraph but as a single node. It is also possible to connect only duplicated instances to the outside in the virtualized device. Conversely, reducing the number of bridges can be accomplished by connecting externally connected device within soldier network.

Objective. The primary goal of our cyber deception approach is to increase the effort of an adversary. From this perspective, the transformation of the graph presented above makes it difficult for an attacker to gain an understanding of the overall graph.

4   Evaluation

To measure the effectiveness of n-gram and cyber deception, we implemented the simulator with python. As earlier mentioned, we adopted the random walk module from *node2vec* [2] and used *networkx* for the graph management.

4.1   Dataset

For the evaluation, we used two kinds of dataset: (1) the peer-to-peer (p2p) topology in real world (2) a random graph generated by stochastic model.

P2P Topology in Real World. First, we tried to find a topology dataset related to IoBT (or IoT) in various repositories, but failed to find one open to the public. Therefore, we carefully selected a distributed p2p topology that seems to have a structure similar to IoT. The selected dataset relates to the topology of the p2p network, Gnutella, which is available to everyone at Stanford Network Analysis Project (SNAP) [11].

Randomly Generated Graph. To demonstrate the generality of the proposed approach, we also performed an evaluation with a randomly generated graph. We employed the Erdös-Rényi stochastic model to generate random graphs.

To generate the random graph G, the model takes as an input n (the number of nodes) and p (the probability that there is an edge between any two nodes). Given that G has n nodes, the probability that G has m edges is [6]:

$$P_n(m) = P(G(n, m)) = \binom{\binom{n}{2}}{m} p^m (1-p)^{\binom{n}{2}-m}, \mathbb{E}_n(m) = \sum_{m=0}^{\binom{n}{2}} m P_n(m) = \binom{n}{2} p.$$

We tried to generate a graph of another structure with the statistics (nodes and edges) similar to those in the Gnutella dataset, so we set $p \approx 0.00067628$ to make $\mathbb{E}_n(m) = 39,994$, where $n = 10,876$. Using the parameters, $n = 10,876$ and $p = 0.00067628$, we generated a random graph with $10,876$ vertices and $40,035$ edges.

Preprocessing. To reflect a realistic environment, we conducted several pre-processing steps to use the two datasets listed above in the evaluation: (1) community partitioning, (2) refining, and (3) labeling.

(1) Community Partitioning. In IoBT, dozens of devices attached to soldiers constitute a small network. To construct this environment, we proceeded with community partitioning on the dataset. Using community detection [1], we obtained 531 and 504 communities for both dataset, respectively.

(2) Refining. The partitioned communities from the previous step contained 1 to 55 member nodes. The focus of this work is only on soldiers on the battlefield where standardized equipment is worn, and this large variation in the number of member nodes is unrealistic. Thus, we filtered the communities with less than 20 nodes or more than 35 nodes out from the graph. We obtained 7,576 nodes, 21,284 edges, and 285 communities in Gnutella, and 7,443 nodes, 21,027 edges, and 291 communities in the random graph, as a result of preprocessing.

(3) Labeling. The final step in preprocessing is to label each node that makes up the community. Assuming that each node in the community is a unique device, we assigned labels such as biochemical sensors, glasses, *etc.* We also assume that the network structures of soldiers networks are similar to one another. This assumption is reasonable, given that soldiers wear standardized devices which operate in an certain embedded way. With respect to the devices interconnections, we also created a consistent degree-based labeling: nodes in the subgraph were sorted according to their degree, and then labels are given sequentially.

4.2 n-gram with Random Walk Strategy

In Sect. 3.1, we discussed the use of n-gram by an attacker to learn features of the whole graph efficiently and accurately. In this section, we demonstrate the advantages of the n-gram based approach by showing the accuracy in various experimental settings.

n-gram with Prior Knowledge. The goal of using n-gram is to extract and learn features using partial prior knowledge. As such, how much prior knowledge an n-gram based system needs in order to learn the whole graph correctly can be considered as an important measure. To evaluate the performance, we selected i communities randomly, where $1 \leq i \leq 60$, and performed the random walk exploration over the selected subgraphs to generate *training data*. The features were extracted as in Fig. 2 and fed to the binary classifier which determines whether the nodes in the given sequence are in the same community or not. The *testing data* is generated through a similar steps. Unlike training data, which is obtained only from vertices included in the prior knowledge, testing data is obtained from all vertices of the whole graph as a starting point. The sequential order recorded during the random walk exploration with a length of 10 starting from each point is used as a criterion for whether the process is done within a community or across different communities.

Figure 3 shows the result of the measurement. The used classifier is based on k-nearest neighbor (k-NN) algorithm with $k = 2$. In this figure, we note two interesting points. First, the prior knowledge is important, but not necessarily large amounts of it. For a small i (i.e., $i \leq 6$), the accuracy increased rapidly with increasing i. However, as i increases beyond 6, the accuracy is not affected by i, in both datasets. Second, we also found that the classifier on the random graph outperformed the Gnutella data. It

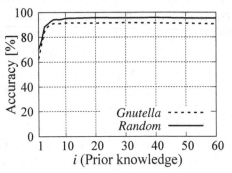

Fig. 3. The accuracy of the classifier with various amount of prior knowledge.

means that the communities in the random graph are highly likely to share common features with each other. Considering that a soldier wears the standardized set of the clothes and devices, the adversarial classifier based on n-gram can achieve a high performance per the random graph.

4.3   The Application of the n-gram Approach

In Sect. 2.2, we discussed two threats in IoBT. Now, we show examples of the threats, the estimation of the number and proximity of soldiers, performed by an adversary.

Counting Soldiers. We conducted the experiments for counting the soldiers using n-grams. With the experiment in Fig. 3 previously showed the result for the exploration with a length of 10 at each node, this time we verify the community detection performance in a single exploration with a length, $l \geq 200$. The value of l was increased from 250 to 2,000 in increments of 250, and the average was calculated after 10 repeated experiments for each case. In the experiment, the prior knowledge (i) was fixed at 20, and the logistic regression with $C = 1$ was used for the classifier model.

Figure 4a shows the result when the classifier counts the number of communities while performing random walk exploration. In this experiment, we can

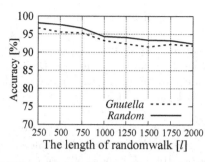 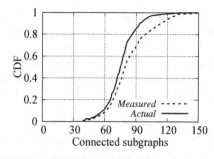

(a) The accuracy of the classifier counting the number of soldiers.

(b) The CDF of the actual and measured number of connected subgraphs.

Fig. 4. The performance of the n-gram based classifier.

see the classifier shows very high accuracy over than 95% for the short lengths ($l \leq 750$). Although, the accuracy steadily decreases as l increases, we can see that the accuracy is above 90% in all cases. Considering that the counted numbers of soldiers in the experiments are below than 250, we can infer that the actual error in the number of soldiers is below than 25 which is 10% of 250.

Proximity of the Soldier. To measure the proximity of an individual soldier, we assumed that the connectivity of a soldier is affected by the geographical distribution of the troop. It means a soldiers' BAN which has a limited range of communication is able to connect to more other soldiers' devices when they exist in close distance. In other words, the estimation the proximity can be considered as an investigation on how a subgraph has a connectivity with other subgraphs.

In this experiment, we measured the number of connected subgraphs from one subgraph. If there is an edge between two nodes in different subgraphs, those subgraphs are considered as connected. By performing the multiple random walk based exploration, the adversary can figure out the connectivity between two different subgraphs.

Figure 4b shows the CDF of the number of connected subgraphs. In the figure, the dash line means the measured number, and the solid line means the actual number. In this figure, we can see that the classifier deduces that about 8.5% of communities have less than 60 neighbors, while actually there are about 11.6% communities with those number of neighbors. The difference between the estimated value and the actual value is then increasingly larger.

4.4 Cyber Deception

To evaluate the effectiveness of cyber deception, as described earlier, we conducted additional experiments for microscopic and macroscopic methods described in Sect. 3.2. In the measurement, we used l-regression based classifier with $C = 1$ and 20 communities as prior knowledge. Moreover, we only use the random graph as a dataset for the evaluation.

Microscopic Approach. The first option the defender can choose is to add/remove nodes or edges in subgraph. By changing the structure of the subgraph, such modification may poison the learning algorithm, and it may make the adversary recognize a community as two different communities. Based on the labeling method, which assigns the label according to the node's degree, the deception that can make the change in the order of the degrees can perhaps be more effective.

To evaluate this approach, we conducted experiments to measure the attacker's accuracy while changing nodes' degrees. We conducted the measurements with four scenarios: no cyber deception, 10%, 25%, and 50% of changed degrees; '10%' means that the degree of 10% of the devices have altered. Such a change in degree causes a change in the order, therefore nodes are labeled differently from the standardized method.

As a result, we could see that the accuracy of 95.73% without cyber deception decreased to 93.57% (10% of degrees changed), to 91.36% (25% of degrees changed), and to 87.27% (50% of degrees changed). That means the more the cyber deception produces more distortion, the less the accuracy of the classifier. Simply changing topology within a subgraph can make the attacker's feature learning measurably difficult.

Macroscopic Approach. The macroscopic approach for cyber deception is the addition/removal of the subgraph or bridges. Using this approach, we cannot only forge the number of soldiers, but also the proximity. As an example of macroscopic cyber deception, we applied the addition of subgraphs and compared the result.

Figure 5 shows that cyber deception significantly degrade the adversary's understanding over the whole graph. When the number of subgraphs increases by 5% or 10%, the accuracy of the adversary's understanding is significantly degraded. In this example, the added subgraph is simply copied from the existing one in the whole graph, which allows us to assume that cyber deception can be more effective when the modification of subgraph is combined. Macroscopic approach can also affect the estimation of the proximity of soldiers. By

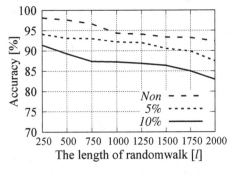

Fig. 5. The accuracy of the classifier counting the number of soldiers when deceptive subgraphs are added to the whole graph.

adding the forged subgraphs, the attacker recognizes the fake subgraph as an individual community, which makes the errors in Fig. 4b larger.

5 Related Work

Feature Learning Algorithm. The conventional approaches for feature learning over graphs depends on manually crafted features [7, 9]. There have been various studies on unsupervised learning through matrix representation of graphs. In general, these kinds of works extracted and learned features using linear or nonlinear dimensionality reduction approaches [3, 17]. However, due to the computational cost of eigen-decomposition, the dimensionality reduction based approach is difficult to use in case of large-scale graph. Recently, a significant improvement has been made in natural language processing. The *word2vec* combined with Continuous Bag-of-Words (CBOW) and Skip-gram learns the features by optimizing the likelihood objective [12]. The significant advancement in natural language processing has also affected other areas. Combined with random walk exploration, recent studies [8, 15, 19] represent the network or graph as a document and learn the features through the approach similar to *word2vec*.

Cyber Deception. Cheswick [5] introduced documented his detecting an attack on the gateway, luring the attacker by feeding the forged data, and tracing him. Inspired by this story, the concept of cyber deception has become increasingly systematized. There have been lots of efforts to create and exploit a trap on the network called Honeypot or Honeynet, which attracts attackers and collects information about them [16, 18].

6 Conclusion

In this work, we modeled threats on IoBT, by formulating the problem as a learning of a graph to extract high-level IoBT context information. We proposed the n-gram based approach combined with a random walk strategy, and explored the effectiveness of cyber deception as a countermeasure against an adversary's activity. From our simulation, we show that fragmentary information can allow an adversary to extract meaningful information over the whole network. In the future, we will explore the effectiveness of the learning approach as well as the cyber deception over various types of graph structures to validate in a more realistic scenario. Moreover, we will demonstrate a cyber deception-based defense against different graph learning approaches.

Acknowledgement. This work is supported in part by NSF grant CNS-1809000 and NRF grant 2016K1A1A2912757.

References

1. Community detection for networkx. http://python-louvain.readthedocs.io
2. node2vec repository. https://github.com/aditya-grover/node2vec
3. Belkin, M., Niyogi, P.: Laplacian eigenmaps and spectral techniques for embedding and clustering. In: Proceedings of the NIPS (2002)

4. Cameron, L.: Internet of things meets the military and battlefield: connecting gear and biometric wearables for an IoMT and IoBT. https://www.computer.org/publications/tech-news/research/internet-of-military-battlefield-things-iomt-iobt

5. Cheswick, B.: An evening with berferd in which a cracker is lured, endured, and studied. In: Proceedings of the USENIX Conference (1992)

6. Erdos, P., Rényi, A.: On the evolution of random graphs. Publ. Math. Inst. Hung. Acad. Sci. **5**(1), 17–60 (1960)

7. Gallagher, B., Eliassi-Rad, T.: Leveraging label-independent features for classification in sparsely labeled networks: an empirical study. In: Proceedings of the SNAKDD (2010)

8. Grover, A., Leskovec, J.: node2vec: scalable feature learning for networks. In: Proceedings of the ACM KDD (2016)

9. Henderson, K., et al.: It's who you know: graph mining using recursive structural features. In: Proceedings of the ACM KDD (2011)

10. Kott, A., Swami, A., West, B.J.: The internet of battle things. IEEE Comput. **49**(12), 70–75 (2016)

11. Leskovec, J., Krevl, A.: SNAP datasets: stanford large network dataset collection (2014). https://snap.stanford.edu/data/p2p-Gnutella04.html

12. Mikolov, T., Chen, K., Corrado, G., Dean, J.: Efficient estimation of word representations in vector space. arXiv preprint arXiv:1301.3781 (2013)

13. Mohaisen, A., Hollenbeck, S.: Improving social network-based sybil defenses by rewiring and augmenting social graphs. In: Kim, Y., Lee, H., Perrig, A. (eds.) WISA 2013. LNCS, vol. 8267, pp. 65–80. Springer, Cham (2014). https://doi.org/10.1007/978-3-319-05149-9_5

14. Pang, J., Zhang, Y.: DeepCity: a feature learning framework for mining location check-ins. arXiv preprint arXiv:1610.03676 (2016)

15. Perozzi, B., Al-Rfou, R., Skiena, S.: DeepWalk: online learning of social representations. In: Proceedings of the ACM KDD (2014)

16. Provos, N.: Honeyd-a virtual honeypot daemon. In: Proceedings of the DFN-CERT Workshop (2003)

17. Roweis, S.T., Saul, L.K.: Nonlinear dimensionality reduction by locally linear embedding. Science **290**(5500), 2323–2326 (2000)

18. Spitzner, L.: The honeynet project: trapping the hackers. IEEE Secur. Priv. **99**(2), 15–23 (2003)

19. Tang, J., Qu, M., Wang, M., Zhang, M., Yan, J., Mei, Q.: LINE: large-scale information network embedding. In: Proceedings of the WWW (2015)

Hardware Security

Ring-LWE on 8-Bit AVR Embedded Processor

Hwajeong Seo$^{(\boxtimes)}$, Hyeokdong Kwon, Yongbeen Kwon, Kyungho Kim,
Seungju Choi, Hyunjun Kim, and Kyoungbae Jang

IT Department, Hansung University, Seoul, South Korea
hwajeong84@gmail.com, korlethean@gmail.com, vexyoung@gmail.com,
pgm.kkh@gmail.com, bookingstore3@gmail.com, khj930704@gmail.com,
starj1023@gmail.com

Abstract. Fast implementation of Ring-LWE is a challenge for the low-end embedded processors. One of the most expensive operation for Ring-LWE is Number Theoretic Transform (NTT). Many works have investigated the optimized implementation for the NTT operation. In this paper, we further optimized the NTT operation on the low-end 8-bit AVR microcontrollers. We focused on the optimized and secure polynomial multiplication to ensure countermeasures against timing attacks and high performance. In particular, we propose the combined Look-Up Table (LUT) based fast reduction techniques in regular fashion. With the optimization techniques, the proposed NTT implementation enhances the performance by 14.6% than previous best results. Finally, proposed NTT implementations are applied to the Ring-LWE key scheduling and encryption operations, which require the only 1,325,171 and 1,430,601 clock cycles for 256-bit security levels.

Keywords: Ring learning with errors · Software implementation ·
Public key encryption · 8-bit AVR · Number Theoretic Transform ·
Timing attack

1 Introduction

The hard problem of traditional public key cryptography algorithms, such as RSA and Elliptic Curve Cryptography (ECC), are based on integer factorization and discrete logarithm problems, which are believed to be secure against classical attacks on traditional computers. For this reason, previous works focused on efficient implementations of RSA and ECC cryptography systems [6, 7, 9–11, 13, 14, 18, 22–24, 26]. However, such hard problems can be solved by using Shor's algorithm in polynomial time when a sufficient large quantum computer is ready [27]. In order to avoid the potential quantum attacks, the lattice-based cryptography is considered as one of the most promising candidates for post-quantum cryptography. The lattice-based cryptography is built based on worst-case computational assumptions in lattices that would remain hard even for quantum algorithms.

© Springer Nature Switzerland AG 2020
I. You (Ed.): WISA 2019, LNCS 11897, pp. 315–327, 2020.
https://doi.org/10.1007/978-3-030-39303-8_24

Furthermore, the future computing platforms, such as Internet of Things (IoT), are widely deployed and used. The low-end IoT devices with many sensors handle important sensor data. For this reason, secure cryptographic algorithms should be implemented on the low-end IoT devices. However, the low-end IoT devices are very resource-constrained, in terms of computing power, energy, and storage. This hard condition introduces a challenge to implement the cryptography algorithm on low-end devices. In this paper, we present the most optimal implementation of NTT computation for lattice based cryptography. The implementation also ensures the constant timing, which is secure against the timing attacks.

The introduction of Learning with Errors (LWE) problem and its ring variant (Ring-LWE) [15,19] provide efficient ways to build lattice-based public key cryptosystems. The following software implementations of Ring-LWE based public-key encryption or digital signature schemes improved performance and memory requirements. Oder et al. presented an efficient implementation of Bimodal Lattice Signature Scheme (BLISS) on a 32-bit ARM Cortex-M4F microcontroller [16]. De Clercq et al. implemented Ring-LWE encryption scheme on the identical ARM processors [5]. They utilized 32-bit registers to retain two 13–14 coefficients at once. Boorghany et al. implemented a lattice-based cryptographic scheme on an 8-bit processor for the first time in [1,3]. The authors evaluated four lattice-based authentication protocols on both 8-bit AVR and 32-bit ARM processors. In particular, Fast Fourier Transform (FFT) transform and Gaussian sampler function are implemented in optimal way. In LATINCRYPT'15, Pöppelmann et al. studied and compared implementations of Ring-LWE encryption and BLISS on an 8-bit Atmel ATxmega128 microcontroller [17]. In CHES'15, Liu et al. optimized implementations of Ring-LWE encryption by presenting efficient modular multiplication, NTT computation and refined memory access schemes to achieve high performance and low memory consumption [12]. They presented two implementations of Ring-LWE encryption scheme for both medium-term and long-term security levels on an 8-bit AVR processor. Liu et al. presented the first secure Ring-LWE encryption and BLISS signature implementations against timing attack [8]. NTT and sampling computations are implemented in constant time to prevent timing attack. Particularly, modular reduction is performed in Montgomery reduction to reduce computation complexity. In ICISC'17, Seo et al. proposed secure and efficient Ring-LWE implementations by using LUT based modular reduction technique and random shuffling [25].

Contributions. This paper continues the line of research on the secure and compact implementations of the Ring-LWE encryption scheme on the low-end 8-bit AVR processor. The contributions are the techniques to prevent information leakage and the efficient implementation to improve real-world performance of Ring-LWE encryption scheme on 8-bit AVR processors.

In particular, we focused on the optimization of Number Theoretic Transform (NTT) based polynomial multiplication. In NTT computation, a number of modular arithmetic operations are required and the optimization of modular arithmetic is highly related with performance. In order to improve the performance of modular reduction, we used the combined Look Up Table (LUT) techniques for modular multiplication. This efficiently performs all reduction with memory accesses.

Based on the above NTT optimization techniques, we present secure and compact implementations of Ring-LWE encryption scheme on an low-end 8-bit AVR processor. All operations are designed to prevent the timing attack. The key scheduling and encryption implementations require 1,325 K and 1,430 K clock cycles for 256-bit security level, respectively.

The rest of this paper is organized as follows. In Sect. 2, we introduce background of Ring-LWE encryption scheme, NTT algorithm, and previous implementation techniques for NTT algorithm. In Sect. 3, we present optimization techniques for NTT on low-end 8-bit AVR processors. In particular, the proposed method ensures the constant timing and reduces the execution time of NTT algorithm. In Sect. 4, we report performance of our implementation and compare with the state-of-the-art implementations of NTT, key scheduling, and encryption on the low-end 8-bit AVR platforms. Finally, we conclude the paper in Sect. 5.

2 Background

2.1 Ring-LWE Encryption Scheme

In 2010, Lyubashevshy et al. proposed an encryption scheme based on a more practical algebraic variant of LWE problem defined over polynomial rings $R_q = \mathbb{Z}_q[\mathbf{x}]/\langle f \rangle$ with an irreducible polynomial $f(x)$ and a modulus q. In Ring-LWE problem, elements a, s and t are polynomials in the ring R_q. Ring-LWE encryption scheme proposed by Lyubashevshy et al. was later optimized in [21]. Roy et al.'s variant aims at reducing the cost of polynomial arithmetic. In particular, the polynomial arithmetic during a decryption operation requires only one Number Theoretic Transform (NTT) operation. Beside this computational optimization, the scheme performs sampling from the discrete Gaussian distribution using a Knuth-Yao sampler. In next subsection, we will first present mathematical concepts of NTT and Knuth-Yao sampling operations, then we will describe the steps used in the Roy et al.'s version of the encryption scheme.

Now, we describe steps applied in the encryption scheme proposed by Roy et al. [21]. We denote the NTT of a polynomial a by $\tilde{a}$.

– Key generation stage **Gen**($\tilde{a}$): Two error polynomials $r_1, r_2 \in R_q$ are sampled from the discrete Gaussian distribution $\mathcal{X}_\sigma$ by applying the Knuth-Yao sampler twice.

$$\tilde{r_1} = NTT(r_1), \tilde{r_2} = NTT(r_2)$$

and then an operation $\tilde{p} = \tilde{r_1} - \tilde{a} \cdot \tilde{r_2} \in R_q$ is performed. Public key is polynomial pair $(\tilde{a}, \tilde{p})$ and private key is polynomial $\tilde{r_2}$.

- Encryption stage **Enc**($\tilde{a}$, $\tilde{p}$, M): The input message $M \in \{0,1\}^n$ is a binary vector of n bits. This message is first encoded into a polynomial in the ring R_q by multiplying the bits of message by $q/2$. Three error polynomials $e_1, e_2, e_3 \in R_q$ are sampled from $\mathcal{X}_\sigma$. The ciphertext is computed as a set of two polynomials $(\tilde{C}_1, \tilde{C}_2)$:

$$(\tilde{C}_1, \tilde{C}_2) = (\tilde{a} \cdot \tilde{e}_1 + \tilde{e}_2, \tilde{p} \cdot \tilde{e}_1 + NTT(e_3 + M'))$$

- Decryption stage **Dec**($\tilde{C}_1$, $\tilde{C}_2$, $\tilde{r}_2$): One inverse NTT is performed to recover M':

$$M' = INTT(\tilde{r}_2 \cdot \tilde{C}_1 + \tilde{C}_2)$$

and then a decoder is used to recover the original message M from M'.

Algorithm 1. Iterative Number Theoretic Transform

Require: A polynomial $a(x) \in \mathbb{Z}_q[x]$ of degree $n - 1$ and n-th primitive $\omega \in \mathbb{Z}_q$ of unity
Ensure: Polynomial $a(x) = NTT(a) \in \mathbb{Z}_q[x]$
1: $a = BitReverse(a)$
2: **for** i from 2 by $i = 2i$ to n **do**
3:     $\omega_i = \omega_n^{n/i}$, $\omega = 1$
4:     **for** j from 0 by 1 to $i/2 - 1$ **do**
5:         **for** k from 0 by i to $n - 1$ **do**
6:             $U = a[k + j]$
7:             $V = \omega \cdot a[k + j + i/2]$
8:             $a[k + j] = U + V$
9:             $a[k + j + i/2] = U - V$
10:        $\omega = \omega \cdot \omega_i$
11: **return** a

2.2 Number Theoretic Transform

We use the Number Theoretic Transform (NTT) to perform polynomial multiplication. NTT can be seen as a discrete variant of Fast Fourier Transform (FFT) but performs in a finite ring $\mathbb{Z}_q$. Instead of using the complex roots of unity, NTT evaluates a polynomial multiplication $a(x) = \sum_{i=0}^{n-1} a_i x^i \in \mathbb{Z}_q$ in the n-th roots of unity ω_n^i for $i = 0, \ldots, n - 1$, where ω_n denotes a primitive n-th root of unity. Algorithm 1 shows the iterative version of NTT algorithm.

The iterative NTT algorithm consists of three nested loops. The outermost loop (i-loop) starts from $i = 2$ and increases by doubling i, and the loop stops when $i = n$, thus it has only $log_2 n$ iterations. In each iteration, the value of twiddle factor ω_i are computed by executing a power operation $\omega_i = \omega_n^{n/i}$, and the value of ω is initialized by 1. Compared to i-loop, the j-loop executes more iterations, the number of iteration can be seen as a sum of a geometric progression for 2^i where i starts from 0 and has a maximum value of $log_2(n-1)$, thus, the j-loop has $n-1$ iterations. In each iteration of j-loop, the twiddle factor ω is updated by performing a coefficient modular multiplication. Apparently, the innermost loop (k-loop) occupies most part of the execution time of NTT algorithm since it is executed roughly $\frac{n}{2}log_2n$ times. In each iteration of the innermost loop, two coefficients $a[i+j]$ and $a[i+j+i/2]$ are loaded from memory into registers, and then $a[i+j+i/2]$ are multiplied by the twiddle factor ω, after that, the value of $a[k+j]$ and $a[k+j+i/2]$ are updated and stored in the memory.

2.3   Previous Implementations of NTT

In LATINCRYPT'15, Pöppelmann et al. optimized the NTT operation by merging inverse NTT and multiplication by powers of ψ^{-1}. Furthermore, bit-reversal step is removed by the manipulation of the standard iterative algorithms. In CHES'15, Liu et al. suggested the high-speed NTT operations with efficient coefficient modular multiplication [12]. They presented the Move-and-Add (MA) method to perform the 16-bit wise coefficient multiplication and the Shift-Add-Multiply-Subtract-Subtract (SAMS2) techniques to replace the expensive reduction operations with the MUL instructions by cheaper shift and addition instructions. In TECS'17, Liu et al. improved the modular reduction by using Montgomery reduction [8]. This improves the previous SAMS2 techniques when the case requires a number of shift and addition operations on low-end devices. The new technique ensures the constant time computation together with high performance. In ICISC'17, the optimized Look-Up Table (LUT) based fast reduction technique is proposed [25]. The main idea is to first reduce the result by using the 8-bit wise pre-computed reduced results, and then perform the tiny fast reduction steps on short coefficients. The results are kept in the incomplete representation in order to optimize the number of subtraction in the reduction step.

3   Proposed Methods

NTT computation uses the majority of the execution time on modular multiplication operation since it is performed in the innermost k-loop of NTT computation. The target 16-bit wise multiplication can be efficiently performed by using previous works [12]. In this paper, we focused on the optimization of fast reduction operations for NTT computation. We chose the prime modulus $q = 12289$ (i.e. 0x3001 in hexadecimal representation) for the target parameters, which are used in previous works [8,12,25].

The modular reduction can be implemented using the bit-shift and add technique (i.e. SAMS2) covered in previous works [8,12], This approach can be accelerated by using the optimized Look-Up Table (LUT) based fast reduction technique for performing the mod 12289 operations [25]. The main idea is to first reduce the result by using the 8-bit wise pre-computed reduced results, and then perform the tiny fast reduction steps on short coefficients. The results are kept in the incomplete representation in order to optimize the number of subtraction in the reduction step.

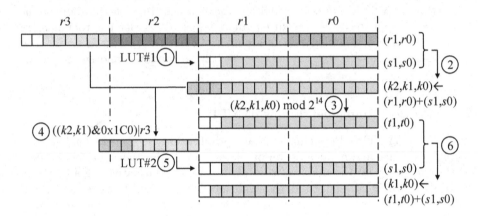

Fig. 1. Look-Up Table based Fast Reduction for $q = 12289$, ①: LUT access; ②: addition; ③: modulo; ④: concatenation; ⑤: LUT access; ⑥: addition.

In this paper, we further optimized the LUT based approach by using combined LUT techniques. For the case of prime modulus $q = 12289$, the variables are always kept in range of $(0, 2^{15} - 1)$ in incomplete representations and the intermediate results (IR) of multiplication are kept in $(0, 2^{30} - 1)$. We set two pre-computed LUTs with (mod 12289) operation. One input variable are ranging from 17-th bit to 24-th bit, which are the values located in $x \times 2^{16}$ where x is ranging from 0 to 2^8. Afterward, the variable is reduced to 14-bit wise results through (mod 12289) operation ($\approx ((IR \ div \ 2^{16}) \ mod \ 2^8) \ mod \ 12289$). The reduced results are added to the intermediate results (i.e. r_1, r_0). The addition of 14-bit results and 16-bit results generates 17-bit intermediate results. With this intermediate results, the other LUT received the combined two input variables (one from 15-th bit to 17th bit and the other one from 25-th bit to 30-th bit)[1]. The LUT ensures that the variable is reduced to the 14-bit results ($\approx (IR \ div \ 2^{14}) \ mod \ 12289$).

After the second LUT based reduction operations, the 14-bit wise results are added to the remaining 14-bit wise intermediate results (1-st bit–14-th bits), which output 15-bit intermediate results. In previous works, they utilize the tiny fast reduction in the last step. The proposed approach only requires LUT based reduction without tiny fast reduction. This ensures the optimized performance than previous works.

---

[1] Two LUTs only require 1.5 KB ($2^8 \times 2 + 2^9 \times 2$) and the LUTs are stored in the FLASH memory. Considering that 8-bit AVR platforms support to write data into the FLASH memory and its size is ranging from 128–384 KB. The storage for LUTs is negligible on the target processors.

Algorithm 2. LUT based modular reduction in source code (mod 12289)

Input: operands R22, R23, R24, R25

Output: results {R24, R25}

1: CLR R26 {MOV-and-ADD}	18: LPM R23, Z
2: MUL R24, R22	19: ADD R18, R22
3: MOVW R18, R0	20: ADC R19, R23
4: MUL R25, R23	21: ADC R20, R20 {Register re-use}
5: MOVW R20, R0	
	22: MOV R30, R19
	23: ANDI R19, 0X3F
6: MUL R24, R23	24: ANDI R20, 0X01
7: ADD R19, R0	25: ANDI R30, 0XC0
8: ADC R20, R1	
9: ADC R21, R26	26: ADD R30, R21
	27: LDI R31, hi8(LUT2_L) {LUT access}
10: MUL R25, R22	28: ADD R31, R20
11: ADD R19, R0	29: LPM R24, Z
12: ADC R20, R1	
13: ADC R21, R26	30: LDI R31, hi8(LUT2_H)
	31: ADD R31, R20
14: MOV R30, R20	32: LPM R25, Z
15: LDI R31, hi8(LUT1_L) {LUT access}	
16: LPM R22, Z	33: ADD R24, R18
	34: ADC R25, R19
17: LDI R31, hi8(LUT1_H)	35: CLR R1

The detailed method is described in Fig. 1. We keep the product in four registers $(r3, r2, r1, r0)$, which has been marked by different colors. Each of register $(r3, r2, r1, r0)$ is 8-bit long. The colorful parts mean that this bit has been occupied while the white part means the current bit is empty. The reduction with 12289 using LUT approach can be performed as follows:

1. LUT access. We first perform the LUT access with variable $(r2)$ to get the 14-bit wise reduced results $(s1$ and $s0)$.
2. Addition. The reduced results $(s1, s0)$ is added to the intermediate results $(r1, r0)$. This addition generates 17-bit intermediate results.
3. Modulo. The intermediate results $(k2, k1, k0)$ below 14-bit are extracted and we obtain the $(t1, t0)$.
4. Concatenation. The intermediate result $(r3)$ and the other 3-bit intermediate result (i.e. $(k2, k1)\&0x1C0$) are concatenated and generate 9-bit wise value.
5. LUT access. We perform the LUT access with the concatenated value to get the 14-bit wise reduced results $(s1$ and $s0)$.
6. Addition. Finally, we perform the addition operation of $(t1, t0) + (s1, s0)$ to get final 15-bit wise results.

In Algorithm 2, the LUT based modular reduction in source code level is described. In Step 1–13, MOV-and-ADD multiplication is used to perform the 16-bit wise multiplication. The 32-bit intermediate results are stored in 4 8-bit registers (R18, R19, R20, R21). Afterward, we perform the LUT based reduction operation. The LUT input and output are 8-bit and 16-bit, respectively. In order to accelerate the memory access, we used two different optimized technique. First method is aligned memory access. We set the higher 8-bit address with one operand and only update the lower byte with different values. The detailed descriptions are as follows:

- 8-bit aligned (init): MOV R30, R24 → LDI R31, hi8(LUT) → LPM R22, Z
- 8-bit aligned (second): MOV R30, R24 → LPM R22, Z

where Z, R24, R25, R1, R30, R31, and R26 are Z pointer, first input value, second input value, zero value, lower part of memory address, higher part of memory address and result, respectively.

Fig. 2. Comparison of LUT construction, (a) previous method, (b) proposed separated memory access. Yellow and green blocks represent higher and lower parts for LUT, respectively. (Color figure online)

Second method is separated memory access. The LUT outputs 16-bit wise results, which requires doubled offsets. In this setting, the aligned memory access is not feasible. We separated the LUT into two parts. First one is for lower 8-bit and second one is for higher 8-bit. The detailed method is described in Fig. 2. Unlike previous LUT construction, the separated LUTs are constructed. Under this LUT setting, the aligned memory access is efficiently performed. The technique is also applied to the following LUT accesses.

In Step 14–15, the 17–24-th bits (R20) is loaded to the lower 8-bit address (R30). Then, the higher 8-bit address of LUT1_L is loaded to the register (R31). In Step 16, FLASH memory access is performed with LPM instruction. From Step 17 and 18, higher part of LUT1 is accessed. Since we used the aligned memory access, only higher address is modified.

In Step 19–21, the reduced results and intermediate results are added. In particular, we re-used the register (R20). The addition with carry can store the carry bit generated from Step 20.

Thereafter, in Step 22–25, two intermediate results are concatenated. In Step 26–32, LUT2 access is performed in aligned memory access method. Finally, the reduced results and intermediate results are added together. This ensures the 15-bit wise intermediate results.

The proposed modular reduction method is generic approach for any primes for Ring-LWE. For this reason, we can easily extend the proposed method to other primes without difficulty. Definitely, the proposed method is working for lattice based PQC candidates, such as NewHope and CRYPSTALS-KYBER [2,4]

Discrete Gaussian Sampling. Discrete Gaussian sampling is an integral part of Ring-LWE algorithm. For fast computation, we adopted the Knuth-Yao sampler with byte-scanning [12,20]. However, original sampling is not secure against timing attack and simple power analysis. In order to ensure the secure implementation, we adopted the random shuffling after random sampling [20]. The random shuffling removes the relation between random samples and timing information.

4 Performance Evaluation

This section presents performance results of our implementation. We first give the experimental platform in Sect. 4.1. Afterwards, we show a comparison with the previous modular multiplication and NTT implementations in Sect. 4.2. Finally, we show a comparison with the previous Ring-LWE implementation in Sect. 4.3.

4.1 Experimental Platform

Our implementation uses ATxmega128A1 processor on an Xplain board as target platform. This processor has a maximum frequency of 32 MHz, 128 KB flash program memory, and 8 KB SRAM. It supports an AES crypto-accelerator and can be used in a wide range of applications, such as industrial, hand-held battery applications as well as some medical devices. The main structure and interface are written in C language while the core operations such as modular arithmetic is implemented in Assembly language. For the LUT based approach, the constant LUT variables are stored in flash program memory, which requires 1.5KB for saving the parameters and 3 clock cycles for each byte access. We complied our implementation with speed optimization option '-O3' on Atmel Studio 6.2. In order to obtain accurate timing, we execute each operation for at least 1000 times and report average cycle count for each operation.

4.2 Comparison of Modular Multiplication and NTT

Table 1 summarizes execution time of modular multiplication and NTT for long-term security levels. First, various works including [1,3,12,17] are not constant-time solutions, which means the attackers can perform timing attack to extract the secret information. Previous work by Liu et al. introduced the secure approach with tiny Montgomery reduction [8]. They perform the Montgomery reduction to reduce the 28/30-bit variables to 14/15-bit results. However, the complexity of n-word Montgomery reduction is generally $n^2 + n$, which is still high overheads on the low-end devices. In ICISC'17, Seo et al. suggested LUT based

Table 1. Execution time of modular multiplication and NTT (in clock cycles), where 256-bit security represents $(n : 512, q : 12289)$ on 8-bit AVR processors, e.g., ATxmega64, ATxmega128.

Implementation	Mod MUL	NTT	Const
Boorghany et al. [3]	N/A	2,207,787	–
Boorghany et al. [1]	N/A	N/A	–
Pöppelmann et al. [17]	N/A	855,595	–
Liu et al. [12]	N/A	441,572	–
Liu et al. [8]	70	516,971	√
Seo et al. [25]	66	403,224	√
This work	47	344,288	√

approach to achieve high performance and constant timing [25]. However, we find that there is still room to improve the performance.

As shown in the Table 1, the proposed modular multiplication with 12289 only requires 47 clock cycles, which are 19 clock cycles smaller than previous approaches [25]. Definitely, the proposed NTT operation also shows higher performance than previous works. NTT operation only requires 344,288 cycles for 256-bit security implementation. Results of NTT for long-term security is 14.6% faster than previous works.

4.3   Comparison of Ring-LWE

With optimized NTT implementation, we evaluated the Ring-LWE encryption scheme with parameter sets (n, q, σ) with $(512, 12289, 12.18/\sqrt{2\pi})$ for security levels of 256-bit. The tailcut of discrete Gaussian sampler is limited to 12σ to achieve a high precision statistical difference from the theoretical distribution, which is less than 2^{-90}. These parameter sets were also used in most of the previous software implementations, e.g., [1,3,5,8,12,25].

Table 2. Performance comparison of software implementation of 256-bit security level lattice-based cryptosystems on 8-bit AVR processors, e.g., ATxmega64, ATxmega128.

Implementation	NTT/FFT	Key-Gen	Enc	Secure
Boorghany et al. [1]	2,207,787	N/A	N/A	–
Pöppelmann et al. [17]	855,595	N/A	3,279,142	–
Liu et al. [12]	441,572	2,165,239	2,617,459	–
Liu et al. [8]	516,971	N/A	1,975,806	√
Seo et al. [25]	403,224	N/A	1,754,064	√
This work	344,288	1,325,171	1,430,601	√

Table 2 compares software implementations of 256-bit security lattice-based cryptosystems on the 8-bit AVR processors. We compare the previous work [1,3,8,12,17,25] with ours. Proposed 256-bit security implementation requires 344K, 1,325K, and 1,430K cycles for NTT, key generation, and encryption, respectively. Compared to the recent work [25], the NTT operation is significantly improved because we used compact modular multiplication routine. The performance improvements of NTT accelerate the key generation and encryption for Ring-LWE implementations. The proposed encryption implementation outperforms previous works by 18.4%. Furthermore, the proposed implementations are constant timing, which ensures a secure computation against simple power analysis and timing attacks.

5   Conclusion

This paper presents optimization techniques for efficient and secure implementation of NTT and its application Ring-LWE key generation and encryption on the low-end 8-bit AVR platform. The proposed NTT implementation achieved new speed records for secure 256-bit Ring-LWE encryption implementation on low-end 8-bit AVR platforms.

Our future works are applying the proposed techniques to the other low-end IoT devices, such as 8-bit PIC and 16-bit MSP processors. Similarly, these platforms also support very limited Arithmetic Logic Unit (ALU) and storage. Second, we will further investigate the side channel attacks for Ring-LWE scheme on the low-end embedded processors.

Acknowledgement. This work was supported as part of Military Crypto Research Center(UD170109ED) funded by Defense Acquisition Program Administration(DAPA) and Agency for Defense Development(ADD).

References

1. Boorghany, A., Sarmadi, S.B., Jalili, R.: On constrained implementation of lattice-based cryptographic primitives and schemes on smart cards. Cryptology ePrint Archive, Report 2014/514 (2014). https://eprint.iacr.org/2014/514.pdf
2. Alkim, E., et al.: Newhope. Technical Report, Technical report, National Institute of Standards and Technology (2017)
3. Boorghany, A., Jalili, R.: Implementation and Comparison of Lattice-based Identification Protocols on Smart Cards and Microcontrollers. Cryptology ePrint Archive, Report 2014/078 (2014)
4. Bos, J., et al.: CRYSTALS-Kyber: a CCA-secure module-lattice-based KEM. In: 2018 IEEE European Symposium on Security and Privacy (EuroS&P), pp. 353–367. IEEE (2018)
5. De Clercq, R., Roy, S.S., Vercauteren, F., Verbauwhede, I.: Efficient software implementation of ring-LWE encryption. In: 18th Design, Automation & Test in Europe Conference & Exhibition-DATE (2015)

6. Liu, Z., Huang, X., Hu, Z., Khan, M.K., Seo, H., Zhou, L.: On emerging family of elliptic curves to secure internet of things: ECC comes of age. IEEE Trans. Dependable Secure Comput. **14**(3), 237–248 (2017)

7. Liu, Z., Longa, P., Pereira, G., Reparaz, O., Seo, H.: Fourq on embedded devices with strong countermeasures against side-channel attacks. Technical report, Cryptology ePrint Archive, Report 2017/434, 28, 29 (2017)

8. Liu, Z., et al.: High-performance ideal lattice-based cryptography on 8-bit AVR microcontrollers. ACM Trans. Embedded Comput. Syst. (TECS) **16**(4), 117 (2017)

9. Liu, Z., Seo, H., Großschädl, J., Kim, H.: Efficient implementation of NIST-compliant elliptic curve cryptography for sensor nodes. In: Qing, S., Zhou, J., Liu, D. (eds.) ICICS 2013. LNCS, vol. 8233, pp. 302–317. Springer, Cham (2013). https://doi.org/10.1007/978-3-319-02726-5_22

10. Liu, Z., Seo, H., Großschädl, J., Kim, H.: Efficient implementation of NIST-compliant elliptic curve cryptography for 8-bit AVR-based sensor nodes. IEEE Trans. Inf. Forensics Secur. **11**(7), 1385–1397 (2016)

11. Liu, Z., Seo, H., Hu, Z., Hunag, X., Großschädl, J.: Efficient implementation of ECDH key exchange for MSP430-based wireless sensor networks. In: Proceedings of the 10th ACM Symposium on Information, Computer and Communications Security, pp. 145–153. ACM (2015)

12. Liu, Z., Seo, H., Sinha Roy, S., Großschädl, J., Kim, H., Verbauwhede, I.: Efficient ring-LWE encryption on 8-Bit AVR processors. In: Güneysu, T., Handschuh, H. (eds.) CHES 2015. LNCS, vol. 9293, pp. 663–682. Springer, Heidelberg (2015). https://doi.org/10.1007/978-3-662-48324-4_33

13. Liu, Z., Seo, H., Xu, Q.: Performance evaluation of twisted edwards-form elliptic curve cryptography for wireless sensor nodes. Secur. Commun. Netw. **8**(18), 3301–3310 (2015)

14. Liu, Z., Weng, J., Hu, Z., Seo, H.: Efficient elliptic curve cryptography for embedded devices. ACM Trans. Embedded Comput. Syst. (TECS) **16**(2), 53 (2016)

15. Lyubashevsky, V., Peikert, C., Regev, O.: On Ideal Lattices and Learning with Errors Over Rings. Cryptology ePrint Archive, Report 2012/230 (2012)

16. Oder, T., Pöppelmann, T., Güneysu, T.: Beyond ECDSA and RSA: lattice-based digital signatures on constrained devices. In: 51st Annual Design Automation Conference-DAC (2014)

17. Pöppelmann, T., Oder, T., Güneysu, T.: High-performance ideal lattice-based cryptography on 8-Bit ATxmega microcontrollers. In: Lauter, K., Rodríguez-Henríquez, F. (eds.) LATINCRYPT 2015. LNCS, vol. 9230, pp. 346–365. Springer, Cham (2015). https://doi.org/10.1007/978-3-319-22174-8_19

18. Qiu, L., Liu, Z., Pereira, G.C., Seo, H.: Implementing RSA for sensor nodes in smart cities. Pers. Ubiquit. Comput. **21**(5), 807–813 (2017)

19. Regev, O.: On lattices, learning with errors, random linear codes, and cryptography. In: 37th Annual ACM Symposium on Theory of Computing, pp. 84–93 (2005)

20. Roy, S.S., Reparaz, O., Vercauteren, F., Verbauwhede, I.: Compact and side channel secure discrete gaussian sampling (2014)

21. Roy, S.S., Vercauteren, F., Mentens, N., Chen, D.D., Verbauwhede, I.: Compact ring-LWE cryptoprocessor. In: Batina, L., Robshaw, M. (eds.) CHES 2014. LNCS, vol. 8731, pp. 371–391. Springer, Heidelberg (2014). https://doi.org/10.1007/978-3-662-44709-3_21

22. Seo, H., Kim, H.: MoTE-ECC based encryption on MSP430. J. Inf. Commun. Converg. Eng. **15**(3), 160–164 (2017)

23. Seo, H., Liu, Z., Großschädl, J., Kim, H.: Efficient arithmetic on ARM-NEON and its application for high-speed RSA implementation. Secur. Commun. Netw. **9**(18), 5401–5411 (2016)

24. Seo, H., Liu, Z., Nogami, Y., Park, T., Choi, J., Zhou, L., Kim, H.: Faster ECC over $\mathbb{F}_{2^{521}-1}$ (feat. NEON). In: Kwon, S., Yun, A. (eds.) ICISC 2015. LNCS, vol. 9558, pp. 169–181. Springer, Cham (2016). https://doi.org/10.1007/978-3-319-30840-1_11

25. Seo, H., Liu, Z., Park, T., Kwon, H., Lee, S., Kim, H.: Secure number theoretic transform and speed record for ring-LWE encryption on embedded processors. In: Kim, H., Kim, D.-C. (eds.) ICISC 2017. LNCS, vol. 10779, pp. 175–188. Springer, Cham (2018). https://doi.org/10.1007/978-3-319-78556-1_10

26. Seo, H.: Faster (feat. ECC PMULL) over F2571. In: A Systems Approach to Cyber Security: Proceedings of the 2nd Singapore Cyber-Security R&D Conference (SG-CRC 2017), vol. 15, p. 97. IOS Press (2017)

27. Shor, P.: Algorithms for quantum computation: discrete logarithms and factoring. In: 35th Annual Symposium on Foundations of Computer Science, 1994 Proceedings, pp. 124–134, November 1994

Low-Noise LLC Side-Channel Attack with Perf

Youngjoo Ko, Sangwoo Ji, and Jong Kim$^{(\boxtimes)}$

Department of Computer Science and Engineering,
Pohang University of Science and Technology (POSTECH), Pohang, South Korea
{y0108009,sangwooji,jkim}@postech.ac.kr

Abstract. Many cache side-channel attacks have been proposed, and they threaten sensitive programs in real-world. The success of the attacks depends on how accurately to decide whether a set of cache lines are in cache or not. However, external factors insert noise into cache attacks, and the noise disturbs the attacks' decision process. Attacks in last-level cache (LLC) have more noise compared with core-dedicated caches.

In this paper, we propose an attack method using Perf—a performance analyzing tool in Linux, attack$_{Perf}$, to achieve low-noise in cache side-channel attacks to LLC. The proposed method utilizes Perf to decide cache hits/misses when accessing memory. Since Perf gets the number of cache hits and misses from hardware performance counters, it can identify the cache hits/misses of memory accesses with the less noise. For evaluation, we compare the performance of attacks$_{timer}$ (existing attack method) and attacks$_{Perf}$ by implementing Flush+Reload and Prime+Probe. For the accuracy of Perf, we compare the clock cycles of the timer and the counts of Perf according to the victim's access.

Keywords: Side-channel · Cache attack · Perf · Hardware performance counter · Multi-core attack

1 Introduction

Cache side-channel is well-known and threaten security applications in broad fields. Many researches have recently reported cache as a critical attack space. Since processes share the cache, attackers can extract victim's sensitive information by monitoring victim's memory accesses in the cache. To decide whether a victim has accessed a target memory region, attackers access the memory region that maps to a set of cache lines congruently hosting the victim's target memory region. If the victim has accessed the target memory in the cache, it brings a change in the set of cache lines and attacker's accesses are going to be cache hits or misses. Most attacks exploit a timer to know the cache hit/miss resulting from the victim's access to the target memory in the cache [9,16]. The cache attacks have been studied widely, for example, Zhang $et\ al.$ [17] conducted the cache attack in a cloud environment, and Chen $et\ al.$ [5] performed the attack on

© Springer Nature Switzerland AG 2020
I. You (Ed.): WISA 2019, LNCS 11897, pp. 328–340, 2020.
https://doi.org/10.1007/978-3-030-39303-8_25

a web browser. Furthermore, many methods have been proposed to exploit last-level cache (LLC) side-channel [8,11,16] to attack across cores and incapacitate defense mechanisms.

However, existing cache side-channel attacks have suffered from many kinds of noise. Especially, extracting accurate cache hit/miss information is not simple because of the noise from external factors and defenses. Several external factors, such as exceptions, context switches, and unexpected timing latency, contribute to the noise that results in inaccurate cache attacks. The noise from external factors causes wrong decisions and false-positives. Note that adding the noise to a timer is an effective countermeasure against cache side-channel attacks, given that the attacks require a sophisticated timer to decide cache hits/misses. The noise to the timer is one of the main difficulties in the success of cache side-channel attacks, which frustrates the performance of cache side-channel attacks. There are relatively few studies devoted to reducing noise for the better decision of cache hits and misses, although it is important to improve the performance and accuracy of the decision.

In this paper, we propose a cache side-channel attack to solve the noise problem by using a performance counter. We call the cache side-channel attacks utilizing Perf as attack$_{Perf}$ and cache side-channel attacks using the timer as attack$_{timer}$ when determining cache hits/misses. Performance counter provides the number of cache hits/misses; hence, the attack process is able to monitor real cache hits/misses with low false-positives. To use hardware performance counters in the program, we use Perf interface to interact with the counters which is provided by Linux by default. Since Perf can monitor hardware events of specified code parts in user mode, it is possible to obtain the cache hits/misses of memory instructions of the code parts. The attack$_{Perf}$ can be used widely, since most Linux kernel includes Perf and most commodity CPUs support hardware performance counters.

We evaluate the attack$_{Perf}$ on two environments: normal environment and the timer defense deployed environment. We implement the attack$_{timer}$ and the attack$_{Perf}$ for two representative cache attacks: Flush+Reload and Prime+Probe on AES T-Table attacks. We demonstrate that attack$_{Perf}$ achieves high accuracy with a small number of AES encryption attempts. Also, we show that attacks$_{Perf}$ can identify victim's memory accesses better than attacks$_{timer}$ using Kuiper's test[1] values [10]. Furthermore, we show that attack$_{Perf}$ accomplishes attacks even on the timer defense deployed environment. We show an analysis of why attack$_{Perf}$ has lower noise than attack$_{timer}$. As a result of the analysis, measured clock cycles of cache hits and misses are heavily overlapped on attack$_{timer}$, while the number of cache hits and misses on performance counters are separable on attack$_{Perf}$.

Our key contributions are:

- We show through the implementation that it is possible to run practical cache side-channel attacks using Perf with low noise in a multi-core environment.

---

[1] Kuiper's test is used in statistics to test whether a given distribution or family of distributions, is similar to another distribution.

- We show that the proposed method improves attack accuracy and performance in measuring cache hits/misses compared with attack$_{timer}$
- We show that the attack$_{Perf}$ can bypass the defense adding noise to the timer.
- We analyze the reason why Perf enables more precise attacks.

The remainder of this paper is organized as follows. In Sect. 2, we provide background about cache architecture, cache side-channel attacks, cause of noise of cache side-channel attacks, and performance counters in Linux system. Section 3 describes attack$_{Perf}$. Further on, in Sect. 4, we evaluate our method by executing a real attack on AES T-table and figure out the reason why Perf achieves high precision. We discuss several pieces of research related to our work in Sect. 5 and conclude in Sect. 6.

2   Background

2.1   Cache Architecture

Caches are hardware components in CPU and store frequently and recently used data and instructions, in order to reduce access time and make memory access faster. A cache consists of multiple cache sets, each of which stores a fixed number of cache lines. A typical cache line is 64 bytes in modern CPU. The caches are hierarchically structured in modern processors—multiple hierarchical levels of caches. Higher level caches are closer to a CPU and faster than lower level caches, but higher level caches have a smaller capacity than lower level caches. Each core has dedicated caches[2], and all cores share one last level cache (LLC). Many commodity processors have an inclusive cache structure; lower level caches include the content in higher level caches. Therefore, the LLC contains all content in higher level caches. If the cache line in the LLC is evicted or flushed, then the cache line in higher level cache should be flushed together. To attack across cores, the inclusive LLC is an essential property, given that a victim might load content from core-dedicated cache without loading content into the non-inclusive LLC.

2.2   Cache Side-Channel Attacks

Most side-channel attacks occur on shared resources between processes, and the cache is a well-known shared resource. Given that processes share the cache, a spy program can observe the memory access of the victim program. The cache side-channel attack consists of three phases: (1) reset, (2) wait, and (3) confirm the victim's access. In the reset phase, the spy program resets a part of cache to make the victim's content out of that part of the cache. Then the spy program waits for the execution of the victim program. As the final phase, the spy program

---

[2] Most processors usually have two caches, L1 and L2 caches. Modern x86 processors typically support a L2 cache for each core.

checks the cache lines by usually cache hits or misses to see if the victim has accessed the memory. Through repeating three phases above, the spy program extracts important information from the victim's memory access pattern. Cache side-channel attacks are launched on the same core target dedicated caches in each core. Furthermore, the attacks can be launched across cores in the multi-core system through the LLC. Although the attack on the multi-core system has bigger noise than attacks on dedicated caches, the LLC attack can target wide areas [5,17] practically. We provide further details about two representative cache attacks.

Flush+Reload: Flush+Reload [16] is one of the well-known methods among cache attacks. This method is mostly used for the Intel ISA because cache flush instruction (*clflush*) is provided and can be executed in user-mode. Flush+Reload targets a specific address, so it requires to share the target address with a victim process. As the reset phase, the method flushes the spy's address from the cache and waits a certain time. After the waiting time, it reloads the address. If it takes a short time to load the content (cache hit), it means that the victim has accessed the address during the waiting time. Flush+Reload can figure out the victim's access accurately, but it requires shared memory and *clflush* instruction.

Prime+Probe: Prime+Probe [12] is the most general method for side-channel and also mostly used in cache attacks. Unlike Flush+Reload, Prime+Probe does not require to share memory between spy and victim processes, so that it can attack any processes. In the reset phase, it fills a certain cache set with spy's content using eviction sets to evicts victim's cache lines. After waiting time for the execution of the victim process, the spy accesses the spy's content again and measures the time to access its content that was filled before in the cache set. If the access time is over a threshold (cache miss), one of spy's content from the cache set is evicted. It means that the victim has accessed its content and loaded it to the cache set. Prime+Probe has the high noise because it does not check one cache line, but several cache lines in the same cache set.

2.3   Cause of Noise on Existing Cache Side-Channel Attacks

Noise is mostly introduced for two reasons. One is a corruption of a target cache set by unexpected events or unrelated processes and the other is timing delay in accessing a target cache set due to unexpected latency. When a timer is used to determine cache hit or miss in the third phase, the noise due to timing delay affects the accuracy and performance of cache side-channel attacks. Many external factors affect the timer delay, for example, context switches, and latency from read/write buffers, which results in long cycles even if cache hits. Therefore, the noise on the timer makes the decision of cache hits or misses confused. To make stable cache side-channel attacks, we need a precise measurement to determine cache hits/misses.

2.4   Perf in Linux for Performance Counters

Hardware performance counters count many hardware events such as the number of instructions executed, cache hits, cache misses, etc. dynamically and save them into counter registers. All current x86 CPUs are equipped with hardware performance counters. Perf is a software tool in Linux that interfaces with hardware performance counters, reads the value, and analyzes the performance. Perf can be performed not only from the command line but also inside the code to monitor certain parts of instructions by using *ioctl* system call. Given that Perf can monitor hardware events that occur in specific code parts, it is possible to observe cache hits/misses precisely. Most Linux kernels support Perf by default in user mode and kernel mode. For our attack, using Perf in user-mode is enough, since we need to count cache hits/misses generated by a process (specially attacker's process) in user mode.

3   Cache Side-Channel Attack with Perf

Most cache attacks exploit a timer to decide cache hits and misses resulting from the victim's access. However, the external factors such as context switches or the full of read/write buffer result in more delay on a timer and make cache hits serve as cache misses even though they are not real cache misses. Existing attacks (attacks$_{timer}$) have been influenced by external factors, therefore, they generate several false-positives in counting cache hits/misses.

In contrast to attacks$_{timer}$, our method is not much affected by external factors while relying on hardware performance counters. The proposed attack method utilizes Perf in Linux to determine cache hits and misses. We use Perf inside the program code using *ioctl* system call that can monitor hardware events in the target code part, in our case, the target code part is accessing spy's memory. For this reason, attacks$_{Perf}$ can determine cache hits/misses only when the spy accessing memory. We expect that the attack$_{Perf}$ can increase attack performance and reduce the noise by reading hardware performance counter, since hardware performance counters count real cache hits/misses occurred while executing a process. Note that hardware performance counters may have the noise due to context switches, event occurrence, etc. during measurement. However, we consider the noise in performance counters is smaller than the noise in timer. Our attack has been conducted in the LLC to run in the multi-core environment if the spy can exploit Perf. We use the same sequence and hardware properties of Prime+Probe and Flush+Reload except determining cache hits/misses.

Listing 1. Prime+Probe attack with timer

```
1       start = rdtsc();
2       access all cache lines in an eviction set
3       end = rdtsc() - start;
4
5       if (end > threshold)
6           victim access
```

Listing 2. Prime+Probe attack with Perf

```
1    ioctl(fd, PERF_EVENT_IOC_RESET, 0);
2    ioctl(fd, PERF_EVENT_IOC_ENABLE, 0);
3    access all cache lines in an eviction set
4    ioctl(fd, PERF_EVENT_IOC_DISABLE, 0);
5    read(fd, &count, sizeof(long long));
6
7    miss_num = count.value;
8    if (miss_num > threshold)
9        victim access
```

We implement attacks$_{timer}$ and attacks$_{Perf}$ in the case of two cache attack methods: Flush+Reload and Prime+Probe. To describe the main difference between attacks$_{timer}$ and attacks$_{Perf}$, we show the simple code snippet in the scenario of Prime+Probe. Listing 1 shows the existing Prime+Probe attack$_{timer}$. It uses *rdtsc* instruction that provides a subnanosecond resolution timestamp to measure clock cycles taken to access cache lines in eviction sets. The measured time is employed to decide whether the spy's content is evicted or not. Therefore, the Prime+Probe attack$_{timer}$ monitors the victim's memory access through the timer. In the measuring part, it is possible that the decision about victim's access can be failed because of delay on the timer. The Flush+Reload code is also similar to the Prime+Probe attack, but it measures the time of reloading one cache line.

Listing 2 shows the code snippet of the cache side-channel attack$_{Perf}$ in Prime+Probe. The difference from Listing 1 is the way to measure cache misses. The attack$_{Perf}$ calls *ioctl* system call to check cache misses using Perf. To eliminate unrelated cache misses, *ioctl* system call first resets the hardware register to zero and then enables to save the number of cache misses. After accessing cache lines in eviction sets, the attack stops counting cache misses. The counter value on Perf is used in our attack instead of the clock cycle on the timer to identify whether the memory accesses have caused cache misses or not. Given that the attack is able to check the cache misses of the desired part, it increases the accuracy of cache misses. In case of Flush+Reload, the attack$_{Perf}$ measures cache hits when reloading a cache line.

4   Evaluation

We perform a comparison between attacks$_{timer}$ and attacks$_{Perf}$ by implementing Flush+Reload and Prim+Probe attacks with/without the timer defense. Besides, we figure out why Perf indicates low noise compared with the timer. To demonstrate the power of the attack$_{Perf}$, we run the cache attacks on the AES implementation of OpenSSL [2,12]. The AES algorithm with T-tables is known to be vulnerable to cache side-channel attacks [1,6,9]. The AES cryptographic algorithm accesses T-tables using the secret key k and the plaintext p. During the first round of encryption, the algorithm accesses the entries $T_j[p_i \oplus k_i]$ with $i \equiv j \bmod 4$ and $0 \le i < 16$. As these T-tables typically map to 16 different cache lines, we can use a cache attack to determine which cache line is accessed during this round. If the attack knows which cache line is accessed by a victim, the cache attack can derive the secret key from $[p_i \oplus k_i]$ in case p_i is known.

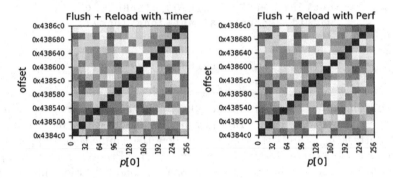

Fig. 1. Flush+Reload attacks on AES (Color figure online)

4.1 Experiment Setup

All of our evaluations were performed on a system with an Intel(R) Skylake i7-6700k CPU @ 3.40 GHz, 8 MB and 16-way set-associative of L3 cache, and 8 GB of RAM. We ran Ubuntu 16.04 with Linux 4.4.0-130. We attacked the OpenSSL 1.0.1e version which is vulnerable to the cache side-channel attack.

4.2 Attack Scenario

We target the AES secret key to extract the four upper bits of each byte. For Prime+Probe, the spy fills a group of target cache sets using the eviction set in the reset phase. Subsequently, the attacker triggers an AES encryption with chosen p_i. The attacker checks whether a group of target cache sets has been accessed or not. The attacker repeats the encryption to gather the number of cache hits or misses for inspection of victim's access. The attacker can learn that a certain target cache set has high counts of cache misses. Based on the target set having high counts, the attacker infers the table index used by the victim. Sine the table index is $[p_i \oplus k_i]$, we can derive upper 4 bits of the secret key k_i using the address of cache line as we know p_i. In the case of Flush+Reload, the attacker resets and confirms a victim's access by an address granularity, not a cache set. Thus, it is possible for the spy to derive 64 bits of the secret key k.

4.3 Effectiveness Comparison of Attacks on AES T-Table

Figures 1 and 2 show the results of Flush+Reload and Prime+Probe attacks on AES T-table with two different ways of measuring cache hits/misses: the timer and Perf. The left side shows the attack$_{timer}$ and the right side represents the attack$_{Perf}$. Each attack does AES encryption 100 times for each cache line to extract the secret key. The y-axis indicates the offset of T-table and the x-axis represents the value of the first byte of plaintext. Each box means the rate of cache hits in the Flush+Reload and the rate of cache misses in Prime+Probe. The dark green box indicates a higher rate of cache hits and misses than white box relatively. Thus, the boxes with high rate imply that the victim has accessed the offset(address) with high probability. To show the visible pattern, we target a cache line used to extract the four upper bits of the first byte of the secret key, and repeat the test by changing the first byte of plaintext $p[0]$ from 0 to 256. Thus, we can observe the pattern according to the index of T-table to which the victim accesses. From the figure, the dark green diagonal boxes show the matching table index offset according to a given plaintext and other non-white boxes indicate that it has the noise. By reading the figure vertically for the given plaintext (x-axis), we can know the offset. In addition, we can extract the secret key by extending all cache lines of the T-table.

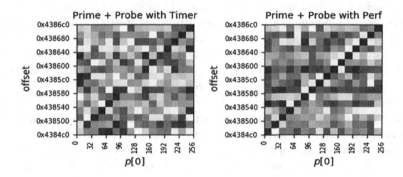

Fig. 2. Prime+Probe attacks on AES (Color figure online)

The performance difference between the timer and Perf in Flush+Reload is small, since Flush+Reload attack targets a specific cache line so that it has the low noise originally. To demonstrate the result statistically, we compare the rate distribution of cache hits for victim's accessing addresses to that of cache hits for victim's non-accessing addresses using the Kuiper's test [10]. The Kuiper's test is used in statistics to determine whether two distributions stem from the same base distribution or not. In other words, if the null hypothesis is rejected due to small *p-value*, usually smaller than 0.05, it means that the attack can distinguish the victim's accessing clearly. Both attack$_{timer}$ and the attack$_{Perf}$ show almost 0.000 on the *p-value* in Flush+Reload. From this, it can be said that there is strong evidence against the null-hypothesis so that two distributions show a clear difference in both attacks.

In the case of Prime+Probe, we can see through Fig. 2 that both Prime+Probe attacks show different cache miss rates. The Prime+Probe attack$_{timer}$ is hard to figure out the secret key, whereas the Prime+Probe attack$_{Perf}$ is able to distinguish the pattern and derives the secret key successfully. With the Kuiper's test, we compare the rate distribution of cache misses for victim's accessing addresses to that of victim's non-accessing addresses. The p-test value in the attack$_{timer}$ indicates 0.213 It means that the two distributions are similar. Therefore, it is hard to distinguish between the victim's accessing addresses and non-accessing addresses. In contrast to the attack$_{timer}$, the attack$_{Perf}$ shows 0.000004 on the p-value. It indicates that there is very strong evidence against the null-hypothesis and the cache miss rate distribution of victim's accessing addresses is not similar to that of victim's non-accessing addresses. Therefore, the attack$_{Perf}$ can succeed in the attack with better accuracy and detect the secret key with fewer encryption attempts practically due to the low noise in Prime+Probe.

4.4 Bypass Timer Defence

One of the cache side-channel defense techniques is to put a timer noise to prevent cache side-channels [14]. To evaluate the ability of attacks$_{Perf}$ to bypass the defense, we implement a system with a timer protection [14] by adding the noise on the *rdtsc* instruction, and test attacks$_{timer}$ and attacks$_{Perf}$.

Figure 3 shows the results of a Flush+Reload attack$_{timer}$ and a Prime+Probe attack$_{timer}$ on the system with timer protection [14]. The results of attacks$_{Perf}$ are the same as in Figs. 1 and 2. In contrast with the result of attack$_{Perf}$, the timer protection has a significant effect on attacks$_{timer}$. Given that the measurement of cache hits and misses in attacks$_{timer}$ does not decide cache hits and misses correctly, it is impossible to obtain sensitive information such as the secret key. However, the attack$_{Perf}$ can bypass the timer protection in a real-world setting; as a result, the attack$_{Perf}$ can still threaten security applications.

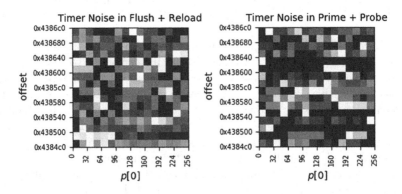

Fig. 3. Noise on timer to existing cache side-channel attacks: Flush+Reload, Prime+Probe

4.5   Accuracy of Classifying Cache Hit/Miss

To analyze the reason of the high accuracy of Perf, we compare how accurately
the timer and Perf decide the victim's accessing. We collect clock cycles on the
timer, as well as the count value on Perf in the case of the Prime+Probe attack.
Figure 4 represents the groups of data. One group is the result that the victim
has accessed and the other group is the result that the victim hasn't accessed.
The left side shows the distribution of clock cycle on the timer, whereas the
right side shows the distribution of count values on Perf. In the figures, the box
means from the first quartile to the third quartile (the data distribution of the
50% between the first and third quartile); the top and bottom values represent
a maximum value and a minimum value respectively.

In Fig. 4, the measured clock cycles of two groups are heavily overlapped,
while the count value on Perf is separable. When using the timer to decide the
victim's accessing, the clock cycles are overlapped 97% in the box area (50%
distribution). In view of all of the data points, 78% data points are overlapped
with two groups. Thus, the high overlapping rate increases the noise and results
in an opaque measurement of the victim's accessing during cache side-channel
attacks. On the other hand, when using Perf, the two groups are separable at
count value two visually in the box area. Furthermore, when considering all data
points, the two groups are 50% overlapped. The results indicate that Perf can
distinguish the victim's accessing more accurately compared with the timer.

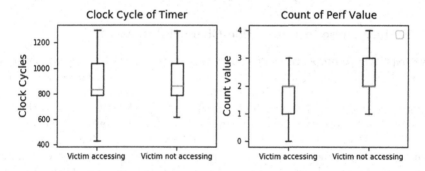

Fig. 4. Cache hit and miss cycles in timer and cache hit and miss count value in Perf

5   Related Work

5.1   Use Performance Counter in Defences and Attacks

Hardware performance counters monitor hardware events and save the monitoring results into registers. They are used for performance monitoring by
researchers in many areas. In security, researches have applied performance counters to defensive cases that allow detection of malware [7] and a control flow

integrity check [15]. Hardware performance counters have also been used for cache side-channel attacks [3,4,13]. Sarani and Mukhopadhyay [3] used Perf to side-channel attack a branch target buffer(BTB) against RSA. Targeting different hardware components except the cache to infer sensitive information is out of the scope of our work. Hence, we have not compared our proposed work with Sarani and Mukhopadhyay [3].

Brasser *et al.* [4] used Performance Monitor Counter (PMC) for the cache side-channel attack in SGX enclaves. Although it has succeeded in the attack on RSA and Genomic attack by targeting processes in SGX the paper did not analyze the difference between PMC and timer. However, we analyzed the difference attacks$_{Perf}$ from attacks$_{timer}$ through distribution of cache hits and misses. In addition, we compared performance of attacks$_{Perf}$ and attacks$_{timer}$ using Kuiper's test in two representative attacks. We have better analysis in comparison between Perf and the timer.

Leif *et al.* [13] did similar work with our attack. However, the main difference is that we have attacked AES encryption practically and extracted specific secret key in the attack. Furthermore, while Leif *et al.* [13] ran cache side-channel attack in a single core, which is impractical in a real world, our work attacks the LLC across cores in the multi-core system. Unlike Leif *et al.* [13], we implemented two representative cache side-channel attacks with the timer and Perf, and compared the accuracy and performance. Therefore, we consider that we have extended the attack surface of Leif *et al.* [13] to the multi-core system and implemented a real attack to extract secret key practically.

5.2   Reduce Noise in Cache Side-Channel Attacks

Some papers have proposed improved cache attacks by eliminating the noise of attacks. Flush+Flush [9] uses *clflush* instruction instead of *Reload* as a transformed attack from a Flush+Reload attack. While checking victim's behavior through the existence of the cache line, utilizing *clflush* contributes to the low noise and fast attacks due to non-memory instruction. To detect victim's access immediately, Prime+Abort [8] exploits Intel TSX extension that triggers abort when transactional memory is evicted from the cache. This scheme eliminates the noise of time gap between victim's access and probing cache lines.

Flush+Flush [9] as a transformed attack of Flush+Reload is not able to reduce the noise of other cache side-channel attacks such as Prime+Probe, whereas our proposed work cuts down the noise on general cache side-channel attacks, which typically use a timer, to increase the success of attacks. While Prime+Abort [8] shows the very low noise, it is only possible in the hardware supporting Intel TSX. Although the cache side-channel attack with Perf requires the hardware performance counter, all CPU manufacturers put such capability in their CPUs nowadays. So, it is safe to assume that that capability is commonly available.

6   Conclusion

This paper presents the cache side-channel attack with Perf, a low-noise cache attack compared with cache attacks using the timer. We compared the attack$_{timer}$ with the attack$_{Perf}$ by implementing two representative existing cache side-channel attacks: Flush+Reload and Prime+Probe. Also, we experimented with two cache side-channel attacks on the timer defense deployed system for comparison.

Given that Perf is able to measure cache hits/misses accurately, the proposed method achieves high performance with fewer AES encryption attempts compared with existing attacks using the timer. In an environment that a timer defense is deployed, our attack succeeds to derive AES secret key, but attacks using the timer do not. To conclude, the attack$_{Perf}$ achieves high performance and accuracy in the AES attack and the precise measurement of cache hits/misses in the multi-core system.

Acknowledgement. This work was supported by the National Research Foundation of Korea (NRF) grant funded by the Korea government (MSIT) (No. NRF-2017R1A2B4010914). MSIT : Ministry of Science and ICT. This work was supported by NRF (National Research Foundation of Korea) Grant funded by the Korean Government (NRF-2018-Fostering Core Leaders of the Future Basic Science Program/Global Ph.D. Fellowship Program).

References

1. Acıiçmez, O., Schindler, W., Koç, Ç.K.: Cache based remote timing attack on the AES. In: Abe, M. (ed.) CT-RSA 2007. LNCS, vol. 4377, pp. 271–286. Springer, Heidelberg (2006). https://doi.org/10.1007/11967668_18
2. Bernstein, D.J.: Cache-Timing Attacks on AES (2005)
3. Bhattacharya, S., Mukhopadhyay, D.: Who watches the watchmen?: utilizing performance monitors for compromising keys of RSA on intel platforms. In: Güneysu, T., Handschuh, H. (eds.) CHES 2015. LNCS, vol. 9293, pp. 248–266. Springer, Heidelberg (2015). https://doi.org/10.1007/978-3-662-48324-4_13
4. Brasser, F., Müller, U., Dmitrienko, A., Kostiainen, K., Capkun, S., Sadeghi, A.R.: Software grand exposure:{SGX} cache attacks are practical. In: 11th {USENIX} Workshop on Offensive Technologies ({WOOT} 17) (2017)
5. Chen, S., Wang, R., Wang, X., Zhang, K.: Side-channel leaks in web applications: a reality today, a challenge tomorrow. In: 2010 IEEE Symposium on Security and Privacy, pp. 191–206. IEEE (2010)
6. Chiappetta, M., Savas, E., Yilmaz, C.: Real time detection of cache-based side-channel attacks using hardware performance counters. Appl. Soft Comput. **49**, 1162–1174 (2016)
7. Demme, J., et al.: On the feasibility of online malware detection with performance counters. In: ACM SIGARCH Computer Architecture News, vol. 41, pp. 559–570. ACM (2013)
8. Disselkoen, C., Kohlbrenner, D., Porter, L., Tullsen, D.: Prime+ abort: a timer-free high-precision l3 cache attack using intel TSX. In: 26th USENIX Security Symposium (USENIX Security 17), pp. 51–67 (2017)

9. Gruss, D., Maurice, C., Wagner, K., Mangard, S.: Flush+Flush: a fast and stealthy cache attack. In: Caballero, J., Zurutuza, U., Rodríguez, R.J. (eds.) DIMVA 2016. LNCS, vol. 9721, pp. 279–299. Springer, Cham (2016). https://doi.org/10.1007/978-3-319-40667-1_14

10. Kuiper, N.H.: Tests concerning random points on a circle. Nederl. Akad. Wetensch. Proc. Ser. A **63**, 38–47 (1960)

11. Liu, F., Yarom, Y., Ge, Q., Heiser, G., Lee, R.B.: Last-level cache side-channel attacks are practical. In: 2015 IEEE Symposium on Security and Privacy, pp. 605–622. IEEE (2015)

12. Osvik, D.A., Shamir, A., Tromer, E.: Cache attacks and countermeasures: the case of AES. In: Pointcheval, D. (ed.) CT-RSA 2006. LNCS, vol. 3860, pp. 1–20. Springer, Heidelberg (2006). https://doi.org/10.1007/11605805_1

13. Uhsadel, L., Georges, A., Verbauwhede, I.: Exploiting hardware performance counters. In: 2008 5th Workshop on Fault Diagnosis and Tolerance in Cryptography, pp. 59–67. IEEE (2008)

14. Vattikonda, B.C., Das, S., Shacham, H.: Eliminating fine grained timers in xen. In: Proceedings of the 3rd ACM Workshop on Cloud Computing Security Workshop, pp. 41–46. ACM (2011)

15. Xia, Y., Liu, Y., Chen, H., Zang, B.: Cfimon: detecting violation of control flow integrity using performance counters. In: IEEE/IFIP International Conference on Dependable Systems and Networks (DSN 2012), pp. 1–12. IEEE (2012)

16. Yarom, Y., Falkner, K.: Flush+ reload: a high resolution, low noise, l3 cache side-channel attack. In: 23rd USENIX Security Symposium (USENIX Security 14), pp. 719–732 (2014)

17. Zhang, Y., Juels, A., Reiter, M.K., Ristenpart, T.: Cross-tenant side-channel attacks in PaaS clouds. In: Proceedings of the 2014 ACM SIGSAC Conference on Computer and Communications Security, pp. 990–1003. ACM (2014)

Optimized SIKE Round 2 on 64-bit ARM

Hwajeong Seo[1]([✉]), Amir Jalali[2], and Reza Azarderakhsh[2]

[1] IT Department, Hansung University, Seoul, South Korea
hwajeong84@gmail.com
[2] Department of Computer and Electrical Engineering and Computer Science,
Florida Atlantic University, Boca Raton, FL, USA
{ajalali2016,razarderakhsh}@fau.edu

Abstract. In this work, we present the first highly-optimized implementation of Supersingular Isogeny Key Encapsulation (SIKE) submitted to NIST's second round of post quantum standardization process, on 64-bit ARMv8 processors. To the best of our knowledge, this work is the first optimized implementation of SIKE round 2 on 64-bit ARM over SIKEp434 and SIKEp610. The proposed library is explicitly optimized for these two security levels and provides constant-time implementation of the SIKE mechanism on ARMv8-powered embedded devices. We adapt different optimization techniques to reduce the total number of underlying arithmetic operations on the filed level. In particular, the benchmark results on embedded processors equipped with ARM Cortex-A53@1.536 GHz show that the entire SIKE round 2 key encapsulation mechanism takes only 84 ms at NIST's security level 1. Considering SIKE's extremely small key size in comparison to other candidates, our result implies that SIKE is one of the promising candidates for key encapsulation mechanism on embedded devices in the quantum era.

Keywords: Post-quantum cryptography · Isogeny-based cryptography · 64-bit ARM processor · ARM assembly · Key encapsulation mechanism

1 Introduction

Initiated by the National Institute of Standards and Technology (NIST), Post-Quantum Cryptography (PQC) has been elevated to a standardization process to solicit, evaluate, and standardize one or more quantum-resistant public-key cryptographic algorithms [17]. To prepare for security concerns caused by quantum computers, in 2016, NIST called for the cryptographic algorithms which were assumed to be resistance against high-scale quantum computers. These proposals provided key encapsulation mechanism (KEM) or digital signature algorithms from different arithmetic structures, resulting in different characteristics and parameters. Recently, NIST announced approved candidates for round 2 which are the most promising candidates in terms of security, performance, and compatibility with current technology. For the key encapsulation mechanism,

© Springer Nature Switzerland AG 2020
I. You (Ed.): WISA 2019, LNCS 11897, pp. 341–353, 2020.
https://doi.org/10.1007/978-3-030-39303-8_26

only 17 candidates made it through to the second round for being evaluated and analyzed from different perspectives.

Different PQC candidates are constructed on hard mathematical problems which are assumed to be impossible to solve even for large-scale quantum computers. These problems can be categorized into five main categories: code-based cryptography, lattice-based cryptography, hash-based cryptography, multivariate cryptography, and supersingular isogeny-based cryptography, see, for instance [7].

Supersingular Isogeny Key Encapsulation (SIKE) mechanism is one of the PQC candidates which is constructed on the hardness of solving isogeny maps between supersingular elliptic curves. In fact, SIKE is the only candidate that offers the quantum-resistance cryptographic construction over elliptic curves, resulting in well-known structures in implementation perspective. The proposed key encapsulation mechanism is derived from the original Jao-De Feo's Diffie-Hellman key-exchange and public-key encryption algorithms [14]. However, constructing cryptographic structures from hardness of supersingular isogeny graphs was introduced by Charels-Lauter-Goren [6].

The first round SIKE submission [4] offered three different security levels known as SIKEp503, SIKEp751, and SIKEp964. According to the best known quantum attacks on solving supersingular isogeny problem by that time, the proposed security levels met NIST's level 1, 3, and 5 requirements, respectively.

However, recent studies on the cost of solving isogeny problem on quantum computers by Adj et al. [1] revealed that the security assumptions for SIKE was too conservative. In fact, a set of realistic models of quantum computation on solving Computational Supersingular Isogeny (CSSI) problem in [1] suggests that the Oorschot-Wiener golden collision search is the most powerful attack on the CSSI problem, resulting in significant improvement on the SIKE's classical and quantum security levels.

Accordingly, the second round SIKE [3] offers a new set of security levels which are more realistic and provide significant improvement on the key encapsulation performance. In particular, decreasing the bit-length of SIKE's primes translates to notable performance improvement, making this scheme suitable for many potential applications on low-end and embedded devices.

In this work, we provide a full report on the highly-optimized implementation of SIKE on 64-bit ARM processors over all the proposed security levels. In particular, the reference optimized implementation of SIKE [3] on 64-bit ARM only targets two security levels, i.e., SIKEp503 and SIKEp751. Therefore, in this work, we address this shortcoming by providing the KEM full benchmarks on different security levels which provide a reference for the performance analysis of this scheme for the second round.

Our proposed library takes advantage of state-of-the-art engineering techniques as well as low level assembly optimizations. We studied different approaches for finite field arithmetic implementation over SIKE's new primes. Our benchmark results offer significant improvement in performance compared to portable implementation, suggesting the possible integration of this scheme on mobile devices in the future.

Alice	Bob
$sk_A : m_A, n_A \in_R \mathbf{Z}/\ell_A^{e_A}\mathbf{Z}$	$sk_B : m_B, n_B \in_R \mathbf{Z}/\ell_B^{e_B}\mathbf{Z}$
$\phi_A := E/\langle[m_A]P_A + [n_A]Q_A\rangle$	$\phi_B := E/\langle[m_B]P_B + [n_B]Q_B\rangle$
$pk_A : \phi_A(P_B), \phi_A(Q_B), E_A$	$pk_B : \phi_B(P_A), \phi_B(Q_A), E_B$

$$\xrightarrow{\quad pk_A \quad}$$
$$\xleftarrow{\quad pk_B \quad}$$

$E_{AB} :=$	$E_{BA} :=$
$E_B/\langle[m_A]\phi_B(P_A) + [n_A]\phi_B(Q_A)\rangle$	$E_A/\langle[m_B]\phi_A(P_B) + [n_B]\phi_A(Q_B)\rangle$
Shared secret: $j(E_{AB})$	**Shared secret:** $j(E_{BA})$

Fig. 1. SIDH key exchange protocol.

2 Background

In this section, we briefly review the SIDH protocol and the required steps for Alice and Bob to generate a shared secret. Furthermore, we describe the SIKE, a post-quantum key encapsulation mechanism from isogenies of supersingular elliptic curves which was submitted to NIST's PQC standardization competition. We refer the readers to [4,14] for further details.

2.1 SIDH Key Exchange

In 2011, Jao and De Feo [14] proposed the SIDH, a quantum resistant key exchange protocol from isogenies of supersingular elliptic curves. Similar to classical Diffie-Hellman key exchange, SIDH protocol is constructed over some public parameters which are agreed upon by communication parties prior to key exchange.

Public Parameters. Fix a prime p of the form $p = \ell_A^{e_A} \cdot \ell_B^{e_B} \cdot f \pm 1$ where ℓ_A and ℓ_B are small primes, e_A and e_B are positive integers, and f is a very small cofactor. We define a based supersingular elliptic curve E over $\mathbb{F}_{p^2}$ with cardinality $\#E = (\ell_A^{e_A} \cdot \ell_B^{e_B} \cdot f \mp 1)^2$, and base points $\{P_A, Q_A\}$ and $\{P_B, Q_B\}$ from the torsion subgroups $E[\ell_A^{e_A}]$ and $E[\ell_B^{e_B}]$ respectively, such that $\langle P_A, Q_A \rangle = E[\ell_A^{e_A}]$ and $\langle P_B, Q_B \rangle = E[\ell_A^{e_B}]$.

Key Exchange Protocol. Alice randomly chooses two integers $m_A, n_A \in \mathbb{Z}/\ell_A^{e_A}\mathbb{Z}$, not both divisible by ℓ_A as her secret key and computes an isogeny $\phi_A : E \to E_A$ using kernel $R_A := \langle[m_A]P_A + [n_A]Q_A\rangle$. Alice also computes the image points $\{\phi_A(P_B), \phi_A(Q_B)\} \subset E_A$ by applying her secret isogeny ϕ_A to the public basis P_B and Q_B. She sends $\phi_A(P_B), \phi_A(Q_B)$ and E_A to Bob as her public key. Bob also selects random elements $m_B, n_B \in \mathbb{Z}/\ell_B^{e_B}\mathbb{Z}$, not both divisible by ℓ_B and computes a secret isogeny $\phi_B : E \to E_B$ from kernel $R_B := \langle[m_B]P_B + [n_B]Q_B\rangle$, along with image points $\{\phi_B(P_A), \phi_B(Q_A)\} \subset E_B$. He sends his public key, i.e., $\phi_B(P_A), \phi_B(Q_A)$ and E_B to Alice.

In the second round of key exchange, Alice uses Bob's public key $(\phi_B(P_A), \phi_B(Q_A), E_B)$ and computes an isogeny $\phi'_A : E_B \to E_{AB}$ from kernel equal to $\langle [m_A]\phi_B(P_A) + [n_A]\phi_B(Q_A) \rangle$; Similarly, Bob computes an isogeny $\phi'_B : E_A \to E_{BA}$ having kernel $\langle [m_B]\phi_A(P_B) + [n_B]\phi_A(Q_B) \rangle$ using Alice's public key. Since the common j-invariant of E_{AB} and E_{BA} are equal, they use this value to form a secret shared key. The entire SIDH key exchange protocol is illustrated in Fig. 1.

2.2   SIKE Mechanism

SIKE mechanism is constructed by applying a transformation of Hofheinz, Hövelmanns, and Kiltz [11] to the supersingular isogeny Public Key Encryption (PKE) scheme described in [14]. It is an actively secure key encapsulation mechanism (IND-CCA KEM) which addresses the static key vulnerability of SIDH due to active attacks in [10].

Alice

Key generation:
$\text{pk}_A = [E_A, \phi_A(P_B), \phi_A(Q_B)]$
$s \in_R \{0,1\}^t$

Bob

Encapsulation:
$m \in_R \{0,1\}^t$
$r = H_1(m \parallel \text{pk}_A)$
$\text{pk}_B(r) = [E_B, \phi_B(P_A), \phi_B(Q_A)]$
$j = j(E_{BA})$
$c = (c_0, c_1) = (\text{pk}_B(r), H_2(j) \oplus m)$
$K = H_3(m \parallel c)$

$\xleftarrow{\quad (c_0, c_1) \quad}$

Decapsulation:
$j = j(E_{AB})$
$m' = c_1 \oplus H_2(j)$
$r' = H_1(m' \parallel \text{pk}_A)$
If $(\text{pk}_B(r') = c_0) \to K = H_3(m' \parallel c)$
If $(\text{pk}_B(r') \neq c_0) \to K = H_3(s \parallel c)$

Fig. 2. SIKE mechanism.

Public Parameters. Similar to SIDH, SIKE can be defined over a prime of the form $p = \ell_A^{e_A} \cdot \ell_B^{e_B} \cdot f \pm 1$. However, for efficiency reasons, $\ell_A = 2$, $\ell_B = 3$, and $f = 1$ are fixed, thus the SIKE prime has the form of $p = 2^{e_A} \cdot 3^{e_B} - 1$. The starting supersingular elliptic curve $E_0/\mathbb{F}_{p^2} : y^2 = x^3 + x$ with cardinality equal to $(2^{e_A} \cdot 3^{e_B})^2$, along with base points $\langle P_A, Q_A \rangle = E_0[2^{e_A}]$ and $\langle P_B, Q_B \rangle = E_0[3^{e_B}]$ are defined as public parameters.

Key Encapsulation Mechanism. The key encapsulation mechanism can be divided into three main operations: Alice's key generation, Bob's key encapsulation, and Alice's key decapsulation. We describe each operation in the following. Figure 2 presents the entire key encapsulation mechanism in a nutshell.

Key Generation. Alice randomly chooses an integer $sk_A \in \mathbb{Z}/2^{e_A}\mathbb{Z}$ and by applying an isogeny $\phi_A : E_0 \rightarrow E_A$ with kernel $R_A := \langle P_A + [sk_A]Q_A \rangle$ to the base points $\{P_B, Q_B\}$, computes her public key $pk_A = [E_A, \phi_A(P_B), \phi_A(Q_B)]$. Moreover, she generates an t-bit[1] random sequence $s \in_R \{0,1\}^t$.

Encapsulation. Bob generates an t-bit random message m $\in_R \{0,1\}^t$, concatenates it with Alice's public key pk_A and computes an e_B-bit hash value r using cSHAKE256 hash function H_1, taking $m \parallel pk_A$ as the input. Using r, he applies a secret isogeny $\phi_B : E0 \rightarrow EB$ to the base points $\{P_A, Q_A\}$ and forms his public key $pk_B(r) = [E_B, \phi_B(P_A), \phi_B(Q_A)]$. Bob also computes the common j-invariant of curve E_{BA} by applying another isogeny $\phi'_B : EA \rightarrow E_{BA}$ using Alice's public key. Bob forms a ciphertext $c = (c_0, c_1)$, such that:

$$c = (c_0, c_1) = (pk_B(r), H_2(j(E_{BA})) \oplus m),$$

where H_2 is a cSHAKE256 hash with a custom length output and a defined initialization parameter. Finally, Bob computes the shared secret as $K = H_3(m \parallel c)$ and sends c to Alice.

Decapsulation. Upon receipt of c, Alice computes the common j-invariant of E_{AB} by applying her secret isogeny to E_B. She computes $m' = c_1 \oplus H_2(j(E_{AB}))$ and $r' = H_1(m' \parallel pk_A)$. Finally, she validates Bob's public key by computing $pk_B(r')$ and comparing it with c_0. She generates the same shared secret $K = H_3(m' \parallel c)$ if the public key is valid, otherwise she outputs a random value $K = H_3(c \parallel s)$ to be resistant against active attacks.

3   Target Architecture

ARMv8 Cortex-A, or simply ARMv8, is the latest generation of ARM architectures targeted at the "application" profile. It includes the typical 32-bit architecture, called "AArch32", and advanced 64-bit architecture named "AArch64" with its associated instruction set "A64" [2]. AArch32 preserves backwards compatibility with ARMv7 and supports the so-called "A32" and "T2" instructions sets, which correspond to the traditional 32-bit and Thumb instruction sets, respectively. AArch64 comes equipped with 31 general purpose 64-bit registers (i.e. X0∼X30) and one zero register (i.e. XZR), and an instruction set supporting 32-bit and 64-bit operations. The significant register expansion means that with AArch64 the maximum register capacity is expanded to 1,984 bits (i.e. 31 × 64, a 4x increase with respect to ARMv7.).

---

[1] The value of t is defined by the implementation parameters.

ARMv8 processors started to dominate the smartphone market soon after their first release in 2011, and nowadays they are widely used in various high-end smartphones (e.g. iPhone, Huawei Mate and Samsung Galaxy series). Since this architecture is used primarily in embedded systems and smartphones, efficient and compact implementations are of special interest.

ARMv8 processor supports powerful 64-bit wise unsigned integer multiplication instructions. Our implementation of modular multiplication uses the AArch64 architecture and makes extensive use of the following multiply instructions:

- MUL (unsigned multiplication, low part):
  MUL X0, X1, X2 computes X0 ← (X1 × X2) mod 2^{64}.
- UMULH (unsigned multiplication, high part):
  UMULH X0, X1, X2 computes X0 ← (X1 × X2)/2^{64}.

The two instructions above are required to compute a full 64-bit multiplication of the form 128-bit ← 64 × 64-bit, namely, the MUL instruction computes the lower 64-bit half of the product while UMULH computes the higher 64-bit half.

For the addition and subtraction operations, ADDS and SUBS instructions ensure 64-bit wise results, respectively. The detailed descriptions are as follows:

- ADDS (unsigned addition):
  ADDS X0, X1, X2 computes {CARRY,X0} ← (X1 + X2).
- SUB (unsigned subtraction):
  SUBS X0, X1, X2 computes {BORROW,X0} ← (X1 − X2).

4   Optimized Field Arithmetic Implementation

There is a number of works in the literature that study the ARMv8 instructions to implement multi-precision multiplication or the full Montgomery multiplication for "SIDH friendly" modulus [12,13,16]. In [12], Jalali et al. implemented 751-bit and 964-bit finite field multiplication. They utilized the Comba method (i.e. column-wise multiplication) for both cases [8]. In particular, they used 2-level Karatsuba for 964-bit finite field multiplication, which shows 23.9% performance enhancements than conventional Comba method. In [16], Seo et al. optimized the 503-bit finite field multiplication for SIKEp503. They also used the Comba method with 2-level Karatsuba method to enhance the performance of multiplication. Furthermore, they optimized the MAC (Multiplication ACcumulation) routines to avoid the pipeline stalls.

Recently, two novel SIKE protocols (i.e. SIKEp434 and SIKEp610) for NIST Post Quantum Cryptography competition were suggested, which meet NIST security level 1 and 3, respectively [3]. However, previous works do not show the optimized results for both protocols. In this paper, we show the first practical implementations of SIKEp434 and SIKEp610 protocols on 64-bit ARMv8-A processors. In order to achieve high performance, the arithmetic for SIKEp434 and SIKEp610 is optimized to utilize the ARMv8-A ability fully. To describe the multi-precision arithmetic, we used following notations. Let A and B be operands of length m bits each. Each operand is written as $A = (A[n-1], ..., A[1], A[0])$ and $B = (B[n-1], ..., B[1], B[0])$, where $n = \lceil m/w \rceil$ is the number of words to represent operands, m is operand length, and w is the computer word size (i.e. 64-bit). The addition result $(C = A + B)$ is represented as $C = (C[n-1], ..., C[1], C[0])$. For the multiplication $(C = A \times B)$, the result is represented as $C = (C[2n-1], ..., C[1], C[0])$.

4.1   Finite Field Addition and Subtraction

In the beginning, the finite field addition and subtraction operations need to perform addition and subtraction operations, respectively. Afterward, the intermediate results are reduced, when the carry or borrow bit is set. In order to avoid the timing attack, both reduction routines are performed without conditional statements (i.e. constant timing). Instead, we used the masked modular reduction approach, which always perform regular routines, regardless of the carry or borrow bit. When the carry or borrow bit is set, the mask value is set to $2^{64} - 1$. Otherwise, the mask value is set to 0. With the mask value, the modulus is determined whether it is modulus or 0.

For 434-bit addition or subtraction operation, we utilized 14 general purpose registers to store the operands (i.e. $2 \times \lfloor 434/64 \rfloor$) since each operand requires 7 registers. In particular, two limbs of 434-bit modulus are $2^{64} - 1$ (i.e. 0xFFFFFFFFFFFFFFFF). We only set one limb to $2^{64} - 1$ and use it twice for computations, which reduces one operand setting overheads.

For 610-bit addition or subtraction operation, we utilized 20 general purpose registers to retain all operands (i.e. $2 \times \lfloor 610/64 \rfloor$) since each operand requires 10 registers. Similarly, three limbs of 610-bit modulus are set to $2^{64} - 1$ (i.e. 0xFFFFFFFFFFFFFFFF). This limb is used three times with only one memory access, which reduces two operand setting overheads.

4.2   Multiplication

In previous works, they used the Comba method (i.e. column-wise method) to improve the multi-precision multiplication. The Comba method performs the partial products in column-wise, which ensures small number of registers for maintaining the intermediate results. In Fig. 3, the part of Multiplication ACcumulation (MAC) routine in column-wise method for 64-bit ARMv8 processors is described. The example performs the three partial products $(A[i] \times B[j]$, $A[i + 1] \times B[j - 1]$, and $A[i + 2] \times B[j - 2])$ and accumulates them to the intermediate results. In each MAC routine, two multiplication (MUL_LOW and MUL_HIGH) and three addition operations (ACC0, ACC1, and ACC2) are required. For one limb multiplication, we need three addition operations. For that reason, n-limb multiplication requires $3 \times n^2$ addition operations.

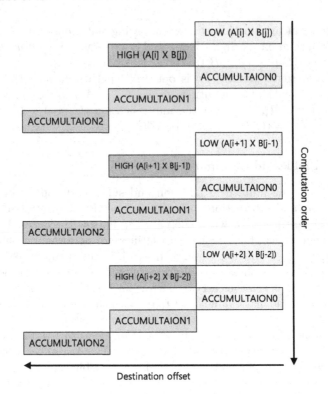

Fig. 3. Part of column-wise multiplication for ARMv8

In this work, we target the relatively shorter modulus (i.e. 434-bit) than previous works (i.e. 503-bit or 751-bit). We decide to use the row-wise multiplication, which requires $2n + 2$ registers ($n + 1$ for operands and $n + 1$ for intermediate results), where n, m, and w are $\lfloor m/w \rfloor$, operand length, and word size, respectively. Under 64-bit processor setting, the n is set to 7 for 434-bit ($\lfloor 434/64 \rfloor$). Considering that ARMv8 supports 31 64-bit registers, the required number of registers for 434-bit can be retained in the registers. In Fig. 4, the part of MAC routine in row-wise method for 64-bit ARMv8 processors is described. The example performs the three partial products ($A[i] \times B[j]$, $A[i] \times B[j+1]$, and $A[i] \times B[j+2]$) and accumulates them to the intermediate results. The number of addition for three partial products in Fig. 4 are 8 (i.e. $2 \times (n + 1)$ where n is 3.). For the n-limb multiplication, it requires $2 \times n \times (n+1)$ addition operations. The comparison of multiplication methods in terms of the number of addition operations depending on the number of limb are given in Table 1. Compared with the column-wise method (i.e. product-scanning), the row-wise method (i.e. operand-scanning) requires less number of addition operations for accumulation routines. For the 7-limb case (i.e. 434-bit), the row-wise method reduces the number of addition operations by 35 times than the column-wise method. The multiplication is performed in original row-wise multiplication rather than row-wise multiplication with Karatsuba method. The Karatsuba method is also working for 7-limb case but it generates a number of sub-routines to perform and store the intermediate results, which requires additional operations and memory accesses [15].

Table 1. Comparison of multiplication methods, in terms of the number of addition operations depending on the number of limb.

Method	3	4	5	6	7
Operand scanning	24	40	60	84	112
Product scanning	27	48	75	108	147

For the 610-bit multiplication, the operands $A = (A[9], \ldots, A[0])$ and $B = (B[9], \ldots, B[0])$ need 20 64-bit registers. Except the operands, we also need registers for intermediate results and temporal storage. Due to the limited number of registers, we only maintain the half number of operands in the registers and load the remaining operands on demand.

We first compute the lower 320-bit multiplication $R_L \leftarrow A[4 \sim 0] \cdot B[4 \sim 0])$ using the row-wise method that requires 25 MUL, 25 UMULH and 52 addition instructions for accumulating the partial products. Second, we compute the higher 310-bit multiplication $R_H \leftarrow A[9 \sim 5] \cdot B[9 \sim 5]$ similarly. Third, we compute the subtractions and absolute values $|A[4 \sim 0] - A[9 \sim 5]|$ and $|B[4 \sim 0] - B[9 \sim 5]|$ and proceed to the last 310-bit multiplication $R_M \leftarrow |A[4 \sim 0] - A[9 \sim 5]| \cdot |B[4 \sim 0] - B[9 \sim 5]|$. Finally, we obtain the result by performing the accumulation step $R_H \cdot 2^{610} + (R_L + R_H - R_M) \cdot 2^{310} + R_L$. Since the multiplication uses all available registers, 12 callee-saved registers $(X19 \sim X30)$ are stored into the stack. The multiplication is also designed to reduce the pipeline stalls. The multiplication and addition/subtraction operations use different instruction group. They can hide each others costs. Based on the above observation, we engineer a multi-precision multiplication to hide the addition costs into the multiplication. At the lowest level, we implement multi-precision multiplication using the row-wise method based on the following multiplication/addition instruction sequence:

$$\vdots$$

```
MUL   X7, X6, X2
ADCS  X18, X18, X13
MUL   X8, X6, X3
ADCS  X19, X19, X14
MUL   X9, X6, X4
ADCS  X20, X20, X15
MUL   X10, X6, X5
ADCS  X21, X21, X16
```

$$\vdots$$

We ensure that the destination of MUL instruction is not used for the source of following ADCS instructions. This approach avoids the pipeline stalls. Second, MUL and ADCS instructions are performed one by one to hide the each costs. As will be shown in Sect. 5, the proposed implementation achieved the high performance (see Table 2).

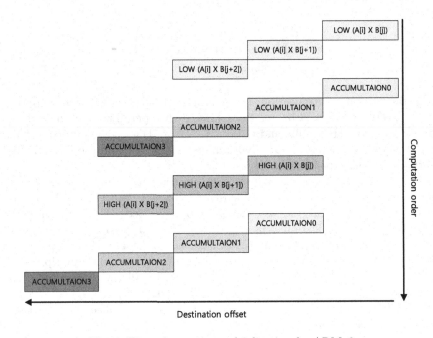

Fig. 4. Part of row-wise multiplication for ARMv8

4.3 Reduction

In this section, we adapt the techniques described in previous sections to implement modular multiplication for the supersingular isogeny-based protocols SIDH and SIKE. Specifically, we target the parameter sets based on the primes p434 and p610 [3].

Multi-precision modular multiplication is the most expensive operation for the implementation of SIKE [9,14]. In particular, Montgomery multiplication for SIKE can be efficiently exploited and further simplified by taking advantage of so-called "Montgomery-friendly" modulus. The advantage of using Montgomery multiplication for "SIDH-friendly" primes was recently confirmed by Bos and Friedberger [5], who studied and compared different approaches, including Barrett reduction. Recent works by Seo et al. also utilized the Montgomery multiplication for SIKEp503 protocols [16].

Based on the observation above, we choose the Montgomery multiplication to implement SIDH-friendly modular arithmetic for SIKEp434 and SIKEp610 protocols. The approach reduces almost half of partial products since the lower part is set to 0. In order to reduce the memory accesses, we keep as many results as possible in the registers. Since the Montgomery multiplication performs the partial products with modulus and quotient (Quotient is intermediate results multiplied by constant m'), we maintained all quotients in the registers and used them directly. The technique reduces the $2 \times (n + 1)$ number of memory accesses for $n + 1$ load and $n + 1$ store operations.

5   Performance Result

In this section, we evaluate the performance of the proposed algorithms for 64-bit ARMv8-A processors. All our implementations were written in assembly language and complied with optimization level -03.

We implemented the multi-precision multiplication algorithm described in Sect. 4.2 and Montgomery reduction in Sect. 4.3. We integrated our implementation of the Montgomery multiplication for ARMv8-A into the SIKE round 2 library [3].

Table 2 summarizes the results of different software implementations of the SIKEp434 and SIKEp610 arithmetic on ARMv8-A processor: a 1.536 GHz ARM Cortex-A53 processor. Since this is first work for SIKEp434 and SIKEp610 on ARMv8-A processors, we compare the results with the SIKE round 2 reference code. The *unoptimized* reference implementation is written in C using the SIKE round 2 library [3]. In this case, the proposed arithmetic implementations show much higher performance than reference work. In particular, finite field multiplication and inversion operations show performance enhancements by 4.96x and 4.98x, respectively.

Table 3 summarizes the results of different software implementations of the SIKEp434 and SIKEp610 protocols on ARMv8-A processor. Compared with reference work, the proposed implementation is between 3.83 and 3.42 times faster for the computation of the SIKE full protocols. Considering that the target processor is 1.536 GHZ, the SIKEp434 and SIKEp610 requires only 0.084 and 0.30 s, respectively.

Compared with the other security levels, the performance depends on the length of modulus. The SIKEp434 shows the highest performance and the SIKEp751 shows the lowest performance as we expected.

Table 2. Comparison of implementations of the SIKEp434 and SIKEp610 arithmetic on ARMv8 Cortex-A53 based processors. Timings are reported in terms of clock cycles.

Implementation	Language	Protocol	Timings [cc]			
			$\mathbb{F}_p$ add	$\mathbb{F}_p$ sub	$\mathbb{F}_p$ mul	$\mathbb{F}_p$ inv
SIKE R2 [3]	C	SIKEp434	172	129	3,110	1,648,372
This work	ASM		71	63	691	380,711
SIKE R2 [3]	C	SIKEp610	257	187	6,599	4,800,694
This work	ASM		100	91	1,329	963,064

Table 3. Comparison of implementations of the SIKE protocols on ARMv8 Cortex-A53 based processors. Timings are reported in terms of clock cycles.

Implementation	Language	Protocol	Timings [cc]	Timings [$cc \times 10^6$]			
			$\mathbb{F}_p$ mul	KeyGen	Encaps	Decaps	Total
SIKE R2 [3]	C	SIKEp434	3,110	114	186	199	499
This work	ASM		691	30	49	52	130
Seo et al. [16]	ASM	SIKEp503	849	38	63	67	168
SIKE R2 [3]	C	SIKEp610	6,599	344	634	615	1,593
This work	ASM		1,329	99	183	183	465
Seo et al. [16]	ASM	SIKEp751	2,450	164	265	284	713

6   Conclusion

This paper presented high-speed implementation of SIKE Round 2 on high-end 64-bit ARMv8 Cortex-A53 processors. A combination of several optimization methods yields very efficient modular multiplications for SIKEp434 and SIKEp610 protocols that are shown, for example, to be approximately 4.96x faster than the normal modular multiplication implementations for "SIDH-friendly" modulus on a 64-bit ARMv8 Cortex-A53 processors. The optimized implementation, which push further the performance of post-quantum supersingular isogeny-based protocols, are 3.42x faster than the previously implementations of SIDHp610 on the same processors. Furthermore, we integrated our fast modular arithmetic implementations, compact prime SIDHp434, and optimal strategy for isogeny computations into Microsoft's SIDH library. A 128-bit full key-exchange execution over optimal prime SIDHp434 is performed in about 0.084 s on a 1.536 GHz ARMv8 Cortex-A53 processors, which shows the practicality of isogeny based post-quantum cryptography over mobile devices.

Acknowledgement. This work of Hwajeong Seo was supported by Institute for Information communications Technology Planning Evaluation (IITP) grant funded by the Korea government(MSIT) (<Q|Crypton>, No. 2019-0-00033, Study on Quantum Security Evaluation of Cryptography based on Computational Quantum Complexity).

This work of Reza Azarderakhsh and Amir Jalali is supported in parts by NSF CNS-1801341 and NIST-60NANB16D246.

References

1. Adj, G., Cervantes-Vázquez, D., Chi-Domínguez, J., Menezes, A., Rodríguez-Henríquez, F.: On the cost of computing isogenies between supersingular elliptic curves. In: Cid, C., Jacobson Jr., M. (eds.) SAC 2018. LNCS, vol. 11349, pp. 322–343. Springer, Cham (2018). https://doi.org/10.1007/978-3-030-10970-7_15

2. ARM Limited. ARM architecture reference manual ARMv8, for ARMv8-A architecture profile (2013–2017). https://static.docs.arm.com/ddi0487/ca/DDI0487C_a_armv8_arm.pdf

3. Azarderakhsh, R., et al.: Supersingular Isogeny Key Encapsulation - Submission to the NIST's post-quantum cryptography standardization process, round 2 (2019). https://csrc.nist.gov/projects/post-quantum-cryptography/round-2-submissions/SIKE.zip

4. Azarderakhsh, R., et al.: Supersingular Isogeny Key Encapsulation - Submission to the NIST's post-quantum cryptography standardization process (2017). https://csrc.nist.gov/CSRC/media/Projects/Post-Quantum-Cryptography/documents/round-1/submissions/SIKE.zip

5. Bos, J.W., Friedberger, S.: Fast arithmetic modulo $2^x p^y \pm 1$. In: IEEE Symposium on Computer Arithmetic (ARITH 2017), pp. 148–155. IEEE (2017)

6. Charles, D.X., Lauter, K.E., Goren, E.Z.: Cryptographic hash functions from expander graphs. J. Cryptol. **22**(1), 93–113 (2009)

7. Chen, L., et al.: Report on post-quantum cryptography. US Department of Commerce, National Institute of Standards and Technology (2016)

8. Comba, P.G.: Exponentiation cryptosystems on the IBM PC. IBM Syst. J. **29**(4), 526–538 (1990)

9. Costello, C., Longa, P., Naehrig, M.: Efficient algorithms for supersingular isogeny Diffie-Hellman. In: Robshaw, M., Katz, J. (eds.) CRYPTO 2016. LNCS, vol. 9814, pp. 572–601. Springer, Heidelberg (2016). https://doi.org/10.1007/978-3-662-53018-4_21

10. Galbraith, S.D., Petit, C., Shani, B., Ti, Y.B.: On the security of supersingular isogeny cryptosystems. In: Cheon, J.H., Takagi, T. (eds.) ASIACRYPT 2016. LNCS, vol. 10031, pp. 63–91. Springer, Heidelberg (2016). https://doi.org/10.1007/978-3-662-53887-6_3

11. Hofheinz, D., Hövelmanns, K., Kiltz, E.: A modular analysis of the Fujisaki-Okamoto transformation. In: Kalai, Y., Reyzin, L. (eds.) TCC 2017. LNCS, vol. 10677, pp. 341–371. Springer, Cham (2017). https://doi.org/10.1007/978-3-319-70500-2_12

12. Jalali, A., Azarderakhsh, R., Kermani, M.M., Jao, D.: Supersingular isogeny Diffie-Hellman key exchange on 64-bit ARM. IEEE Trans. Dependable Secure Comput. **PP**, 1 (2017)

13. Jalali, A., Azarderakhsh, R., Mozaffari-Kermani, M.: Efficient post-quantum undeniable signature on 64-Bit ARM. In: Adams, C., Camenisch, J. (eds.) SAC 2017. LNCS, vol. 10719, pp. 281–298. Springer, Cham (2018). https://doi.org/10.1007/978-3-319-72565-9_14

14. Jao, D., De Feo, L.: Towards quantum-resistant cryptosystems from supersingular elliptic curve isogenies. In: Yang, B.-Y. (ed.) PQCrypto 2011. LNCS, vol. 7071, pp. 19–34. Springer, Heidelberg (2011). https://doi.org/10.1007/978-3-642-25405-5_2

15. Montgomery, P.L.: Five, six, and seven-term Karatsuba-like formulae. IEEE Trans. Comput. **54**(3), 362–369 (2005)

16. Seo, H., Liu, Z., Longa, P., Hu, Z.: SIDH on ARM: faster modular multiplications for faster post-quantum supersingular isogeny key exchange. IACR Trans. Cryptogr. Hardware Embedded Syst. 1–20 (2018)

17. The National Institute of Standards and Technology (NIST). Post-quantum cryptography standardization (2017–2018). https://csrc.nist.gov/projects/post-quantum-cryptography/post-quantum-cryptography-standardization

Selected Security Issues

Shedding Light on Dark Korea: An In-Depth Analysis and Profiling of the Dark Web in Korea

Jinhee Lee, Younggee Hong, Hyunsoo Kwon, and Junbeom Hur[(⊠)]

Department of Computer Science and Engineering, Korea University,
145, Anam-ro, 136-701 Seongbuk-gu, Seoul, Korea
{akrso93,gee308,hs_kwon,jbhur}@korea.ac.kr

Abstract. The Dark Web sites are operated over anonymity-preserving protocols like Tor, making users of the Dark Web services more resilient to identification and monitoring. Although some previous works have focused on understanding the size of the Dark Web services and investigating their criminal activities, there is a lack of research on chronological analysis and in-depth profiling of the Dark Web sites, particularly in South Korea. Therefore, in this study, we implemented a Dark Web crawling system, and collected seed and sub Dark Web URLs using it. Then, the 3,000 Dark Web sites from the seed URLs were selected and their web pages were captured for profiling. An in-depth analysis was then conducted on the collected 3,000 Dark Web sites, and an intensive categorization was performed on the basis of their major criminal activities. We then carried out an in-depth profiling for top 3 Korean Dark Web sites to investigate cyber criminal activities in South Korea. In the profiling, criminal activities were collected and analyzed in a chronological point of view. Personal information leakage and Sybil IDs in the Dark Web were also identified based on the PGP keys we collected.

Keywords: Dark Web · Deep Web · Profiling · Sybil identity detection

1 Introduction

The Surface Web is comprised of web sites that are visible and readily accessible by normal users using standard web search engines such as Google [3], Yahoo [8], and Bing [1]. Whereas, the Deep Web is composed of special web sites that are invisible to normal users, and only accessible by specific users who have the authority. For example, it can include personal email, and online services requiring authentication or payment. The particular part of the Deep Web featuring anonymity through the use of special software is called the Dark Web [9]. The Dark Web is developed for liberty of expression and free consumption of media initially, but it is also widely used in illegal activities such as trading illegal drug and personal information using cryptocurrencies such as Monero [24] and

© Springer Nature Switzerland AG 2020
I. You (Ed.): WISA 2019, LNCS 11897, pp. 357–369, 2020.
https://doi.org/10.1007/978-3-030-39303-8_27

Zcash [14], and maintaining forums and media exchange for pedophiles and terrorists [22]. Thereby, several studies [12,18,19] focused on how to discover, access, crawl Tor hidden services of the Dark Web. While the other studies focused on how to analyze the illegal transactions of cryptocurrencies in it [13,15,20].

While the previous studies have helped to better understand the hidden services and structure of the Dark Web, a comprehensive analysis of the current Dark Web services and its chronological implications is still missing. To achieve it, in this paper, we conduct an in-depth analysis of the Dark Web services by gathering more than 90% web pages from approximately 3,000 Dark Web sites we have found. Then, we focus on the top 3 Dark Web services in Korea, and carry out detailed profiling of them.

Our study has the following contributions:

- We developed a Dark Web crawling system to find hidden Dark Web services. We collected about 40,000 seed Deep Web URLs using our crawling system, and identified and extracted 3,000 Dark Web services from them. Page collection accuracy was measured in comparison to a reference set and an existing normal search engine.
- An in-depth analysis of the criminal activities occurring in the 3,000 Dark Web sites was performed. Then, they are categorized based on the major activities.
- Among the 8 Dark Web sites in South Korea we found, we carried out an in-depth profiling of top 3 Dark Web sites, which constitute most of the cyber criminal activities in South Korea. In the profiling, criminal activities are collected and analyzed in a chronological point of view. Then, personal information leakage was measured, and Sybil identities (IDs) were also identified based on personal PGP keys we collected. To the best of our knowledge, this is the first paper to detect Sybil IDs using PGP keys in the wild.

This paper is organized as follows. Section 2 summarizes the previous works that are related to our research. Section 3 introduces our Dark Web crawling system and its implementation issues. Section 4 shows the analysis results of the Dark Web data we collected using our crawling system. Section 5 analyzes South Korea's top 3 Dark Web sites and performs profiling of them. Section 6 concludes.

2   Related Work

In order to understand the attack landscape and structure of hidden services in anonymous networks, many studies have analyzed Tor traffic [17,21,23] and activities [10,11,25,26].

Van Wegberg et al. [27] observed the increasing commoditization of cybercrime via online anonymous markets, which lows entry barriers for aspiring criminals, and facilitating further growth of cybercrime. Ciancaglini et al. [10,11] analyzed criminal activities in Tor hidden services. They classified features such as language, items to study the criminal activities in Tor hidden services.

Soska and Christin et al. [26] analyzed the types of products sold on 16 Tor sites between 2013 and 2015. They also found that vendors are likely to use PGP keys to hide criminal activities by encrypting communications.

For understanding the structure and illegal activities of the Dark Web, Iskander et al. [25] collected Dark Web data from 7,257 sites and analyzed them. In this study, keyword extraction and clustering were performed using a categorization program. They found that the Surface Web was very commonly connected in the onion domain. Xiangwen et al. [28] attempted to cluster multiple identities across three Dark Web sites. Using photographic information posted on the Dark Web sites, similar angles and backgrounds were determined by machine learning.

While the previous studies have analyzed the hidden services and structure of the Dark Web, a comprehensive analysis of the current Dark Web services in Korea and its chronological implications is still missing. Thus, in this paper, we conduct an in-depth analysis of the Dark Web services by gathering 3,000 Dark Web sites which are currently working, and carry out detailed profiling of the top 3 Dark Web services in Korea.

3   Dark Web Data Crawling and Validation

3.1   Design of Dark Web Crawling System

We developed a Dark Web crawling system using Selenium [6], a web development library that is also capable of collection. Especially, two kinds of crawlers were developed to collect hidden data from the Dark Web. One crawler collects only seed URLs, while the other collects only sub URLs of seed URLs. The seed URL refers to the top-level URL of a site, and sub URLs refer to various pages derived from the top-level URL. Our crawler was divided into two crawling systems because one crawler collecting both the seed URL and sub URLs together, would become trapped in an infinite loop. Therefore, two independent crawlers were implemented collect many Dark Web pages in a more reliable way. Our Dark Web crawling system consists of the following two collectors.

- Seed URL collector: the seed URL collector stores only the seed URLs for the Deep Web sites, not the specific web pages. It stores the seed URLs collected by periodically visiting the public Dark Web services such as the Hidden Wiki [4], Dark Web ad sites [7], and Dark Web directory services [2]. During the periodic visits, if any new seed URLs are found, seed URL collector extracts and stores them in the seed URL database.
- Sub URL collector: the sub URL collector stores all Dark Web subpages related to each seed URL. The URL address, collection time, page title, and page contents are saved for each page, and all of the web page screens are captured as image files for situations in which the data is not directly accessible. Since many Dark Web sites are frequently changing their URLs to deter traces to them, converting the Dark Web pages into the image files are useful for the later forensic analysis.

Table 1. URL exposure and security pattern

Type	Pattern	Ratio
URL exposure	HTML code	85%
	JavaScript functions	15%
Security	None	99.3%
	Login and membership certification	0.42%
	CAPTCHA	0.28%

3.2   Dark Web Data Crawling

In order to analyze and understand the hidden activities in the current Dark Web environment, we collected approximately 40,000 seed URLs using the seed URL collector from Oct. 17, 2017 to Dec. 3, 2018. Then, we directly accessed those 40,000 seed URLs, and extracted 3,000 Dark Web URLs from them. Furthermore, applying the sub URL collector to those 3,000 URLs allowed 586,536 pages to be collected in total.

Table 1 shows the URL exposure and security pattern. In the table, 'URL exposure' shows the ratio of the two exposure pattern through which URLs are exposed. Approximately 85% of the URLs are simply exposed through HTML code, which can be simply parsed and extracted by the crawler. The remaining 15% are extracted through execution of a JavaScript function.

In the table, 'Security' indicates the access control pattern of the Dark Web sites. On the basis of our analysis, 99.3% of the Dark Web sites did not employ any user authentication mechanism for access control. However, for 0.42% of sites a deeper level of access is only achievable after membership certification. For these pages, an automatic data gathering by the crawler is almost impossible. Thus, we developed an autonomous login function and applied it to our crawling system to reduce manual efforts. Specifically, the xPath of the login button of the site is extracted and registered, and the login is carried out in the prescribed order before starting data collection. This feature is helpful to increase the Dark Web data collection ratio[1]. Finally, the remaining 0.28% of sites demanded CAPTCHA authentication. Since CAPTCHA authentication is hard to automate, it had to be solved manually.

Several remaining issues about the Dark Web data crawling are briefly discussed. First, although crawlers generally have to solve code obfuscation, the crawlers used in this study did not consider it because they are represented in the web browser itself. Second, Dark Web sites have URLs, such as shopping carts, writing, and logouts which are not meaningful as Dark Web data. Thus, we set patterns in advance to avoid crawling such web pages for the Dark Web data. Third, Dark Web sites may be inaccessible at a specific time because many

---

[1] For example, when we applied this approach to HiGH KOREA, which is the largest Dark Web site in Korea, we could increase the number of the collected web pages from 792 to 7,740.

Table 2. Overall Dark Web page collection rate

Site name	Category	The number of pages	
		Actual	Our crawler
Under videos	Porno	49	41
DUMPS Market	Finance	13	11
NLGrowers	Drugs	5	4
Ninja's LR Casino	Gambling	377	311
Cocaine Citizens	Drugs	74	62
...	...	...	...
Crime	Violence	18	14
Clone CC Shop	Finance	22	18
Average collection rate for 1500 sites : 90%			

Table 3. Korean Dark Web page collection rates

Site name	The number of pages		Result
	Actual	Our crawler	
HiGH KOREA	1675	1341	80%
666LETOM	514	334	65%
HiddenGOD	1	1	100%
Beetgames	58	47	81%
Agora	483	382	79%
Hidden Wiki Korea	2321	1841	79%
UNKNOWN CREW	43	36	84%
Freespg	74	67	91%
Average collection rate for the 8 Korean Dark Web sites: 82%			

Table 4. Korean keyword search rate

Keyword		마약 (Drug)	코카인 (Cocaine)	대마초 (Marijuana)	헤로인 (Heroin)	비트코인 (Bitcoin)	살인 (Murder)	도박 (Gambling)	음란물 (Porno)	Total
Collected pages	Our crawler	626	85	702	62	596	340	145	121	2,677
	Not Evil	179	31	224	31	452	89	40	51	1,099

of them are temporary and the connection is unstable. Hence, we did not try to reconnect to URLs found to be inaccessible. Finally, the maximum wait time is set to 10 s per page.

3.3 Performance of Dark Web Crawling System

The page collection rate of the crawler is measured to verify its crawling performance and accuracy for both Dark Web pages in general and specific Korean Dark Web sites. The keyword search rate is also compared with existing search engines. To measure general Dark Web page collection rate, we made a reference set for comparison. Specifically, we randomly selected 1,500 sites from the 3,000 Dark Web sites we collected, and manually checked the exact number of pages per site. We then compared the manually created reference set with the number of pages collected by our Dark Web crawler. As shown in Table 2, our crawler achieved an average page collection rate of 90%.

We also measured the page collection rate for the 8 Korean Dark Web sites among the 3,000 Dark Web sites as shown in Table 3. As before, a reference set was created by manually measuring the total number of pages by taking advantage of the post numbers at each site. According to Table 3, our crawler's average page collection rate is 82%.

Next, we measured the crawling accuracy by comparing Korean keyword search results of our crawling system with existing search engines. We chose Not Evil [5] as a comparison since Not Evil can support Korean keyword search and return only the Deep Web results. For comparison, we selected the top 8 crime keywords and compared search results between the pages collected by our crawler and Not Evil. The comparison is shown in Table 4. In the experiment, Not Evil collected 1,099 pages for the Korean keywords, while our crawling system collected 2,677 pages.

4 Dark Web Data Analysis

4.1 Structure Analysis of Dark Web Sites

Figure 1 shows the size of each seed URL on a log scale. This analysis is conducted on 7,257 onion sites in [25], which is compared with 3,000 Dark Web sites we collected. While 46.07% of the existing Onion sites consist of a single page, only 27.19% of the Dark Web sites consist of a single page. 135 Dark Web sites have more than 256 sub-pages, which accounts for 4.6% of the total. Among the 135 Dark Web sites, we selected the largest top 5 Dark Web sites, and analyzed their sizes and major activities. The Dark Web site, with the highest number of pages, is a porno site, mostly child porno. The second and fifth sites are dealing mainly with counterfeit credit cards trade. The third and fourth sites are created for the study of socially regulated technologies such as illegal hacking techniques. The site information is shown in Table 5.

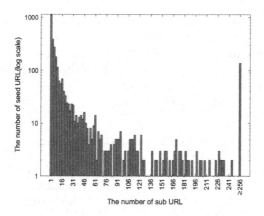

Fig. 1. Size of Dark Web sites

Table 5. Top 5 Dark Web sites

URL	Size	Category
http://alicedbdh5xixwai.onion	14,997	Porno
http://26z56lc5zszmadnm.onion	11,899	Commodity
http://rvy6qmlqfstv6rlz.onion	11,183	Community
http://dob3bs7dgnzd7r7a.onion	9,250	Community
http://x7giprgefwfvkeep.onion	8,389	Commodity

Table 6. Number of sites by category

Category	Example	Size	Category	Example	Size
Finance	Counterfeit notes	655	Social	Anarchism	89
Drugs	Cocaine, Heroin	337	Violence	Murder by contract	83
Hacking	Hacking programs, Malware	298	Gambling	Casino	52
Private info. trading	Trading stolen ID/PW, SSN	274	Forgery	Fake identification card	49
Porno	Adult, Child pornography	246	Arms	Illegal weapons	39
Community	Illegal forum	238	Extremism	Radicalism, fanaticism	3
Cryptocurrency	Mixing service	106	Portal	Links to various Dark web sites	441
Commodity	Trading stolen goods	90			

4.2 Classification of Dark Web Sites

We classified 3,000 Dark Web sites by their major activities. Even if many of the sites handle multiple illegal subjects simultaneously, they were classified on the basis of a couple of the top-interest subjects of the sites. Although a similar analysis was carried out in the previous study [25], we tried to improve reliability of classification by using more precise manual categorization. The classification results are shown in Table 6. According to our analysis, illegal financial trading such as counterfeit notes is in the majority of the Dark Web sites, which is followed by drugs, hacking, forgery, and so on.

Table 7. Top 3 Korean Dark Web pages

Site name	Total number of pages	Number of pages containing crime keywords
HiGH KOREA	51,403	29,565
666LETOM	1,044	526
Agora	34,756	15,330

5 Profiling of Korean Dark Web Sites

In this section, an in-depth analysis of the criminal activities and profiling are conducted on the Korean Dark Web. Especially, among the 8 Korean Dark Web sites in Table 3, we select the three most popular ones, which are HiGH KOREA, Agora, 666LETOM constituting most of the cyber criminal activities in South Korea. In the profiling, criminal activities are collected from 2017 May to 2018 August, and analyzed in a chronological point of view. Then, personal information leakage are also measured in comparison to the general Web environment.

5.1 Chronological Analysis of Criminal Activity

To analyze criminal activities, a list of keywords including criminal jargon was prepared in advance. Specifically, 41 keywords were provided by the Korean National Police Agency and 240 keywords were selected by the authors. In order to carry out profiling of the three Dark Web sites in an autonomous way, we developed parsing techniques to extract only the criminal keywords from all of the postings in the sites periodically. As a result, crime keywords are found in a total of 45,421 of the 87,203 pages from the sites. Detailed results are shown in Table 7.

In order to conduct a chronological analysis of them, we classify the crime keywords into four big categories: Drug including keywords such as cocaine and heroin, Porno including keywords such as child pornography, and Org including keywords such as radicalism, and the rest classified as Etc. Then, we analyze the criminal activities over time as shown in Fig. 2. Chronological analysis results by hour of day and by month are shown in Fig. 2(a) and (b), respectively. As shown in Fig. 2(a), activities related to drugs are most active during the afternoon, while those related to Porno is more active at night than in the afternoon. In terms of the monthly trend between May 2017 to August 2018, overall activities increased between August and September, and declined in November or April as shown in Fig. 2(b). Because the monthly activities are analyzed for a limited period of time, that is approximately 16 months, we believe it is hard to interpret them with great meaning in practice. Statistically more meaningful monthly trend could be analyzed by collecting more data, e.g., for a couple of more years.

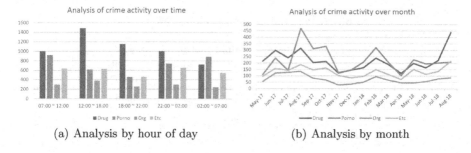

(a) Analysis by hour of day   (b) Analysis by month

Fig. 2. Chronological analysis of criminal activity

5.2   Personal Information Leakage

In order to understand how much personal information are leaked and illegally traded in the Korean Dark Web sites, we collected cell phone numbers, e-mail addresses, Bitcoin addresses, and social security numbers of people. As a result, 893 cases of personal information leakage are detected. In the procedure, we only counted unique cases and removed any redundant ones among multiple postings. That is, if any personal information is found in multiple postings, it is counted as one case of personal information leakage. The detailed results are shown in Table 8. On the other hand, we have observed that if some personal information exposed to the Dark Web are combined with any public information revealed in the Surface Web, much more fine-grained private information could be identified, such as name, social security number, home address, occupation, and so on. Thus, in order to understand how much the personal information exposed to the Dark Web have practical impact in the real world, we crawled the Surface Web sites using Google search engine to see if the personal information exposed to the Dark Web is also searchable on the Surface Web. As a result, 460 cases of personal information were also retrieved from the Surface Web. The Surface Web search results for each item are shown in parentheses in Table 8. As a result, 62 of the 261 email addresses were also retrieved from the Surface Web. Of these, 6 emails are linked to a personal SNS page revealing daily private information and social relationship, and 3 emails are able to uncover resident area information. For Bitcoin addresses, 373 transaction records are found from the Surface Web out of the total 404 addresses identified from the Dark Web. The Bitcoin addresses obtained from the Surface Web can be used as a means to identify the owner's identity in the real world for some specific Bitcoin transactions by applying clustering [16], or anonymous network fingerprinting [17, 21, 23] technologies. In the case of phone numbers, 19 out of 44 cases are also found on the Surface Web. By combining partial information independently crawled from Dark and Suface Webs, for example, we could identify some cases that disclose the other private information such as specific person's residential address, occupation, salary, age, SNS, and so on, which may lead to phishing or financial fraud in the real world.

Table 8. Personal information detection results

Site name	Phone number	Email address	Bitcoin address	Social security number
Agora	$44_{(19)}$	$219_{(45)}$	$33_{(6)}$	$130_{(0)}$
HiGH KOREA	0	$42_{(17)}$	$371_{(367)}$	0
666LETOM	0	0	0	0

5.3   Finding Sybil Identities

In the Dark Web, identifying Sybil identities (IDs) among the multiple Dark Web sites is one of the most challenging problems. Therefore, several heuristic and machine learning-based techniques exploiting posted contents such as pictures about drugs [28] have been proposed. However, since it is practically infeasible to get the corresponding ground truth data in the real world, demonstrating the efficacy or accuracy of the solutions remains unsolved.

With this regards, we observed one interesting trend during the analysis of the Korean Dark Web sites. That is, most of the information needed for trading between vendors and buyers, such as the amount of drugs, prices, Bitcoin addresses, are exchanged via encrypted email using PGP key to hide the contents of them. When making illegal transactions, the email sender encrypts the messages with the public key of the receiver so that the receiver can decrypt it with his private key. Since a PGP key is unique information corresponding to each ID, we develop a parsing technology to separate and store PGP keys for individual IDs among the Dark Web sites. Then an attempt is made to cluster the IDs using the collected PGP key information to identify Sybil IDs in the Dark Web sites. If one person posts using multiple IDs in the multiple Dark Web sites using the same PGP key, it is decisive evidence demonstrating the IDs belong to the same person. It is important to note that, as far as we know, our idea is the first to find Sybil IDs using the PGP keys in the Dark Web as opposed to the previous heuristic approaches.

We examined the number of such cases and the duplicate PGP keys. Overall, 123 of the 1,468 PGP keys collected from HiGH KOREA were duplicated. Surprisingly, the most widely used PGP key was used by 24 IDs, which means one

Dark Web user are using 24 different Sybil IDs in the 3 Korean Dark Web sites. Detailed results are shown in Table 9. On the basis of our analysis, we found 347 Sybil IDs among the top 3 Korean Dark Web sites, and on average 2.84 Sybil IDs are used by a single user. It is important to note that our idea is very effective to provide decisive evidence for identifying Sybil IDs, especially in the Dark Web environment where getting ground truth data is almost impossible.

Table 9. The number of Sybil IDs based on PGP key

# of Sybil ID	2	3	4	5	6	7	9	10	24
# of users	81	21	9	6	1	1	1	1	1
Total # of Sybil IDs :									347
Average # of Sybil IDs per user :									2.84

6 Conclusion

While the previous studies have helped to better understand the hidden services and structure of the Dark Web, a comprehensive analysis of the current Dark Web services and its chronological implications is still missing. To achieve it, in this paper, we conduct an in-depth analysis of the Dark Web services by gathering more than 90% web pages from approximately 3,000 Dark Web sites in the wild using our Dark Web crawling system. Then, we focus on the top 3 Dark Web services in Korea, and carry out detailed profiling of it. In the profiling, criminal activities are collected and analyzed in a chronological point of view. Then, personal information leakage including personal PGP key are also measured in comparison to the general Web environment. According to our analysis result, we found non-negligible amount of illegal trading are carried on in the Korean Dark Web, and personal information are exposed, which may reveal much more fine-grained private information when combined with publicly known information on the Surface Web. In order to find Sybil IDs in the Dark Web, we also proposed a novel idea to exploit PGP keys in the Dark Web sites, and demonstrated its efficacy by investigating every redundantly used PGP key in the Korean Dark Web.

Acknowledgment. This work was supported by Institute of Information communications Technology Planning Evaluation (IITP) grant funded by the Korea government (MSIT) (No.2018-0-00269, A research on safe and convenient big data processing methods), (No.2019-0-01697, Development of Automated Vulnerability Discovery Technologies for Blockchain Platform Security).

References

1. Bing (2019). http://www.bing.com. Accessed 14 June 2019
2. Deepweblinks (2019). https://deepweblinks.net/directories/. Accessed 14 June 2019

3. Google (2019). http://www.google.com. Accessed 14 June 2019
4. Hidden Wiki (2019). https://thehiddenwiki.org. Accessed 14 June 2019
5. Not Evil (2019). https://hss3uro2hsxfogfq.onion.to. Accessed 14 June 2019
6. Selenium (2019). https://www.seleniumhq.org. Accessed 14 June 2019
7. Thedarkweblinks (2019). https://www.thedarkweblinks.com. Accessed 14 June 2019
8. Yahoo (2019). http://www.yahoo.com. Accessed 14 June 2019
9. Catakoglu, O., Balduzzi, M., Balzarotti, D.: Attacks landscape in the dark side of the web. In: Proceedings of the Symposium on Applied Computing, pp. 1739–1746. ACM (2017)
10. Ciancaglini, V., Balduzzi, M., Goncharov, M., McArdle, R.: Deepweb and cybercrime. Trend Micro Rep. **9**, 1–22 (2013)
11. Ciancaglini, V., Balduzzi, M., McArdle, R., Rösler, M.: Below the surface: exploring the deep web. Trend Micro pp. 1–48 (2015)
12. He, B., Patel, M., Zhang, Z., Chang, K.C.C.: Accessing the deep web: a survey. Commun. ACM **50**(5), 94–101 (2007)
13. Hong, Y., Kwon, H., Lee, J., Hur, J.: A practical de-mixing algorithm for bitcoin mixing services. In: Proceedings of the 2nd ACM Workshop on Blockchains, Cryptocurrencies, and Contracts, pp. 15–20. ACM (2018)
14. Hopwood, D., Bowe, S., Hornby, T., Wilcox, N.: Zcash protocol specification. Technical report 2016-1.10. Zerocoin Electric Coin Company, Technical report (2016)
15. Kappos, G., Yousaf, H., Maller, M., Meiklejohn, S.: An empirical analysis of anonymity in zcash. In: 27th {USENIX} Security Symposium ({USENIX} Security 18), pp. 463–477 (2018)
16. Koshy, P., Koshy, D., McDaniel, P.: An analysis of anonymity in bitcoin using P2P network traffic. In: Christin, N., Safavi-Naini, R. (eds.) FC 2014. LNCS, vol. 8437, pp. 469–485. Springer, Heidelberg (2014). https://doi.org/10.1007/978-3-662-45472-5_30
17. Kwon, A., AlSabah, M., Lazar, D., Dacier, M., Devadas, S.: Circuit fingerprinting attacks: passive deanonymization of tor hidden services. In: 24th {USENIX} Security Symposium ({USENIX} Security 2015), pp. 287–302 (2015)
18. Liu, W., Meng, X., Meng, W.: ViDE: a vision-based approach for deep web data extraction. IEEE Trans. Knowl. Data Eng. **22**(3), 447–460 (2009)
19. Madhavan, J., Ko, D., Kot, Ł., Ganapathy, V., Rasmussen, A., Halevy, A.: Google's deep web crawl. Proc. VLDB Endowment **1**(2), 1241–1252 (2008)
20. Miller, A., Möser, M., Lee, K., Narayanan, A.: An empirical analysis of linkability in the monero blockchain 2017 (2017)
21. Mittal, P., Khurshid, A., Juen, J., Caesar, M., Borisov, N.: Stealthy traffic analysis of low-latency anonymous communication using throughput fingerprinting. In: Proceedings of the 18th ACM Conference on Computer and Communications Security, pp. 215–226. ACM (2011)
22. Moore, D., Rid, T.: Cryptopolitik and the darknet. Survival **58**(1), 7–38 (2016)
23. Murdoch, S.J., Danezis, G.: Low-cost traffic analysis of Tor. In: 2005 IEEE Symposium on Security and Privacy (S&P 2005), pp. 183–195. IEEE (2005)
24. Noether, S.: Ring signature confidential transactions for monero. IACR Cryptology ePrint Archive **2015**, 1098 (2015)
25. Sanchez-Rola, I., Balzarotti, D., Santos, I.: The onions have eyes: a comprehensive structure and privacy analysis of tor hidden services. In: Proceedings of the 26th International Conference on World Wide Web, pp. 1251–1260. International World Wide Web Conferences Steering Committee (2017)

26. Soska, K., Christin, N.: Measuring the longitudinal evolution of the online anonymous marketplace ecosystem. In: 24th {USENIX} Security Symposium ({USENIX} Security 2015), pp. 33–48 (2015)
27. Van Wegberg, R., et al.: Plug and prey? measuring the commoditization of cyber-crime via online anonymous markets. In: 27th {USENIX} Security Symposium ({USENIX} Security 2018), pp. 1009–1026 (2018)
28. Wang, X., Peng, P., Wang, C., Wang, G.: You are your photographs: detecting multiple identities of vendors in the darknet marketplaces. In: Proceedings of the 2018 on Asia Conference on Computer and Communications Security, pp. 431–442. ACM (2018)

An SGX-Based Key Management Framework for Data Centric Networking

Minkyung Park[1], Jeongnyeo Kim[2], Youngho Kim[2], Eunsang Cho[1],
Soobin Park[1], Sungmin Sohn[1], Minhyeok Kang[1],
and Ted "Taekyoung" Kwon[1($\boxtimes$)]

[1] Seoul National University, 1 Gwanak-ro, Gwanak-gu, Seoul, Republic of Korea
{mkpark,escho,sbpark,smsohn,mhkang}@mmlab.snu.ac.kr,
tkkwon@snu.ac.kr
[2] Electronics and Telecommunications Research Institute, 218 Gaejong-rho,
Yuseong-Gu, Daejeon 34129, Republic of Korea
{jnkim,wtowto}@etri.re.kr

Abstract. As the Internet has evolved from host-to-host communications to content distribution, data-centric networking platforms are gaining a momentum. Especially, as the cloud computing becomes the norm, there is a consensus that data is to be distributed over some potentially untrusted servers to which its publishers/subscribers are connected. While data-centric networking platforms have been an area of active research, there have been few studies on how to distribute and manage keys for data protection in such platforms with untrusted servers. We present a key management framework in which symmetric and asymmetric keys are securely managed. A writer publishes not only his (encrypted) data but also the symmetric key for the data. Likewise, a reader retrieves the symmetric key as well as the data of interest. To make the key distribution securely between a writer and a reader via an untrusted server, we introduce a key server running on top of the Intel SGX technology. In this way, we can manage and distribute keys for data protection in an efficient and flexible manner. We demonstrate that the prototype of the proposed framework is running with the negligible overhead.

Keywords: Data-centric networking platform · Key management ·
Intel Software Guard Extension · Named Data Networking · Global
Data Plane

1 Introduction

As increasingly more traffic in the Internet is attributed to content-centric application (rather than host-based ones), data-centric networking platforms are gaining a momentum for scalable and efficient solutions. One of the clean-slate approaches is Named Data Networking (NDN) [12] whose key components are data names not host locations. To receive data in NDN, a data request is routed

© Springer Nature Switzerland AG 2020
I. You (Ed.): WISA 2019, LNCS 11897, pp. 370–382, 2020.
https://doi.org/10.1007/978-3-030-39303-8_28

by its name, and then any entity in the path that has the data can send it back. Recently, the Internet of Things (IoT) has accelerated the research and development of data-centric networking platforms since a growing number of the IoT devices will require efficient and scalable solutions for data dissemination. For instance, Global Data Plane [7] is a log-based data-centric IoT platform in which append-only logs are written on a potentially untrusted distributed infrastructure.

While the current host-based applications can rely on credentials (like ID/password) and certificates (with public keys) for security measures, the security solutions for the data-centric networking platforms are still elusive. In the host-based applications, a publisher (or a writer) can control where and how long his data are stored, which means that he decides the container of data and secures the access to the container for data protection. In the data-centric networking platforms, however, the data may be disseminated through some entity outside the control of the publisher[1]; thus, the publisher himself may have to encrypt the data for access control and/or confidentiality. Henceforth, we refer to both access control and confidentiality collectively as data protection, which is the focus of this paper. In host-based security systems, the access control can be done by simply checking the credential (e.g., ID/password) of a reader (or a subscriber) at a given host under the control of the writer. This method should be changed in data-centric networking platforms since there is no designated host holding the data. Instead of checking the credential of the reader, the data protection for the data-centric networking platforms can be achieved by distributing keys for the encryption/decryption.

In this paper, we introduce a secure and efficient key management framework for data protection in the data-centric networking platforms. The proposed key management framework addresses both symmetric key and public key distributions. For the purposes of secure key distribution, we introduce a key server that leverages Intel Software Guard Extension (SGX) to serve as a trust anchor. That is, the Intel SGX-enabled server can play the role of a gatekeeper that thwarts an adversary who tries to access with a revoked public key. Thus, a writer or a reader with a valid public key can encrypt/decrypt the symmetric key (by its private key) by interacting with the key server. Also, the writer and the reader can trust the key server with Intel SGX by a remote attestation.

In addition to the above features, the proposed framework devises a symmetric key generation technique to support flexible data protection and efficient key distribution. Suppose that the writer is generating his data in a sequence, and hence updates his symmetric key (for data encryption) periodically. The flexible data protection means that the writer can control when (and how long) each reader can access (or decrypt) data. As to the efficient key distribution, the writer does not need to distribute keys for each data generation. Our hash-based symmetric key generation technique can significantly reduce the number of keys to be distributed.

---

[1] We interchangeably use a writer and a publisher to refer to an entity who generates the data; likewise, a reader or a subscriber will consume the data.

2   Intel SGX

Intel SGX (Software Guard Extensions) is a technology to protect code and data from disclosure or modification by leveraging an isolated container, called an enclave. The enclave protects a memory page that consists of code, data, stack and heap areas by strict access control mechanisms supported by the hardware.

Remote Attestation. The enclave provides an attestable proof for the protected memory of the enclave. Any other party in a remote platform can request the target enclave to demonstrate its status by publishing a report, which is called a *remote attestation*. An enclave can generate a report that contains the hash of the internal log, the hash of the authority certificate, and other security-related status information. A dedicated enclave (called Quoting Enclave) signs the report using a group key. The signed data structure is called a quote. Then, the challenger can ask a validity of the quote by connecting to IAS (Intel Attestation Service) that holds the key. The IAS responds with a verification report that proves the quote is valid or not.

Sealing. There exists a hardware-protected encryption key system that can be accessed and derived only by the enclaves. With an encryption key, the data inside the corresponding enclave can be "sealed" (i.e., encrypted) and stored securely even in an untrusted system.

TLS-SGX Integration. Knauth et al. [5] proposed to integrate the Intel SGX remote attestation with the Transport Layer Security (TLS) protocol by binding the report and his certificate. The server includes the hash of the server public key in the Intel SGX report and requests the IAS to issue a verification report for its quote. The server can create a self-signed X.509 certificate with the verification report as an X.509 extension. By verifying the certificate and the verification report, the client (challenger) ensures that it is connected to the genuine Intel SGX enclave. The client can verify the verification report inside the X.509 certificate using the Intel's public key. Then the self-signed certificate can also be trusted based on the verified report.

3   Networking Models and Design Goals

3.1   Data-Centric Networking Platforms and Its Key Management

First, we illustrate a general model of the data-centric networking platforms. The examples under consideration are Named Data Networking (NDN) [12], Global Data Plane (GDP) [7], and blockchain [6,13].

In a data-centric networking platform, every data is labeled with its identifier, and is normally assumed to be immutable. Hence, secure replication and efficient validation of the data is implied. That is, any copy (of the data) is identical to the original, and its integrity can be validated (e.g., with a digital signature). Accordingly, each data can be distinguished by its identifier, which is of fixed or variable length.

We present a data structure, called a log, which consists of the data and its identifier, at minimum. Depending on applications and operating environments, a log may also contain the length of the data, a timestamp, and other attributes. The identifier is globally unique and independent of its (storage) location and its application. Once a log is generated (or written), it is impossible to rewrite or modify the log.

In a general data-centric networking platform, there are three types of entities participating in data distribution: a writer, a reader, and a storage server. We may refer to a writer and a reader collectively as a client. The writer publishes a log to the storage server(s) using a publishing mechanism of the platform. The log can be distributed over multiple physical machines (i.e., storage servers) of which the writer may not be aware. For data protection of the log, the writer encrypts the log (i.e., its data part) to control accessibility.

A log's identifier is publicly visible to any entity, but its data part is encrypted. That is, its data is decrypted only by authorized readers, who can read from any storage server. The reader can request a log of interest by using its identifier. There may be an overlay network to route a request or its response (e.g., [7]) or a network that directly supports name-based routing (e.g., [12]). A storage server, a reader, or a writer may be co-located with another entity depending on operating environments. For example, in the case of blockchain, the three entities are co-located and there is no routing (in the overlay network) since every machine has a copy of all the logs.

In addition to the three types of entities, we introduce a key server that manages a binding of an identifier of an entity and its public key. The key server also acts as a gatekeeper for the symmetric key distribution. The key server is the only entity that needs to be equipped with the Intel SGX hardware. The software of the key server runs in the enclave and its code is publicly available so that its integrity can be verified by the remote attestation. Our proposal for key management framework will be detailed in Sect. 4.

3.2 Design Goals

We rely on Intel SGX by assuming that the enclave behaves with integrity. Therefore, any client can verify the integrity of the behaviors of the key server through TLS-SGX including the remote attestation. We assume an adversary is a malicious client to impersonate another client to access an unauthorized log.

Under the threat model, our key management framework aims to satisfy the following criteria. In this subsection, the symmetric key means the key used for encrypting the original data, and the public/private key pair is bound to each client.

Periodic Key Updates. By periodically updating a key, the damage can be mitigated even if the key is leaked.

Flexible Data Protection. The writer should be able to control when and how long individual readers can access its data log depending on the reader's contract and so on. Also, the moment at which the data log is published should be irrelevant to the one at which the reader accesses the data, which is called the flexible data protection.

Efficient Key Distribution. Updating the symmetric key for each period may be burdensome as the period becomes shorter. Therefore, we should seek to balance the enhanced security and the key updating overhead for the efficiency in the key distribution.

Forward and Backward Secrecy. The keys of the unauthorized (data) logs should not be available even if the reader knows the previous or the following keys. This is called the backward secrecy and the forward secrecy, respectively.

Actions Against Key Compromises. Even though a compromised private key is revoked, some symmetric keys encrypted by the compromised private key can be decrypted by an attacker. This is important since the key logs cannot be deleted in case of append-only data-centric networking platforms (e.g., GDP and blockchain). Therefore, we should mitigate the damage if an attacker compromises the reader's private key.

4   The Proposed Key Management Framework

We propose a key management framework considering the above criteria. We first explain the public key management. Next, based on the public key management, we detail how the symmetric keys are managed and distributed. We denote by $E_k(m)$ a ciphertext of a message m using a key k. Also, the encryption scheme depends on the key k, which means that if the key is symmetric or asymmetric, then the encryption scheme is also symmetric (e.g., AES) or asymmetric (e.g., RSA), respectively. Likewise, we denote by $Sign_{Priv_X}(m)$ a message m's signature generated using the private key (of entity X) $Priv_X$. We represent a digest of a message m as $H(m)$, and a result of hashing a message m x times as $H^x(m)$. That is, $H^x(m)$ can be derived by $H(H^{x-1}(m))$. The hash function $H(\cdot)$ is a cryptographic hash function such as SHA-256. Apart from a private key used for TLS-SGX in Sect. 2, the enclave $encl$ randomly generates a master secret key msk, which is kept only inside the enclave $encl$.

4.1   Public Key Management

Every client C has a publicly verifiable identifier, $\mathcal{ID}_C$, and a newly generated public/private key pair $(Pub_C, Priv_C)$. To register its public key, C sets up a session using TLS-SGX (without client authentication) with an enclave $encl$ in the key server. C can verify whether $encl$ is securely created and running using the remote attestation and TLS-SGX. If TLS-SGX fails (say, the remote attestation fails), the registration fails. Otherwise, by sending the identifier $\mathcal{ID}_C$ and Pub_C, C proves to $encl$ the ownership of (1) the corresponding private key $(Priv_C)$ using a signature $Sign_{Priv_C}(\mathcal{ID}_C || timestamp)$ where $timestamp$ is used to prevent replay attacks and (2) his identifier. Then, $encl$ stores '$\mathcal{ID}_C$ and Pub_C' in its local storage, which is protected by the sealing.

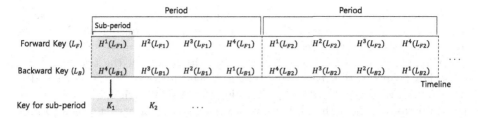

Fig. 1. A symmetric key for a sub-period is generated by using a hash function in two opposite directions for the two long-term keys of the period.

The enclave manages not only the public key binding but also the public key revocation. Like the PKI system, the enclave can revoke the relation between an identifier and its public key. As soon as a public key is revoked, it is recorded as 'revoked' and a new public key can be registered using the above process. In this vein, the key server serves as a certificate authority (CA). It maintains all valid and revoked public keys for registered identifiers.

4.2 Symmetric Key Generation

Before publishing a log, a writer W generates a symmetric key. Considering the criteria in Sect. 3.2, we divide a period into sub-periods; its rationale will be explained later. Figure 1 illustrates the case in which there are 4 sub-periods in a period. We call a key for a period a long-term key, and one for a sub-period a short-term key, both of which are generated based on the following rules.

- The writer decides the durations of a period and a sub-period.
- For every period, the writer independently and randomly generates two long-term keys. We call them forward and backward keys, L_F and L_B.
- Let d be the number of the sub-periods for a period.
- The writer computes two chains of hashes: one is a forward chain using the forward key $\{H(L_F), H^2(L_F), ..., H^d(L_F)\}$, and the other is a backward chain using the backward key $\{H(L_B), H^2(L_B), ..., H^d(L_B)\}$.
- To generate a symmetric key, the derived hashes in the forward chain are used in order, and the ones in the backward chain are used in reverse order.
- A symmetric key for x-th sub-period is generated using a pair of hashes $H^x(L_F)$ and $H^{d-x+1}(L_B)$, i.e., $H(H^x(L_F)||H^{d-x+1}(L_B))$. We may use an exclusive-or operation instead of the concatenation depending on the required key length.
- If any short-term or long-term key is compromised, the writer has to update long-term keys for remaining sub-periods, then the derived short-term keys will by automatically changed. The writer will encrypt the data logs in the following sub-periods with the updated keys. The writer adds some metadata (in plaintext) to the data log to notify that the long term keys are updated, so that the readers can figure out they should fetch the updated keys.

As the symmetric (short-term) key is changed in each sub-period, the reader should know or derive all the keys for the sub-periods during which he can access the logs. To give a reader the keys for some consecutive sub-periods in a period, the writer only needs to distribute the hashes of the two long-term keys. For example, the reader who has a hashed forward key $H^x(L_F)$ and a hashed backward key $H^{d-y+1}(L_B)$ can derive the symmetric keys from the x-th sub-period to the y-th sub-period. In each period, the writer needs to give a reader two long-term keys (or their hashes depending on the allowed sub-periods). When the writer generates the long-term symmetric keys, he should also specify the period and the sub-period to inform when a new symmetric key is updated. Such information can be also deemed as the metadata (*metadata*).

Let $ek = \{H^i(L_F), H^{d-j+1}(L_B)\}$ be a pair of hashes of the long-term keys to distribute the symmetric keys for the corresponding sub-periods. That is, using ek, symmetric keys $\{ek_i, ek_{i+1}, ..., ek_j\}$ can be derived where ek_s is for s-th sub-period and $i \leq s \leq j$. To publish the data $\mathcal{D}$ for s-th sub-period, the writer $\mathcal{W}$ encrypts $\mathcal{D}$ using ek_s, and the ciphertext is denoted by $E_{ek_s}(\mathcal{D})$. $\mathcal{W}$ publishes the encrypted log $E_{ek_s}(\mathcal{D})$ using the primitives in the underlying data-centric networking platform. In this way, the writer $\mathcal{W}$ can allow the reader to access the logs from the i-th sub-period to j-th sub-period by giving the symmetric key ek. Note that this key encryption is for a particular reader. The key should be delivered to the reader securely as follows.

4.3   Key Delivery to Key Server

Delivering ek to each reader is not simple due to the following reasons. As the writer can be a resource-limited device (e.g., IoT) with the vulnerabilities, we rely on the key server to securely distribute the keys to readers. However, we seek to hide the keys from the key server as well. For this, $\mathcal{W}$ encrypts ek using reader $\mathcal{R}$'s public key $Pub_\mathcal{R}$, i.e., $E_{Pub_\mathcal{R}}(ek)$. To securely publish $E_{Pub_\mathcal{R}}(ek)$, $\mathcal{W}$ connects to the enclave *encl* in the key server using TLS-SGX with client authentication. It authenticates the writer $\mathcal{W}$ as well as the enclave *encl*.

For the client authentication, the writer $\mathcal{W}$ constructs a self-signed certificate *cert* that includes the registered public key $Pub_\mathcal{W}$ and the registered identifier $\mathcal{ID}_\mathcal{W}$. $\mathcal{W}$ uses the certificate in the TLS-SGX handshake. As the public key is already "pinned" in the key server, *encl* can authenticate the client. If the public key in the writer's certificate is not valid or the certificate verification fails, the TLS-SGX fails and the process stops. Otherwise, the legitimate writer $\mathcal{W}$ sends $\mathcal{ID}_\mathcal{R}$, $E_{Pub_\mathcal{R}}(ek)$, $Sign_{Priv_\mathcal{W}}(H(ek))$ and *metadata*.

After receiving the above materials, *encl* encrypts them using its master secret key msk (i.e., $E_{msk}(\mathcal{ID}_\mathcal{R}, E_{Pub_\mathcal{R}}(ek), Sign_{Priv_\mathcal{W}}(H(ek)), metadata)$), which is returned back to the writer $\mathcal{W}$. The writer publishes it in the same way the writer publishes a data log. If there are multiple readers, $\mathcal{R}1, \cdots, \mathcal{R}n$, the writer can send a request to *encl* for encrypting $\mathcal{ID}_{\mathcal{R}1}$, $E_{Pub_{\mathcal{R}1}}(ek)$, $\cdots$, $\mathcal{ID}_{\mathcal{R}n}$, $E_{Pub_{\mathcal{R}n}}(ek)$, $Sign_{Priv_\mathcal{W}}(H(ek))$ and *metadata*.

4.4 Key Delivery to Reader

Although any reader retrieves the encrypted data log $E_{ek_s}(\mathcal{D})$ and the corresponding encrypted key log, only authorized readers can decrypt the log $\mathcal{D}$. In our framework, $encl$ is the only entity that can generate the key log. That is, $encl$ uses its msk to decrypt '$E_{msk}(\mathcal{ID}_\mathcal{R}, E_{Pub_\mathcal{R}}(ek), Sign_{Priv_\mathcal{W}}(H(ek)), metadata)$'. The reader $\mathcal{R}$ and the enclave $encl$ mutually authenticate each other using TLS-SGX in the same fashion as the key publishing process. As soon as the TLS-SGX handshake is successfully completed, the reader sends a request to $encl$ for decrypting '$E_{msk}(\mathcal{ID}_\mathcal{R}, E_{Pub_\mathcal{R}}(ek), Sign_{Priv_\mathcal{W}}(H(ek)), metadata)$'. After decrypting it, $encl$ checks whether the plaintext (i.e., $\mathcal{ID}_\mathcal{R}$, $E_{Pub_\mathcal{R}}(ek)$, $metadata$) contains the reader's ID, which indicates that the reader is authorized. If it contains, $encl$ sends the corresponding encrypted key ($E_{Pub_\mathcal{R}}(ek)$, $Sign_{Priv_\mathcal{W}}(H(ek))$, $metadata$) to the reader. The reader decrypts the key ek by its private key, and checks the validity of the metadata and the signature.

5 Analysis

Let us elaborate on how the framework can satisfy the design goals in Sect. 3.2.

Periodic Key Updates. In case of asymmetric keys, the key server can make the clients update their public/private key pairs by enforcing the expiration dates of the public keys. The key server does not accept expired public keys by making the TLS-SGX handshakes fail. On the other hand, the update of a symmetric key is managed by the writer. Thus systematic primitives for key updates should be prepared by the platform to prevent update failures.

Flexible Data Protection. In data-centric networking platforms, the moments of data publish and consumption are irrelevant. For this, the writer can distribute the log of a symmetric key regardless of when the corresponding data is published.

Efficient Key Distribution. Recall that the same symmetric key may have to be reused for a series of data for a certain duration to lessen the key update/distribution overhead. In addition to that, we devise the hash-based symmetric key generation for efficient key distribution. That is, we adopt the two-level hierarchy in key update periods: a *period* and a *sub-period*. Even though a symmetric key is different in each sub-period, two long-term keys (to be published) are randomly generated at each period. The reader need not fetch symmetric keys for every sub-period, which mitigates the overhead of key distribution as well as key publication.

Forward and Backward Secrecy. Our framework solves the forward and backward secrecy problems by the symmetric key generation using two hash chains. Suppose that a writer generates two long-term keys, L_F, and L_B for a period. Also, an adversary has $ek = \{H^i(L_F), H^{d-j+1}(L_B)\}$ that can be used to decrypt the logs from the i-th sub-period to the j-th sub-period. To read logs before the i-th sub-period, the adversary has to know $H^{i-1}(L_F)$. Likewise, to read logs after j-th sub-period, he has to know $H^{d-j}(L_B)$. However, we assumed that the hash is cryptographically secure, and it is impossible to find a pre-image of any hash value. Therefore, even if a reader has the symmetric keys of a range of sub-periods, it is impossible to guess other symmetric keys beyond the range.

Actions Against Key Compromise. Even if any public/private key pair of a reader is leaked to an adversary and revoked, the adversary should not be able to get the symmetric keys for the data logs. In the proposed framework, the SGX-based key server is responsible for denying any access from an entity with the revoked key. Suppose that an adversary obtains a client's private key $Priv_\mathcal{R}$. The adversary may fetch the encrypted data (i.e., $E_{ek_s}(\mathcal{D})$) and the encrypted symmetric key (i.e., $E_{msk}(\mathcal{ID}_\mathcal{R}, E_{Pub_\mathcal{R}}(ek), Sign_{Priv_\mathcal{W}}(H(ek)), metadata)$) from the data-centric networking platform. To get the original data $\mathcal{D}$, the adversary has to acquire ek, which is encrypted twice: one by the reader's public key and another by the key server's msk. Thus, to acquire ek, the adversary should first request the key server to decrypt the symmetric key by msk. Recall the msk is protected by the corresponding enclave. However, in the process of the TLS-SGX handshake, the enclave filters out the adversary since it keeps track of the revoked keys.

6   Experiments

In this section, we show the feasibility of the proposed framework by demonstrating a proof-of-concept prototype. Since the SGX-enabled key server acts as a gatekeeper, its performance may be of concern in deployment; we seek to shed light on how many key servers (or enclaves) should be operating for a given workload. Thus, we measure the performance overhead of TLS-SGX (running on a key server), key publishing, and key retrieving.

Experiment Setup. We use a Linux machine with an Intel Core i7-6700K CPU and 32 GB RAM for running server applications and Raspberry Pi 3 with a Quad Core 1.2 GHz Broadcom BCM2837 ARMv8 64bit CPU and 1 GB RAM for the client applications. All measurements are reported over an average of 5 runs. The implementation code is modified based on the TLS-SGX implementation [5] using the WolfSSL library [1].

TLS-SGX. When establishing a TLS-SGX session, the key server creates a certificate when the enclave is created since the client requires the server certificate which is used in the remote attestation. Therefore, we measure two steps of the certificate generation. The first step at which the server generates a quote by communicating with the quoting enclave takes about 4.7 ms. The next step where the server sends a quote to the IAS to obtain a quote verification report that verifies the link between the server's public key and the server's SGX identity takes about 2.8 ms. The total generation time including all other sub-steps is about 3.2 ms. However, this may have little effect on the overall system performance because the server performs the certificate generation once per system boot. We also measure the computation overheads for the TLS-SGX handshake

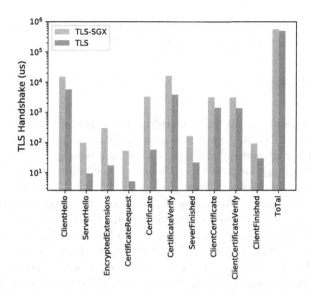

Fig. 2. The computation time of each step of TLS handshake using TLS-SGX is plotted at the server. The results are compared with those of the vanilla TLS handshake.

Table 1. The response time corresponding to the Key Publish/Key Retrieve request.

μs	Computation overhead		Communication overhead	
	Publish	Retrieve	Publish	Retrieve
Server	92	26,548	635	13,962
Client	93	295,155	253	47,821

by comparing each handshake message in the TLS-SGX compared to the one in the vanilla TLS. At the server, in Figs. 2, the TLS-SGX increases the computation time at each step, which adds up to about 70 ms overhead. At the client, the TLS-SGX similarly adds about 70 ms total computation time. While there is some small overhead, this result shows that the proposed framework is practical considering that the total computation time is about 600 ms.

Key Publishing and Key Retrieval. The key server seals or unseals the symmetric key in response to the corresponding request. Thus, we measure the response time both at the server and at the client as Table 1. The response time at the client-side is the time from the sending the key-publish/key-retrieve request to the sealing/unsealing symmetric key. At the server-side, the response time is the interval from receiving the key publish/key retrieve request to sending the sealed/unsealed symmetric key. The computation overheads are sealing and unsealing computation times for the key publish and key retrieve requests, respectively. At the client, the computational overheads are mainly due to the asymmetric encryption/decryption operations. However, the actual overhead added to the whole operation may not be critical since the key publishing and the key retrieving operations are performed only once per period.

7 Related Work

Key Management when Membership Changes. Cloud storage systems have similarities to data-centric networking platforms in the sense that they need to manage continuously changing reader membership. Therefore we investigate the key management in cloud systems. In cloud storage systems, every data stored in cloud storage is encrypted since the cloud is usually managed by an untrusted third party. Thus managing a group key in such a way that satisfies forward secrecy and backward secrecy is an important issue in cloud systems. Sherman et al. [8] suggested an efficient group key management GKM scheme called One-Way Function Tree (OFT) for groups whose membership changes frequently. The OFT scheme obtains a new group key in a bottom-up fashion from one-way hash trees. However, this approach still requires all members of the group should be on-line when the protocol is implemented. Lam et al. [9] proposed an invitation-oriented modification of Tree-based Group Diffie-Hellman (TGDH) [4]. Unlike original TGDH where a new member has to wait for a designated sponsor to come online, a new member can join the group without waiting for the sponsor. Also the proposed scheme assumes that members use asynchronous channels, so that the members may not be online simultaneously all the time when updating the group key. When the offline members come into online, then each member calculates the new group key. Xue et al. [11] suggested an enhanced TGDH scheme which transferred most of the computational complexity and communication overhead to cloud servers. Thus suggested scheme can update group key even if not all the group members are online together, with the help of the cloud server.

Trusted Hardware-based Key Management. Leveraging the TEEs serving as the root-of-trust, various key management systems have been proposed to solve the problem of building trustworthiness among multiple parties. Knox [3] is a mobile security platform based on the ARM TrustZone, which is a TEE technology supported by the ARM processor. An Android application that requires a key generation for sensitive data management or computation in the secured environment can utilize the platform by using Knox APIs. The root-of-trust chain is always a device root key (DRK) that is stored after being encrypted with a device-unique hardware key (DUHK). Because the DUHK is only accessible by the cryptography module running on TrustZone, the integrity of the trust chain is guaranteed [2]. Also, all signing keys, encryption keys, or keys for specific applications generated by the Knox platform are managed in a secure key store with the help of the TrustZone. [10] is another example of the key management system based on the hardware supporting TEE. [10] proposed a secured SSL private key management system STYX for cloud-based content delivery network (CCDN) applications. In CCDN environment, secured key protection and key distribution are challenges due to that the CDN nodes are running on the cloud environment, an untrusted platform. In STYX, SGX powered key management modules in Key Distribution Center (KDC) and Key Sub-Center (KSC) securely authorize each other and build a trusted channel through the SGX remote attestation process. The KDC can provision the SSL key to the KSC's enclave as key store, which guarantees the key protection.

8 Conclusions

Delivering data between a writer and a reader via untrusted servers will be popular. For efficient and scalable data distribution, data-centric networking platforms are gaining a momentum. In this paper, we focus on how to manage keys securely in data-centric networking platforms for data protection. The proposed framework considers the management of both symmetric and asymmetric keys. We introduce a key server that leverages Intel SGX to serve as a trust anchor against adversaries. We also devise a novel symmetric key generation technique based on hash chains for efficient and flexible key distribution. We implemented and evaluated the proof-of-concept prototype to reveal that the overhead of the proposed framework is negligible.

Acknowledgement. This work was supported by Institute for Information & communications Technology Promotion (IITP) grant funded by the Korea government (MSIT) (No.2018-0-00231, Development of context adaptive security autonomous enforcement technology to prevent spread of IoT infrastructure attacks). In addition, the ICT at Seoul National University provides research facilities for this study.

References

1. Wolfssl library. https://www.wolfssl.com/. Accessed 31 May 2019
2. Technotes:hardware root of trust, pp. 1–3 (2016). https://kp-cdn.samsungknox.com/bb91024cad9080904523821f727b9593.pdf. Accessed 31 May 2019
3. Samsung knox (2018). https://www.samsungknox.com/en. Accessed 31 May 2019
4. Kim, Y., Perrig, A., Tsudik, G.: Tree-based group key agreement. ACM Trans. Inf. Syst. Secur. (TISSEC) **7**(1), 60–96 (2004)
5. Knauth, T., Steiner, M., Chakrabarti, S., Lei, L., Xing, C., Vij, M.: Integrating remote attestation with transport layer security. arXiv preprint arXiv:1801.05863 (2018)
6. Mattila, J., Seppälä, T., Holmström, J.: Product-centric information management: a case study of a shared platform with blockchain technology, p. 1 (2016)
7. Mor, N., et al.: Toward a global data infrastructure. IEEE Internet Comput. **20**(3), 54–62 (2016)
8. Sherman, A.T., McGrew, D.A.: Key establishment in large dynamic groups using one-way function trees. IEEE Trans. Softw. Eng. **29**(5), 444–458 (2003)
9. Szebeni, S., Butty'n, L., et al.: Invitation-oriented TGDH: Key management for dynamic groups in an asynchronous communication model. In: 2012 41st International Conference on Parallel Processing Workshops (ICPPW), pp. 269–276. IEEE (2012)

10. Wei, C., Li, J., Li, W., Yu, P., Guan, H.: STYX: a trusted and accelerated hierarchical SSL key management and distribution system for cloud based CDN application. In: Proceedings of the 2017 Symposium on Cloud Computing, pp. 201–213. ACM (2017)

11. Xue, K., Hong, P.: A dynamic secure group sharing framework in public cloud computing. IEEE Trans. Cloud Comput. **2**(4), 459–470 (2014)

12. Zhang, L., et al.: Named data networking. ACM SIGCOMM Comput. Commun. Rev. **44**(3), 66–73 (2014)

13. Zyskind, G., Nathan, O., et al.: Decentralizing privacy: using blockchain to protect personal data. In: 2015 IEEE Security and Privacy Workshops (SPW), pp. 180–184. IEEE (2015)

Author Index

Printed in the United States
By Bookmasters